THE VANISHING HECTARE

CULTURE&SOCIETY
AFTER SOCIALISM
A SERIES EDITED BY
BRUCE GRANT&NANCY RIES

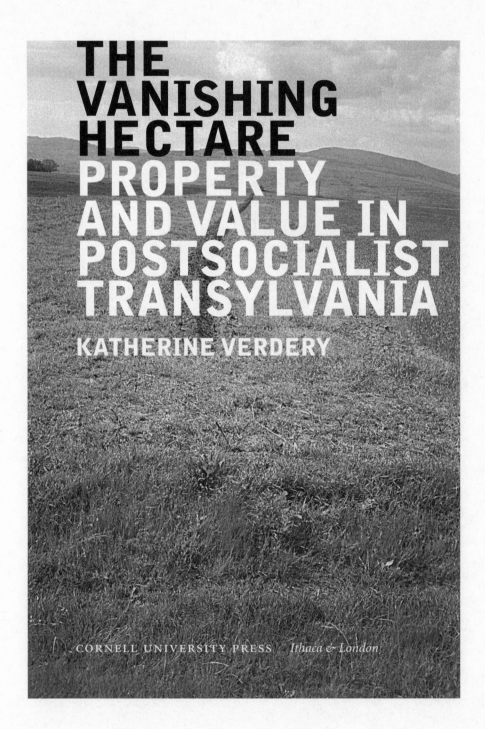

THE VANISHING HECTARE

PROPERTY AND VALUE IN POSTSOCIALIST TRANSYLVANIA

KATHERINE VERDERY

CORNELL UNIVERSITY PRESS   *Ithaca & London*

First published 2003 by Cornell University Press
First printing, Cornell Paperbacks, 2003

Printed in the United States of America

Library of Congress Cataloging-in-Publication Data

Verdery, Katherine.
   The vanishing hectare : property and value in postsocialist
Transylvania / Katherine Verdery.
      p.cm.—(Cuture and society after socialism)
Includes bibliographical references and index.
   ISBN 0-8104-4197-8 (cloth : alk. paper)—ISBN 0-8104-8869-9 (pbk. :
alk. paper)
   1. Land reform—Romania—Transylvania. 2.
Peasantry—Romania—Transylvania. 3. Transylvania (Romania)—Rural
conditions. 4. Post-communism—Romania—Transylvania. 5. Social
change—Romania—Transylvania. I. Title. II. Series.
   HD839.T7V47 2003
   333.3'14984—dc21

                              2003012516

Cloth printing   10 9 8 7 6 5 4 3 2 1
Paperback printing   10 9 8 7 6 5 4 3 2 1

For Phyllis

To understand how land is owned, it is above all necessary to know how it is used and why it is valued.

(Bronislaw Malinowski, *Coral Gardens and Their Magic*)

> What do you have buried here?
> Wheat? We have forefathers and fathers,
> Our mothers, sisters and brothers.
> > Strangers, out of the way!
> Holy and dear this is our land,
> Our cradle and our grave.
> Our warm blood defended it,
> And nothing more has watered it
> Than tears poured from our eyes—
> > We want land!

(From "We Want Land!" by Romanian poet George Coşbuc, 1896)

CONTENTS

ILLUSTRATIONS

TABLES

FIGURES

MAPS

PHOTOGRAPHS

PREFACE

This book is about a subject vital to everyone who eats: the rights to the land on which food is grown. No matter—other than the *way* in which that food is produced, with all its toxic potential—is more central to human well-being. Despite the subject's significance, however, an author cannot count on a passionate response to it from readers in Western Europe and North America, where a mere 3–6 percent of the population handles the business of feeding millions of people.

Quite the contrary is true in the countries of Eastern Europe and the former Soviet Union, where the fall of communist party-states in 1989–1991 meant the possibility for individual households to own land. For the large majority of the rural populations there, that possibility had not existed for several decades. The only people who had the privilege of owning land during the previous regime were small numbers of hill-dwellers, along with most villagers in Poland and Yugoslavia—unique in having not collectivized agriculture. Everywhere else, decollectivization, or the return of land to private ownership, appeared very early on post-1989 political agendas. It led to lengthy, confusing procedures, often chaotic and rife with complex political maneuvering. Passions flared on all sides, both in the parliaments that legislated the return of land and in the rural contexts that were host to it. In that part of the world during the 1990s, if you wanted to have an animated conversation, land was a very good bet.

This, indeed, was how I was drawn into the subject. In the summers of 1990 and 1991, I traveled to two Transylvanian villages in which I had lived during the socialist period to see how they were faring. What villagers wanted to tell me about was land. I had never paid much attention to property before, but participating in these conversations showed me a fascinating world, filled with deep longings, antagonism and revenge, shady dealings, prideful accomplishment, toil, constant squabbling and tension, devious speech, violence and threats of it, determination, ingenuity, and rage. Then, as the decade of the 1990s wore on, these gave way to bewilderment, loss of heart, and resignation.

The present book chronicles some of these feelings and events for one Transylvanian community, Aurel Vlaicu, during the years 1990–2001. I attempt to bring to life the concerns, hopes, strivings, and disappointments of this small world, while not losing sight of the ever-more-inclusive contexts and processes that framed them. Beyond this, I suggest that contrary to those who see decollectivization as a process of *(re)creating private* property, it is better understood as a process of *transforming socialist* property. Socialism was not a property void; it had its own structure of property rights, a structure that had a long afterlife in the course of dismantling socialism and was little appreciated by those charged with that task. Their disregard contributed much to the difficulties that decollectivization brought about.

For readers disinclined to spend this much time on agriculture in an insignificant place, I remind them that in the 1990s stories comparable to this one were unfolding in thousands of rural settlements across the former socialist bloc—and more broadly, as emerging markets ensnared would-be cultivators in country after country in the course of "development." Worldwide, property rights have come onto the agenda, with economists and politicians thinking that if those can just be created, then development will naturally follow. One of my tasks is to show, for one case, why this is not so. Each case has its specificity—a major theme of the book—but each is worth attending to for what it reveals about the predicaments of being human in the disarray accompanying the turn of the millennium.

The processes I describe make the book worth reading, however, even for those who prefer their units more macro. Read it if you wonder how old power structures renew themselves in radically changed circumstances; how an object of value was transformed in different ways for different sorts of people, vanishing for some of them; how and why people once deprived of land ownership struggled to regain it, even when they could not make use of it; why people might continue to work land even when they lost money doing so, thus resisting the World Bank's intention that land ownership be consolidated and made more efficient. Read it if you wonder how a community of rural people managed to live through the twentieth century's second greatest upheaval (the creation of Soviet-style socialism being the first): the *departure* from that socialism.

ACKNOWLEDGMENTS

Intellectual production, like socialist and peasant agriculture, is a collective endeavor pursued through networks in fields of relationships, often involving debts. My first and greatest debt is to the people of Vlaicu, especially the families introduced pseudonymously in these pages (they will know who they are). They have put up with my inquisitiveness on and off for three decades, with rather little to show for it. I mention by name the entire Boşorogan family who adopted me in 1973 and passed me on from one generation to another, always welcoming me and teaching me more than anyone else about whatever I wanted to know. Another great teacher and loved friend is Teodora Cărăban, the first person I ever interviewed at length (on numerous occasions) by transoceanic cell phone.

Four mayors of Geoagiu commune suffered my presence among them with grace, as did judicial personnel in the Hunedoara county court in Deva and in Orăştie; the notarial staff in Deva; employees in the county's Department of Agriculture, Office for the Cadastre and Territorial Organization in Agriculture, branch of the state archives, and office for implementing Law 18; and the directors of the Orăştie Agricultural Bank, Romcereal, the Geoagiu Agromec, and several state farms. In Bucharest I was fortunate to meet with a number of senators and parliamentary deputies, as well as with government officials in the ministries of Agriculture and Public Administration, who were involved in the reform of agriculture and helped me gain a broader view of the process. I received further assistance from the Bucharest offices of USAID and the World Bank and from the commercial officers of the U.S. Embassy.

A project that lasts ten years enters into far more collegial conversations than can be properly acknowledged. I recognize some of these colleagues in the chapters to which they contributed but wish to mention here those who have offered special encouragement. Liviu Chelcea, Jane Collier, Gail Kligman,

Daniel Lățea, Phyllis Mack, Oana Mateescu, and Doug Rogers read most or all of the manuscript and saved me from myself in numerous ways. Among other Romanian scholars, I benefited particularly from discussions with the late Ivan Aluaș, Sorin Antohi, Daniel Dăianu, Mihai Gherman, Liviu Maior, Alina Mungiu-Pippidi, Alec Niculescu, Aurel Răduțiu, Simion Retegan, Stelian Tănase, the late Pompiliu Teodor, and Liviu and Marieta Ursuțiu, as well as from the research assistance of Emanuela Grama, Sidonia Puiu, and Magdalena Tampa. Ray Abrahams, Michael Burawoy, Gerald Creed, Elizabeth Dunn, Ashraf Ghani, Chris Hann, Caroline Humphrey, Martha Lampland, Elinor Ostrom, Marilyn Strathern, and Nigel Swain offered me valuable ideas and information. The bulk of the manuscript was written while I was a fellow at the marvelous Wissenschaftskolleg zu Berlin, where members of the FIASCO reading group offered useful criticism, especially Peter Bernholz, Richard Bernstein, Francis Snyder, Patricia Springborg, Robert Wade, and Wang Hui. My thanks to all these colleagues. Among my friends in Ann Harbor who gave me good reason to leave my office were Gillian Feeley-Harnik, Shirley Neuman, Ann Stoler and Larry Hirschfeld, Erik Mueggler and Min Kim, Alvia Golden and Carroll Smith-Rosenberg, Fernando Coronil and Julie Skurski, Webb Keane, and Kelly Askew. My wonderful staff at the Center for Russian and East European Studies thoughtfully refrained from telling me just how lousy a boss I was at times.

Several organizations supported the research on which this book is based. They are the International Research and Exchanges Board (IREX, 1993–94), with funds from the National Endowment for the Humanities, the United States Information Agency, and the U.S. Department of State, which administers the Russian, Eurasian, and East European Research Program (Title VIII); the National Science Foundation (1996–97), grant #P420-C20-2020-2000; the American Council of Learned Societies; the National Council for Soviet and East European Research; the Stanford Center for Advanced Study in the Behavioral Sciences; the University of Michigan, for additional field research funds; and the Wissenschaftskolleg zu Berlin. Without holding them responsible for any of the book's contents, I express my gratitude to each of these organizations, the personnel who assisted me, and the funders who enabled their support.

At Cornell University Press, I am very thankful for the enthusiasm and careful readings of the series editors, Bruce Grant and Nancy Ries; the encouragement of Fran Benson; and the fine editorial assistance of Catherine Rice and Karen Laun. The cover photograph of the land registry map for Vlaicu is from Arhivele Naționale Deva (Fond Inspectoratul Tehnic Cadastral, 1884/6, tubul nr. 10). Except where noted, Karin Steinbrueck provided the volume's fine photographs; Sean Cotter translated the poetry used as an epigraph; and Ron Fraker did the illustrations.

Phyllis Mack knows all too well how much work went into writing this book, and how much foregone enjoyment. I dedicate it to her, deeply grateful for how much she has enriched my life.

NOTE ON PRONOUNCIATION, ROMANIAN NAMES, TERMS, AND TRANSLATIONS

Romanian is pronounced more or less like Italian, with the following additions:

ă = *u* as in *but* [schwa]

î (also â) = a high central vowel with no English equivalent; the final *e* in *intelligent*, spoken quickly, approximates it.

ş = *sh* as in *shoe*

ţ = *ts* as in *fits*

final *i* is often not pronounced, becoming voiceless and/or palatalizing the preceding consonant. *I* before another vowel usually becomes a glide (thus, *Ion* is pronounced "Yawn").

As in Italian, front vowels soften *c* and *g* (to č and dj); hard *c* or *g* before front vowels is spelled *ch* or *gh*.

Phonetic approximations for the four place names used most often are:

Hunedoara = hoo neh DWA ra
Orăştie = aw rush TEE yeh
Geoagiu = jo AH joo
Vlaicu = VLY koo (*vly* rhymes with *fly*)

The inhabitants of a settlement are often indicated by the suffix *-eni;* hence Vlaicu's inhabitants are *Vlaiceni* [vly-CHEŇ; the final *i* palatalizes the preceding *n* and the *-eni* takes the word stress]. I use this form of reference but do not complicate it by using the proper definite and indefinite endings (-*enii* as opposed to -*eni*). In the singular it is Vlaicean [vly-CHAN].

Concerning Names. Except for those in photograph captions, all names of villagers in this book are pseudonyms. I created some of them; others were suggested by the individuals themselves, perhaps as a favorite name (some of these choices produced odd anachronisms, as if one were to assign the name *Mindy* to a person born in 1900). To assist readers, I have chosen fairly simple names, most of which can be pronounced by stressing the penultimate syllable. The names are consistent within this book but not always with other publications. In an effort to protect identities, I assigned some of the characteristics of a few highly identifiable people to others.

Concerning Transylvania, Banat, and Regat. Romania consists of several named regions, among them the Regat, Transylvania, and the Banat (see map 1). The Regat includes all of Romania south and east of the Carpathian mountains. The Banat is the westernmost part of the country, bordering Hungary and Serbia. *Transylvania* is used in two senses: an expansive one, which includes the Banat, and a narrower one, which excludes it and refers to the area surrounded by the southern, eastern, and western Carpathians. For some purposes lumping Transylvania and the Banat makes sense; for others it does not. Specifically with reference to the agrarian economy, the two differ in terrain and in land use, the Banat being a flat plain and Transylvania an intermontane plateau, but with respect to ethnic composition and property history, they are very similar. I generally use *Transylvania* in the expansive sense; to signal the restricted one, I use *Transylvania proper* or *central Transylvania*.

Concerning Quotations from Interviews. The communist era created very unpleasant associations with the idea of tape recording. I did not tape interviews but took handwritten notes in a mix of English and Romanian, trying to stay as close as possible to people's own words. Inevitably a lot was lost. Quoted passages should be read as very loose translations of what my respondents actually said. All translations from Romanian are mine.

A glossary of terms and abbreviations follows the endnotes.

THE VANISHING HECTARE

INTRODUCTION
PROPERTY, VALUE, AND GLOBAL TRANSFORMATION

> Privatization is when someone who doesn't know who the real owner is and
> doesn't know what it is really worth sells it to someone who doesn't have any
> money.
>
> *(Polish Privatization Minister Janusz Lewandowski)*

To get to Aurel Vlaicu,[a] you take the train (or, by car, the international highway) from Bucharest north and westward toward the Transylvanian cities Timișoara, Arad, or Cluj. You pass through stretches of flat plain
and the oilfields of Ploiești; then you begin to climb up toward the old German city of Brașov in the southern Carpathian Mountains, whose watershed
demarcates the plains from the Transylvanian plateau. The mountains rise
grandly to their glistening peaks. Continuing through Brașov and the city of
Sibiu, the train is now moving westward toward Hungary, through the flood
plain of the river Mureș. Here, the land lies flat and then curls upward into the
low foothills of the western Carpathians, on your right. On your left, and
more distant, you can still see the much taller southern Carpathians. If you arrive in summer, a haze probably hangs heavy in the air, spoiling the view; otherwise the landscape has a lovely definition, not too confining but with clear
edges.

As you approach Vlaicu you see a single immense field planted with corn
and then some dilapidated buildings with antique tractors in the courtyard—a
former state farm, now worked by its director. To the right is a field bearing the
short stubble of recently harvested wheat (this is July), and then many narrow
strips of land, at most 1–2 ha in size, distinguished from one another by crop or
color and by evident care. A few strips have huge stacks of hay amid other cut

---

a. Pronounced ow-RELL VLY-koo. This is the full name of a famous aviator born in the village in
1882. Locals usually leave off the first name and use simply *Vlaicu*, as I do here, reserving the full name for
mention of the actual person.

Entering Vlaicu.

hay loose on the ground, with some long branches carefully inserted into the soil ready for more hay once it has dried. You turn off the main road at the sign, coming at once upon houses clustered together. The houses, most surrounded by wrought iron fences, stand fairly close together and are set off from the asphalt road by heavy gates. Tile roofs cap structures made of brick with a stuccoed exterior, painted in various colors—mustard yellow, green, dark red, gray (but not white or blue, the colors of serf houses a century and more ago). Ducks waddle along the roadside ditch; occasional herds of geese hiss at you; an oxcart laden with hay lurches past.

Looking at this seemingly bucolic landscape in the year 2000, you might not realize that across its variegated surfaces have flowed conflict and recrimination, despair, determination, endless measurings and remeasurings and dueling furrows, hope, usurpation, and disillusionment—not to mention thousands of kilograms of manure and chemical fertilizer, pesticides that did not work because they were misapplied or sold outdated, herbicide applied sparsely because it was too expensive (and, besides, we can weed the corn ourselves), seed of widely varying quality and price, many many liters of gasoline at upward-spiraling prices, and rivers of sweat—all provided by these villagers at ever-increasing personal cost. This book is about that landscape: how it was made, to whose benefit, and toward what future.

Overview of Vlaicu from the lookout point of its former feudal lords.

Themes and Events

The Vlaicu you just encountered was undergoing, like all formerly collectivized villages in Romania, a process of decollectivization. Its once-unbroken huge fields had been divided and returned to the former owners—that is, made into private property. This process was part of a larger one, privatization, that followed the collapse of communist party-states in 1989. Both international and national actors had perceived that collapse as an opportunity to reverse one of socialism's defining features: the absence of private ownership. Such actors—including experts sent by the World Bank and International Monetary Fund (IMF), national politicians (such as Poland's Leszek Balcerowicz, Czechoslovakia's Václav Klaus, and Russia's Stanislav Shatalin), and hired consultants such as Jeffrey Sachs and Anders Åslund—saw the restoration of private property as essential to developing socialism's failing economies and as better suiting human nature than does collective property. Many envisioned the task as a fairly simple one: remove the hand of the state, and private property would naturally emerge.[1] Emphasizing the creation of property rights, they imported blueprints for a western-style property regime and they made the privatization of socialist firms a condition for countries such as Romania to receive loans and credits from the IMF and other capital sources. Rarely mentioned was that these infusions would enable new forms of western colonization through transferring expertise, employing Eastern Europe's cheap skilled labor force, and flooding markets hitherto closed to western products.[2]

The experience of the 1990s, however, showed that recreating private ownership was vastly more complicated than this. Inevitably, the blueprints provided opportunities for some internal actors and constraints for others. The various responses modified the blueprints, shaping the postsocialist property order differently from the one envisioned. For instance, obtaining rights often failed to generate ownership that was effective, in which owners could actually do something with their land—the ostensible point of the whole exercise. Yet many failing smallholders nonetheless refused to sell land to others consolidating larger farms. Both advisors from western countries and the politicians and economists of formerly socialist ones were unprepared for these outcomes.

One reason they were unprepared, I believe, was that the very concept of private property was so deeply ideological, for both westerners advising the process and East Europeans clamoring for it, that no one was able to think clearly about its logistics. Because private property is not natural but profoundly social, it requires a degree of planning and deliberation that no one had time for in the rush to develop these countries and integrate them into the late-twentieth-century world economy. One of my goals in this book is to show the effects of trying to institute a certain conception of property that very few in Eastern Europe fully grasped and very few in the west saw for what it was: a symbol, a schema only loosely related to how it actually works, even in market economies themselves. If the results of the process were different from the expectations, this was not because policy somehow distorted the creation of secure property rights and functioning markets such as those in western countries; it was because all property-making, including our own, is not a natural but a historical and political process.

Privatization and the Global Context

That process was taking place in a global context. For postsocialist property reform, this setting had a number of important characteristics, sometimes discussed under the heading *globalization*. They include increased inequality on a world scale; a devaluation of labor power; changes in the nature of the state; an intensification of worldwide flows of capital, people, and goods and services of all kinds; a simultaneous concentration of capital and diversification of responses to it; the replacement of manufacturing by finance capital as the global economy's central coordinating mechanism; the much-expanded influence of international financial organizations such as the IMF, World Bank, European

Investment Bank, and European Bank for Reconstruction and Development (EBRD), as well as of international accounting firms such as Deloitte and Touche, Ernst and Young, PricewaterhouseCoopers, and KPMG. All participated in a global economic reorganization that numerous commentators have seen as a shift in modes of capital accumulation.[3] Privatization was part of this reorganizing, as governments withdrew support from activities in which they had held financial stakes, turning those over to private interests. Although Margaret Thatcher's Britain was the capitalist showcase for this process, it occurred as well in the United States, France, and elsewhere.

Global transformation is closely linked with the collapse of socialism in 1989–91, although opinions vary as to how. The end result was that East European countries entered the periphery of the capitalist world, their paths diverging from one another with their differential insertion into it. Here, too, privatization was a basic element, but on a scale vastly outstripping that of the cases just mentioned. Whereas in the 1980s the number of firms privatized worldwide was approximately 6,800 and in Britain a mere two dozen, the number to be privatized in Poland alone was 7,500 (Adams and Brock 1993, 76–77). There was also the fundamental difference that whereas the privatizations in capitalist countries (as well as land reforms in countries such as Mexico) took place in societies already governed by the principle of private property, postsocialist privatization required putting that very principle into place.

Postsocialist privatization took two main forms. The first was to dissolve state ownership over goods and objects that had been newly created during the socialist period by socialist means. These included the millions of apartment buildings and new sites of industrial production constructed by communist parties, using the labor of citizens and forced surpluses from agriculture as a basis for state investment. None of these goods had previous owners, and one could see whatever value they represented as belonging to the whole society that had supported their creation. Postsocialist governments usually offered housing stock for sale to the present occupants at subsidized prices and distributed rights to the industrial assets in the form of shares. This process was *private property creation*, since the objects in question had never been held privately. The second form of privatizing was to restore private ownership over *preexisting* goods and objects, such as land or houses, that the communists had nationalized or collectivized after they took power. Because these goods were usually returned to the people from whom they had been taken, the process is aptly called the *recreation of private property* or the *restitution of property rights*—sometimes called *property restitution*, for short. It implied questions of justice, for the prior owners recovered property rights partly in the belief that they had been harmed by the loss.

This second form of privatization was not unique to Eastern Europe. Rather, it participated in a much broader trend toward restitution and retributive justice involving groups as diverse as South Africans, native peoples of North America, Holocaust survivors, and descendants of slaves in the United States.[4] In many of these cases, redress was sought for harm of a nonmaterial nature—imprisonment, torture, murder, and educational opportunities denied. For harms such as these, property restitution is not necessarily an appropriate remedy or to make it so requires a broader definition of what property is—for example, cultural practices, versions of history, or objects in museums. In the postsocialist cases, as scholars such as Claus Offe, Jon Elster, and Stephen Holmes have argued, the return of ownership rights to land did not compensate for the many other forms of loss suffered in the socialist period (see Offe et al. 1993).

Both property restitution and retributive justice use an accounting metaphor to create a balance sheet of losses and compensation. Because the people formerly in power have lost their positions and thus their impunity, they and the regime they served must be called to account; this account then becomes a narrative of who is to blame. Such a settling of accounts is a way of talking about a transformation in values, and that leads us to consider another global trend in which privatization participated: changes in the assessment of value, or revaluation. In the most general terms, revaluation appeared as an increasing separation of apparent (or virtual) from actual values, as stock prices increasingly diverged from firms' actual profitability. The trend was evident in the emergence of new forms of speculation such as junk bonds and derivatives, in the 1987 stock market crash, and in the Japanese real estate bubble of the 1990s. That decade was a time of wildly gyrating stock values as U.S. stock indexes broke several previously unbreachable thresholds in the space of a few years and as the stock values of technology firms greatly outstripped their productive worth. Various market corrections, alongside the corporate scandals that began with the bankruptcies of the Enron and WorldCom corporations in 2001–2002, wiped out huge stores of value in savings and pension plans. The scandals revealed the excesses of an asset society shot through with unacceptable levels of risk, in which what had come to count was inflating assets and the price of corporate shares, while hiding losses and liabilities. That the major players in these unfolding scandals were accounting firms—the chief arbiters of financial worth—makes clear just how fundamental a reorganization of value was taking place.[5]

Postsocialist property transformation participated in this global process of revaluing, but in postsocialist contexts the process was far more thoroughgoing than elsewhere. Socialism was a system based on values, both ethical and financial, that were contrary to those of the system toward which these societies were now supposedly moving. Two years after the 1987 stock market crash, the crash of the Berlin Wall opened a massive influx of capital into formerly protected socialist states, along with pressures to re-evaluate enterprises in market terms. The matter of evaluation was not at issue in land-rights restitution (initially, at least), but it was the main dilemma in privatization methods designed to sell off state assets to private (including foreign) buyers, who reasonably enough wanted to know what their prospective purchase was worth. In other words, the dilemma of those methods was to determine values in a market-oriented financial sense for firms not subject to such evaluation before. Polish Privatization Minister Lewandowski, quoted in the chapter epigraph, expressed the dilemma succinctly.

Specifically with respect to the revaluation of assets in agriculture, this too participated in yet another aspect of global transformation: the continued decline of agriculture everywhere as a site for accumulating value.[6] Literature on international development is full of accounts, like the one I give here, of small farmers bankrupted by widening price scissors between the cost of inputs and agricultural commodity prices. Euphemized as *emerging markets* stories, these accounts show the devastating particulars of long-term structural change in capitalist economies, as each discovery of a new domain of profit (first agriculture, then manufacturing, then service industries and information technology, and so on) eventually renders the older ones less and less profitable. This is as true in highly developed regions as elsewhere. Arguments within the European Union concerning the fate of the Common Agricultural Policy, for example, show that without sizable subsidies, profitable agriculture cannot exist.

The response to this decreasing profitability has been a change in the kind of ownership that matters. In turn-of-the-twenty-first-century farming, the ownership that gives significant control and generates value is control not over land but over chemical inputs, through the patents held by chemical, biotechnology, and oil industries—in short, intellectual property rights. These inputs include genetically engineered seed that can be used only once; complex pesticides and fertilizers, fabricated to be effective only with specific seeds; animal fodder, the subject of much criticism with the outbreak of mad cow disease; and so forth. (Their cost, however, may preclude their use by smallholders, as I show in chap. 5.) Land has become a neutral medium for absorbing manufactured inputs so as to manufacture crops; its own qualities grow insignificant as it becomes but a platform for chemical products that are closely integrated with one another. I emphasize this transformation in farming and the worldwide decline in agriculture to underscore the fact that much of the story I tell is not peculiar to postsocialism but partakes in global trends.

❧

Within this context occurs the subject of the present book: how land in a Transylvanian community moved out of the property regime of socialism, becoming the private property of villagers whose families had previously owned it, and how its value for different groups of people changed over time. The principal actors in my account are (1) international organizations and consultants, together with Romanian politicians, who pushed for restoring private ownership by making a law for land restitution and creating policies that affected what people could do with the land; (2) the former collective farm members who petitioned for return of their rights, as well as those who received none; (3) the local authorities and former elite of the collective and state farms who obstructed restitution; and (4) a host of organizations such as banks, courts, notaries, fertilizer factories, seed companies, restitution commissions, and retailers of herbicides and pesticides. Influencing their actions were the history of land and property in socialism, the rapid but uneven integration of the former socialist bloc into the global economy, and the need for Romania's political elites to secure both external and internal support for reform programs that many Romanians would find extraordinarily taxing.

Particularly important in this story was that Romania had relatively few prospects for rapid economic development, compared with Hungary, Poland, or the Czech Republic. Among the reasons were that the government from 1990 to 1996 was dominated by former party apparatchiks and that the Nicolae Ceauşescu regime had largely ruined the economy, far more than had occurred in those other countries (as reflected for instance in the per capita GDP in Romania in 1989—less than half that of Czechoslovakia).[7] The result was not very attractive to foreign investors, particularly because property rights remained very unstable throughout the decade. Indeed, Romania was about the only country in which the first round of privatization did *not* result in a substantial foreign contingent in the newly forming entrepreneurial classes. The networks remaining from the former Communist Party were strong enough—because the Romanian revolution had not expelled from power all the former communists but only their top echelon—to prevent foreigners from buying into the economy, had they wanted to. As an economist specializing in Romania put it, "Romania is the only country where the Marriott hotel chain could bid on a hotel against Bucharest's Păunescu brothers and *lose!*"[8] (He was referring to the celebrated privatization of Bucharest's centrally located Intercontinental Hotel, for which two Bucharest entrepreneurs, the Păunescu brothers, bid approximately half the amount Marriott offered but were awarded the sale anyway). The situation changed somewhat with the neoliberal government elected in 1996, which made the opportunities for foreign investors more enticing. In general, however, undesirable investment conditions plus entrenched domestic interests meant that outsiders posed less of a challenge to the position of the old/new Romanian elites than occurred in other countries, and this in turn retarded the restructuring of Romanian enterprises and of the communist-era managerial elite.

One result was that effective landowning proved elusive. Because international financial organizations militated against protective tariffs and subsidies for agricultural products, Romanian farmers entered the global economy with few of the supports enjoyed by farmers in the European Union. Many could not keep their heads above water. Meanwhile, local mayors and the former managers of socialist agriculture struggled to retain or fortify their power base by retarding decollectivization, as well as by diverting into their own pockets the credits and benefits the state did provide, which villagers needed in order to make viable farms. The privatization blueprint failed to take into account a crucial effect of the collapse of the party-state: by weakening the political center, it hobbled the government's ability either to finance the transition or to control the population, especially those charged with implementing the land law.

Throughout the decollectivization process, rights to land held multiple and conflicting significances for different actors. For foreign advisors they meant the possibility of efficient agricultural production and for Romania's leaders a symbol of change and a potential source of value to be transferred into industry. For some agrarian elites they provided a vehicle for retaining power, for others a low-risk launching pad into commercial farming. Villagers saw land rights as a means to assert their dignity and worth and as a basis for current livelihood and future security. All these hopes intersected in tiny parcels, claimed by smallholders such as the people I introduce in these chapters.

Research on Postsocialist Privatization

The transformation of socialism has produced a mammoth literature in a variety of fields, particularly around that ubiquitous troika, privatization, marketization, and democratization. Predictably, economists, political scientists, and legal scholars flocked to these subjects, with sociologists, geographers, and anthropologists hovering at the margins. Concerning the problems of privatization in particular, all these scholars produced many illuminating accounts, too numerous for me to summarize here.[9] Neoinstitutionalism was particularly prevalent, although among the European agricultural economists who dominated the study of decollectivization that approach was vigorously debated by two others: neoclassical economics and political economy.[10] Much of the economic literature took it as axiomatic that creating private ownership was both an unalloyed good and a necessity (but cf. Meurs 2001; Murrell 1992, 1993). This was so much the case that a paper advocating the benefits of leasing agricultural land rather than owning it presented the findings as a surprise (Hagedorn 2000).

Particularly influential was the work of several sociologists: Michael Burawoy, Jadwiga Staniszkis, David Stark, and Iván Szelényi (three of whom joined argument in a review symposium in the *American Journal of Sociology* clarifying their different points of view; see Burawoy 2001a). Among these scholars, the question of postsocialist elites emerged as central: whether the old ones were blocking property reform, whether they were reproducing their position or being replaced, what path dependencies we could discern in their trajectories, on what forms of property and other assets these trajectories rested, and so on. Stark's (1996) seminal paper on recombinant property was one in a series of fine papers that placed fuzzy property boundaries and intraelite networks at the center of analysis; some of these papers appear in his *Postsocialist Pathways* (Stark and Bruszt 1998). A significant disagreement emerged between the early position staked out by Staniszkis (1991a, 1991b)—that the driving force for change was the conversion of party elites' political capital into ownership and wealth—and the one developed by Szelényi and collaborators in their *Making Capitalism without Capitalists* (Eyal, Szelényi, and Townsley 1998). These latter authors rejected the political capitalism hypothesis and saw cultural capital, instead, as both the defining trait of postsocialism—"a unique social structure in which cultural capital is the main source of power, prestige, and privilege" (6)—and the basis for converting social and political capital into other forms of wealth and status (see also Maurel 1994b, 353).

Scholarship using *capital theory* can be confusing because the term has three distinct sources in the work of James Coleman (1990), Robert Putnam (1995), and Pierre Bourdieu (1977, 1984); each means something different by it. Nonetheless, one or another conception of different and interacting capitals appears in much of the writing on postsocialism (e.g., Böröcz and Róna-Tas 1996; Lampland 2002; Maurel 1994b; Róna-Tas 1998; Róna-Tas and Böröcz 1999; Sandu 1999; Stoica 2004; Thelen 2001). Although I do not organize my discussion around this framework, I sometimes use its terms, following the interpretation of those, such as József Böröcz, who see property transformation as arising from conversions of social capital by previous elites.

By contrast with these scholars, Burawoy has focused less on the behavior of elites than on the experiences of the workers subject to privatization (e.g., Burawoy 2001b; Burawoy, Krotov, and Lytkina 2000; Burawoy and Lukács 1992). He has also criticized the others for seeing the different trajectories of East European countries as indicating alternative capital*isms*, whereas he sees them as indicating the differential insertion of these countries into a global capitalist economy (Burawoy 2001a, 1116). Among his goals is to counterbalance excessive emphasis on socialist legacies and path dependency with greater attention to contemporary capitalist processes. Do we continue to have socialist elites in postsocialist elite structures because of legacies from the past or because of something about how the world works *now* to produce that pattern? Upon inspection we often find that what might look like legacies are better seen as responses to quite contemporary processes. (Gerald Creed 1995b, 1999, for instance, does this beautifully in explaining why Bulgarian villagers after 1989 continued to vote socialist). A complete analysis will of course incorporate both: aspects of the past deeply affect how a country is drawn into "combined and uneven development" in the global economy.

For example, in chapters 5–8, I argue that decollectivization in Vlaicu reproduced the hierarchy of privilege in socialist agriculture, with state farm directors at the top, collective farm staff below them, and village households at the bottom, holding very few resources for surviving in the new environment. Yet this is only in part to argue that socialist legacies determined the post-1989 outcome. As I have previously indicated, owing to Ceaușescu's devastating policies Romania's economy was in far worse shape in 1989 than were those of the northern tier; this discouraged foreign investment, which in turn meant that would-be Romanian entrepreneurs had less competition from outsiders. It was this, more than a lingering socialism, that dictated the continued utility of socialism's cultural, social, and political capital endowments after 1989. In Romanian conditions, well-educated state farm managers who were accustomed to working on a large scale, managing large budgets with substantial investments, and throwing costs onto the state still found these talents useful, and they were generally better endowed with such skills than were the staff of the collectives (see also, e.g., Maurel 1994b, 352; Swain 1995). By the same token, after 1989 villagers who commuted to skilled jobs in nearby towns, thus benefiting from socialism's favoritism of industry, found themselves privileged with off-farm incomes (their industrial pensions) that enabled them to work their land and find value in it that others without such pensions could not. These are not just legacies of socialism but the adaptive use of existing resources to survive in Romania's particular postsocialist context. Both legacy and insertion arguments, then, have their place.

Let me broaden this point to justify the suitability of how I interpret my material. Romania's position relative to global investment enabled former apparatchiks to retain power longer there than elsewhere, which they used to exclude foreign investors further. Yet the government's ongoing involvement with programs of the World Bank, IMF, the European Union's Phare Programmes, and so forth placed constant demands on policy formation concerning property rights. No one could be certain that ways of getting by today would work tomorrow. That uncertainty encouraged actors to plan over the short rather than the long term and increased their motivation to make off with anything they could. Such behavior, practiced by people at every level of Romanian society, contributed to a tremendous devaluation of the socialist infrastructure. Managers alienated or ruined the assets of their firms—letting tractors rust and selling off entire pieces of machinery as scrap metal—in hopes of privatizing them on the cheap. Scavenging, in Romanian conditions, became a way of life—conforming to Prime Minister Petre Roman's declaration in 1990, "The Romanian economy is just a heap of scrap iron!" (Mateescu 2002, n. 21).

My point is that socialist-era elite advantage and processes of devaluation, although present all across the region, are also variables tied to a country's place in the world economy. Romania's economic unattractiveness to foreigners gave its socialist managers more support in retaining their positions and more incentives to scavenge, dissipating the wealth accumulated under socialism while having little to put in its stead. Therefore, an account that emphasizes prior endowments of political, social, and cultural capital and that focuses on value transformation makes especially good sense for the Romanian case. This case offers a perhaps extreme example of Staniszkis's thesis in *Post-Communism* (1999, 349) that what distinguishes the peripheral situation of postsocialist Eastern Europe from other peripheries is elites' use of elements of the legacy of socialism to fight against capitalist competition. For this case in particular, socialism's endowments were especially consequential; thus, I begin with a discussion of property in socialism (chap. 1).

I have been discussing some arguments in the sociology of postsocialism. What does anthropology have to offer? Although few debates have yet emerged, anthropologists such as Creed, C. M. Hann, Caroline Humphrey, David Kideckel, and Martha Lampland have been amassing valuable descriptions of postsocialist change, especially in agriculture. These appear in some collections,[11] in parts of monographs and a small number of complete monographs,[12] and in an ever-expanding archive of papers (which I do not list here). Perhaps because so many of the researchers employ the perspective of political economy and do not employ a hypothesis-testing mode, conflicting interpretations have been slow to develop. The principal conclusion these works suggest is that responses to decollectivization exhibit tremendous diversity, not just from coun try to country but from region to region and even village to village. A comparison of work on Hungary (e.g., Hann 1993a, 1993b; Lampland 2002) or Bulgaria (Creed 1998, 1999; Meurs 2001) with work on Romania (Kideckel 1992, 1995a; Verdery 1994) or Albania (de Waal 1996, 2001) gives a sense of the range. In addition, this body of work reveals a number of themes that appear in the present book, such as the increased social conflict and rural impoverishment that decollectivization produced in many areas, the extraordinary legal and logistical challenges it posed, the resuscitation of earlier kinship norms, and the hesitancy of many villagers to leave cooperative forms.

Specifically concerning decollectivization in Romania, David Kideckel is the only ethnographer besides myself who has published on this theme (Kideckel 1990, 1992, 1993a, 1993b, 1993c, 1995a), and to similar effect. Further afield, the main argument that has developed concerns whether decollectivization has led to a return to traditional peasant agriculture or, rather, a forced retraditionalization (the position I take here). Andrew Cartwright (a lawyer) in *Return of the Peasant* (2001) and Beatrice von Hirschhausen (a geographer) in *Les nouvelles campagnes roumaines* (1997) take opposite sides on the issue, whereas Mircea Vultur (a sociologist) in *Collectivisme et transition democratique* (2002) sees the tradition in which Romanian cultivators are chiefly enmeshed as the collectivist tradition of the socialist period. Among publications in Romanian, those by Alina Mungiu-Pippidi and Gérard Althabe (2002), P. I. Otiman (2002), and Vladimir Pasti, Mirela Miroiu, and Cornel Codiță (1997) are more general, although all are dedicated to showing the post-1989 government of Ion Iliescu as the enemy of private farming and the agent of further oppression for Romanian peasants. As will become apparent, I share some of these concerns about the fate of the peasantry, but my attention is centered elsewhere.

Concepts

I understand decollectivization in Frederic Pryor's terms as "the conversion of state and collective farms into either private (corporate or individual) farms, or tenant farms with long-term leases, or genuine producer cooperatives" (1992, 265). Although this understanding of the term lumps together all forms of socialist property in agriculture—inaptly, because collective and state farms differed from one another in many respects—in the interests of simplicity I follow Pryor in using *decollectivization* for the dissolution of both. Among the other terms I use to speak of the process is *unmaking socialist property*, which reminds us that property is a process (of making and unmaking certain kinds of relationships); that its end point is not known; and that socialism indeed had a property system, even though different from those of most developed countries. Also appropriate is *land reform,* which suggests a process of altering both the status of land as an object of social relations and the organizational forms of agricultural enterprise; it also encourages comparison with the broader set of land reforms worldwide. And finally, the term *restitution,* which is often used with respect to property in land—specifically, people's "getting their land back," as they put it. Although restitution was of *rights* to land, I write more simply of land restitution.

Thinking about Property

> The word "property" is best seen as directing attention to a vast field of cultural as well as social relations, to the symbolic as well as the material contexts within which things are recognized and personal as well as collective identities made. —*(Hann 1998a, 5)*

A book about transforming socialist property forms requires a word about the concept of property: what it is and how we might think about it most usefully. As Hann (1998a, 1–47) has shown in a comprehensive discussion, this is not a new task for anthropologists; we have engaged in it for decades—inheriting it, indeed, from disciplinary forefathers Sir Henry Maine, Lewis Henry Morgan, and Numa Denis Fustel de Coulanges. Work by such scholars as Ernest Beagelhole (1931), Max Gluckman (1943, 1965), A. Irving Hallowell (1955), E. Adamson Hoebel (1942, 1954), Edmund Leach (1961), Robert Lowie (1920), and Bronislaw Malinowski (1926, 1935) established the study of property as central to the discipline. Following a lapse in the 1970s and 1980s, the topic returned in a flood of publications (e.g., Coombe 1998; Fine-Dare 2002; Greaves 1994; Hann 1998b; McCay and Acheson 1990; Strathern 1999) on themes as diverse as property in body parts and intellectual and cultural property rights. Not even the study of socialist property transformation is wholly new, having begun with Sally Falk Moore's (1986) work in Tanzania.

Despite this interest, and despite (or because of) the centrality of property to our own social order, providing a definition of it is not a simple matter. The concept has been defined in a variety of ways even within western legal traditions—as things, as relations of persons to things, as person-person relations mediated through things, and as a bundle of abstract rights. Extrapolating from Thomas Grey (1980), we should probably see most existing definitions of property as specific to a given time period and form of (capital) accumulation rather than as a universally valid conception of it. Indeed, scholars such as William Maurer, Annelise Riles, and Marilyn Strathern have questioned whether there is any utility at all to the property concept—other than to take it as yet another object of interrogation, something we study rather than employ analytically. These scholars offer their field material from the Caribbean, Fiji, and Papua New Guinea so as to undo property for us.[13] We should concentrate, they suggest, on the power and operation of the property idea, not look for better definitions of it.

Should we even continue to speak of *property* at all? Is it not preferable to abandon a term so heavily populated with commonsense meanings as to be analytically useless? For some purposes, this would indeed be the best route, but there are circumstances in which it is important to keep the word anyway. For instance, Frank Speck, writing about Algonkian peoples in the early 1900s, felt it necessary to speak of property so as to challenge evolutionist assumptions about that institution, as well as to critique the premises of colonization (Nadasdy 2002, 250). Similarly, in his work in Africa beginning in the 1930s, Max Gluckman (1943) insisted on writing about property precisely to counter British imperial conceptions about the "savages" they ruled: finding property among such "savages" should make them worthy of greater respect.

For comparably political reasons I think it necessary to talk about property for 1990s Eastern Europe. First, among my desired audience are various economists, political scientists, and policy-makers who were actively involved in promoting private property for the eastern bloc. By using the word, I hope to persuade them to see it more complexly for postsocialist countries in particular and to understand socialism itself as having had property arrangements that influenced the path of transformation (rather than regarding the property scene in 1990 as a *tabula rasa*). Second, during the 1990s, *property* was the language into which the phenomena I discuss were being sucked. *Property* was the idiom used by international organizations, which made economic assistance conditional on changes in property rights, as well as by Romanian politicians wanting either aid from abroad or symbolic capital against the former party apparatchiks who exercised power from 1990 through 1996; villagers, too, had a property discourse, speaking of "my land" and "my rights." In a word, property was an important political symbol, a point to which I return in chapter 2.

If I prefer to use rather than avoid the word *property,* how do I understand it?[14] I offer not a generic definition but modes of approach that help with the material I consider in this book. I see property variously as a western "native category," a symbol, a set of relations, and a process. As a western native category, the idea of property acts powerfully in the contemporary world. It contains its own implicit theories, which contribute to its ideological character as a native category, and its conceptual content varies from case to case and discipline to discipline. Most of its implicit theories have two elements, economic and political. Economists generally understand property as a means of regulating access to scarce resources and increasing their efficient use by assigning persons rights in them relative to other persons—a premise common to many political and legal scholars as well.[15] Underlying this notion is the axiom, in my view highly questionable, that resources are naturally scarce a priori and that all we have to do is figure out how to get them and exclude others. Once we do that, once we create property rights and deliver them to people, property ideology says that those people will have an incentive to work well and to use assets efficiently, disciplined by the market. I hold, rather, that resources are *made* scarce within a given system of values and power relations (skeptics may want to read Marshall Sahlins's 1972 essay on "the original affluent society," which raises doubts that scarcity is always present). Thus, property as an institution often establishes scarcity rather than arising in response to it.

The second ideological element is the connection of property with liberal democratic practice, a connection dating at least from the writings of John Locke. He theorized property as a particular relation between state and citizens, a form of subjection to which property entitlements were central. In his work as well as in subsequent political theory, this became an association between democracy and property—the property-owning citizen is the responsible subject of a democratic polity. Linked with this is an additional element in the property concept: it always hints at a morality—something we see clearly from Locke's using interchangeably the words *property* and *propriety*.[16] What is the proper relation of people to one another with respect to things? How should property claims be judged? Tied to this moral or normative aspect is yet another piece of the native theory implicit in western property concepts: it emphasizes rights or entitlements and sees the subjects of property relations as inherently rights-bearing, hence the prevailing language of property rights. A final pseudotheoretical element is that if property involves persons, things, and their relations, then those persons and things are clearly bounded, have integrity, and are easily recognizable as separate kinds of entities. That is, standard western property concepts have long presumed an object-relations view of the world.[17]

That such ideas are native theories, rather than analytical concepts, is evident from any anthropological comparison. Concerning the person-object separation, for instance, anthropologists have found rather different relations of persons and things from those common to nonaboriginal North Americans. Let us consider land, that seemingly most objective of things—surely it is there and we are here? Because land is the subject of this book, let us dwell on this question for a moment. Human beings have always had complex relationships with land. In Australia and in ancient Rome, for example, it could be part of them; ancestors might be both part of land and part of living communities.[18] Elizabeth

Povinelli (2002, chaps. 5–6) writes concerning the group of aboriginal Australians she worked with that via conception, sweat, and ancestral spirits, land and people constitute one another mutually (our language already posits them as separate, but here they are not). Sweat from ceremonies, for example, travels underground among sacred sites, deepening the land-person unity; the land will then recognize a person's sweat. The interchange of bodily fluids and spirits makes a group of people "stick" to the land. In parts of Romania, views reminiscent of these are documented as late as the 1930s and leave traces in fascinating etymologies around the root *mos-*, implicated in words for giving birth, landed estate, and inheritance.[19] Similar linguistic parallels exist in Russian as well (see Paxson n.d., chap. 2).

This is not all. Land may in fact own people, rather than the other way around (e.g., de Coppet 1985). For certain Siberian peoples, land is a person, with intentionality and a soul; it can choose the humans who will live on it (Vitebsky 2002, 185–87). In such circumstances, animals, humans, and land may be understood as forming an organic whole of interconnected beings—not a great chain of being, but something more like a great stew (cf. Stephens 1986; Anderson 1998). As Marcel Mauss observed long ago, many human beings believe that material objects exchanged as gifts carry traces of the people who gave them (Mauss 1965; Malinowski 1922). Some objects, indeed, so embody individual or group identities that to see them as separate—such that one could establish relations among persons with respect to them—is an error. Never mind the further possibility that persons themselves may be divisible, not integral (Strathern 1988). Examples such as these suggest that land may not be an object at all but a site at which many forms of beings intersect. We should avoid an image so impoverished that land seems only a material thing and that its essence is unaffected by changes in people's rights to it; the kinds of labor and the substances people put into land affect its essence and can be functions of those rights.

I have been discussing some of the elements of western property notions as a particular native category that underlies its historical form. With privatization, the mistake was to see this historically contingent property form as universal, natural, and neutral. This is what I mean when I say that complicating privatization was the ideological nature of the property concept on which it rested. That ideological quality, in turn, leads to the invocation of property as a political symbol. Because (private) property is so deeply rooted in the consciousness of westerners, peoples who come into contact with them may find that manipulating the word *property* brings advantage. Literature on native land claims shows exactly this process, as peoples to whom such a concept was not indigenous nonetheless found that using it enabled them to make substantial claims on the polities that incorporated them (see, e.g., Nadasdy 2003 for the Canadian

Yukon; and Povinelli 2002 and Williams 1986 for Australia). East European governments also manipulated the property idea in dealing with international financial organizations, as well as in their own electoral politics. Part of my argument in this book is that governments such as Romania's successfully wielded the property symbol to gain western aid but were then unable to make the concept a reality.

What kind of reality does property become? The standard anthropological approach emphasizes its linking persons to one another with respect to things, goods, or values (the nature of these and their separateness being not premises but empirical questions). Lawyers would add that this linking usually happens through the notion of rights. That is, property indicates particular sets of social relationships—such as relations of use, of exclusive owning, and of obligation. Culturally speaking, property specifies what things have what kind of value and who counts as a person, and it then positions these in wider sets of social relations.[20] Property in its cultural and social aspects also makes boundaries. It sets up inclusions and exclusions—*belongings,* concerning what belongs to whom and who belongs to or has affinities with some larger entity (such as a clan or corporation) that occupies a relation to specific things or goods. As such, property is a powerful idiom in processes of appropriation. Appropriation is, of course, the central issue in privatizing, which transforms the property order so as to reduce appropriation by state authorities and increase that by the individual owners or larger corporations. In this way, privatization creates a new arena for making claims on the social product. I discuss several kinds of appropriation in this book, including socialism's mechanisms for extracting the social surplus, collective farmers' efforts to appropriate the products of their effort, the different means by which the state appropriated the social product after 1989 (such as pricing mechanisms and auctions that devalued objects other people had endowed with value), the appropriation of political capital by mayors who delayed land restitution, and the appropriation of profits by newly emerging commercial farmers.

If the elements I have pointed to—values, cultural meanings, and social and power relations—are sufficiently stable and coherent, we might speak of a *property regime* . I use the word regime in the sense of a regular pattern of occurrence and do not wish to imply that it is something imposed from above. A property regime is a heuristic concept that may help in our thinking about transformations of property from socialism to postsocialism. Roman Frydman and Andrzej Rapaczynski (1994, 169–70) employ the notion in just this way. Property regimes are multiple and can coexist in any one society or situation. Among those most often mentioned are private property regimes, open access regimes, commons, collective property, public goods, state property, and socialist property; each may have its variants. All organize persons with respect to one another and to things, goods, or values. The devices for this organizing vary—rights held in bundles will be one way, birth on clan lands another, and purchase in a market yet another. For any given case, empirical analysis must show what the central values are and through which relations and devices their appropriation takes place. Also to be discovered are the characteristic idioms for making claims. Among the possible idioms one might use to lay claim to land, for instance, are, "Our lineage is bigger," "We got here first," "I'm stronger," "I inherited it from my parents," or "I paid good money for it and I have the deed." Some of these claims find greater acceptance in one property regime than in others. Still another variable is how claims are adjudicated, such as by using mediators, court trials, uncountered force, or divine sanction.

In these paragraphs, I have proposed treating property as simultaneously a cultural system, a set of social relations, and an organization of power. They all come together in social processes. I accentuate the word *processes* because this book examines several, beginning with the processes of appropriation at the center of my property conception. Another is the process of transforming one set of property forms into another. Related to it are the processes through which a new class of proprietors was emerging and its composition was being shaped—processes of accumulation and dispossession. I also explore processes that concentrated power over land rights in the hands of commune elites, and other processes that devalued the new property objects. In the most global terms, this book is about the processes that transformed villagers' local worlds following the collapse of communist parties.

Three final points, concerning rights, risk, and ambient conditions, are particularly significant for the case I discuss. First, rights: Although in general I believe that property is not best understood in terms of rights, I use this word here because Romanian actors do—especially the villagers I worked with, who often spoke of trying to obtain their rights *[drepturi]*. The decollectivization process was conceived in exactly this way: restoring the property rights of people who had lost them, and creating new rights to land for some who had never had them. But unlike legal scholars such as Michael Heller, I do not limit my subject to rights and their bundling, which I think provides an impoverished understanding of what decollectivization is about.[21] If we move beyond rights, we are more apt to see the kinds of processes I just mentioned—and to see how amazingly simplistic was the design of the entire project, given the vast panoply of absurdly framed procedures, unintended consequences, and unrealized intentions it produced.

Second, I reveal some of this by using a word my respondents did *not* often employ: risk. Under the cover of restoring rights, Dunn (2004) has argued, privatization is about introducing risk into societies unfamiliar with it, given that the socialist state had protected people against economic (although not political) failure. New owners now faced risks for which not even activities in the informal economy could have prepared them. Unfortunately, however, the instability of the decade was so great that most people had inadequate parameters for predicting so as to manage risk; they could only suffer its consequences (see chapters 5–8). The instability had several sources. One was the changes in world markets, especially financial ones, that repeatedly threatened disaster (e.g., the Asian crisis of 1997–98, and the collapse of Long Term Capital hedge fund in 1998). Another source of instability, for Romania in particular, was the continual fluctuations in government policy, changing in response now to international pressure, now to internal discontent. No policy was left in place long enough to assess its effects properly. Not only were external conditions unstable, but so was the matrix of values within which property was to have meaning, a matter I take up shortly.

Third, these observations about instability lead to noting the ambient conditions within which people sought to make their property rights and relations effective. Daniel Bromley (2000) observes that the problem of the postsocialist transition was not just to privatize control over assets, but to figure out how they could be mobilized for human aims, and he decries the failure of postsocialist governments to do that (see also van Brabant 1998). For instance, in Romania, former owners received property rights to land that their families had given to collective farms in the 1950s; presumably, they would use it to grow crops. Governing their relations to that land and their ability to use it, however, was their not having received other necessary means of production, while the state made it nearly impossible for most of them to acquire those means. The unstable economic and political environment aggravated their difficulties further. Throughout this book I argue that such ambient conditions must be part of a property analysis: we must show not only the struggles through which people gain rights to land (e.g., Berry 1993) but also how the powers of ownership are then realized. This leads us to see that in property restitution, obtaining rights proved far less important than controlling the context in which those rights could be exercised and value obtained. That control lay in the hands of international organizations and state actors, interacting with the policies of each postsocialist government.

Thinking about Value

What I have just said leads to the theme of value, a central one for my treatment of property, and for postsocialism as well. The notion of value is integral to property: no one wants to establish property relations with other people over something they do not value. I have already indicated the centrality of value questions for privatization in my comments about its de- and revaluing wealth within a global trend of the same kind. From this point of view, my subject here is the circumstances under which land acquires value—and value of what kind and for whom. What forces come together, and how, to shape the value that land holds, so that people want to manipulate it, invoke it, own it, belong to it, identify with it? What kinds of resources need they have in order to realize the value they attribute to that object? Do they need to control capital, and what kind of capital—money, political position, wide social networks, experience and knowledge, formal education?[22] Such questions are central to my discussion in Part II.

What, indeed, do we mean by *value*? This is a very complex matter over which anthropologists, philosophers, economists, and others have meditated at length. In anthropology it has received its most extensive treatment in the ethnography of exchange (e.g., Appadurai 1986; Mauss 1965; Munn 1986; Strathern 1988; Thomas 1991; Weiner 1992), as well as in the abundant ethnographic literature examining discrepant estimations of value in cross-cultural encounters. The matter of exchange underlies Karl Marx's famous distinction between two kinds of value: use value and exchange value. David Graeber's book on the subject discusses three ways of understanding value—in the sociological sense, as conceptions of the desirable; in the economic sense, as how much something is desired; and in the linguistic sense, as meaningful difference (2001, 1–2). To these he adds others, most of which boil down to meaningfulness in context. This understanding makes values a part of what we often mean by *culture*, seen as not just mental models but practices. However we conceptualize value, the mechanisms that define it are extremely complex.

I use the term in both the meaningfulness and the economic senses, seeking to show how the imposition of certain economic definitions of value on formerly socialist societies after 1989 diminished other conceptions of it. In my view, the creation or definition of value is a process, often highly political: in speaking of values, I mean to point to the process of attributing value to property objects and of struggling to impose one's own definition of it over others. This very process lies at the heart of Eastern Europe's property transformations, as I will show. Sometimes I use *value* in preference to words such as *thing* or *object* because what counts is not the object per se but the value people attribute to it. The values at issue may refer to objects or things such as land, shares in a firm, information, assessments of budgetary worth, or political capital. I also use the word to mean the kinds of priorities around which a social order is organized—for example, the commodity form, or the hierarchy of property types instituted in socialism. As with property, considerations of value often intersect with questions of morality—especially, in postsocialist cases, as people question the morality of increased commodification when monetary values begin to define value *tout court* (see Mandel and Humphrey 2002).

Finally, like Graeber, Nicholas Thomas, Nancy Munn, and others, I see value(s) as a function of context. Economic profit is unlikely to be of interest to someone in a noncapitalist environment, the exchange of slightly grubby armshells and necklaces to someone outside the Trobriand Islands, the location of oil to communities living from solar energy, or the accumulation of followers to a wealthy capitalist. Similarly, cultivators in a small village may care a great deal about the connection that land forges between them and their ancestors, but for managers of firms in town this value is nil. The late twentieth century saw fascinating changes in what was to be considered valuable and made subject to property interests—for example, gene sequences from a kernel of rice in Africa or the chemical composition of some weed in the Amazon jungle, a shift in valuation evident in the shift from *jungle* to *rainforest* as the name for their habitat (Sawyer 2004). Items that had been valueless now became possible assets and the quest for new assets a way of life. Indeed, concern with assets and asset values made huge inroads into the consciousness of many Euro-Americans, daily checking the fortunes of their stocks.[23] Property language penetrated the domain of culture (yielding *cultural property*) and flourished in the complex world of electronic and other new technologies, establishing values and then seeking to lock them into the straitjacket of ownership.

If values have something to do with context, then any alteration in context perforce changes values. The collapse of socialism radically altered contexts—those in which national politicians made policy, those in which their policies might affect the formation of value, and those in which various kinds of actors in local settings tried to strategize their way into an uncertain future by valuing things in new ways. With the fragmentation of the state and the reorganization of the political field, the configuration of interests that might influence policy shifted, affecting who would get values and who junk. In socialism, a central value lay in relations of reciprocity and obligation (see chapter 1); privatization now threatened to individualize these relations, which would change the context for establishing values. The support systems of socialism had somewhat equalized life chances in the name of a radiant future; privatization involved constructing a dark past that must be eliminated, thus removing most of the contexts in which the increasingly dispossessed could find help. They were unlikely to find value in this new context.

As part of this global reorganization of property and valuing, privatization imposed budgetary calculations of value on a system not based on them.[24] The value of socialism's state enterprises had been assessed in completely different terms from those of KPMG or Arthur Andersen. It was not just that a socialist firm's revenues and costs were calculated differently (Dunn 2002); these firms had offered their workers far more than simply a wage, and for people who worked in them these additional offerings were a crucial part of their value. In a detailed presentation of this issue, Catherine Alexander (2004) observes that socialism's factories and farms saw to the manufacture not only of goods but of workers and consumers, providing such services as hostels, polyclinics, day care, vacation spas, perhaps even children's summer camps, sanatoria, and houses of culture (see also Kotkin 1995). Although not every enterprise offered all these services, most of them offered benefits that could not easily be monetized. After 1989, when international accounting firms evaluated the assets of these firms toward privatizing them, those functions were regarded as not assets but liabilities. The discrepancies between different modes of valuing is the subject of other important work, such as that by David Woodruff (1999; n.d.). William Tompson's (1999) title, "The Price of Everything and the Value of Nothing" (concerning Russia's "virtual economy"), nicely captures the result.

The opacity of socialist firms to capitalist accounting was one of several things that led to a kind of valuation roulette, the net effect of which was that the declared sale price of a firm could oscillate wildly over time for no apparent reason. In chapter 7 I present some of the machinations that could affect the assessed value of state farms, processes common to other kinds of state enterprise as well. Other literature has described the processes of asset-stripping and cherry-picking, which had the same end result: a massive devaluation of the wealth accumulated during the socialist period as it was recast into market values that a foreign capitalist or local manager might be willing to pay. Firms that had previously employed thousands and created millions in state revenues might now be sold for the equivalent of an expensive house, leaving their employees astonished and dazed. Time and again my friends in Vlaicu who had been employed in state industry expressed to me their bewilderment that factories capable of producing goods and making money before were now reduced to heaps of scrap metal, employing almost no one. How, they demanded to know, was this possible?

Alongside these complex movements of assets and outright devaluations were many practices designed to snatch assets from the jaws of liability, as one person's write-off became another's source of income. Devaluation and revaluation thus went hand in hand. For example, scrap metal—the rusting metal supports for the guide wires of a hops farm were a liability for whoever wanted to farm the land differently but an asset for laid-off farm workers, who sold the pipes on the international scrap-metal market.[25] The physical destruction of many state assets had this substrate, as factory or farm directors and employees found value in what western accountants judged a liability. Among managerial tactics was to separate assets from liabilities and throw the latter onto someone else, a practice common in turn-of-the-millennium capitalism as well. Stark (1996), for instance, writing of recombinant property, reveals the strategies through which managers of state enterprises in Hungary loaded their state firms with all the liabilities while creating private satellite companies that made off with the assets. Dunn (2004) describes how a multinational firm sought to shed the perceived liabilities of the Polish company it had bought. Thus, central problems for many actors were to discover what was valuable now and how one could get it, what practices were relevant to the valuations newly emerging, and how one could escape from things whose value was now plunging or make such things into assets—what or whom did one have to know and what did one need to have, so as to find value in someone else's liability. I take up this question in chapters 7 and 8.

Accompanying these reassessments of assets and liabilities was much talk of accountability. The idea was to put property rights in the hands of responsible actors, who would use them efficiently or bear the consequences. To monitor this, governments introduced new forms of accounting, replacing socialist accounting practices with French, Anglo-Saxon, or international ones. Peter Miller and Nikolas Rose (1990) argue eloquently for the importance of accounting practices in forming a new governmentality, but in the postsocialist cases they were above all a central means of devaluation. Through them, East Europeans obtaining property rights became subject to processes far beyond their control, whose effect could generate unprecedented risks, devalue their property object, and open them to debt. They were made accountable, for instance, for the government's inability to subsidize agriculture effectively, as do most governments in developed countries, or to adopt appropriate credit arrangements for cultivators; for its removing tariff barriers, to the ruin of local producers; for its ongoing subsidies to nonviable industries so as to reduce unemployment; and so on. In short, creating accountable owners placed all the cost-benefit burdens on people who rarely had the resources to bear them. It drew them into a much wider process in which responsibility and liability are individualized while corporations appropriate the assets and rewards.

In this light, we can understand some of the so-called corruption scandals of postsocialism as practices designed to evade accountability, to protect their perpetrators against the imposition of these budgetary accounting rules, and to aid them in insulating their own domain of values. So-called corruption, Elizabeth

Dunn argues, is a form of protectionism, by which Eastern Europe's insiders help one another to resist the new mechanisms for determining value. The size of the bribe necessary to clinch an insider deal is an index of a firm's value, albeit different from its book value. A bribe establishes value in terms difficult for outsiders to penetrate—through the cultivation of personal connections, "through intimate negotiations, and especially through knowledge of local practices (giving a bribe is a delicate matter which requires knowing not only whom to bribe, but how to deploy cultural values, social statuses, and the etiquette of corruption)" (Dunn in press).

I have been emphasizing the ways in which de- and revaluation involved reassessed monetary worth, but more than just this, they involved the loss of other valued aspects of things. A workplace no longer served additional needs beyond the paycheck. At the same time, certain things acquired new value. Land, for instance, was being returned to its former owners and now acquired a kind of value it had lost with collectivization in the 1930s (for the Soviet Union) and 1950s (for Eastern Europe). As I show in chapter 5, there was a sharp transformation in the value of land in the area of my research. It began as a store of wealth—recipients could not imagine ever selling it—and an embodiment of social relations and status values. Yet this too could fall victim to revaluation, as people increasingly failed in their cultivation plans, for reasons unrelated to their talents. By 2000, land had ceased to be a store of value in both financial and social senses, and some people were selling it. Questions of de- and revaluation form the core of Part II of this book.

By asking about the transformation of value, I place myself in the excellent company of Nancy Munn's *The Fame of Gawa,* centered on precisely that question. Indeed, I find inspiration in her analysis of how Gawans convert their control over valuables into circuits of fame. Unlike Munn, however, who is dealing with noncommodified forms of value, I deal with forms of value that are moving from a noncommodified to a (re)commodified situation. This situation requires, I believe, an account of micropolitics, for people's actions reposition values in a wider matrix of value that is itself changing. Land had one cluster of values before it was collectivized, another after that, and after 1989 yet a third cluster. This is so not only because the societal context in Romania changed each time but because, as I have noted, the value of land has itself been completely transformed in global terms, becoming no longer productive on its own but only by the widespread application of purchased inputs. In this sense, to speak of restitution as restoring people's ownership rights to land is inaccurate—rather, it reshapes the entire field of values in which both persons and land have been positioned.

Usually conceived as a matter of institutional design (to use the expression from Elster, Offe, and Preuss 1998), the reform of socialist property forms participated in a larger project of engineering intended to completely revamp macroinstitutions: the system of political parties, constitution-making, the courts, economic institutions such as the market, and so forth.[26] Institutional design and "making capitalism" tended to focus on policy and rules formed at the top, although there was some recognition that these policies might have unintended consequences when actually implemented. The actors pushing these changes tended to perceive impediments to them in macro-level balances of power or legacies of socialism, rather than in the strategies of ordinary people trying to survive or in the obtuseness of the policy-makers' own conception. What that conception overlooked was that post-1989 change would occur at all levels of society simultaneously; it did not begin with policies initiated from above whose effects would gradually cause people to alter their behavior. People were not waiting for that but were behaving all the time, and in very uncertain circumstances guaranteed to wreak havoc on rational top-down planning.

The assumption behind this social engineering was that by establishing the rules that enable playing the game in some sort of concert, institutions help to create the predictability within which actors can strategize and act. Notably, this assumption rests on another: that the normal state of society is for rules and procedures to be clear, although outcomes may be uncertain. But this is only one way of organizing power in society, a way that sees organization and predictability as "good" power at work. What, however, if people at the top do not want rules and predictability but opacity, to keep others off balance? This is how Jan Gross (1988) understands the "spoiler state" of socialism. Valerie Bunce and Mária Csanádi pose the matter slightly differently; for them, in capitalist democracies rules and procedures are certain and outcomes are uncertain, whereas in socialism it was the other way around—outcomes were certain, and the rules and procedures were not (1993, 266–72). This alternative view of society does not deny that people may seek order and predictability but suggests that the political system or other institutions will not necessarily help them find it—both in socialism and afterward.

In modern farming, for instance, farmers have to find sources of cash to purchase equipment and manufactured inputs such as herbicides, pesticides, growth hormones, and antibiotics. In earlier times, they might have bought a new oxcart with the proceeds from selling a cow that same day and they reused seed for many years; there were no manufactured inputs. Now they must involve themselves with marketing institutions far more complicated than a simple cart ride to the weekly marketplace with their corn. They may have multiple relations with the government, if their product is subsidized, and with the law, which guarantees their property rights or their various contracts. In developed economies, most of these institutional relationships promote predictability.

In postsocialist contexts, however, they often made life ever less predictable, increasing rather than mitigating uncertainty and risk. Government subsidies and bank credits failed to reach their targets, market prices were not free, courts often failed to uphold legitimate property claims, and marketing institutions were nonexistent. The goal of institutional design was to rectify precisely these conditions, but in the meantime people had to figure out their own ways of either avoiding or domesticating the uncertainties they encountered with financial institutions (banks), courts, retailers of inputs of markets for crops, land commissions, and so on. The more of these sources people were vulnerable to, the more complex became their fields of maneuver. Their efforts to survive might not connect, however, with broader institutional arrangements, especially if these were seen as part of the problem and if people's way of reducing uncertainty was therefore to withdraw from them. Daily life rested on constant improvisation, generating routines and networks that could at length produce their own social infrastructure, which would then shape outcomes at the top at least as much as the other way around. The result might be contrary to power-holders' intentions.

In Romania, for example, once the interest rates on bank loans began to gyrate, as is common in inflationary times, villagers who had loans to repay might be forced to reduce their capital stock by selling a cow from their new dairy farm to pay off the loan, so as to remove themselves from that source of unpredictability. People planning to take out loans might either find other ways of financing their large purchases, perhaps through pyramid schemes, or simply not purchase anything; this decision, multiplied by the thousands as smallholders chose to keep away from banks, might then affect what banks could do. Again, if aggrieved parties went to court to contest the status of their land and found themselves repeatedly rescheduled (yet another expensive train fare to court, yet another day taken from other activities), they might cease to show up, leaving yet another set of uncertain property rights unresolved. The experience might diminish their sense that the legal system could serve them impartially—a worrisome outcome for any policy-maker hoping to institutionalize the rule of law.

Finally, as time went on and new smallholders increasingly found themselves incapable of making ends meet, they called on the state to help them. Such demands ran counter to the plans of international organizations to reduce the power of postsocialist states and convinced policy-makers that these populations were prisoners of a socialist mentality. As it happened, however, village farmers understood the situation very clearly: if the state did not help them as western European states help their own farmers, these villagers could not succeed. It was not a socialist mentality that made them a dangerous political force, it was the very workings of the new institutions in unpropitious contexts.

For all these reasons, to understand postsocialist transformation it is crucial to realize the fallacy of the assumption that if institutions are created properly, they will function as planned (see also Kennedy 2002, 9; Lampland 2002, 32, 36). This assumption drove conversations I had during the 1990s with the representatives of international lending organizations, who evidenced no appreciation for local practices or for how people were trying to accomplish what they were used to being able to accomplish.[27] Working only with elites in the newly formed institutions, such foreign observers were then baffled by why these institutions were not taking—why Hungary, for instance, which all considered to have made a successful transition, could reelect the Communist Party, or why financial blockages persisted when market mechanisms were supposedly in place.

To understand postsocialism, then, requires attention to the micro level—the sort of thing anthropology is good at. There we can see more clearly how it is that policies made at the top are subverted or modified, thereby constraining what is possible at the top. In the context of institutional instability, local actors had to find ways of stabilizing their existence that might not accord with those planned in national and international politics. By concentrating on cultural understandings and social relationships at the micro level and by getting inside daily practices through which new property arrangements can take shape, anthropology contributes ways of understanding property change that institutional approaches miss. It also greatly complicates the assessment of costs and benefits that might enter into "rational calculation."

Research Site

My vantage point for investigating all these matters is Aurel Vlaicu (Vlaicu, henceforth), a village of about 820 people in 274 houses, located in Geoagiu commune, Hunedoara county, in the Transylvanian region of Romania (see map 1).[28] I conducted research there throughout the socialist period and returned during the 1990s to explore land reform.[29] During several trips I not only spent time talking and occasionally working with Vlaiceni but also attended court sessions, sat in on land transactions at the county notary, and discussed with judges and notaries the kinds of problems they were encountering. I was present at several events around the attempted sale of some state farms, and I

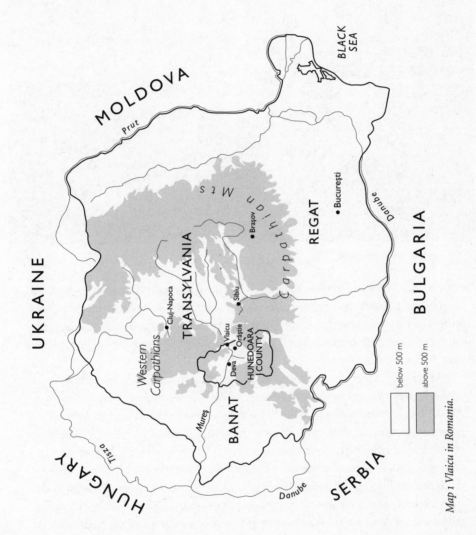

Map 1 Vlaicu in Romania.

The author doing fieldwork.

interviewed officials in Geoagiu and in all the main institutions with which villagers had contact (the Agricultural Bank, state grain procurement center, suppliers of plowing services, county land registration offices, and so on). I supplemented these data with statistical information from the Ministry of Agriculture and other, published sources.

This study is therefore largely a village study, although one that follows wider connections throughout. Anthropologists repeatedly run up against the objection, "But is your village typical? What can we learn about the global process of privatization from your one village?" In other words, "So what?"[30] There are several responses to this question. One is that there is no global process of privatization, only specific instances of it, and that following any instance provides insight into how the abstract idea of privatization might occur. Another is that there is no typical village—all have their peculiarities, and to describe those is to show a point on a broad continuum of possible outcomes of the national legislation that broke up socialist agricultural forms. It is precisely in local settings that we see how people negotiated their way through the tremendous challenge this legislation set them. The idea is not to use the local as an illustration of larger forces but to show which issues these rural cultivators (as opposed to elites) confronted and how they tried to reshape their worlds, so unexpectedly gone awry (see also Kideckel 1995a, 2).

A third response to the "So what?" question is that it is misleading to ask whether the findings from a single village are typical or generalizable. What counts, rather, is the analytic framework in terms of which its story is told so as to make its significances apparent. What kinds of things do we want to know or think about in order to grasp the privatization process? What construal of these processes best makes sense of what the people involved in it saw as important, while also making some kind of sense in our own analytic terms? Therefore, readers should take from my account a set of principles or variables useful for thinking about property reform, a way of putting data together. This does not mean forgetting the data themselves, for such an approach works only if I offer sufficient data to persuade readers that my conception of the process does make sense. The particulars matter because, organized in a given way, they provide a dense texture of the processes taking place, one that throws up questions not imagined by those whose data lie at a much higher level of aggregation. For these three reasons, then, I do not worry about whether or not what I describe for Vlaicu is typical or generalizable; I worry whether it is both persuasive and productive of further questions.

❧

I organize the book around the theme of value in thinking about property. Creating property rights was one thing, creating effective ownership another. Finding value in land would come from the ability to put together all the necessary production factors. In Part I, I discuss the socialist and postsocialist environments in which private property rights were made, and in Part II the attempts of various groups to make satisfactory use of them. Chapter 1 sets out the property order of socialism, with its emphasis on rights in people and the hierarchy of values in socialist agriculture. In chapter 2 I describe how Eastern European governments using private property as a symbol crafted policies for creating it. Chapter 3 shows how decollectivization took place in Vlaicu and how the situations of commune authorities permitted their subverting central designs, finding value in land as a source of political capital. Meanwhile, village elites who valued it differently subverted other aspects of central politics, by denying land to the landless. Chapter 4 assesses the major changes in village social relations as a result of decollectivizing and asks what land meant to the smallholders who received it.

In Part II, I disaggregate the units spun off from socialist agriculture and pursue each in a separate chapter. Chapter 5 treats former collective farm households, arguing that whatever the government's intentions, smallholders' inability to bring production factors together limited the forms of value they could realize. Chapter 6 turns to the collective farm infrastructure, which became a cooperative association. I describe its function and its failure, which I attribute in part to the place of collectives in the hierarchy of values in socialism, as well as to villagers' lack of trust in it. Chapters 7 and 8 show how state farms could lose their economic value while enabling their managers to strategize toward potentially viable farming as tenants of the rentier smallholders. In all these chapters, we can see hectares vanishing—as diminutions of people's expected allotments, as false entries on property deeds, as reduced sites of personhood and economic value, and as diminished grounds for the experience of locality.

As is clear from my lengthy catalog of themes, this book—like property itself—is about everything: power, practices, institutions, land, the transformation of value, social relations, privatization, class formation, and so on. In short, it is about the adventures of a concept, property, moving from one context to an entirely different one. It is about how local practices interact with political processes at higher levels—that is, its actors are not just elites but the people whose lives those elites attempt to shape in particular directions. It is about possession and dispossession, accumulation and disaccumulation, as ownership by "the whole people" gave way to ownership by village households.

PART I
MAKING, UNMAKING, AND REMAKING OWNERS

To grasp transformational processes in Vlaicu since 1989, we must situate the village in the various fields that shape the experience of its inhabitants. If Vlaicu is not typical, how does it differ from other villages around it? What distinguishes the county (Hunedoara) and region (Transylvania) in which it lies from Romania's other counties and regions?

One thing that does *not* distinguish it is that, like many other Romanian villagers, Vlaiceni have long been influenced by international forces both in the past (what, if not international influence, was the entire communist system!) and in the 1990s. Indeed, I think of Vlaicu as a "world village," so extensive have been its international connections. These are people used to talking with U.S. anthropologists and to watching *Columbo* and *Dallas*—which they did assiduously throughout the 1970s and 1980s—and since then *Santa Barbara,* along with soap operas from Latin America and films from many other countries. Emigration and marriages abroad have created multiple ties linking Vlaiceni with kin not only across Romania but farther afield in Germany, France, Spain, Italy, and the United States. Other contacts made after 1990 took a few of them on visits into Western Europe, where they saw what prosperous small farms might look like and were stimulated to attempt something similar at home.

Vlaicu in Transylvania

The most significant element of Vlaicu's specificity is its location in Transylvania, rather than in the southern and eastern regions of Romania, known jointly as the Romanian Kingdom, or Regat (kingdom). For land restitution, this made a difference so substantial as to determine the title of this book—

"in Transylvania" rather than "in Romania." Of what did this difference consist?

To begin with, Transylvania had been part of the medieval Hungarian Kingdom and thence the Habsburg Empire, whereas the other regions were Ottoman dependencies until the mid- to late 1800s. Thus, historically Transylvania had large populations of Hungarians and Germans, whereas the Regat lacked these national minorities. Romania's Germans, who numbered about 350,000 at the end of World War II, had their lands confiscated and given to Romanians in a 1945 land reform; in some biethnic villages, the consequence after 1990 was dual land claims, as both the German owner and the Romanian family subsequently settled on the land sought to get it back. In short, Transylvania's land restitution was more likely to be complicated by ethnonational issues than was true elsewhere in Romania.

Second, the landforms and climate of Transylvania differ significantly from those of the Regat. Transylvania proper is a plateau with substantial forests and an accidented terrain, some of it unsuitable for mechanization, whereas much of the Regat is flat grainland adjacent to the Danube River. In consequence, more Transylvanian villages remained uncollectivized, and complex relations between people in the collectivizing and uncollectivized zones complicated the process of restitution there in ways less common in the Regat. Central Transylvania's population density per arable hectare is higher—3.3 people per arable hectare, as against 2.0 for the Regat—and its agrarian economy rests more on raising livestock than on grain-farming.[1] Its farms are more like the continental European pattern of mixed grain and livestock farms, while the south, east, and west of the country specialize in extensive cereal-growing on immense latifundia. Transylvania's collective and state farms tended to be smaller than in the Regat (see table 6.3, in chapter 6), and its poorer soils required heavier capital investments. In consequence, the agrarian elite of collective and state farm managers was much more powerful in the Regat, the amounts of land to be taken over more substantial, and the possibilities for wealth from agriculture much greater—all of which augmented the likelihood that after 1989 powerful agrarian elites in the Regat would find ways to usurp smallholders' rightful share, an outcome less likely in Transylvania.

Furthering that tendency were two other very significant differences between the two regions: the history of smallholding and the form of land registration. From these two factors come the major reasons why a study of decollectivizing in a Transylvanian village cannot be taken as typical for all of Romania but only as representing a more limited set of processes. If we imagine that people are more likely to fight for their land where long-term family ownership has instilled a property mentality or ownership habitus, then Transylvanian villagers are more likely than Regățeni to have had one. In 1848 serfdom was abolished in the Habsburg realm (which included Transylvania) and ownership rights to the land were given to a large group of serfs on feudal estates; these joined an already existing stratum of free Romanian peasants who held land in the German areas. Others who received no land at the time or were not effectively emancipated could buy their way out of servitude and into proprietorship, although that was not easy to do (see Verdery 1983, chap. 2). From the mid-19th century, then, we find an emergent class of Transylvanian peasant owners, while high population densities compelled most others there to struggle for ownership as well (which many did by temporary emigration to the United States).

In the Regat, however, the situation was otherwise. Some villagers in the Carpathian foothills had remained free of feudal relations, often living under a communal regime rather than as individual proprietors (see Stahl 1958–65). The rest of the peasantry had endured a form of serfdom less burdensome than that in Transylvania, but the emancipation in 1864 left many peasants still in relations of dependence on large Regat estates rather than making them owners (see also Lampland 1995). Most of them did not become full owners until the land reform that followed World War I, in which over 6 million hectares, or one-third of Romania's agricultural surface, was taken from large owners and some 3.9 million of them distributed to cultivators.[2] Because that reform was not completed until 1930 or later, when collectivization occurred in the 1950s many Regat families had been owners for barely three decades.

Here is where the other significant factor—forms of land registration—comes in. Systems for registering land ownership vary and are not always homogeneous even within a given country; such is the case in Romania, reflecting the different histories I have mentioned. When Transylvania became part of Romania in 1918, its registration system was left intact despite major contrasts with the system in place in the Regat. I call the two titling arrangements the Transylvanian and Regat systems.[3] Fascinating as the intricacies of these systems are, I limit myself to their implications for tracing landownership in post-1991 restitution claims. Transylvania used the Habsburg land registry system based on numbered plots corresponding to a map, each parcel having its own file; entering a transaction into the land register's multiple dossiers constituted title, and the history of ownership was fairly easy to trace. This registry system thus guaranteed the property right, although it made the circulation of land more cumbersome. By contrast, the system used in the Regat consisted of a single large register into which each day's transactions were entered as they occurred; the entry numbers did not correspond to sites on a map. This facilitated the free circulation of land but it complicated ownership, because the status of the person who claimed the right to sell a piece of land was not verified with each transaction, as it was in Transylvania. The Regat system makes it much easier to assert false ownership. Obviously, the two systems have major implications for the kinds of proof they offered to those seeking to reclaim land in the 1990s. The Transylvanian system enabled proofs the other did not, but it also generated a more protracted restitution process, often involving the courts.

❧

To these peculiarities resulting from Vlaicu's Transylvanian location we can add others relating to the county in which it lies, Hunedoara. The most important facts about it are its mountainous terrain and its high level of industrial development compared with most other counties in Romania. The terrain predisposed it to extensive coal-mining and the associated steel industry—the steel complex in Hunedoara city was one of Romania's largest—and also accentuated the Transylvanian pattern of livestock farming over grains. Because Hunedoara's high industrialization drew large numbers of people into well-paid factory work, labor shortages in agriculture was more likely there, and this weakened its collective farms. Finally, the county's terrain also meant that an even larger proportion of its villages than usual was uncollectivized. During the communist period, Hunedoara had Romania's highest percentage of agricultural land in private ownership—fully 41 percent, against a national average of 9.5 percent (Rizov et al. 2001, 1259). In consequence, its collective farmers were in frequent contact with numerous uncollectivized ones, the latter keeping alive the habits of private property cheek by jowl with the former.

All these facts meant that after 1991, less of the county's total surface had to be restored to former owners in villages such as Vlaicu, but a larger percentage of its labor force became vulnerable to unemployment from industrial restructuring. Those unemployed workers found themselves pushed back into at least temporary reliance on land, and this perhaps made them especially eager to secure their rights to it. That Transylvania and especially Hunedoara were well suited to small-scale mixed farming of grain and livestock made it feasible for people to get by on the small patches of land they received after 1989. Overall, because most state investment in Hunedoara went to industry, its collective and state farms were less successful than those in the predominantly agrarian counties on which the regime depended for the food supply. Hunedoarans were therefore more likely to press for the complete dissolution of their collectives, which had offered them rather little (see Swain 1999). In sum, then, Vlaicu's inclusion in Hunedoara county affected its collective farm and land use under socialism in ways that suggest a more fraught process of land reform in that vil-

lage than might be true in areas where agriculture had provided a better livelihood before 1989.[4]

Vlaicu among Its Neighbors

Vlaicu's Transylvanian and Hunedoara locations lend it certain peculiarities;
others come from its own characteristics among surrounding villages. It differs
from those first of all by the reason for its name: its native son Aurel Vlaicu is
among Romania's most famous twentieth-century heroes, and no neighboring
village had anyone like him (see Verdery 1983, 226–27). Ever since his death in
1913, native villagers have taken great pride in him and, according to their crit-
ics, have acted as if they too partook of his genius. Vlaicu also differs from most
nearby villages in having a minority of Germans, who formed about 20 percent
of the village in 1910, 15 percent in 1948, and 10 percent in 1973.[5] When they had
arrived as colonists in the 1890s, they had had much better agricultural technology than Romanian villagers. During the 1970s Vlaiceni readily acknowledged
to me that they had learned improved farming methods from the Germans and
that this was one reason why Vlaicu was a comparatively wealthy village. Combined with their pride in being the home of Aurel Vlaicu, this sense of themselves as a rich village with better farming technology gave Vlaiceni the reputation of being haughtier and more arrogant than other villagers in the region (a
reputation I did not find justified).

Vlaicu is a lowland village among other lowland villages, lying next to hill
villages. Like many other villages in Hunedoara, not all its neighboring villages
were collectivized—in particular, nearby Homorod across the Mureş,
renowned for its ţuica (plum brandy) (see Verdery 1994, 1079, 1083). Because
Vlaicu shares borders with a number of collectivized communities—Gelmar,
Şibot, Băcăinţi, Vinerea, Pişchinţi, and Vaidei (see map 2)—and because collectivized villages had often exchanged land, the borders among all these settlements were problematic. Another peculiarity is the large number of state farms
in Vlaicu's perimeter—five—probably owing to the fertility of the Mureş valley
in an otherwise hilly region and to Hunedoara's numerous industrial workers,
who had to be fed. In all of Romania in 1990 there were only 411 state farms,
about one-quarter of them in Transylvania with its 4,700 villages; this makes
Vlaicu with its five state farms highly unusual. They complicated restitution in
Vlaicu because state farms were not initially dismantled, as collectives were.

An important fact about all these villages is that they are divided among four
different local administrative units (communes)—Geoagiu, Romos, Cugir, and
Şibot—and two different counties—Hunedoara and Alba. One of Vlaicu's state

Map 2 Vlaicu among neighboring settlements.

farms actually sits astride the county line, and three of them overflow into other communes. No other village in the area has this administratively complex a location, and this fact caused tremendous headaches both for those implementing the land reform and for those trying to obtain land, as well as for would-be foreign buyers interested in taking over the state farms that straddled village and county boundaries.

Because Vlaicu lies on both the highway and the railway, like Şibot but unlike others such as Geoagiu, Gelmar, or Vaidei, it was a prime location for people wanting to work in Hunedoara's growing industries. With a maximum 15–minute walk one can reach buses or trains (or catch a ride with a passing truck) headed for one of four industrializing towns: Cugir (25 km distant), Orăştie (9 km), Deva (35 km), and Hunedoara city (40 km). Not only did a large percentage of Vlaicu's labor force commute to these jobs (52 percent, in 1973), but the village was a particularly attractive spot for would-be factory workers from the poorer hill villages. Industrial jobs gave them generous pensions, which proved crucial after decollectivization. The influx of these migrants brought extra labor to the collectives of Vlaicu and other villages on transport lines, but with the collectives' end came severe problems because the migrants claimed a share of the land too, even though they had not owned any previously. Vlaicu had far more such problems than did most of its neighbors.

Because it is so complex a place, Vlaicu offers the perfect spot for gaining insight into privatization, a process that was itself of the utmost complexity. I have suggested earlier that this process does not exist in the abstract, only in specific cases. What I have said about Vlaicu, however, makes clear that a specific case is not limited to the physical space of one community but spreads out into courts, banks, the parliament in Bucharest, the IMF in Washington, D.C., and so forth. Vlaicu is a site at which numerous linkages, processes, and institutions intersected to produce the dismantling of socialist landed property. Yet within the physical space of this one community we see the effects of those intersections on people's daily lives—the conflicts among co-villagers, neighbors, and kin; the dispossessions and consolidations; the joy of those repossessing family land and the rancor of those excluded from it; and the efforts to cultivate it in unpropitious circumstances. That is decollectivization.

CHAPTER 1
PROPERTY IN SOCIALISM
COLLECTIVIZATION, ADMINISTRATIVE RIGHTS, AND THE CIRCULATION OF GOODS

> The theory of the Communists may be summed up in the single sentence: Abolition of private property.
> *(Marx and Engels 1968, 35)*

> [T]he socialist economies of Eastern Europe did not have *any* property system . . . governing their productive activities. It is not surprising, therefore, that in all East European countries it is nearly impossible to answer the question of who owns what in the state enterprises: the legal determination of ownership was simply irrelevant under the old system, which relied instead on directly prescribing the conduct of factory officials.
> *(Frydman and Rapaczynski 1994, 11)*

> Ownership is the back-bone of the economic system of Socialist countries.
> *(Knapp 1975, 64)*

"Property," Proudhon wrote, famously, "is theft." Among those agreeing with that opinion were Karl Marx and Friedrich Engels, who placed the rectification of this injury at the heart of their communist program. From there it ultimately justified what might qualify as the greatest theft in history: the nationalization of assets in the Soviet Union, including all its land, which was turned into collective and state farms. Variants of the same process were carried out later in the satellite countries of Eastern Europe, although they did not nationalize land fully. This theft occurred in the name not of Proudhon's bourgeois capitalists but of "the whole people," the new kind of owner that communist parties brought into being. They strove to create a new mechanism for appropriating the products of people's work in the name of redistributing that product equitably, as capitalism had not.

In Romania (as in most of Eastern Europe), private property was not abolished outright with the communist takeover, even though expropriations as early as 1945 made it clear that private property was no longer sacrosanct.[1] Right up through 1990, the property provisions of Romania's Civil Code of 1864 remained in force (Firoiu 1976, 359–60). Article 480 of that code, however, affirmed its property rights only *within the limits set by law*. Over the next several decades, new laws and decrees made these limits ever more stringent. Land, for example, could no longer be sold and was inheritable only in uncollectivized areas; the size of the courtyard left to house-owners gradually shrank from 1,000 to 250 square meters. Likewise constrained was producers' freedom to dispose of the produce from their small plots—that is, their right to appropriate their own product.

Property remained important—the word occurs throughout party documents—but now it was socialist property that counted. This socialist property instituted a wholly new system of values, beginning with the eradication of bourgeois property. Instrumental in creating the identity of socialist states, the construct *socialist property* announced that property was indeed important and these party-states were doing it differently. Among the values this order established were that property was made an administrative rather than a legal matter, and that different kinds of owners—the state, cooperatives, and individuals—formed a hierarchy, with the state privileged as owner over all others.

For the builders of socialism, land in particular was valuable for several reasons. Socializing it would facilitate plans for rapid industrial growth by (1) seizing a major means of production and transferring its surplus directly into industrialization; (2) controlling the rural population, the food supply, and thereby the price of food; and (3) creating a proletariat for industrial work. A closer look at the fate of land in socialism shows us some processes by which socialist property was made and lays the groundwork for subsequent chapters.

Collectivizing Land

Land initially became socialist property by one of two means: nationalizations/confiscations, and collectivization. Across the region, once the communists took power they began confiscating the land of certain individuals deemed "enemies of the people," including political prisoners, wealthy landowners, and those considered war criminals. Many of the owners were deported or sent to labor camps; in this way, the state came rather quickly into possession of sizable amounts of land. Collectivization, by contrast, was a much more protracted and arduous process, ostensibly voluntary, that occurred in several waves. It began in most East European countries as early as 1948 but was pushed through to completion only in the early 1960s (in Romania, 1962). In its most benign form, it occurred through sentences phrased in the future tense, having imperative force:

When they enter the collective farm,[a] members will bring into the farm's patrimony all their land.

The boundary paths separating parcels will be abolished, the land being consolidated into one or a few large masses.

The terrain of the farm will be divided into fields according to the rotation adopted and will be worked in common by the farm members.[2]

The illocutionary effect of these decrees was to create a new property form, and implementing their provisions would confound the restitution process later.

There was little room for negotiation in the decision to join. Here are some brief excerpts from Vlaicu villagers, recalling the experience (my interventions are in parentheses).[3]

M.G. (male, born 1924):

Collectivization actually began in 1945, when the Russians took over. In 1946 the authorities began to make a preliminary cooperative. After a while they came to get our family to sign up, but we didn't want to. Then they assigned us huge grain requisitions, so big we couldn't meet them, but we still didn't sign up. In '53, they confiscated everything we'd grown, and again in '56. In '58–59 right after New Year, they began taking people (I was one) to the Secret Police in Cugir, and they beat us. They took people from [neighboring villages], about forty of us—those who owned the most land. Our family had 8 ha. They beat us and told us they have to make a big farm and we should sign up. I said, "I can't, the land belongs to my father-in-law." We signed up only at the end. They took our cattle, they took our cart, they took our horses. We signed that we gave these "of our own free will" but it wasn't true. In one week almost the whole village signed up. (How did they convince you to join?) We had no choice! There was a huge tax, and they exchanged people's land for parcels 20, 30, 40 km away, on the hillside. Mine was exchanged too—they took my field in the Plain and gave me one in the Swamp.[b]

The cadres who made the collective told us, "The land belongs to all of you!" But the harvest? Who did *that* belong to! They told us, "Give us your land, and you'll get the harvest." But it wasn't like that.

U.V. (widow, b. 1935, family had ca. 7 ha at collectivization):

a. Although in some languages of the region (including Romanian) the word used is *cooperative* farm, I prefer *collective* farm, which is more widely used in English and carries connotations more appropriate than does the word *cooperative*.

b. These are local field names. They show that because he would not sign up, he lost his best land and received poor land in exchange.

We were among the first to sign up, because my father had been a prisoner in Russia and knew collectivization was inevitable if we ended up on the Russians' side. No one would believe him when he said we would have a *kolkhoz*.[c] When they started with the requisitions, he said this was how collectivization started in Russia. We had two cows and the collective took one. They'd take it to pasture, and on the way back it would try to come home, into our courtyard, and it would bellow outside the gate—my mother-in-law stood at the entry, crying after it.

There was a big communist, Bera. He worked for the railway and had come here from the north; he was really poor. People like this—miners, railway workers, people who had nothing—they made the Party. Bera would say, "If I haven't got anything, others shouldn't either. Everyone should have the same." There was another communist, Todor, who married here from Blandiana. One day he came to make my father join the Party. My father locked himself inside the house, and Todor tried to break down the door. But my father had an axe and shouted to Todor that if he broke in he'd kill him with it. Todor left.

I.B. (male, b. 1925, ca. 6 ha):

What really got to me was the petition:[d]"*Please* accept me into the collective." That was just too much. When I saw it, I said "Never!" I went into hiding. From the loft I could hear the parade—they were inaugurating the collective! But we weren't in it yet. We'd been forced to exchange some of our land with people who had joined. My father never signed up; he was in the hospital, sick, and he said, "I worked so hard for this land! I just can't do it." Though they got me to sign up, he stayed out for two more years, until finally he told me to sign for him because he couldn't do it himself. So I signed. (How did you feel about it?) Terrible! We cried until our blood vessels burst. Your whole life's work! None of it was left. *Everyone* in this house cried until we had no more tears.

Except for Poland and Yugoslavia, which renounced collectivization early, we could elicit stories of this kind from thousands of villages in Romania and

---

c. The Russian term for collective farm.

d. To join the collective one had to write a petition [*cerere*], one variant of which read as follows: "I the undersigned _____ and my family request that we please be accepted into the collective, with the following surface areas. . . ."

other East European countries. The events they report occurred in countless places, as local authorities sought to compel villagers to "donate" their land by arresting, beating, or even killing them; by deporting people from their homes to some distant place, often for no clear reason; by huge requisitions and taxes beyond people's ability to pay; by confiscating some land to smoothe the way for further donations; and by repeated harassing and fines. Villagers bearing old grudges denounced others, bringing them hardship and ruin; authorities used kin to apply pressure, threatening to throw one's child out of school or factory work if one did not join. Especially vulnerable to humiliation were the most influential villagers, those tied in to wide networks of kin or those whose wealth or occupation made them employ others' labor. Labeled *chiaburi*, or exploiters (the *kulaks* of Soviet collectivization), they were assigned impossible quotas or tasks—to plow their entire ten hectares in a single day, for instance—being imprisoned if they failed. Along with these accounts one also heard of occasional acts of resistance, much more substantial than anything that happened in Vlaicu. There, cadres had waited until very late in the campaign, expecting resistance; villagers had had time to get used to the idea and to know that resistance would be futile, so collectivization was accomplished more easily than in other settlements. Many of Romania's villagers were far less fortunate.

Lacking the space for a full account of collectivization—a subject worth several books—I will briefly recapitulate some of the differences among the socialist countries in how collectivization proceeded and then continue my account of how socialist property worked.[4] With collectivization, the early architects of Soviet socialism hoped to bring into being a new property order; their clients in Eastern Europe emulated it to at least some extent after 1945. Instituting it, however, required imposing a novel set of forms on populations that were not just exceedingly recalcitrant but very diverse, their social relations and property conceptions varying greatly from one country to another. In some parts of Russia, for instance, much of the land had been held not in full private ownership but jointly by the whole community, the *mir*. Only with the Stolypin reforms of 1906–7 had peasant landowning become more widespread, but when collectivization began in 1929, ownership had not yet sunk deep roots. The collectivization drive therefore encountered a peasantry for whom the idea of communal ownership and management was part of recent memory.[5] Not so in most of Eastern Europe, dominated by either peasant smallholding or large landless populations dependent on postfeudal estates. Also variable was the proportion of small to large owners; for instance, in Bulgaria and Romania in the 1930s, 89 and 92 percent of all land, respectively, was held in farms of *under* 10 ha, whereas in Hungary in 1935, 81 percent of the agricultural surface was held in farms of *over* 10 ha.[6]

These differences, in turn, related to prior differences in the extent of pre-communist land reforms (see Verdery 2001). In Romania, for example, collectivization was not the first land reform but the fourth. The first one, accompanying the end of feudal relations in the mid-nineteenth century, produced some peasant smallholding in Transylvania. The second and most extensive followed World War I; it distributed to peasants 3.9 million hectares, one-fifth of the country's cultivated surface, leaving only 8 percent of the surface in farms of over 10 ha.[7] In 1945 there was yet another reform, in which 1.4 million ha were expropriated and 1 million distributed (Roberts 1951, 374–75). Then in the 1950s came the fourth reform, collectivization, which dispossessed all who had received land in the previous ones. Thus, Romania's 1991 decollectivization—its fifth reform—had a venerable line of precedents.

The Romanian pattern of land reform was not, however, common in the region. Hungary, Albania, eastern Germany, and Poland[8] had no significant reform until 1945 or later. Those reforms broke up and redistributed huge surfaces—in Hungary, fully 64 percent of all agricultural land, and in Poland 50 percent (Swinnen, Buckwell, and Mathijs 1997). Czechoslovakia legislated an extensive reform after World War I but because its implementation was spread out over thirty years, its effects were not felt until the mid-1930s. Those five countries therefore lacked a substantial peasantry long accustomed to owning land—the kind of peasantry found in Transylvania. Bulgaria diverges from all these cases because its property structure even before World War I was already so egalitarian that subsequent reforms changed proprietorship very little. These differences influenced the course of collectivization.

Partly on account of these reforms and partly because of prior economic development, East European countries differed in the numbers of people collectivization affected. In southeastern Europe and Poland, the percentage of the population employed in agriculture was much higher than in the northwest. For instance, in the late 1940s, 74 percent of the population in Romania and Bulgaria was employed in agriculture, 57 percent in Poland and 53 percent in Hungary, but only 38 percent in Czechoslovakia and 29 percent in eastern Germany.[9] Thus, in the first two countries, collectivization involved a much higher proportion of the citizenry than in the last two. And, as a result, post-1989 decollectivization involved far more people in Romania and Bulgaria than in Hungary or the Czech Republic.

Countries differed, as well, in the manner and speed of collectivizing (see Pryor 1992, chap. 4). It proceeded in fits and starts, some communist parties abandoning it altogether, others slacking off only to resume later. Because all party leaders in the region knew how disastrous collectivization had been in the Soviet Union—with terrible violence, humanmade famines, millions of people killed outright or dying from forced labor in Siberia, and so on—they adopted methods that were less extreme. In Romania, owing to sharp conflict among the top party leaders as to whether and how to collectivize (Levy 2001), the campaign went slowly at first. By 1952 less land was collectivized there than in any other East European country: 3.1 percent, compared with 3.5 percent in Poland, 8.1 percent in Hungary, 19 percent in Czechoslovakia, and 51 percent in Bulgaria (Cătănuş and Roske 2000, 31). As of 1957, however, the Romanian leadership determined to conclude the process, declaring it officially closed in 1962. Except for Poland and Yugoslavia, other countries completed it around the same time.

In sum, the variations among East European party-states and their differences from the Soviet Union precluded their being strict copies of the Soviet blueprint—itself unrealizable even in the Soviet context. None of these regimes was fully capable of overturning property relations on so vast a scale. Thus, making socialist property in agriculture was a protracted process of struggle, attempted imposition, and modification of the rules, all occurring within a field of existing relationships. What emerged from the process everywhere was that the tie between peasant households and their land was broken; kinsmen and co-villagers had been used against one another, rupturing earlier solidarities; the influential members in each village had been humiliated and dispossessed; the former poor now held political advantage; and land was no longer the main store of wealth or the means for villagers to manifest their character, skill, or diligence.

At the same time, from the Party's point of view, collectivization had established mechanisms for the reliable seizure of grain. In James Scott's assessment, despite the failure of many of the aims of Soviet collectivization its achievement was "to take a social and economic terrain singularly unfavorable to appropriation and control and to create institutional forms and production units far better adapted to monitoring, managing, appropriating, and controlling from above" (1998, 203). Collectivization did not just transform property rights as an instrument of appropriation; it superseded them, putting in their place a system of appropriation based in administrative methods. Yet it still insisted on the importance of property for doing so.

In the remainder of this chapter I describe the workings of the property system in which the organizational forms created for agriculture (state and collective farms) were embedded. I argue that within the hierarchy of property types, the main administrative mechanism created to manage socialist property—the allocation of administrative rights—worked only through a complex system of informal exchanges and reciprocity. That system of exchange enabled managers to procure what they needed for production and to deliver goods for their central plan, but it also required their appropriating vast quantities of the product to exchange with other bureaucrats. This set them at odds with the people at the bottom of the food chain, the collective farm peasantry, who engaged in constant struggle to appropriate some of that product for themselves.

The Organization of Socialist Property

I begin with a schematic discussion of how property in socialism was organized, outlining some of the basic rules of property in socialism and then describing the social processes that went on by means of and often in spite of them. Although my initial outline applies to both industrial and agricultural production, I draw my examples of social process from Romanian agriculture.

Even to speak of *socialist property* already oversimplifies, homogenizing a reality that was much more complex and varied across both space and time, with several parallel property arrangements coexisting at any given moment. Some Eastern European regimes were more willing than others to depart from canonical forms of socialist ownership. Hann's studies of property relations in the Hungarian village of Tázlár and in Polish Wisłok, for example, illustrate the point.[10] In addition to noting such cross-national differences, we ought as well to track modifications in the theory and practice of socialist property over time—for example, in his analysis of socialist political economy, János Kornai (1992) insists on distinguishing two periods, the classic system and its reform variants. The example of China after 1978 shows how thoroughly a socialist regime might diversify its property relations while still calling itself socialist or communist. Unfortunately, I cannot do justice to these complexities and variations here and must offer a fairly schematic account, aimed at clarifying how new property forms might be made from the property relations of socialism. The picture I present is more coherent than were the actual processes, and my discussion understates the proliferation of proprietary claims.

Rather than limiting myself to the questions of ownership that Frydman and Rapaczynski emphasize in the second chapter epigraph, I follow Bronislaw Malinowski's dictum and ask how socialism's resources were used (Malinowski 1935, 323). This strategy enables me to examine socialist property in something like its own terms, instead of as a failed form of western property. Toward this end, which I believe is the best path toward understanding privatization, I emphasize the strangeness of property in socialism, suggesting analogies from anthropological literature on Africa rather than drawing on the more obvious similarities of socialist property to capitalist theory and practice (such as the shared connections among property, work, and entitlement). I do this to render socialist property more visible than it would be if we compared it with property in market societies. Nonetheless, I do not want readers to see in my procedure a brief for capitalist private property, as something both familiar and natural, superior to the "primitive" forms of property in socialism. Precisely this assumption on the part of privatization's architects—that with appropriate intervention, private property will naturally spring forth from the ashes of socialism—is what the evidence of the 1990s seems to refute.

I have already discussed in my introductory chapter how I understand the notion of *property*: as simultaneously a cultural system, an organization of power, and sets of social relations, all coming together in social processes. Using this framework, I look first at the categories socialist systems created for property. What kinds of property subjects did they posit, and what kinds of objects? Second, I consider it as an organization of power and social relations. How did a system based in ownership by the whole people break that entity down into smaller ones interacting with one another to make property rights effective? Through what social processes did interrelating actors animate the property regime, making its rigid constructs workable? Here I turn specifically to the socialist treatment of land and bring in material from my research in Romania.

Socialist Property as a Cultural System and Organization of Power

Although Marx is not generally the best authority for "actually existing socialism," I might invoke a sentence from the *Communist Manifesto* to justify my inquiry into socialist property: "The distinguishing feature of communism is not the abolition of property generally, but the abolition of bourgeois property" (Marx and Engels 1968, 34–35). Property relations, in the self-conception of communist parties, were crucial to distinguishing socialism from capitalism.[11] As a result, socialist societies institutionalized the construct *ownership* at their very heart, naming principal actors and specifying these in clear relation to property. For example, article 10 of the 1977 Soviet Constitution states, "Socialist ownership of the means of production . . . constitutes the foundation of the economic system of the USSR" (cited in Feldbrugge 1993, 230). Likewise, from a Romanian law textbook: "Socialist property constitutes the foundation of our national economy, the fundament of all socialist social relations and the indispensable condition for constructing a multilaterally developed socialist society" (Lupan and Reghini 1977, 11). Soviet and East European textbooks in civil law gave considerable space to forms of socialist property.

We should exercise care in reading these texts, for law did not occupy the same place in socialist societies as in western ones, and property was no exception. Property in socialism was more an administrative than a legal issue; it was governed by administrative measures rather than by legal procedures aimed at creating regularity and certainty. Although laws relevant to property were indeed made, more important were decrees and administrative procedures, re-garded as having the force of law but not created through a legislative process backed by courts. The archives of the 1950s, for example, are full of documents recording the donation of a piece of land or exchanges of one piece for another, such documents attesting to the regime's determination to keep track of the ownership status of those pieces.[12] In no society do formal laws tell us what is actually going on, but the gap was especially wide in socialism. We might say that an administrative decree acquired the force of law and was applied as such,[13] although perhaps it is preferable simply to call the party-state a fiat state rather than translating it into the terms of law.

This said, however, it is worth inspecting the law because the categories em-ployed in a society's laws help to reveal its conceptual foundations, giving a sense of its universe of both power and meaning, as well as of how these differ from those of other property regimes. Socialist legal categories begin with an expected definition of *property*[14] as a historically determined social relation connecting people with material goods, especially means of production (Lupan and Reghini 1977, 12). To specify this requires identifying objects of property (means of production, items of consumption); kinds of property relation (ownership, control, use); and potential subjects of these relations (the state, cooperatives, individuals, etc.).[15]

Western economic and legal systems divide property into types such as real and personal property, tangible and intangible property, and state, commons, and private property. Socialist property categories, by contrast, emphasized a different set of property types based on the identity of the owners and the social relations among them (Heller 1998, 628). Socialist law recognized four property types relating to three main property subjects (three types of owner/actors): (1) the state (technically the whole people in whose name the state acted), (2) so-cialist cooperatives together with other nonproducing socialist organizations, and (3) individuals or households.[16] (We might contrast this set of recognized actors with others that could conceivably be recognized as property subjects but, in these societies, were not, such as lineages, clans, sovereigns, and corpo-rations.[17]) These three actors were distinguished from other possible actors in that they alone were empowered to own, unlike actors such as ministries and commissions, individual state-owned enterprises (SOEs), or central, regional, and local administrations.

Significantly, these three actors were defined as jural subjects precisely by their property status; that is, they were made real actors by being made subjects of property. As W. E. Butler puts it (speaking of the Soviet Union), "Juridical persons are those organizations which possess separate property, [and] may ac-quire property and personal non-property rights and bear duties in their own name" (1988, 179). Thus, jural personhood was a function of property status, and to be a jural person automatically entailed having certain property rights. Defined as a jural person, an entity could further allocate rights to specific sub-units—crucial to the system's operation, as I will show. For instance, the state could parcel out rights to use state property both to cooperatives and to other lower-level actors, such as SOEs, socialist organizations (trade unions or Councils of National Minorities), or lower-level territorial units (such as republics, in the Soviet case; counties; and municipal governments).

The three types of property subjects were distinguished from one another by the type of property they were empowered to own. There were four recognized property types: state property, cooperative property,[e] personal property, and private property, each having its own legal regime. In all Soviet-type socialist societies, the most valued productive resources were held in state property. This was particularly so where land was owned by the state regardless of whether it was in state or collective farms, as was true in the Soviet Union and Albania; but even where land was owned by the collectives whose members had formed them (as in Romania and Hungary) or by individual farmers (as in Poland), state property still encompassed most of the social wealth and the means for generating it. Among the objects in this category were the major means of production and certain other things restricted exclusively to state ownership. These included subsoil raw materials and mines, forests, waterways, and public buildings, as well as other items such as factories and manufacturing sites, banks, means of communication and public transport, energy companies, agricultural machinery stations, much of the housing stock, and so on. Some of these are things that western states too claim and regulate; indeed, the state in capitalist democracies can monopolize and regulate property matters—such as what you can do with land you own—every bit as closely as did socialist ones.

Cooperative property was one of those compromises life so often forces on grand designs. The Bolsheviks intended the category *state property* to encompass all values in Soviet society, but they were unable to implement that intention, owing both to popular resistance and to their own incapacity. In consequence, an additional category came into being, *cooperative property*. It consisted of means of production "donated" or pooled by individuals who had formed a cooperative—most commonly, land that people were compelled to give into collective farms or other means of production for various trades' cooperatives. Unlike state property, which belonged to the whole people, cooperative property belonged only to those who had pooled it. Their property rights

e. I use the term *cooperative* in referring to the category that includes both agricultural and nonagricultural enterprises of nonstate type. When I wish to speak of nonstate agricultural enterprises, as already noted, I use the term *collective*—as in *collective farm*—rather than speaking of *cooperative farms*.

resembled those of shareholders in a capitalist firm. State property coexisted uneasily with this form and was always meant to absorb it. Because different factions in the Communist Party might favor one or the other form at different times (see Armstrong 1983, 4–5), however, cooperative property failed to wither away. The categories state and cooperative property together made up the supercategory *socialist property*, which included nearly all society's major means of production; the interaction of its two subsidiary categories gave that supercategory an unexpected dynamism.

A third type, *private property*, also concerned means of production but consisted of those owned and used by petty-commodity producers such as uncollectivized peasants and tradespeople (e.g., tailors, cobblers, and carpenters); such property was likely to be organized in households. Not included in that category were the misnamed private plots of collective farmers. Those formed, rather, part of the socialist property of collective farms, which assigned members use-rights to them. Viewed as a residue of the bourgeois order, private property was of minimal importance in all but Poland and Yugoslavia, where private-property-owning cultivators formed the large majority of the rural population. In all socialist systems, private property was slated for eventual elimination. By contrast, socialist regimes viewed the fourth type—*personal property*—as closely linked with socialist property and planned to increase it continually, in raising the standard of living. This category consisted primarily of objects of consumption; laws constrained their use to keep people from turning them into means of production. For instance, one could own one's car but was prohibited from using it as a taxi to generate income; one could own a house, but not a second house that might bring income from rent. To party planners, increasing personal property indicated progress in the development and use of socialist property.

Crucial to the state's being an entity, an effective actor, was the notion that state property formed a unitary fund, inalienable, immune from attachment for debts, and indivisible. Not even the state itself could alienate state property (Kornai 1992, 74). Rights to use its resources might be allocated downward, but this did not compromise the integrity of the whole. It was because any values that remained outside the sphere of state property—forms such as cooperative property and remnant private property—diminished the putative unity of the state and its whole people that socialist regimes aimed, in theory at least, to bring cooperative and state property forms into ever closer integration, while gradually eliminating the private remnants.

This long-term intention underlay the hierarchical relations of property forms—state property was prior to all others and enjoyed the fullest legal protection, followed (in order) by cooperative, personal, and private property. The hierarchy had both its normative and its practical facets. For instance, from the legal point of view each of these levels of owner held rights to possess, use, and dispose of its goods, but the rights held at each level constrained those held at levels below it. The subordination of lower to higher was clearest with personal and private property: the state could prevent uses of either that were not to the liking of party planners, and there was no recourse concerning such decisions. Although things were somewhat murkier with cooperatives, which maintained a modicum of autonomy, they too were constrained from above. For instance, they had ownership rights over their buildings and means of production—but only concerning objects relevant to the social objective for which they had been created. A clothing cooperative would have no reason to own food-processing equipment, nor a baker a stock of leather. Furthermore, cooperatives were expected to use their property rationally, as determined by the centrally set production plan (Păunescu 1974, 195). This placed serious limits on how they might use the goods their cooperative owned, and their capacity to dispose of their products was conditional on first fulfilling state delivery contracts at fixed prices.

The state could own goods that it prevented all other actors from owning (such as forests, banks, and mines); cooperatives likewise could own things individuals and households could not. The means available to the state for augmenting its property fund—nationalization, expropriation, and confiscation, for instance—were far more extensive than those available to cooperatives or individuals. Similarly, cooperatives but not individuals could acquire property through coerced voluntary donations or through extended socialist reproduction, while the personal or private property rights of individuals or households could come only from purchase, inheritance, or (occasionally) long-term possession and use; the kinds of objects they could hold in this way were limited. In sum, using the words of a Romanian judge with whom I spoke, "Socialist state property was *more* inalienable, *more* exclusive, *more property* than any other form, and judicial practice was to shore it up, buttressing its status over that of other kinds." This superior status empowered planners to treat cooperative property as if it were part of the unitary fund of state property, despite its theoretically belonging only to a cooperative's members. Whenever there was a conflict between the state's needs for appropriation and those of some lower unit, the state always won out.

State and Collective Farms

Socialist property in agriculture followed these general organizational principles, with some variation.[18] From land confiscated and redistributed after 1945, the new party-states withheld large surfaces (in Romania, almost half a million hectares) with which they would inaugurate state farms (SFs) and collective farms

(CFs). These two kinds of farm were central to socialist agriculture everywhere; alongside them was a small amount of land left in private farming (usually in mountainous terrain difficult to mechanize or control). The proportion of land in these various forms differed from one country to another, and that meant variation in the importance of the main forms. In the mid-1980s, for instance, 68 percent of land in the Soviet Union but only 8 percent in East Germany was held in state farms; 82 percent of land in East Germany was held in collectives but only 30 percent in the Soviet Union; 78 percent of land in Poland but only 0.5 percent in Albania was held privately (see table 2.1, in chapter 2). A second source of variation concerned the agricultural machinery stations (AMSs) or machinery parks, which served collective farms in some countries (Romania, Albania, and Russia into the 1950s); in others the collectives owned their own equipment.

The extent to which land was owned as state property rather than some other type differed greatly among the socialist countries. In the Soviet Union, for example, a 1917 decree abolished private property in land and nationalized it, expropriating all noble and church estates. Owing to peasant resistance, however, evident in constant battles over grain procurement during the 1920s, Stalin decided on another form of socialist ownership: collective (as opposed to state) farms, which could often be created at one stroke by collectivizing entire communal villages through a vote of the members (Fitzpatrick 1994, 44). The Soviet state continued to be the sole owner of land, but now it granted different kinds of rights to different lower entities, including free and permanent grants of usufruct rights to collective farms. This solution satisfied the ideological demand for social ownership of land, which now took two forms. Except for Albania, however, the Soviet example was not followed in Eastern Europe. There, communist parties nationalized only the land of "enemies of the people," reserving some of it for state farms and redistributing some to poor peasants and war veterans. All other land remained in private ownership until collectivization was completed, at which point it became jointly owned by the members.

Despite this regional variation, a general similarity emerged in the nature of the socialist landscape and in the differences among its organizational forms. There was one nonstate entity—collective farms—and one or two kinds of state entities—state farms and (sometimes) machinery stations to serve the collectives.[f] Each had a different profile, state farms differing from collective farms in a number of ways consonant with the hierarchy of forms already presented:

f. In Romanian these three forms are known as *Cooperativă Agricolă de Producţie* (agricultural production cooperative), or CAP, in common parlance; *Intreprindere Agricolă de Stat* (state agricultural enterprise), or IAS; and *Staţiune de Maşini Agricole* (agricultural machine station), or SMA. Instead of using the abbreviations common in Romanian literature, as I have in other publications, I use here the names (and accompanying abbreviations) common in English: state farm (SF), collective farm (CF), and agricultural machinery station (AMS).

(1) the way they were formed, (2) their property status, (3) their relation to the state budget, and (4) their ways of remunerating workers.[19] First, as already mentioned, the land in SFs came chiefly from confiscations, that in CFs from "voluntary" donations of land by villagers. (Just how voluntary the donations were is clear from the recollections cited earlier.) Second, related to this was the different property status of their assets, as already explained. The assets of SFs were considered part of the entire national fund of state property, belonging to the whole people. They could be managed only by people who were appointed from above and were thus local agents of the Party's agricultural bureaucracy. The assets in CFs, by contrast, were the joint property of the former owners who had donated land and implements and whose work underlay acquisition of further assets. These assets did not belong to any larger group, only to the members of that specific CF. In theory the only persons entitled to manage CF assets were chairmen elected by the members.

Third, as state property, SFs held the most privileged status among agricultural organizations. They received much greater investments and direct subsidy; they had their own equipment, which was better than that in the machinery parks; they had the best land available in the area, with the best access to transportation networks. Compared with the collectives, they received more timely delivery of other kinds of inputs (fuel, chemical fertilizer, select seed, herbicides, pesticides, and so on), of better quality, and in more adequate amounts. CFs, by contrast, were more likely to be left with land of poorer quality and to receive late and inadequate deliveries of supplies. Instead of investments, they were given credits that—unlike the resources distributed to SFs—they were supposed to repay. In some countries they owned capital equipment—tractors, combines, seeders, and so on—but not in Romania, where each CF had to make contracts with the machinery parks, paid by in-kind deliveries. Their lack of machinery left them open to abuse by AMS personnel, who would work for their favorites first, leaving other farms to be plowed or harvested after the optimal time might have passed. It also subjected the CF to the exorbitant fees of AMSs, set so high that there was not much left for paying CF members. (This pattern continued even after 1989.) Thus, the state sector encroached on the collective sector, draining its resources outward to the detriment of the members whose land it cultivated. Table 1.1 indicates some of these differences, showing that Romania's SFs were on average twice the size of CFs (land per farm), had a lower ratio of employees per hectare, and held nearly seven times the fixed assets of CFs.

Fourth, additional evidence of the privileged position of state farms was their employees' pay. SFs were run as state enterprises with salaried labor, the wage was paid regularly regardless of the year's harvest, and both managers and workers were much better compensated than those in collectives; the wage of full-time SF

Table 1.1

Indicators for Romania's State and Collective Farms in 1989

Indicators	State Farms	Collective Farms
Number of farms	411	3,776
Average land per farm	5,000	2,374
Agricultural land (in 1000 ha)	2,055	8,963
Employees (in thousands)	261	1,910
Employees per hectare	127	213
Fixed assets (in millions of lei)	121,848	84,624
Fixed assets/hectare	59,000	4,700
Investments/hectare 1989	9,440	663

Source: Adapted from Brooks and Meurs (1994, 22); von Hirschhausen (1997, 50), after
   Romanian Statistical Yearbook for 1990.

employees (electricians, tractor drivers, accountants) about equaled that of factory workers.[20] Collective farmers, on the other hand, received instead of a fixed
salary various forms of remuneration in cash and kind. In every country, CF
members enjoyed use-rights to a personal or usufruct plot of varying size, which
they could generally use as they wished, to supplement their household income or
their food supply.[21] Beyond this, they received wages calculated according to the
farm's production—and only after all its obligations to the Five-Year Plan had
been fulfilled (as well as all the "special deliveries" to friends of the chairman). The
methods for calculating members' pay varied both by country and across time. By
the late 1980s, in some countries CF members earned reasonably well, especially
in Hungary, but in Romania they earned very little (one reason for the savage destruction of most Romanian CFs after 1989). An important consequence of CF
workers' low pay was their efforts to supplement their official wages with informal appropriation, officially known as *theft*, to which I return later.

Hierarchies of Estates of Administration

So far, I have presented a static picture of types arranged in a hierarchy. Now,
to clarify the relations among the types and put this picture into motion, I introduce a second hierarchy; I call it, after Gluckman (1943), a hierarchy of estates of administration. Understanding this hierarchy is essential to understanding how state ownership worked. What could it possibly mean, in practical
terms, for the state to own and effectively use a unitary fund of values?[22] How
were all those state-owned means of production put into production in an ef-

fective way? What sorts of social relations both facilitated their doing so and emerged as a result? Answers to these questions come more readily if we stop asking about ownership per se, which is far from the only way of organizing property, and look at the distribution of various kinds of rights and relations, as well as at patterns of actual use (see also Humphrey 1983).

In socialist property regimes, the most important relationship after the ownership prerogatives of the state was based in what was officially termed the *right of direct (or operational) administration*, which I call *administrative rights*. Following Humphrey, I find anthropologist Max Gluckman's meticulous description of the Lozi kingdom in central Africa (Gluckman 1943, 1965)—a redistributive system, like socialism—very helpful in understanding this arrangement (see also Ferguson 1992).[23] Among the Lozi the king was known as *owner of the land*, and people in his kingdom obtained land by kingly grants. Any recipient of such grants could create further grants downward to others in what Gluckman refers to as a "hierarchy of estates of administration." Recipients at each tier in the hierarchy exercised rights of disposal over both the land and the land's products. They were empowered to allocate elsewhere use-rights to it, to control or regulate its use, to transmit rights to it to their heirs, to defend it against trespass or against unlawful incursions even by the king himself, and otherwise to behave like owners, subject only to two constraints: they could not alienate it permanently, and in exchange for the rights granted them they were obligated to make gifts of food, service, and allegiance upward. Gluckman resists the term *usufruct* to describe the rights allocated, because they went well beyond merely enjoying the fruits (1965, 85–86). He sees the rights accorded as attributes of status, and he emphasizes that neither the king nor his subordinates saw these downward allocations as in any way diminishing or dismembering ownership at the center.

In observing that it is better to talk of a hierarchy of estates of administration than of the king's ownership (Gluckman 1943, 34), Gluckman seems to me to characterize state-socialist ownership as well. Compare Heller's description of socialist property:

> Instead of assigning an owner to each object, socialist law created a complex hierarchy of divided and coordinated rights in the objects it defined. . . . The law integrated ownership of physical assets within overlapping state structures, often linking upward from a state enterprise, to a group of similar enterprises, to the local and then central offices of a ministry responsible for that branch of industry. (1998, 629)

Intriguingly, Humphrey points out that in Soviet conceptions of power, "the term *khoziain* [proprietor, master] was used at each hierarchical level of the Soviet system, such that the directors of enterprises, and the Party bosses of districts and provinces were all called 'proprietors,' and at the apex of the system Stalin in his time was called *nash khoziain* ('our master')" (2002a, 28).

Just as the Lozi king allocated rights downward without compromising his power, so the party-state retained its claim to supreme ownership but exercised that ownership by passing the rights downward to lower-level entities, assigning various kinds of control over parts of the property of the whole people to inferior levels in the bureaucratic hierarchy. Recipients of these rights could further parcel them out to others still lower down the scale—for example, a ministry to its regional branch, thence to county-level planning structures, and finally to a state farm director (see table 1.2). The heads of these lower units were to use the rights to generate products for the state to appropriate and redistribute; meanwhile, complex rules of accounting aimed to prevent them from obtaining the information they would need in order to become fully autonomous (see Dunn 2002).[24]

An administrative right was not simply a use right. According to Knapp, "it has no analogy in the law of capitalist countries. . . . Neither does the right of administration of property . . . resemble the institutions of *usus* or *usufructus*"(1975, 50). Its *sui generis* character comes from the dual nature of SOEs in socialist economies—they were simultaneously subordinate to the state and autonomous legal entities distinct from it. Directors of SOEs and other holders of administrative rights exercised these not as state agents but in their own name. The rights were so extensive as to approximate those of ownership (including possession, use, and disposal short of full alienation), yet the power to exercise them was premised on the prior existence of the state's power as owner, from which the administrator's power was derived (Knapp 1975, 51).

In explaining the relationship between administration and use, Gluckman distinguishes between estates of *administration* and estates of *production* (1965, 89–93). Superiors hold estates of administration, allocating rights downward, whereas those at the base hold estates of production, using the rights granted them to fructify collective assets. Although Gluckman does not explore possible

Table 1.2
A Hierarchy of Administrative Estates for Socialist Property[a]

Central Committee, Politbureau of the Communist Party
Ministries, regional governments
Subministries, local governments
State-owned enterprises

---

[a] At each level, the entities hold from the level above them the rights to manage socialist property.

sources of tension between these two kinds of estates, a consequence of these latter rights in the socialist case was a steady erosion of the center's capacity to grant the former, administrative ones.

The system of multiple and overlapping administrative rights over the state's unitary fund permitted myriad transactions to occur without the forms used in capitalism, such as mortgages or sale contracts, to effect changes in ownership (Feldbrugge 1993, 231). For instance, if a state farm director made a contract with a brewery to deliver a product—say, 100 tons of hops—the hops was at all times state property. Its owner did not change; all that changed was who held the power of administrative rights over it. Thus, the SF director held the power to dispose of the product to the brewery—a power common to ownership relations— but ownership did not change thereby.

A concrete example will clarify how ambiguous the situation could be. In chapter 7 I introduce an SF director, Radu, who ran a state farm in Vlaicu. In 1997 Radu explained to me that he had always found uses for land that had been declared marginal. For instance, he had cleared a piece of unused land not included in his cultivation plan, given a strip of it to each of his employees, and used a strip to plant vegetables for himself. When he harvested his beans, he noted, villagers might accuse him of stealing them from the state. He also offered to let his workers cut the grass that grew up along the roadside—another unused surface—keeping half of it for themselves and giving him the rest. He sold the bulk of that to the dairy farm down the road, using the income to obtain something needed for his SF, and kept some to feed the calf he was raising there. Radu saw this as legitimate use of state property: "Yes, the grass on the land belongs to the SF. If I didn't cut it and use it, no one else would claim it. But is it preferable to leave the grass unreaped or to do what I did? *It's true I'm not the proprietor, but I'm the administrator*" (emphasis added). In this case, he took extra product from the socialist patrimony and used it to enhance the SF's budget, to shore up his workers' allegiance so they would work better on the SF, and to feed his own private calf. Where are the boundaries here?

The right of socialist managers to move items of socialist property around at will was essential to one of the hallmarks of these political economies: inter-enterprise barter and trading of the goods necessary for production, as I describe later. Technically speaking, only the managers holding administrative rights to state property could do this with one another, but in practice they were linked in giant trading networks with the managers of cooperative enterprises such as CFs as well (although SOE directors had richer networks than others). A major consequence of these practices was that the boundaries within the unitary fund of property became blurred, and objects might move among numerous people exercising rights to them that were akin to ownership rights but were not consecrated as such. This fact vastly complicates assigning both asset values and ownership rights during privatization.[25] Because the units receiving this right thereby entered as jural persons into direct relation with the means of production, their managers could come dangerously close to infringing on the state's property right. Here we see that the behavior of those holding Gluckman's estates of production can put them at odds with those allocating estates of administration above them. The legendary hoarding, dissimulation, plan bargaining, and other manipulations of state property by lower-level managers produced internal contradictions in the notion of the state as a unitary actor and state property as an object of coherent planning.

Indeed, the inability of the political center to keep these actors in check, and their gradually increased autonomy in consequence, were critical elements in socialism's transformation. Various scholars have pointed to changes taking place up to two years before 1989, as the holders of estates of production ceased to respect the hierarchy of command and began to usurp the state's rights of ownership.[26] Especially once central control began to disintegrate, these managers arrogated state powers, even selling off state assets—often to themselves. By the time privatization officially commenced, many of socialism's erstwhile directors were well on their way to being private owners, a process that socialism's hierarchy of administrative estates had facilitated. For this reason, it would be inadvisable to see administrative rights as an insignificant form of property relation. Their exercise in practice constituted state firms as powerful actors—particularly the directors of these firms, organized into robust networks that themselves became real social actors, as the aftermath of 1989 amply showed.

Socialist Property in Process

My discussion of administrative rights has begun to give life to the official property categories of socialism; I now expand on the processes that unfolded within these confines. How did actors' behavior within socialist organizations give socialist property flexibility and produce a working property regime, with consequences that affected the exit routes from that system?

Evidence concerning these questions is somewhat limited because ethnographic research inside socialist enterprises was rare. Most of it comes from Hungary, whose economists also produced studies having strongly ethnographic implications.[27] Other illuminating work came from Soviet emigrés, often with the aim of showing the extent of "corruption" in the Soviet system (e.g., Simis 1982). These works explore managerial behavior but without linking it specifically to socialism's property regime, which is my objective here. I concentrate on agriculture, emphasizing collective rather than state farms because anthropological data are richest for these sites and including anecdotal material from my research in both Vlaicu and its commune center, Geoagiu.[28]

I take up three kinds of questions: vertical relations of farm directors and the bureaucratic hierarchy, horizontal relations among collective and state farms with respect to land, and attitudes of villagers toward socialist property. In standard anthropological fashion, I emphasize not ownership rights but institutionalized statuses bound together by reciprocal obligations among socialist property managers. This is not to distinguish rights from obligations—which are in effect two sides of the same coin—but to emphasize the system of social relationships and the obligations that bind them together. An emphasis on rights too often focuses on the person making a claim, rather than on the system of relations in which someone else is obligated to that person.

Hoarding, Bartering, and Networks of Obligation in Shortage Economies

Socialist managers did not live merely in a hierarchy of estates; they lived in economies of shortage, a very special environment that I have described elsewhere (Verdery 1991), drawing on the work of Kornai (1980), Bauer (1978), Burawoy (1985), and others. Fundamental to shortage economies is that producing units operated within *soft budget constraints*—that is, firms doing poorly were bailed out and there were few financial penalties for what capitalists would see as irrational and inefficient behavior (excess inventory, overemployment, and overinvestment). In other words, the notion of *liabilities* was weak—a major problem for eventually assessing the value of these firms after 1989. Firms also operated within plans, which assigned them production targets that were orientative if not obligatory (varying by country and time period). Managers of firms usually tried to bargain their plan, seeking lower targets and higher quantities of inputs; planning authorities, for their part, strove to ratchet targets upward and to extract greater productive capacity by various means. The process of bargaining within plans pitted segments of the economic bureaucracy against one another, as those most essential to the Party's goals—the military and heavy industry—secured more resources than did sectors judged less crucial—agriculture and light industry.

In this environment, managers hoarded both labor and materials, including not just those provided by the state but also materials they themselves produced above plan targets. They struggled to secure extra resources—Humphrey (1983) calls these "manipulable resources"—and to hide these from state agents who came expressly to squeeze them out into the state property funds. Because glitches in socialist planning and distribution could prevent managers from mobilizing the necessary raw materials for the level of production expected of them, they not only demanded more inputs than they needed but held onto any excess they received or were able to produce. Managerial bargaining and hoarding produced shortage, as hoarding at all levels froze in place resources needed for production somewhere else.

But although enterprise managers helped to generate shortage by hoarding, they also strove to reduce its effects by widespread barter. They traded with other managers whatever they might have in excess supply—and even withheld supplies from production so as to have materials to trade—in exchange for inputs they needed. Although these practices did not fully alleviate the problem of obtaining resources for production, because one could not always count on covering all one's needs through one's network at the necessary times, they became an integral and time-consuming part of socialist production in both agricultural and industrial settings. A Romanian state farm director gave me a sense of the magnitude of these efforts: "On average, I spent one hour of every six-to-eight-hour day on the telephone, trying to scare up what I needed or being asked for things by someone else." Reforms introduced in each Eastern European country during the 1960s and 1970s modified economic organization and sought to make managers more accountable for their production costs, without, however, eliminating these horizontal trading networks. After 1989, those networks proved to be sources of social capital.

Therefore, plans, targets, and hoarding set the parameters of a far-flung system of obligations intimately related to production within socialist property. Such obligations are far from unique to socialism, but what distinguishes these from other cases is the context provided by socialism's political economy. The obligations were of several kinds. First were two forms we might call *socialist tribute* that were primarily vertical: (1) obligatory deliveries of a firm's product upward to state procurement centers in fulfillment of the plan and (2) (especially in the case of cooperatives) returns on contracts made with the state for inputs the enterprise did not directly control.[29] For collective farms, these included special seed grown in state research stations, fertilizer produced in state factories, pesticides and herbicides made in other state firms, and the machinery—tractors and harvesters—supplied from the machinery parks. A third kind of vertical obligation, much less substantial, moved downward: the pay that managers were required to give their workers. In collective farms, this was often shortchanged because other obligations diminished the total fund available to distribute.

Next were forms that could be both vertical and horizontal but, unlike the three just described, were not part of the formal requirements of socialist production. These included the obligations entailed in barter: if I give up inputs you need today, I have a claim on your inputs (you have an obligation) for what

I need tomorrow. Because managers who did not know how to manage this sort of reciprocity soon found themselves unable to mobilize enough inputs for production, the obligations of barter were highly binding. They were not requirements of the formal system, but it could not operate without them. For example, collective farm chairmen and their technicians had to cultivate immense and far-flung networks in order for their farms to function. They needed to induce the AMSs to work for them at the optimum time, to obtain inputs when these were hard to find, to anticipate and adapt to changes in the county political environment, to influence the people at the state warehouse not to apply rigorous standards to the quality of the crops they delivered, and so forth. Filling each such need incurred social debts that had to be honored.

That might be done through nebulous obligations of a general kind that helped to oil the joints of the hierarchy of administrative estates. They involved gifts to superiors, status equals, and inferiors and gifts to equals for their superiors. Whether the debts were vertical or horizontal was not always clear; as a state farm director put it, "Our bosses were always coming around for products they needed. We were in relations of collaboration, not of subordination." The gifts often came from the production process itself, especially in agriculture, where immense quantities of apples, vegetables, or grain went from farms to the cronies and party superiors of the farm directors. The return on such gifts might be looser plan targets, special bonuses, access to raw materials otherwise hard to obtain, or generalized goodwill.[30] Moreover, as Caroline Humphrey (1983) has brilliantly shown, participation in such exchanges might be crucial to obtaining effort from those in one's workforce. What made the exchanges possible to begin with, however, was the granting of administrative rights, which entailed managerial discretion over the use of various kinds of socialist property. This far-flung system of exchange involving gifts and favors justifies seeing socialism as a complex form of gift economy,[31] one in which the aim was to collect followers, supporters, and allies—in other words, to *accumulate people* on whom one could rely in moments of need. We must not, however, lose sight of the fact that all this bargaining and trading, aimed at facilitating the production of goods to be appropriated for central redistribution, itself appropriated tremendous amounts of the product so destined.

This movement of resources gave substance to a vital actor: networks of exchange partners. Socialist firms were not units at at the end of a chain of command but were linked in extended webs of managers and politicians, all striking bargains to optimize their situations. If we stop with the allocation of administrative *rights,* we miss this crucial aspect of socialist property, so dependent on a corresponding system of *obligations.* In other words, the central actors of socialism's property regime were not just the state, cooperatives, and individuals, but also networks (see also Stark 1996). These networks extended across the field of socialist enterprises and could enjoy considerable stability over time; they were real enough to become the postsocialist "clans" or "mafias" so widely noted in the transformation of socialist property, particularly in Russia.[32]

Managing Socialist Property

SF directors and CF chairmen with their supporting staff of officials (agronomists, veterinarians, technicians, and accountants) had to accomplish a number of things.[33] They had to respond to plan indicators, whether or not those suited local conditions, and to deliver something like the amounts recommended to them obligatorily from above. For this they had to obtain sufficient inputs and then secure yields sizable enough to cover their delivery contracts and their various other obligations. Because prices were set administratively in a way that made profit nearly impossible, their success depended instead on cushioning their relations with the party bureaucracy in the manner I have just described, improving their chances for good production results. In addition, they had to obtain sufficient labor from their members or from other sources, often by participating in a gift economy and system of patronage involving fellow villagers, as well.[34] What were some of their means for managing all these demands successfully? I emphasize those that had implications for the process of decollectivization later, using examples from my fieldwork.

Rationalizing Cultivation through Horizontal Exchanges

Early in the process of collectivization, both SF directors and CF chairmen engaged in certain practices that had consequences decades later when those farms were disbanded. Because the early collectives had to show good results so as to attract more members, farm heads consolidated the pieces already donated to make compact fields of good quality that they could cultivate rationally. That both SF and CF heads were able to allocate rights to land at will, enjoying priority over private property rights, enabled them to reorganize the landscape for their convenience through numerous land exchanges. These were of three kinds: between CFs or SFs and individuals, between CFs and SFs, and among CFs or SFs. That is, the exchanges occurred across three of the four main property types and all three kinds of owners.

In Romania, for example, Decree 151 (1950) enabled collectives in formation to create contiguous parcels by exchanging land with individual private owners. Often, the land of villagers who had joined the collective or its precursor did not form contiguous blocks; officials had the right to create these by compelling nonmembers with land in the middle of a good field to exchange it for parcels at the edge. SFs seeking to consolidate their fields had the same prerogative. Individuals could not refuse these exchanges,[35] having to accept parcels much inferior to those they had been compelled to turn over. Indeed, the decree stated that the contracts for such exchanges were valid even without the signatures of the owners thus displaced, as long as the local authorities invoked Decree 151 in their records. Technically speaking, farm officials were supposed to make and archive such contracts, but often—from haste, or carelessness, or confidence in the supremacy of their own property form—they did not. Their cavalier treatment of land enabled farm members after 1989 to challenge the jural status of such earlier exchanges in order to recover their better-quality parcels.

In the same spirit of rational cultivation, state and collective farms often exchanged their donated or confiscated lands with one another. Because directors administered the property rights to the land (albeit via different mechanisms), they could dispose of it as necessary to pursue their objectives; the wishes of the former owners had no place in such exchanges. They could even enforce exchanges on private owners living in uncollectivized areas, whose private property lay at the bottom of the hierarchy of property forms.

All these exchanges altered the landscape fundamentally, creating large undivided fields from the intricate patchwork of tiny parcels owned by people from multiple places. Farm managers could do this, moving parcels formerly owned by myriad individuals like so many pieces on a chessboard, precisely because they enjoyed far-reaching rights to acquire and dispose of landed property, indifferent to the possible rights of the former private owners (and even to the different legal statuses of the land as state or cooperative property). Treating all collective lands as a single fund, farm managers could trade them with other units at will, without having to record a property transfer. After 1989, these deedless exchanges created havoc in the process of reconstituting private ownership.

Hoarding and Hiding Land

Managing socialist property in land meant not just moving it around among production units but also finding ways to get more of it, toward filling ever-higher plans. For example, farm heads tried to expand the surface areas they could use, bringing new land into cultivation by filling swamps, plowing pastures to make them arable, draining wetlands, and so on. These practices augmented a collective's property fund, although not necessarily to its members' benefit because what motivated chairmen was concern with their vertical and horizontal exchange relations. The lands thus reclaimed were a site of argument after 1989, as they usually had no prior owner but many claimants.

The same pressures also pushed farm chairmen to other practices that had major effects on property reconstitution after 1989. One such practice was hiding land, something already being done by peasant owners as well. Among the reasons for this were the onerous delivery quotas mentioned in my opening section. Because the quotas grew heavier the more one owned, households had an incentive to declare less land than they had or to sell with a secret understanding that the sale was a fiction. After 1989, however, these tactics proved difficult to reverse. Local cadres had further concealed the land that peasants had hidden before, using it to swell their productivity by planting and harvesting areas that were officially recorded as smaller than they actually were (see Rév 1987). Thus, even as commune mayors and collective farm presidents created land by clearing and draining, they also hid some from higher authorities. These kinds of hiding show that the "vanishing hectare" of my title existed well before the 1991 land restitution.

Practices such as these involved manipulating collective property to ensure production and thus depended on the position and good relations of farm officials with their superiors in a chain of command. A consequence, of course, was to introduce permanent uncertainty into the system of information and planning because figures relating to means of production at the disposal of farm heads could not be trusted. Indeed, as I have argued elsewhere, during the socialist period such maneuvers could place the actual surface area of villages such as Vlaicu wholly in doubt, with published statistics from before and after 1945 being completely inconsistent (see Verdery 1996, 144–45). Party officials treated land as a movable rather than an immovable good, its transfer made as easy as a simple trade between two friends. Land pertaining to any given collective or state farm had no firm boundaries that distinguished each such entity from others like it: all were fungible within the unitary property fund of socialism. And of course there was no need to record land exchanges and transfers because they all occurred within that unitary fund. These manipulations and failures to record all contributed to making presocialist agricultural holdings almost impossible to reconstitute after 1989.

Theft: The Struggle over Appropriation

> Old Uncle George slaughtered his calf [illegal, in those days]. His neighbor denounced him, and the collective farm took him to court. There the judge admonished him, "Why did you kill your calf?" "Because it's mine," he replied. "No," said the judge, "it's not yours. The *cow* is yours. The calf is *ours*." "If I'd known that," said Uncle George, "I'd have slaughtered the cow." —(*Romanian joke from the 1980s*)

My discussion so far has shown how socialist managers used the official system of administrative rights to accomplish their goals while oiling it with unofficial exchanges so it would work. I also observed that these exchanges required removing from circulation large portions of the goods their units produced. What about the members of these farms, the people whose land made everything possible? How did they feel about about socialist property and all those managerial shenanigans? In this section, I suggest that at the bottom level of the hierarchy of estates—where estates of administration became estates of production—the struggle over conflicting forms of appropriation came to a head. It was here that managers' strategies for making their enterprises produce set them at odds with their direct producers. We see this especially well in the concept of *theft*.

The total product of a collective farm was finite and could support only so many destinations. If farm directors gave priority to delivering on contracts and to the gift economy, there would be little left for paying members. Indeed, the chronic complaint of collective farm members I spoke with—both from Vlaicu and from elsewhere in Romania—was that their work was woefully underpaid. This fact led them to leave agriculture for industry, if they could, and, in a natural form of counterappropriation, to take things from the collective. Inspiring this was the example of their superiors, whose behavior made it fairly easy to see the collective product as "ours" for the taking. Although theft of socialist property was punishable by much heavier penalties than theft of personal property, villagers never saw their farm president sanctioned for the uses he made of their collective product. How could one distinguish theft from gifts, in such circumstances?

A villager of my acquaintance put the problem thus, as she described her exploits in stealing from the collective—for which she had been arrested. I asked if she thought she was stealing: "In my opinion I was bringing stuff home, not doing something bad. Look at my neighbor [the CF president]; he built two houses! Everyone was doing it. . . . When I was arrested, the judges seemed *embarrassed* at having to try a lawsuit for three bales of hay! Meanwhile, THEY [the authorities] were stealing *whole cartloads* [*care intregi*]!" Others I spoke with made similar points. "We'd see the bosses come and take whole cartloads, and we'd think, 'If they can do it, why can't we?' But we only used sacks, just enough to take home." The theme of "whole cartloads" appeared constantly. Again: "Political officials would come and steal all the time, whole cartloads! Half those people didn't even work there, but *I* did; I had more of a right to steal than they!" Another observed, with sarcasm, "We who worked in the farm were 'stealing' small amounts in our clothing, but the big communists here . . . they *took*. They just 'took,' but they said we were 'stealing.' They walked out with this stuff in plain sight; no one did anything to *them*."

In this way, when the heads of socialist firms unofficially moved goods into the socialist gift economy, they further blurred the boundaries within socialist property. Their self-interested notion of collective ownership, or at least collective entitlement, generalized downward from those who were not prosecuted for it to those who were. Collective farmers might be prosecuted for stealing just a few potatoes or a sack of corn from their places of work; a 1981 law mandated six months to five years in jail no matter how small the theft. Even if this law was in fact rarely applied, abundant anecdotes attest to a climate of constant vigilance by farm officials and constant concern of members about being caught. (Among my own respondents, several told of narrow escapes from the law, in which their court cases were dismissed only through timely intervention by a well-placed friend or relative.)

Vlaiceni insisted to me, however, on their *right* to take from the collective—indeed, some claimed that it was inappropriate to use the word *theft* for such behavior. Similarly, Humphrey reports that the Soviet villagers she worked with used the word *theft* to refer only to stealing from one another (1983, 136.)[36] Most of my respondents presented themselves as recovering things that were rightfully theirs, either because they'd worked on those things (harvested corn, pulled potatoes, or collected fruit) for inadequate pay or because they had once owned the land for growing these things and they were not getting enough to live on. For example, "No one thought of this as theft—if you worked to collect fruit, or if you spent a whole day at the vegetable garden pulling up peppers and carrots, then taking a pocketful was not theft, after a day of work." "How could it be theft? *We worked* there." "[I wasn't stealing], I was *taking*. I was taking my work, because we worked and didn't have enough." "I knew it was *my land*; we worked and we didn't have anything. I was just taking what belonged to me."

All these comments suggest that villagers saw their collective property as producing goods that belonged to them and to which they had a right, even if they sometimes had to appropriate those goods on their own. In this respect, theft of CF products was a defense of their personal property right against what they saw as illegitimate appropriation by farm officials. Recall M. G.'s statement quoted earlier in this chapter: "The cadres who made the collective told us, 'The land belongs to all of you!' But the harvest? Who did *that* belong to! They told us, 'Give us your land, and you'll get the harvest.' But it wasn't like that." Taking was their response.

Theft was a common topic—both spontaneous and elicited—in my fieldwork during and after socialism. In the 1990s it even evoked much merriment, as well as nostalgia. For example, in November 1993 I sat talking with three women; it was a cold day, and they were warming themselves with some brandy. They started to reminisce about life in the collective. One of them began, "We set out one night to go stealing,[37] my husband, sister-in-law, and I. My sister-in-law was carrying the sacks, but somehow she dropped them. We were crawling around trying to find them, but we couldn't. It was pitch dark. My husband tripped on a pipe and fell into the swamp . . ." All laughed at the recollection. We recalled a story I'd heard long ago from another woman who had stolen some wheat from the CF one day and put it in a three-liter water jug. Then she ran into a policeman, and he asked for a drink. For this she suffered months of ridicule, although she was not arrested. Another told of how she'd go to the CF to sow wheat, carrying in her lunchbox a plastic bag that she'd fill with wheat seed to take home. I learned also of the common trick of wearing a tight-waisted skirt so you could stuff corn into your blouse and it would not fall out. Once a friend recounted with great amusement and verve how a co-villager would go to work at the farm and fill her blouse with corn seed *before* going out to the fields for the day. "We'd ask her, 'Rica, why are you doing this *now* and not later? Why work all day with a blouse full of corn?' She'd reply, 'I'm worried that when it's time to go home, the brigadier will be watching and I won't be able to get anything.'"

An important theme in some of these stories was that the farm officials often connived in this. "I worked with a team of about six women in the vegetable farm, and we had a lot of fun, laughed a lot. We were the head engineer's favorite group. He'd send the others home and keep us to load the trucks, then he'd drop us off at our gate, closing his eyes to whatever we might take with us. No, he didn't encourage us, just closed his eyes." Another recalled how the brigade leaders would tell them to take their share. "He gave us permission. Once when he did this, the driver refused to transport all our sacks of corn—we were twenty women and we each had several 30- to 40-kg sacks. You should have seen us all going home across the fields, staggering under the weight of these huge sacks, because none of us would give up what we'd been encouraged to take." Thus, although their unofficial appropriation might be severely punished, its source could in fact be the farm leaders, once again using farm products to help the farm run better—this time, by cementing good relations with its workers.[38]

Other conversations revealed further ambiguities in these villagers' property conceptions. During the 1990s I discussed with Vlaiceni what they thought about the personal plots they worked as CF members—to whom did these belong?[39] Many began by saying the plot was theirs, and in some cases the connection was indeed close because the plot they were given had once belonged to their families. As we talked more, however, they changed their minds—the plot was theirs only to use, not to own. This emphasis on use is what Alexandr Vysokovskii, writing of Russia, calls "pseudo-ownership": "People tend to 'acquire' what they use, without considering who really owns it" (1993, 277). It is not only Romanian or Russian collective farmers who think this way, of course; we find it in many other times and places. Indeed, the ancestors of these very people thought the same: in the 1820 feudal census carried out by Habsburg authorities, serfs in this village spoke of the land to which the feudal lord had accorded them use-rights as "theirs."[40]

When villagers were prosecuted for theft of collective farm produce, two fundamentally different conceptions of ownership came into conflict. *Theft* as a construct presupposes a system of clearly defined persons, objects, and boundaries that separate them; theft is a violation of those boundaries, as one agent takes something from a bounded fund of objects to which another agent lays claim. The official organization of socialist property employed a three-tiered system of boundaries. The strongest one separated the patrimony of the whole people (the entire country) from that of other countries. Inside that boundary was another one separating socialist from private property; for this discussion, that boundary was the most consequential. Within socialist property there was yet another boundary, very weak and rarely observed in practice, separating state from cooperative property. Actors could appropriate the socialist product by moving things upward (across the boundaries between private and socialist or collective and state) or laterally within a given category. What was unacceptable to the authorities was any movement of goods downward across the boundary between socialist property and lower types. That was theft. Party officials did plenty of it, but those appropriations disappeared into the much larger flow of gifts and tribute upward. In equating their own appropriations with those of officials, collective farmers made the mistake of not realizing that the direction of movement mattered.

In taking from the collective farm, villagers were producing something rather different from what officials produced with their own takings. The networks of exchange and their associated obligations, I have argued, were crucial to making socialist property work. Although many officials were also undeniably feathering their own nests, their appropriations lubricated the planned economy, nourished officials' positions of authority within it, and constituted them as certain kinds of persons—effective communist cadres. By contrast, villagers taking from the collective were constituting themselves as persons of a different kind: members of households, kin, and people who resisted the oppressions and sacrifices socialism imposed on them. They were draining socialist property downward into personal property in order to behave as they thought self-respecting persons should. Historically, property relations have long been implicated in defining how persons should be, and this case offers us no exception. Although from the official point of view their behavior qualified as theft, from the viewpoint of the villagers themselves it qualified them as proper human beings.

Implications

The collectivization of agriculture was the single most far-reaching administrative act of those socialist countries that pursued it. It affected more people in a shorter time, to what most of them perceived as ill effect, than any other policy. It made the peasantry dependent and prepared them to become proletarians by dispossessing them—although not fully, because it kept them in collective farms that offered them at least a minimal livelihood. It assured central control over the food supply, toward building up industry and the urban working class. By creating a new, noncapitalist means for appropriating the social product, it laid the foundation for the redistributive project of communist parties.

Concerning the property order in which collectivization participated, I have been arguing that contrary to Frydman and Rapaczynski's claim (see the first chapter epigraph) about socialism's "not having *any* property system," it had a very complex one. To grasp that system has required setting aside questions about ownership and looking at patterns of use, administrative rights, and social networks of exchange and reciprocity. Laws and administrative measures defined a specifically socialist property regime encompassing both agricultural and industrial production, in both state and cooperative enterprises. To solve the problem of producing within a system of centralized appropriation, party-states established hierarchies of administrative and productive estates, held together by delegating administrative rights. These rights (the most important form of property right in socialism) were intended to link the different legal property types and to establish specific relations to values and goods.

Translated into practice, however, these ceased to serve as rights over *things* but entered into social relations that privileged rights over *people*. Extended networks of reciprocity moved products upward, laterally, and downward, all in the service of collecting people whose goodwill, trades of raw material, protection, patronage, and effort would put socialism's productive means into motion. Those patterns, however, placed multiple demands on the social product and generated an ongoing struggle—more intense in countries such as Romania than in others—around appropriation at the bottom, as villagers found that the official redistributive economy was just not working out for them.

This is the argument of the present chapter. What are its implications for chapters to come? The policies of *de*collectivization initiated after 1989 aimed to undo the system I have described and to create or recreate private property, the form most disdained in socialist planning. How does my discussion here prepare us for the problems this transformation caused? I suggest three general points related to the theme of value, raised in my introductory chapter, which I believe are applicable to some extent to all postsocialist countries. The points concern the values inherent in socialist property, specifically the priority of administration over legal regulation, the matter of asset evaluation, and the hierarchy of property types.

As a property regime, what did socialist property do? For one thing, it helped to institute an entirely new set of values, based in an ideological opposition be-tween socialism and capitalism. The values I have emphasized here are (1) an administrative over a juridical basis for property and (2) a hierarchy of actors and statuses: the state itself as managing the patrimony of "the whole people"; below that, smaller cooperative entities holding resources in common; and, at the bottom, households and individuals as private entities engaging in property behavior, whether "good" (consumption-based) or "bad" (continued owner-ship of means of production). Each of these sets of values had consequences for postsocialist property transformation.

I begin with the party-state's preference for politico-administrative over legal procedures. This preference entailed making decrees and administrative deci-sions about the use of resources but not necessarily ratifying these decisions by the legal procedures that had governed property transformation in precommu-nist times. Regionwide, 1989 initiated a reversal of this set of priorities, attempt-ing to create the "law-governed state." The logistical nightmares encountered in that process were legion, as we can see, for example, inquiring into the owner-ship status of the land held in collective farms—which, in most countries, was not state-owned but belonged to the members jointly. During the socialist pe-riod, as I have observed, land was administratively moved around more or less at will among CFs, SFs, and noncollectivized households; because who owned it was rarely an issue, officials who exchanged parcels or modified land use gener-ally did not record the alterations in the land registers.

But after 1989, ownership suddenly mattered very much. Had the members relinquished ownership rights altogether upon joining the collective, or did those rights maintain some kind of shadow existence throughout? What did the joint ownership of cooperatives actually mean from a legal point of view? Did membership mean transferring actual title to physical land or rather transmut-ing that into ownership of shares, comparable to the rights of membership in a corporation? Post-1989 legislators argued these questions at length, and the an-swers differed by country, as did the ownership status of CF land (see Knapp 1975).[41] Lawyers with whom I have discussed the issue give contradictory ac-counts, as do Romanian law books. Writing about the status of cooperative land as part of their account of decollectivization, two Ministry of Agriculture legal specialists state both that "the cooperative appeared as the titulary of the prop-erty right and thus exercised possession, use, and alienation over lands of any kind in its patrimony" and that "the land continued to remain the property of the cooperative member" (Scrieciu and Chercea 1996, 524, 534).

There seem to me three possibilities for understanding the status of land in cooperative farms. One is that member households forfeited access to their land both de facto and de jure when they signed it over to the CF—the lay perception of the matter. Another is that member households retained ownership title but ceded the basic rights of ownership (possession, use, alienation) to the collective farm management—in a word, they held empty title. In this connection I adduce an interesting item from a discussion with a former president of the Vlaicu CF about how the collective had run in his time:

> People would ask us, "Why are you keeping so many animals, when they're all dying because they're not getting enough food?" The CF agronomist had thirty-three cows die on him one year, it was terrible. But we kept them to use as *collateral*, when we wanted loans from the World Bank or IMF; we couldn't use land, because it belonged to the members. So we kept animals in order to say, We have 700 cows. . . . This was the *only* reason to keep them, because so many died.

If this man is credible, then we have excellent practical evidence that the land belonged to the collective farmers, in some sense, at least. The final possibility is the suggestion of Linda Miller, a lawyer, based on extensive reading of Romanian legal texts and decrees: on the analogy with a corporation, joining a collective was a transaction in which you made a capital contribution (your land and implements) and received an ownership interest in return. The appropriate model for collective farms is therefore the corporation with a large number of shareholders relatively uninvolved in its actual management. In support of this idea, anyone wishing to withdraw from a collective had the theoretical right to claim a piece of land equivalent to that she had brought into it, but not necessarily her original parcel.[42]

Why did this matter?—because the answer to the ownership question affected the policy options for decollectivizing. If farm members had renounced in perpetuity all legal claim to their land, then the process of decollectivizing could take certain forms. Romania's parliament, representing all collective farmers, could undo the collectives in one single act (as indeed it did), perhaps distributing the land only among resident villagers able to work it, rather than trying to return it to former owners. It could cap the amount of land any one family might receive and could auction off CF buildings without compensating prior owners of the land under them, rather than requiring buyers of those buildings to pay ground rent. And so on. If, on the other hand, joining the collective had left members with title, howsoever empty, or with ownership interests in the corporation, then after 1989 a new law-governed state would have to confirm their ownership by restituting or reconstituting prior ownership rights, rather than by distributing the land exclusively to people who lived in villages. Indeed, in that case restitution would require no separate law, merely the members' joint declaration to dissolve the collective, at which point everything would revert to the status quo ante. (Never mind the complexities of discovering what that was after so many years of exchanging land, erasing boundaries, and transforming the landscape; see Verdery 1994.)

The more significant, underlying issue, however, is this: From the vantage point of which mode of regulation—legal or politico-administrative—should the question be answered? Although law did have its place in the socialist system, increasingly so as time went on, legality simply did not have the same status or legitimating function in the socialist property system that it has in market democracies. Property law was a supplement to the more active principle, property administration. Moving from such a regime to one supposedly grounded in law and judicial process raised innumerable difficulties concerning whether and how to translate administrative decrees into the language of the law in order to formulate policy. Can we select out the law-governed aspects of the socialist system and build a new one on those? Or must we retroactively legalize that system—even though the premise of the 1989 events was its illegitimacy—in order to proceed?

For those who regard the entire communist period as illegitimate, none of its acts has legal status. Hence, trying to determine and reverse the legal effects of an administrative decree is pointless; one need only make new laws. The weaknesses of this position include the following. To declare the acts of the socialist period illegal ignores the judicial maxim of *tempus regit actum*, which posits that the status of an action in its original context should govern how it is regarded now. If an administrative decree "acquired the force of law," as we might translate it, then those effects should be taken seriously in disposing of present ownership claims. Moreover, dismissing the entire socialist period as illegal wreaks havoc on a notion of law-governed practice rooted in predictability and continuity: how can one simply hop over the intervening illegal forty-five years and assert new ownership, without compromising the principle of a just claim?

The alternative is to recast the acts of that period in terms that permit continuity, even if to do so is to legitimize the system one seeks to displace. That is, restitution builds political legitimacy paradoxically: instead of playing up the illegitimacy of the old regime, it may require first legalizing the status of property under socialism so as to return rights to previous owners. The status of land in Transylvania offers a particularly clear example. There, the form of land registration meant that no transaction could be performed except on the basis of a previous legal transaction recorded in the land register. For me to receive back a parcel of land on which the collective farm built a structure, I must first have the structure and the parcel it stands on written into the register as belonging to the collective farm and then reregister it in my name. This procedure effectively legalizes the seizure of my parcel and the new use to which it has been put—that is, the procedure runs directly counter to the premise of unlawful seizure on which restitution rests! Michael Heller and Christopher Serkin make a similar observation: "Privatization of a factory by sale or auction partly legitimizes the prior socialist ownership of the factory" (1999, 1398).

The work involved in retroactively legalizing forty-five years of transformations, however, would be unmanageable. Any reader who has bought even one house involving a complex title search will gape at the prospect of multiplying that procedure a millionfold. The complexities relate not only to the legal status of different kinds of resources but also to the weak or fuzzy boundaries that characterized socialist property. Lacking clear edges, it was held together by social relations that were reticular and rhizomatic, that worked across property types. Those uncertain edges could be advantageous, as David Stark has argued (1996). In agriculture, they could also produce chaos. All the moving around of resources, the exchanges of parcels, the hiding of land, the erasure of field boundaries; all the uncertainties about the ownership status of collective and state farm land; all the failures to write land transactions into the land register—these made it extremely difficult to reestablish ownership rights, as I show in chapter 3 (see also Verdery 1994). The problems were particularly great in countries such as Romania, which adopted restitution on owners' previous sites.

A second point concerning the values instituted in socialist property has to do with commodification. Whatever else we might say of it, socialism's property regime established among people and goods a set of relations that did not rest mainly on a commodity basis. One goal, of course, was to erect a bulwark between the socialist and capitalist worlds, to protect local resources from being sucked into external capitalist markets. The strictures against any form of alienating socialist property, even by the party-state itself, and the insistence on the integrity of the unitary fund belonging to the whole people worked toward that end. Thus protected from the market, the resources controlled within socialist property relations were subject to evaluative criteria driven not by the market but by politics (e.g., what kinds of production would best fortify the Party's power, rather than how profitable an activity might be). It became exceedingly difficult to assess the book value of firms being privatized because the state, as the ultimate holder of financial obligation, had absorbed most of the liabilities of its subordinate firms and the materials a given firm used in production were so often not those the state had allocated to it. After 1989, the problems of evaluating the assets of SOEs defeated even the smartest economists. Questions of value, from the most basic (what kind of life do people want to live) to the niggling details of a firm's purchase price, joined with questions of morality to dominate public consciousness. Who ought or ought not to be profiting from the wealth accumulated under socialism—the former managers of state firms? foreigners? the general public?

Some answers to these questions came from a third aspect of the socialist property regime: its creation of a ranked hierarchy of forms, with those of the state at the top, cooperative/collective forms second, and individuals/households (especially those with private property) at the bottom. This hierarchy produced a very powerful class of state-enterprise directors benefiting maximally from state resources and from their control of administrative rights over estates of production. Even before 1989 they had begun using these rights to decompose state property from within, thereby weakening the political center. As that center grew weaker, the power of these directorial networks intensified. In short, socialism's property regime gave a decisive edge in the postsocialist era to a specific group of actors—SOE directors. They were accustomed to manipulating the fuzzy boundaries of socialist property, to moving resources around to maximum advantage. They disposed of large funds of social capital, in the form of their networks, and of cultural capital, in the form of their higher education and more extensive experience with the most modern farming their national economies could support. In agriculture specifically, we see the advantage of state over collective property in the greater cultural and social capital of SF heads over CF heads. SF directors had wider circles of connections, more complex managerial experience, greater familiarity with recent technology, better-endowed farms from which to strategize their exit, and so on, all owing to the higher position of state over cooperative property forms. Although international blueprints called for privatizing ownership rights, these socialist managers began by privatizing only their administrative rights, enabling them to avoid the liabilities of ownership by shucking those off onto the state, while still drawing central investments.

In this they were aided by socialism's overlapping estates of administration, which had socialized responsibility so thoroughly that the buck never stopped anywhere but continued to circulate in gifts. They were aided, as well, by the alliances these circulating gifts entailed. Networks of directors, as Stark has shown, could use their administrative advantage to resist competitive privatizations—quite successfully, in places such as Romania and Ukraine (see, e.g., Stark 1996; Stark and Bruszt 1998; Johnson and Minton-Beddoes 1996). Indeed, Stark (1996) suggests, the unit for privatization ought never to have been made the individual firm but instead, the interfirm network. In some countries, these networks generated viable capitalist firms; in others, they obstructed the privatization process, even using it to fortify their power by continuing to surround themselves with retinues of petitioners. This resistance made it difficult to create the property bundle so dear to the advocates of private property and perpetuated use-right arrangements similar to those of the hierarchy of administration. Although it is not surprising that SOE directors tended to fare well in the postsocialist period, my purpose here has been to show how their future success, as well as the disadvantage of certain others, was already inscribed in the property regime of socialism.

In agriculture, socialism created three kinds of social actors, hierarchically ranked, each of which spun off particular kinds of postsocialist progeny. From state farms came new enterprises and associational forms, run by well-endowed technocrats—sometimes as new managers, sometimes as what I call *supertenants*. Collective farms spun off, first, the farm infrastructure and its leadership, endowed with some of the resources of SF directors but in lesser degree, and second, households poorly endowed in knowledge, resources, and networks. In Romania, the former initiated producers' cooperatives, or associations; the latter became private owners engaged largely in subsistence farming, as they had done before on their usufruct plots. Chapters 5–8 describe how each of these progeny fared in one Transylvanian village.

❦

The architects of property restitution envisioned it as an act of recuperation, a return to a just order based in individual ownership that would permit more efficient economic action. Legislating the restoration of ownership rights would overturn the grand theft that had made socialist property possible. This conception failed to grasp how deeply embedded that system had been in social relations of exchange and obligation, not so easily modified by passing a few laws. Those social relations now served as the basis for yet another round of theft: as a society based in collecting people gradually gave way before one based in accumulating things, a lot of those people—particularly the ones at the bottom—were sloughed off. Underlying the rise of responsible owners and entrepreneurs, as I show in chapters 5–8, lurked forces that dispossess. In Eastern Europe, the twentieth century passed, from start to finish, under the sign of Proudhon.

CHAPTER 2
UNMAKING SOCIALIST AGRICULTURE
CONTEXTS OF RESTITUTION IN THE 1990S

We must prevent the concentration of land in the hands of one proprietor, for that would discourage the formation or the preservation of village communities as spaces of the authentic national spirit.
  (Romanian Prime Minister Petru Roman, 1990)[1]

It's just a fad, this business about sacred private property as the basis of social life.
  (Romanian President Ion Iliescu, 2001)[2]

In 1989, the entire property order I have summarized in chapter 1 was suddenly called into question. If, as the epigraph to that chapter asserts, the central idea of the communists was the abolition of private property, then the overthrow of communists might logically mean abolishing that abolition. And indeed, plans to accomplish precisely this absorbed tremendous political energy in every formerly socialist country, as well as in their relations with foreigners. Something like a western private-property blueprint was the assumed end point, with the restoration of precommunist property relations a good beginning, but there was little agreement on how to go about it.

By far the most telling obstacle to property transformation was that no one had ever done anything like it on so massive a scale. The preprivatizations that had been going on covertly under the socialist umbrella, mentioned in chapter 1, were nowhere nearly comprehensive enough to qualify as property transformation, although they might pave the way. There were two other possible precedents: (1) prior land reforms, some of which had distributed large quantities of land while facing tremendous logistical difficulties that resembled those of the 1990s, and (2) the privatizations going on in Western Europe and the United States during the last quarter of the twentieth century—the model for advisors to East European governments. Yet both precedents were distinct from postsocialist property reform in that they were accomplished within systems already dominated by the principle of private ownership. Not so the transformations of postsocialism. Moreover, western privatizations embarked from totally different initial conditions, and their volume was minuscule by comparison with postsocialism. In short, there was little to guide policy-making for this momentous process.

What engaged the most political energy was the dismantling of state-owned enterprises (SOEs) in industry. In countries that had relatively large populations residing in the countryside or employed in agriculture and/or where agriculture provided a sizable percentage of the gross domestic product (such as in Bulgaria, Romania, and Albania), however, the politics of decollectivization had very high stakes. Rural people constituted an important electoral resource; it was important to gain their gratitude by giving out land, to avoid excessive landlessness, and to win those people over as a counterweight to the political opposition. Nonetheless, rural residents could never be as important as the more sizable (and potentially organizable) urban population, who wanted their food cheap even as farmers wanted it expensive. In this way, the rural populace became a political football.

Although various kinds of political actors strove to realize their objectives in crafting decollectivization policies, internal constituencies were far from the only ones to consider. Fundamentally constraining what national politicians could do were the prospects for accession to the European Union, with its various benchmarks in pricing, tariffs, privatization, and other indicators. Likewise, hopes for more immediate economic transformation required submitting to the conditions of international financial actors: the IMF, World Bank, USAID, European Bank for Reconstruction and Development (EBRD), and so on. The various East European countries were differently drawn into these various bodies, as well as into international capital flows—further reason for wide variation in what they could attempt to do. Thus, as Hanisch (2000) suggests, to see the voter market as the main influence on decollectivization policy is insufficient because, to a considerable degree, the agenda was being set elsewhere.

In this chapter, I provide the post-1989 context for my ethnography of decollectivization in Vlaicu, first describing the restitution process as it occurred across the former socialist bloc and then concentrating on the Romanian land law of 1991. I argue that given the myriad groups who had a stake in the outcome, privatization policy was an eminently political process (rather than, as some foreign observers seemed to believe, just a clear economic necessity). The multiple political pressures behind reform legislation, together with the parlous state of Romania's economy, compromised the success of decollectivization from villagers' point of view. Ultimately, the government's inability to support the creation of property rights in land with policies enabling its recipients to use the land effectively limited the forms of value they might find in it.

Comparative Decollectivizations

The literature on postsocialist privatization and on the subset of it dealing with land restitution is vast, including both general overviews and case studies. Its volume spares me the work of an extended presentation. In this section, I briefly discuss trends in postsocialist restitutions, emphasizing points relevant to decollectivization in Romania.

Justifications

The justifications for decollectivizing, and for privatization more generally, were numerous and complex, with various arguments emphasizing the symbolic and moral, the economic, and the political dimensions.[3] For postsocialist elites, the symbolic and moral arguments were crucial because they bore on the legitimation of the emerging order. The creation of socialism's property system had intimately touched everyone in these countries; reversing that system was an act of great symbolic power. It announced (whether truthfully or not) to publics both internal and external that the new rulers were different from the old. Presented as at least partly an act of reparation for wrongs done in the name of socialism, it would validate the new governments in Eastern Europe both to their own populations and to actors in the international environment— states, foreign investors, international financial institutions, and so forth. By raising questions about justice and accountability, it symbolized a commitment to instituting the rule of law, which the communists were accused of having violated. The hoped-for result of wielding the privatization symbol was both domestic support and foreign aid.

Concerning the economic arguments, their principal advocates were the consultants and policy-makers from the United States and Western Europe who poured into the region after 1989. They saw private property as essential to both fixing the problems of these economies and creating markets there—processes that would also integrate the region into the global system to the region's benefit, they assumed. Meanwhile, such integration also facilitated the entry of foreign capital into places long relatively isolated from it, at a time when finance capital was increasingly the dominant coordinating power in the world economy. Creating private property rights was the cornerstone of western advice to

Eastern Europe, but postsocialist governments, for their part, were also largely persuaded that secure property rights were essential to redressing their countries' economic decline and ending the inefficiencies of socialist plans. Some of them also saw privatization as a source of revenues (from the sale of state firms) and thus as a way of paying for new policies and servicing debts.[4]

Here the economic arguments shaded into several political ones. National elites saw economic growth as a way to develop a broad base of support, as well as new forms of livelihood and political patronage for themselves and their allies. Dismantling socialist property would give political constituencies new shape. For example, legislators might manipulate restitution laws so as to exclude and thus weaken ethnic minorities as a politico-economic force. In countries such as Poland, Czechoslovakia, and Hungary in which a noncommunist opposition had come to power, the new leaders feared socialism's reinstatement, given the large numbers of socialist-era bosses who still ran state institutions. Crucial to thwarting that possibility would be to divest the state of its socialist institutions for gaining revenue (i.e., state property). Breaking those up would also free resources for the new political parties, which (unlike the successors to the Communist Party) had no war chests. Here, again, the goals of new elites converged with those of foreigners, who had their own plans for those liberated resources.

These various justifications indicate the multiple sources of value that the property question might hold for people in positions of power, who legislated the breakup of socialist agricultural forms. The political and economic circumstances of postsocialist states, including their politicians' dependence on international financial circuits, gave the notion of property rights special meaning. In the remainder of this chapter, I describe how they sought to create property rights in land; subsequent chapters show how these rights proved insufficient to enabling many of their holders to own successfully.

Restitution Politics

As with other forms of privatization, the possible goals of land reform were numerous, fundamental, and sometimes contradictory.[5] They included issues of historical justice, political expediency, ethnic empowerment, equality, buying off the losers, economic efficiency, distributive effects, and accumulating political capital. The logistical problems of restitution were legion and the debates concerning them very heated; they were fought out in protracted political battles among groups in a constantly shifting field of forces, with the balance among contenders in continual flux. Hard-won decisions could be revisited or overturned as that balance changed. The trick, then, was to chart a course that would garner as much political support and as little opposition as possible. Because the relevant groups, their initial power positions, and the balance of political forces differed from case to case, the results differed for each country and reduced sequential learning from one to another.

These groupings cannot properly be called political *parties*—certainly not at the time when the laws were being debated and written (1990–94)—and therefore could not represent specific constituencies. Among those who sought to influence the outcome were all who hoped to attract votes and build political careers, people who expected to retrieve sizable estates, the managers of socialist farms (whose interests were not, however, uniform), and members of the state agricultural bureaucracy that ran those farms. Very few participants in the national debates, I think it is fair to say, sought to represent the concerns of prospective smallholders (see also Maurel 1994b, 157, 162). Although a few ad hoc organizations of farmers sprang up, these more readily catered to the restitution hopes of the wealthier landowners, not the immense one- to five-hectare crowd.

One fundamental question, extensively debated, was to what degree the socialist state should be dismantled and replaced with a less activist one. Should the state be "brought back in" or "back out"? On the "back out" side were those economists and international organizations eager to create leaner postsocialist states whose bureaucracies would immobilize fewer resources than had socialist ones. Forgetting the state-led growth of countries such as Japan and Taiwan, these groups worried that a strong state would attract rent-seeking, to the detriment of economic growth. In contrast to this opinion were the proponents of "back in," encouraged by numerous studies of economic development in nonsocialist contexts that saw a strong state as necessary for development, especially for the formation of markets.[6] To transform socialist societies, these scholars believed, required strong states that would actively manage state-sector decline. But this leads to what Frydman and Rapaczynski (1994, 13, 200–201) call the "paradox of transition," with the state both playing the game and making the rules. Observing that for political as well as economic reasons the speed of transition required a level of state intervention that usurped decision-making usually left to the private sector, they conclude, "All in all, the activism of the state, attempting to manage the process of the state sector's decline, prevents the establishment of a private property regime, which is the whole purpose of the transition" (Frydman and Rapaczynski 1994, 201). Although we may disagree with that last phrase, their summary nicely captures a predicament found to greater or lesser degree all across the region.

In addition to such big questions, there were endless debates concerning the specific procedures to be followed. Without exploring the nuances, I list here a number of them to show which options were on the table.[7] The first was whether property rights that had been given over to socialist forms should be returned through restitution to previous owners, compensated in some other form, or distributed without respect to prior ownership. In general, Eastern European countries, including the Baltic states, opted for some form of restitution or compensation, whereas the other former Soviet republics went for distribution. Underlying this difference were the facts that (1) in many parts of Russia and Central Asia, land had never (or only very briefly) been held in individual ownership and (2) collectivized agriculture had begun much earlier in the Soviet Union, before the memory of most living farmers. Because both facts vastly complicated reconstructing the precollectivization property order there, distributing land seemed the only option if the socialist forms were to disappear. For Eastern Europe, however, restitution was the preferred policy, debate centering only on how it would proceed.

One issue was whether restitution should be preferential or equitable. Should it privilege some over others on particular grounds (they had owned it, they lived there, or they could work it) or should it treat all in a community equally? If land were given to nonresidents, leaving numbers of villagers landless, that might sharpen conflict in rural areas. The same question was also crucial to the future success of agriculture: if land were given only to people living in the countryside, it was more likely to be used than if given back to everyone who had lost it, many of them now urbanites. In the latter case, there would be a large number of absentee owners, a situation that might cause agricultural output to drop in the short to medium run but then promote a faster consolidation of holdings thereafter.

Then, if rights to land were restored, should they be returned in full or only in part? Some countries set a limit on the amount of land any one recipient could recover (although elections might later open those limits to revision, as happened in Romania and Bulgaria). Should land sales be restricted, to keep people from losing their land to speculators or the old communist elites? Should land rights be returned directly in their original form or in some other—that is, should people receive title to actual land or, instead, vouchers representing its value? If actual land was given, should it be returned in its *historical* boundaries (that is, in exactly the fragmented parcels that the communists had seized) or in *comparable* boundaries (that is, land of equivalent quality but in a different location, or in fewer and more compact parcels)?

Still other questions concerned the difference between collective and state farms. Should land in state farms be treated in the same way as land in collectives, given the different methods for creating them and the different status of their land, as explained in chapter 1? In many countries, the distinction between

SF and CF land ownership explains why land in collective farms but not in state farms was usually given back, as well as why land was treated differently from other assets of the disbanding CFs, which were under collective and not individual ownership.

And how about nonland assets that the CFs and SFs had acquired during the socialist period—the farm buildings and machinery, above all? Such assets were critical to future farming success, so how should they be treated? A common solution was to assess the contributions of members to the collective, sell the nonland assets, and divide the proceeds proportionately. Different countries created different algorithms for this compensation, based on the amount of land people had given their farm and the labor they had contributed to it; these algorithms were—like solutions to all the other questions we have considered—politically motivated.[8] The assets in state farms, however, would have to be treated otherwise. Should these be sold, thus privileging the agrarian elites who had money to buy things, or given away, precisely so as to obstruct accumulation by those elites? If they were sold, how should one arrive at a value suitable for setting their price? It was precisely the difficulties of determining the worth of state assets in a nonmarket environment that led even the World Bank finally to advocate giving them away.

From among the many other logistic dilemmas, I consider one more: Which precommunist property order should restitution recreate? This was far from an idle question in a region where before World War II, all the states were multinational, many of them had contained Jewish populations as well as sizable German minorities, and several had very unequal property structures, having undergone no land reforms since the end of serfdom. Into this varied context had come postwar communist land reforms that redistributed the property rights of both nationals and ethnic minorities, in ways I discussed in chapter 1. Per capita, the most land was redistributed in Hungary and Poland, then Albania, then Romania and Czechoslovakia, then Yugoslavia, and last Bulgaria. The German minorities figured prominently in these postwar reforms because expropriating them had yielded large surfaces—almost one-third of the total land area in Poland and one-quarter of it, in Czechoslovakia.[9]

The 1945 reform thus had ethnonational significance, and so did the restitution of land rights after 1989. That is, restitution became entangled with the process of forming postsocialist national identities.[10] Key to this outcome was the choice of the baseline date for restitution: some dates would enhance the percentage of land held by the majority group; others would impropriate minorities at the expense of the majority. In Czechoslovakia, the baseline date for restitution was February 25, 1948, after the expropriation of, first, Jews and then 2 million Sudeten Germans. Clearly, the new landed classes would be Czech.

Likewise, Hungarian law initially set the date at June 8, 1949, which excluded Jews and Germans. In the Baltic countries, the problem was not pre-1945 minorities so much as the many Russians who had later moved in for industrial work; land laws set the restitution dates to exclude them. Politicians in all countries, then, tried to select baseline dates that left out significant ethnonational others, who could be sacrificed because they had little electoral weight (Heller and Serkin 1999, 1406; Swinnen 1997b, 376–79). The dates shaped the electorate in other ways as well, such as by impropriating the poor and landless, who would receive nothing if the law chose a date when wealthy landowners had not yet been expropriated.[11]

Comparative Restitutions

How did restitution look, across the region as a whole? How did Romania differ from its neighbors, so we might see what is peculiar about the case treated in this book and what is more generally applicable? I begin with some tables. Table 2.1 shows the percentage of the population that was employed in agriculture in the 1940s and 1990 as well as the share of that sector in national budgets, and table 2.2 the percentages of land held in collective and state farms. Table 2.3 summarizes the procedure chosen (restitution vs. distribution) for the two farm types by country.

At the time of collectivization, the various countries had differed considerably in their levels of industry and thus in the percentage of their population that was employed in agriculture—an indication of how many people were vulnerable to collectivization. Table 2.1, column 3, shows these percentages before collectivization, indicating that far more people in Albania, Bulgaria, and Romania were likely to suffer from collectivization than was true elsewhere. During the socialist period, the rapid development of industry reduced these percentages, as indicated in column 4; the differences among the countries nonetheless remained, along with differences in the proportion of their GDP that came from agriculture (column 5). All these numbers are relevant to decollectivization. The figures in column 3 indicate in which countries the 1990s land reform touched more of the population, even if they were no longer resident in the countryside. The figures in columns 2 and 4 suggest how large that population might be—an issue of some political consequence, pushing governments with larger rural populations to different decisions from those with smaller ones. The share of agriculture in the GDP shows the potential risk to the state budget if decollectivizing resulted in a sharp decrease in output. In Romania, this figure probably influenced the decision not to privatize state farms at first. As these numbers show, Romanian communists inherited an economy still

Table 2.1

*Share of Agriculture in Employment 1940s and 1980s and in State Budgets
1990/1991, Eastern Europe*

Country (1)	Population ca. 1990 (in millions) (2)	Population Employed in Agriculture (%)		Agriculture as Percentage of GDP 1990/91 (5)
		Late 1940s (3)	1989 (4)	
Albania	3,256	88	49	39
Bulgaria	8,989	76	18	18
Czechoslovakia	15,650	38	10	6 / 7
East Germany	16,028	29	11	10
Hungary	10,355	53	18	14
Poland	38,183	57	26	8
Romania	23,190	74	28	20

Source: Europa Publications Limited (1994) and World Bank (2001) (cols. 2, 3, and 5); OECD
    Center for Cooperation with Non-Members (1998) and Commission of the European
    Communities (1992) (col. 4).

heavily agricultural and, despite their intense efforts to industrialize, in 1989
they left it more agrarian than most.

Table 2.2 shows the tremendous variation in the average sizes of socialist farms,
as well as in the amount of land held in the three main farm types. For the Soviet
Union, the much larger farm sizes reflect the vast expanses of farms in Central
Asia and of nomadic animal-herding farms in Siberia. The size difference makes it
clear why Soviet farm chairmen were so powerful, relative to their Eastern European counterparts. As we see from the table (columns 3 and 5), the USSR had the
bulk of its land in state farms or huge state complexes; those with land mainly in
collectives were (in descending order) East Germany, Albania, Hungary, and
Czechoslovakia/Romania. In Bulgaria large agro-industrial complexes predomi-
nated until the late 1980s, making the distinction between state and collective
farms somewhat moot. Poland had almost no collectives at all; its land was largely
in private farms. Thus, Romania's farm organization most closely resembled that
of Czechoslovakia, although with a much larger rural population. From columns
4 and 6 we see evidence of the restructuring that decollectivization might entail,
given that the average farm size in the United States is 300–400 ha and in Western
Europe 70 ha—well below socialist farms (Lerman 2000b).

These two tables provide evidence of the variation across the region with respect to the initial conditions facing decollectivizers. Some countries (including

Table 2.2

Comparison of Collective and State Farms by Average Size and Proportion of Agricultural Land Occupied, Eastern Europe and the Soviet Union, mid-1980s

Country (year of data source)[a] (1)	Land Farmed Privately (%) (2)	Land in Collective Farms (%) (3)	Average Size (ha)[b] (4)	Land in State Farms (%) (5)	Average Size (ha) (6)
Albania, 1983	0.5	78	1,300	21	n.a.
Bulgaria, 1989[c]	13	70	4,000	17	1,615
Czechoslovakia, 1987/1985	6	64	2,600	30	6,200
East Germany, 1987	10	82	1,200	8	1,000
Hungary, 1987	14	71	4,400	15	7,400
Poland, 1987	78	4	300	18	2,700
Romania, 1987/1985	9	61	2,400	30	4,900
USSR, 1987/1986	2	30	9,300	68	34,600

Sources: Pryor (1992, 101, 144–45); I have rounded off Pryor's figures, so as not to produce an impression of exactitude that would be inappropriate for the socialist period. Figures for Romania are from Turnock (1986, 184). Figures for Bulgaria in columns 2 and 5 are from OECD (2000, 72, 78). The first column is worded so as to include both land that is privately owned and the personal plots of collective farmers.

Note: n.a., not available.

[a] If the data come from different years, the first date refers to the percentage of land in each type, the second to the average size.

[b] In nearly all cases these figures are larger in the 1980s than they had been 10–15 years earlier, reflecting a uniform trend toward concentration.

[c] During the 1970s, Bulgaria amalgamated its state and collective farms to produce huge agro-industrial complexes; it is thus somewhat artificial to separate SFs from CFs, although by the late 1980s that policy had been reversed. Subtracting the 13 percent in col. 2 and 17 percent in col. 5 (figures from OECD 2000, 72, 78) from 100 leaves 70 percent as an approximate figure for cooperatives (col. 3).

Romania) had more people to restore land to than others and were thus likely to find the process more complex and time-consuming; some were more concerned than others about the possible effects of decreased agricultural production on the national budget and therefore more likely to try to retain a category of unrestituted state land (as in Romania); some contained a larger state-based agrarian elite than did others—in Romania, a powerful group of state farm directors from the southern and eastern parts of the country, where state farms had been much larger than in Transylvania. Although Eastern Europeans are heartily sick of being told that they formed a natural laboratory, the variation shown in these tables does encourage seeing them as a kind of live experiment (Lerman 2000a).

A further source of variation in outcomes was the extent of socialist-era reforms in agriculture. In the countries where reforms went furthest, such as Hungary and to some extent Czechoslovakia and Bulgaria, collectives sometimes worked sufficiently well that villagers came to accept and even benefit from them (e.g., Creed 1998; Swain 1985). In others, however, such as Romania, Albania, and the Baltic countries, reforms were minimal, and farm performance was mostly unsatisfactory. Why is this important? Nigel Swain (1998) has argued that reforms in socialist agriculture were inversely proportional to destruction of the collectives after 1989. In many areas in Albania and Romania, farm members spontaneously took over cultivation, divided up farm inventories, and, in acts of startling fury, demolished collective farm buildings and vandalized the assets—even though these represented a huge labor investment and were still useful. Asserting their ownership rights, they either began farming the land themselves or turned over its management to newly formed cooperative associations, in hopes of receiving better pay than they had from the previous collectives. In Hungary and the Czech Republic, by contrast, collective agriculture had brought sufficient benefits that villagers were less eager to break it up. Instead, collectives were transformed—without first dismantling them—into new cooperatives or corporations that retained the collectives' assets.

How were alternative solutions distributed across space? During the early 1990s, each government passed a land reform law providing for the manner in which collective farms and state farms would be dismantled. These laws were subsequently amended to adapt to problems that had arisen. Table 2.3 shows the year of the main law plus basic methods adopted, by farm type. Were the table to include more of the non-Baltic Soviet republics (such as Ukraine, Kyrgyzstan, and Uzbekistan), where distribution rather than restitution was the policy, the contrast between them and Eastern Europe would be more apparent (see Wegren 1998b, xx). As is evident, in two-thirds of the cases the procedures for dismantling state and collective farms differed in at least some respects. The table does not show the tremendous degree of fragmentation that resulted where land was returned to former owners rather than passing directly into some more sizable unit. In Albania, for example, there were an average of 3.3 plots for the average 1.3-ha holding; in Romania the average 2.2-ha holding was in an average of four to eight pieces.[12]

Across the region, land laws restored property rights in one form or another to those who had previously held them. In some cases, they created property rights for people who had not held any before. To restore or create rights was one thing; to produce ownership titles, however, was vastly more complex. The

Table 2.3

Manner of Breaking up State and Collective Farms, with Year of First Land Law

Country	Year of Land Law[a]	Chief Means of Disbanding Collective Farms	Chief Means of Disbanding State Farms
Albania[b]	1991	Distribution, some restitution	Distribution, some restitution
Bulgaria	1991	Restitution	Some restitution, some left intact
Czech Republic	1991	Restitution	Sale/leasing[c]
East Germany	1992	Restitution	Sale/leasing
Hungary	1991	Restitution, distribution, and sale for compensation bonds	Sale for compensation bonds, plus sale/ leasing
Latvia	1990	Restitution	Restitution
Lithuania	1991	Restitution	Restitution
Poland	1991	—	Sale/leasing
Romania	1991	Restitution, some distribution	Delayed restitution, some sale/leasing
Russia	1990	Reregistering as CFs, distribution	Reregistering as SFs, distribution
Slovakia	1991	Restitution	Sale/leasing

Source: Columns 3 and 4 are modified from Swinnen (1997a, 365). Data for Russia are from Wegren (1998b, xx).

[a] This date refers to the first major law regulating socialist agricultural forms. In nearly all cases, relevant laws continued to be issued over a longer period, sometimes revising and sometimes completing the earlier ones.

[b] The Albanian land law provided only for distribution, but in the northern and more mountainous areas of the country many recipients insisted on having their former plots (i.e., restitution). See de Waal (1996).

[c] The category Sale/leasing refers to leases accorded pending sale.

process usually began with a preliminary measurement that yielded provisional titles, to be replaced by final titles based on measuring more systematically. Most figures on the pace of decollectivization derive from the former of these—the figure most governments wanted to emphasize, so as to convince others of their commitment to private property. From the provisional to the final title, however, there could be many a slip. Moreover, some government statistics (Romania and Bulgaria for certain) tended to overreport the percentage of the land held in individual farms and to underreport cases in which the former collectives had simply reorganized into cooperatives, their individual-farm owners leaving their land with the new form. Such governments' desire to show rapid progress in creating private property, together with their not actually knowing what was happening in the countryside, make statistics for this period every bit as untrustworthy as for the period preceding.

In general, four main forms emerged from dismantling socialist agriculture: (1) individual private farms, either small plots cultivated for subsistence by owner-families or larger individual farms oriented to the market; (2) producers' cooperatives or associations, often created by reorganizing the collective farms; (3) new private farming companies or corporations oriented to profit (some of which overlap with the individual-farm category); and (4) remnants of socialism (chiefly state farms or land retained for agricultural research). For a variety of reasons, however, it is difficult to compare countries in terms of these four forms, notwithstanding publications that do precisely that (see Verdery 2001, 146). For this reason, I offer few figures in the following paragraphs, and they are at best approximations.[13]

The restitution process was simplest in Poland and former Yugoslavia, where agriculture had not been collectivized. There, the task was to dismantle only the state farms, which in 1990 occupied only 18 percent and 15 percent, respectively, of agricultural land.[14] The dissolution of socialist forms proceeded fastest in Albania. Within eighteen months, collective and state farms were disbanded and their land distributed to the residents of villages, without regard to prior ownership—a policy that distinguished Albania from all other Eastern European countries. Only in the mountainous north did villagers force restitution to previous owners. Contributing to the speed of this outcome was that central policy remained consistent—unlike that in, for instance, Bulgaria, Romania, or eastern Germany. Moreover, because all land had been state-owned, there was no legal argument for restitution, with the lengthy gathering of evidence about previous owners, measuring, and so forth that occurred elsewhere. By distributing land equally to village residents, the government could complete the process rapidly. Almost as radical for similar reasons (nationalized land and a dismal experience with socialist agriculture) were Latvia and Lithuania. By 1995, 79 percent of all agricultural land in Latvia and 67 percent in Lithuania was in full- or part-time family farms. Latvia distinguished itself by being the only country that restituted land to former owners even if they were no longer Latvian citizens, so as to keep it out of Russian hands.[15]

The remaining example of radical reform was Romania. There, destruction of collective farm buildings was so extensive as to compel the government to cancel all collective farm debts (in contrast, for example, to Hungary and Czechoslovakia) because there was often nothing left to recover them from. Unlike the examples mentioned so far, Romanian law disbanded only the collectives, not the state farms—a function of the heavy weight of agriculture in its GDP and labor force, the substantial areas held in state farms, and the weight of the agrarian elite in policy-making. Only later were state farms dismantled as well; meanwhile, they were to provide food in case the restitution of CF land diminished agricultural production. The restitution process was slow, for many former owners insisted on receiving exactly the same parcels they had owned; lawsuits dragged out the process.

In other countries, there was less interest in completely breaking up socialist agriculture. Instead, many of the collectives persisted, often under slightly different cooperative guise, and only some of the prior owners withdrew their land. In the Czech Republic, for example, there was considerable resistance to decollectivization; a 1992 survey by Maurel of 2,500 people found that fully half did not want individual farming, the low demand for it probably related to the fact that only 17 percent of those who stood to receive land were still active in agriculture. For this reason, policy emphasized the smooth transposition of collective-farm land into new cooperatives or corporations. Cooperatives became the dominant form there within three years of restitution (Maurel 1994b, 247, 279). Complications nonetheless attended the effort to restore land (for those who wanted it) on the old sites, as in Romania and Bulgaria.

Bulgarian farmers also resisted decollectivizing but national politics prevented a Czech solution. Precisely because there was great popular support for the collectives, the reformist parliament elected in 1991 forced them to dissolve, so as to destroy these "bastions of communist sentiment" (see Creed 1995b, 1999; Hanisch 2000; Meurs 2001). Political struggle between the nearly matched reformist and neocommunist forces soon reversed this, however, when the latter took power in 1992; in the next three years, there was a sevenfold increase in the (re)formation of cooperatives. As of 1995, official statistics showed 53 percent of Bulgaria's land as privately farmed, 41 percent in cooperatives (probably too low a figure)[16] (Davidova, Buckwell, and Kopeva 1997, 29, 39). When the government changed again in 1997, things were up in the air once more, and Bulgarian property rights remained insecure for most of the decade. Meanwhile, as in Romania, abundant lawsuits arose from the difficulty of restoring land on its old sites, both immobilizing land transactions and occasioning tremendous legal expense for cash-poor villagers.[17]

The more spectacular case of dissolution from above was, of course, the German Democratic Republic. There German reunification resulted in the rapid dismantling of collective farms, which were turned into new capitalist corporations (see Buechler and Buechler 2002). State farms, however, were not broken up but remained state property; to have returned them would have resurrected the huge estates that were broken up in the 1945 land reform. Instead, the government of the Federal Republic became the owner of the state farms and rented the land out to capitalist farmers—a nice source of revenue that diminished government interest in privatizing it.[18] Between 1990 and 1995, the government in Bonn sank 17 billion deutsche marks into support for East German agriculture, an extraordinary sum compared with what all other governments in the area were able to provide. The subsidies, along with free access to European markets that accompanied Germany's EU membership, made East Germany's land reform wholly distinctive from other Eastern European cases.[19]

Hungary, long the exception among Eastern European economies, was also exceptional in its ingenious and complicated restitution program.[20] It was the only country in which former owners could not claim land directly; instead, all were given privatization vouchers reflecting the value of their previous landownership. They could use the vouchers to bid not only at the land auctions held for this purpose but also for other goods, such as shares in firms. Rightly viewing the return to old sites as a nightmare, this program meant that people seldom recovered the specific parcels their families had owned before.[21] In short, the Hungarian restitution plan gave priority not to historical justice but to creating an agriculture that would be viable in the future. They were able to do so partly because they already had one, from two decades of market-oriented reforms (see Hann 1980; Swain 1985). Because the collectives had nurtured a flourishing household-based agriculture, farmers had none of the incentive of those in Romania or Albania to destroy the farms and start new private ones; the impetus went rather to modifying the collectives or turning them into companies. Moreover, many of Hungary's farmers were reluctant to repossess land as individuals. For example, in the village of Boly, Maurel's survey found that 90 percent of those who had owned land before collectivization refused to pull out and become independent farmers because they saw the future of agriculture as too chancy (1994b, 245).

The situation in Russia differs substantially from the cases already summarized.[22] Socialist farms there were generally much larger than elsewhere (see table 2.2) and their directors were more powerful relative to members—a situation only accentuated by the collapse of the Soviet state and the emergence of local suzerainties inadequately controlled from the political center (Humphrey 1991). Collectivization had occurred so much earlier, and on the basis of very unstable private ownership, that restitution was never a possibility. After passage of the 1990 law "On Land Reform," providing for the dissolution of socialist agricultural organizations, all farms were reregistered in one form or another: unchanged, as ongoing state or collective farms; as various kinds of new associations, cooperatives, partnerships, or joint stock companies; or as individual private farms, although serious obstacles were placed in the way of withdrawing land from CFs for this end (see Humphrey 1998, chap. 9). Voting patterns showed that villagers did not generally support land reform, and both they and farm chairmen undermined private farmers' success—as did the end of agricultural subsidies.

This last point underscores something I have scarcely mentioned: each country's economic policies concerning agriculture. It was difficult enough to transform property relations, but far from sufficient for enabling successful farms. In his 1992 book on collectivization, Frederic Pryor indicates the magnitude of the problem, explaining why he thinks collectivization would be difficult if not impossible to reverse. Successful individual farming required numerous institutional prerequisites, such as a reliable and accessible source of inputs, including equipment; available credit; basic infrastructure (barns and silos that were not too big and a good road network); conditions for marketing farm products; and ways of cushioning the problems of risk that individual farmers faced—for example, by setting up cooperatives (Pryor 1992, 268–75). In other words, Pryor's conditions include not just re-creating private ownership rights in land but creating conditions in which the owners could actually make use of it. There was little advantage to exiting the collective farm if one could not make a meaningful living after that. The point is important for my emphasis on value: if the new owners could not bring other production factors together, land would lose value for them.

Throughout the region, everything Pryor mentioned proved a major obstacle. The infrastructure for delivering inputs to individual farmers, a system for providing credits so people could buy equipment, distribution channels enabling sale—none of these was even remotely adequate for the growth of commercial farming. Not only could governments facing budgetary crises do little to create suitable conditions, but if they promised subsidies, their handlers in international finance objected, pressing instead for free markets with no subsidies and low tariffs—right next door to an EU agriculture built on subsidies and protection. The results, claims Szelényi (1998, 12), were an economic crisis in the former socialist bloc that between 1988 and 1993 was more profound than the Great Depression of 1929–33. Like that earlier Depression, it entailed a reversion to subsistence farming, but now under circumstances in which the price scissors cut deeper.[23]

We can see the outcome in greater detail in Swinnen's (2000) conclusions from a decade of studying Eastern Europe's agricultural transformation. He notes, first, a sharp decline in gross agricultural output everywhere except Albania for the first half of the 1990s; it then mostly leveled off in Eastern Europe, although not in Russia and Ukraine. (Note that in Poland, the country with the least extensive land reform, there was less of a drop than in the others.) Second, he observes, the main causes of this decline were institutional disruption, reduced demand, and the effects of freeing prices and cutting agricultural subsidies. These produced an ever-widening gap between the cost of resources necessary for cultivation (inputs) and the sale prices of agricultural products—that is, a widening price scissors. Aggravating the trend was widespread inflation that in some countries resulted from continued subsidies to state-owned industry. In addition, major problems with securing credit in rural areas prevented rural producers from acquiring loans for investment and even for working capital. Despite gains in yields and aggregate labor productivity in some countries, there was a regionwide decline in the use of productivity-boosting inputs such as fertilizer, down to as little as 20 percent of its 1990 use—in Russia, down to as little as 11 percent (Swinnen 2000).[24] This indicated the shortcuts that cash-poor farmers were having to take. Further evidence is an increased amount of land left uncultivated, especially in southeastern Europe, in part because the owners could not afford to work it. Official figures for Bulgaria in 2000, for instance, put the amount of unworked land at 28 percent of the total surface.[25] Although things might improve after 2000, the costs of bringing land back into cultivation might be too high for farmers struggling to compete with EU agriculture.

Because of the difficulties individual farmers faced, in several of these countries large-scale production units continued to be dominant throughout the decade, although they were decreasing in size. Since many of these units rented land from individual owners who could not manage to farm it themselves, the trend could persist for some time. Although Swinnen does not note this, leasing has the advantage that tenants can leave with the owners any liabilities associated with the asset. Rentals of that kind were the principal form of land market, owing to unresolved ownership rights, government moratoria on sales, owners' hesitancy about selling in such insecure times, and other obstacles that made sales of land sluggish.

In sum, a significant effect of restitution was to separate ownership from control and use once again, as was true in the socialist period (and as is true of the United States as well, where land leasing is widespread). Indeed, as Szelényi (1998,14) points out, a decade of unmaking socialist agriculture left many similarities to what went before. The postsocialist landscape resembled that of socialism (and of feudalism as well), with large latifundia alongside small garden plots. These latifundia were in many cases the same old collectives in a new guise; much of the equipment was the same and so were the managers.

❦

From this summary of land restitution regionwide, I can now turn to its particulars in Romania. To recapitulate: because 70 percent of Romania's population had worked in agriculture at collectivization, much larger numbers of Romanians were affected by decollectivizing than was true in countries other than

Albania and Bulgaria. Like those two countries, Romania derived a larger percentage of its GDP from agriculture than other East European countries and had a fairly large proportion of its population employed in agriculture—28 percent in 1989 and rising to 40 percent over the next two years. Agrarian interests therefore counted heavily in leaders' political calculus; the high percentage of land in state farms, together with their relatively large size, gave weight to the lobby of SF directors even as CF presidents lost their jobs. Combining these facts helps to explain why SFs were not included in the land restitution law, as they were almost everywhere else.

The Romanian economy was in the worst shape of all except Albania, indicating the distance to be traveled in the reform process (see, e.g., Pop-Eleches 1999). Under Iliescu's leadership through 1996, that reform process was slow. Foreign investment was weak, and internal power struggles often ended by further retarding outside influence. The country's position in the global economy remained more peripheral than that of Hungary, Poland, or the Czech Republic. Because the Ceauşescu regime had brought the economy nearly to ruin, the new government had to obtain loans from the IMF, World Bank, EBRD, and European Investment Bank, and those lenders established conditions that promoted more reform than powerful insiders might have wished. The result was that pressure for privatization went with serious limits on what the government could do to support private enterprise. That was particularly true for farming, and it constrained the possibilities for realizing value from land ownership. In Romania this outcome mattered more than elsewhere because a fairly large percentage of people—fully 46 percent, in 1990—lived in rural areas, even if many commuted to towns for work.

To shorten what could be a too lengthy review, here I say relatively little about the ins and outs of Romanian politics or the general climate in the country during the 1990s, focusing on the restitution law, the measures for implementing it, and subsequent policy toward agriculture.

Legislating Decollectivization in Romania

> Thus, the agrarian reform laws left to the authorities the power to establish parcels so small that in practical terms they could not ensure the economic independence of the peasantry. —(Şandru 1975, 147, concerning Romania's 1921 land reform)

The disorganization of Romanian politics beginning in January 1990 can scarcely be overstated.[26] The Communist Party's first successor was the National

Salvation Front, a hodge-podge of second-tier apparatchiks, dissidents, members of the army and secret police factions who had turned against Ceauşescu, and miscellaneous others.[27] Forming in opposition to it were fragile resuscitations of political parties from before World War II, the so-called historical parties, which eventually formed a loose coalition calling itself the Democratic Convention (DC). Although elections in May 1990 gave political control to the Front under the presidency of Ion Iliescu, a former first party secretary at the county level, the next several years saw perpetual flux in political entities and affiliations. The Front split more than once, its core of ex-apparatchiks morphing into the Party of Romanian Social Democracy (PRSD). I refer to these two groupings as the postcommunists (PRSD) and the neoliberals (DC), a simplification that leaves out various nationalists and others and that understates changes in the PRSD over the decade.

To call these groupings *parties* would be to stretch the usual meaning of the term beyond recognition; I have referred to them elsewhere (Verdery 1995) as "unruly coalitions." Heir to both the main resources and the integrating networks of the Communist Party, the PRSD was the best organized and financed of them. Throughout the 1990s it remained the most powerful but by no means stable political force. In my opinion, the pulsating field of opportunity and uncertainty containing the PRSD prevented its achieving the firm hegemony many commentators attributed to it. When the neoliberal coalition replaced it in late 1996, the center's political control over lower levels declined even further.

For much of the decade, politics consisted of continual reorganizations and of struggles between central and local authorities, with a marked disjuncture between what was legislated at the center and what happened down below. Romania's chaotic land reform and its aftermath reflected that disjuncture. In part it resulted from disestablishing the Communist Party, which had organized politics from top to bottom, but the Party's central control was always weaker than it pretended to be.[28] With the end of its formal monopoly, lower-level authorities became even harder to control than before. This was the truer given the frenzied scramble for power and resources that was unleashed at the national level, from which emerged a jumble of contradictory policies and utterances on which local authorities could draw selectively. In such a situation, I find it unwise to write as if there were "a state" with a recognizable and enforceable intention. Not just between electoral mandates but within any one government (and there were many), people were constantly at one another's throats. This was the context in which the law for property restitution was debated, promulgated, and implemented.

In 1990, although the Iliescu government was not in favor of undoing social-ist agriculture, several things compelled them to do so even before pressure began from international financial organizations. Perhaps most important, widespread action in the countryside dramatized the necessity for change, as some among each village's CF members destroyed the buildings of CFs and walked off with animals and implements.[29] (A resident of one such place de-scribed it as "a kind of Hiroshima," so complete was the destruction; Mungiu-Pippidi and Althabe 2002, 69.) The government had tried to head off such ac-tion by decreeing Law 42/1990 in January 1990, after barely a month in office, giving all CF households the use of one-half hectare (rather than the usual 0.15–0.3 ha), but this did not prevent spontaneous seizures. These actions were especially common in the transitional foothill zones between the plains and the mountains where, we should note, private farming had persisted during the so-cialist period—that is, collectivized farmers in the foothills always had the ex-ample of private ownership nearby.[30] The spread of violent actions might also owe something to what people were seeing on television as appropriate revolu-tionary behavior.[31]

Added to forcible occupations were other reasons for the government to concede on restitution. One was the symbolic significance of decollectivizing: as a countermeasure to the collectivization process that had implicated three-fourths of the population in the 1950s, decollectivizing would send a signal that the new government was anticommunist. Given how much of it was in fact dominated by the second-tier apparatus of the widely hated Communist Party, this was an important (if misleading) signal to send to both the Romanian pop-ulation and the international community. Indeed, Béatrice von Hirschhausen and Florence Gerbaud assert that "The symbolic dimension obliterated the pro-ductive dimension of the problem" (1998, 154). Second, in the overwhelming political disorganization it was uncertain just how powerful the forces pushing vociferously for property restitution would be; the Iliescu government did not clearly have a mandate to refuse it, and the opposition made it a rallying cry.

In February 1991, then, around the same time as in other formerly socialist countries, the Romanian parliament passed a land reform law known as Law 18/1991 or *Legea Fondului Funciar* (the Law on Land Resources). (For a more ex-tended presentation of this law, see Cartwright 2001, 110–23.) It received much subsequent invective and countless amendments. This law provided for liqui-dating all collective farms, which occupied 61 percent of Romania's agricultural surface, and giving the land in them to the households that had donated it at collectivization. There was a proviso for giving some to people who had not given their CF any land but had worked in it, but (as I show in chapter 3) local land commissions—dominated by landowning villagers—did not necessarily pursue this option, which might have required reducing their own share.[32] Law 18 did not just distribute land to villagers who lived on or had worked it; the law attempted to restore ownership to those who had lost it at collectivization. Therefore, people could receive land even if they did not live in the countryside and/or were incapable of working it. Another proviso aggravated the resulting absentee ownership: land could be claimed by anyone related to the original owner up to the fourth kinship degree.[33]

The timing the law envisioned was, to put it gently, naive. From the moment of its publication, claimants had thirty days (later extended to forty-five) in which to register their claims. If one failed to act within that limit, one's rights automatically became invalid. Registering a claim meant producing proofs of prior ownership, from any of several sources: the official land registry books, documents of sale or inheritance, the petitions of entry into the CF, the commune agricultural registers of the 1950s—both of these had been based on verbal declaration—and so on. Claimants also had to submit copies of the relevant birth, death, and marriage certificates to prove their eligibility. To marshal such evidence took time, and people who lived far away from their natal places might be unable to do so quickly. Following this, the law set ninety days as the period in which all claims should be ratified. After ninety days, however, the situation was completely chaotic; the limit was abandoned and no new one set. Evidence of its sheer lunacy is the number of court cases the law provoked: over 1 million—in a 1998 interview, the Romanian Minister of Justice stated that Law 18 had produced the largest number of court cases in the history of Romanian jurisprudence.[34] As late as 2002, there were still many people without property titles (see also Mungiu-Pippidi and Althabe 2002, 172).

Had the drafting committee known the history of previous land reforms, they might have reckoned more soberly. For example, following the emancipation of Transylvania's serfs in 1848–54, court cases to resolve problems with impropriation dragged on for fifty years. Two decades after the 1921 land reform, 17 percent of large estates had not yet been expropriated, and two-thirds of all peasants eligible to receive land had received none.[35] Moreover, neither of those reforms attained the magnitude of the 1990s restitution, which involved about 6,200,000 claims for recognition of ownership rights, resulting in about 4,900,000 provisional titles for a surface area of about 9,200,000 hectares (compared with 3.9 million hectares for the 1921 reform). I say "about" because the inconsistency of official figures makes it impossible to do otherwise (other figures cited here should also be taken loosely). Indeed, an article in the Romanian daily *Ziua* in 1998 under the headline "The Government Has Expropriated a

Million Romanian Peasants!" compared several sets of figures from the Ministry of Agriculture. The article concluded that the surface area of Romania was changing by the day and that the number of people impropriated had *decreased* by a million in the previous two years, thus justifying the headline.[36]

Law 18 was drafted by a committee of the Ministry of Agriculture that solicited extensive input from economic and agricultural research organizations, the Ministry of Education, state and collective farms, lawyers, notaries, politicians, and agricultural specialists. The draft then underwent lengthy debate in parliament and emerged with numerous compromises. Among the points at issue were the following.[37]

1. Should the law effect an agrarian reform, which would require first nationalizing all land and then distributing it, or should it rather reconstitute previously held property rights? If the latter, should there be any limit on the amounts to be recovered? The compromise was part reform, part restitution, with a 10-ha cap on returned holdings so as to have extra land to distribute to those who had brought none into their CFs. The postcommunists prevailed with the cap and the distribution to landless villagers (phrased as equity measures), their opponents with the basic restitutional principle. Although the 10-ha cap would indeed produce land reserves wherever there had been large estates—particularly in the Regat—it would be harder to find reserves where estates had been smaller and land had gone to the landless in 1945, the situation more common in Transylvania. Two effects of the 10-ha cap were that it obstructed the rapid formation of commercial farms and undermined the potential resources of those in the opposition parties who had previously owned large estates. Therefore, when those parties gained power in 1996, they revised precisely that stipulation.

2. Should all land in socialist enterprises be given out or only that in collectives? Here the Iliescu group's preferences for retaining large-scale agriculture prevailed, and they pressed to leave intact the state farms that worked 30 percent of Romania's land (this policy contrasted with that in Bulgaria, for example, which dismantled both forms). They argued that since dismantling the CFs would inevitably cause dislocation and a drop in output, the state must ensure continued food production on the SFs. Equally plausible is that the state farm lobby was sufficiently powerful to keep SF privatization off the table, giving state farm directors time to fortify their positions. In consequence, however, many people whose land had been confiscated in the 1950s did not get it back; instead, the SFs were declared *commercial companies* with former owners perforce becoming their shareholders, entitled to dividends (but not to any say in running the farms). The shareholders did not always accept this status, some of them forcibly occupying their SF lands. Beginning with the 1994 land rental

law, which specified that former owners could claim their land in SFs as of 1999, further measures regularized their situation.

3. Should free circulation of land be permitted at once or only after a delay? Neoliberals argued for free land sales, while the Iliescu group argued that to permit them might worsen land fragmentation and also make smallholders vulnerable to a new bourgeoisie bent on accumulating land. Similar arguments had accompanied the 10-year moratorium on land sales following the 1921 reform, as well. Added to Law 18, then, was an Agency for Rural Development, which would organize improvements to the land and infrastructure and also mediate land sales, promoting those that consolidated terrain and exercising the state's right of preemption toward that goal. Iliescu's opponents saw the government's tardiness in creating this agency (it never did appear) as intentional, to prevent the emergence of a land market—a plausible although overly simple view.

4. Exactly how should land be returned? This matter was connected with the fragmentation/consolidation problem. Should owners repossess land rights in precisely the same locations as before or not? According to the law, only in hilly regions would restitution occur as a rule [*de regulă*] on the old sites [*vechile amplasamente*]—that is, the exact parcels that families had once owned. There was no such expectation for those in plains villages, where the law gave local commissions the option of consolidating parcels instead of returning prior holdings, so as not to regenerate the fragmented property structure of the 1930s.[38] On this question, however, villagers had the last word: in many plains settlements, people forced a return to old sites as the norm, arguing that this was the only way they could be certain of not being pushed aside for someone else. It was also, incidentally, the form that favored those with the best-quality land (often the instigators), who tended to be people long resident in a given village and often owning more than the average amount. Their insistence on the old sites produced numerous lawsuits. (On multiple occasions Senator Vasile Lupu observed that two words, *de regulă*, were all it took to cause millions of peasants to undergo torture in tribunals.)

5. Should land restitution/distribution occur immediately or only after creating a new cadastre? Here the neoliberals seem to have won out, pushing for immediate restitution—perhaps from fear that if they waited for a cadastre, restitution might never happen. The provisions for setting up a cadastre were removed from Law 18 prior to its passage. The failure to create a cadastre before implementing the law, however, had some devastating consequences. One was that nobody thought to subtract from the totals for redistribution the surface areas occupied by roads; thus, parcels were allocated to a certain number of claimants who could not, in the end, all fit in. Another was that awarding land to people within boundaries that had not been fixed guaranteed endless remeas-

uring and a long backlog in recording transactions. Despite pressure and promises of assistance from international organizations (the World Bank accorded a substantial loan for it, as had Europe's Phare program and USAID), only in 1996 was a cadastre law passed, and even then its implementation began only in 1999.

Although the Iliescu government caused much of this delay, such as by failing for almost two years to provide USAID surveyors with the necessary cartographic points for satellite mapping,[39] the question of making a cadastre was more complex than this. First, there was a serious dearth of trained surveyors— a profession not much in demand during socialist times. Second, the huge number of tiny parcels made it impossible to map by satellite, so measuring required even more surveyors, precisely what was lacking. Third, Romania had no unified cadastre. Ever. As I explain in the introduction to Part I, there was one system of property registration in Transylvania and another in the Regat, and even after the regions' unification in 1918 the differences endured. To create a cadastre in the 1990s, then, was not simply to measure and number terrain but also to decide how to combine these two irreconcilable systems, each backed by its own local practices and interests.[40]

Procedurally, Law 18 set up two kinds of commissions as the agents for undoing the collectives. First were the liquidation commissions, whose job was to evaluate and sell or otherwise dispose of the nonland assets of the collective and then to distribute the money among the former CF members. I say more about this process in chapter 3. Second were land restitution commissions, whose job was to restore rights to former owners and create some new holdings for the landless. There were three levels of land commission— at the county, the commune, and village levels, with the mayor as head of the latter two. Each village elected three people who, together with an agronomist from the commune and a surveyor, formed its land commission. The three villagers were also members of the commission of the commune, which consisted of all that commune's village representatives, the commune's mayor and secretary, and several others—a legal counsel, the head of the local forestry division, an accountant, and additional agronomists. All communal land commissions in a county were unified under a single county commission, which (together with the county judiciary) was the final arbiter of conflicts.

Of the three levels, the 2,949 commune commissions were by far the most consequential because they controlled the implementation of the law. Crucially, these commissions had remarkable autonomy: the law contained no sanctions compelling commissions to decide fairly and no time limit for their work. They had no effective oversight unless a disgruntled villager brought suit—and even then, they received no penalties for their errors. The only form of sanction was that the elected mayors who headed the commissions might be thrown out in the next election, other candidates accusing them of shady dealings in the restitution process. Often a person with experience in the socialist hierarchy, a mayor might have strong backing from his former cronies in the county capital—including the prefect, appointed from Bucharest—who might be his allies in schemes to corrupt the law.

As of June 1994, 6,236,507 claims had been filed, of which 4,897,573 were accepted, for a total returnable surface of 9,168,386 hectares, two-thirds of Romania's entire agricultural surface.[41] A claimant might consist of more than one person because siblings inheriting a parental farm had to file a single claim; therefore, the number of people implicated was far greater than 4.9 million. Once the commission ratified a claim, the new owner received a certificate (*adeverință*), a provisional title enabling use of the newly restored rights. Although these were awarded rather quickly, with 93 percent of them completed by 1994 according to Ministry of Agriculture statistics, final titling proceeded more slowly. Figures from mid-1997 indicate that 69 percent of final titles had been completed by then; by December 2001 that figure had barely increased, to 70 percent.[42] In my research area in that year, there were still whole villages in which not a single title had been given out.

Besides the delaying tactics of Iliescu's government, the chicanery of local officials, and the shortage of properly trained and equipped surveyors, another source of delay was that the move to restore the old sites produced extraordinary fragmentation. Forty-five percent of all holdings were under one hectare in size,[43] and 82 percent were under five hectares—a larger percentage than after the land reforms of 1918 and 1945! (See Teşliuc 2000a, 100; Mungiu-Pippidi and Althabe 2002, 69). The full extent of fragmentation is unclear. I have seen figures ranging from 23 million to 45 million parcels for the restituted 9.2 million hectares, with average numbers of parcels per holding ranging from 3–4 to 7–8.[44] In my field area, one village had an average of over twenty parcels per holding. No matter what the figure, to measure out and title that many parcels with an inadequate corps of surveyors would certainly take time.

Some Effects of Law 18

The application of Law 18 produced a multitude of effects. First, some demographics. With 46 percent of the population residing in rural areas in 1992 and 70 percent agriculturally employed in 1956, decollectivization immediately touched half or more of all households. In 1990, 29 percent of the working population was employed in agriculture, and this figure rose to nearly 40 percent by the mid-1990s, indicating that agriculture was absorbing people from industry.[45] Decollectivization might therefore cushion Romania's transformation, contributing to political stability.

Its contribution to people's economic prospects, however, was more dubious. The average holding restored was 2.2 ha of arable and up to another hectare of pastureland, varying by county from a mean of 1.0 to 5.2 ha. The law produced an unprecedented number of owners who lived in towns rather than in the villages where they had received land: 43 percent of recipients holding 40 percent of the agricultural surface area. Many of these (although by no means all) would have difficulty making productive use of their land.[46] It also produced a generational ownership structure: only 9 percent of those receiving land were under 40 years old and 57 percent of new owners were over 65.[47] In 1997, pensioner households were 41 percent of the rural population, had received 65 percent of the land, and worked 63 percent of it (Teşliuc 2000a, 120). At that age, few new owners would be eager to invest in modern means of production or in anything but subsistence agriculture.

This relates to a further effect of Law 18: it returned one vital means of production without any provision for people to acquire the others. A 1991 World Bank survey found only 9 percent of owners had some kind of tractor, 28 percent a horse or buffalo, and 12 percent a plow; nobody had seeds to plant (Jackson 1997, 312–13). This situation had several consequences: (1) the new agriculture would be more "traditional" than that which it superseded; (2) to prevent this would required heavy subsidies for purchased inputs that cultivators could not otherwise afford; and (3) the alternative was to continue agricultural cooperation in a new guise—but this would support the retention of the old-style managers of the former collectives. Indeed, according to Jackson (1997, 315), villagers complained of being forced into cooperative associations as a condition for having their land claims recognized (see also Cartwright 2001, 111).

A third set of effects came from the peculiarity that Law 18 implicitly reconstituted a social landscape—the village and its households—as of the year of collectivization (between 1949 and 1962, depending on the place). But that landscape no longer existed. Household heads had died—without dividing the land because it was not then inheritable. Offspring had grown up and moved away, presumably but not formally renouncing interest in village properties. Now, however, they might reconsider, making unexpected claims on locally resident siblings (see also Berdahl 1999, 165–66, for eastern Germany). Law 18 was not designed to resolve inheritance disputes; it restored the precollectivization status quo and left heirs to fight it out among themselves. Quarrels over division could end in court. There, joining with the multiple lawsuits against commissions, usurpers, neighbors, and other villagers, they further delayed the implementation process. Many villagers spent more time in court than in their fields and wasted all their savings on court costs. (At the same time, however, they were also becoming familiar with the courts, an institution they had long feared.) Thus, Law 18 produced ongoing conflicts among kin, among members of different ethnic groups, between villagers who had had land before and those who had not, and between village residents who had remained in the village and those who had emigrated to an easier life in town (see Cartwright 2001, chaps. 8, 9).

The matter of villagers' encounters with the system of justice leads us to consider how Law 18 affected villagers' relations with the Romanian state more broadly. The matter has two separate angles: the way decollectivization was legislated and the petitionary status of land recipients. As I explain in chapter 1, the state was not the owner of land in CFs; only the members were, jointly. Because the collectives were constituted as "voluntary" acts, in theory only the voluntary agreement of the members could bring them to an end. Yet in creating Law 18, the Romanian government did not ask villagers for their agreement; it simply declared liquidation of CFs unilaterally. Collectivization was therefore ended exactly as it was begun, through force. This final act of force amounted to acknowledging the "free consent" of the founding of the collectives as a fiction: there was no point in obtaining villagers' consent to break up the CFs because they had not in fact given it in the first place. Just as villagers had been forced to donate their land, they were forced to take it back even if they now saw it as a burden (as indeed it proved to be).

Moreover, they had to take it as a gift. First, in 1990, the state gave villagers one-half hectare—as a favor, not as something they had a right to—and then local commissions gave them back their land. Prepotency stood behind both transformations of rights to land. This is apparent in what was required of would-be owners. As Cartwright points out (2001, 113), they had to petition for return of their land, just as they had petitioned to give it away before. Only if they asked for it and passed the tests of proof would their rights be restored. Under Law 18, the default option was for land to remain in associational or state property unless the prior owners petitioned for it; ownership rights did not accrue to them automatically. The requirement of a petition seems to me to confirm the premises of socialist property underlying the law, which—like the procedure for dividing an inheritance [ieşire din indiviziune]—required individuals to break out of a jointly held estate. That is, even in the restitution law, the socialized form was prior to and the condition of individualization.

These provisions of Law 18 suggest a striking resemblance to the previous order with respect to the relation between persons and the state. Because the group in power consisted largely of people who had benefited from that order and were used to thinking in its terms, the resemblance should not surprise us.

To what extent would the postcommunist government in fact support private agriculture, then? This is a crucial question, for without adequate support, obtaining title—property rights—would not generate effective private property in which the owners might realize the values they saw in their new property object. That would be possible only if new owners could obtain access to implements and sources of capital enabling them to bring together all the necessary production factors. Decollectivization had given them land but no more; at the advanced age and low incomes of most recipients, acquiring the rest was a serious problem. Thus we come to the topic of the government policies that facilitated or retarded their access.

Government Policy Toward Agriculture

In my presentation so far, I have already indicated the government's possible bias in favor of socialized agriculture, evident in its making some form of cooperative the default option and not returning the land in SFs, in its delays in giving out titles and the necessary cartographic information for a new cadastre, in villagers' being pressured to join new cooperatives, and in comments such as the chapter epigraph from President Iliescu. Many observers, both Romanian and foreign, interpreted these as signs that the postcommunists intended to prevent the development of individual ownership, on a small scale at least (see, for example, Otiman 2002). Although agricultural policy would seem to further that interpretation, my own is somewhat different. Despite good evidence that the postcommunists preferred larger-scale farming of one sort or another, it is likely that not the government *tout court* but the powerful agrarian lobby based in the Regat and led by Senator Triță Făniță shaped agricultural policy from 1990 onward, as did the international lenders who objected to agricultural subsidies. Throughout the 1990s, we see successive Romanian governments constantly squeezed between their desires for electoral support and social peace, the demands of the World Bank and IMF, and the influence of the agrarian lobby. These governments treated villagers not as potential farmers but as voters, weighed them against urban consumers and against workers in industry, and struggled over their relations to both the postsocialist agrarian elite and international financiers, thereby further politicizing the land question. The result was highly inconsistent policy, which added to the already enormous uncertainty new owners faced. In my view, if agricultural policy failed to support village farming for all but a few, the reason is not simple government recalcitrance but the constantly shifting balance among the various groups. Politics made it impossible to support the creation of meaningful private property for village smallholders.

Romania's agricultural policy during the 1990s is a topic much too large to cover here. I limit myself to a few observations on prices and the problem of subsidies and credits, indicating the groups that influenced policy and its effects on cultivators' ability to combine production factors so as to farm.[48]

Let us begin with prices. The Ceauşescu regime had kept prices of agricultural commodities and (hence) of the urban food supply very low, a plan the first Iliescu government (PRSD) hoped in part to continue—one reason for its not disbanding the state farms. It imposed price controls on a number of essential food items (such as grains and dairy products), which applied to any transactions through state procurement centers. Producers who wanted to find their own buyers could charge whatever they could get. The result was a dual pricing system in which the state price initially exerted downward pressure on the market price, although inflation tended to obscure this fact. Inflation was a serious problem throughout the decade, worst in 1991–93 and 1997. Between 1990 and November 1996 the Consumer Price Index rose 17,000 percent; over the next twenty months alone, it increased to 53,000 percent.[49] Among its principal causes were continued subsidies—despite the pressure of international lenders against these—to SOEs in agriculture and, especially, industry, in hopes of reducing unemployment and popular discontent.

When the neoliberal Constantinescu government (Democratic Convention, DC) came to power in December 1996, it first modified and then abandoned the price controls—a condition of the structural adjustment loan it negotiated with the World Bank. For the next three years the economy experienced negative growth and a rise in unemployment (from 6.3 percent in late 1996 to 11.5 percent in 1999). The government failed to reduce inflation below 45 percent (Pop-Eleches 2001, 159); between December 1996 and June 1997 the consumer price index doubled. Although this might have been good news for rural producers, it was not because during the decade the prices of agricultural goods rose more slowly than those of industrial inputs, such as equipment and chemical substances for boosting yields. In addition, at just about the time that Romanian wheat prices reached world market levels (1997), world wheat prices fell by almost half.

I turn now to subsidies and credits. If food prices were to remain manageable for urban consumers, producers would need some system of credits, loans, or subsidies lest they go under, given the negative terms of trade for agricultural goods relative to industrial inputs. They had to have some way of not only making ends meet but also acquiring capital equipment that almost none of them had at the outset. During the socialist period, rural people had been able to save money, but it rapidly disappeared as inflation took off. Thus, they needed state assistance. The postcommunists proved friendlier in this respect than the neo-liberals, allocating subsidized loans for both equipment purchases and production costs and channeling the funds through the (state-owned) Agricultural Bank. Indeed, a World Bank report stated that the failure of the Romanian National Bank to meet the credit requirements of IMF standby loans came largely from directed agricultural credits (World Bank 1997, 10–11).

For a variety of reasons, however, the overwhelming majority of these credits never made it into the hands of smallholders but went instead to state farms (see Teşliuc 2000b)—bank directors were so instructed; they were likely to have friends and old-boy connections with SF directors; and, as the director of the Agricultural Bank branch in eastern Hunedoara county explained to me, any intelligent loan officer would lend to the borrowers with the most secure collateral. Those borrowers were state farms, with their large inventories of fixed capital. Because land could not be used for collateral and few small cultivators had substantial fixed investments, banks required them to put up their houses—something almost none were willing to do—and this too made SF managers the more likely recipients of loans. Reflecting the hierarchy of forms from the socialist period, then, huge sums were transferred to certain privileged actors in agriculture, sums amounting to 11 trillion lei by fall 1998 (double the entire budget of the Ministry of Agriculture for that year).[50]

As a result, credits were available, but only to a select few, leaving out the bulk of the smallholding population. Further handicapping them was that banks not only funneled the largest credits to SFs, they often preferred short-term loans for starting a production cycle rather than longer-term loans for equipment. The bank director already mentioned had stopped giving loans for tractors as of 1992, because in inflationary times he did better with short-term loans than by locking up his funds in tractors for five years. Moreover, Vlaiceni complained to me, he made them repay the loans immediately at harvest when grain was cheapest, so they could not wait for a better price. A final problem with bank loans was that the IMF's macroeconomic stabilization program created positive and floating interest rates, which (to quote only the experience of Vlaiceni) might vary between 40 and 125 percent without warning. Few smallholders were prepared to brave these waters. Probably for this reason, when villagers wanted to obtain means of plowing, they acquired horses. Although from 1989 to 1995 the number of farm animals in general declined, horses were the one exception, increasing in number by 18 percent (Pasti, Miroiu, and Codiţă 1997, 53). Considerably cheaper to obtain than tractors, they did not require bank loans.

What about agricultural subsidies of other kinds? These too fluctuated throughout the decade, as budgetary support for agriculture ranged from 9 to 18 percent of the gross value-added in agriculture (this excludes the hidden subsidies of the preceding paragraphs) (Teşliuc 2000b, 52). The principal instrument for delivering subsidies was a state monopoly organization called Romcereal, formed in 1991 in response to the confusion following the land reform. A makeover of the state grain procurement centers of before, Romcereal controlled all Romania's state storage capacity. It was to be the main supplier of inputs, to distribute subsidized credits for them, to purchase grain, and to serve as a storage and marketing agent. For a time it provided fertilizer free of charge, although only to its clients. It contracted with state farms, new producers' cooperatives, or individual farmers to organize mechanical services and deliver subsidized inputs, against a portion of the harvest (one could also sell it more than that portion). Whatever was delivered to Romcereal, however, was paid at the state-controlled rather than the higher market price.

In the absence of any effective distribution and marketing channels, adequate storage, or readily available machinery services, something like Romcereal was clearly essential. It enabled producers of all types to start their production cycle without having to take out bank loans and to sell their product when they otherwise might not have had time to search for buyers. In the opinion of the World Bank, EU advisors, and the IMF, however, Romcereal prevented the growth of markets for inputs, services, and sales; in consequence, these organizations applied pressure to dismantle Romcereal, a process the neoliberals completed in 1997 with effects I describe in chapters 5 and 6.

Beginning in 1997, the DC government substantially reorganized the system of agricultural subsidies, arguing that it was necessary to eliminate the kind of corruption that had delivered most of the PRSD's credits to the state farm mafia rather than to the individual farmer. Hoping to lure the PRSD's rural constituency,[51] they distributed coupons worth 135,000 lei each (for each hectare cultivated, to a maximum of five); these were to be used for acquiring inputs, thus subsidizing some part of the cost.[52] The coupons were fungible and could be used for fertilizer, herbicides, gasoline, seed, or even equipment. In 1997 the DC allocated 1,400 billion lei for these subsidies, which should also help to develop markets for input suppliers. To avoid their reaching the hands of the rural elite, the coupons were delivered through the post office, which had lists of legal owners. The Ministry of Agriculture official who explained the system to me concluded proudly, "For the first time in Romanian history we have direct support to the owner of a peasant farm!" (In my research area, only in 2000 did these coupons begin to make a difference.) In the 2000 election campaign, the PRSD promised they would continue the system at a higher amount.

One other form of subsidy was the PRSD's moratorium on agricultural taxes, initially valid until 1994, then extended, over the objections of the IMF. Proponents of the moratorium argued that it was absurd to tax cultivators when they had not been given either their property titles or the necessary conditions for producing.[53] In fact, however, a World Bank report found that even with no formal tax, agricultural production *was* effectively taxed by the combined effects of transfers, price controls, subsidies to industry, and other measures. The report estimated the effective taxation rate for 1995 at 15 percent, higher for private producers than for state farms (World Bank 1997, 9–10, rubric 37). The same report criticized the government's inconsistent policies that created high uncertainty and instability in agriculture, making it impossible for cultivators to plan. These frequent changes of course persisted under the DC government as well.

I conclude this section by asking whether the various Romanian governments, particularly those of the PRSD, were purposely inhibiting the development of small-scale private farming, as many Romanians and foreign observers maintained. The question is important because it bears on cultivators' evolving relationship to the new state—to its legitimacy, first of all. As my village respondents struggled to get by, in the late 1990s, many thought the state should be doing more for them and was intentionally pushing them out of business, in favor of cooperative forms. The PRSD probably did prefer agriculture on a larger scale than two- and three-hectare holdings scattered in multiple parcels (as would I myself) and officials gave off numerous signals to this effect. At the same time, however, it did try to help smallholders, probably because they were essential to its electoral base. That many of the benefits went into the pockets of the agrarian elite is a separate matter, one that does not necessarily reflect government intention. It may, rather, indicate the center's inability to control what went on below—as well as insufficient funds for the purpose, in the opinion of former Finance Minister Daniel Dăianu.[54]

The level of subsidy remained too low to keep smallholders afloat, but there were other causes as well: the skill and power of the agrarian elite in skimming off what was available, the demands of international lenders, and the government's relative poverty owing to the economy and standard of living it had inherited. In his review of the government's agricultural policy, Romanian economist Emil Teşliuc argues against two faulty opinions: that agriculture was inadequately subsidized, compared with elsewhere, and that it was unprotected against imports, including dumping. I myself heard these opinions frequently from villagers with whom I worked. Without disagreeing that Romanian support for agriculture was low, he notes that a higher level was neither financially nor socially affordable, given international pressure, the government's tight budget, and the low GDP per capita. Controlling for these, Romania's agricultural supports through 1997 were surprisingly high, he says, even though they were half the level of subsidies in the EU (Teşliuc 2000a, 112–13). Moreover, because agriculture's share in the GDP and in employment was relatively large, higher levels of subsidy would have literally broken the bank—precisely the point of EU debate about ending the Common Agricultural Policy for new members. Thus, Teşliuc concludes, in the 1990s Romania subsidized its agriculture as much as it could.

I have one final speculation concerning the inadequacy of agricultural policy. Regardless of how much money a government has to dispense, the various ministries always fight to increase their share, but several observers have suggested that the Ministry of Agriculture was very weak, relative to other ministries—just as it had been under Ceauşescu.[55] Indeed, one parliamentarian declared to me, "The Ministry of Agriculture doesn't exist! [He formed intersecting horizontal planes in the air.] Diverse interests cut across it in such a way as to nullify its organizational definition—financial interests and so on." If true, the implications of this idea for agricultural policy are substantial: a weak ministry could not effectively lobby either the parliament or the council of ministers for a larger share of the budget, for stronger laws against diversion of funds, or for other things advantageous to its smallholding constituency, had it wished to.

What was the influence of international actors such as the EU, the World Bank, and the IMF on Romania's agricultural policies during the 1990s? They exerted pressure that narrowed the government's maneuvering room considerably, given its need for development loans. On the whole, that pressure was directed toward creating free markets (at a time when protection and government regulation were on the rise in Western Europe[56]). My conversations with employees of the U.S. Embassy, USAID, the World Bank, and others made it clear, however, that—as with so much foreign aid—the market they were concerned with was less the Romanian one than the market for western goods and services.[57] External loans would pay western firms to supply Romania with irrigation works, for instance. Financing the new cadastre would help to clarify ownership so that land could be sold and used as collateral for loans, often to acquire western equipment, pesticides, or herbicides (if anyone could afford them). From this (western) point of view, insisting on an end to subsidies made good sense because subsidies made it more difficult for outsiders to compete on the Romanian market. Taking Teşliuc's argument to heart, I believe, enables us to see Romania's policy-makers as promoting support for agriculture partly so as to keep foreigners out.

It bears noting that small cultivators were trying to take advantage of whatever opportunities they could in an environment of constant public scandals about misuse of funds, bribery implicating top government ministers in illegalities, siphoning off of subsidies intended for cultivators, shady bank deals, abuse of power by mayors and local land commissions (not to mention the judiciary and police), and so on. This is not the place to discuss the climate of scandal in 1990s Romania; the allegations were far too numerous and the motives of those decrying them always suspect. But because some of them bore directly on the ability of smallholders to assemble production factors—the theme of the preceding section—I briefly illustrate the climate with a couple of examples.

Throughout the 1990s, bank scandals were legion, with several major banks collapsing under the weight of unrepaid loans. The usual explanation was that bank directors and loan officers had given loans to their cronies, who had then taken the money and used it to build villas rather than for the declared purposes and not bothered to repay it. (As already noted, sometimes these cronies also had better collateral and therefore appeared safe, in comparison with the hordes of small borrowers with inadequate security.) A variant of this was reported for the nationwide Agricultural Bank, a very important institution for cultivators: it was initially the only bank through which the government directed (better said, misdirected) credits for them. In 1998, the Court of Accounts, which prosecuted cases of financial malfeasance, found that in 1995–96 this bank had given subsidized credits to agents who either had no connection with agriculture or used the funds for nonagricultural purposes; the figure given was 53 billion lei.[58] All too often the money had gone to state entities rather than to the cultivators who were the supposed destination. For example, a large sum was loaned to Romcereal (hardly an agricultural producer), with which it bought gasoline to resell to both agricultural and nonagricultural entities; other sums had gone to paying the salaries or vacations of State Property Fund personnel.[59] In such an environment, it is not surprising that smallholders had limited access to agricultural credits. Other institutions could be equally cavalier with smallholders' subsides—Romcereal was found to have exported up to 40 percent of the fertilizer given it for free distribution to cultivators.[60] While the state was protesting that it had insufficient funds to support agriculture at a higher level, then, billions of lei were being drained from the budget through actions of this kind.

Just such practices caused the neoliberal government elected in 1996 to set up the coupon system already mentioned, which bypassed banks and other agricultural interests by delivering credits directly to local producers through the post office. Here, however, scavenging intervened again, this time by postal officials. In one 1998 report, a postmistress stole a total of 626 coupons worth 74 million lei.[61] Even the direct recipients could not be counted on to use the funds as intended: often, producers sold the coupons, used the money for something else, and rented out their land to someone who did not benefit from the subsidy.[62] Others too profited from the coupons, taking advantage of smallholders' ignorance and charging hefty commissions for accepting the coupons (one supplier of fertilizer, for example, pocketed 3.3 million lei from villagers in his commune); or they would accept the coupons but only at less than face value and then pocket the difference. Various swindlers xeroxed copies of coupons and sold them; others bought up coupons for less than face value and sold them at a premium to cultivators wanting extra; still others used coupons to buy items not covered by the government decree covering what they could be used for.[63] Scavenging state resources for agriculture took place from top to bottom. The effect, however, was a demodernization of agriculture, because by the end of the decade smallholders could assemble only the cheapest production factors.

A final set of abuses in agriculture concerned the efforts of local agrarian elites and officials of communes to pervert the restitution process at the point of its implementation: in village and commune settings. Directors of state farms, former staff of the collectives, heads of the newly created agricultural associations, mayors, commune councils and land commissions, and even villagers elected to them strove to delay the process of giving out land, to usurp the place of rightful owners, to compel smallholders into the new associations, and in general to interfere with the process of restoring property rights to their proper recipients. Stories of such abuses were legion; certain newspapers (such as *România liberă*) specialized in them, as did the weekly television program *Village Life* (*Viaţa Satului*). By far the most numerous complaints concerned abuses in implementing Law 18 at the local level, the sphere of operation of commune mayors and commune or village land commissions. Having access to all the information available, they could manipulate it, cause maps and pages and entire registers to disappear, and withhold facts that claimants required.[64] They could threaten anyone who complained; they could charge fees illegally or extort bribes for doing their jobs. Taking advantage of the nebulous situation of lands that had been hidden or exchanged during the socialist period (see chapter 1) enabled them to give good land to their friends at the expense of the real owners; the friends would then sell their freely acquired land and pocket the money.[65] Villagers who lodged their claim and received nothing might later find that the mayor himself was working what they should have received. In some villages, frustration with commune mayors led to efforts to split off from the commune so as to cut loose from the abusive officials. More extreme responses were also possible: the TV evening news on January 30, 1994, showed villagers from two Moldavian settlements who had threatened to march on the county prefecture with their pitchforks if their grievances were not resolved.

In chapter 3 I take up this issue directly, presenting specific examples of mayors interfering with restitution. To anticipate that argument, I revisit once again the matter of government attitudes toward smallholding: Was the PRSD leadership encouraging mayors to drag their feet, so as to force smallholders into associational forms? That is not out of the question, but I think it is not necessary in order to explain why local officials delayed implementing Law 18. Equally important, I believe, was that the political center was not able to exercise adequate control over them—in brief, that it was weak. Although I agree that there is good evidence of a PRSD intention to retain central control of the economy, including a push for larger farming units, I doubt that this intention was easy to translate into practice. To think otherwise presupposes both a central government with more power than I believe it had and a local sphere obedient to central directives (a laughable image). Procrastination did not have to be ordered from above; local officials had their own reasons to procrastinate, as chapter 3 shows. Open abuses of power in implementing Law 18 imply the center's ineffectual control over its subordinates or perhaps its collusion, but not necessarily that it was directing them to obstruct the process.

In arguing for a weak rather than a strong state, I do not deny that members of the "new red bourgeoisie" represented by the Party of Romanian Social Democracy (although not by them alone) might have opposed dismantling the planned economy from which they had profited before. There is plenty of evidence for that (see, e.g., Mungiu-Pippidi and Althabe 2002, 172–75). I deny, rather, that these forces were sufficiently concerted to achieve such an objective and, above all, that they had the institutional means necessary for doing so through the state. The field of politics was too fragmented, with groups and individuals constantly shifting sides, coalitions, and party identities. Some red bourgeois (such as the agrarian elite) supported the Democratic Party, which for a time was an ally of the PRSD's chief opponents, the National Peasant-Christian Democratic Party. Other red bourgeois from state-owned firms went with the PRSD or with one of its splinter groups or a nationalist party. Occasionally an issue polarized the field such that no legislation could be passed because the opposing forces were so nearly matched—the fate of nationalized housing and state farm privatization are prime examples. In this way, the non-formation of the Agency for Rural Planning and Development, which was to organize land sales, was less likely the result of a central directive than the result of political battles over whether to modify Law 18. Rather than indicating a purposeful attempt to slow the circulation of land, it reveals a paralyzing balance of political forces over the land question.

Postsocialist Romanian politics, then, bears the monstrous stamp of the Ceauşescu period, its state not strong but weakened by parasitism, barely controlled anarchy, and scavenging on the part of virtually everyone.[66] That behavior, in turn, was a function of the ever more straitened circumstances of people's lives, as Ceauşescu's self-imposed austerity program had drained the country of resources and his skillful manipulations turned people against one another. More than a decade after his fall, Romanian politics had not yet overcome the free-for-all of the socialist period, for which some of the supporting conditions still obtained. In a highly unstable environment characterized by tremendous risk and uncertainty, everyone was trying to create islands of certainty by any means possible. These included sabotage of central intentions, as local-level struggles overturned the political compromises struck in Bucharest.[67] Under such circumstances, I submit, it makes little sense to explain restitution's chaos in the countryside as government obstruction. Just as analysts failed to perceive the signs of decomposition in socialism by attending only to central party policies, I think attributing too directive a role to state actors after 1989 leads to the same misperception.[68]

Property and Politics

Decollectivization, like privatization in general, proved to be extraordinarily complicated. It challenged the understanding of people who had thought they knew what property was and how to create it, confronting them with unanticipated contingencies, unpredictability, a huge gap between theory and practice, and the intrusion of multiple unintended consequences. It also proved to be a preeminently political process (see also Frydman and Rapaczynski 1994, 173–76). In a 1994 interview, Romania's Minister of Agriculture remarked that the agricultural question was too important to let it become politicized.[69] The reality to which this disingenuous observation referred was precisely the opposite: "the agricultural question" was politicized, as was all privatization, from the moment of its imagining. Although western advisors tended to present creating property rights as not a political question but a technical and procedural one and the market as a strictly neutral mechanism unaffected by politics, it was precisely through politics that Romania's new institutions would be forged. That was true not just in the national arena but at the level of small villages.

Indeed, the question of ownership was politicized in the international arena even before it entered into domestic struggles that politicized it further. Daniel Bromley (2000) puts the matter bluntly: the insistence on creating private property rights began in the ideological struggle between "East and West," with property the basic demarcational metaphor. Although some dissenting economists suggest that if economic efficiency really were the bottom line then pushing private ownership was probably the wrong tack (e.g., Murrell 1993), the men from Harvard, Chicago, and Washington continued to peddle their dogma. No surprise, then, that national elites and former communist bureaucrats politicked with property too. The consequence of the two sets of politicking, however, was repeated conflict between political bargains made within and dictates from without (see also Dunn 2004). For the state to satisfy all these conflicting demands while being expected to divest itself of its main source of revenue was simply impossible.

As a political phenomenon, decollectivization was more than a set of policies with distributional implications. As I have just implied, it also had symbolic and ideological, or some would say mythical, elements. By this route we return to the questions I raised early in the chapter about decollectivization's ideological significance. It symbolized a new order, and it was saturated with ideological premises both domestically and internationally that amounted to powerful myths. The domestic premise was that private property mattered precisely because communism had abolished it—this recoil animated its politicization. The international one was that private property would naturally flower once the oppressive hand of the state was removed. In this respect, the experience of Eastern Europe offers a powerful demonstration of how blinding an ideological premise can be: the premise that private property rests on a natural instinct and that socialism had squelched it, producing a property vacuum. But there was no *tabula rasa;* socialism had a property order, one to which the myth of its unmakers made them blind.

The politics around decollectivization gave the impression that land was still a source of economic value and a worthy property object that afforded its owners important forms of control—a view I call into question in my Introduction. At the same time, these politics obscured the fact that (as is true elsewhere in the world) smallholders could do little without the off-farm incomes sufficient to pay for inputs. Otherwise, land could become a negative rather than a positive asset. In all the urging by the World Bank, EBRD, IMF, and other organizations that private property rights in land be created, left unsaid was that land would now become a carrier of liabilities as people proved unable to purchase all those inputs at the prices international firms were charging. In this way, land lost economic value.

Perhaps institutional instability and the stakes in the national and international arenas contributed to a final aspect of decollectivization politics—the chasm between politics at the center and how reforms were implemented locally.[70] Often, the latter process overturned the bargains fought at the center. In

Konrad Hagedorn's view, governmentally produced laws and decrees that emerged from bitter political struggle amounted to little more than proposals, at the implementation stage; local processes might or might not confirm them (an outcome reminiscent, he believes, of socialism's top-down planning).[71] That argument offers a strong rationale for ethnographies of the process, such as the one I offer in this book.

The burden of subsequent chapters, then, is to show for a small Transylvanian community how restitution, conceived partly as a reparation of injustice, was locally implemented in ways that produced injustice anew. That injustice had many facets: people not receiving their family plots, some people receiving more and others less than they were supposed to, assets of CFs and SFs being frittered away or simply pocketed at others' expense, local officials usurping the rights of owners, and recipients being unable to realize economic value from land that was becoming a liability. These difficulties eroded alternative forms of value land might hold: manifesting skill as a farmer, retrieving land rich with family associations, or even enabling subsistence. In Vlaicu, a decade of smallholding produced a handful of commercial farmers precariously generating profits and a large mass of smallholders forced to withdraw from all but subsistence farming on small plots, just as in the socialist period, while turning their land over to tenants who worked it in farms resembling the state or collective farms of before. I describe, in other words, the specific processes—part of a much larger, global process—through which the agricultural sector in one place further declined as a source of value, in multiple senses, and therefore as a site of significant property relations.

CHAPTER 3
HOW HECTARES VANISHED: DECOLLECTIVIZATION POLITICS IN VLAICU

> I've been looking for Mrs. Iuga's .8 ha that she wants the Association to work, but I can't find it anywhere—it's in the book, but on the ground, no. So how can I plow it for her?
>
> *(Head of Vlaicu producers' cooperative)*

> I can't understand where my land has gone! It was there on Monday and by Wednesday it had vanished!
>
> *(Complaint to Vlaicu land committee)*

In 1996 the Romanian comedy team Divertis released its version of decollectivization, a skit entitled "Where's There's No Law, There's a Theorem." The central character (T) is describing how he responded when the peasants came to him and asked him to divide up the land; his interlocutor (D) expresses periodic astonishment and derision. Here is an extract, which follows their discussion of whether the geometry appropriate to the task should be Euclidean or non-Euclidean.

T: It was a big problem, because there wasn't any law then, so we decided to do it by a theorem—the Theorem of Pythagoras. I taught it to them in a week: "The sum of the squares of a triangle's two sides equals the square of the hympontenuse [sic]." So I made a plane with three points on it. I put point A on the village's eastern border and point B on the opposite border, at the base of a precipice; then I put C at the top of the precipice, to make the horizontal and vertical lines for our triangle. A-C is the hympontenuse, running from the valley to the top of the precipice. Then I asked, "Who wants land, and where?" And where do you think everyone wanted it? On the hympontenuse!

D: But that's impossible! The hypotenuse is an imaginary line!

T: No, I hung some stuff on it so people could see it. They wanted their land there because they said it's bigger, longer. They wouldn't listen to my objections.

D: But those who got land on B-C, the precipice—how can they sow their crops?

T: I gave them pistols. For those on the hympontenuse, the Ministry of Agriculture issued some guidelines about how much to plant and advised them that at the harvest, they should multiply their yield by the cosine of alpha.[1]

This skit appropriately introduces us to the chaotic implementation of Law 18 in villages across Romania, the subject of the present chapter. It was a process in which misguided expertise and the imaginary played an undue role—in which land stretched and shrank, as I suggested in my paper "The Elasticity of Land" (Verdery 1994), and hectares vanished inexplicably. What Law 18 initially conceptualized as a project taking three months dragged on for years. To the delays that resulted from the politics I described in chapter 2 we should add further sources of delay that came from the complexity of the process itself and from the passions, confusions, and ambitions it aroused.

Consider, for example, the following notes taken at meetings of the Vlaicu land committee between April and early June 1994.[2] During these two months, arguments among Vlaiceni heated up because this is the time for planting, when they discover that others have encroached on their land; this was also when the committee happened to measure household gardens for the definitive cadastre. In these notes, "Agron" is the land commission's agronomist, "Map" its surveyor, and "Com't" one of its Vlaicu members. The participants refer often to specific locations in the village using the names of fields (most of them identical to those on maps from the 1880s). Because many field names are untranslatable, I leave them in Romanian.

Sîvu comes in and is very noisy about what terrible things he's going to do if his case isn't settled. He has a piece in Filigore, claims it must be measured, Map says it already has been—they repeat this several times. Map gets mad because people want remeasuring: "We'll never finish this job if people make us remeasure all the time!" One woman wants him to go measure in Lunca; he says, "We already did it there, if we have to go back we won't get out for two weeks." Sîvu says loudly, "I don't want anything except what's *mine!*" He accosts Com't: "Look into my eyes, you're my godfather, I'm not asking for anything except what's *mine*. I bought it from Gheorghe, it's next to Ana and to Constantin. If you don't give it to me, I'll . . . I'll do what no one's done in all of Vlaicu!"

A woman arrives, an urbanite, niece of Lazar B. She wants Map to go and measure a piece in Lunca. He says no. "You have to resolve it with your uncle, or with the courts, not with me." She: "It's nothing to do with him, I have my own piece." After much resistance, Map looks it up, says, "There should be 15 meters for you, 15 meters for him." He says he'll go and see— this only after Com't has insisted several times, "*She's* the owner, we should do justice." He says this to me too, several times, "Look how hard this job is, but we have to do justice!" He says this to everyone who comes in: "If it's yours, we'll give it to you, never fear." He's drunk, as is obvious when he sits near me and breathes—he even comments to me that when he drinks, his mind is not affected. The woman wants to go with them right now and have them show her exactly where it is so she can plow a furrow at once—"If I just go and plow on my own, my uncle will hit me over the head!"

Cousins Andrei and Emil come, one says to Agron, "They measured yesterday, but it isn't right." Agron: "I can't help you." "But it's not right!" Agron: "You'll have to remeasure. Then if you move the stakes and can't agree, that's your problem. Your mistake is, you shouldn't just use the stakes, you should use some other sign—a path, some trees, a ditch, make a pile of rocks . . . .We can't guard your stakes!" They're all shouting now: who pushed into whose land, who pushed whom over. They start comparing lists—Ion has 10 meters, Iosif has 10 m, Elena has 14 m, Petru has 18 m, Pavel has 3 m . . . .Map: "We don't have Pavel anywhere. Ion came into your field." Andrei: "Well, *I* wasn't the one who divided the land!" Agron: "Ion made a mistake." Emil: "I have .21 ha from uncle Luca and .21 from my father, my brother had .07 and gave it to me. If Ion with his .29 ha has 10 m, then how can I with .42 ha have only 12 m?!" Agron: "Your neighbors must have come over onto you. Come on Tuesday, we're measuring gardens then." Andrei: "We don't want to quarrel with each other." Agron: "Map doesn't want to keep measuring over and over again. There's no point in fighting, since the land is *there!*" Emil: "He said he'd cut my head off!" Andrei: "How about the land in Vaidei [village]?" Agron, exasperated: "You have to go to the commission there and insist. We don't give land to people in Romos commune." Andrei: "You as the committee are *obligated* to give us our land!" Agron: "But not in *other communes!*"

Mimi comes from Bucharest, she wants land where the Germans are now, and she wants the garden at house 221. Agron: "We assigned you some elsewhere." She is upset that they did this without letting her know. She: "You oblige me to go to court!" Map: "Please do!" She: "*The entire village knows* that I was there!" Map: "Then you can bring the entire village as witness for your lawsuit." Agron has walked out. Map—he is steaming—answers my question why a Bucharest person wants a garden: "She just wants to get it to sell it back to that miserable fellow! He's handicapped, too, but she wants to get more out of him." Mimi, apoplectic: "I'm not quitting! I'll go to the highest fora! As long as the country is run by Gypsies and Russians, nothing good is happening—Iliescu's wife is Gorbachev's sister and his mother was the daughter of the Gypsy King! Bucharest is a garbage pit because of them. You people will pay for what you're doing to me! I'll sue for damages for all the time I was unable to use that land, plus all the trips from Bucharest plus moral damages!"

Aurica had asked to have her aunt and uncle brought in "because I'm sick of quarreling with them. If we can't resolve it here, I'm going to break in on their land and plow it!" First is the aunt; she's yelling at the top of her lungs. Agron has exited and is holding his head, says this is what happens each time they try to resolve Aurica's situation. Then comes the uncle. Agron admonishes him, "Sometimes we joke but now we're serious: why are you on more land than you're supposed to be?" Lots of yelling on both sides. Agron: "The law is the law! You have to respect it!" Uncle: "I was supposed to get more land than I did." Agron: "You should have lodged a protest if you weren't happy." Uncle says he did, Agron asks the outcome, uncle gives a long story about his health, when he got out of the hospital the term for contesting was over. Agron keeps asking him for his certificate, "Bring your certificate for that land!" Uncle: Long story . . . .Agron: "Stop treating us like kindergartners and bring the certificate!" Uncle: "I lost it." Aurica crows, "He doesn't have it!" Aunt: "I just want my father's land, nothing else." Agron: "But your father's land belongs to the Germans!" Uncle argues loudly about the injustice of the Germans' getting their father's land and says that's why he occupied land he wasn't supposed to. "I'm not giving up my father's land! I'm sick of coming around and asking, 'Pretty please, give me some land.'" Agron: "Are you agreed to divide that piece with your sister and your niece?" Uncle: "No!" He walks out.

Agron tells Aurica that she'll get a piece in compensation when they go back over the measuring and take a little from everyone for cases like hers. She: "You think people will actually give up a piece for me? You're deluded!" Agron: "*They have* to give it up!!" Aurica: "The hell they will! I'll bet on it. Just you wait. I can see it now: you take .21 ha from someone in the plain and say, 'We'll put Aurica in here,' but when I go to plow, the owner will say, 'Aurica!? *Their* family never had land in here!! Her father was poor, he never had anything down here!!' and they won't let me in. The problem is that those of us with the least land are all the ones with land at the Germans, we're deprived of it for two, three years, and when you give us something elsewhere after everyone is in place they'll drive us out of those plots. It's discrimination!" She is, of course, exactly right.

Map tells me that Iulia from Deva called him at home one night and said, "You know that parcel of mine on the hill: who's working it?" "How am I supposed to know?!" he asks, "Do you know where it is?" "No," she replies. "Then how can you say someone's working it!?!" People call him at home all the time and disturb him. It's driving him nuts.

Law 18 was passed in February 1991, yet nearly three years later scenes such as these were still very common. Even during my visits in 2001 many cases had not been resolved, although by then a number of the aggrieved had simply given up and accepted the loss of some of their entitlement because they lacked the proofs, the money, or the time to bring suit. What were the mechanics of restitution, so clearly laid out in Law 18, that made it so difficult to complete? How did its intrinsic difficulty intersect with the schemes of local elites? Why did hectares vanish, and how did Vlaiceni seek to recover them? In the present chapter I address these questions, describing how the collective farm was dismantled and pointing up some of the issues in the excerpts presented: repeated measuring; people's constant demands on the commission because they did not understand the rules; undercurrents of violence; conflicts among kin; and the themes of justice, law, and knowing. I emphasize that my subject is only the dismantling of Vlaicu's collective farm, not its state farms, which I discuss in chapter 7. My account is meant to complement that of my earlier publications (Verdery 1994, 1999, 2001), which provide material not included here.

In presenting how these processes unfolded, I emphasize the politics through which village elites and the commune commission altered the agenda that Law 18 had established. They failed to give land to the village's most disadvantaged members (the PRSD had hoped to make such people its social base), they gave land to ethnic minorities over locals (the former inconsequential, in electoral terms), and they delayed completing restitution until various local elites were well taken care of. Continuing my argument from chapter 2, I show how local officials could distort the restitution process with little or no encouragement from the PRSD—and not only could, but had every reason to. Together with the design of Law 18, action by these and other kinds of people in local contexts had the effect of concentrating power in the hands of commune officials, who were thus able to delay the completion of the reform. What drove the outcome was the power to allocate land and control over it, which enabled officials to accumulate allies—precisely the dynamic of socialist property. Land, that is, had value for them as a route toward political capital.

Village Particulars

Before I proceed, I must give some information about Vlaicu, its land, and its inhabitants. Although not all the data are from the same year, the differences are not essential to my story. The complexities of decollectivizing begin with the village's crossroads location, mentioned in the introduction to Part I, which created several problems for returning land. For example, during socialism, collectives sometimes exchanged land at their margins for one or another reason. A field I might have had in Vlaicu might now be in Şibot—which had completely different local, communal, and county land commissions than Vlaicu. Therefore, if I want to claim my land I have to go to both Vlaicu and Şibot village land commissions, both Geoagiu and Şibot commune offices, and both Alba and Hunedoara county offices to find the necessary documentation. This means I need a plethora of personal connections to help me find the information I need—or, more likely, that I will never obtain the information. It also means, as chapter 7 shows, that the administrators of the state farms that fell across this border had to deal with two county prefects and four different mayors in trying to resolve problems that arose with the reform.

A second complexity comes from Vlaicu's size: just how much land was to be given back? It was contained in six different entities—a collective farm (CF) and five state farms (SFs)—of which only the CF was initially slated for restitution. All the entities had land beyond the village's precollectivization borders, although this was least true of the CF. Of the five state farms, only one was fully contained within Vlaicu, the others straddling other villages/communes as well as the county line. The sizes of all six entities had changed over time, the SFs increasing in number and size at the expense of the CF. That fact produced much confusion and ill will as villagers whose land fell in the perimeter of the SFs watched their kin and neighbors repossess land from the former collective. Meanwhile, they themselves received instead dividends from the SFs—each SF paying, if anything at all, different amounts that declined over time at varying rates.

As I have explained elsewhere (Verdery 1994, 1084–85), figures for Vlaicu's surface area are inconsistent, especially from 1948 on, reflecting the exchanges of land described in chapter 1. In 1991 the land commission determined that it had either 599 or 631 ha available for redistribution, later revised to 759 ha. This represented only the land held by the collective, excluding the five state farms; the totals for those appear in various lists as 801 ha and 675 ha. Exactitude not being necessary for my purposes here, I use my best guess on the basis of comparing several contradictory numbers:[3] a total surface area of 1,434 ha, 631 of them from the former CF and 803 from the five SFs.[4] Thus, 44 percent of Vlaicu's total surface was to be returned in the first round and the remainder only as of 1999, when SFs were to be finally broken up.

The commune archive contains a list of all the people who received provisional titles, or certificates [adeverinţe]. There are 267 positions on that list, but many of the positions have more than one name; those people would have to divide their allotment on their own, at the notary or at court. Counting all the names on the list, the total is 352, many of them not resident in Vlaicu. This initial list was subsequently much amended. In the first phase of restitution, when the commission thought it was distributing 631 ha, someone made a note on the charts saying, "Vlaicu, total area requested 674 ha, actual area available 631 ha." Soon thereafter Vlaicu's Germans reclaimed an additional 70 ha, making the gap between claims and actual surface 113 ha. When I write later in this chapter of the problem of Vlaicu's having no "reserve lands," something like this figure is what I mean.

As for the total population of Vlaicu itself, as I have previously indicated, this number is not very certain either: both of the official figures I received from the commune office and the Orăștie police were questioned by the people who gave them to me. My own highly tentative figure from autumn 2000 is 820 residents, in 274 households.[5] This total comprises several different social groups, which fall into two broad categories: those born or married into the village, whom I refer to as *locals*, and those migrating in with their spouses as adults, whom I call *venits* (veh-NEETS), one of the terms villagers used for them.[6] (The distinction blurs in the 1990s younger generation, with marriages of venit and local offspring.)

In the category of *locals* were people born in Vlaicu (as well as in-married spouses), who had given land to the collective when it was formed and now received it back. The amounts they recovered from the CF ranged from a fraction of a hectare, held by a sizable number of people at the bottom of the scale, to the 17 ha belonging to a couple who had combined their ten-hectare allotment with their son's seven. Figure 3.1 shows, very approximately, the distribution of the reconstituted holdings as of 1995.[7] While not great, this range was sufficient to encompass people of quite different prospects. Amounts that any household might have in a state farm do not appear in these tables or in my discussion in chapters 3–5 because until 2001, when titles to land in the SFs finally began being distributed, those with land there had no choice as to how to work it. They were shareholders and accepted whatever the farm paid them, in what was effectively a nonnegotiated rental arrangement.

According to my figures from 2000, the category of those with land contains 51 percent of all Vlaicu households. I include in this tally all local-born Vlaiceni who had not actually received any land yet but stood to inherit some from their parents. It is clearly not a uniform category. I divide it loosely into those who would have been classed as wealthy in the presocialist period (anyone with more than six or seven hectares), middle (anyone with between about 2 and 6 or so ha), and poor (anyone with under about 2 ha).[8] The numbers should not be overemphasized, because soil quality, what a household did with its farm, how many members it had, how much other labor or extra income it disposed of,

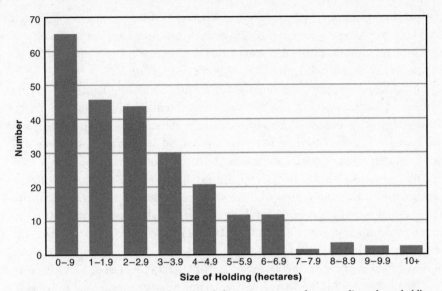

Figure 3.1 Amounts of land returned to Vlaicu's former owners as of 1995, pooling a household's parcels.

and how fragmented the farm was were more important than sheer amounts; still, farm size did set limits. I refer to these respectively as poor, middle, and wealthy *smallholders,* a term I use to distinguish them from the tiny stratum of commercial farmers who were emerging from both local and venit families; their trajectories are the subject of chapters 7 and 8.

An additional group is the Germans (they call themselves *Benzenzers*[9]), whom I include among the locals, as do Vlaiceni. They made up 3 percent of Vlaicu's households in 1992 and, following deaths and emigrations to Germany, barely 1 percent by 2001. All but two of the families living in Vlaicu in 1991 had owned land from when their families arrived in the 1890s until they were expropriated and their lands given to others in the land reform of 1945. I call these others, all Romanians, the *'45ers.* I reserve further information on them until later in the chapter.

The category of venits consisted almost entirely of people who had moved in for industrial jobs during the 1960s and 1970s, after the collective was formed. They had joined it only as laborers, the wives often engaging in the arduous work of the CF dairy sector while the husbands commuted to work in one of the industrial towns to which Vlaicu had ready access. Some venits retained a claim to land in their natal villages—land that was uncollectivized, generally of poor quality, and divisible among many siblings, but that held economic value for them during the socialist period because they might bring hay, brandy, and fruit down for use or sale. As I explained in chapter 2, Law 18 provided for such people to receive some land in their lowland homes after 1991, but in Vlaicu this did not happen, for reasons I discuss later. Venits constituted 49 percent of all Vlaicu households in 2000, an unusually large proportion.

I include in this figure one other group without land: approximately twenty families of Roma, who lived in two small apartment buildings built in Vlaicu during 1975–76 to house workers for one of the state farms. Because Roma did not have land in the CF, they, like venits, got none after 1991;[10] since they had not been members of the CF even though they provided day labor for it, they did not even receive the tiny CF pensions. Being of the stigmatized Roma identity meant that the venits (who are all Romanians) did not welcome them. These Roma were the people most disadvantaged of all by property restitution, which broke up first one and then the other socialist organization that had employed them. After 1989 they continued to work on the state farms, but as those declined they began working as day labor for smallholders or at best as share-croppers who weeded and harvested corn for 25–30 percent of the harvest. (Some were also involved in the brisk scrap-metal trade between Romania and Western European countries.) In 2000 the PRSD government began giving them welfare, which caused a number of Roma to withdraw from the village labor pool—to the distress of smallholders.

The trajectories of people in all these categories were exceptionally varied. For example, in 1997 I went to visit one family that in 1994 had been among the most destitute Vlaiceni; they had no land and lousy pensions, and they were too frail to work as sharecroppers for someone else. To my surprise, they were now living comfortably and talked of buying a bit of land: their daughter had met and married a German and now regularly visited them with gifts and infusions of deutsche marks. Similarly, venits with nothing used hard work and hay from the uplands to raise and sell animals in order to buy land that other poor locals could not afford. Some Vlaiceni who had received sizable amounts, by contrast, were having so much difficulty finding anyone to work their land that it became almost useless to them, requiring huge cash outlays they could not cover. Villagers' resources were not necessarily restricted to Vlaicu—far from it. A few families had international connections, such as one household I often visited, who I thought had achieved a very careful balance that permitted them to work their land without losing money—until I remembered about their son in Canada. In addition, as was true in the socialist period when fully 85 percent of Vlaicu's men of working age were employed in urban industrial jobs (see Verdery 1983, 58–59), many in the 1990s did also. Industrial restructuring made their jobs insecure, however, and contributed to villagers' desire to obtain at least subsistence from their farms.

By the end of 2000, what had a decade of restitution produced in Vlaicu? Breaking up the collective farm had created legal owners, most of whom held property deeds, for perhaps 85 percent of the people who expected them; the average holding size was 2.7 ha. As of 2000, when people began claiming their land in the state farms, both figures changed. These owners, however, were but 51 percent of village households, and a fair number of them either had little land or were insecure in their proprietorship. A full 49 percent of households had no land at all. Thus, the reform brought approximately one-fifth of village households, at most, into a situation of relative well-being (by their standards). Restitution had therefore produced rural inequalities that the postcommunists in Bucharest had hoped to avoid.

I turn now to some of the processes whereby the distribution of land took place. Because I did not begin serious work on this topic until September 1993 and had not visited Vlaicu since July 1991, I missed some of the most exciting events. These included people's beginning to occupy their former holdings, the CF liquidation process, and the measurements of parcels (I attended these only for household gardens, in spring 1994). With the help of people involved, I have reconstructed the events through interviews conducted in 1993–94 and thereafter.[11]

Undoing the Collective

Vlaicu's collective farm had an unprecedented harvest of corn in fall 1989 and of wheat in summer 1990; it not only paid off all its debts but gave people amounts they had hardly ever seen before, worth up to 25 percent of the yield.[12] Perhaps partly for this reason, Vlaiceni—unlike villagers in many other parts of Romania, including those in Geoagiu down the road—did not destroy the CF buildings and cart off the materials, for they were not as disaffected with their CF as were villagers elsewhere.[13] They began working the half hectare the Iliescu government gave them that winter and waited to see what would happen. Although in some other Romanian villages people were already starting to break up the collectives, during a brief visit that summer I heard a number of villagers rejecting the very idea: "Who wants to go back to farming! Having to get up at the crack of dawn! All that work!" This echoed what I had often heard during the 1970s and 1980s: "Who needs land? Not me!" Such people had no use for recovering private ownership of their land and were satisfied with the government's gift of one-half hectare (larger than their old usufruct plots). They would leave the rest with whatever cooperative form emerged, as long as it paid better than the old collectives.[14] In fall 1990, the CF plowed and planted for its last production cycle.

Around this time the new mayor of Geoagiu (previously vice president of the

Geoagiu villagers rapidly took apart their collective farm buildings and carted off the materials (photo by author).

Vlaiceni left their CF buildings intact; the proceeds from selling them went to the new cooperative (photo by author).

People's Council) called a meeting of the general assembly of Vlaicu's CF, where he announced that following the next harvest, the CF would be dismantled and a producers' association formed for those who wanted one. For now, they would divide up the CF's animals and vote on a commission to oversee that process. My respondents could not recall whether an actual vote was taken specifically on the question of disbanding the CF and recovering land; the vote on procedures for returning cattle was tantamount, they thought, to a vote on that larger question. Vlaiceni set up a procedure for dividing the dairy herd: each family drew lots for the number of cows it had given to the collective, as recorded in the entry petitions for the CF, and took home the corresponding cows. The remainder of the herd was sold, the money going into the liquidation fund from which villagers were each to receive a share. After the fall harvest of 1991, the crops were completely divided among the members.

A small number of households, however, about ten in number, decided they wanted to repossess their land. Already in fall 1990, one of them went and reaped clover the CF had planted on land he considered his; another asked that he be given his share of the CF's wheat harvest *from his own former holding*, rather than from the total take; still others began plowing their fields. All were from families that had previously owned a fair amount of land by local standards, and all were certain they knew where their land was—not automatic, given how radically the collective had altered the surface and erased boundaries, as I show in chapter 1. The first to plow was a man from the village's former wealthy families who had spent many months in jail at the time of collectivization for being a *chiabur* and for actively opposing collectivization. Like him, nearly all the others who soon followed his lead (or their parents) had suffered persecution at that time. Once these few had plowed, then a number of others whose land abutted theirs did so as well. By the time Law 18 appeared in February 1991, then, the process of recovering rights to land was already underway spontaneously.

That process would continue under the charge of the two commissions I describe in the previous chapter: the liquidation commission, charged with selling off the CFs' assets, and the commune land commission and village committee, charged with returning land. For simplicity, I distinguish among the various levels of land commission as follows: I reserve the word *commission(ers)* for the most important level, that of the commune; I refer to the county level in Deva as the *county board* and the village level as the *committee(men)*. Outside (or *Geoagiu) committeemen* refers to the surveyor and agronomist from the commune commission; they were the ones actually empowered to return land.

A final clarification. In what follows, I sometimes use the word *elites,* as in *village elites* or *local/commune elites*. For Vlaicu, the category *village elites* is not

Private property comes to Vlaicu, with fences and variegated fields.

clear-cut. I use the term to refer mainly to the village elite from before 1959, people with more than 6–7 ha, some of whom now held themselves above others, especially venits. Although only two of Vlaicu's seven or eight (total) committeemen had this status, they too qualify as elites for this discussion, as do the two delegates elected to the commune council. When speaking of *local* or *commune elites,* I include primarily the ones involved in the politics of Law 18, not other elite figures such as doctors, school principals, priests, heads of various commune organizations, and so on. The local elites of restitution were the Geoagiu administration (mayor, vice-mayor, secretary, and chief accountant), the head of the local forestry division, and the most important members of the land commission (largely excluding the representatives of the commune's constituent village committees), such as its technical and professional personnel (the surveyor, legal consultants, and agronomists). Many in this category had held comparable elite positions in the socialist period.

Land and Liquidation Commissions

The core of the liquidation commission was not elected but emerged from conversations among the mayor and the office personnel of the old CF (a fact that later drew much acid commentary about rigged auctions and insider sales). It comprised five people from the CF staff, including its three accountants. Then the CF general assembly elected four other members; there was no overlap between this commission and the land committee. On the other hand, two of the liquidators also figured on the leadership council of the new Association, which was gradually taking shape in a haphazard way (see chapter 6).

Village land committees were technically part of commune commissions, but in any given village the people who actually showed up to handle land were but a subset of the larger commission. For Vlaicu, they consisted of three village committeemen elected by the village as a whole, as well as a surveyor and an agronomist from the Geoagiu commission, with the very occasional presence of the mayor, its ex officio head. Table 3.1 gives the composition of these various bodies, including the county board.

Liquidation

The final harvest of the CF in summer 1991 was distributed in its entirety to the members. Liquidation proceeded with auctions of the remaining cows, some equipment, three barns, some outbuildings, and so on, most of them bought by Vlaiceni. Proceeds from these sales were to be distributed to former CF members according to an algorithm sent from Bucharest that assessed each member's contribution to the CF. In deciding how much of the proceeds each

Table 3.1

Organizational Levels of the Restitution Process

Administrative Unit	Law 18 Executive Body	Composition[a]
Village	Committee	3 village residents plus 3 from commission: mayor (head), agronomist, and surveyor
Commune/ Municipality	Commission	The above 6 plus other villages' committee members, jurist from county capital, and other administrative personnel from commune/ municipality and former collective farm
County	Board	County prefect, other county administrative personnel, head notary, and directors of cadastre office, state farm trust, and other offices concerned with land resources

[a] As given in Law 131/1991, published in *Monitorul Oficial al României* 3 (43), 1–23.

person would get, land and labor counted for 40 and 60 percent, respectively. That is, the amount of land one had donated to the CF was worth 40 percent of one's compensation and one's total labor contribution to it 60 percent, based on people's accumulated work-points for all their years in the CF. The algorithm reflects the priority given to labor over kin-based entitlements, a point I take up again in chapter 4. Although the percentages had been dictated from above, the chief accountant appears to have manipulated work-points, favoring friends or taking bribes (villagers called it selling or stealing work-points). Many people came off with fewer points than they knew they had worked and some others with considerably more. Since the calculations also affected people's pensions from the CF on into the indefinite future, the accountant's math was a subject of much complaint throughout my research.

The Ministry of Agriculture set the starting prices for auctioned items, evaluating all fixed capital according to the costs of construction, by date and materials used, minus depreciation. As inflation worsened, the figures were modified—always from above, with no confirmation on the ground. Inevitable rumors accompanied the auctions, such as that the chief accountant was pocketing bribes and selling things to her friends. Three of the CF's five barns went to locals, without much competition. A few items were assets the future Association might have wanted, such as a tractor, but only in March 1992 did the Association finally hold its first meeting, draw up a statute, and elect a council (which then proceeded to interfere in the auctions, as I have described elsewhere; Verdery 1999). On August 1, 1992, the liquidation council made a full inventory of the CF's remaining assets (see appendix) and turned them over to the Association, as Law 18 allowed. The chief accountant then left; her assistant, Anda (see chapter 6), took over the books for the new Association.

From that time on, the Association sold any CF assets it did not want, again supposedly distributing the proceeds. I heard frequent complaints, however, that villagers did not receive the money from the sale of CF assets. Although they all assumed Anda and others were pocketing the funds, I believe the problem was, rather, Anda's procedure for giving out the money, in the context of inflation. Deciding, reasonably enough, that people with land were better protected than those without, she gave all the money from the first round of sales to the landless and venits; she entered the entitlement of the others as shares in the Association, thus encouraging them to join it. The next major sale two years later—a barn—brought a large sum. Owing to problems with registering the land under it, however, the buyer put the sum in an escrow account, where inflation reduced it to nothing before it could be distributed. One way or another, few Vlaiceni saw anything from the sale of the CF's fixed assets, and this diminished their confidence in the entire procedure.

Land Restitution

The liquidation process had a short life and a natural end once the Association formed, but this was not true of resolving people's claims to land—the job of the commune land commission and its village committee. The composition of the latter was crucial to the outcome of restitution, and it changed a number of times over the first two years. When Vlaiceni voted in their first committee, they chose three men in their early sixties who had reputations for being honest and fair-minded. All were locals, for venits lacked the necessary knowledge of precollective field boundaries. Two were from middle-peasant families of before, the third of slightly higher status; the first two had worked in industrial jobs rather than the CF, the third as a SF tractor driver. One of them explained that their mandate was never clear—the mayor had told him he was not to decide problematic cases but only to verify that person X or Y was claiming land in the right place, yet soon he found himself adjudicating conflicts as well, a job he did not relish. He then resigned. After that, the other two were replaced in a way I describe later, their replacements being the former CF president and its veterinary technician, plus a former factory worker (and reputed police informer); the first two were from middle-peasant families and the third of low status. None had any reputation for probity and all a sizable lust for drink. When the former CF president died, he was replaced by someone of comparable character. Further measuring and assigning of land, then, proceeded under these auspices.

The logistics Law 18 set in place were of nightmarish complexity. As explained in chapter 2, the law gave all who wanted to claim land forty-five days, later extended to ninety, to get their papers in order and write the petition to lodge their claim. They had to assemble not only the required proofs but birth, marriage, and death certificates for any kin from whom they claimed descent. The upheaval that followed is scarcely imaginable, for many villagers, Vlaiceni among them, had thrown away all evidence of their former holdings. Moreover, many people had moved away to cities during the socialist period and had difficulty meeting the deadlines for putting their claims together. (Collective farm and commune officials often found ways of putting off such people, in hopes of making them miss the deadline so their land would remain available for other uses.)

Vlaiceni were luckier than some, however, because the two main sources of information—the entry petitions for the collective farm (which stated how much land each person had brought in) and the 1959 agricultural register (giving not just amounts but general locations)—had not disappeared, as had happened in many communities. Furthermore, as Transylvanians, they had access to the land registry book that had constituted formal title prior to 1948, although obtaining information from it could be difficult. Access to this registry book was in fact a mixed blessing. From the 1930s to the 1950s, for various reasons people had not always registered their land transactions in it; thus, it gave a far from accurate picture of ownership—but at the same time it had higher legal standing than the other two forms, both produced within the knowledge framework of the party-state. I return to this point later.

Beginning in February 1991, Vlaiceni frantically sought to put together their claims. The first step was to write their claim petition, based on their own knowledge, on consulting elderly villagers, or on checking the agricultural register and the petitions with which they had joined the CF, located at the CF office. Understandably, this period was utterly chaotic. People who had moved away telephoned for information, others showed up after the deadline, staff had to explain over and over what the procedures were and why someone might be receiving less than expected, every dissatisfied claimant wanted help with the claim, people turned vague recollections into certainties, and so forth.[15]

Meanwhile, two former CF staff members drew up lists showing the amounts recorded for each household on the entry petitions and in the 1959 agricultural register. They then compared these figures with those in each person's claim, consulting with Vlaicu's committeemen about discrepancies and about kinship connections linking claimants with their owner-ancestors. If the two official figures were the same, they became definitive; if they differed, the staff members made discreet inquiries to try to establish an accurate figure (gossip had it that they favored their friends and relatives). Discrepancies were legion. When I asked one of these two women what was the hardest part of her job, she replied, "Adding up all the claims and discovering they didn't correspond at all to the total surface area." Countless problems arose from a number of people who had bought or inherited land in Vlaicu but were absent from the village; the lists naming them had somehow disappeared, leaving the staff uncertain as to how much land to reserve for them.

When the claims had all been gathered, the commission met and made some crucial decisions. The first concerned field consolidation: Law 18 encouraged commissions not to recreate the patchwork landscape of tiny fields that collectivization had erased but to consolidate each household's allotment into two or at most three fields, in different ecological niches. Vlaiceni, however, refused this solution—better said, those with high-quality land refused it, for Vlaicu's fields vary significantly in quality and no one with good land wanted to exchange it for larger chunks of worse quality. The result can be seen on the cover of this book: scattered small parcels resembling those on the 1886 cadastre. Map 3, drawn by the proud owner of a 9.45-hectare holding, shows the dispersion of his twelve parcels.

The committee's other two decisions related to the reserve fund of excess land, which Law 18 had invited land commissions to create so as to resolve problem cases or give small amounts to landless villagers. The law's 10-ha cap on restitution aimed partly to create this fund, to be augmented by any land that no one had claimed; if this did not produce a reserve large enough for all needs, then a fixed percentage—the reduction coefficient—would be subtracted from the reconstituted holdings. For a variety of reasons, creating the reserve fund proved difficult in Vlaicu. The soil was good, virtually all of it was being claimed, and the mayor had his eye on pieces of it. Moreover, the number of landless (venit) families was so large that owners would have to give up a sizable amount if all were to receive some land. Unsurprisingly, the committeemen—being locals of middling status—did not want to give up a large chunk of their families' land. They voted to create only a small reduction coefficient (and ultimately did not apply even that), inadequate for giving land to all those venits. The decision had consequences for intravillage conflict and for the labor supply available to the new owners (see chapters 4 and 5).

The second decision concerned the land that had been expropriated from Germans and given to Romanian '45ers. Article 16 of the law provided that descendants of Germans should receive land from the reserve fund, if there were any—that is, not necessarily their old lands or even any land at all. At least one of the original three committeemen and two subsequent ones being '45ers, it is scarcely surprising that they opted not to accept Benzenzers' land claims. And

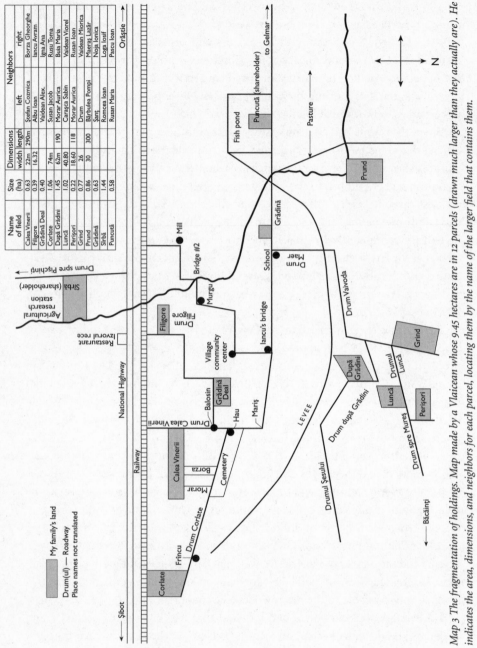

Name of field	Size (ha)	Dimensions		Neighbors	
		width	length	left	right
Calea Vinerii	0.63	22m	290m	Ştefan Cozmica	Borza Gheorghe
Filigore	0.39	16.32		Albu Ioan	Iancu Avram
Grădină Deal	0.40			Vaidean Alex.	Igna Ana
Corlate	1.06	74m		Susan Jacob	Rusu Toma
După Grădini	1.45	62m	190	Morar Aurica	Buia Maria
Luncă	1.02	40.80		Caraşca Sabin	Vaidean Viorel
Perişori	0.22	18.60	118	Morar Aurica	Rusan Ioan
Grind	0.77	30		Drum	Vaidean Miorica
Prund	0.86	26	300	Bărbulea Pompi	Maeraş Lazăr
Grădină	0.63			Şanţ	Noja Ionica
Sîrbă	1.44			Romcea Ioan	Loga Iosif
Puncută	0.58			Rusan Maria	Pascu Ioan

Map 3 The fragmentation of holdings. Map made by a Vlaicean whose 9.45 hectares are in 12 parcels (drawn much larger than they actually are). He indicates the area, dimensions, and neighbors for each parcel, locating them by the name of the larger field that contains them.

by not creating a substantial reserve fund, the committee had no cushion if somehow their decision were reversed, as it later was. This decision too affected conflict in the community.

On July 14, 1991, a list appeared on the door of the CF headquarters, giving the names of all villagers who were to receive land formerly held in the CF, with the amounts returned to them. Not everyone received rights to land; a substantial number, including many who thought themselves entitled to land, instead received shares in a state farm, even if none of their former holdings had been located in it. (Their situations were to remain in limbo for several years.) Then followed a period for contestations by anyone wishing to challenge the allotments. They might bring two witnesses or two people whose fields abutted theirs to swear that they had had more; or, if they had bought land from someone still alive, that person might agree to testify to the purchase (though he or she might prefer to claim the land instead). Those who got nowhere with their contestation at the commune level could lodge a complaint with the county board, and, if dissatisfied there, they might bring suit in court. Because the initial lists gave only the amounts to be returned, not the precise sites, people could contest only the former, not the latter. The most impressive of the contestations was that lodged by Vlaicu's Benzenzers when their claim was denied: a group lawsuit based on legal advice and extensive documentation (unlike many Romanians, most Germans had not discarded evidence of their landholdings). I discuss it later.

Bounding and Assigning Land: The Village Committee at Work

At the end of the period for contestations, villagers picked up their property certificate, although they might still face years of discord or lawsuits. Now began the vexatious process of measuring out specific plots—a process called "putting in possession" [punerea în posesie], which I call *assigning* land—after which a definitive title might be issued. I say vexatious not only because each person's holding might be divided into many small parcels but because the socialist land management practices described in chapter 1 made it often impossible to establish where borders lay (Verdery 1994). Collective farms were worked in huge blocks, not in the maze of tiny fields of the 1930s. To create these huge blocks, CFs had obliterated all distinguishing signs from the landscape, cutting down trees and hedgerows and removing boundary stones between fields. To rationalize and reorganize cultivation, they had bulldozed old ditches and dug new ones; plowed over dirt paths and roadways and carved out roads more suited to the new, expanded use of fields; and plowed crosswise across what had been tens of strips plowed lengthwise—this alters the land's very conformation. Most of the signs whereby people had recognized their property disappeared. In olden times, field boundaries had been imprinted onto people's bodies by the practice of *beating the bounds*: taking one's children around one's fields and beating them so as to emblazon the memory of the sites on their neurons. But no one with this kind of memory was alive any longer. For all these reasons, the process of assigning parcels to claimants was fraught with difficulty.

We might visualize the land surface of Vlaicu's CF as initially retaining a core collective identity—the land of all prospective owners who were not sure they could work their land and waited to see if an association would form to work it for them. Because government directives had urged that associations work compact blocks, what now happened was precisely the reverse of collectivization: people not wanting to join the Association were given parcels on the margins so the Association could cultivate large fields. Gradually this concentrated core shrank, as people increasingly decided to take their land out.[16] As long as there was a large number still waiting for a collective solution, however, there was no urgency about assigning the land to these latter owners because the Association would work it all together. Thus, the committee at first had to assign land only to those who wanted to withdraw from the collective pool of land and work it themselves. During 1992, however, as increasing numbers of owners insisted on occupying and working their original family parcels, it became clear that the Association could no longer maintain a single compact area for the roughly 200 ha it was working. Now the committee would have to measure every single parcel—which in 1948 (the baseline for restitution) had numbered 1,339 for this one small settlement, and many of those would now be subdivided among heirs. The first set of measurements, then, was no longer valid, and the surveyor began all over again.

Given the moves toward people's old sites, the multiple parcels, the uncertain boundaries, superimposed ownership claims, and disagreements as to who should be where, the process of measuring was already complex enough. The way this committee worked, however, made it impossibly so, leading to the kinds of scenes I reported early in the chapter.[17] Its procedures invited accusations of malfeasance, often justified. Ideally, all the people to be assigned land in a specific field would show up, certificate in hand, at the place where they thought they should be. The surveyor would begin at one end of the field—as demarcated, say, by a stream or a roadway—and proceed person by person, parcel by parcel, each person then erecting a makeshift marker. This ideal was rarely achieved. Because the committee often failed to announce its workdays, owners—especially if they lived in towns, as a large number of them did[18]— could be absent when their fields were assigned. An owner could find that her plot had already been measured and staked out, without her having had any

Encroaching on one's neighbors was not difficult, given the flimsy boundary markers.

chance to disagree. Such owners were very likely to return to the committee and complain that they were in the wrong place or needed to have their parcel measured again because a neighbor had encroached on their space. Remeasuring one parcel, of course, jeopardized other measurements, leading to repeated requests for measurement for years thereafter.

When the committee measured household gardens (that is, land near houses rather than out in the fields), Vlaiceni brought on the hospitality. In my brief experience with this exercise, almost every household that was quarreling with a neighbor who had a stronger case would invite the committeemen in for something to eat and, especially, drink; or they might put a package of meat or some eggs or cream into the satchel of one or another member. Households without problems were unlikely to do this. One of the Geoagiu committeemen openly encouraged such practices, telling people in a joking way that if they'd slip him some brandy or a freshly killed chicken he'd arrange things for them.

All these practices left plenty of room for people to be favored in the group's decisions. Because measurings were unannounced, committeemen could privately inform their friends to show up and then stake out a few extra meters for them, at the expense of the absent neighbors. I was not in a position to witness what numerous Vlaiceni alleged: that later in the process, the committeemen cared only about getting more land for themselves and their friends and that once they had done so they stopped showing up for meetings. "*You* know that

A claim is established by plowing a furrow, which might stray from the proper boundaries (photo by author).

[committeeman] Ralea's family was poor, but look at him now: he has 10 ha, and another 2 ha written directly in his son's name!", I was told. My friend Victoria Iancu (see later discussion) put the same point more wryly, "Mrs. Bora's family had five hectares, of which she has now recovered six." One early committeeman, thrown off for being too honest, observed of another, "Wherever Ionel said he was interested in a piece of land, the Geoagiu people would write down 'reserve land,' and later you'd see Ionel working it. If you asked him why, he'd say it belonged to some distant relative."[19] At first, villagers did not necessarily notice that they had been shortchanged. As one committeeman put it to me, "They were so glad to get land that they didn't bother about a few square meters." Later, however, these discrepancies could generate lengthy conflicts and even lawsuits, the fault of the committee's procedures. (Other lawsuits developed, of course, from the sheer complexity of the process, the possibilities for multiple claimants, the contradictory forms of proof, and so forth, as I indicate in chapter 2.)

Naturally, Vlaicu was far from the only place where such things happened—or the 1990s the only time. For example, Konstantinov (2000) reports similar behavior in a number of Bulgarian villages surveyed for the World Bank (56 percent of those surveyed accused their committee of favoring its friends), and Cartwright (2001) and von Hirschhausen (1997) for other Romanian villages. For a quite different case, I examined the maps from the 1921 land reform and found a wealthy Vlaicean receiving a number of parcels; villagers I asked about this said he was the mayor in charge of the reform. Concerning the later reform in 1945, the biggest beneficiaries were reportedly the sons of the then mayor and his various girlfriends. None of this is unexpected.

Even in June 2001 there were still Vlaiceni whose cases remained in question because of ongoing suits or from the failure of the committee to adjudicate quarrels and give out titles (it had essentially ceased to function). Worst of all, even where the bulk of land in collective farms had been distributed by the end of 1999, now the law concerning the break-up of *state* farms kicked in, permitting people to take their land out of those as well. The same circus began all over again. With even more land in SFs than in the collective, Vlaiceni could anticipate yet more months and years of chicanery. In a flurry of activity in summer 2000, a newly elected village deputy gave out a few titles for SF land. He managed to label many parcels belonging to urbanites "commune reserves" and set himself up on them, ceasing to give out other titles. By summer 2002 the entire process was stalled.[20]

I turn now to ways in which the process concentrated local power in the hands of mayors and commune commissions; this continues my argument in chapter 2 that the political center was unable to control restitution. Beginning with evidence of the power and maneuvering of commune officials, I show how both superior and inferior levels abdicated their decision-making power, throwing it to commune mayors. My examples come from the way the village committee and the commission dealt with problem cases and the different kinds of knowledge held at each level.

Chicanery in the Commune

> The land is here, but *whose is it*? That's the question. —(*Geoagiu's Mayor Lupu*)

As is already evident, Law 18 delivered a powerful instrument into the hands of local political elites and opened tremendous opportunities of which they would have been fools not to take advantage. For these elites, the process of land-rights restitution was a windfall. Law 18 handed them a resource everyone wanted and ordered them to distribute it. If some village committeemen had turned this opportunity to their advantage, what might be possible for the people actually in charge of restitution: the commune commission and the mayor? I answer this question using the example of Geoagiu's mayor during the most critical phase of the process, 1992–96. Although I cannot prove the allegations I report here, given their frequent repetition I find them very plausible.[21]

La Jigoaia and Mayor Lupu

The Geoagiu land commission responsible for giving land back in Vlaicu was headed by a man I call Mayor Lupu.[22] A long-time party bureaucrat with many friends in high places, he was reported to have good relations with Hunedoara county's prefect, county board, and legal establishment. After his election, he seems also to have consolidated an alliance with those members of the commune office who had survived the "revolution" (the secretary, treasurer, etc.), at least two of whom had already occupied land belonging to others and therefore had every reason to cooperate with him. Joining them on the land commission were some additional supporters of Lupu and a relative or two, as well as the kinds of people listed in table 3.1. Mayor Lupu was not from Geoagiu but from one of its component villages, a hill settlement with relatively poor soil. Probably for this reason, he was interested in good land, of which there was a fair amount in the floodplain of the river Mureş that flows through both Geoagiu and Vlaicu—land that had claimants, of course, because it was the best land in both settlements.

The mayor's game was apparently to obscure the status of large land surfaces, some of which he worked himself and some of which he gave out to his allies, thus securing their complicity. One tactic reported by a state farm director from a nearby community was this: Lupu had asked him to pay SF dividends for 8 ha to a person not listed among the people owning land in that SF's perimeter—the rightful recipients of those dividends, whose share would thereby decrease. The two men had argued, and when the director offered instead to work those 8 ha so as to have something to pay the dividends from, Lupu became angry and left. The director later learned that Lupu himself had been working the 8 ha while telling the owner that it was impossible to resolve the case and trying to mollify him with SF dividends that diminished other villagers' dividend income. According to another report, Lupu's fellow villager, Sabin (not from Vlaicu), owned 5 ha in Vlaicu's floodplain. Hearing from someone on the commission that he was to receive 6.2 ha, Sabin asked in surprise where it was. The commissioners became angry. The plan, apparently, was to give people more on paper than they actually owned, then give them a property title with the correct amount, and keep the difference.

Still other means toward the same end were repeated failures to measure parcels that were contested in the murkiest of Vlaicu's fields. The ownership status of this large field, about 25 ha on Vlaicu's western border, was very unclear. It had been passed back and forth between the collective farms of Vlaicu and Geoagiu during the socialist period; at first it was not even included in the land to be returned in Vlaicu. Known as La Jigoaia (the nickname of the former owner), much of this area had belonged to someone thought to have no heirs. Although this was precisely the kind of land that should have formed the reserve fund, somehow that never happened; the mayor and his allies had taken it over. Whenever villagers in or near this field complained about improper measurement, the surveyor would always promise to come and measure it but he never did.

One such owner found that the land was worked every year—and worked in rotation (now wheat, next year corn), evidently by the same usurper. One day he found an unknown person there, who claimed to be working the land as a sharecropper from Mayor Lupu and his vice-mayor. A villager with extensive knowledge of that same area observed to me that Lupu was filling it with his own people. For example, according to her, a newly employed cleaning woman for the commune headquarters had agreed to hire on only if given one-half hectare, and the next day she had a piece in La Jigoaia. "So the mayor gives land in Vlaicu to his employees from other villages," she concluded, "and right next to that piece the vice-mayor is working another one!"

That the mayor was usurping land in Vlaicu's floodplain seems beyond doubt. Even the commission's surveyor, in a moment of candor (I had recently given him a bottle of scotch), waved his arm at the huge expanse of La Jigoaia running from the road down to the river and confided, "This should all have been the committee's, to redistribute for problem cases. But who do you think was the first person in here after the revolution, before he became mayor? Lupu. Then-mayor Cristea came to tell him to get out, but he said, 'Forget it. I'm here to stay.' After that he stood for election, and there'll be no getting him out now."

Then Mayor Lupu had a nasty surprise: an heir had appeared, Iulia, who sued the commission. Although he obstructed her lawsuit for two years, she eventually won the right to nearly 10 ha. For another two years he postponed measuring it out for her, disappearing whenever she came to the commission or keeping her waiting in the hall for hours and then leaving by the back door. Finally he measured the land, improperly and in inconvenient locations, when she was not present. Soon thereafter, he told her that if she did not work it, as she had not the previous year, he would follow the stipulations of Law 18 and take it away. When Iulia protested that she could not have worked it until he gave it to her, he replied (according to her), "You should have occupied it anyway and worked it!" This hapless woman concluded my discussion with her in 1994:

So many trips to Geoagiu! I think about it all the time; I think "If the mayor says this, I'll say that." My son says I'm nuts, because I spend all my waking time on this problem. If, if, if . . . . For four years he's led us on! I'll be in his office, and these [landless villagers] from Vlaicu come and say, "Mr. Mayor, please give us 20 ari." He says, "I've nowhere to get it from! I haven't a single gram of soil." So I say, "Give them something from *my* land, I'm not getting it all, give them something down there." He looks daggers at me! I've spent so much money on this . . . but it's the time as well—countless trips to Vlaicu, Geoagiu, Orăştie . . . .

None of this, we can assume, mattered to Mayor Lupu, who saw the land as his own resource.

The mayor's relationship to La Jigoaia wrought far more havoc, however, than Iulia's wasted time and sleepless nights: it generated considerable social conflict. To show this I must briefly explain about Vlaicu's German minority (Benzenzers). I have discussed elsewhere the history of German-Romanian relations in Vlaicu (Verdery 1983) and note here only that Benzenzers had owned considerably more land than the Romanians. The wealthiest family among them had held 80 ha (compared with the wealthiest Romanian's 14 ha); when expropriated in 1945, they collectively lost 250 ha, 31 percent of Vlaicu's total arable surface. In 1991 those who still lived in Vlaicu anticipated receiving a total of 70 ha and had arranged with a group in Austria to obtain implements in good condition, so as to work the land jointly. It was not they, however, who received their land back in the first round in 1991 but the '45ers who had been impropriated on it, for those were the people who had signed it into the CF. Instead, Benzenzers collectively received gardens totaling only 10.3 ha for nineteen claimants. The remainder was assigned to them as shares in a state farm.

Because they had had no land in that state farm, however, they first appealed to the county board and then, in February 1992, sued it for their rights; thanks to the timely warning of one of the committeemen, they had been able to mobilize their case rapidly and won it.[23] The Geoagiu commission awoke to a court order awarding Benzenzers 70 ha. As they had requested, the land was to be given in two large blocks (formerly owned by the wealthiest Benzenzers) so they could work it in common. With most of the village land already distributed, the committee had now to find seventy additional hectares. Even though Law 18 stated very clearly that Germans claiming land would receive it *only* on reserve lands *if there were any*, not on their old sites, the land committee decided to give them formerly German land, as they had asked. This meant pushing off those 70 ha some fifty-six families of '45ers, for whom land would have to be found elsewhere.[24] Following this, Benzenzers (3 percent of village households) collectively held about 10 percent of the land from the former CF, with an average holding size of 4.7 ha, as against the average 2.6 ha for Romanians. The discrepancy was a major source of resentment on Romanians' part.

The report, signed by all members of the Vlaicu committee as well as the mayor, stated that the land for '45ers was to come from two places, one of which was La Jigoaia. Had the letter of Law 18 been followed, Benzenzers rather than '45ers would have received that land. The problem was that, as we know, Mayor Lupu himself had already illegally occupied the land with which he ought to have impropriated one or the other group. He had good reason to give the Germans land where they asked for it, so he could continue the unlawful practices that both put money in his pocket and gave him a distributable resource. Moreover, the lawsuit was convincing evidence that the Germans were better organized to resist him than were the '45ers. That he gave the former two large fields on their old sites does not require us to believe, as '45ers did, that he or the county board had been bribed. Lupu's own motives are sufficient explanation.

From 1992 until 1996 or later, Lupu delayed resolving the situation of the '45ers he had uprooted by his handling of the Germans. He gave '45ers dividends from the state farms (not yet dismantled), promised each year to find them a plot next year, and responded piecemeal, suddenly finding land for people who brought suit against the commission, for instance, but not for the more patient others. Some local officials and perhaps also he himself apparently encouraged the '45ers to resolve the matter by force. Here, at least, is the court testimony of one Mihai, head of a group of '45ers who in fall 1993 broke in and plowed over the already-plowed field of the Germans. (The Benzenzers immediately sued for damages.) "I went to the prefecture, and they told me they couldn't give us the land as long as the Germans are there. Only if we entered by force . . . That's what they told us, and that's what the mayor told us too, that he can't resolve the problem unless we enter by force. 'Enter by force and seize your rights!' he told me." A disaffected '45er observed, "If he gives us land at the state farm, then we'll be fighting with the other Romanians who own it. He'd rather we Romanians should fight with Germans, so he keeps postponing resolution."

The result was indeed much bad feeling between '45ers and Benzenzers, manifest not only in this forcible occupation but in numerous '45er threats of violence, such that Benzenzers came to fear leaving their courtyards. Hostility increased as many of them began to emigrate to Germany, leaving their land in the agricultural cooperative they had formed (see chapter 6) and receiving money after each harvest—while '45ers, most of whom had little if any other land to use, stood helplessly by. Lupu's actions, in a word, had seriously disrupted ethnic relations in Vlaicu. But the disruption went beyond this, for Romanian villagers who had received ancestral land tended to side with Benzenzers against the '45ers, whom they derided for having gotten the land "for nothing" in the 1945 land reform, rather than through purchase or inheritance—as had both Benzenzers and they. Even worse, Lupu's usurping the reserve lands meant that landless villagers were left completely without. As he gradually began satisfying aggrieved '45ers by pushing them onto the land of people even less powerful than themselves, such as widows and urbanites, bad feeling spread throughout the village, poisoning the atmosphere.

By the time Mayor Lupu was voted out of office in 1996, he had already been working land at La Jigoaia for four years and keeping the proceeds, and he stood every chance of receiving title to part of that area. Meanwhile, he had created chaos and social conflict by not resolving superimposed ownership claims in Vlaicu that would have required him to turn "his" land over to someone else. In Geoagiu he had avoided giving out titles altogether, a situation his successor perpetuated. He had also built a large villa in a nearby resort, apparently by illegal means, and would be able to rent it out for permanent income.[25]

Lupu's actions, then, had a number of effects. First, they contravened the plans of the central government, which wanted landless households to receive land so they would be reliable supporters; for this it would happily have alienated a few Germans, who had little influence on national politics. But Lupu saw things differently. He coddled the Germans and alienated the landless in pursuit of his own aggrandizement. Second, toward the same end he sacrificed social harmony. Discord in Vlaicu served him well by keeping the committee weak and the village unlikely to organize against him. Third, perhaps the most serious casualty of all was people's confidence in the restitution process. Instead of finding solutions that would uphold everyone's rightful claims to private property, even if only in part, he blatantly demonstrated his own prepotency.

Commune/Center Relations

Why, we might wonder, could people such as Lupu continue in this way? Part of the answer lies in the structural relations of communes with central authorities after 1989, particularly the institutional hiatus between national and local governments. In each election cycle, Romania holds two sets of elections, one for the president and parliament and another for mayors of communes and cities. The party or coalition that wins the national elections appoints, from above, the prefects of Romania's forty counties, whereas the mayors are elected from below, by the people in the units they administer. In the socialist period, mayors had been selected by their superiors, but the new election laws had snapped the formal bureaucratic chain connecting them with the level above them. This is not to say that a mayor had no reason to curry favor with his prefect: to do so might enable him to secure more funds or help him be reelected and, in addition, cultivating his superiors could help to ensure that the surveillance over his activities was not too great. Nonetheless, with the Law on Local Government Autonomy (Law 69/1991) mayors gained significant powers that reduced their dependency on higher levels, because their budgets were not wholly determined from above but were a function of their local economy. Only if that afforded them insufficient revenue were they dependent on the prefect for help.

It is important that Parliament passed Law 69/1991 *before* legislating the constitution; this fact contributed to mayors' sense that they had to answer to no one.[26] More significant still, however, was a feature of Law 18 and amendments to it: there were no sanctions if local officials failed to implement the law, and the reorganization of political responsibility had provided no alternative levers. Judges and lawyers with whom I discussed the question all agreed that this was the main problem with land restitution; so did Romania's prime minister in a television interview in 1993.[27] Asked why the state did not enforce Law 18 more vigorously, he replied, "We ought to be firmer. But we have a separation of powers, especially at the local level. There's not much the prefects can do. . . . We no longer have direct government control [over what goes on]." The only way any sort of pressure had been put on the process was that as of about 1994, surveyors were no longer to be paid a regular salary but only a piece rate according to how many titles they had completed in a given month.

The entire enforcement mechanism returned final authority to the mayors and commune commissions. If a claimant brought suit against a commission and won, the courts or prefects referred execution of the sentence down to the mayor, for prefectures and county boards did not have the authority to award titles. Although commissions could be sued, they were not liable for damages. As a judge told me, "I can find all sorts of infractions but have no means available to punish them." Another observed that she had resolved to fine the mayors who headed these commissions; then she learned that (unsurprisingly) many of them had not been reelected and there was no way to extract a fine from them. It seemed that local authorities were virtually unpunishable.

It is possible, of course, that judges and the prime minister were claiming their powerlessness over mayors as a way of justifying their inaction—or their unwillingness to act on behalf of the powerless against the more powerful, who might be in their own networks. Nonetheless, when the political opposition came to power in 1996, it behaved as if the problem of inadequate sanctions were real. It attempted to rectify the problem by proposing legislation to give judges full jurisdiction over land-rights cases, which they would no longer have to refer to commune land commissions for execution; to fine recalcitrant mayors for every day of delaying the resolution of a property claim; to assign penalties to not only mayors but entire commissions; to require all owners to declare the surfaces they held and to present documents justifying their ownership, with 1- to 3-year jail sentences if they could not; and so on.[28] Passage of these measures proved exceedingly difficult, however, because one of the coalition partners (the one representing the agrarian elite) bolted. Even after a version finally passed, implementing it, too, proved arduous, and when the coalition fell from power in November 2000, things reverted to the status quo ante.

Accumulating Clients

Law 18, as I have previously observed, was a political treasure trove for local elites. These included the commune administration and the most important members of the land commission described earlier, many of whom had held positions in the socialist period. Also connected to them was the retinue of former presidents, technicians, and agronomists of the collective farms, plus directors of still-functioning state farms and other state agricultural units. Although many of these people had lost some or all of their ground as a result of Law 18 and might be expected to block its application, their obstructionism was not just a matter of defending past privilege; it was also a response to the new opportunity that restitution offered. By failing to give out titles or to resolve the myriad problems associated with Law 18, these elites could both use the land themselves (or give it to cronies, as I have shown with Mayor Lupu) and also keep land claimants in a petitionary and dependent posture. In doing so, they were behaving like socialist bureaucrats, who established a power base by accumulating clients and dependents and by cultivating far-flung networks through reciprocity. This clientele might help a mayor to build himself a villa (as did Mayor Lupu), to be reelected, or at least to obscure the machinations behind his building and land-use projects.

I believe the titling process was much slower than expected all over Romania in part for this reason: land was a political asset *only as long as it was not given out to its owners.* Why should local elites give out titles, destroying their patronage base? By exploiting the absentee status of many recipients, people's ignorance about the procedures, and other ambiguities, mayors could create clients, following the well-hewn path of capital accumulation so vital in the socialist political economy. Because they could no longer count either on maintaining their positions for long or on having stable relations with their prefects, who might be of a different party, they would have to enrich themselves from their local political base. Creating a web of allies with whom they could collectively exploit land belonging to others was one good way of doing just that. For these reasons, giving back land and resolving titles became anything but attractive options. A marvelous illustration of the mentality of such mayors appeared in a 1993 TV program, in which a mayor explained to the interviewer that he gave land to people who had helped with asphalting the roads and improving the local water supply. In other words, he saw people's land as his to use in rewarding those who cooperated with him.[29]

The commune's power to allocate property rights thus enabled accumulating people, as in socialism. Having such power was also a pure sign of the prepotency that raised mayors above other local officials—after 1989 as well as before it. Local elites, then, treated agriculture as a source of political capital rather than seeking to develop its economic potential. Yet the structural situation of mayors and the impetus to persevere in the habits of the socialist period are only part of the story of how commune commissions acquired their power over restitution. Other forces were at work also, including the tendency of both superior and inferior bodies to throw restitution problems down or up to the commune for resolution.

Restitution Practices Empower Commune Elites

I have already indicated that higher fora usually returned cases to the communes, noting for example that judges sent their decisions down to mayors. Both the county board and the courts to whom claimants appealed tended to respond in this way. When I asked the Geoagiu agronomist how much freedom they had in their decisions, he replied that higher authorities gave the commissions a free hand in settling local cases and intervened very little. He observed that although villagers had the right to appeal local decisions to the county board, "those guys don't know anything about circumstances here, who's who, who's credible. So they tend to throw the cases back down to us to settle." When we realize that the next level of appeal was the county court, whose sentences were (until 1999) also referred to the communes for execution, we see that villagers were largely trapped into accepting the decisions of local elites. Vlaiceni perceived the commission's independence clearly. One person complained about the committee's improper measuring, "If you were rich, the 'horse' [two-legged measuring device] could take an extra step in several directions, but if you were poor, they'd knock off a bit instead. And the Geoagiu people went right along with it. Who keeps an eye on these guys? No one. They have free rein, no one checks up or supervises what they do."

Vlaicu's committee members themselves, however, contributed further to the commune's independence. They simply avoided making difficult decisions, sometimes aggravating conflict among villagers in the process and sending them to the commune to appeal. For complicated cases, they might say, "We'll have to come back with the mayor," or "We have to wait until we solve the problem with Germans, then we'll see what we can do for you," or "Once we give out all the land these local owners are entitled to, we'll see if there's any reserve left for you," or "We have to end now, but we'll take care of you next time." The most egregious injunction was, "If you don't want to wait, then break in and occupy the land yourself!" Urging villagers into direct conflict was a way for the committee to avoid the problem, because the parties would then most likely end in court. (It was a risky tactic, however: in a 1997 TV program called *Crimes for Land,* I was told by some who saw it, a villager had killed a member of the commission. Others interviewed said this was good: "because of him, half this village is in court.")

In addition, the committee suffered from the problem that unlike the two outsiders, all three would have to live in the village long after restitution was over, and by refusing to take sides in complex cases they were protecting their future relations. A revealing example concerns a villager, Petru, whose garden someone else was claiming. The first time around, the committee had awarded it to Petru, but now the former owner had angrily challenged that decision. After an extensive discussion of who actually had the right to the garden, the surveyor asked the group, "What should we do?" The agronomist answered, "The *committee* must decide," to which a committee member immediately objected, "But I'm on good terms with *everyone*!" Without any vote, the surveyor decided to assign the garden to the former owner. The episode exposed the delicate relations between Vlaicu committeemen and the ones from Geoagiu—the former refused to decide the fates of fellow villagers, thus forcing the latter to make the decisions and, of course, take the blame. The agronomist assessed this incident for me in precisely those terms: "We have to help the locals with one another. It's very bad that villagers are asked to settle quarrels of others they have to live with. So we come in and say it's not the *committee* that decides but the *law*, something bigger than all of us. But the same motive makes the Vlaicu committeemen *blame us outsiders* for problems and say *we're* the ones who are messing things up." Although the less-forgiving surveyor railed against the committee's failure to exercise leadership or to "have the guts" to decide complex cases, he would not have to live out his days among rancorous Vlaiceni.

The consequence, of course, was to endow the commission and the mayor with even more power as local committeemen abdicated their responsibility. Villagers' constant criticism of their local committee had the same effect. Deeply acquainted with the character flaws and scheming of their own committee's members, they accorded it no legitimacy. Moreover, villagers' encounters in other spheres reinforced the idea that the commission was the locus of power over land reform. If they went to the county board, court, or land registry office, they were told, "Go to the commission, go to the mayor; they'll fix it for you." To empower the commune commission in this way, however, was to increase the likelihood that locals would become victims of the machinations of the mayor and his allies; this further undermined the Vlaicu committee in favor of the commune commission.

There is yet more to be said, however, about Vlaicu's "gutless" committee: it was appointed by Mayor Lupu and not elected by villagers. In 1991, Vlaiceni elected the three honest committeemen I mentioned, but as the process of measuring got underway the best of them resigned, reportedly over the illegalities he was being asked to ratify. The other two were abruptly replaced in fall 1992 at a village meeting conducted under the old socialist rules: the mayor's representative read out three names, asked, "Are these OK?" and when there was (understandably) no dissent, he declared them the new committee. The best-liked of the three was a heavy drinker who never wanted to offend anyone; he would agree with whoever was immediately present and was always impressed by people with titles or well-placed relatives. (Once, a fellow Vlaicean disgruntled with the committee's work admonished him in these terms: "You act like a mannequin! You never object to what the surveyor or others are doing with the land. *You're* supposed to be the one with knowledge that outsiders don't have. Don't just ratify everything they do!') With this composition, the committee was weak because its members were not respected and, moreover, could not agree on anything. The surveyor asserted to me that the discord among them was making his work virtually impossible.

Thus, Mayor Lupu and his allies had rid themselves of committeemen who offered resistance in favor of others more malleable. This created a committee whose new members owed their position to him, rather than to their fellow villagers. In other words, the mayor was again behaving like a party apparatchik, ensuring clienteles and treating the commune as his fief. Significantly, he controlled the committee in yet another way: its agronomist was his nephew. This nephew reportedly encouraged the three members' impulses to acquire land they were not entitled to, thus making them complicit in behavior the mayor too was engaged in, which they would accordingly be loath to expose. It is no surprise, then, that Vlaiceni had nothing but complaints about this committee that they had had no say in appointing. The result of its practices was to fortify control by the mayor and commune commission over the process of handing out land. We can see more of this process in the different kinds of knowledge held by each level in the commission hierarchy.

Local and Official Knowledge

The top two commissions relied on forms of knowledge very different from that of the lowest level: the commissions and county boards relied on the various official records held in commune archives, and the committees on local knowledge derived from years of having observed fellow villagers at work in their fields before 1959. Although Law 18 privileged the records, it also left room for adjudication according to local memory. Both sources of knowledge are unreliable, of course—the records because they could be falsified or disappeared, the recollections because memory is partisan. Nonetheless, by according legitimacy to the latter, Law 18 created at least some friction against misuse of the former. What were these different kinds of knowledge?

Returning land rights to previous owners required both the knowledge held in formal records and many other forms of knowledge and information. They included knowledge of the law, of the procedures it required, of the necessary timing, of the bureaucratic competence of different institutions, and so on. All of these were in some sense formal institutional knowledge, held by judges, county and commune authorities, some land commissioners, and notaries. None of it was generated, and little of it held, in village communities. In court, in the notary's office, and in everyday conversations, I repeatedly witnessed villagers' ignorance of the formal procedures for restitution. For instance, during my rounds with the committee and my attendance at the county court, I saw a number of misunderstandings about the period allowed for filing a claim.

People would protest that they wanted to file a claim or were supposed to have more hectares than appeared on their certificate, only to learn that they should have filed the claim or contested the assignment in summer 1991; now it was too late. "But I just now found the paper I need! I couldn't have contested it sooner." In these circumstances the outside committeemen would admonish them that the terms for submitting a petition, a protest, and so on had all been very clearly publicized and if they had not paid attention, there was nothing to be done now. (For their friends or for a little consideration, however, something might be arranged. . . .)

In addition to these official knowledge forms generated and held from without, there were various kinds of informal knowledge, particularly about ownership patterns in space and time and about kinship links between past owners and present claimants. These forms of knowing were generated and held locally; almost no one beyond the community had them (except me).[30] Their repositories were elderly Vlaiceni, who were old enough in the 1950s to have become familiar with the cultivation patterns of their fellow villagers and could (or thought they could) remember those in the 1990s. Thus, a man in his early seventies in 1991 would have worked the fields from his teens to age forty; it was possible that he might recall who had cultivated which parcel next to whom, and if several of these old men got together they might collectively be able to put together the village ownership map of 1959.[31] Their genealogical knowledge connected that map with 1990s Vlaicu.

It was this map, in fact, and not those based on formal figures, that best approximated the true situation on the ground at collectivization, because, as I have indicated elsewhere (Verdery 1994), the self-declarations underlying figures in the official sources were distorted by failures to record transactions in them or by the interests and stratagems suited to those times. The shortcomings of the official statistics justified putting elderly villagers on the land committees: they were assumed to have an essential form of knowledge otherwise lacking. What would happen if they forgot, disagreed, or used their knowledge in partisan ways, as happened not just in Vlaicu but everywhere, was another matter.

Throughout my research, questions abounded as to whose knowledge was authoritative, beginning with everyday conversation but emerging most loudly during land assignment and contestations, when both confusion and claims to knowledge proliferated. (We can see some of this also in the field notes quoted earlier.) An 82-year-old woman was telling me why she was not satisfied with her 41-year-old nephew Traian:

I wouldn't have to bother myself with all this, because the land isn't mine any more—I gave it to him. But he doesn't know exactly where things are.

Even Nicu [his father] doesn't know—Nicu keeps saying he had a piece in Bârceana, but where I knew we were, he says is wrong. Maybe he went there when he was little, before he married; but I don't remember it the way he does, and I'm older. These guys do God knows what, they assign people in the wrong order, not as things used to be. People don't remember. There used to be stones, but with the collective, the stones were taken away, they made it all one big field. Now we can't find where the land was. Look at what the Bible says, it's just like that now: "When the end of the world is coming, you'll go out into your field and you won't know where it is!'

An owner might claim that she knew exactly where her land was, only to be contradicted by an elderly Vlaicean, or her neighbor or cousin. "It was by this tree." "No, it was by the stream." "I shared a boundary with Lazar's Ion." "No, he was farther down. Your boundary was with Iosif's Maria." "We had three hectares." "No, you had three *yokes*, they didn't use hectares then." "What makes you think you know anything about this? They were still wiping snot from your nose while I was already out working the land." Then there was recourse to putatively common knowledge: "*The entire village* knows [ştie tot satul] that I was there and you weren't." Listening to these arguments by the hour, I was struck by the variety of claims to know authoritatively, by the constant contradictions among the three committeemen, by the influence that any one of them (the others absent) could have on the outcome even when dead drunk or obviously drawing as much on his imagination as his knowledge, and by the tremendous amount of detail the two Geoagiu-based committeemen would have to control in order to do their job properly—control that they as outsiders simply could not have. Lacking this, they had to rely on the locals with their own axes to grind. Sometimes the axe included *not* applying knowledge (if indeed they could agree on what it was), lest one alienate a friend or relative. In other words, there could be social constraints on the exercise of local knowledge that tended to push the quest for information toward the more formal sources, held in the commune.

For appeals and lawsuits, arguments not only concerned alternative local knowledge claims, of course, but combined these with more formal ones. Appeal to the commission, the county board, or the court could involve bringing in figures from different sources or pitting one official source against another or against a person. People might accuse one another of having bought their witnesses' testimony or falsified an official document. The problem was especially bad in Transylvania, with its multiple sources of proof. As the surveyor observed,

Law 18 was very poorly thought out, especially for Transylvania. It was made for the Regat, where there's no evidence, where there's plenty of land, and where land can be given out more or less as the authorities like. Here things are very different. People have all these records. They can go to court, someone says, "The agricultural register says you didn't have land there," and the other one pulls out his other proofs and says, "Look here, man!"

For villagers to claim land successfully meant mobilizing several different kinds of information. They had to know when and where the committee would be working; the official figures in the entry petitions or agricultural register as well as the topographic number and file number in the land registry book (or how to get those), in case of a lawsuit; who their kinsmen were and how they were related; what land they had, in which locations, with which neighbors; how long they had for filing a claim and contesting their assignment; how to appeal to the county board; and how to bring suit effectively. Most of the requisite knowledge was not simply lying around. It had to be mobilized. One had to know at which sites to mobilize it and to have the contacts for doing so. Otherwise one was likely to fall victim to the machinations of the commission, with its control over all the formal sources.

For example, Achim Rusan, a former party activist living in Geoagiu, had land in his natal community about 40 km distant. In 1991 he was dismayed to find that he had not received the most valuable piece of it. With some difficulty and by using his old party contacts to get in by the back door, he was able to bring the commission documents from the land registry to support his claim. They told him, however, that the papers were inadequate—he needed to bring witnesses and neighbors to say he had actually worked there (this requirement was abusive; the law demanded no such thing). Although he brought some, the commission was still not satisfied. A cousin who sat on it took him aside and told him he needed much more documentation, including the land records of all his neighbors, which he secured after long effort and expense, again with higher-level assistance. Meanwhile, on the advice of a county official whom he reached through personal connections, he had filed suit, supported with further documentation. Perhaps most important, he also worked out a deal with his cousin to give her a piece of the land if he won it, as he eventually did. This brief example shows the power of the commune commission, which made its own rules, forced Achim to jump through its hoops and bring ever more documents, and waited to see if he would somehow manage. If so, then he might receive his rights. That is, he would have proved to them that he could defend himself and therefore would be likely to win a lawsuit because he could mobilize the necessary documentation. But Achim had well-placed help—without which he would never have won.

To contest or to bring suit successfully required having extensive proofs of a formal sort, which were largely in the hands of officials who might want to prevent clarification. It also required extensive knowledge of the system of justice. Did Vlaiceni too have such resources? Some did, on the evidence of the over thirty lawsuits in which they were involved. But they also had to have nerve, for in socialist times not only did villagers have no confidence in the courts, they viewed going to court as shameful. You went to court only if you were accused of something, not by bringing suit yourself. In the early 1990s, then, bringing suit required a certain fearlessness that not all villagers possessed—initially, at least.

To show what it took for an average villager to bring suit successfully, as well as how many impediments the commission might place in their way, I introduce Victoria Iancu, a remarkably brave and intelligent peasant woman who was seventy years old when decollectivization began. In 1950, her family had owned just under six hectares of good land; in 1952 party cadres confiscated that land, which they later used in starting the collective. The family endured much suffering over the next few years, and this hardened Victoria's already substantial will. When she discovered, in 1991, that because her land had been confiscated (rather than "donated") she was not receiving it back, she immediately contacted her son for help in contesting the decision. This son, Aurel, lived in town, held a state job, and had good access to legal advice. After consulting with well-placed lawyers, he filed a complaint in July 1991. That Victoria had kept the family's land records from before, including the topographic and file numbers in the land registry book, facilitated their complaint.

For the next year, Victoria was constantly on the road to press her case. She made innumerable trips to the county capital, to the notary in Orăştie, and to the commission in Geoagiu. Under Aurel's regular guidance, she gave packages of coffee, other presents, and a tip to the functionary who was supposed to authenticate her claim so he would bump her up ahead of the swarms of other people seeking the same service. For the first court date in January 1992, the commission failed to submit the papers on time; the case was postponed a month. This time the papers arrived (she and Aurel had pestered the mayor continually to be sure he was sending them), although only at the last minute. Upon inspection, the papers—signed by the mayor and the Vlaicu committee members, two of them her relatives!—averred that her land was under the buildings of the state farm and was thus unreturnable. Since this was completely false, Aurel advised her to postpone the date again. With yet more effort, she obtained a declaration from the state farm director that her land was not there and then resubmitted the complaint. Although she told me she had not tried to bribe the judge (as Vlaiceni assumed), she admitted to paying off the person who scheduled the hearings so she would not waste an entire day waiting in court.

Following the election of a new mayor, Victoria finally received a positive judgment in June 1992, but the saga continued. No one came to assign her land, and her formal property title turned out to be for almost one-half hectare less than she expected; it had been labeled "reserve land, commune council." Although the commission tried to intimidate her into accepting the title, she refused. More trips to Deva, to the notary, to the cadastre office; these were now more difficult because arthritis had severely crippled her. Countless phone calls to try to find the surveyor, now transferred to another job. Back to Geoagiu, where they stonewalled again, until she threatened to sue; that seemed to move things forward. Finally the commission remeasured her parcel and gave her a supplementary title for the remaining amount.

Victoria could not begin to estimate for me the time and money that had gone into securing this result, and she was convinced that without Aurel's intervention it would never have happened. "He was the one who knew what we had to do, that we had to postpone when that false paper came from the commission. When the new mayor asked me how I knew the correct legal form for all these papers, I told him my son did it. He congratulated us!" But equally important, she believed, was that they had all the formal proofs. "If my papers were all in order, the court *had* to rule in my favor, no?" In other words, Victoria relied not on the local knowledge of village elders but on the formal sort, and she exerted great effort to break through the commission's monopoly on it.

Note what this success required: access to extensive knowledge of many kinds, connections, money, mobility, stamina and determination, a conviction of her rights (and of the probity of the courts, a view that is rare), and a sense of moral purpose. She justified her repeated interventions: "This land was from my ancestors! How could I let the commune council keep the field I got from my ancestors? I'd have become a laughingstock! There was one huge field that belonged to my grandfather; how could the commune council have a strip in the middle of it? People were even making jokes about that." At issue, then, were her dignity and her feelings of connectedness to her own past. Victoria's success also required a refusal to be cowed by the commission—its delays, its falsified papers, its intimidation. Even though she could obtain adequate proofs by going around them, that took time and effort. Thus, the commune's control of knowledge forced villagers to go to great lengths in pursuit of their rights—the same message we drew from the case of Achim Rusan.

I have already mentioned some of the ways that commissions and commune officials might modify information to their own advantage; here are others. They might, like the secretary of Geoagiu commune, write their own families into some of the best land (protected by the mayor, he was not prosecuted but encouraged to retire). They might obliterate parts of the archives, especially agricultural registers and maps. When one villager obtained from the county archives a detailed map of village land, Mayor Lupu was furious—he had lost his monopoly control. Moreover, for purposes of implementing the law, communes obtained sources of knowledge they did not usually possess. The county's chief notary explained to me, for instance, that although it is strictly illegal to copy the maps of the land registry book, in the present circumstances he had permitted commune officials to do so to help them in their work. This, of course, further enhanced their ability to monopolize and manipulate knowledge. Using official data as well as the genealogical knowledge they gained *from village land committees*, local officials could easily identify areas that had no heirs, so as to make use of these themselves, as I have shown.

In thinking about such struggles over knowledge, we should recall the context from which they emerged. This point was brought home to me by the committee's agronomist, as we talked about how my accompanying the committee had enlivened my persistent reputation as a spy. "People can't imagine what anyone could be doing here with us. They know all these data about surface areas used to be *secret*. Not even two agronomists could talk about areas! If another one asked me how big my collective farm was, I wouldn't tell him." In the socialist period, there were continual struggles over information: at each level, party cadres hoarded it and falsified it so they would look good to their superiors, who therefore had no way of knowing the actual situation.[32] The general population responded to all that information hoarding with perpetual gossip and rumor.

For elites to manipulate information and subordinates to counter with knowledge of their own was commonplace; it is hardly a revelation that this conflictual relationship to knowledge was part of decollectivizing. Given the unsupervised void in which commissions worked, however, they clearly had the upper hand. They knew the law's complex procedures (as villagers did not) and controlled access to proofs; county boards lacking local information urged them to resolve problem cases, and villagers did too, so as to protect delicate social relations. In consequence, local knowledge gave way before more official knowledges. All these pressures served to concentrate power in the hands of commune officials and their commissions.

Compromised Legitimacy

In this chapter I have shown how the organizational hiatus between communes and the political center helped to give Geoagiu's commission a life of its own. The lack of sanctions in Law 18 energized it, as did the weakness of village committees, which resulted partly from the commune's interference and partly from committee members' reluctance to alienate their fellows by being decisive. In consequence, local knowledge gave way before more official knowledges, and hectares could more easily vanish in the process.

In addition, I have suggested that in Vlaicu, and I believe in many other places, commune authorities, especially mayors, continued behaving like Communist Party officials: accumulating political capital in the form of allies and clients (such as the Vlaicu committee), who colluded in turning the restitution process to their own benefit. Land was valuable for them as a means toward this end. There were three essential ingredients in that outcome. First, unlike Russia, for instance, Romania's legislation disbanded all collectives outright, even though also making provisions for cooperative forms thereafter. This gave commissions lots of work but also lots of room for maneuver. Second, given the size of Romania's agrarian sector in the 1950s and the consequent magnitude of decollectivization, the only way Law 18 could be implemented was by empowering lower-level officials to do so. Because the election laws made them less beholden to their superiors than they had been in communist times, they now occupied veritable fiefs. Third, with prospects for rapid economic development in doubt, continuing to trade favors and accumulate clients looked like the best way to get ahead in uncertain times.

The casualty of all these practices, however, was that wherever they occurred in Romania, villagers became cynical (as did those in Vlaicu) about the emerging property regime. People such as Mayor Lupu and his clique in Geoagiu commune had failed to do justice at a moment when justice was critical to consolidating the new order. Such officials did not just usurp the land of others: they compromised the very idea of a justly acquired hectare of one's own, guaranteed by the state. More than this, they compromised the very legitimacy of the private property institution that was taking shape. The attempt to institute new values—rectifying past injustice, the rule of law, and so on—foundered on the means devised for instituting them.

CHAPTER 4
NEW KIN, NEW SERFS, NEW MASTERS
TRANSFORMED SOCIAL RELATIONS AND THE MEANINGS OF LAND

As producer the Trobriander values his land . . . because his gardening, if good, enhances his renown, an incentive which makes him take pride and pleasure not only in the quantity of his produce but in the lay-out and beauty of his gardens.

(Malinowski 1935, 331)

For agriculture to develop, we must have an association of economic interests. Instead, we've generated a huge fund of emotions, and this means not evaluating land according to its intrinsic value. It becomes a talisman—"my father's hectare" and so forth—and people fight over this kind of thing.

(Romania's Deputy Minister of Agriculture, 1994)[1]

Despite the chicanery, delaying tactics, and struggles for information that Law 18 produced, eventually about half of all households in Vlaicu obtained ownership rights to land formerly held by their families. What happened then? French geographer Marie-Claude Maurel concludes her excellent study of post-socialist property transformation in East-Central Europe by observing that decollectivization overturned social relationships and called the entire social order into question. Its premise was a rupture with the ideology of egalitarianism and a return to the principle of inequality as the foundation of village life (Maurel 1994b, 347–48). The present chapter explores some of the social and cultural dimensions of these changes in Vlaicu: transformations in kinship and other social relations, in forms of inequality, and in how people understood land's value and their relations to it as persons. Decollectivizing altered the basis of appropriation from social to individual, and it drew a new set of boundaries among villagers, including and excluding in ways rather different from before. It completely reconfigured the connections among persons, things, and the values attributed to them. It transformed notions of what *persons* are and provided new resources for constituting them.

All these processes were confusing and often painful. They altered patterns of social conflict, as I already illustrated with the case of Benzenzers and '45ers, and they brought into contention opposed idioms for justifying ownership claims. The two primary idioms—kinship and labor—emerged directly from the law itself, but different groups used them from different vantage points. The distant past (one's forebears) suddenly became a resource for some but not for others, who argued instead that their present and future potential for working the land justified their receiving it. Some villagers sought new self-affirmation in the status values of presocialist times, transposed into a very different context. Others vigorously resisted the imposition of those traditional values that would leave them at the bottom of the social hierarchy. Although the contrasting views tended to correspond to the division between locals and venits, poorer locals were likely to side with the latter in an emerging class struggle.

I begin with a discussion of the priorities Law 18 was intended to promote—values relating to kinship and labor, justice and equity. Then I discuss transformations in how people understood kinship in daily life, as well as its contradictions with labor. Turning to the question of property and personhood, I show other kinds of meanings landownership held, relating to status, dignity, work, autonomy, and mastery. When land symbolizes these kinds of things, the matter of making private property becomes far more complex than merely awarding rights and titles.

Kinship, Labor, and Social Conflict

As I explain in chapter 2, Law 18 emerged from fierce political debate as a hybrid of barely reconcilable values: historical justice (restitution to former owners), and equity (the 10-ha cap, the 1948 baseline date for restitution, and the reserve fund for landless villagers). Justice was the concern largely of the neoliberal parties and equity of the postcommunists. These two goals were to materialize from the application of three criteria: prior ownership, kinship, and labor. Being former owners or their kin governed reconstitution of *prior* rights, and having labored in the collective governed the constitution of *new* rights. Each was both an idiom for justifying a claim and the potential grounds for changed relations. How did the two fare in Vlaicu's decollectivization? Because prior-owner claimants were less numerous than the heirs who claimed land in their name, I collapse prior ownership into kinship. Both kinship and labor, as well as justice and equity, were important to Vlaiceni, but not in quite the same way as to the law's framers.

Kinship

The priority Law 18 gave to claims based in kinship fell on fertile soil, for kin relations lay at the heart of village life. Households were the basic unit of activity, kin-based cooperative work in the fields had continued in the socialist period from the years before it, and family was a primary value for all. Indeed, Law 18 itself began with the household, recreating the landscape of family holdings from the time of collectivization and proceeding from there. To make kinship a prime determinant of restitution claims made particular sense, given that the neoliberals believed they were rectifying injustice done to the family members of present-day villagers. The law permitted return of rights to anyone related to the original owners by kinship to the fourth degree (see figure 4.1). That is, in theory one could claim land donated to the collective by one's great-great-grandparents; great-grandparents and their siblings; grandparents and their siblings and children; and parents and their siblings, children, and grandchildren. In practice, land was not likely to have been donated above the level of Ego's grandparents, at most.[2]

Significantly, claims based in kinship were largely gender-neutral, for in Transylvania women have long inherited equally with men (cf. Pine 1998, for Poland). When a woman brought dowry land to a marriage, it entered into the couple's joint possession; should they divorce, she could claim it back. I knew several couples who spoke of "his land" and "her land," although this was not common. For instance, someone asks Mihai about "your piece of land down in Lunca," and he replies, "That's not mine, it's my wife's." In consequence, anyone claiming land in the 1990s could claim it equally through women and men—and this further proliferated the possible claims. In both Transylvania and the Regat, couples who had married after collectivization had no provisions about land in their marriage contract; thus, men could have no basis for claiming the land their wives might receive after 1991. Daniel Lățea suggests that this gave women all over Romania an occasion to reconsider power relations in their families.[3] The principal respect in which women suffered disproportionately from decollectivization was, as I have noted elsewhere (Verdery 1994, 1103–4), that widows were the people most likely to be victimized by others wanting their land—in part because without a husband's support they were less likely to bring suit, assuming they would not be taken seriously.

As the results of decollectivization in Vlaicu would show, however, it was naive for legislators to give such weight to an institution that was the stuff of villagers' daily life and still expect to achieve their own goals. The reason was that for these people, Law 18 made restitution preeminently what Chelcea (2003) calls a "genealogical practice." It became the vehicle for reconnecting with par-

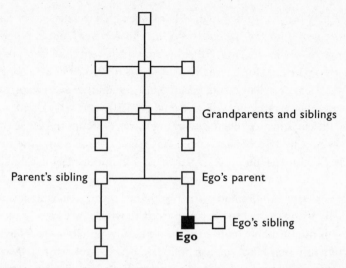

Figure 4.1 The four degrees of kinship enabling land claims. Ego can inherit from all the persons shown (four squares away from him/her).

ents and grandparents, central to the reorganization of kinship relations that followed 1989. During socialist times, vertical ties had been weakened relative to horizontal ones. Collectivization had completely transformed kinship patterns in rural areas, undermining the authority of elders. Wealth ceased to be primarily a matter of inheritance (Humphrey 1998, 270), and household patriarchs no longer organized the labor of their units—the collectives did that. Moreover, the organization of work in CFs privileged horizontal relations among kin and neighbors over vertical ones between ancestors and heirs (who could no longer inherit land).

Law 18 restored the emphasis on vertical kin ties, since having these was the main criterion for filing a claim. Land brought people ancestors, and ancestors brought them land.[4] The law gave elderly recipients a strong asset in conflicts with their children, potentially restoring the pension system of presocialist rural society when promises of land had secured an old person care and income from expectant heirs. My elderly Vlaicu respondents all planned on this (as one of them told me, "Land is my hope"). The emphasis on these vertical links accompanied not only a deep shift in the value of horizontal kin ties, as I will show, but also a sudden solicitude toward elderly kin who now had a value their relatives wanted.

Kinship was both the basis on which Vlaiceni claimed land and also the justification of their rights to receive it. Many people, in response to my asking why they thought they had a right to this land, replied, "Because it's my inheritance! It's from my forefathers!"[5] (Recall Victoria Iancu's observations in chapter 3 about how people would laugh at her if she failed to retrieve her ancestors' land). Moreover, some regarded it as a duty to recover land that had caused their parents so much suffering, either because the parents had lost it or because they had been punished for having had it. As one urbanite put it to her prospective tenant, "Please work my land, because my grandfather went to prison for it. I don't want much from it, just to have it worked." The return of land, then, rectified a historical injustice. Even if working it was difficult, the sense that one's forebears' suffering had been avenged was some consolation. One might say that restored rights to land represented an asset in both genealogical and ethical terms.

For those whose families had owned land, the kinship criterion gave them an advantage by fixing people to specific parcels to which they could prove a connection. This might enable them to withstand usurpation by others having connections of a different kind, such as political ones. In other words, land restitution brought two different kinds of social capital into conflict: connections defined through blood across time and those defined by clientelism and intraelite exchanges within the socialist and postsocialist contexts. The phrasing of Law 18 gave villagers some hope of using the former to withstand incursions by people having the latter. A nice example of this comes from an urbanite born but no longer living in Romos, near Vlaicu, who told me how his neighbors there had urged him to be more aggressive in pursuing his rights to his family's land: "You have to do it out of respect for your parents, who worked so hard for this land. You *have* to get it back! Only that way can you have dignity. You have to get it back because otherwise these pigs [local officials] will get it, since you live far away. They'll trick you out of it."

The privilege accorded kinship had, however, a number of negative effects as well. First, using kinship rather than residence as the governing principle gave rise to multitudes of owners living away from the site of their new holdings (over 40 percent of all Romania's recipients). Although some of these were fully capable of attending to their land, many such holdings helped to fill the coffers of unscrupulous local officials and provided major headaches for new associations, as I show in chapter 6. Second, the kinship principle enabled a return to the old sites, undermining the possibility of field consolidations that might make land easier to work. Returning to old sites, in turn, increased not only dispersal of fields but the number of parcels to be measured and titled, thus further delaying that process. Two additional effects deserve lengthier discussion and illustration. These concern, first, transformations in both relations among kin and understandings of what kinship meant, and, second, the implications of not having the kinship ties that Law 18 favored. Both were sources of social conflict that disrupted village life and could even end in violence.

Changing Kinship Relations

The return of land to people defined as kin led to social conflict among siblings, cousins, and other villagers with rival kin-based claims to land. This outcome was not, of course, peculiar to Romania or other bloc countries: land titling has produced similar conflicts in other contexts as well, such as the British Virgin Islands as described by Maurer (1997). In the worst case, reported periodically in the Romanian media, one sibling might kill another because they could not agree on the division of the parental holding (this happened in Geoagiu, although not in Vlaicu). In the best case, a group of siblings jointly received their parents' few hectares, which they were to divide among themselves; if they could do this peaceably, they went to the notary and registered the division. But often, they found themselves at odds over who should inherit how much land, particularly over who was entitled to more because of having cared for elderly parents or for some other relative in exchange for land. Alternatively, siblings who had moved to town during the socialist period and informally renounced any claim to the parental estate (which then consisted mainly of a house) might now rescind that understanding and push for their own share of land (see also, e.g., Konstantinov 2000, 38–39, for Bulgaria; Berdahl 1999, 165–66, for eastern Germany).

Some of these disputes ended in litigation, contributing to the million court cases I mentioned earlier and thus to further delays in obtaining title. Suits did not necessarily resolve the problem, for bad feeling was likely to persist whatever the judgment. Even without trials, however, relations among kin might be permanently disrupted, as one person repeatedly occupied a few meters of a kinswoman's land or spread nasty rumors to humiliate her.[6] Vlaicu during the 1990s, like many other Romanian villages, was full of examples of such discord among kin.[7] At least four cases produced lawsuits (in addition to the over twenty lawsuits not directly involving kin) and another ten or more resulted in a marked cooling of relations. Lawsuits were perhaps more likely among cousins than among siblings, who had a stronger sense of the indivisibility of a family holding they might have jointly worked in earlier times.[8]

Many of the quarrels concerned how to divide the land among heirs, others merely the location of field boundaries. To give the flavor of village kin relations at this time, I illustrate with a case of the latter kind. Five households, four of them claiming relatedness through their great-grandparents, could not agree on the borders separating them in a particular area that had clear boundaries on all sides—thus, expanding into the land of non-kin was not an option. The quarrel centered on three, whom I call Cornel, Nistor, and Traian, occupying parallel strips in that order. Although all agreed on their order in space and the width of their parcels, the problem was that garbage-strewn strips of uncultivated land at each end reduced the available total, and both Cornel and Traian were too young to know whether the strips were part of their land. Because neither wanted the trouble of clearing the strips unnecessarily, each encroached on Uncle Nistor. During the winter and spring of 1994 I heard constant complaints from each of the three. "He's nuts!" complained one of them, "He's so bent on enriching himself with his land that he's prepared to throw away a half century of good kin relations!" "She ploughed too far away from the edge!" he defended himself to me. "There's a strip that hasn't been ploughed for years, and she just left it and came in on my land. What am I supposed to do?" During my earlier visits these three families had been the closest of friends. Now I heard nothing from them but disgruntlement and carping.

Nistor's position in the quarrel was delicate, for his wife, the one with the actual kin connection, kept telling him simply to accept a few meters less rather than fight with her kin. Nistor, however, had been one of the first to break into CF land in 1990, and he hungered for every square meter. He therefore had to choose whose side to take, Cornel's or Traian's. Initially, although he lived next door to Traian's aunt, he sided with Cornel, to whom he had long been emotionally closer; therefore, he plowed his furrow fifteen meters into Traian's land so as to get his proper surface (350 square meters). This initiated a skirmish of reciprocal plowings-over. The quarrel was seriously disrupting this once-tight kin group, however, and at length—whether from his wife's pressure or from general discomfort—Nistor did something very unexpected. Having vowed never to give the Vlaicu Association a millimeter, he turned his strip over to it, saying that now *it* would have to figure out where the boundaries were so it could plow. Then, when the Association had clarified the matter, he took his strip back out. Nistor's brilliant solution shows how averse Vlaiceni were to prolonged conflicts with kin and how readily they would throw the problem into someone else's yard if they could not resolve it easily themselves. Further proof of this aversion is that very few quarrels among village-based kin actually went to court; instead they smoldered, while protagonists assured me and others, "I'm not taking this to court because he's my kin." Important in this story is that Nistor's decision was not an individual one but one made in the context of his family obligations. This is the sort of thing an institutionalist model would have difficulty factoring in.

Quarrels of this kind had several effects. First, they might finally end in lawsuits, where people would squander much time and money they could have been using for cultivation. Second, solutions like Nistor's (others used it too) increased the insecurity of the Association that was supposed to be helping Vlaiceni work their land. Third, the pattern of throwing problems upward—

which we saw in chapter 3 also—strengthened higher-level actors' capacity for action while diminishing that of locals. And fourth, quarrels among kin strained the networks of cooperation essential to both agriculture and village life more generally, because kin who had fought could no longer expect one another's help in weeding, harvesting, preparing wedding or funeral feasts, and so forth.[9] Quarrels therefore undermined the participants' social capital. The emphasis of Law 18 on kinship thus created unforeseen conflicts that might delay the titling process and hamper people's use of land thereafter.

These effects came in part from a larger transformation of kinship that Law 18 produced: a change in how kinship was understood. That law understood kinship as only a matter of blood and marriage, something like the kinship diagrams of anthropologists (as in Figure 4.1). Villagers, however, had not understood kinship that way; for them, it was performative. To be kin meant *behaving* like kin. It meant cooperating to create marriage, baptismal, and death rituals; putting flowers on relatives' graves; helping out with money or other favors; and caring for the elderly (who might not even be one's parents) in exchange for inheriting their land. In this conception, kinship is—as Collier (1997) puts it—something one *does*, not something one *has*; the doing makes one a pious person in relations with ancestors (Fortes 1961). This performative view does not reject the bloodlines view, on which kin performance usually builds, but broadens it, turning it into practical rather than abstract kinship. Practical kinship was precisely what socialism strengthened—even in agriculture, through the contract-payment system, in which the unit for contracting with the CF was the household (see Kideckel 1993c).

With Law 18, however, this changed. Although kinship was a venerable and robust local institution, villagers' desire for land compelled them to accept a definition of it narrower than before. Instead of understanding kinship as a special kind of embedded social relationship that involved specific behaviors and expectations, the law understood it strictly as a set of abstract statuses at the intersection of blood and marriage. Vertical links among positions gained priority over the horizontal ties among persons that had prevailed during the socialist period, precisely as land quarrels among kin eroded horizontally based practical connections.

These different conceptions of kinship came up over and over during my discussions of land conflicts in Vlaicu: "I was the one who fed her on her deathbed and organized the mortuary feast; her son didn't do a thing for her. I'm the one who should get her land now." "Everyone knows I [a neighbor] was the person who wiped old Aunt Ioana's butt, while her 'nephew' never came to see her at all. Why should *he* get her land?"[10] In all such cases, unless there were written testimony expressly willing a caretaker not just the house but land, commissions awarded land to the blood relative, not the performing one. Perhaps this shift underlies something I heard numbers of Vlaiceni say over the decade: that in accepting claims by kin to the fourth degree, Law 18 had allowed "*too much kinship*," fostering claims by people who had never performed as kin.

If blood rather than behavior were the criterion, then conflicts were inevitable because almost everyone was related to someone, whether or not the connection were actualized in behavior. Performative kinship narrowed the range of practical kin (Aunt Ioana needed not the entire kindred but only one or two people to wipe her butt), whereas the abstract kinship of Law 18 broadened it. Precisely this broadening obstructed implementation of the second criterion recognized in Law 18: one's labor contribution to the CF. The law meant to have that criterion impropriate people who had worked in the collectives without necessarily having kin-based ties to land. What happened to it in Vlaicu?

Local-Venit Relations

Kinship, however conceptualized, works to include and to exclude. It excluded those who could make no claim to land by either blood ties or performative ones, both of which favored the locally born and excluded most venits. Moreover, the matter of the fourth degree widened the claims that locals could make, further diminishing the possibility that land might be left over for anyone else—the law's provisions notwithstanding. Locals dominated the land committees; they were unlikely to award land to the landless unless there were enough to go around after every local land-holding family had received its full due. Oddly, the framers of Law 18 seem not to have imagined that the land-owning locals running village committees would shortchange people they viewed as outsiders rather than deprive themselves of land. The result was much-increased social conflict in this village and others of similar circumstance. Because Transylvania had both more industry than the Regat—industrial jobs being the reason for venits to move in—and higher population density (with correspondingly greater competition for land), this problem afflicted Transylvanians more than other Romanians.[11]

By basing restitution on kinship, Law 18 empowered locals whose way of implementing it confounded its postcommunist framers' goal of greater social equity. As we saw in chapter 3, this is precisely what happened in Vlaicu: when the committee realized that overlap among claims exceeded any possible reserve land, the venits were the first people to be shunted aside. Instead of being given the land that the law allowed them, they received nothing; even the one-half hectare given them in 1990 (by Law 42) vanished. I discussed venits' landlessness repeatedly with locals during the 1990s, and the responses always invoked kinship in one way or another: "Why should I give them a piece of my ancestors' land so they can have some down here, when their families still have land in the hills?" "People see that someone gets land and they ask, 'Why not me too?' They blame me for getting land from my parents, but it's not my fault if his left him nothing!"

Venits vociferously objected to the "too much kinship" of Law 18 and continually invoked that other criterion recognized in the law: justification by labor. Over and over I heard from them complaints such as these: "When we moved in here, all the local women were on 'sick leave' all the time. They were too sick to hoe and weed; we were the ones who did that. Now they have their own land, and suddenly they're healthy! They work until they pop! But we were the ones who worked in the collective all those years, and now we're getting nothing." "We venits deserve the land that the law promised us because we kept the CF going, we suffered the daily grind of caring for dairy cows twice a day for thirty years. Shouldn't we get something for that?" "All these locals whose kids got city apartments just so they wouldn't have to come and weed! They had no time for agriculture before, but now when there's land they're here in droves."[12]

Locals, for their part, took the labor argument seriously, but in a quite different way. Here's how one local, Iacob, replied to my asking whether he would be willing to give up a small piece of his five hectares—more than he needed to live on—so the venits could have some. Becoming very agitated, he replied, "My ancestors were servants! They worked and worked to buy the land I have now! I'm going to give this up so venits can have some?!" In innumerable conversations with locals this was a frequent line of argument: not only do I deserve the land that belonged to my ancestors, but they too deserved it because they worked so hard to obtain it, and that obligates me to fight for it now. (A variant was, I deserve the land of my uncle because I worked to care for him when he was failing.)

The same kind of argument could justify why people were not selling land they were having evident difficulty working. Every year I asked an elderly couple, Iosif and Ioana Borza, why they kept working land and did not sell it. One or other would reply, "Because my parents were poor and worked so hard to buy it. I feel it's up to me to care for what they bought and left to me." Labor appeared yet again in locals' distinction between land that had been worked for [*muncit*] and land that just fell into people's laps [*căpătat*], such as in the 1945 land reform and the free houseplots given out by the CF. One's claim to land was stronger, they insisted, if it was land *muncit*. Therefore, the labor argument might serve the landless and venits to whom the Iliescu group in Bucharest had wanted to give land, but it served just as well the locals who intended to prevent that.

In order to understand better the transforming relations between locals and venits, perhaps we might step back and consider more fully the nature of those relations over the past thirty or so years. Before the CF was formed, there were almost no venits in Vlaicu; there were only people who had married in from other places (and even these people felt that their nonlocal origin handicapped them socially). Like all plains villagers, Vlaiceni regarded hill people as backward country bumpkins. Beginning in the late 1960s, venits moved in (with already constituted families) because the growth of industry in the area offered them factory work and better living conditions. The CF's largely female labor force was divided between the dairy farm and the field brigades (grain, vegetables, and potatoes); most in the field brigades were locals, whereas dairy workers were venits and people from once-poor local families. Although pay was much better in the dairy, the work was arduous and lasted 365 days a year, whereas work in the field brigades was seasonal and could be avoided with medical certificates. Locals' frequent resort to this form of sabotage made CF leaders prefer the venits, whose work enabled leaders to give products upward, whereas locals who were always "sick" contributed nothing.

The majority of venit families moved in around 1970. When I first arrived in Vlaicu in 1973, according to a recent census venits made up 27 percent of the 264 households (as compared with 49 percent in 2000), and relations between them and locals were not good.[13] Locals disdained and resented them, and they were resentful right back. Locals often complained to me during the 1970s and 1980s that whereas they, as collective farmers, were practically destitute, venits always had hay, fruit, firewood, brandy, and other goods that came from their families' uncollectivized land in the hills: "They're rich while we suffer." Having hay, venits could raise more livestock than Vlaiceni with their tiny plots; having firewood saved them the tremendous expense locals had for fuel; and having fruit enabled them to make excellent brandy that Vlaiceni (lacking fruit trees) could not make. Venits could sell all these products to make even more money. What this meant was that the well-being of venits depended much less on the collective farm than was true of locals (and as we see later, dependence was something to be avoided). For lowland villagers to feel themselves inferior to hill people, when it had always been the other way around, stuck in the craw of local Vlaiceni.

By the time of my later visits to Vlaicu in the 1980s, the mutual hostility had subsided a bit. Locals recognized certain venit families as nice, hardworking people and made fewer gratuitous slurs about them in daily conversation. But that situation was reversed with the implementation of Law 18. Now the tables were turned, as locals avenged their years of felt inferiority by finding no extra land for venits. The intransigence of the Vlaicu land committee on the matter of giving them land enraged many of them, and although they made several trips to the prefect in Deva and were promised that their situation would be resolved, it never was.

Compounding their bitterness at receiving no cropland was that they were also losing out to locals on another front—household gardens. The law specified that people who had bought houses or built new ones on land allotted by the collective could claim only a total of 1,000 square meters for their house, courtyard, and garden. Anything over that amount reverted to the original owners or their heirs, who could decide to give it or sell it to the present occupant, to request the equivalent amount elsewhere, to work it themselves, or to sell it to someone else. Many houses in Vlaicu have large gardens, much larger than 1,000 square meters. Venits, having no other land, were especially eager to retain as much garden as possible, by threats and aggression if necessary. But they did not fare very well; during the 1990s, they lost nearly every lawsuit over gardens. Particularly galling was that most locals wanted these gardens mainly to sell back to them. Not caring to work the gardens themselves, locals nonetheless saw no reason why venits should get those for nothing; they should buy that land, as they should buy other land if they wanted it. This attitude infuriated venits, who complained that being forced to buy their gardens was part of a new form of class struggle.

To indicate how such conflicts might unfold, here is an extract from notes I took while accompanying the Vlaicu land committee on its measurement rounds in spring 1994. As in chapter 3, "Map" is the committee's surveyor, "Agron" its agronomist, and "Com't" a village committeeman; "M" stands for mother.

We get to Elena B, whose garden is claimed by Vasile D; Com't has sent for Vasile to come. Map asks Elena if she worked in the collective: no, only her parents. When was the house built? twenty years ago. How big was the garden then? Maybe 500 square meters, 800 . . . [plus the house and courtyard]. Map: "If you want the garden, you have to come to an agreement with Vasile, the former owner of the land." Elena becomes furious: "In Vlaicu justice will never be done!" Her mother comes, much shouting. Vasile: "Why don't you want to sharecrop the land?" Elena and M: "A boss is a boss! We won't work for you 'aristocrats,' for *chiaburs!*" They go on and on: "You people with land are the worst there is. You take everything and leave us with shit! We have six kids, and nothing to plant food on. . . ." Vasile: "I didn't ask you to move here or have six kids! Get land from your parents, like everyone else!" He too is shouting, mad.

Now Agron is trying to calm things: "The law is the law, we have to do it by the law. The laws of before have changed now, we're not doing things

as in Ceauşescu's time. The law says . . ." Vasile: "I didn't intrude on anyone! It's mine, period! I have the documents, I'll take you to court, you'll
have to pay costs and I'll sue you for three years' harvest!" . . . Elena and
M: "You're on the side of the Americans!" [I had shaken hands with Vasile
when he showed up]. Vasile: "Well, it's clear you're on the side of the Russians! I'm simply not going to give away this land! It's been worked for
[*muncit*], not just gotten for nothing [*căpătat*]!"

Shouting could escalate into threats of violence. For example, one venit
being sued for a garden had threatened to beat up both the owner and the land
committee, should they come to measure it. I discovered this because on the day
the committee was to measure there, most of its regular members failed to show
up. The two who did appear argued to postpone the measuring until the mayor
could come, but the surveyor scoffed at them. Because no one would go with
him, he handed one end of the tape measure to me and told me where to stand,
while the remaining members and the aggrieved venit looked on. Only later did
I learn of his threat. Like most venits, he lost his lawsuit.

There is an irony to this outcome: because venits would have to buy, a market for land would develop around precisely the group to whom PRSD politicians were trying to give it. That market began with household gardens but
soon expanded into field parcels as well, even though the PRSD hoped to delay
that outcome. Village politics had once again subverted central designs.

These are some of the elements of the reorganization of the field of social relations that restitution provoked. Property-making verticalized kinship and divided the community into haves and have-nots. Thenceforth the haves strove to
engage the have-nots as laborers, while the have-nots did everything in their
power to become haves—a story I tell in chapter 5. At the heart of the conflict
was the contradiction among the priorities instituted in Law 18—kinship and
justice versus labor and equity. The contradictions provided arguments for
Vlaiceni of different kinds, agitating their relations with one another.

Meanings of Land

It was not just social relations that restitution reorganized; it was also meanings of land and notions of person, all of them important in understanding
property. I turn now from the diverse significances of kinship and labor for the
creators of Law 18 and its various targets to additional meanings that gave land
value for Vlaiceni. What did recovering land mean to people? What kinds of
symbolic capital could it provide? What kinds of persons could ownership

make? How were the values of land shifting through the decollectivization process? My discussion carries forward the theme of inequality that pervaded the previous section and is a basic issue in land restitution.

In chapter 3 I argue that for commune elites land had value primarily for its capacity to attract clients and build up elites' social and political capital. This is not to say that they recognized no economic value in it. Clearly they did, for the proceeds from cultivating might enable them to construct fancy villas—although even those were as much a display of capacity as an object of economic value. Likewise, smallholders saw land as potentially enabling wealth or at the very least as having subsistence value; that possibility is the subject of the next chapter. Especially given the likelihood of factory closings in this highly industrialized county, none could deny the subsistence value of a family holding. Here, however, I look at values of other kinds. Why did people in their sixties, seventies, and even eighties pursue their rights with such determination in the face of the kinds of obstacles described in chapter 3? Was it only so they could have something to sell or eat? My answer is that, as important as eating is, there was more to it than that.

Land and Social Status

In describing the locals' view of land as reconnecting owners to their ancestors, I have neglected to say what venits and landless locals thought of this: not much. In my conversations with them they would scoff at it, saying, "My ancestors! My ancestors!" in sarcastic tones. According to a poor local, those who emphasized ancestry were wanting to get back family land not because it was ancestral but because it was good land. They wanted the certainty of believing that they could not be removed from land that was their inheritance because "*the whole village* knows that's where we were." Those without land saw the entire inheritance discourse as a piece of cant supporting the return of the formerly rich to high status.

They had a point, because this was precisely what the genealogical connection did: it affirmed the superior status of the formerly landed over those with less or no land, thus asserting a claim to the prestige one's family had held in the presocialist rural stratification system. This was not simply a smallholder's view. Here is how Lucreţia, an agronomist friend from a once-wealthy peasant family in neighboring Şibot, explained the same idea, referring to herself:

> Our family had a *position* in the village. Now that we're getting our property back, we want to hear people say, "Those Morarus are rich people!" the way they used to. The communists made us all equal, all the same

within the village, except for those who sent their kids to university. Otherwise there was no distinction. Now we make distinctions through our material status. Not everyone accepted the idea of equality—richer people were compelled to, but equality was a big burden for them. Only those lower down didn't find it so. They liked equality better.

I heard Lucreția's observation from a number of Vlaicu's once-important families, too. Venits could only lose, of course, from the imposition of these values; as one of them said to me defensively during a discussion of how much land people had, "We venits have *our own* scale of what makes people respectable."

Although this might seem merely the recreation of traditional rural status system and its accompanying ideology, I believe more is at stake than that. We should bear in mind that the villagers most responsible for pushing this line were from formerly respectable families who had suffered the most during the socialist period. They and their values had been constantly ridiculed; they had been deported or jailed for having had "too much" land. Persecuted in the rural class struggle, many were excluded initially from the collective farm, which meant they went hungry and had to beg from others. Iosif Borza described to me how during collectivization, once-wealthy villagers would be crying because they had no way to provide their requisition quotas; they'd approach him for loans because his quotas were lower. "One woman came to me, sat down on the step, and said, 'If you won't lend me money to buy my quotas, I'll drown myself in the Mureș.'" Those still alive and the family members who endured their misfortune with them have a vivid memory of those humiliations. It is no surprise that such people should want to reassert their earlier prominence, so as to vindicate themselves and their families and to reconfirm a positive self-identity. Rather than simply recreating a traditional value system, they were making use of a familiar idiom to find an identity more appealing than that of collective farmer, in circumstances that afforded them very few resources for creating new identities. Let me explore this theme further, by asking how land might form certain kinds of persons.

Propertied Persons

Writings on property, from philosophers such as Locke and Hegel to anthropologists such as Strathern, often link it with aspects of character, identity, and the person. Property, being a relation among persons with respect to values, is a critical component of how persons are defined. What sort of person–entity is it that enters into social relations? Precisely because property is person-forming, the century's two abrupt changes in the status of land brought changes in the quality of the persons attached to it. How did restitution not only transform people's relations to one another and to land but also create new kinds of property subjects, new sorts of persons, constituted differently from those of socialism?

A rather abstract answer relates to the temporal and spatial implications of claiming land through one's ancestors. Before collectivization, identity had had deep temporal roots for families owning a few hectares of land: we are the descendents in X place of A or B respected families. Land was the objectification of this identity. Its permanence and our ongoing relation to it give us continuity—as kin, as locals, as beings in and of this particular place. Collectivization had ruptured that kind of self-concept, interrupting continuities and disrupting people's sense of locality. To some extent, recovering land meant reasserting those ways of being-in-the-world for Vlaiceni who had been raised in them. Even if one did not work it, just retrieving it reconstituted people as locals, as valued persons, as people who shared a past with their kin. Land objectified that kind of embedded self, and recovering it enabled them to be somebody again. This is not simply a return to traditional values but rather the use of a familiar idiom for making new present identities.

Thus, property restitution privileged a kind of personhood that was defined by *having things* and being embedded in kin relations extending into the *past*. Venits, by contrast, who emphasized their entitlement through labor—through *doing* rather than having—were defining themselves in a much shorter time frame (their years in the collective) and with respect to their *present and future* capacities: we can work the land from now on, whereas those old locals are too decrepit and the urbanites are too far away. Both kinds of personhood differ from that of socialism, which derived from connections—the social capital that was essential to distinguishing the haves from have-nots (cf. Berdahl 1999, chap. 4). The persons of socialism were embedded in dense networks of relations extending far beyond kinship; they were what Strathern (1988) calls "dividuals." It was precisely this social embeddedness that the new property-based market-economy-in-the-making challenged (see Dunn 2004).

Vlaiceni had rather more concrete ways of talking about how owning affects one's character, a topic they engaged in sometimes spontaneously and sometimes in response to my questions. One man with whom I spoke was very thoughtful on this subject. We had been talking about why people had struggled so hard to get their land back and why he thought it important to own property. "Because it gives you a sense of responsibility," he said, as if fresh from a seminar with neoclassical economists. "You have something you have to take care of; it makes you more cautious, more hardworking, more thrifty. Without it, you just do what you please, without any sense of responsibility." (KV: Did you lose

Mărioara and her husband won the lawsuit that recovered her ancestors' land.

your sense of responsibility when you lost your land?) "No, because I was raised to have one. Even when we had no land, I'd think about it, and if I was walking near it I'd notice if it was being worked well. That's how I was raised." Views such as this came not only from a few other smallholders but also from aspiring entrepreneurs.

A second and related point about self-conception came from Victoria Iancu, introduced in chapter 3. I asked her if she felt that recovering her land had changed her in any way. "YES!" she replied emphatically. "I feel more powerful, prouder, because it's mine, because I'm rich, because things are going well. I hold my head up higher. I'm different now, completely different! Without land I was always anxious." She as well as others saw it as a question of dignity—the return of their land was a return of their dignity, enabling them to feel like respectable persons. Such self-respect was a special theme among those who took land cases to court. Victoria explained why she had gone to such lengths to get her land back by saying, "The important thing is not to let those people *rip me off!*" An idea expressed even more often, when I asked friends why they thought villagers were fighting so hard to get their land back, was some version of this: "Because people were trampled on for so long under the old system that they want to recover possession now even if they don't work it, just so they know it's theirs."

Another central component of a propertied identity was labor. I noted above that both locals and venits accorded labor high priority, even while making different arguments around it. And it was not just that both were simply manipulating an idea brought up by Law 18. Long before Marx's name became a household word for them, the importance of labor in defining the person had been a crucial ingredient in self-conception, especially for middle peasants. In researching collectivization, I asked my elderly respondents to describe what kinds of people their parents had been (an effort to get at prior conceptions of *person*); I heard over and over that their parents had been hardworking and diligent and had enjoyed respect for it. Almost none of the thirty people to whom I put the question failed to use these terms.

At issue was not just labor per se, however, but control over it. For this, land represented autonomy, the possibility of working for oneself rather than for others. Writing about peasants in Hungary prior to collectivization, Martha Lampland (1995, 35–46) explores in detail the significance of work in self-definition, showing that the ability to control their labor was what mattered to them most. "One's relative independence in work, particularly for men, was important for one's sense of social respectability and honor. . . . [B]eing forced to work for others was demeaning and deprived one of initiative and integrity. . . . The more one controlled one's labor, the more prestige one enjoyed. Conversely, the less one was master of one's own labor, the less respect one was accorded. . . . The central concern of villagers was to be one's own master" (35, 41). And she quotes from Ferencz Erdei's 1941 work on the peasantry that the necessary condition of "a full peasant lifestyle was that he possess his land without interference, disturbance, and supervision, and that he control his produce without fixed obligations" (45). Vlaiceni subscribed to very much this set of conceptions, perhaps because their ancestors and Lampland's villagers had lived under the same feudal system. My conversations about decollectivization showed the same idea: both venits and locals saw autonomy, independence, and not having to work for someone else as the ideal. Even if one did not actually work one's land, simply having it was a value because it represented one's independence. For the very richest, a sign of their high status was to have other people work for them (although not many had this luxury), much like the feudal lords.

I believe this cluster of values relating to the self underlies venits' violent reaction to becoming the "serfs" of the local "nobles" as a result of receiving no land. We have seen this in the fight between Vasile D. (a local) and Elena B. (a venit), when the latter replied angrily to the former's question as to why she would not sharecrop the land from him, "We won't work for you 'aristocrats,' for *chiaburs*!" Working for the collective was one thing, and it ought to entitle them to land, but working for locals was something else again. I heard the same idea in discussing with venits how they thought they would get by without land if they also lost their factory jobs. "Will you sharecrop from the people with land?" I asked, receiving the following kinds of answers, always in a heated tone: "We don't want to be serfs for the local nobles!" "I'm not going to make *someone else* a gentleman!" "You think I look like a servant? People with lots of land are waiting for us to come and support them while they rest in the shade. Some people here have 20 ha, while others of us have none at all. If we go and work for them, it will be just like the days of serfdom! No way!"

Their reaction was not exaggerated. Consider the many locals I spoke with who described their experience with sharecropping in terms such as these, from one well-to-do owner:

> I've never been so relaxed! I've given 3 ha of corn in sharecropping to four people. They're getting only 30 percent of the harvest, since I already plowed and planted. The main problem is transport: because they're few, they can't do much in a day so our son has to make more frequent trips to bring in harvest from the fields. We suggested that the four get together and work on successive days, to make less effort for our son. We've turned into gentlemen![14]

It was not only venits who expressed hostility to working for the landed; poor locals did so as well. I asked one woman whose land was tied up in court why she was not sharecropping until the case was resolved. She replied with vigor, "I don't want to! I don't want to! I don't want to enslave myself on someone else's land! It's one thing to work my own, but I'm not working for anybody else!" People like her were just as acutely sensitive to the possibility of being considered serfs—a status with which their grandparents had been all too familiar. (Indeed, during my work prior to 1989 I often heard Vlaiceni invoke the feudal past, sometimes as a metaphor for their life in the collective farm.) In Vlaicu, the division between potential serfs and lords was expressed in terms of the venit-local division because it happened that most locals had received some land. Underpinning that division, however, was the one between the landed and the landless, and in villages without venits it took that form.

I believe there may be more behind these feudal metaphors than simply the idea of independence. In our conversations, Vlaiceni almost never used the word *property* [*proprietate*] with respect to their land; they spoke not of "my property" but of "my land" [*pământul meu*]. It is not easy to find words in Romanian that translate the concept *ownership* or *to own*. Aside from *proprietate*, dictionaries give *a avea* ("to have") or *a poseda* ("to possess"), not quite the same as "own." One other word caught my attention, however, appearing both in dictionaries and in daily speech: *a stăpâni*, or *a fi stăpân*, "to be master." Widows describing how someone else had tried to usurp their land were likely to say, "He came and made himself master [*s-a pus stăpân*] on my land." When I asked villagers if the personal plot of the CF was theirs, many initially replied yes. After discussing for a while what they could and could not do with their plot, some would change their minds: "No, I wasn't master of it [*n-am fost stăpân pe el*]."

Among the meanings of *stăpâni* as a verb are "to rule, to govern, to master, to dominate," and, as an abstract noun [*stăpânire*], "domination, reign, sovereignty, command." Both the sovereign and the feudal lord were called *stăpân*. Even a law school textbook uses this language in defining property as "relations that are established among persons relative to appropriating the means and the products of production and exercising mastery [*stăpânire*] over them" (Lupan and Reghini 1977, 12). Hudečková, Lošt'ák, and Rikoon (2000, 104) suggest something similar for Czech cultivators: the importance of behaving "as owners *sovereign*." This idea offers an image very different from the roots of our English words *property* and *ownership*: whereas those two words have at their core the idea of self,[15] the core of *stăpânire* is the idea of dominion.

Mastery does not mean just owning but being effectively in charge. Consider Nistor, telling me how he felt about getting his land back: "Very happy! Because I thought, I'll be *stăpân* over it. But it hasn't worked out that way, I'm not *stăpân* over it. . . . I'd be *stăpân* if I had my own implements and a tractor." Mastery is also something interactive, not a unilateral imposition of the will. As Victoria Iancu said, explaining to me why her urban daughter would never be good at agriculture, "You can't just come and go as you like. You have to be *stăpân* on the land, work it *now* when it needs to be worked, not only when you happen to have time and money for it." Land thus elicits mastery through its requirements. In other words, restitution brought villagers an opportunity to reconstitute postsocialist selves that rested on having a sense of mastery and control, as well as independence—things they had mostly not enjoyed during the socialist period.

I explored some of these issues in a quite different conversation with Traian, a former state farm director and party member. Discussing why communist officials had taken so many cartloads of produce from collective and state farms, he said, "There's a deeply rooted idea that if he's a leader, it's his due. He has no shame about taking stuff, because he's thinking his position entitles him to it since he's the one who resolves problems." Then I asked whether he saw any connection of this to the notion of *stăpân*: Did such a party official see himself as a representative, or rather as a *stăpân*? He responded, "Not a representative but a *stăpân*. 'We give you food, we do everything for you. . . . ' They saw themselves as the determining factor of everything that happened. First Secretary Cucu was this kind of big *stăpân*. They were *stăpâni* of the whole county, over all its people, all its immovable property; all possibilities were open to them."

What I took from this set of conversations was the idea that owning land does not merely give one control over one's work, although that is vital: it makes its owner a kind of lord, understood as an active or ordering principle. I am reminded of Humphrey's brief but fascinating discussion of Russian ideas about power, as revealed in the words *khoziain* ("master, proprietor") and *gosudar'* ("sovereign"). Linking the term with an older idea in Russian thought, she continues: "According to this idea, socio-political order is brought about by the exercise of centralised and personified power, not by law, the observance of principles, or the existence of civil society.... [T]he cultural concepts of the 'domain' (*khoziaistvo*) and the state (*gosudarstvo*) encode in themselves from the beginning the reification of political entities in which a central personification of power creates order" (Humphrey 2002a, 28). Although I lack so comprehensive a sense of the meanings of *stăpânire*, it seems clear from my examples that a master is an ordering principle. I believe this is how Vlaiceni saw themselves in relation to their land: it was something that enabled them to create order, to control their own labor and its products, and to feel a sense of mastery.[16] I refer to this as their having *effective ownership*.

The Visible Economy

The value placed on mastery was not just a personal matter but a social one. Mastery was something others could see; they could see laborers working on your fields, and they could see how competent a master you were by the state of your crops. In other words, mastery was part of what I call a *visible economy*. In my travels through Vlaicu's fields during the 1990s, visibility was a constant theme. Whoever was with me would comment on the fields we passed, "Oh, there's Sandu's wheat, look how beautiful it is!" or "See those ugly weeds? those stunted cornstalks? That's Dumitru's lousy work." This same personalization of the landscape is found in other rural ethnographies as well (for one among many, see Donovan 2001, 283). In the late 1990s, when smallholders were beginning to think they were losing money by farming, they continued to cultivate it because their reputations as good farmers and competent persons would suffer if they did not (see chapter 5). Families from whom I was trying to learn crop yields were disconcertingly vague on how many kilograms of corn or wheat they had harvested, instead emphasizing the number of cartloads they had brought home. When I asked how many kilograms a cart held, they became exasperated, as if I just did not get it. (They were right; I didn't.) The yield figures

The visible economy: "That's Dumitru's lousy work!", indicated by its weeds and unkempt appearance.

some of them gave me were preposterous—not, I think, because they were lying but because they were seeking to answer a question posed in terms alien to them. By the same logic, to sell land was anathema because it deprived you of autonomy, but it was also shameful because it showed that you were a lousy farmer.

In this system of values, having a field of fine and well-weeded crops that all could see was a way of exhibiting mastery and asserting superior status over those with less or no land, or with poor labor capacity. Likewise, having an outdoor storage loft bursting with corn, much like the bursting yam houses of Trobriand Islanders (Malinowski 1922, 1935). Especially given the low grain prices, corn sold in the market was less of an asset than corn everyone in Vlaicu could see: it proved you were an industrious and competent master. Indeed, an official of the former collective told me that in 1990 the farm had distributed huge amounts of grain to villagers—whose first move was to build outdoor storage sheds for it, visible to all.

This attitude could cause intergenerational conflicts. For example, one evening a commercial farmer, Mihai, had a colossal fight with his mother and aunt, whose fields he had been working. The two women were angry that he harvested the grain and sold it; then they had to use their pensions to buy bread, whereas if they gave the wheat to a local baker, they got bread for free and could

The visible economy: a large corn harvest, stored where it is easily seen, with its proud owner.

use the pension money on something else. Continuing the conversation, his aunt asked him how to save money. "The best thing," he said, "is to sell grain and turn the money into dollars." She snapped back, "I never sold grain in my life, and I'm not going to start now! I always kept it to use." Mihai concluded, to me, "These women are happy only if they see their granary full! It means more to them than money in the bank." The example reveals generationally different modes of investing in property: older people, whose investment was deeply symbolic, and younger ones, who thought of themselves as investing economically or rationally (and no doubt wished that their elders would just pass the land over to them so they could work it in terms of scientific farming and profit or loss).[17]

The matter of seeing, which includes not just surface areas but the work put into them, is therefore key in thinking about status. The farmers' goal was not simply to have land but to have it worked (cf. Lampland 1995). In this view, land was an asset in social and symbolic terms; if it were left unworked, those capitals were devalued. Such a status system rests on visibility and thus on a particular conception of what constitutes property. It had to be concrete, particular, and bounded, identifiable as distinct from everyone else's. It and its products had to be visible—and visibly linked to their particular holding. In short, land had to be property as a concrete physical object, not as abstract shares in some state farm. Seeing was a value for venits and poor locals as well, although with a critical edge. In expressing their impatience with locals' self-promotion, they would say, "Just walk the fields! Wherever you see weeds, that's where the rich people are working! Beautiful fields are usually the work of us venits."

Some venits, however, advocated different values altogether. Marica, a widowed venit in her sixties and a person of generous and nonjudgmental spirit, had a salaried son and daughter-in-law, so they were not dependent on land. They had struggled to buy one-half hectare, but she was not interested in buying more. When I asked why in winter 2001, she replied: "Life is *better* without land because you have fewer worries! Will it rain, will there be a flood, and so on. You're working so hard you haven't time to sit and chat, knit, relax. That's not for me. And besides, we calculate that with cereal prices so low, it's cheaper to buy wheat than grow it." Hers was yet another view—admittedly rare—of the value of land, which saw it as not worth the trouble. Just what that trouble amounted to is the subject of the next chapter.

Local Values and Central Directives

There were several ironies in the way restitution worked out, ironies that included subverting some of the goals expressed by those who made the law (see also Cartwright 2001, 133). First, because venits did not receive land, they were compelled to find ways of buying it, even including the gardens right behind their houses. Together with urbanites and others who had land they could not use, venits helped to create a land market, contrary to postcommunist intentions of suppressing it.[18] Second, the criteria privileged in Law 18 as bases for land claims—kinship and labor—entered into a process that, in Vlaicu, ultimately thwarted the equity goals of the postcommunists. Many of those whom kinship favored received historical justice for the sufferings of their ancestors, as the neoliberals had hoped; these people dominated village land committees and prevented nonowners from receiving land. That sharpened rather than diminishing the inequalities of presocialist times—something the postcommunists had wanted to avoid. Locals overwhelmed venits' arguments about the value of labor with their own counterarguments about the labor of their ancestors, while seeking to engage venits as labor for themselves.

Therefore, local action by both native-born Vlaiceni and venits worked against the postcommunists' aims, even as the law's framing modified villagers' conceptions of what kinship meant. At the same time, the conflicts that emerged reduced village solidarity, thus contributing to the tendency I discussed in chapter 3: the concentration of power in the commune administration. In addition, the preoccupation with kinship aggravated the problem of fragmented fields, slowed the process of awarding titles, and further played into the hands of commune power-holders with their own reasons for delaying restitution.

These tendencies in Vlaicu would not necessarily appear everywhere. First, in Vlaicu the superimposed ownership claims of local '45ers and Germans had decreased the chance that venits would get land, whereas in other settlements with larger surfaces and fewer claimants (such as in much of the Regat), this would not happen. In general, Transylvania's higher population density made claims and quarrels proliferate. Second, not every plains settlement had as many venits as Vlaicu did; in two others nearby, where the percentages were much smaller, venits did get a piece or two of land. Vlaicu's venit population was a function of its especially favorable place on transport networks and of its location in one of Romania's most highly industrialized counties. Third, the widely varying soil quality in Vlaicu underlay well-situated locals' insistence on receiving their old sites, thus preventing a field consolidation that would have eliminated conflicts over field boundaries and speeded up titling. Because villagers elsewhere sometimes accepted field consolidation, they avoided some of the problems that plagued restitution in Vlaicu. Nonetheless, interest in the old sites was widespread enough that the difficulties we saw in Vlaicu would be echoed in other places.

In this chapter I have described some of the ways in which relations among people with respect to things of value were reorganized as land became private property. Implementing Law 18 created social conflict both among kin and among different categories of villagers, a situation exacerbated by the broad extent of permissible kinship claims. The law reasserted over space the predominance of certain social relationships based in shared local identity, privileging people born in Vlaicu over those born elsewhere and making that a class difference. I have also indicated what land meant to smallholders who received it, beyond being a means of subsistence. For the middling and wealthier smallholders, it meant an assertion of status, identity, and a sense of mastery after three decades in which land could not play that role. Its value was not just economic, but tied to notions of self and to one's life in community, through the idea of mastery that others recognized.

What would happen if they found it impossible to experience this sense of mastery in their efforts to work their land—if they felt, as Nistor did, that they did *not* control the production process, were not effective owners, and could not produce goods? The idea of property restitution was a powerful one for collective farm members, who believed that they would now appropriate more than they had when the state organized extraction. But what if the situation they found themselves in obstructed mastery and, despite all the propaganda about private property rights, they could not appropriate more product? Then land would lose value for them. In the next chapter I show how this devaluation occurred.

PART II
REALIZING THE POWERS
OF OWNERSHIP

In Part I, I described the previous property order and the process by which it was taken apart; in Part II I present what emerged in Aurel Vlaicu from its state and collective farms. Part I showed how owners were made; Part II shows how they were thrown into a world of total uncertainty and high risk, in which they were to make effective ownership. A few preliminary points will make chapters 5–8 easier to read as part of the larger story into which they belong—a story about devaluing and revaluing the wealth in Transylvanian agriculture as one set of property forms gave way to another.

First, some brief reminders of information presented in chapter 2. There I discuss the price controls that kept food prices low but allowed prices of industrial inputs to approach world market levels. The resulting price scissors widened during the decade, along with inflation, which reached 300 percent in some years. These trends put a brake on rural accumulation. Government subsidies and bank loans for agriculture rarely reached village smallholders but were pocketed by people higher up. The circumstances were so unstable—with inflation, government policies changing every few months, constant questions as to whether Law 18 would be modified, and so on—that in the words of an economist I spoke with, any "normal risk-taking capitalist" would find it totally hostile. I also note the dismantling of the state monopoly Romcereal, between 1994 and 1997, despite its important role in the early phases of transformation as a mediator of government credits and a warehouser and distributor of crops. In this high-risk environment, Transylvanian smallholders expected somehow to create viable private agriculture.

From chapter 1 we should recall the distribution of organizational forms in agriculture: collective farms that were labor-rich and capital-poor, agricultural machinery stations (AMSs) that were machinery-rich and land-poor, and state farms relatively rich in land and all capital inputs. These spun off four organizational entities: agricultural machinery stations now renamed *Agromecs*, state farms, and two successors to the collectives—(1) individual households of former CF members, which might become small agricultural enterprises, and (2) the organizational infrastructure and personnel of the CF itself, which in many cases morphed into associations. That is, the CF's land and labor went into one kind of entity (individual households), while its organization, networks, expertise, and large buildings went into another (associations). In contrast to this fragmentation of CF assets, state farms were to remain intact, at least for a time. They might ultimately become commercial farms, but meanwhile, their personnel and organizational infrastructure remained unified, and they retained control of both their labor force and the land they had worked all along.

The way decollectivization was conceived thus led immediately to peculiar imbalances. CFs returned land to member households but could not provide them with capital inputs. Agromecs were to continue working for both members and associations, but a 1994 law on tenancy prohibited their directors from renting land. That is, units having land and labor had trouble obtaining machinery, and units having machinery could not easily accumulate land. Agriculture requires land, labor, machinery, and other inputs; only the SFs had access to the full set—and precariously, at that. Thus, decollectivization was so conceived as to create serious problems in bringing production factors together—the basis for creating value in agriculture.

How the various entities strove to do this is a main theme of the remaining chapters, in which I describe three of these organizational forms in detail. Concerning the fourth, the Agromecs, I wish to note a few points necessary to following these chapters. Instead of breaking up the AMSs immediately and turning their equipment over to the newly forming associations, the Iliescu government left them as state-owned enterprises. The new Agromecs would provide machinery services to both associations and households, for a fee; eventually they were to be privatized. One way for old directors of these Agromecs to survive, instead of being put out of business by the death of the CFs, would have been to form their own associations to rent villagers' land, but the 1994 tenancy law precluded that. These directors had nothing but a lot of old equipment and scores of pen-pushers. Acting as a group, they figured out how to support their myriad functionaries and maintain their aging and decrepit equipment: they set exorbitant prices for the services they provided for cultivators and associations. The prices were uniform by county. Each county's Agriculture Department called all its Agromec directors together annually to discuss the prices they should set to cover all their costs—gas, oil, and parts; depreciation; ordinary operating expenses; and salaries, using socialist piece-rate norms at new labor rates set by the unions for an excessive number of personnel. (In the case of the Agromec near Vlaicu, that number amounted to one staff member for every 29 ha, whereas the ratio for the Vlaicu Association was one staff member for every 50 ha.) In short, the Agromec's rates were high because they were administrative prices, as in socialism.

Although a few villagers bought tractors and began to compete with the Agromecs, this did not reduce prices by much—surprisingly, given that these individuals did not have a load of functionaries to support—because they used the Agromec prices as a yardstick and dropped their fees just slightly. That is, they did not charge according to their actual costs but to obtain maximal gain, at their fellow villagers' expense. Agromec prices were among the factors that prevented both associations and smallholders from quickly accumulating funds to buy their own machinery (which would put the Agromecs out of business). Instead, these prices pushed associations into assuming bank debts so as to buy their own machinery, debts that could cause financial problems for them down the line. In assessing the causes of rural decapitalization, the Romanian government's handling of the AMSs is high on the list.

Connected with the fate of Agromecs and state farms is another noteworthy phenomenon of the late 1990s: trade on the international scrap metal market. Scrap metal is an important ingredient in making steel products, and steel producers worldwide import it. After 1989, East European countries proved a significant source; between 1998 and 2000, for example, income from Romania's scrap-metal trade increased from $96 million to $295 million (Mateescu 2002, nn. 18, 19). Agromecs had derelict equipment, which their own directors could sell to line their own pockets. In addition, many state farms had not only aging tractors but extensive if rusting irrigation works. As the performance of state farms worsened through the decade, both the directors of those farms and their former workers pulled up the irrigation pipes to sell. In fact, not only did people associated with state farms participate in this westward drain of scrap metal, but so did directors of socialism's industrial behemoths, noncompetitive on the world market and loaded with debt. Hunedoara's large and aging industrial infrastructure made it a very good source of used iron. Thus, people of all kinds participated directly in one little-noted aspect of the collapse of East European socialism; where farms and industries were not bought up for restructuring, the systematic devaluation of their assets took the form of a steady westward drain of the physical infrastructure.

All these points about context affected how the three main actors of subsequent chapters—households, leaders of associations, and state farm directors—proceeded. These actors differed in the time horizons according to which they operated and in the kinds of resources on which they could hope to draw so as to absorb and redistribute risk. Households tended to operate on very short time horizons—getting their land plowed now, obtaining a crop this season—without having the luxury of planning further into the future. Associations operated on both short and medium time horizons, trying to manoeuvre their way through the obstacles to each season's successful crop while strategizing how to bring more production factors under their control over a longer term. State farm directors enjoyed the longest time horizon—initially, at least, until the same 1994 tenancy law brought their continued existence into question (see chapter 7). At that point they might find themselves strategizing across all three time horizons so as to envision a place for themselves in a fully postsocialist agriculture.

Second, managers of these forms differed greatly in the social and cultural capital with which they were endowed and on which they could draw to solve their problems. Those endowments were a direct function of what the socialist system had provided them. Heads of CF member households had been given virtually nothing. As they were subsumed within the larger organization of work in the CF, they had lost the authority they had held before collectivization. In addition, their knowledge of farming was belittled, and they were given no instruction in the arts of modern farming; expertise was to be monopolized by the farm leadership. CF members also had little opportunity to develop extensive social networks beyond those they already held in their community.

As I show in chapter 1, both state and collective farm chairmen and their technicians, by contrast, had to cultivate immense and far-flung networks in order for their farms to function at all. CF chairmen needed to be able to influence the AMSs to work for them at the optimum time, to obtain fertilizer or seed or other inputs when these were hard to find, to anticipate and adapt to changes in the county political environment, to influence the people at the state warehouse not to apply rigorous standards to the quality of the crops they delivered, and so forth. The reach of state farm directors was likely to be even wider. To begin with, they were integrated into multifarm systems grouped into large regional structures. In addition, the range of endowments they enjoyed also meant a wider purview of operation. They might appeal not just to other SF directors when they needed a product but to the heads of distant fertilizer factories, to the heads of cement factories when they needed to construct a new outbuilding or make a major repair, or to the fodder conglomerates that served a multifarm network of SFs. Finally, SF directors not only drew on horizontal networks of patronage but could themselves have clients over a wider range than CF chairmen could (whose clients were mainly within their farms). SF directors, and CF leaders to a somewhat lesser degree, thus had a rich array of allies and contacts on whom they could call. To use different language, they were well endowed with social capital.

Both groups also benefited from extensive education and expertise, as well as from managerial experience. Although CF chairmen might not be trained professionals (none of those in Vlaicu were), they directed a staff of trained agronomists and veterinary technicians. These chairmen and their staff might spend years in the job, acquiring valuable organizational skills and contacts that might be convertible to success in a postsocialist agriculture. That was even truer of SF directors, who had the experience of managing huge budgets that accustomed them to numbers terrifying to the average farm member. Their privileged position made them more likely to know of and to have tried the latest complex technology, with which CF agronomists might have less experience. In short, the same hierarchy of social connections—household, CF, SF—obtained in the realm of expertise and experience as well. These differential endowments enabled the former CF and SF leaders to confront the extraordinary uncertainty of the post-1989 economic climate with more resources than were available to most individual households.

In the discussion that follows, I organize my material according to the order implied in these points. I begin in chapter 5 with those most disadvantaged in resources, even though they had just received land—individual member households. I concentrate on their time horizons, their difficulty in putting together production factors, the limited resources through which they tried to mobilize these, and their ultimate loss of both the economic and the social asset value of what they had received. In chapter 6 I move to the Vlaicu Association, discussing its time horizons, its leaders' links with the Agromecs and Romcereal, and its inability to overcome the obstacles placed in its path by both nature and government policy. In chapter 7 I turn to the state farms, showing how some of their directors participated likewise in a massive devaluation of state farm assets; chapter 8 shows how they and a handful of others were able to launch themselves into commercial agriculture. Here the longer time horizons and greater managerial experience and expertise seem decisive in their ability to salvage some value in a sector that was generally in even worse decline than it had been under socialism—and that says a lot.

CHAPTER 5
THE DEATH OF A PEASANTRY
FROM SMALLHOLDERS TO RENTIERS

You loved the land, isn't that so?
—Yes sir! We loved it.
You longed to have it, didn't you?
—Yes, we did!
Well, wasn't it like that when you were younger and you'd see a pretty girl go
by? You'd love her and long to have her . . . But now you're too old for it. Get-
ting land back is like that: being too old for what you used to like to do.
> (*Supertenant to villagers, hoping to rent their land*)

A man keeps complaining he's thirsty. Then after he dies, you give him some
water.
> (*Vlaicean commenting on government agricultural subsidies,
> autumn 2000*)

The people whose values I discuss in chapter 4 came from the units
least privileged in the hierarchy of socialist agriculture: the member households
of collective farms. Would this fact influence their ability to realize their values?
Would they be able to farm effectively as masters of their land? Would they at
least derive economic benefit from it? If property is a relationship enabling appropriation, were they now able to appropriate differently from before? To do
so would require bringing together the main production factors: their land;
control of an adequate labor supply; implements for working the soil and harvesting the crop; structures for storing their goods; funds for inputs such as
seed, fertilizer, and perhaps pesticides and herbicides; and so forth. In this respect, village households were woefully underendowed (cf. Neményi 2000b, 10,
for Romania and Bulgaria). As CF members they had had no reason to build or
maintain storage structures. They owned no implements except tools for gardening, although some had a cow or two, but most had no other means of plowing. In 1990 some of them had substantial savings with which they could buy
these things, but anyone who did not quickly use that money soon saw it disappear in inflation.

In this chapter, I discuss the trajectory of member households out of the collective farm and their retreat into subsistence agriculture (see also Humphrey 1998, chaps. 9–10). I describe some of the problems they encountered and their strategies for trying to manage the tremendous uncertainties they faced. In showing how they sought to obtain the necessary production factors, I bring together several lines of argument. One line concerns the devaluation of land, another the decomposition and recomposition of the property rights in the bundle they had been awarded, and a third the question of the "return of the peasant."

I might schematize the processes in this way. After Vlaicu was collectivized in 1959, many of its men took factory jobs and no longer worked much in the CF. This produced a labor shortage for the farm, which combined with the labor needs of Hunedoara's rapidly industrializing economy to draw people from the hill regions—the venits—down for unskilled work in CFs or factories. The timing of their respective entries into the urban workforce endowed them differentially after 1989. Many locals had industrial salaries or pensions big enough to enable them to work their land, whereas venits, having been in worse jobs, were less likely to have such good income.[1] Moreover, they of course had no land. Although at first they served as a labor force for locals, hostility and their own desire for autonomy led many of them to stop doing so as soon as they could. This forced locals to pay for expensive inputs, pushing some of them to sell land, which venits then bought at subinflationary prices. Tied into their own labor-rich networks, they were better able than locals to manage subsistence farming without losing money.

Alongside these processes, unfavorable price trends over the decade of the 1990s caused land to become a negative economic asset for most smallholders, who could not assemble the necessary production factors within their limited budgets. Despite diminishing economic returns, however, owners kept cultivating their land because of its other values to them, connected with status, self, and mastery. Still, by early 2000 many of them had given up subsistence cultivation and were renting their land to large tenant farmers (the process invoked in my chapter title). It is not, *pace* Cartwright (2001), a story of the return of the peasantry but of its death, as economic difficulties overwhelmed land's other meanings, devaluing it as an asset. In this sense, the "vanishing hectare" of the book's title vanished not as a property object but as a set of values surrounding it.

Important in this result were the kinds of social linkages and other resources smallholders were able to draw on and the time horizon within which they were able to plan. Unlike the leaders of the Vlaicu Association, considered in chapter 6, few of these people had personal contacts with banks, fertilizer factories, the fellow who sells herbicide, or customers for their produce. As collective agriculture had been professionalized, members had become deskilled; their kind of knowledge was no longer useful in running the CF, and they received little training in modern farm techniques (see also Lampland 2002; Pasti, Miroiu, and Codiță 1997, 49). CF leaders and specialists made all the technical decisions; members were there only to supply labor. The farm's managers developed broad networks essential to survival as a socialist enterprise, but farm members did not. Events after 1989 mostly reproduced these households' lowly position under socialism.

One caveat concerning the ethnography in this chapter. Much as Nancy Ries (1997) observed in her discussion of laments as a cultural form in Russia, I often found myself the object of laments and complaining. Romanian sociologist Ioan Aluaş, my research collaborator on this project before his untimely death in 1994, once warned me, "Peasants are *always* complaining." In a similar vein, researchers Daniel Lăţea and Oana Mateescu cautioned me that the villager who one moment proudly displays to his fellows his beautiful crops and newly painted house may at the next moment protest to an outsider that things are dreadful and he can barely survive. I have attempted not to be too gullible, collecting numbers as a way of assessing the validity of their protests (see table 5.1 later in the chapter); other literature on the region also reports many of these same findings. Nevertheless, even allowing that the lament is an important Romanian cultural form, in my judgment Vlaiceni did have something to complain about, and accordingly I seek to present their views with sympathy.

Working Land

Victoria Iancu, whom we met in chapter 3, is from a family that has lived in Vlaicu for at least 150 years. Beginning with my first year there in 1973, both she and her mother taught me a tremendous amount about Vlaicu, past and present, and especially about decollectivization. I have described earlier her determined struggle, including two lawsuits against the land commission, to recover land she had not been awarded in 1991 because it had been confiscated, not donated to the CF. When I first discussed her lawsuit with her, I asked what she planned to do with the land. "Give it to the Association, of course!" she replied. "I haven't got a horse or tractor to work five hectares with, and I'm too old to buy them! My children have moved to the city; they have no interest in farming the land." For her, recovering it had been a matter of recovering her dignity, not of becoming a farmer.

By the time I returned to Vlaicu in 1993, Victoria and her husband Aron had changed their minds; they were laboriously working their 5.7 ha themselves and bringing forth harvests that were a great source of pride. "No one else in this village has a harvest like ours!" Aron boasted. They told me at length how hard they'd worked, how he'd carried home countless bags of chemical fertilizer on his bicycle, two at a time; how they'd gone out in the snow to sprinkle it on their land, in freezing weather, worrying that they'd catch cold. Justifying this effort, Aron said, "We couldn't do anything under the communists; now at last we can do something." Then he gleefully described bringing home a huge truckload of wheat and dumping it in their courtyard to form an immense pile. "Everyone came to look, and their eyes popped out! How resentful they were of us! (KV: Why?) Because we had such a good harvest. (Couldn't they have one too?) No, because it's all these people who don't have land to work."

Although Victoria and Aron sometimes received help from their urban children, they knew their farm would die with them because the children did not intend to make a living from agriculture. One had a good state job and the other had joined the growing stream of people who traveled twice a month by bus to Hungary to buy cheap goods for resale at home. When Hungarian products became too expensive, she went (less often) to Turkey for the same purpose. She also talked longingly of going to the United States and encouraged her son's romance with a French girl.

Over the next eight years as I visited Victoria, they were having more and more trouble working their land. She referred constantly to the prices of various ingredients they needed—plowing and harvesting services, seed, fertilizer, and so on—as she described the shortcuts they were having to take. As time passed and they grew older, she stressed the difficulties they had mobilizing enough labor, since they could no longer do everything themselves. Paying for workers was making it even more costly, indeed prohibitive, to cultivate their land. Although (like most Vlaiceni I spoke with during this time) Victoria and Aron did not calculate their costs and incomes precisely, she had the feeling that they were not making money. "Thank heaven for our pensions!" she repeatedly observed. "Without them we couldn't afford to work our land at all." In summer 2000 their pensions amounted to 2.3 million lei/month; it cost 600,000 to plow one hectare of wheat, another 600,000 for harrowing and planting, and then 800,000 to harvest that hectare—all this without adding in the cost of seed, fertilizer, herbicide, and day labor at 70,000/day/person, not to mention other household expenses. She concluded her comments, "We're being forced to abandon our land by these high costs." Their main hope now was that some tenant or other would rent the land from them, paying them enough to live on.

In contrast to this well-entrenched local household was a family of venits, Iacob and Cornelia Rusu, ten years younger than the Iancus. In 1968 they moved into Vlaicu from the hills so Iacob could take an industrial job. Cornelia joined the CF as a laborer and accumulated a large number of workdays; both earned reputations as extremely hardworking people. Their very bright children won scholarships, the eldest (Valeriu) obtaining an engineering position in a state enterprise. With industrial restructuring after 1989, however, he was forced to return to Vlaicu, where he opened a store, tried his hand at various other activities, and finally settled down to helping his parents with agriculture. His married brothers commuted from the village to jobs in town. Unlike the Iancus, then, this family had local labor they could count on. In 1999, they also acquired an international connection when another son competed successfully for a two-year work contract in Italy, whence he sent back good money.

What the Rusus lacked was land. Along with everyone else, in 1990 they received Iliescu's one-half hectare, but they subsequently lost it—along with the garden behind their house, which was returned to the former owner with her other land. Unlike some venits, their natal village was too far for them to bring in resources from there. Thus, the Rusus entered the postsocialist period with no land at all—and were very bitter about that fact. As Cornelia said to me, following an acid diatribe on the newly rich members of the Vlaicu land commission, "Those who didn't have anything before are making out even worse now." They began by sharecropping 1.3 ha from the former owner of their house, using their share to fatten and sell livestock (also fed with hay reaped from around Vlaicu). Lacking both a horse and the money to buy farm equipment, they were unable to increase the amount of land they could take in sharecropping; this limited the pace of their accumulation and fed their resentment. Each year from 1993 until 1996 Cornelia complained to me about the ill will of locals: "I worked 27 years in the collective, when all these local women were home 'sick' with medical certificates. But they don't want to give us land. (KV: Why not?) They want us to be their servants! To work as their serfs, to be their day laborers! In other villages venits got land, but not here!"

In 1996, however, and again in subsequent summers, I learned that the Rusus had begun buying land with the money they made raising livestock. The only sure thing these days was means of production, Valeriu told me, and he was going to make sure he had some. He bought nearly four hectares at once and began reading technical manuals on agriculture. Meanwhile, his parents had not renewed their sharecropping arrangements and his mother no longer complained. They filled all their labor needs themselves and used manufactured inputs sparingly, for the moment, so as to accumulate more rapidly. Although Cornelia would not tell me how much land they had bought by 2001 (someone else guessed it was 12 ha), they were clearly much more sanguine about their prospects than they had been in 1993, and their son intended to make a success of commercial farming, even though on a modest scale.

These two contrasting examples show us the main ingredients of life in Vlaicu's households during the 1990s: a constant struggle to bring together production factors amid ever-rising costs; concerns about obtaining labor; efforts to recover lost social status and senses of personal identity, somehow wrapped up with land; the simultaneous pursuit of subsistence and commercial agriculture (the latter by younger, better educated people who had some leadership experience under socialism); recourse to forms of temporary migration for income otherwise unavailable; and the transformation of local class relations alongside the new property arrangements, a theme of chapter 4. These different processes produced some contrasting trends: one toward the devaluation of land as an economic and social asset, one toward the emergence of commercial farming and land concentration.

Because the people involved in this latter process are significant players in the narrative to follow, I say a brief word about them now. For the decade of the 1990s, in addition to two from nearby villages I count six people in Vlaicu as rising commercial farmers. All but two had some degree of higher education, and four had been involved in running state and collective farms. One was a venit, two lived elsewhere, and the rest were locals. Although not always land-rich, they had skills and social or political positions that enabled them to work land beyond their own at a profit. As of 2001, one of the original eight had failed; the others were still functioning, some precariously, and another venit was joining them. Meanwhile, two other venit families were working abroad and buying land in Vlaicu with the intention of starting commercial farms. Three of these people appear in this chapter as supertenants. They rented owners' land from a position of advantage, thus differing from the more common agricultural tenant because they had so much more social and cultural capital than the owners. Their peculiar situation arose from the peculiar *rentier* society decollectivization had created: instead of many tenants seeking land from a few large owners, we have many owners and few tenants. I call them *supertenants* to indicate that even though they rented means of production belonging to others, their social situation was superior to that of their lessors.

Resources for Cultivation

Some 51 percent of Vlaicu's households had either land of their own or local kin who did; Law 18 obligated them to cultivate it. That required bringing it together with other factors of production, most of which were expensive. Given that few Vlaiceni had the necessary ingredients, how could they proceed? How were they to obtain the basic capital inputs, and how would they work their parcels? Where would they store their harvest? How could they pay for all this? Because my conversations with Vlaiceni during the 1990s indicated that ideally almost all wanted to work their land themselves, any departure from this already indicated a concession to the difficulties of doing so. The solutions adopted varied both from family to family and over time for any one of them.

First, a word about what these villagers grow on their land. The main crops have long been corn and winter wheat; villagers eat corn and feed it to animals, and they use wheat for some household needs while marketing the rest. Planted in smaller amounts are two kinds of barley [orz and orzoaică], sown in the spring along with corn; additional hoed crops on small surfaces include sugar beets, sometimes fodder beets, and potatoes. Every household also has a vegetable garden, and many like to plant squash (as food for animals) among their corn; a few have some fruit trees (cherries, plums, or apples). Each household has chickens and maybe some geese or ducks, as well as at least one pig—some as many as ten or twelve—fed with corn, squash, potatoes, wild greens, bread, and table scraps. Many have one or two cows, which they feed with a mix of grains plus hay, grown and reaped on their own land or from other sources.[2] For the summer months all cattle are sent to Vlaicu's large common pasture. A few villagers market dairy products in Orăștie, but most sell them to cowless neighbors.

In Transylvanian conditions, smallholders generally profit more from selling fattened livestock than grain, although calculating the profit never includes the cost of their labor, which is considerable. Some also say they like the psychological lift of receiving a huge sum from a single market transaction, rather than the dribs and drabs of selling grain. Throughout the twentieth century, even under socialism, these villagers used their produce both for household consumption and for fattening livestock, but before 1989 their private livestock feasted in part on appropriated goods such as hay from the collective. Once Vlaiceni had to produce their own fodder, the number of cattle began to fall.

❧

The principal inputs smallholders needed were plowing services to plow and sow their land; combines to harvest wheat; seed, some herbicide, and perhaps fertilizer and pesticides; and labor for hoeing, weeding, and bringing in corn, potatoes, sugar beets, and vegetables, as well as for reaping hay. Initial providers of plowing and harvesting services were the Agromecs or the few villagers who had bought equipment, or sometimes cattle or horses belonging to oneself or a neighbor—all of which, even the horses, were very expensive.[3] Although the best way to plow cheaply was to buy one's own means, bank interest on loans made this difficult. Putting land in the Vlaicu Association was also a way of obtaining machinery, but as of 1998-99 members had to pay cultivation costs up front, so joining the Association was a solution only for those with cash. At first, Vlaiceni could use Romcereal to begin a new production cycle on credit and arrange for all the materials and machinery services, but after 1997 this was no longer possible. Initiating production required either selling well enough during the winter to have made some money or having additional sources of income. Selling was problematic, given the underdeveloped distribution systems, and until 1997 the government held down the prices of basic food commodities, making it difficult for farmers to come out ahead. Subsidies in the form of coupons toward production costs were inaugurated in 1998 and covered about 235,000 lei/ha. for production costs that in Vlaicu that year were at least 2.5 million/ha—thus, subsidies covered 9 percent of the total.[4]

The main source of off-farm income for many in Vlaicu was their prior jobs in industry, which had endowed them with pensions; given the jobs they had held in Hunedoara's strategic industries, those pensions were at first quite generous. They put their recipients on an entirely different footing from Vlaiceni who had only pensions from the collective farm, which were completely inadequate to the financial demands of the 1990s. For the only time in Romanian history, industry in the form of these pensions actually supported agriculture rather than depleting it. Two households of virtually identical means (age, fitness for work, and land endowments) might deal with their land in completely different ways if one but not the other had industrial pensions. As the decade wore on, however, pensions did not keep pace with inflation; by 2000, households that had managed with them before could no longer do so.

Although the expense of chemical inputs such as fertilizer, pesticides, and herbicides was one impediment to applying them, it should be said that not everyone wanted to work with these substances, which they believed the CF had overused. Nearly all with whom I spoke found the fields they had recovered from the collective farm to be in lousy shape—"tired" [*obosit*], as they put it, and in need of nurturing or "rest." Some believed that the CF's excessive use of herbicides (owing to its labor shortage) meant that now things did not grow well; others asserted that because the collective planted too much wheat and not enough corn and other root crops, it had relied too much on chemical fertilizer and in this way it had run down the soil. Fertilizer makes things grow, they said, but it does not build the soil up as manure does. "People who work this land now have to work it with a lot more care, do proper rotations even though those crops require labor, and put lots of manure to bring it back up to scratch. It'll take ten years to restore it to proper fertility after the treatment it's had." (The one person who did not agree with this was an agronomist of the former CF.)

Petru and Ileana manure their "tired" field. He bought his tractor new in 1992 (photo by author).

The amount of land each household received was no indication of its prospects for success: some had sources of cash or labor that others with more land did not, some were younger and could imagine taking on loans whereas others could not, and some were willing to plow with horses rather than tractors whereas others were not. Households with more land faced somewhat different problems from those with less for the wealthier needed greater amounts of labor and cash for inputs, which most did not have immediately available. (Households with no land at all, of course, faced problems of yet other kinds.) For all these smallholders, the 1990s marked gradual retrenchment, devaluation of land, and increasing recourse to supertenants in rental arrangements that were rare in 1993 and frequent by 2001.

Spreading Risk

Although I did not survey every household, I believe that most of those with up to two or three hectares of land tried to farm their land completely on their own, whereas those with more adopted a mixed strategy. They farmed some on their own, placed some with the Association, and gave some out in sharecropping. I asked one woman who was complaining to me about hoeing corn why she had not put the land in the Association: "I'm not rich, I just have 3 ha, so I work it myself." I heard the same thought from others: "We haven't much land, we can work it," or "Why should I let someone else take my harvest, if I can work it myself? We get more of it this way." The more land you had, the more likely you were to divide it among all these arrangements, thus spreading your risk. Other ways of spreading risk included having land in several different micro-zones of the village—even if this meant having numerous small parcels rather than a few large ones. Thus, when the river flooded you would still have some crops in a place that was dry, and if hail flattened them in one area some would still be standing in another. Field fragmentation, generally seen as a liability, in this case was an advantage and was one reason why many communities chose not to consolidate their fields, as Law 18 recommended.

Placing land in the Association was perhaps the principal means of spreading risk. First, the Association paid members not according to the harvest taken from their particular parcel but according to the mean yield for the whole 200 or so hectares it worked. This arrangement benefited everyone over the medium run (flood, drought, and hail could strike rich and poor alike), but it was especially advantageous to those with poor-quality land. As one woman explained it to me: "You know what's great about the Association? Maybe you have a parcel that's not very good, but they give you the *average yield* for the whole farm, so you come out better than if you worked it yourself." This system meant, of course, an open opportunity for free riders, and it broke down when repeated flooding in one part of the village caused those with land elsewhere to withdraw it from the Association so as not to keep supporting those with parcels in the floodplain. Second (and perhaps in part for the same reason), people usually gave the Association their land of poorer quality, more vulnerable to disasters, or farther away from the village center. They retained for themselves the better and nearer parcels. In this way, they reduced their labor input (in the form of travel time), their costs of fuel if they worked by tractor, and the uncertainty associated with farming land that was difficult or marginal. They also thereby saddled the Association with scattered parcels of problem land, thus contributing to the difficulties I describe in chapter 6.

Third, villagers used the Association to cushion labor scarcity, pulling land out when they had enough labor and putting it back in when they did not. If a family member was ill for a time, land would go into the Association; when she recovered, it would come back out. Although this strategy was more likely to be used by wealthier households that had greater labor needs, it could be used by anyone. All such practices, although advantageous for individual households, naturally undermined the prospects of the Association as a whole. It had lower-quality land, its tractors had to travel farther and use more gasoline, and its uncertainty over whose land it would control precluded long-term planning. That is, the strategies of individual households undermined the very organization that had been formed to help them solve the problems of working their land. Ultimately, the Association was unable to handle the uncertainties it faced, including repeated floods; as I show in chapter 6, it fell apart in summer 2000, leaving many villagers stranded.

Getting By in Independent Family Farms

According to its accountant, during the 1990s about 60 percent of all village landowners had at least some land in the Association, as did most of Vlaicu's absentee urban owners. Those who did not had various reasons: they did not like the pay arrangement, they had so little they could work it themselves, or they wanted the whole crop rather than some portion. A few had stronger principles—for example, Iosif and Ioana Borza. Iosif had claimed every patch of land to which he had even a remote claim and had been awarded 9.5 ha, two of them in SFs. This made his one of the village's seven wealthiest households. From the outset, Iosif and Ioana were determined to work their available 7.5 ha themselves, one way or another. Although no longer young (at the time of our initial conversation he was 69, she 63), they were both very strong, hard workers. They refused to put any land in the Association, likening it to the former CF. When I pressed him for details in 1993, he replied more or less like this:

My family was not rich before collectivization; they worked very hard to accumulate land. My mother had only three pairs of shoes to her name, and my brother and I were always in rags so they could buy more land. When the collective farm was made, my father and I both refused to sign up; we went into hiding. Finally they got to my wife and she had to do it. So now the CF is breaking up, but I see the same jerks there, and I have no intention of ever spending another minute in a collective situation. All the people running the Association are the ones who got used to standing around and not working, telling us, "Go on over to that field there and pick some corn. . . ." Even if it's hard for us, we'll do it on our own. I want to repay my parents for all that hard work by not putting our land back in that sort of thing. Besides, when they finally made us join the collective, we had to put our name to a petition that said, "I the undersigned *request that my land be graciously received. . . .*"[5] I want nothing to do with any organization that has this in its past—that after all the suffering of collectivization they made you *beg* to get in.

I heard some version of this opinion from them many times, always justifying their determination to succeed at farming without joining any collective.

This left Iosif with a lot of problems to solve on his own. To illustrate concretely how villagers such as Iosif tried to get by, let me summarize how he handled things over the decade, before describing the situation more schematically. Immediately after collectivization, Iosif had taken a factory job, rising to a good position among skilled workers there. From it he received a sizable pension—and this was fortunate, for Ioana's pension after years of work in the CF was ridiculously small. Their children, both with university degrees, lived in a city about two hours away and had no interest in taking over the parental farm. Thus, the couple had to secure labor, along with everything else—a prime reason others joined the Association. Using Iosif's industrial pension, they paid both the Agromec and a village Rom (hoping he would be cheaper) to plow and plant some of their land. Their labor being insufficient, they also gave two hectares in sharecropping, first to a Vlaicean who asked them for it and then, through him, to a family from a nearby town. They worked with them every summer for six or seven years, gradually taking on more. The two couples split the costs of cultivating and the harvest 50-50; the sharecropper was to cover the costs of fertilizer, herbicide, and pesticide (if used). Iosif was happy with the arrangement, partly because (as he put it) all sharecroppers steal from you, but these people come by car. Their car's trunk is a lot smaller than a villager's ox-cart. He worked to develop a trusting relationship with his sharecroppers in hopes of keeping theft to a minimum. Indeed, they made a deeply emotional entrance at Ioana's wake when she died suddenly in 2001.

Iosif and Ioana also gave one hectare to a supertenant, who paid them 1,100 kg of wheat for its use. They would have given him more had he been willing, for they found it harder and harder to obtain tractorists who would plow on time and do a good job. Although they had bought a horse, it just was not enough. In 1993 Iosif confided sheepishly that he had considered buying a tractor (Ioana's comment was, "Don't be an idiot! Grandpa on a tractor!") because he saw owning a tractor as the best way to make an income from his land. Since he was too old to take on the huge expense and uncertainty of a bank loan, he was thinking of putting money in the pyramid scheme Caritas to pay for his tractor (see Verdery 1995). Had their farm not been fragmented into several small parcels, the supertenant might have taken another four hectares.

For the first several years, Iosif and Ioana bought almost no inputs, other than to pay for plowing, sowing, and harvesting. They and their sharecroppers sowed with Iosif's own corn seed, which (he boasted in 1997) had been in their family for ages; they bought no herbicides except for wheat, doing all the weeding of other crops by hand, and no fertilizer, using only crop rotation and manure from their horse and two or three cows. Instead of marketing their grain, they fed it to pigs and cattle, occasionally selling one of these when they needed

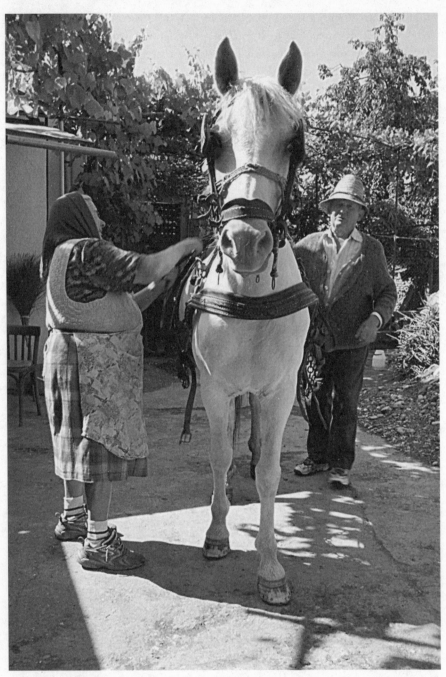

Maria and Octavian used only their horse to plow their fields.

cash. Otherwise, their production went largely to their own and their children's consumption. Working at this level, they were able to cover all the costs of production with their pensions.

Gradually over the decade, however, they began intensifying their use of capital inputs to increase yields and reduce the burden of labor that they were growing too old to provide. In 1999 Iosif renounced his family's corn seed and bought hybrid seed (Pioneer, which—contrary to instructions—he reused for two subsequent years), supplemented his manure with chemical fertilizer, and began using herbicides to limit the amount of hoeing necessary for his corn. These inputs were extremely expensive, however, and became proportionately more so during the decade. To pay for them he began going to the weekly market with sacks of grain instead of farming mainly for subsistence, as had been their plan. But even with their pensions and these sales of grain and animals, he was losing his ability to cover costs; by 1999, he told me, he was no longer making back what he put in. Once the tax moratorium ended, in 2001, their land would cease to be a positive asset and become a negative one. "So why do it?" I asked. "Because I feel bad for my parents, for how hard they worked to buy this land." When I asked what they would do once they could no longer work it, they replied that the only solution they could envision was for a supertenant to take it. Otherwise, it would go uncultivated. Would he give it to the Association? "Ten years ago I wouldn't, but now that I see how difficult it is to work the land myself, I would—if it weren't collapsing."

We can draw a number of points from this example. First, we should bear in mind that the Borzas were wealthy, by Vlaicu standards: they had 7.5 hectares of usable land as well as a good cash pension. If by 2000 they had trouble making ends meet, then what might we expect for others? Second, what we see initially is that because of Iosif's pension, their biggest problem was not cash for inputs but labor. Refusing to solve this problem through the Association aggravated it. They solved it by working like dogs and by engaging sharecroppers, being fortunate to find some whom they liked and who continued to accept the arrangement. For the future they put their hope in supertenants, who would eliminate most labor needs by working with advanced technology Iosif and Ioana could not afford. Third, as for their cash needs, they strove to protect themselves from risk through the following devices. They sought inexpensive arrangements for the preparation of their land (using their own horse for some of the work), tried to maintain soil quality by careful crop rotation and use of manure, and exposed their budget as little as possible to market prices for both raw materials and their products by using what they had and consuming what they grew— that is, by aiming solely at subsistence. Only when they acknowledged that working without high-quality seed, fertilizer, and herbicides was harming their yield did they begin assuming more financial risk, always cushioned by Iosif's pension (their urban offspring were, if anything, still a drain on their income rather than a supplement to it). Although he was owed dividends from the state farms that held two of his hectares, he never knew whether the dividends would be paid; after 1996 they stopped coming altogether.

Iosif and Ioana's example provides some evidence concerning the issues I raised in my opening section—time horizons, networks, and devaluation. Iosif's time horizon was relatively short, one or maybe two years. He could think in slightly longer terms when planning crop rotation and manuring, but otherwise, given constant inflation, he could not know from one season to the next what he would be able to afford. Even though he saw a tractor as a necessity, he could not envision paying for one; he could not imagine that in inflationary times his debt for it might rapidly shrink. His sociospatial horizons were similarly constricted: he neither had nor required extensive contacts as long as he was subsistence farming. He purposely refrained from using banks, where he would need connections in order to get a good loan. A fellow villager brought him his sharecroppers, and local Roma plus the Agromec his plowing. Once he ventured into higher technology he needed advice on how to apply it, but this was available locally too, from the Association's agronomist. Recourse to such technology, of course, brought him to the limits of his accumulated knowledge and experience. As long as he was farming like his father, he had all the knowledge he needed. The application of chemicals, however, was something else again, something for which neither his experience in the factory nor his wife's in the collective had prepared him. Contemplating it made him think about supertenants, who had that kind of expertise.

As for the value of his land, what he experienced over time was that, economically, it declined more and more; to maintain it cost him more than if he left it unworked. Most of its devaluation, as I show later, came from factors well beyond his control, but he contributed to it as well, in small ways. Although he strove to build up his land with manure and rotation and by keeping it cultivated, he also compromised it to some degree by expecting his sharecroppers to pay for costly fertilizer, herbicide, and pesticide. Their underuse of these inputs ultimately diminished the yields, which reduced his possible income.

Brief comparison with another family, Vasile and Veta Barbu, helps to show how delicate was the balance among labor, cash income, and farm size. Two or three years younger than Iosif, Vasile brought his wife Veta from Homorod, across the Mureş. Both were healthy and strong; in addition, for much of the decade their urban-employed daughter and son-in-law lived with them and could provide some labor. Like Iosif, Vasile had a good pension. They worked 3.5 ha, also aiming at subsistence, and they did it themselves, with no recourse to either sharecroppers or the Association. Aside from requiring less labor and less cash up front than the Borzas, they were able to do more of the work of the plowing and planting for their smaller farm with their own animals, saving money Iosif had had to spend on tractors for his larger holdings. Like Iosif, Vasile used mainly his own seed and manure, purchasing almost nothing.

Each year that I visited them, they claimed to be doing well; even when Iosif began complaining that he was losing money, the Barbus were content. They kept as many animals as the Borzas or even more, which they fed grain as well as hay that Vasile regularly carted from Homorod. They sold pigs and dairy products for cash. By being frugal, they were able to make enough money to install central heating at tremendous cost, without any help from their son, who lived abroad. In 2000 they described their strategy to me (a bit tendentiously) like this:

> The secret is to make spending for agriculture your number one priority and use your cash for almost nothing else. We buy cooking oil and salt, but we raised sugar beets for sugar, as well as potatoes and grain, and animals for manure and for the dairy products we sell. We don't use much gas or electricity, so our bills for those are small. People who complain of hard times [and this was almost everyone I spoke with that year] either don't know how to manage money or don't know how to work hard. If you do these things, you get along fine.

This fortunate arrangement was suddenly endangered, however, in summer 2000, when Vasile had a minor stroke that impaired his ability to work, and a fight with their children led to the latter's departure. Now they had to hire labor, and it was expensive. For that year they enjoyed the help of some neighbors to whom they had given grain earlier, but from then on they would have to budget not only for hired hands but also for tractors because Vasile would no longer be able to plow with his animals. When I visited them in January 2001 they were expecting to use venits for their labor needs, "though many of them are now buying land and don't want more work." In that case, the Barbus too were facing large cash expenditures for herbicides. Perhaps it was the excellent Homorod brandy we drank together that made them seem optimistic about a future they were obviously seeing in a harsher light.

Capital Inputs and the Devaluation of Land

I can now step back and discuss more generally the problems that Vlaiceni faced during this decade in trying to be not just owners but *effective* owners of their land. Holding one production factor, land, they had to acquire the others. Let us begin with the larger items of capital equipment: buildings (barns and storage facilities) and implements such as tractors, seeders, fertilizer spreaders, and combines. Their cost far exceeded the savings of nearly everyone and rose vertiginously. Only in the first year or two, before macroeconomic stabilization policies had wiped out the monetary overhang (that is, people's savings), could a few households take on this kind of large purchase without recourse to bank loans. Otherwise, banks were the main solution, but they had serious drawbacks.

First was the problem of collateral. Since one could not yet use land for that purpose, the only alternative was to use one's house, something almost no one was prepared to do in these uncertain times. Second, it was possible in theory to obtain state-subsidized loans, but for this one had to pay a 10–20 percent commission (that is, a bribe) and needed very well-placed connections even so, for the amounts the state allocated for this purpose were a tiny fraction of the need. Third, even with the subsidy one faced fluctuating interest rates. One person who had taken a loan to buy a tractor told me his monthly interest payments varied so wildly that he never knew how much money to take to the bank. The loan, borrowed initially at 62 percent interest, fell to 42 percent, then rose to 75 percent, and then to 110 percent! Under these circumstances, very few villagers took bank loans; instead they bought used equipment with cash saved up or borrowed informally, and often via special and not wholly legal arrangements.[6]

Throughout the decade, prices kept going up. A small tractor bought new in 1992 cost about 900,000 lei; the same tractor in October 1993 cost 3.4 million. A large one that in November 1994 cost 9.5 million was 75 million in June 1997 and 150 million in August 2000—a sixteenfold increase. Or, to phrase it relatively, whereas a tractor purchased in 1994 cost the equivalent of 50 ha of harvested wheat, the same purchase 1.5 years later required the wheat harvest of 100 ha, reflecting both the ballooning cost of equipment and the stagnation of crop prices. The same inflation occurred with old tractors also, at a lower level. One family bought a used tractor from the Agromec at auction in 1990 for 41,000 lei and sold it in 1991 for 200,000. Under these circumstances, that twenty-seven Vlaiceni bought tractors in the 1990s is surprising, until we learn that these were mostly very old and were paid for with savings or loans from friends.[7] Many of the buyers rented out their services to other villagers (from whom they recovered the tractor costs through unduly large rental fees). As for buildings, three villagers with big plans bought three barns from the collective farm in 1991, borrowing from relatives to do so. Other families renovated their old barns or built more modest outbuildings, mostly by saving up cash.

Inflation affected the other production factors too, as the following figures indicate. The figures are approximations; a difference of one or two months in *when* I noted prices during the year could mean the difference between a twenty-fold and a thirty-fold increase in comparing 1994 prices with those for 2000. During this time, for example, the price of gasoline increased thirty- to fortyfold, as the government under IMF pressure allowed petrol to rise to world prices. The cost of hiring someone to plow increased twentyfold, and so did chemical fertilizer. I do not have figures for herbicide early in the decade, but between 1995 and 1997 the most effective herbicide, Titus, increased from 1.4 million to 14 million lei/liter, a tenfold increment in just two years.[8] The television program *Village Life* aired a segment on 14 February 1994 that gave even more alarming figures: the price of a specific fertilizer had increased 62-fold (presumably since 1989— no baseline was given). Perhaps this explains why in the decade of the 1990s, fertilizer use in Romania dropped to 20–30 percent of its levels in 1989.[9] The same trends appeared in other countries of the region as well.[10]

Against these increased costs, incomes rose less rapidly. A top industrial pension increased eighteen-fold, slightly behind the increment in most inputs; as we see in two of the cases I described, industrial pensions were the principal source of income that enabled many of these villagers to pay for inputs. Those lacking them fared much worse. From 1994 to 2000 the sale price of wheat and pigs increased fifteen- to sixteen-fold, lagging further behind.[11] To give a more pointed example, between 1995 and 1997 the state price of wheat increased from 240 to about 1,100 lei/kg—a 4.6-fold increase[12]—less than half the rate of increase of Titus. Different evidence on the price scissors came from the director of Orăștie's Agricultural Bank, who told me in 1996 that since 1990, the cost of inputs had increased by 301 percent, output prices by 195 percent.

In considering these figures, we should remember that for forty years, Romania's villagers had experienced virtually no inflation at all. Against that background, the perceived risk entailed in the 1990s inflation was far greater than it would have been for someone accustomed to periodic increments. Indeed, for many the price trends were not just bewildering but terrifying. They affected Transylvanians more than farmers in the Regat because the relatively less fertile soils in Transylvania (and especially in Hunedoara) required more fertilizer and additional plowings to produce good yields. Whereas Transylvanians were paying 800,000 lei/ha for production, an agronomist explained to me, Regățeni might be paying only 500,000 lei/ha; they could therefore make money if wheat was selling at 900 lei/kg, but Transylvanians would go under (see table 5.1).

What I have said here gives an idea of how people sought to protect themselves against these risks: by putting land in more than one arrangement; by avoiding bank loans to reduce their financial exposure; by reusing seed; by manuring, with chemical fertilizer as at most a supplement to be cut if money was

Table 5.1

Approximate Increases in Some Agricultural Costs and Incomes, South-Central Transylvania, 1994–2000

Service/Good	Increase (in lei)	Increment
Costs		
Gasoline	300–400 → 12,000 per liter	30- to 40-fold
Plowing services	25,000 → 500,000 per ha	20-fold
Fertilizer	1,000 → 20,000 per kg	20-fold
Tractors	9.5 million → 150 million	16-fold
Income		
Top pension	130,000 → 2.3 million per month	18-fold
Wheat sale price	200 → 3,500 per kg	16-fold
Pig sale price	1,200 → 18,000 per kg	15-fold
Sale price of land	1.5–2 million → 7–10 million	3- to 5-fold

Source: Author's interviews.

tight; by using little or no herbicide and instead weeding by hand; and by using old-style pesticides (such as copper sulfate) on new-fangled pests. These were "traditional" practices, but the cost of the manufactured alternatives—which many would have preferred—obviated anything else. Not using those inputs, however, also had its costs; it increasingly compromised cultivation in the village as a whole. When some villagers failed to apply appropriate pesticides, a huge invasion of Colorado beetles resulted—the worst the Association's agronomist had ever seen—that destroyed potato crops all over. It did little good to use pesticide if your neighbors did not. The bugs would settle into a more hospitable parcel and spread at the slightest opportunity. Similarly with weeds—that many households used no herbicide made everyone else's fields vulnerable to the seed the resultant weeds threw off. In 1997 someone complained to me of a newly entrenched weed that spread swiftly and was very hard to pull out. "Why didn't you use herbicide?" I asked her. "The Association did the work, and they didn't use it because they said it's too expensive and members won't pay that much."

Thus, smallholders found themselves increasingly in a box. All but those with very little land had difficulty doing subsistence agriculture without losing money, and as time went on many had increasing problems with labor. It made sense, then, to resort to more expensive inputs that would reduce labor needs and increase yields; the resulting excess beyond household consumption could be sold, perhaps compensating for the increased cost of cultivation. Then the problem was to find markets, and that was not easy. Moreover, serious flooding followed by drought in the late 1990s increased the exposure of those who had bought expensive substances and then lost their crop. Finally, because many smallholders did not understand the complexity of applying some of the more specialized products, they would purchase these at great expense and later find that the products did not work.

All these above considerations contributed to a trend: over the decade, government policies and the widening price scissors increasingly undercut the value of land. The risks of farming had become so high for smallholders that fewer and fewer of them could manage, and their inability to cultivate it well devalued it further. By 1999–2000, some of my respondents were borrowing money from various sources simply to pay for plowing; many others were leaving large portions of their land uncultivated—and this devalued land by making it much more costly to bring back into cultivation. Still others were trying to sell, even though the price of land was inordinately low and the money obtained would soon disappear in the continuing inflation, unless they converted it to dollars. The repeated floods brought the Association to a standstill; by the summer of 2000, it too left three-fourths of its land uncultivated before shutting its doors. It was not only Vlaiceni or even Romanians who experienced these difficulties. The same trends are reported for Estonia (Abrahams 2001) and Bulgaria, to name only two. Konstantinov (2000, 24) reports that in a Bulgarian community he surveyed, people were asking themselves, "Why did we reassume ownership over our land?" Many did not bother to complete the titling process, and villagers left two-thirds of the land unworked that season. Where we do *not* find such difficulties is in eastern Germany. There, according to the Buechlers (2002, 208–27), the EU and Federal Republic subsidized agriculture heavily, and independent farmers fared rather well.

Clear evidence of land's devaluation is the trend in the price of land over the decade, shown in table 5.1. As against the fifteen- to fortyfold increase in production costs and incomes noted in the table, the price of land increased only three- to fivefold. A parcel of land might sell for 1.5–2 million lei in 1994; in 2000 it would cost 7–10 million. We might compare this with the cost of a top-quality milk cow: in autumn 2000 it was about 7 million lei, the price of a poor-quality hectare of land. To sell land, then, amounted to trading away one's hectare for a cow.

Vlaicu's Venits

There were two groups for whom this was good news, however: one was the emergent commercial farmers mentioned earlier and the other was Vlaicu's venits. Many of the latter responded to their landless situation by struggling to buy a patch of land, if only a hectare, so as to plant a household garden with some vegetables, potatoes, and corn; this would at least cheapen their costs of living and remove the burden of being "serfs" and "servants," as Cornelia Rusu put it. Their main route to ownership was to raise animals for sale and to use that money to buy land. Because the price of land increased at one-third to one-fifth the rate of increase in the sale price of livestock, what local smallholders saw as devaluation was a boon to venits. Their preference for animals resulted in part from the fact that at least some of them could still return to their natal upland villages and bring back hay, which was much harder for them to obtain in Vlaicu. If they sharecropped locals' corn crop, they could use their share as animal fodder.

The Rusus were not the only venit family who began the decade complaining bitterly about their landlessness but who ended it with a hectare or two. In 1994 Cornelia Rusu suggested I go talk with Filip Moga, whom I had not yet met, if I wanted to know what venits were doing to try to get land from the land commission. The Mogas had been living in Vlaicu since 1975; Filip had worked for a number of years in a factory. When I first visited them, he and his wife were sitting in their kitchen with their son and two nephews, all three of whom also have houses in Vlaicu. Soon after they had welcomed me, they began criticizing locals for having prevented their getting any land. A year earlier they had gone with a delegation of venits to protest their situation to the county prefect; he had told them to wait patiently. Now they had just returned from another such trip, where they had told the prefect, "We've lived here for over twenty years, we worked hard in the collective farm when all the locals were out 'sick' with medical certificates, and now we don't even get a few square meters of land so we can plant a potato!" They were convinced there was enough land for them but were beginning to face the fact that no one was going to give them any.

The Mogas went on to tell me how hard life was now, all of them having lost their city jobs in the first round of firings (like most venits, they were unskilled workers.)[13] They were collecting unemployment, but it was too little and would soon end. Without land in Vlaicu, they had no alternative livelihood. When I asked whether they wanted to buy land, they said they would but no one was selling, and they had no money to buy it with anyway. Instead, they were share-cropping from various locals, their share of the crop being just about enough for them to feed some animals—all emphasized the importance of this. "How about your land in your home village?" I asked. "It isn't any good," they replied. "We had to leave there because of the mudslides. At most, we can bring some hay down for our animals." They did not mention that it also produced the excellent plum brandy with which they (like Valeriu Rusu above and all the other venits I visited) welcomed me on several occasions. Selling it was a good source of income for Filip's nephew Remus.

In 1996 I returned for another shot of it and learned that the Mogas had bought some land, maybe two hectares (it was hard to learn from any Vlaicean how much land he had bought). The sellers were locals who had moved away to town; one was a person from whom Filip had sharecropped and who finally offered to sell to him instead—a pattern I encountered with others, too. Filip had paid for it with his pension, with the proceeds from animal sales, and by selling their land uphill, which meant they now had to find a new source of hay (I wondered about the brandy) to supplement the clover they had planted. Given all their local relatives, they had no trouble working the land themselves, although they complained about the tractor services of the Agromec. As for expensive inputs, they did not use anything except a bit of herbicide on their wheat.

A year later they had bought another hectare, this time with money they got from selling the stocks of a cement factory in which they had invested their privatization vouchers. They had quit sharecropping altogether; their former patrons, for want of alternatives, had had to put that land in the Association. "This is what happens when people buy land and quit sharecropping!" they observed merrily. Moreover, they had bought some farm equipment, which they used with their horse. They admitted that only one of their pieces of land was of really high quality; the others had been less expensive. When I commented on the low price of land, they demurred. From their point of view, relative to salaries, it was high. You could buy land only if you lived in a village and could keep a pig, cows, and so forth. But they did agree that compared with other things (such as a house), land was cheap.[14]

Despite their success, they complained that the difficulty with agriculture was that the state did not support it with credits or by stabilizing prices. They now plowed with private tractorists, not the Agromec—or even with a horse, as nephew Remus was doing with the two widows for whom he sharecropped and who had decided to stop paying the plowing costs they had covered before (they were too broke). Like the Borzas and Barbus previously described, the Mogas hoed and weeded rather than apply herbicide, and they used manure rather than fertilizer. They were fortunate to have five families of kin in Vlaicu, who helped one another out. (Indeed, they and other venits cooperated so closely that when Remus's horse died, all chipped in to buy him another.) When they needed cash, they used Filip's pension or sold an animal.

Other venits with whom I spoke had similar stories to the Mogas'. They sharecropped from locals, did everything possible to buy (sometimes from those same people) at least a hectare for household use, paid for with money derived in part from their ties to their former villages (brandy, or hay for the animals they sold), from pensions, or, for those few who still held urban jobs, from salaries. As soon as they bought some land, they stopped sharecropping, an activity for which all expressed considerable distaste. Significantly, they preferred to do this work for Vlaiceni who were absentee owners rather than those resident in the village (perhaps because the absentees would have had no role in the decision to deny them land). Venits were more likely to use animal traction for work that locals did with paid tractor services, and their cultivation strategies were if anything even more labor-intensive than those of locals. They benefited from very close relations of exchange with other venits, especially when those were kin or had come from their own villages. Although venits did have ties with locals, it is my impression that the networks within this group were much tighter than those either across the local/venit line or among locals. This was especially true of those venits who were neo-Protestants, rather than of the majority Romanian Orthodox Church; their minority status may have further increased trust among them.[15] That is, venits' social capital was centered on ties within the village and with kin in hill settlements, whereas the networks of locals extended not into the hills but more into the cities.

To clarify this requires us to look more closely at the problem of securing labor, which has been a theme in most of my examples. Obtaining inputs for the production cycle set one kind of challenge; securing labor set others. I have just indicated how venits solved that problem. Now I return to the locally born smallholders for whom, as we have seen, venits were so unwilling to work.

The Crisis of Labor

A serious difficulty emerged during these years: a crisis in the labor supply, perhaps worse in this area than elsewhere.[16] I dwell on it at some length, for if the possibility of realizing value from land depended on working it and labor was the production factor smallholders were most likely to control, then any failure to do so would compromise their experience of restitution. Moreover, the high cost of capital inputs would compel villagers to substitute labor for them as much as possible. They perceived this trade-off clearly. Augmenting the labor problem was that many smallholders saw certain labor-intensive practices as preferable to modern capital-intensive forms. They resisted using herbicide on their corn and preferred to hoe by hand because they liked to plant squash and beans under the corn stalks; the herbicides they knew of prevented this.[17] And then, too, they thought of the land as "tired" from so many capital inputs.

Normal field preparation for smallholders in this area consisted of plowing after the harvest in the autumn and then harrowing and sowing in the spring—

that is, three passes for each hectare sown. Fertilization could require another pass, and herbiciding yet another. After this, wheat had to be harvested and taken home, usually in cartloads. Corn required two separate hoeings, the first of which might be done with a special implement that could be horse-drawn; some people followed this by one hoeing, others by two. Then the corn had to be harvested—almost always by hand, even in CF times—and its stalks cut before the fall plowing. Both crops had to be hauled in from the fields somehow. Other work included cutting, drying, and hauling hay for animal feed; planting, weeding, and harvesting vegetables and potatoes; carting manure to the fields and spreading it; and perhaps hoeing and harvesting small amounts of sugar beets. In addition, anyone who kept animals had the considerable work of feeding and cleaning them, work that was less time-consuming for pigs and more so for cattle.

What corners could be cut to reduce cash outlay, even if at the cost of intensifying labor? You could sow and apply chemical fertilizer at the same time; you could leave out fertilizer and/or herbicide to cut down both on buying them and on paying the tractor fees. But then you would have to haul and spread manure and/or do a lot of hand hoeing and weeding, and in either case the crop would suffer. Likewise if you omitted these operations entirely or used smaller amounts. Although years of experience in the collectives had mostly convinced people that tractors were superior, you could use not a tractor but a horse or oxen for some of this work, cheapening your costs substantially—yet lengthening the time necessary for the work. You could hire the cheapest tractor services, which might also be not very good. If you had family labor, you could use that instead of paying for day labor.

Mobilizing Labor

All these solutions presuppose, of course, that one has the manual labor to substitute for cash inputs. In 1990s Vlaicu, however, this was not always true. The households with land were aging and their children mostly gone. The other possible source of labor—people with no land to work—diminished as the decade progressed and they were able to buy some land of their own. During my eight years of visits, complaints about finding labor were second only to complaints about inflation. It was a problem not just for individual households but for the Association as well, as I show in chapter 6. So how could labor be mobilized? Given the precarious budgets of most of these smallholders, the best way was through creating relations of social obligation, perhaps through time-honored practices from the precollective period. We would be mistaken, however, to see this simply as a revival of traditional agriculture. These practices were, in monetary terms, cheap, and that made them good adaptations in the present, not simply resuscitations of the past. That they were also part of some families' repertoire from earlier times meant chiefly that people had some idea of how to do them. If you had land, you should be able to obtain labor either from social equals or from inferiors, accumulating people as sharecroppers and day laborers from among neighbors, kin, the village landless, and Roma SF workers.

Before collectivization, in an equally labor-intensive rural economy, families of similar means had regular labor partners (*ortaci*) with neighbors and kin working in reciprocal obligation: we all work my field today, yours tomorrow. Among equals the problem was mainly one of choosing the kinsmen or neighbors you could rely on; anyone who failed to reciprocate labor would not be selected another year. The remaining kinds of social obligation (between unequals) involved mechanisms not only for creating trust but for collecting people: creating a relationship in which one (the superior) party gathered around him dependents who were in some way beholden, and they would pay off their debt with labor. The debt could be anticipatory—you worked for a person who contracted (often in writing) to make you his or her heir—or it could be based in past and present relations. Elderly people could use this arrangement with their offspring or some other person (see chapter 4). Wealthier households would periodically hold a work party [*clacă*] at which co-villagers would come and hoe or weed or harvest all day, the party-giver obligating himself to provide a big meal. An especially important means was ritual kinship, in which families of lesser means asked those with more to serve as marital sponsors [*naşi*] or godparents to their children's baptism.[18] In this way high-status families created a retinue of dependents, and it was these people, such as their godchildren [*fini*] and their kin of lesser means, who attended the work parties. Finally, people might take on sharecroppers from among the poorer villagers, the partner bearing all the expense and labor of cultivation and bringing the owner half the crop.

These were the main models available from earlier times to secure labor through social relationships, instead of through money. Most of them were predicated on differential land endowment, just as became true after 1991, but now many of these devices no longer worked. Younger people were less interested in agriculture and less willing to care for their elders in exchange for land that was of dubious value; a number of Vlaiceni had alternative sources of income and preferred to avoid these obligatory entanglements; much of the village population was too old for regular labor exchange; and almost no smallholder had a social position enabling real patronage. The wealthy of before had become small-fry in a larger industrialized environment and no longer had many godchildren to call on, because new couples preferred someone from town who could give them more help than could a local smallholding family.

In suggesting that the grounds for securing labor through social obligation had weakened, I am not saying that all forms of reciprocity disappeared. The problem was primarily with labor in agriculture—that is, sustained patterns of exchange that required considerable effort. If a woman's husband died, she could instantly mobilize neighbors and kin to help her prepare the mortuary feast. That, however, is a rare event and its cycle of reciprocity very long term. For the more sustained agricultural work, however, villagers without adequate labor would have either to pay for it or to substitute by giving land they could not work to the Association or to sharecroppers.[19] The usual sharecropping arrangement was that both parties would split most or all of the costs of cultivation, the sharecropper would provide the labor, and they would split the harvest. (A common variant was that the sharecropper would do only the weeding and harvesting, leaving the owner with 70 percent of the take.)

A sharecropping strategy assumed that there were potential sharecroppers who were both financially able and willing to pay those costs and to do the work. To a fair extent this assumption was incorrect, and one reason was a serious deficit of trust. Although some land-poor locals took on sharecropping, the main source of labor for it was the venits, who were not of charitable mind. First, locals had prevented them from getting land, and now those same people wanted their labor; it was not a situation conducive to good feeling. Some venits bridged the gap because they had to. As one put it, "Some [of us] say, 'We shouldn't work their land! We shouldn't work it!' But of necessity, you work it." Many, however, refused to "work for the local nobility," as we have seen with the Rusus and the Mogas. They preferred working for one another.

Once venits began acquiring land, they stopped sharecropping, thus deepening the labor crisis for smallholders. Now, they reserved much of their labor capacity to exchange among themselves—and it was *better* labor because they were on average considerably younger than the smallholders. Their solidarity and cooperation were enhanced by their having no reason to quarrel over land, as locals did. In a word, their stock of social capital was more robust.[20] The two groups sought to mobilize different pools of social reciprocity: locals wanted a villagewide pool incorporating venits; venits wanted one restricted to their own group, or, at most, extending into their natal villages. Hoarding their labor was even more crucial to the average venit family given their economic adaptation. They were more likely to concentrate on raising livestock, which is far more labor-intensive than growing cereals.

From the many conversations I had with venits, it was clear that their solidarity was in part a reaction to having been excluded from land restitution. It may also have owed something to years of socialism. One venit, Lina, put the matter clearly: "Things are tough for us nonlocals because we couldn't start out with land

Tica, a venit, sharecrops from Aurel some land he hopes eventually to buy. Here they do the first weeding together.

as a support. We have to *work* to get the money to buy land. We have to sharecrop for other people—but that means I give them my work. That's exploitation! Here I hold with the communists' view." Venit families differed in the extent to which they felt this way, some continuing to work as sharecroppers or to cooperate with their local neighbors; others were pleased that they had the leverage to create a problem for the people who had excluded them from owning.

In addition to these motives, however, there were two others, related to both work and pay. The German association (in existence until 2001) and supertenants both cultivated corn and needed workers to hoe and/or harvest it. They paid slightly better than locals were inclined to, which is probably why one supertenant told me he had had no trouble getting labor to harvest the corn he had planted. In short, these other opportunities were more attractive than was sharecropping for locals. (In addition, however, neither of those employers had played a part in excluding venits from land.)

Troubled relations between locals and venits were, of course, not new. Years of contempt and resentment by locals toward venits had not endeared the former to the latter. That resentment had contributed to locals' unwillingness to find any land for venits in 1991—they were getting revenge. But by doing so, they had created not a labor supply but a labor crisis because venits now refused to play their game. Increasingly, locals had to seek workers among the village

Roma, who, once the state farms stopped producing (as of about 1996–97), needed work. Most locals complained that Roma were lousy workers and that they stole. When the government began giving Roma welfare at 1 million lei or more per month, however, locals saw even this labor pool drying up. In 2001, Iosif Borza assessed the situation concisely:

> When they gave us our land back, they gave us no implements. Then they took apart the Agromecs, removing the only implements available. Now they're taking away our labor force as well, by giving Gypsies welfare so they don't want to come and work. One fellow I worked with before is now getting 1.6 million a month, and when I saw him on the street he said, "Don't bother calling me to come and work, because I'd rather sit for the 1.6 million I'm getting." I'm convinced the government is giving Gypsies welfare on purpose to keep us from having a labor force, because Iliescu never did want private agriculture.

Although we should beware of attributing to Roma the characteristics smallholders did (laziness, chiefly), the calculus he attributed to them has its logic.[21]

The increased antagonism between venits and locals indicated that the balance of power was shifting away from the owners in favor of labor, compared with the 1930s. Smallholders complained, "You can't find good people. In the past the sharecropper did all kinds of work for you. Now you have to do a lot of it too, and give them a lot of the harvest. We have to go afterward to cut the cornstalks because they won't do it!" For much of the decade, however, smallholders seemed oblivious to the fact that there might be a problem with their long-term expectations. If I asked a family what they would do when they could no longer work their land or if the Association collapsed, surprisingly many—sometimes the very people who had grumbled about the difficulty of finding people to sharecrop even now—said, "I'll give it out in sharecropping," as if they would have no problem finding someone.

By 2000 a new pattern for labor was emerging, one that mixed leasing and sale. Many venits would no longer sharecrop, instead renting land on multiyear contracts—but only from people (usually urbanites) willing to sell it to them. Each year they would pay a portion of the purchase price along with their rent. In this way they might spread the price of the land over five years, meanwhile using it to generate income for the purchase.[22] Valeriu Rusu had reportedly leased some 15 ha in this way, alongside the 12 ha or so that he had already purchased. Not surprisingly, this new pattern was finally raising the price of land relative to other production factors—a tendency augmented by the reform politics of the neoliberal government, which led Hunedoara's industries to lay off massive numbers of workers. For these people, land now acquired new significance. In winter 2001, sellers renegotiated one supertenant's purchase from an earlier-agreed average of 9 million lei/ha to an average of 12 million (also reflecting a falling exchange rate). The shift in the price of land reveals something about the specificity of Vlaicu and Hunedoara: as long as industrial work was available, villagers were less mindful of land's subsistence value. In areas without industrial alternatives, perhaps the price of land reflected that value more fully.

In the meantime, Vlaiceni unwilling to sell land found fewer and fewer people to help them with it. The main countertrend involved Roma more than venits, and it was based on the creeping poverty that by the late 1990s was being felt everywhere. I began to hear that during the year, people who had too little land to feed their families or too little cash to buy food would come to small-holders and ask for corn or wheat. The locals would give it to them but refuse to accept money, instead asking for labor during the next season. Whether under this arrangement or in regular day labor, the host was obligated to provide the two meals for a day's work that was part of a day laborer's wage. The bargaining power of labor was now felt in negotiations over food: locals were indignant at how much food the workers expected and at how costly it was—some of them even demanded coffee (very expensive relative to incomes)! I was visiting the Barbus one day when their neighbor, a woman from a poor local family, stopped by to chat. She had spent the previous day hoeing for someone, and she was not happy with how things had turned out.

Four other women and I went to hoe for Petru's Ana. At noon she came by with three tiny *sarmale* [stuffed cabbage leaves], about as big around as your finger, and some bread. We complained to each other, but then at 7:00 in the evening when we wanted to go home, Ana got angry. I said to her, "You expect us to work until dusk on three sarmale?!" She said, "I gave you enough for seven people!" Another time she gave us a couple of pieces of cheese, one of them was already stinking and yellow with age. It had mouse shit on it! And she had the nerve to be irritated when we complained!

Clearly, food had become a weapon in the struggle over labor—and in the emerging class conflict.

❧

There was one more drain on the local labor supply, which developed around the mid-1990s—emigration. While smallholders had trouble making a decent livelihood, Hunedoara's numerous factories began to close, affecting all

Vlaiceni with family members who commuted to them. In consequence, young and able-bodied Vlaiceni facing dismal local prospects turned their thoughts elsewhere. In 1992, a local Vlaicean whose family had not received enough land to support everyone arranged a short-term work contract in Germany. From there he went to Spain with two friends. In classic fashion, this started a chain migration that gradually picked up speed, until by autumn of 2000, 12 percent of all Vlaicu households had at least one family member working or married either in Spain or, more rarely, in some other Western European country. All of them could see no other way to get ahead; land had become something to escape from (cf. Vitebsky 2002, 182).

More were from local families with land than from the landless—14 percent of landed local households had migrants, and only 10 percent of venit/landless households. The reason is probably that migrating cost money, and venits generally had less of it. In summer 2000, the price for black-market visas was $1,000 and rising steadily. Targets of police raids and border controls, the would-be migrants also had to be ready with extra cash for bribes, especially at the border crossings into Hungary, Austria, and Spain itself. Some of the migrants bought land in Vlaicu with their earnings or rebuilt their houses and courtyards, with an eye to returning and setting up modern farms. Others planned some sort of commercial venture, such as opening yet another village store. Still others, however, planned to settle in Spain permanently, asking, "What's there to return to?" Summarizing the entire situation that had produced this migrant stream, Victoria Iancu's daughter said, "The only way to help your kids these days is to help them *leave*."

The experiences of these migrants warrant another chapter, filled with adventure, heartache, and the generosity as well as perfidy of their hosts abroad. My point here, however, is that emigration both reveals villagers' sense of constricting local horizons and contributed further to Vlaicu's labor shortage because with this migration stream, local smallholders lost labor that Spaniards gained. Vlaiceni were striving to work their land under conditions that turned some of them into an international proletariat, where they often performed the same kind of labor they had left behind—unskilled work in agriculture, such as picking olives—but earned enough to help their families at home. The larger process in which they participated was the transformation of an international pool of migrant labor, newly augmented by refugees from the changes in East European socialism.

From Labor to Money

I have been showing why it had become very hard in the 1990s to collect people by nonmonetary means. Therefore, smallholders had to pay for work,

and the wage was high because that labor was scarce. In addition, they intensified their own work. Those with urban jobs took part of their vacation time to
stay home and hoe or harvest corn, and they labored for long hours after their
workday as well. Sandu Bogdan, a man in his early fifties, had worked in a factory for thirty-five years, but after 1991 he developed a taste for agriculture, buying a small tractor to work his 4.5 ha. In 1993 his wife (who also worked long
hours in town) grumbled to me, "My husband is crazy: he works all the time.
He gets home at 4:00 P.M. and right away—without even eating—gets on his
tractor, goes to plow, sow, harvest corn, cut the stalks. One Friday evening last
week he went out to plow at 5:00 and came back at 11:30—and he has to get up
at 5:00 A.M. to go to the factory." Finally, when his factory began offering early
retirement in 2000, he leapt at the chance even though he knew that inflation
would outpace his pension; now he could work full time with his tractor, cows,
and pigs.

Already in 1993 I frequently heard litanies such as the following: "We have so
much work! We have to bring in stuff from the garden, harvest corn and grapes,
press wine. . . . We're old, this is very tiring, we can't do it all." "It would be
much cheaper to buy corn on the market—and a lot less effort!" By 1997, people
were telling me more and more often that they were exhausted with so much
work.[23] First it had been the land that was "tired," now it became the owners. By
the late 1990s, villagers were often saying that they wished they'd never gotten
their land back. One man age seventy commented to me one day, "Things
would be so much better if we hadn't gotten land! I'm an old man now, and I
find myself working harder than I have in years. I certainly didn't work this
hard in the collective farm!" Had they merely remained with the one-half
hectare given them in 1990 and somewhat better pay from the collective, many
said, they would have been satisfied.

Increasingly, then, smallholders were pressed in several directions, most of
which departed from their ideas about proper farming technique. First, they
began skimping on the labor-intensive crops, just as the collective had done;
they planted too much wheat, which required less labor than corn. By interfering with proper rotation, however, this solution furthered the tendency toward
devaluing land because it made the soil "tired" again. Second, they spent money
to bypass labor altogether, using that most costly of inputs, herbicide. A supertenant in another village saw this as progress, telling me in 1997 that when she
began renting land, her father had given her a tiny chunk. Gradually he increased the amount he entrusted to her as well as what he permitted her to do
with it. "Finally this year he gave me all of it and said curtly, 'Put herbicide.' I
made him repeat it. Seven years it took! I never thought he'd come around to
the low-labor solution." From smallholders' point of view, however, this solu-

Maria hired two venits to help hoe her corn; she complained about the cost of having to feed them.

Drying and carting hay to feed livestock (photo by author).

tion was disastrous because of the cost. As prices for herbicides in particular increased exponentially, well above inflation, smallholders could not afford this kind of expense. Third, they considered selling their land, although its low price made this very imprudent and the law still forbade land sales.[24] And fourth, they could lease their land to supertenants, who would work it with advanced technology and give them a small rent.

At this point, national politics finally intervened (howsoever briefly) in smallholders' favor. Facing dismal reelection prospects, in early 2000 the Constantinescu government beefed up its agricultural subsidies: farmers would now receive coupons worth 500,000 lei for each hectare that was worked, to be used for purchasing inputs of any kind. In Vlaicu, the amount would cover the entire cost of plowing that hectare, or fertilizer for about half of it, or most of the cost of harvesting it (at 800,000/ha). Although Aron Iancu dismissed the possibility, in his remark about the thirsty man (quoted in the second epigraph of this chapter), that kind of assistance might enable paying for herbicides to reduce labor needs. Inevitably, a brisk trade in coupons sprang up and, with it, a coupon mafia and various coupon scams.[25] Those Vlaiceni who used them as intended found that they made the difference that year between being able to work or not work their land. For the same political reasons, the PRSD promised to double the coupons' value for 2001 if it were elected, again enabling people to cultivate land in that year.

Devaluation and Revaluation

Up to this point, I have been describing the loss of land's value in primarily economic terms: what things cost, who could afford them, and how that compromised what land was worth in market terms. With all this loss of economic value, why did people keep farming—even after keeping accounts and proving to themselves that it was a sorely losing proposition? Even to cultivate it for its subsistence value was becoming unaffordable. The answer to why people kept farming lies in some of the other values of land, as I described them in chapter 4, values related to mastery and the visible economy.

In 2000, Sandu Bogdan calculated that it was costing him almost twice as much to grow produce as it would to buy it with his pension. When I asked him why he was still throwing money away by working his land, he replied animatedly, "*De ruşinea oamenilor!*"—from shame before other people. "What will people say if they pass my field and see it full of weeds, or with corn a half-meter high in September? They'll say, 'Look! There's Sandu's field, and what a mess! He should be ashamed!'" Similarly, in January 2001, after telling me how much he had lost by cultivating his land, Iosif Borza replied to my question as to why he continued to do it, "People will look at my land and say, 'Isn't this terrible! That's Iosif Borza's land, and it's unworked!'" I heard the same rationale from several other villagers who likewise complained that even though the costs of production exceeded their revenues, they continued to work their land so as not to be ashamed before other villagers. Even commercial farmers expressed something similar. My agronomist friend Lucreţia from Gelmar put it this way, referring not just to villagers but to other specialists such as herself: "I was born here, and I'm embarrassed before the people around me. I don't want them to be saying, 'Look! Is *that* the best she can do, with all her schooling?'" Those who might think of selling hesitated because to sell would similarly advertise their incompetence.

The land and agricultural infrastructure that were negative assets from a budgetary perspective, then, still held value in status terms. Perhaps these observations throw some light on possible reasons—for Transylvania, at least—why the process of land concentration proceeded too slowly, in the opinion of the World Bank experts who repeatedly chided the government for this reason. Villagers sold with reluctance because land was more than an economic value for them. Moreover, the land that was sold went not just to commercial farmers who would concentrate it but to people who could afford only a tiny patch yet were determined to have it to free themselves from exploitation by "the local nobility."

For land to retain these kinds of values fully, however, required that it be cultivated, and if smallholders could not do this, they imperiled their ability to manifest their character and social status visibly. If economic circumstances prevented their exercising effective ownership, the state of their fields could no longer provide evidence of their mastery. Thus, for these smallholders, land experienced a double devaluation. No amount of mastery could reduce the sources of risk that increased people's financial exposure, sources that included the global devaluation of agriculture in comparison with other sectors, the macroeconomic stabilization programs of the IMF, the Romanian government's subsidies to industry, and so on.

The only solution open to them other than selling was to rent their land to supertenants, whose specialized knowledge and other endowments gave them a better chance at viable commercial farming. To rent to such people, however, meant to abandon the visible economy, for supertenants operated according to different values. They erased the land's individuality, pooling all parcels into a single field and all harvests into uniform piles from which owners received a fixed rent. If they worked your parcel as part of a single large field, then you lost your source of pride: fields *better* worked than those around them, crops *more* resplendent, *more* carts piled high with the harvest. As they erased your particular visibility, the value of your hectare as a basis of personhood therefore vanished. The move toward supertenants was a move toward abstraction, something villagers had been fighting for most of the decade. Following thirty years of not being able to think of a specific parcel as theirs, they had clutched tenaciously at their land, its concreteness being their recompense for years of its having been treated as an abstraction under socialism. But if they could not work it, its concreteness ceased to matter. Here, then, was an unexpected source of devaluation, from their point of view: land lost its social and symbolic value when it lost its particularity.[26] Helena Hudečková, Mihal Lošt'ák, and Sandie Rikoon note a similar finding from the Czech Republic, "The distance (spatial and social) of an owner from the place of his or her fields degenerates the meaning of fields to one in which they are viewed solely as means of production. As Max Weber noted, the land loses its magic character" (2000, 109).

For many families, by this time finding someone to work their land was good enough. It spared them the shame of unworked fields—even if those fields were worked by someone else—and it provided them with some income as rentiers. Renting out their land might even afford them one final pleasure: now, just like the feudal lords, they had people working for them. Now they could put their feet up and wait for the rent to come in. Unfortunately this final consolation was meager because they saw the terms of their contracts as very unfavorable. Whereas in the mid-1990s such tenants had paid owners the money equivalent of 800–1,000 kg of wheat per hectare, by 2000 the inflated production costs and stagnant prices had brought this down to at most 350–500 kg per hectare. Given that in a good year a well-farmed field might produce 3,500–4,000 kg of wheat, owners found the rent bewilderingly small. They did not realize how much higher the costs of production were for supertenants than for themselves, as I show in chapters 6 and 8. Receiving such low rent diminished the satisfaction they might feel from the one value they could still enjoy: having someone else work for them. Perhaps in other parts of Romania smallholders on rental arrangements fared better,[27] but in Vlaicu I heard few expressions of satisfaction at this new form of mastery. They were nonetheless compelled to it, for by 2001 Geoagiu's mayor was beginning to follow the instruction in Law 18 that owners who could not work their land would be fined. Moreover, the mayor would then assign the land to someone else (doubtless some friend or client) to work, in yet another abuse of the village population.

One essential consequence of becoming rentiers was one further change in the relationship of Vlaiceni to locality. As serfs they had been tied to the soil; as smallholders prior to World War II they had embedded themselves in it; as collective farmers their tie had been broken and the land had become an abstraction, but they were not free to leave.[28] After 1991 they sought to re-embed themselves, but for those who finally became rentiers or otherwise could not farm on their own, land became an abstraction once again. This time, however, they *were* free to leave, heading for Spain and Italy, where they might finally settle.

Demodernized Peasants

> The return to ancestral modes of production has less to do with a voluntary re-anchoring in traditional peasant values than with the collapse of the socialist framework of the food industry. —*(von Hirschhausen 1997, 14)*

In this and the two previous chapters I have offered an analysis of property barely mentioning the word *rights,* so common to property discourse, and instead emphasizing the social relations in which the property object is embedded. Here I have shown transformations in the value of land from several angles as part of transforming relationships, particularly those between locals and venits. If I were to recast things in the language of rights, the processes I have described might look like this. We began with three groups: locals, venits, and supertenants straddling these two categories. Locals theoretically received the full bundle of property rights to their land—rights to use, to control revenues, and to alienate—although technically, they were not to alienate it for ten years. Then followed a period in which the rights bundle decomposed: sharecroppers, the Association, and supertenants all acquired partial use-rights and claims on owners' revenue. These claims were least for sharecroppers and most for supertenants, who assumed all managerial decisions, which the other two did not. Over the decade the groups with weaker claims fell by the wayside for one or another reason, leaving supertenants holding all use-rights and claims to the bulk of the revenue for many smallholders. Owners were left with some revenue, liabilities such as taxes, and the right to alienate the land altogether, an option their circumstances increasingly favored even if the law and their values did not. The ownership bundle would be recomposed in the hands of new owners, polarized between holders of very small parcels and entrepreneurs—both venit and local—accumulating larger farms.

Missing from this rights-oriented summary are the differing contexts, meanings, temporalities, and resources, both social and symbolic, in terms of which the various actors operated. These enable us to understand the outcome as not a return of the peasantry—contra Cartwright (2001) and Pasti, Miroiu, and Codiță (1997)—but its death, for the values and practices we associate with traditional subsistence agriculture no longer held in the new context. To the extent that Vlaicu's cultivators appeared traditional, they were, rather, demodernized. Noronha writes, "The small farmer is not given much of a chance: he is being starved of assistance. The strategies he adopts at the moment are survival strategies. Thus, there is a self-fulfilling prophecy: the output of the small farmer is low, therefore he cannot be a modern farmer" (1996, 17). This is what I mean by demodernization.

For example, the Agromec fees, price controls, and persistent inflation, all arising from government policy, made it impossible for most cultivators to accumulate so as to buy modern farm implements. If both the number and the price of horses kept rising, it was not from a traditional mentality but because horses were all that some villagers could afford. It was not that they insisted on recreating interwar subsistence farming rather than use complex inputs; they had no choice (Pasti, Miroiu, and Codiță 1997, 51). Owing to the unstable environment caused by government policy, they could not plan on anything longer than a one-season time horizon, shorter than that of other actors (the Association or supertenants). This temporality might look like a traditional value, as it did to supertenant Mihai, who quarreled with his parents over the advisability of buying a still to make brandy. His parents did not like the deal, he said. "They have a completely old-fashioned outlook, which calculates benefits only over the short term—tomorrow, next week. They can't see the point of having a still that I can pay off in a few weeks of light work, and after that it makes me money for ages with practically no maintenance costs." In my view, his parents' attitude reflects less a traditional outlook and more the realities of their circumstances, just as his attitude reflects the realities of his.

Those realities boil down to the reproduction of smallholders' place in the socialist hierarchy: at the bottom, giving their asset over to someone else's management for rather little pay. I agree with von Hirschhausen (1997) that this is the best way to understand these smallholders' seeming return to tradition. Their lives in socialist agriculture had endowed them with very little that would be useful once they emerged from the collective. As Pasti, Miroiu, and Codiță put it, "Throughout the communist period, the social status of the peasantry was one of semi-serfdom" (1997, 49). Economically, they were the worst-paid group in the socialist labor force. Educationally, their farms did nothing for them; expert knowledge about agriculture remained the special preserve of qualified specialists, not something to be systematically passed on to lowly farm members. In status terms, they knew they occupied the last rung of socialism's prestige ladder.[29] Socially, the CF gave them few ties beyond their community that would help them function as independent cultivators. Higher-level connections were not for them but for farm managers, whose networks hindered smallholders' access to low-cost credits; a resource distributed downward from the top tends to be snagged by the nets immediately below, as happened repeatedly with the sums designed for low-interest loans to agriculture. Despite the appearance of major agricultural transformation, then, villagers' marginal place in Romanian society had scarcely changed. And despite all the early promises that owning land would enable them to create value, their situation obviated their doing so.

Cultivators in Vlaicu would have liked to do better, and they argued that their government should have helped them. That it failed, from their point of view, undermined their confidence in it (cf. Wegren 1998a, 17). Although outside observers might see their expectations of the state as evidence of a socialist mentality (an opinion evident in numerous World Bank reports, for instance), these people in fact understood the problem very clearly: if the state did not help them, they could not succeed alone—any more than can subsidized farmers in Western Europe or the United States. But instead, "Politics between 1990 and 1996 bore the distinctive stamp of the Romanian transition, in which various interventionist laws produced contrary effects that succeeded in canceling each other out or in creating undesired consequences" (Mungiu-Pippidi and Althabe 2002, 174). Partly from internal political struggles and partly from the exigencies of the global environment, the result, as Pasti, Miroiu, and Codiţă put it (1997, 209), was Romania's "bananization."

In the next chapter I add to this discussion of smallholding the second form spun off by the disintegration of collective farms: the Aurel Vlaicu Agricultural Society, which arose to help them work their land. Some familiar themes appear there—the prohibitive cost of inputs and the problems with labor—alongside others, such as the complexity of obtaining credits and marketing agricultural produce. We revisit, as well, the legacy of the disadvantage of collective farms in the hierarchy of socialist property forms. That story, too, is largely a story of decline rather than flourishing, for the Association ultimately fell apart.

CHAPTER 6
OF CREDITS AND CREDIBILITY
THE RISE AND FALL OF THE VLAICU
ASSOCIATION

Our hands are tied by the members: as soon as we talk about withholding income for investments, they say, "It's the collective farm all over again!" If we proposed fixing a barn and buying twenty pigs, telling members they'd get nothing this year in order to get a lot next year, they wouldn't buy it: "The collective again!" Even now, they clutch: they wanted this land so much for so long, and now they have it, but they can't work it as they'd want to. So they give it to the Association, but they can't conceive of letting us actually work it as a long-term proposition without seeing that as "More collective farm!"
(President of the Vlaicu Association)

I never got the feeling that people really wanted it to work. If we'd expected them to bring their labor to it, that would have seemed like the collective farm, so our only solution was to work with cash. But we simply could not figure out how to do it, even if we used the money members themselves provided, so we gave up.
(Association accountant)

In the spring of 1994, I took several rides through Vlaicu's fields, jolting along deeply rutted dirt roads in one or another friend's tractor, aging jalopy, or horse-drawn cart. The guide of my most extensive such tour began by noting one large field and commented that the Vlaicu Association was working it as an unbroken expanse—in his opinion, for the enrichment of its officers, whereas the area should have been given to Romanian '45ers. Then came an area of former pasture that the CF had earlier brought under plow—another area for abusive farming, since technically it belonged to no one, yet there were crops in it. Then another area of the same kind. This place here was sold by the former president for a bottle of brandy to people from Homorod, that one there is contested by villagers from Vlaicu and Băcăinţi, and so on.

As we continued, my guide frequently pointed out the fields being worked by the Association and compared them with fields he and other villagers were working. Its wheat, he observed, was quite nice, as was its barley, but its corn crop was decidedly inferior to that of a number of individual households. When wheat was planted the previous fall, the Association had enough money from the year's harvest to buy fertilizer, good seed, herbicides, and pesticides. Moreover, the tractorists it employed did their job properly because of colder weather and fewer side jobs to distract them. By the spring, however, when corn was planted, the Association had much less money, the price of inputs had gone way up, and the tractorists had too many side jobs and did not plow as they should.

A longer ride and greater discussion of village topography would have yielded other things to consider in explaining the Association's visibly mixed results. First, although it worked several parcels in single large blocks (for instance, 7 ha, 18 ha), most of its land was in tiny pieces because fields had not been consolidated; thus, the Association suffered from the same fragmentation as did smallholders. This reduced whatever efficiencies of scale it might have enjoyed and increased the time necessary for working the land (as well as the wear and tear on equipment). Moreover, for reasons I indicate in chapter 5, the land people gave it tended to be farther from the center of the village and of lower quality—often very demanding soils that required painstaking effort to bring a good yield. Corn in particular posed a problem, for the Association did not have the labor necessary for manual weeding of any but small areas of corn, nor did it have the money for the top-quality herbicides that would eliminate the need for manual weeding altogether. The high number of its absentee owners—almost half—aggravated that situation. Over time, it had trouble planting enough of the labor-intensive corn and root crops for adequate rotations with wheat, thereby compromising the wheat harvest long term. But my guide commented on none of this. He dismissed the Association's shortcomings as the result of its "communist legacy."

These brief observations from the dusty paths of Vlaicu's landscape help to move us from descriptions of individuals' efforts to recover and use their land rights to an organization that was for many of them the first resort, as they lacked either labor or implements to farm on their own. This is the Aurel Vlaicu Agricultural Society—known by all as the Association—one of two such organizations in Vlaicu.[1] Whereas my unit of analysis in the previous chapter was individual households in the village context, here it is the Association in both its village and its interorganizational environments. I present my material in considerable detail, for although we find ample literature describing the process of smallholder decollectivization, there are as yet no ethnographies of the cooperative forms into which so many cultivators chose to place their land.

Two women are central to this chapter: the Association's accountant, Anda Drăgan, a very intelligent young woman who had mid-level education in accounting and had worked in the collective farm for its final three years, and (from 1993 to 1999) its university-trained agronomist, Nica Marcu, who had served for many years in a CF in nearby Vaidei. They did nearly all the work of running the Association—a time-consuming, exasperating, and frustrating job—until it collapsed in 2000, at which point Nica (who was not from Vlaicu) found work in another community and Anda entered Vlaicu's migrant labor stream to Spain. Both seemed to enjoy explaining to me how the organization was run, exposing its problems openly. Although Vlaiceni often muttered complaints about them, I portray the Association's struggles chiefly from their point of view—not because they did everything right but rather to reveal in a sympathetic way, as I sought to do in chapter 5, the thinking of the two people most deeply involved in creating this new organizational form, a postcollective cooperative.

Context

As before, I must underscore the tremendous uncertainties all agricultural actors faced in this period, which made planning on more than a short time horizon very difficult. But at least as important, the attempt to form and maintain the Association was occurring in a time period in which not only was agriculture a decreasingly profitable sector worldwide but agricultural cooperatives were everywhere running into trouble from the onslaught of agribusiness, in both less and more economically developed settings. In this context, we might expect that Vlaicu's Association would run into difficulty also. Nonetheless, the conditions that gave rise to it and the factors contributing to its decline are partly specific to the postsocialist situation.

Cooperatives are very important wherever the market environment is imperfect, as economists say—definitely true of 1990s Eastern Europe. In such contexts, people form cooperatives to protect themselves, at least temporarily, from unexpected risk. If markets develop further, commercial farming usually proves more efficient than cooperatives and tends to kill them off; nonetheless, they are significant as forms that solve certain kinds of problems other forms do not (Lerman 2000a, 14; see also Meurs 2001). The context that made them a meaningful solution in Eastern Europe was a specific constellation of problems and interests peculiar to postsocialism. First among these was that decollectivization created owners of land who tended to be elderly and who lacked other production factors. Although aspects of this problem are also common to land reforms elsewhere in the world, socialist patterns of industrialization had produced an age structure in villages that was unfavorable to both providing the labor and acquiring the implements necessary for effective cultivation. This was probably the single most important reason why all across the former socialist bloc, land restitution—whatever its modality—so often resulted in recreating cooperative forms.

Another difficulty resulted from socialism's suppression of market mechanisms, more extreme than in other world areas. In consequence, distribution channels outside the state procurement system were very weak, making it difficult for small farmers to find outlets for their goods. Unfortunately, this difficulty bedeviled the new cooperatives too, making them tend toward serving largely as producers' cooperatives: they organized the preparation and cultivation of people's fields and brought in the harvest, some of which they paid to the members in kind. Figuring out how to sell the rest so as to cover cultivation expenses or pay members posed sufficient headaches for many of these cooperatives that they were loath to assist the members with marketing as well. This was certainly the situation in Romania.

Two other peculiarities of the postsocialist situation concern people's attitudes toward cooperatives and the availability of agricultural experts. Wherever collective farming had not gone well, as in the Romanian case, the years of the CF had left a very bitter taste in the mouths of rural people. They were likely to view any new collective form with some distrust even when dependent on it, and this fact constrained its options. Land reforms elsewhere have usually had other antecedents less burdensome to the idea of cooperation. Finally, it is rare in other contexts that land reform follows some other agricultural organization containing numerous agricultural specialists, such as those whom decollectivization freed from Eastern Europe's collective and state farms. The employees of the old CFs—their presidents, their accounting staff, and their armies of technicians, agronomists, and veterinarians—were suddenly out of work. Their need for jobs and the new owners' need for assistance merged to generate producers' cooperatives. (Concerning Hunedoara county, the accountant of the Vlaicu Association informed me that every association she knew of had been started at the initiative of former collective farm personnel.) This motive for their formation was found in all East European countries to varying degrees (see, e.g., Lampland 2002, 43–51). In Romania, the Iliescu government in some ways encouraged their formation, such as through Law 18's proviso that associations could freely obtain the material endowment of the CFs without buying it at auction. Thus, at least some associations could begin with a partial farming infrastructure, especially buildings and other items that they might sell to enhance their budget. Other government policies, however, worked against the associations, as I show in this chapter.

The Vlaicu Association, formed in 1992, did well for its first few years and then began a downhill slide that ended with its collapse in the summer of 2000.

I describe what happened, asking what problems the Association had to solve in order to bring together land, labor, and inputs so as to create value; how it sought to resolve those problems, and through what circuits of connectedness; what role it played in the creation of a new class of entrepreneurial farmers; and in what ways it contributed to the process of devaluation discussed in chapter 5.

Creating an Association

Even before Law 18 decreed their end in February 1991 there had already been talk in Romania of disbanding the collective farms. Many agronomists in collectives moved to the new Agromecs, where they could draw good state salaries. Others anticipated forming one or another new agricultural enterprise. Romanian legislation after 1989 provided for several kinds of these. Among them were limited liability companies, firms incorporated as joint-stock companies, agricultural societies (cooperatives having jural status but not organized as joint-stock companies), and family associations of up to ten families, having no jural status. In addition, in many settlements people simply created cooperatives that had no legal status but were too big to be family associations; I call these *informal associations*. They and the family associations had much looser requirements than the others: they did not have to pay value-added tax for inputs or tax on equipment, and they were not required to maintain salaried employees year-round or to pay taxes on those people's wages—both of these being required of the more formal arrangements. For this reason, many who initiated associations preferred these less formal and less costly varieties (which they did not necessarily register with the chambers of commerce in county capitals).[2] That choice also freed them from the surveillance of their practices that the more formal arrangements incurred.

As already described, a few Vlaiceni began pulling their land out of the CF on their own even before the implementation of Law 18. They claimed to be certain where their holdings lay and had no interest in any kind of cooperative venture. Most villagers, however, waited to see what would happen. Forming the nucleus of a potential association, a collective continued to function with some of the old CF staff (especially its accountants). During 1991–92 they gradually consolidated it so as to organize cultivation for the new owners. Although in many settlements associations took over the headquarters of the old collective farm, in Vlaicu that building was under litigation and could not be occupied. Instead, they took over a small rather delapidated kiosk the CF had used for roadside sales. A major problem at first was high turnover in its agronomists. The one

The office of the Association (left). Invisible behind it is the former collective farm headquarters (photo by author).

working there in 1989–90 moved to an Agromec; then came a second one who stayed only a year; and then a third who did likewise, after presiding over the Association's formal founding. Only the fourth stayed for more than a season.

During 1991 and early 1992, while this informal association was still in embryo, the collective farm was liquidated. Its entire inventory was evaluated according to prices announced by the government, and many of the items were put up for auction. The money was gathered in three rounds. Then it might sit for a while, to be chewed up by inflation—a major source of the devaluation of CF assets all across the country—or it might be given out to people according to their labor contributions to the collective, as determined by the number of days they had worked in it. Thus, at the time when an association might be forming, some of what it needed had already been bought by other people. According to Law 18, it would have been possible to liquidate the CF and turn everything directly over to the Association, but this did not happen at the outset owing to the delay in forming it[3]—and, according to one of those present at the auctions, owing to the absolute confusion that prevailed during these months.

The process of liquidation ultimately forced the Association to take on a more formal shape than its agronomist and accountants might have wished. As I have described elsewhere (Verdery 1999), one of the auctions resulted in a lawsuit, brought by the Vlaicean who lost his bid—this was for the CF granary, without which the Association could not have operated at all. A lawyer advised that the Association could win the suit only if it became a jural person—that is, ceased being an informal association and registered as an agricultural society. That meant adopting certain organizational characteristics, among them an elected administrative council, salaried employees, new tax liabilities, and a large set of reporting requirements. All this entailed greater expense in its operation. For the lawsuit they prepared a complete list of all remaining items from the CF, which at this point the Association took over (see appendix).

There were two serious consequences of the Association's having to adopt legal forms that drew it (unlike informal associations) into state revenue streams and bureaucratic oversight. These concerned its costs and its governance structure. Concerning its costs, the requirement to maintain a salaried work force and pay taxes meant that from the outset, the Association would have much larger cash needs than it had before, and these would add to the burden of paying for expensive inputs, as described in chapter 5. That fact put pressure on what it could pay its members—the expenses would have to be subtracted first. In turn, that pressure aggravated the Association's vulnerability to members' changes of heart about the disposition of their land, worsening the legitimacy deficit indicated in the epigraphs to this chapter. Any association that took on formal status had these difficulties, whereas informal ones did not. Although formal status facilitated their access to certain subsidies for a time, overall the Association lost money from being formally registered.

Second, concerning governance, the bureaucratic reporting requirements burdened the tiny staff, chewing up much time that should have been spent in other ways. For example, the accountant observed to me that they could earn a great deal more if they had other markets than Romcereal, but the two staff people did not have the time to explore other avenues. (The association in nearby Vinerea, in contrast, had fourteen employees, precisely to hunt for markets.) More important than this, however, was the administrative council that Law 36/1991 mandated for agricultural societies. In the case of Vlaicu and other villages with many absentee owners, this council made most of the decisions because there was rarely a quorum at the Association's semiannual general assembly meetings. The composition of this council was therefore crucial; in Vlaicu it proved disastrous.

At the first formal meeting in March 1992, members elected nine councilors in open vote. A member would nominate someone, the presider would ask, "Is she/he OK?" and then, hearing no opposition (no one proposed was rejected), would move on to the next. There was no consideration as to whether those nominated were willing and able, or whether they knew anything about agriculture. Of the nine elected, only two had been employed in agriculture (one a former CF president); the remainder were two retired army officers, two former party secretaries from a nearby factory, and two retired factory workers, plus the council president, who had worked his entire life as a tailor, as mayor, or as party secretary.[4] Thus, six had been visibly active in Communist Party politics from before. Although it was not a foregone conclusion that this would be the council elected, the result was fully in keeping with the electoral practices villagers were familiar with from the CF: open votes, nominations of people already in powerful positions, and no candidates rejected. As one person put it, villagers were used to thinking of party leaders as people who know how to do things (the active principle I refer to in chapter 4), and they had not yet gotten into "democracy."[5] Under normal socialist circumstances, knowing how to do things included having the networks to accomplish your goal, but these gentlemen's networks had nothing to do with agriculture—that is, their social capital was wholly inappropriate to their new position.

This council created endless problems for the accountant, Anda, and the agronomist, Nica, whom I refer to throughout as the Association's leaders (as distinct from its council). These two women were the only ones whose networks and connections were useful. Responsible for the daily operations of the Association, they could take no significant action without consulting the council or the membership as a whole. According to Nica, the council's excessive experience with communist leadership and their ignorance of agriculture proved a constant hindrance to sound economic management, thus setting up an ongoing struggle between expertise and ill-informed managerialism. Nica and Anda made their decisions ever aware of potential challenge from people who understood little about the task at hand and would have to be repeatedly persuaded.[6]

Several characteristics constrained these women's prospects from the outset. To begin with, they were relatively young (early thirties and forties), whereas the average age of the council was over sixty-five—a veritable patriarchy. Nica was new, which meant that villagers had not had time to develop trust in her leadership; thus, her credibility was precarious. Moreover, Anda suffered a certain lack of respect, owing to her very humble background in one of Vlaicu's poorest families. A final obstacle was their gender. Although it was possible for women to command successfully in agriculture (I give examples in chapters 7 and 8), that required some breach of normal gender expectations as well as a forceful temperament Nica did not have. I believe that all these factors put the two leaders constantly on the defensive, particularly with respect to their council, and compromised their effectiveness with members too. Their expertise was always open to doubt.

For example, the most influential councilors—those who had held party positions before—were used to administrative prices, not the give and take of market exchange. Anda had soon realized that if she sold the Association's produce to Romcereal at fixed prices, she made much less money than if she took it to the Saturday or Sunday market. Not having the personnel to do so regularly, she made a practice of holding back a certain amount of grain each season and then selling it in the market when she needed an infusion of cash. One day in 1999 she headed off to market, asking two councilors to accompany her so no one could say she was stealing. As she reported to me later, the experience was disastrous. First, the two councilors decided that if they were going to market with a truck, they should take some of their own wheat to sell, thus becoming competitors of their organization. Then they sat around giving Anda orders. They had decided that this grain must sell for 2,100 lei/kg if they were to obtain the funds they needed; but there were no buyers at that price. Anda kept urging them to let her drop the price to 2,000, but they refused. They returned with the truck almost full. A week later she reported something similar, this time concluding, "We went with four tonnes of grain, sold a couple of sacks, and didn't even cover the cost of gasoline. We took the same four tonnes twice to Cugir and twice to Orăştie! It sat in the truck so long that the mice had babies, so we sold wheat with meat!"

A second example concerns leaders' and councilors' repeated disagreement over the time horizon for planning their activity. Because the Association controlled none of the basic production factors, ideally the leaders would not only bring members a crop each year but also formulate a medium-term plan so as to acquire greater control over those factors. Therefore the two women worked simultaneously with at least two temporal horizons—short and medium term—whereas most individual farming households worked with only one— how to get a crop this year. The difference in time horizons caused a number of problems, including what balance to strike between paying the members each year and saving to buy inputs, as well as what kinds of equipment to buy and when. On such questions the council was pivotal: most of the nine men held to a short time horizon, resisting any idea of spending money for future benefits (which would require reducing members' payment, including their own), and it was Nica's job to convince them otherwise. She often, although not always, succeeded in this, but the different time horizons and their accompanying rationalities were a constant source of friction. The two leaders' problem, of course, was that long-term planning required members' trust in the leaders and commitment to maintaining the organization, and these would have to be built through short-term decisions that might compromise the longer-term future.

Worsening its problem was the lawsuit. Although the Association won, thus retaining control of the granary essential to its operation, that outcome had depended on its adopting an organizational form that proved very costly in financial, organizational, and legitimacy terms. Without that (i.e., without a council) all this would never have happened. The two women's authority would not have been continually in jeopardy; they could have taken a number of actions—such as buying equipment early on, as did other associations nearby—that would have given the Association greater momentum and enabled them to win the confidence of villagers, who were instead rightly skeptical of a council packed with former Party officials. In short, the Association emerged straight from the structural space of the collective farm, and this diminished from the start people's trust that it would benefit them. Informal associations did not have such problems. The most important effect of its trust deficit is captured in the second epigraph of this chapter: because the leaders knew they could not expect to run the Association with members' labor, right away they were pushed toward risky capital-intensive means, adding to the financial strain already imposed by the legal form. The Association differed from the individual households treated in chapter 5, then, in encountering its labor crisis at the outset and in being forced earlier into full participation in (imperfect) markets, for both sales and costly inputs, that most individual households for a time avoided.

These are the themes of the present chapter: problems with labor, markets, pay for members, and cash requirements, all in the context of the same price scissors discussed in chapter 5—and above all, problems with members' trust in the organization. I begin with the forces that pushed people to give their land to it and then examine the effects of its labor shortage on the rest of its operations. Throughout, readers should bear in mind that the Association was conceived not as a profit-making firm but rather as a means for villagers to work their land. In this sense, its orientation resembled that of the collective farm that spawned it, only now there were no delivery contracts to higher-level party bodies. The organization's leaders tried to obtain as good a yield as possible so as to keep the members content; making a profit was not, however, its goal. In many other associations around Romania the goal was to make money for the leaders at members' expense, but I believe that was minimally the case in Vlaicu.[7] Simply figuring out how to make a success of this arrangement—unprecedented, to them—was challenge enough.

I argue that although the Association was launched to serve villagers' needs, in order to do so it took on a life of its own. Beginning with owners' allocating partial use and revenue rights to land, its leaders strove to turn those rights more to the organization's advantage. They sought expanded control over all production factors and also over the use-rights they were given, as well as over the income. In buying implements to reduce the costs of cultivation, they accrued assets and liabilities. Their expansionism was motivated not by a desire for greater gain but by organizational imperatives, partly related to the problems attendant on its specific legal form. These imperatives ran counter to the strategies of member households—that is, the Association's story is one of conflicting rationalities based in different situations and kinds of resources. Starting out as a cross between tenancy and a cooperative, it moved closer to tenancy over time.

As the heir of the collective farm—the poorest agricultural enterprises in the socialist period—the Association was handicapped from the outset in the Transylvanian context. It had problems with both credit and credibility, rooted in its earlier life as an unsuccessful collective. Moreover, the kinds of knowledge and networks its leaders disposed of were not sufficient to ensure its economic success. When it collapsed, the reason was not that it was outcompeted by more efficient forms, as agricultural economists might argue. Rather, inflation, government agricultural policies, and its market dependence in a situation of weak market development all contributed to its demise. Its role was to create a space for the accumulation of value in the hands of the supertenants I mention in chapter 5, who were then able to step into the void left by the organization's fall.

Securing Land and Labor

Like smallholders, the Association's leaders had to solve the logistical problems of bringing together sufficient production factors—land, labor, and capital in various forms—in order to obtain a crop in any given year, but they also had to do so in a way different from the collective farm. Initially they controlled almost none of these factors: individual households now controlled land and labor, and funds to acquire the inputs and equipment were to be found in various credit arrangements and exorbitant bank loans. Then they had to resolve technical problems such as pest control and proper crop rotation. Each of these involved struggles with members and, often, with councilors.

Land

Land entered the Association without having to be mobilized, as its dazed owners cast about for ways to manage their unexpected acquisition. The first members were people who had little choice; they had insufficient labor to work all their land themselves (or did not want the bother) or lived in cities and could find no local relative to work their holdings for them.[8] The latter were the people most likely to have their land—all of it—in the Association from the start. For them, its existence was all that permitted them to benefit from their land at all. (As I explain later, they also caused the Association's leaders much bother.) Most of the Association's total surface area came from local Vlaiceni and urbanites, almost evenly divided in numbers. Urbanites' land occupied a disproportionate share of the Association's surface, however (about 70 percent), because most locals put in only some of their land, whereas absentees gave all of it. At no point did the organization include a large percentage of all the village's households. Besides venits and Roma, who were nearly half of village households, other villagers not in the Association included the Germans, who had their own association; some of the '45ers who had left it when the Germans won their lawsuit; a number of people still involved in litigation; and numerous households who, one way or another, found it possible to work their land.[9]

Developments over the decade both brought more land and subtracted some. Vlaiceni grew older and could work less; venits bought land from the urbanites, thus removing it from the Association, while those from whom they would no longer be sharecropping had to join (see chapter 5). Throughout these changes, the one stable element was great fragmentation of holdings. In the first year, before individual titling got underway, the land the Association worked was in a few large blocks, but thereafter in fragments. The Association register for 1994 gives 1,067 parcels for its 207 ha; because some were adjacent, the number of separate pieces it worked was smaller—eighty-six pieces for the 192 ha worked in 1997, for instance. Had village fields been consolidated, the Association's work would have been far simpler, but stubborn locals had prevented that possibility.

The Association did not actually have to acquire land and members; its goal was to work land for people who could not do so themselves. But once it got going, it had to retain enough land and members to justify both its activity and the purchase of implements. This meant it had to hold onto its members, to win their confidence. One means toward that end was the amounts it paid them from the land they gave it. I refer to this as *payment* or *returns*, reserving the word *rent* for supertenants, even though the Association too was a form of rental arrangement. Returns consisted of a fixed amount per hectare given to all members each year, based on the average yield for the entire harvest; the amount varied from year to year according to costs and weather. Decisions about payment were always decisions about relative priorities and different time horizons. To win members' confidence, the Association should pay well, but that meant spending today what might go tomorrow toward buying inputs for next season or purchasing vital equipment that would save money down the road. Between 1993 and 1997, members' payment varied between a respectable 1,200 kg of wheat per hectare (1993) and a dismal 100 kg/ha (1998), after floods inundated 130 out of 186 ha. Reduced returns were a regular motive for people's withdrawing land.

The 1992–93 agronomist established the unfortunate precedent of distributing as payment nearly the entire value of the year's harvest after costs, reserving almost nothing to pay for production in the following year. This decision was less stupid than it may seem: because some villagers were ridiculing those who had joined and were depicting it as "just another collective farm!", it was important to give members a sense that they were not in another CF but in something better. Paying well would certainly distinguish the two forms in people's minds. Nica, who followed him, thought differently, emphasizing the need to buy equipment by deducting the cost from members' returns. Here, however, she ran up against her councilors, who saw no reason to diminish the returns just so the organization could have, for example, a machine to pulp cornstalks.

Over the eight years of its existence, the Association's control of use-rights to land fluctuated. According to its 1992 statute, it had 167 hectares of land (the number of member families was unspecified) but its annual report for 1992–93 gives the total surface as 233 ha with 121 member families; these numbers varied somewhat over the next seven years (see table 6.1 later in the chapter). As of 1997, when floods began destroying crops, the numbers fell from 108 households (192 ha) in 1996–97, to 86 (186 ha) by spring 1998, to 38 (50 ha) in 1999, to about 27 (45 ha) in 2000. Many members had not actually withdrawn; they simply failed to pay what the leaders required in order to cultivate their land.

The Association wanted most of all not more members giving use-rights but greater stability of use-rights and control over the production process on what it held. Throughout the decade the extent of its control of use-rights changed. At first, for example, they were only partial because, although the leaders managed the entire cultivation process, they had to submit to the desires of owners for what they were to plant where. Each year Nica would try to persuade members to make three-year contracts, which would have enabled her to plan ahead; each year the members refused. As she observed to me, "They need to get more confidence before they'll make three-year contracts." The issue was not, however, simply confidence—although that was important—but also that household strategies and time horizons were at odds with those of the leaders.

This was least true of absentee owners, who were largely a captive audience. Although they too might take their land out—to sell it, or to express their displeasure at reduced pay for capital purchases—unlike locals they could not make the constant comparisons with other villagers, other associations in the area, or other options for land use, because they were not around. Therefore these absentees tended to be more stable than others and to adopt a less immediate timeline. Because Nica often used their land to resolve problems of various kinds, they provided a valuable cushion for planning even as they constrained it in other ways.[10] (This did not mean, however, that they were equitably treated. Not only in Vlaicu but across the country, absentee landowners were the ones most regularly cheated by either village associations or local people with whom they arranged for use of their land.)

Local members, however, were another matter. As I indicate in chapter 5, they were constantly trying to maximize their take from the Association and minimize their effort and costs by taking land out and putting it back in. They experimented with whether to put land into the Association or not, which of several parcels to give, and how long to leave them there; they gave it land that was of lower quality, harder to work, or in distant places. Members would put it in, wait for the Association to plow it, then announce that they were taking it out—yet refuse to pay for the work of plowing. If the land commission came late to measure or to resolve outstanding conflicts and thereby delayed planting, those affected would decide to give the land to the Association, and, when (expectably) the harvest was poor, they would say they had no reason to pay for the inputs because there was no crop. People quarreling over borders between fields would give pieces to the Association (recall Nistor, in chapter 4) and then take it back out once the Association had resolved the quarrel. One man put land in when he saw the Association had gotten great yields in the area where his land was; when the yields went down, he took it out.

In short, villagers accorded the Association use-rights to their land so as to throw their risks onto it as much as possible. This was a crucial function, which the Association filled in a way that commercial farmers did not—a very important reason for having associations at that time. People's reasons for taking land out or putting it in were idiosyncratic, but all had the same goal: improving their chances of getting by. To some extent their attitude paralleled that of collective farmers in earlier days: the CF was not something to be built up but something to be plundered, insofar as possible, in one's own interests. Receiving one's land rights merely widened the scope for this sort of plunder. Such stratagems caused the leaders perpetual headaches as they strove to develop a rational cultivation plan, such as one that included crop rotation between wheat and hoed crops—impossible if people kept taking out land that had been prepared for wheat and putting in land that had already been overplanted to it.

In most of these examples, the motives for switching land in and out were idiosyncratic. Not surprisingly, however, there was one motive that appeared over and over in my interviews: people moved their land in and out to resolve problems with labor, the difficulty I discuss in chapter 5. Some might move land longterm (people who had become too old to work it); others did so temporarily, for example, when someone was ill for a season or when an unemployed son-in-law came from town to help at home. For the Association, a death could signal an acquisition, a marriage a loss. Sometimes the reasoning could be quite intricate. Nica told me about Iacob, who had a parcel in a field where yields were usually not very good. But then in 1994 the Association obtained a terrific harvest in that area. Iacob came and said that next year he wanted to take out his parcel there and plant it himself; at the same time, he gave them another parcel where he had had wheat and asked them to put corn on it. She concluded, "So he was getting us to do the labor-intensive work of corn rotation to enable him to get a better wheat yield after that on his own!" In all these instances, however, the principle was the same: any amount beyond what one could manage oneself usually went to the Association—fulfilling, of course, its raison d'être.

Its raison d'être, however, had become more complicated. The organization itself had needs, chief among them greater certainty in its resource base. Anda and Nica never knew exactly whose land they would have to work—from one week to the next, initially, and then from year to year. Only in 1996—in the fifth year of the organization's life—did the members vote any rules at all on exit and entry, but these merely restricted changes to the end of the agricultural season, in autumn. Here we see the clash of different strategies and time horizons, long and short term. Members were thinking from one season to the next, at best, trying to determine the optimal use of their land, whereas the leaders thought in larger blocks of time. Villagers' financial situation made it impossible for them to think like corporate shareholders—to postpone revenues now so those could be plowed back into the Association, increasing its future capacity. Focusing on the question of their need for payment, members prevented the organization from ensuring its control over production factors.

Although Nica sought to regularize her control over land by repeatedly asking for three-year contracts, she never achieved sufficient leverage to get her wish. Part of the cause was the endless delay in regularizing people's property situations (see chap. 3). There was also the matter of credibility. In 1994 the council finally consented to buy two tractors, thus reducing payment below the 1,000 kg/ha minimum in terms of which villagers were thinking, but for some this reduction fanned questions about whether the leaders were cheating them. Their commitment evaporated with the Association's downward trajectory from 1997 on, as calamities befell it and returns dwindled. By 1999–2000, more and more members (largely absentees) were removing land to sell it to buyers who had other long-term plans. These sales cost the Association the land that had been the most stable and the best quality. Far from improving their control over access to land, then, Anda's and Nica's attempt to introduce a longer-term planning horizon failed. Unable to create greater certainty—for both themselves and their members—and unwilling to jeopardize the future by distributing gains in the present, they lost credibility with their members. The short term trumped the long.

Labor

The problem with labor that might drive smallholders into the Association was a critical problem for it as well, although in different and more complex ways. These stemmed from some of the same causes that afflicted individual households: the lack of adequate capital to substitute for manual labor, and the need to plant labor-intensive crops such as corn and sugar beets for crop rotation. Over the long term, the solution to scarce labor was heavy technologization, a goal toward which the leaders continually strove as their finances permitted. The reason they did so was that the Association had a labor problem from the start, because to require members' labor would have made it look like the old collective farm. Smallholders then aggravated the labor problem, for their ideal was that it would not only reduce people's labor needs but allow them to work hardly at all. Although some of my respondents justified their membership in terms of their inadequate labor supply, others said simply, "We don't want to work so much." In 1994, when things were going fairly well, two women commented in my presence that the best deal of all was to give your land to the Association, because "they give you 50 percent and you don't have to do anything but a bit of weeding."

Another labor issue came from the incomplete use-rights the Association held from its members—again, a result of the trust deficit. In order not to look like a CF, the leaders invited members to participate in the cultivation plan by saying what crops they wanted to receive at the harvest (see Verdery 1998, 173). They could opt for various combinations of wheat, barley, corn, and sugar beets, subject only to two conditions. If they wanted labor-intensive corn and beets they had to pay in advance for the cost of plowing and planting those crops, and they had to find a way to provide the necessary labor for hoeing and harvesting by hand (the reason being that the Association had no implements for this work). In exchange, they could take home the entire harvest. After paying for corn preparation, some members provided the remaining labor themselves, while others subcontracted it to sharecroppers (the usual venits, landless, and Roma) for 25–30 percent of the total crop.

I dwell here for a moment on corn, which brings the Association's labor problem most clearly into focus. Corn has long occupied a central place in Transylvania's agricultural economy (and in Romania's, more broadly). It is an important element in rural diets for both people and animals, especially pigs and fowl. For this reason, all villagers—whether in or out of the Association—wanted to plant some of their land to corn. Moreover, in Transylvanian conditions corn can be more lucrative than wheat, which is riskier. Corn can absorb manual labor better than wheat; for example, one can use little or no herbicide with corn and then weed it by hand, whereas that is impossible with the more densely sown wheat. In addition, one can harvest corn by hand but not wheat.

Above all, however, corn is crucial for crop rotation, which in turn is the only way to economize on expensive fertilizer and to maintain the relatively poor Transylvanian soils in decent condition. Indeed, the collective farm's overreliance on wheat (because it too had labor problems) had contributed after 1991 to villagers' finding the soil "tired," in need of special care.[11] According to Nica, on a given parcel one should plant wheat no more than two years running before putting hoed crops such as corn, but given the technological level at which most smallholders and associations in the area were working, hoed crops required higher labor inputs than wheat. Members whose labor problems had driven them into the Association in the first place, however, could not supply labor for more than a small amount of corn. Having people sign up for it and assume the labor burden helped to contain that burden but was totally inadequate to the requirement of rotation: when Nica added up all the members' crop preferences, the result was disastrous for good farming technique. Moreover, if people kept taking land out, it was impossible to plant corn this year so as to prepare for wheat next year. Only three-year contracts could ensure proper rotation, but members would not agree to them.

Concerns about rotation led to numerous conflicts. First, if the aim was rotation, then members could not be given corn on their own parcels: corn would have to be planted all around, not just where members wanted it. But there was wide variation in the soil quality best for corn, so the process of allocating corn for people to hoe and harvest was fraught with opportunities for favoritism and complaint. All the members hoped to get the most productive corn land for themselves, leaving the worst for people they disliked, and they invariably found fault with Anda and Nica's allocation of it. A second problem came from the high percentage of Association members living away from Vlaicu. These urbanites did not want the Association to plant corn for them because they found it difficult to arrange for the labor. But since absentees constituted half the membership and 70 percent of the Association's surface area, their refusal of corn compromised the rotation program for the entire farm.

Corn and its labor requirements caused yet other problems for the leaders' cultivation plan. One was that most members (especially absentees) who took corn failed to do all the labor necessary for freeing the terrain for the next production cycle. The difficulty was this: when corn is left to ripen until completely dry and then harvested by hand, as is normal in this region, the cornstalks [*tulei*] are left standing and must be removed before the soil can be plowed for winter wheat, otherwise they quickly jam the plow. Corn is usually harvested in early to mid-October and wheat is sown in November after one or two plow-

People harvesting corn from the Association often left the stalks standing.

ings. Standing cornstalks either delay the planting of winter wheat and thus compromise the crop or they postpone it so long that only spring barley can be sown, in March. This not only creates problems for the regular cultivation cycle but also costs more. Mechanical harvesting eliminates the problem because the corn is taken stalks and all; but the Association was always short of money, and anyway there was only one corn harvester in the entire county.[12] Unfortunately, the arrangement of having members opt for corn, provide the labor, and take the harvest home meant that most did not bother to go to the extra effort of removing the stalks. Because they already had their pay (the harvest), there was no way to make them do it.

The problem of rotation shows a sharp discrepancy between the strategies of members and leaders. It reveals members conserving labor and costs over the short term, whereas leaders tried to take a longer-term view of soil husbandry. It was not that villagers did not understand that rotation was important: those who plowed their own fields were quick to remove the stalks. Those who failed to do so for the Association were landless day laborers sharecropping the work for locals, or else locals who either did not identify with the organization's long-term needs or simply could not afford to respond to its labor problems. In general, if the farm is working about 200 ha and hopes to plant wheat after corn every third year, at least a third of the surface each year should go to hoed crops. This rarely happened, as we see in table 6.1. The Association's records list the

Table 6.1

Crop Rotation and the Problem of Corn, Vlaicu Association, 1991–2000

Year	Surface Worked (ha)	Corn (%)
1991–92	303	21
1992–93	233	14
1993–94[a]	207	18
1994–95[a]	196	21
1995–96	193	23
1996–97	192	31[b]
1997–98	[186/68][c]	n.a.
1998–99	50	[41][d]
1999–2000	45	[66]

Note: n.a., not available.

[a] The figures for 1993–1994 and 1994–95 refer to the total area worked by the Association itself.

[b] In this and the next year the Association began planting extra corn using high-cost herbicide in place of manual labor.

[c] Because of floods, the Association was able to work only 68 ha of that year's 186.

[d] In this and the next year flooding destroyed much of the wheat crop; some corn could be planted on land not affected.

total area it worked and the surfaces for the crops it planted, for 1991–97. Only in 1996–97 did the percentage approach the desired level.[13] Unless the Association employed unusual methods, it would never rise above 20 percent corn, to the 33 percent plus that was minimally necessary. The consequence was that if the Association planted only as much corn as members wanted, it would risk degrading the soil—just as the CF had done.

Nica therefore resorted to strong measures to resolve these organizational imperatives, which rested in the technical requirements of large-scale farming on a tight budget. First, in 1996 the labor crisis for hoed crops led her to wrest control from members over the cultivation plan. She curtailed the prerogatives of ownership by no longer allowing owners to dictate what they wanted to have sown, beyond signing up for corn if they wanted it. "If they won't obligate themselves to work, they can't expect us to take their orders." Second, without consulting the members, she and Anda began to act on their own to enlarge the amount of land planted to corn, thereby furthering the divergence between their strategies and those of smallholders.

The process had two stages. Beginning in summer 1994, Nica subcontracted 25 ha to Lascu, the head of a nearby state farm, to plant with corn that she could not manage. He worked it with chemical inputs, kept all the corn he harvested, and paid the Association a rent of 800 kg wheat per hectare or the cash equivalent (this from a probable harvest of 3,000 kg/ha on his wheat fields). Thus, Nica received 25 ha ready for rotation, but the Association made nothing at all from the deal toward its future production costs; Lascu received significant benefits at the expense of Vlaicu's Association members. Adding these 25 ha to the input figures for table 6.1 raises the percentage of corn land that year from 18 to 27 percent. Nica repeated this the following year with 20 ha, raising the percentage from 21 to 30 percent.

Here, however, she began running into opposition from Anda, who thought there must be a way to work corn land to greater advantage for the members. As Anda put the matter to me, archly, "Nica doesn't like corn. She prefers wheat because it is less trouble all around. Nica would rather fulfill her rotation plan by letting someone else go to more trouble, even at a sizable loss to her budget." In 1996 they changed tactics. Now they planted 25 ha more corn than members had signed up for and hired workers for the manual labor of weeding and harvesting it.[14] The problem was finding people to do it, given that most village households also needed labor at the same time. When I walked into their office one morning they were discussing with Toma, a rising commercial farmer, how each of them planned to get labor for corn. After several calculations using different figures for probable yields, probable prices, and so forth, the best pay they could come up with was that the workers would weed, harvest, and remove the cornstalks for 30 percent of the harvest—a figure below what smallholders might offer them. "Who will do it?" I asked, provoking much laughter. "We've no idea!" They joked about bringing the students from the nearby agricultural high school (an echo of the Ceauşescu days, when schoolchildren, urbanites, the army, and so on would all be mobilized for the harvest because the collectives did not have enough labor to do it all themselves), and they discussed the possibility of bringing soldiers from the military garrison in Orăştie. Then Toma said he was planning to do his with prisoners from Deva, "because prisons need corn too."[15] To my astonishment, it turned out that now he was not joking at all.

Although the two women stated they would check this out, they ultimately decided against it, having seen what a nuisance it was for Toma to go and pick up the prisoners, bring them all the way to Vlaicu (35 km each way), work with them, and then take them back, on several different occasions. "Besides," Anda said to me, "they *are* convicts, after all!" Instead, they used employees of the nearby state farm, whom they lured away for three days by offering more than that farm could pay them. "They were mad at the farm because it hadn't paid them on time, and besides, we offered them 10,000 lei/day without subtracting taxes as the farm does."[16] This experiment had an unfortunate end; a few days after they had paid out 500,000 lei for the labor, a hailstorm flattened 30 ha of corn land, for which they had no crop insurance.

In 1997 the two women tried something else. Once again, villagers signed up for less corn land than was required. Nica dug into the coffers, bought expensive herbicide, planted 30 ha of corn with it, and used no manual labor except for the harvest. This brought the corn surface up to 31 percent. Moreover, their yield was excellent, and they cleared a 32 million lei profit with which they bought more equipment. If herbicide were not so exorbitantly expensive (even using cheap local brands), they would have done this more often. Further experiments with balancing available labor, needs for rotation, and capital-intensive solutions were ended, however, by the Association's slide into ruin over the next two years.

In these ways, the Association began taking on its own independent life, moving away from its members and working for itself. By subcontracting with Lascu and then using members' land to plant corn regardless of whether members wanted it or not, the two leaders were ceasing to be strictly a producers' cooperative. They were also using much more expensive technology, in hopes of obtaining larger yields to cover those costs. In addition, they were making other decisions, unrelated to the labor question, that had the same effect. They made a contract with a seed supplier and sold some seed, which sold better than cereals, so as to have extra cash for buying inputs, and they rented out the Association's implements so members could plow their other land that was not under its management. Although Nica and Anda justified all such decisions as serving the organization's long-term viability and its members' incomes, my point is that they were increasingly making those decisions independently of the members, in the manner of tenant farmers. Yet their manipulations of crops that members were not receiving, along with the increasing sums they were having to charge to work members' land (discussed later), raised suspicions, fueling the inevitable rumors that the leaders and council were enriching themselves to the members' detriment. The trust deficit was insurmountable.[17]

The entire series of difficulties started with the way property rights had been restored: by giving land back in the absence of other means for cultivating it, in a context of persistent inflation, thus leading to the problems I explore in chapter 5. The Association suffered from the effects of those policies too, particularly the labor shortage, and smallholders aggravated its difficulties. They used it to compensate for their labor shortfall, when possible, and by withholding their labor they pushed it toward costly capital-intensive strategies in an environment too unstable for such planning. In the end, the Association failed exactly where the collective farm had failed before it: given its weak finances in inflationary times, it had to accumulate enough people to do the work of the farm and this proved impossible.

Anda and Nica did manage, however, to solve a few other problems, if only temporarily, by making use of networks and resources beyond the reach of most individual farmers. Nica, like most agronomists, had contacts with state farm directors (such as Lascu) who could take some of her land or give her information about new technologies; she had connections with the suppliers of seeds, fertilizer, and other inputs that might bring her the occasional good deal, and access to the occasional piece of gossip that might lead to a bank loan on better terms than individuals could get; and she had a sufficient volume of business to bargain with harvesters for a better price than they charged smallholders. These connections helped the Association for a time to confront successfully its chief remaining difficulties: how to fund the production cycle for the land and labor available to them, and how to gain greater control over the sources of funding.

Capital Inputs: Equipment, Materials, and Tillage

The divergent strategies of individual households and the Association's leaders with respect to land and labor appeared in a third arena of struggle, around problems of securing other capital inputs essential to farming: buildings, equipment, tilling services, and basic raw materials such as seed, fertilizer, pesticides, and herbicides (henceforth, 'cides). Here, the struggle was three-way, involving leaders, members, and the council, which played a more vigorous role in approving large purchases than it did in the cultivation practices already discussed. By 1997 the leaders were gradually gaining the upper hand, sometimes with the members as allies against the council, until repeated floods brought the organization down.

Tremendous growth in production costs that made smallholder farming a losing proposition also affected the Association, but it worked on a much larger scale and had to mobilize huge sums each year. In addition, it was run by a specialist whose cultivation standards were more stringent than those of most Vlaiceni: no agronomist worth her salt would be caught skimping on herbicide, plowing, or fertilizer, as individual households might do. Therefore, even though the leaders sometimes obtained lower prices for some things than smallholders did, the Association's production costs per hectare were generally higher than was possible for smallholders in financial straits. Finally, the former had marketing problems the latter did not. Smallholders interested in selling grain could do so fairly easily with a few weekend trips to the market in Orăştie or Cugir. The Association, by contrast, managed large volumes with a small staff, and this precluded regular market trips for anything except occasional cash needs.[18] Even after its in-kind distribution of payments, it was left with sizable amounts that had to be sold in order to pay members (especially urbanites) who wanted money. The parlous state of distribution channels, however, worse in Transylvania than elsewhere in the country,[19] gave them few good options. Problems with marketing kept revenues down at a time when the organization needed every leu it could get. How, then, did the Association's leaders resolve these difficulties?

Securing Farm Equipment

From the very first, the process of liquidating Vlaicu's collective farm disadvantaged anyone coming after it because the liquidation committee sold a number of important items from the CF inventory, including, crucially, its one tractor.[20] Things might have worked out had the items been sold and the proceeds immediately reinvested in new equipment, as happened in a few other associations, but owing to its transient agronomists, Vlaicu's association-in-embryo did not yet have anyone in charge to make such decisions. In consequence, the Association had to rely on the overpriced services of the Agromec for all its plowing, harrowing, planting, application of fertilizer and 'cides, and harvesting. Worse, the services of the Agromec were not always good. To be served at the optimal time and with equipment that was working, you had to bribe the director or be his buddy. Its tractor drivers were often drunk, owing to the time they took off from their assigned jobs to plow for individual households, in exchange for a good tip and some brandy. Reliance on the Agromec, then, increased an association's risk by eroding both its budget and the quality of its tillage.

For this reason, Nica began a campaign to buy two tractors, and the story of how she succeeded is revealing both of the organization's governance structure and of how information traveled. Initially, the council's reaction to her request was, "What do we need tractors for?! We can work with the Agromec." Councilors were unwilling to assume the debts required to buy equipment. In fall 1994, however, she obtained a record harvest; while depositing it at Romcereal, she learned from another agronomist that 15 percent credits for such purchases had just arrived at a new bank ("You have to *hear* about these things," she said, "otherwise I'd never have known."). She and Anda sounded out some councilors, who laughed them off. Then, by chance, on a trip to town the Association's president met that same agronomist (a male), who explained to him why it was essential to have one's own tractors. The president replied, "This will never go over with my people," but the other insisted that it was in their interests. The other councilors still said it was an insane idea.

At this point Nica and Anda called a meeting of the full membership and managed somehow to scare up a quorum. There, two urbanites living in Orăştie—one a veterinarian, the other a school principal, thus both of very high status in village terms (and both male)—argued heatedly in favor of the purchase. The members opposed the council and voted in favor, even at the expense of a large cut in their payment. It was the only time, I'm told, that members actually took a decision instead of merely saying, "Do whatever you want." Striking while the iron was hot, Nica decided to buy several other implements necessary to using the tractor effectively. The full loan was 26 million lei (an astronomical sum, to everyone involved), with the two tractors totaling 19 million. Now all they needed was collateral for the loan. The Association did not yet own equipment usable for that purpose, and the buildings it owned were excluded because they had never been recorded in the county land register; therefore, from the legal point of view they did not exist. The only other thing the bank would accept to cover the loan was two houses. Each councilor had some reason why he could not do it, until one army officer (whose daughter had a second house in town) offered his and another followed. Nica paid off the loan two years later, having been thoroughly terrified by the oscillating interest rates (see chapter 5).[21] As they had found themselves taking out further loans simply to pay their interest—and beginning to have insomnia—she and Anda decided that bank loans in this climate were simply too risky.

Especially noteworthy in this story are the networks of specialists and the decisive role of the council, without whose approval the leaders could not proceed. Information does not flow freely in this society; one has to find it through chance meetings with other specialists one knows. Although Nica did not tell me how she managed to obtain a bank credit once she learned of it, I imagine that too required connections. Bank credits rarely went just to anyone who needed them.

To overcome the council's obstructionism, I suspect that in this important instance the two women had worked frantically behind the scenes (mobilizing a quorum, which was not easy to do, and persuading some influential members ahead of time) to create a membership vote that would override the council. Meanwhile, however, a precious year or more had been lost during which both tractor prices and interest on loans had been lower relative to agricultural commodity prices than they would be in late 1994. Dominated by the councilors most ignorant of agriculture, the council's delay cost the Association money that would have helped it gain momentum and win acceptance. I also believe that the council's gender bias made it more difficult for the staff to persuade them to a course of action. Only the president's chance meeting with Nica's male agronomist-colleague (who was no better trained than she) kept the entire matter from being buried. Despite her success with the tractors, Nica continued to find the council an obstacle to her plans. There were still implements she needed in order to save costs and complete necessary work on time, but the council purchased instead items of lesser importance.

Therefore, I return to the point I made in introducing this material: without the liquidation lawsuit that forced the Association to register formally, none of this would have happened. Whoever led the more informal Association would have had more or less free rein to plan as they liked, perhaps through some consultation with members. (It is possible, of course, that without council oversight, an association's leaders would also have had free rein to defraud its members.) When I discussed the organization's problems with a couple of commercial farmers, they both pointed to the "communist" council as the main cause, a situation not unique to Vlaicu. "Because of the administrative council, they have no flexibility," said one. "They have three bosses [he named three former Party secretaries] perpetuating the communist system of agriculture while knowing nothing about it."

Although Nica had managed to bring some production factors under her control, she remained dependent on the Agromec for other items of equipment, combines for harvesting wheat, and so on. There, she was hostage to the Agromec's excessive prices, but also, following her purchase of tractors, to the Agromec director's pique. He had never imagined that the Vlaicu Association might tire of his fees and shoddy service and buy its own tractors, thus depriving him of a large piece of his business. When the two women came to negotiate with him to obtain combines for the harvest, he shrugged them off, saying he was not sure when he would have some and quoting an exaggerated price if he did. Mobilized by this, they began looking to the private individuals who had bought combines and were harvesting for less money. They were contributing, in their small way, to breaking up the state monopoly on agricultural services.

Material for Crop Production

Not all aspects of that monopoly were detrimental. Indeed, a source of political controversy concerned Romcereal, which (as I have explained earlier) disbursed government credits and inputs and stored or bought harvests too large to be taken to market. The government chose to mediate credits solely through

Romcereal, fearing that if they gave aid for agriculture directly to associations it was likely to be lost. To work with Romcereal, producers had to contract at least 1,000 kg of wheat per hectare; then they would receive fertilizer, seeds, and other inputs on credit against the harvest price for the 1,000 kg. Moreover, they could have the land worked by Agromecs—also linked to Romcereal—without having to pay at the time of the work. In the inflationary conditions of the 1990s, this was a great boon to entities such as the Association. Indeed, associations were its main customers, forming 90 percent of all contracts with the Orăştie Romcereal in 1994.[22]

The main drawback to these arrangements was that Romcereal paid a government-fixed price well below the price available on the market. In addition, because you had to bring the crops immediately after the harvest, you lost the chance of holding grain until the price went up. This, of course, was the point: because the government was worried that food prices would rise too fast for urban populations, it fixed agricultural commodity prices very low and required recipients of its credits to use Romcereal. This said, the arrangement did enable Romcereal's clients to avoid taking out bank loans at the high prevailing rates, guaranteed a certain level of low-cost grain delivery into state supplies while the change to individual farming took place, and ensured a market for producer units not yet accustomed to finding their own buyers (one could sell Romcereal as much as one wanted over the 1,000 kg/ha contract, but only at the state price).

Because Romcereal was a state monopoly, however, beginning in 1994 the IMF and World Bank insisted on its being dismantled as a condition of further loans. Although from cultivators' point of view the policy was disastrous, given that there was nothing yet to take its place as a purchaser or bulk storage facility, it is also true that Romcereal had hindered the development of alternatives. It had assumed certain risks for producers, but it had also used state credits to pursue plans for which those credits were not intended, and it had perpetuated in agriculture a system of privilege, with preferred clients who were paid on time and others who were not. Between 1994 and 1997, Romcereal was gradually broken up. First the state limited the credit system and then, in 1997, it ceased sending the money with which Romcereal was to pay for the wheat already contracted. Without this, its clients were unable to pay for the inputs they had taken that spring.

How did Vlaicu's Association weather the disappearance of Romcereal? When word began to spread that there would be no money for Romcereal to buy wheat, I asked Anda whether she would sue for breach of contract (the idea had not occurred to her). She checked her contract for its provisions in such a case and was shocked to discover that, as she put it, "This contract is to our disadvantage! It specifies *our* obligations but not Romcereal's. It says we have to deliver our harvest within ten days, but it doesn't say they have to take it. So *we're obligated, but we have no rights*." This setback was just the beginning. Soon thereafter, the river flooded and the wheat crop was spoiled. Anda sold twenty tonnes of their best wheat to the director of mills for a derisory 900 lei/kg, sold another 180 tonnes cheap as animal fodder, and still had 100 tonnes left, which they sold through special connections at below market price. The nastiest surprise, however, came when they went to file an insurance claim (the Romcereal director was friends with the director of the insurance company, Anda said, so Romcereal required insurance for all its contracts). There they were informed that only if 80 percent of the crop had been completely destroyed would they be indemnified, but in this case they would receive nothing because the insurance covered only "calamities" and flood damage qualified instead as a "catastrophe."

Romcereal's credit system had enabled the Association to minimize the price scissors by paying for inputs with sales from the same price year. Now, however, the leaders faced those price increases differently; they would have to pay part of the inputs with the previous year's income. Thus, they felt the effects of inflation more acutely. If they did not have enough income in the fall to buy all the necessary seed, fertilizer, and 'cides and to pay for the fall plowing and planting, then the costs of all those would be much higher the following spring. Although I have already given some figures in the previous chapter, I provide here a few more, relevant particularly to the Association.[23]

In 1994 Nica had spent 9 million lei on one new tractor; in 1998 the same amount bought two tractor *tires*. In 2000 you might find a used tractor at auction for 40 million. Between 1995 and 1997 the state price of wheat increased from 240 to about 1,100 lei/kg—a 4.6-fold increase—while the most effective herbicide, Titus, went from 1.4 million to 14 million lei/liter, a 10-fold increment. Increased gasoline prices affected the Association even more than smallholders because it plowed fields that were more distant and plowed them more often. When the government removed import tariffs on wheat from Hungary, it flooded the market, underselling local wheat.[24] The price for tillage had also risen: Nica estimated that in 1997 it cost them 1–1.2 million lei to get a hectare of wheat from plowing to harvest, whereas in 1999 it cost more than double (2.7 million) and, in 2000, quadruple (4 million).[25] Given a 1999 wholesale wheat price of 1,700 lei/kg and the Association's dismal yield of 1,670 kg/ha, Anda calculated that their revenues (before paying salaries and taxes) would be 140,000 lei/ha—barely 5 percent of the cost of starting the next production cycle at current prices! (If she were lucky enough to obtain instead the market price of 2,000 lei/kg, her take would be 640,000/ha, or 24 percent of that same cost.)

Their yield would improve if they had better weather and could afford more inputs, but the Association had entered a vicious circle in which it could not afford inputs to increase its production and therefore could afford even fewer inputs on the next round. It was small consolation to the two women that other associations in the neighborhood had already gone bust for similar reasons.

Trying to contain these increases, Nica resorted to her extra-village networks, hoping to find inputs whose price had not yet risen. Further motivating her was the 15 percent commission Romcereal was now putting on inputs it sold after 1997. For instance, she would buy fertilizer in December (when it was a lot cheaper than it would soon become), bringing it straight from the factory where her brother was director. For seed she and Anda went to a firm with whom they had struck up a good business relationship because it had found them serious and reliable. The director would send word when he was about to run out of seed at the old price; sometimes they would even get next year's seed when it was ready this fall. In addition, if they happened to be having money troubles, he would wait to be paid. With herbicide they were fortunate that Nica had a close connection with the supplier from earlier times, whom she had helped with a major problem a number of years earlier and who never forgot it. He would give them the material for 10 percent down and the remainder in three months. All these connections brought them inputs at prices lower than those they would have paid otherwise.

Among the beneficiaries of such relations were the members, who were charged for the Association's work at cost. Nonetheless, they paid for work of higher quality than they might have permitted on their own. That is, an individual household might take shortcuts the Association could not, and this raised its cultivation costs relative to those of an individual working cheaply on his own—skimping on fertilizer and herbicide, reusing seed, reducing the number of plowings, and so forth. In other words, there was not one set of prices for agriculture: there was the minimum threshold for individual households, a higher figure for Associations, and (as we see in chapter 7) an even higher one for commercial farmers, whose situation made them even more technologically exigent. Those who worked with the Association were thus compelled to a higher level of technology and expense, taken from their total returns. The harvest might be better, but in a year when calamity struck they lost correspondingly more money than the individual smallholder. In a word, by insisting on the specialist's higher standards, Nica was placing a potential burden on their budgets. She was spreading the risk of her higher standards across the whole organization, just as its members were doing to her.

Collapse

The disappearance of Romcereal was one in a string of disasters that afflicted the Association. First, in spring 1996 floods ravaged the crop of winter wheat. Then with Romcereal's impending breakup, suddenly the problem of finding their own markets loomed large. "What are we to do with 100 or 200 tonnes of wheat, take it bag by bag to the Sunday market in Cugir?" Anda exclaimed. "We haven't the personnel for it. But there's no alternative! Bakers buy only a month at a time, and we need most of our money all at once." More flooding in the spring of 1997 had the effects already described, but this time it had more serious consequences for the members. When Romcereal provided credits, members had not been directly implicated in the costs of beginning each year's production. With the end of that arrangement, however, the Association began charging members up front for the cost of tillage and planting. It had no alternative—banks now avoided giving loans for production because they saw associations as a bad risk, with small chance of profitability and lack of guarantees. Anda herself had become unwilling to take on loans because she feared there might be no crop to sell; the natural disasters had compromised her credibility. Members would have to pay, then, before their land could be worked. Anyone who failed to ante up the amounts being charged that year would get no returns.

Although the fees were sizable and had to be paid all at once, some members managed to do so despite their anxiety over the flooding. But in 1998 when floods once more destroyed what had been planted, people were unwilling to pay again for replanting, and that autumn far fewer members signed up. The result, as is clear from table 6.1, was that an increasing proportion of land under the Association's management remained uncultivated, and what they did work was poorly prepared. Trying to cultivate when the adjacent parcels of other owners were unworked or inadequately protected worsened their situation. For instance, if the Association was working a parcel of 1.5 ha near other strips worked privately by people who did not use pesticides or herbicides, then the increased pests and weeds all around it compromised its use of these costly substances. And now members began forcing them to cut corners, refusing to pay for sufficient fertilizer, 'cides, or tractor runs.[26]

Predictably, yields suffered, and this naturally meant ever-lower pay to members for use of their land—from 500 kg of wheat per ha in 1996 to 400 in 1997, to 100 in 1998. Table 6.2 gives approximate figures for the Association's mean wheat yields between 1992 and 2000 (comparable figures for corn yields are not available because members took the harvest directly home). The numbers show clearly the consequences of flooding on yields and of requiring members to pay

Table 6.2
Association Wheat Yields, 1992–2000

Year	Surface Planted to Wheat / Total Surface Worked (ha)[a]	Yield (kg/ha)	Comments
1991–92	165/303	3,005	Agronomist 2
1992–93	127/233	2,126	Agronomist 3
1993–94	80/207	3,670	Nica's first full production cycle
1994–95	78/196	3,900	Normal average yield is 3,000
1995–96	85/193	2,344	Floods
1996–97	75/192	2,500	Floods
1997–98	68/186	2,000	Floods
1998–99	13/50	1,670	First time that members pay; no fertilizer
1999–2000	15/45	2,100	Some fertilizer, but small amounts

Source: Figures for 1992–97 from annual reports for Aurel Vlaicu Agricultural Society; later
figures from staff interviews.
[a] For example, 165 ha of wheat to a total worked surface of 303 ha.

in advance (less land worked and shortcuts in cultivating it). In 1999, the yield
fell to almost half the normal yield for this region because even those few who
signed up did not have the money to pay for fertilizer. For the next cycle the leaders insisted on using some fertilizer (although they continued to cut corners in
other ways); the number of participants dropped to twenty-seven and the wheat
surface to 15 ha. It was not that people were withdrawing from the Association;
they simply could not afford the price of cultivating. In this way, then, the Association contributed to the same process discussed in chapter 5: the devaluation of
land, as it was left unworked. Hectares were in place, but their value was vanishing. The organization had insufficient funds to maintain its granary and tractors
in good repair, and it was overusing its equipment with rentals to members.

In December 1999 Anda and Nica declared themselves unemployed, so as to
avoid deducting from the budget the costs (health insurance and taxes on their
salaries) occasioned by their employment, and Nica found work elsewhere. A
few months later, Anda did a complete inventory, reconciled the accounts, and
took off for Spain as migrant labor. When the council president died soon after,
no councilor proved up to the task of succeeding her. As of November 2001,
desperate members had found one supertenant to take on 100 of the 200
hectares once under Association management, and a few other commercial
farmers in the area took on some as well. Meanwhile, more and more urbanites

decided to sell their land. Along with every other association in the area but one, the Vlaicu Association had ceased to exist.

My village respondents gave several reasons for its demise: the floods, the terrible inflation, the collapse of Romcereal and the consequent necessity for people to pay in advance with money most did not have, the problems of finding markets, the entry of low-priced Hungarian wheat, and the "communist" council that insisted on deciding things it knew little about. Each of these doubtless contributed to the result. Many of them were not local but arose from problems in the macroeconomy, such as internationally influenced government policy concerning credits, agricultural prices, distribution channels, and tariffs. In addition, despite constant pressure from international lenders, the Romanian government did not manage (did not want?) to bring inflation under control, in order to continue subsidizing loss-making state firms. For agriculture, this choice had unfortunate consequences all the way down the line, captured in the ever-widening price scissors between costly inputs and cheap agricultural commodities. All these factors suggest that the Vlaicu Association was not alone in the difficulties it faced. To see this we look next at Vlaicu's other association, that of the Germans.

Comparative Associations

As happened in many other biethnic villages, Vlaicu's Germans (Benzenzers) formed their own association, the Cervenka Society,[27] whose complex and interesting story I briefly review here. Created after their successful 1992 lawsuit that brought them land, it initially numbered sixteen families and controlled 69 ha (one less than the original petition). The Cervenka soon became a transnational enterprise when after 1991 Benzenzers began emigrating to West Germany but, as dual German-Romanian citizens, the emigrants could keep their land. It was to work the 69 ha and divide the proceeds among the members, sending deutsche marks to the ones abroad. Unlike the Association, the Cervenka had no storage space—a major drawback. Thus, it was compelled to sell all its crop at harvest (at the state price) rather than hold the crop for a better price, and without storage it could not buy inputs in the fall to hold until the spring. These lacks made it more susceptible to the price scissors because it could never get the best price for either its grain or its other needs. But it had advantages over the Association. First, it had a manageable amount of high-quality land that was not susceptible to flooding, so it was not ravaged by the Association's calamities. Second, the Cervenka had assumed the least expensive organizational form.[28] Although it had a statute drawn up by two members, it was not registered. It paid its accountant (Gretchen) and president (Hans, a retired factory worker) 2 percent of each year's crop but was not obliged to have year-round salaried employees or pay their taxes. It hired tractorists and labor for corn harvesting as needed. It did not even have a bank account; Gretchen simply used her own.

Third, the Cervenka's 69 ha were consolidated in two large chunks, one containing 11 ha, the other the rest; therefore, it avoided the problem of land fragmentation that caused the Association so much trouble. As one respondent explained when I asked if she had had problems with her land, "It makes no difference whether it's *my* land or *Müller's*: it's *ours*, not mine. If each of us took our own land, then who would work it? We *have* to think of it as ours and work it together." Finally, the Cervenka began with a capital of goodwill much greater than the Association's. Being an "association of the German ethnic group" (as its statute said), it benefited from internal solidarity and support for its leaders—distrust and suspicion emerged only late in the decade—and it was not plagued by constant worries that it was too much like the old CF.[29] Its ethnic character, age structure, and higher proportion of absentees meant that people were not constantly switching their land in and out, as with the Association.

Almost as soon as the Cervenka began to operate it fell out with the agronomist it had employed and fired him, deciding that agronomists were an expensive luxury. The relative lack of expertise mattered little at first because it made contracts with Romcereal and the Agromec, which provided not only the services and materials but the expertise for using them properly. Later, when those contracts were no longer possible, Gretchen and Hans did their best to learn, asking Nica for advice[30] or drinking coffee with the personnel of Romcereal to pick up the occasional tidbit. Their yields fluctuated widely, from a high of over 4,000 kg/ha of wheat in 1995 down to 1,700 the following year, but were generally higher than those of either smallholders or the Association. They kept assiduously to crop rotation and seemed to have less trouble obtaining labor for corn than the Association did. Initially working with Roma (whom they, in contrast to Vlaiceni, found reliable and hardworking), they were then besieged by Romanians wanting to work for them. The reason was that their higher yields meant higher take-home pay for the same 25–30 percent of the harvest the Association gave. Notably, all the applicants were venits, not landless Romanian locals, most of whom (the '45ers) had lost land to Benzenzers. Thus, we see two intersecting sets of resentments affecting labor questions: '45ers would not supply "rich Germans" with labor, and venits angry with "rich Romanians" were glad to do so.

The Cervenka had a number of problems parallel to the Association's, including a lawsuit, constant pressure to pay members rather than support the organization's further development, and a distressing relationship to machinery in particular and production costs in general. Concerning the lawsuit (Benzenzers' second), I mention in chapter 3 that in November 1993 some '45ers broke into the Cervenka's land and plowed across furrows it had already planted—a deeply hostile act. The Cervenka sued for damages and, although it won, the episode both aggravated an already tense situation and cost them time and resources, as well as a crop on the affected land.

On the matter of pay, we see something similar to the Association. The Cervenka made all decisions collectively with its members and their representatives, a group as inexperienced and full of unsuitable ideas as the council of the Association. This group's most powerful members insisted that each season the crops should be harvested, bills paid, and the remainder divided among them proportionate to their land, leaving nothing with which to begin the new cycle. As long as Romcereal and the Agromec were working on credit, this was not a problem; once that began to change in 1997, it became one. No Cervenkan wanted to ante up the money as the Association was making its members do, and because they had no jural status they could not take out bank loans. Gretchen now began withholding around 30 percent to cover production costs for the following season, despite members' objections. Expenses grew continually, however, yielding more pressure to distribute returns and much complaint that someone must be pocketing the money. In short, like the Association, the Cervenka struggled to negotiate between rising costs and members who did not think in the long term, wanting immediate gain. Having fewer members to deal with—and, for a time, more credibility with them—helped it keep going despite the odds. Those for whom trust began to dissipate were all absentees.

Finally, concerning their relationship to machinery, Gretchen and Hans had been content with the Agromec's arrangements because they found it very conscientious in its work for them. If they asked it to send nine combines at noon on a given date, nine combines showed up at noon, completing the entire harvest in one day at the optimal humidity for a good sale to Romcereal. I heard no complaining about the Agromec's prices or service, such as I heard from Anda and Nica (perhaps because the Cervenka always paid on time or because its compact fields were more attractive to the Agromec than the Association's fragmented ones). Nonetheless, with the rumored end of the credit system, Cervenkans began to see that they too should get a tractor. They were making this decision at the same time as the Association, but under very different circumstances because, as Germans, they had access to special arrangements through the German Forum and other German ethnic organizations. These connections brought them their tractor. When it arrived, however, its repayment terms were an annual sum fixed in Austrian schillings, not Romanian currency. The arrangement proved ruinous, for the latter fell continuously against the former for the rest of the decade.[31] Gretchen was bitter about the experience, saying that she thought they were being helped by their German connections but instead found themselves skewered.

By 1998 Gretchen had practically nothing left to distribute to members and not enough to renew production on the full 69-ha surface. In 2000 she sowed only 40 ha. She had stopped using fertilizer and now reused the Cervenka's seed rather than buying treated seed that would be pest-resistant; as could be expected, her yields were falling. Then disaffected emigrants began to sell their land, further narrowing the Cervenka's resource base. The crowning blow came when, in search of the markets Romcereal no longer provided, Gretchen gave their entire crop to the director of a state pig farm, who promised to pay her 5 million lei and never did. In consequence, the Cervenka left uncultivated even more of its surface than before.

Despite significant differences in their starting points, then, the fates of the two associations were similar. Both found themselves overwhelmed by the price scissors, although for somewhat different reasons. Both had to sacrifice growth to pay shareholder dividends. Both cut back on the proper technology and were feeling the effects in decreased production. Both were forced to leave land unworked and were then faced with members selling land. The Association's leaders showed greater ingenuity and skill in holding down costs and increasing revenues; as former participants in socialist agriculture they disposed of more social and cultural capital (connections and knowledge) than Benzenzers, all of whom had worked in industry after 1945. Although the Cervenka had better land,[32] they paid more for services on it and sold grain at a lower total price. Their major asset—international social capital—actually turned into a liability. By late 2001 the Cervenka was on its way to joining the defunct Association.

※

As the Cervenka example shows, two associations in the same village facing similar problems might solve them in ways specific to their situations. Indeed, even a cursory glance at the literature on decollectivization indicates remarkable diversity in how associations were organized, both in Romania and elsewhere. Even settlements within a small compass might differ substantially, a fact borne out by my investigations in villages around Vlaicu—such as Romos, Geoagiu, Şibot, and Vinerea. Lacking the space to explore their differences here, I summarize these and the many conversations that I had with agronomists and other association leaders concerning interassociation variability. It appears that a conjuncture of three things set Vlaicu apart from associations that were still functioning in 2001: the lack of field consolidation, the late acquisition of implements, and the nature of leadership.

First, some neighboring associations managed to keep members from insisting on their original family parcels, partly because soils were more uniform than those in Vlaicu (making differences in the location of one's holding less important), partly because prospective association leaders immediately pushed for consolidation. Working consolidated fields facilitated their obtaining good results that won further assent. In Vlaicu, turnover among agronomists meant an absence of effective leadership at that critical moment. Second, the same was true concerning when and how associations bought equipment. Some sold the CF patrimony and bought new equipment right away. Vlaicu's Association, having auctioned off the CF's few implements and three barns without using the money at once to obtain farm equipment, was relatively late in acquiring it and paid more for it. Moreover, its first agronomist had distributed too much of the revenue to members, leaving the till empty for such purchases, and that pattern continued. Vlaicu's Association therefore lost the fast start gained by some others. This difference was related, third, to its "communist" leadership, an element several of my specialist-respondents underscored: a collective leadership of nonexperts who first decided what they were going to give to people, rather than first deciding what the organization needed to stay afloat as a business and then giving members the rest. Other associations benefited from leaders who made their economic decisions themselves, on the basis of specialist knowledge, even at the risk of alienating members with lower pay. And the most prosperous neighboring associations also had leaders who had been in leadership positions in their (relatively successful) CFs for a long time and had some credibility with villagers. By contrast, Nica was new and Anda had been just a lowly functionary in the former CF.

As I have already indicated, I believe the leadership question also had a gender aspect to it. Although Anda did not put it in these terms, she offered me a revealing comparison of how the Vlaicu Association and the leaders of Vinerea's allocated corn land. "Their leadership is different," she said. "They were firmer with people than we were here." She continued,

> We'd spend a half-day with people just trying to give out corn for hoeing. Everyone would crowd into the office. We'd [point to the map and] ask, "Who wants this piece?" No one. "We'll give it to Lina, she wants some this year." Lina's friend Ana would object, "Lina doesn't like it here. Put her over there." At the next strip, the person who wants to work it says, "But I forgot my money [to pay for plowing]." I had insufficient authority, and Nica didn't want to use hers—she didn't want to make people mad. In Vinerea, though, people came in one by one, not all in a bunch.

The boss asks, "Did you bring your money?" "No." "Next person! Did you bring your money? . . . Next!" They exercised their authority.

The two women's gender did not help them exercise authority, especially given their council of elderly men whose Party leadership experience had accustomed them to giving orders. How could two much younger women prevail against such patriarchs? Sometimes Nica could persuade them, but she could never simply say, "This is how it has to be done if we're going to succeed," behavior appropriate for a male agronomist but less so for a woman. It was not just that these two women failed to exercise their authority: they did not *have* much. Under these circumstances, Vlaiceni subjected any action Nica or Anda took to careful scrutiny and the most uncharitable interpretation. The idea that women might not have sufficient authority for this kind of work also appears in ethnographic work from a Russian village, where many of Douglas Rogers's respondents told him that women are just no good at being in command (*khoziain*).[33]

The ingredients for a successful association, then, seem to be (1) fields consolidated early, (2) (male) agronomists with long and positive experience in the settlement and a capacity to wield authority, and (3) an early decision to use the CF's fixed capital to buy new equipment before the price scissors gaped so wide, enabling minimal exposure to loans and credits.[34] Vinerea's association, for example, met all of these criteria; Vlaicu's met none of them. The fact that it outlasted most others in the area that met more of the criteria is evidence of its two women leaders' unappreciated skill. Ultimately, however, not even these criteria could guarantee an association a solid future because the really critical ingredients were those over which local agronomists and villagers had no control whatsoever: the interest charged on loans, the IMF-influenced lowering of tariff barriers that brought in an avalanche of Hungarian wheat, the Romanian government's repeated failure to create stable subsidies for its agriculture, and the inferior soils and climate that made agricultural production in Transylvania more expensive than in the south. Within these constraints there was a small space for maneuvering; association leaders lucky enough to get the early moves right had a chance of surviving the millennium, but those were few.

A brief final comparison with some associations in Olt county (southern Romania) will help to situate the Vlaicu Association even further. According to research by Daniel Lățea,[35] more than half of the communes there had one large association (600–1,000 ha, as compared with the Vlaicu Association's 200), usually run by an agronomist from the former CF. Each of the two associations Lățea investigated had not only a trust deficit, but also a high concentration of power in its leader; its council was his people, who received sizable returns in exchange for their loyalty. Running the association as their fiefs, these leaders could threaten with expulsion anyone who complained about the running of the association or the terms of payment.

In areas such as western Hunedoara, where farms were smaller and supertenants had appeared who were independent of the CF-based associations, that threat would merely drive smallholders to look for someone else. Such competition within a small space, however, was much less likely in southern Romania with its immense state and collective farms (see table 6.3). In the Regat both kinds of farm generally had fewer claimants relative to the available land because they had been created on large estates whose owners could recover no more than 10 ha after 1991, leaving large expanses at the authorities' disposal. The size difference meant that villagers with land were likely to have fewer alternatives than those in Transylvania, where farms and their accompanying personnel were closer together. Although the leaders' abuse of members through falsified production figures might result in protests, in general people found that (owing to richer soils in the south) they received adequate amounts without having to work very much, so in the end they accepted the arrangement. Encouraging this was the fact that when association leaders were sued, they usually won, probably through collusion with the judges.

Aside from enjoying much more power over smallholders than did Transylvania's association leaders, those in the Regat also benefited from much better soils that lowered their lower production costs, making them less vulnerable to the

Table 6.3

Average Sizes of Collective Farms and State Farms by Region, 1966[a]

Region	Total Number of Farms		Average Agricultural Surface (ha)		Average Arable Surface (ha)	
	CFs	SFs	CFs	SFs	CFs	SFs
Regat	2,836	459	2,095	3,027	1,794	2,498
Transylvania[b]	1,465	162	1,654	2,372	1,182	1,427
TOTAL	4,301	621	1,924	2,842	1,575	2,230

Source: *Anuarul Statistic al Republicii Socialiste România*, 1967.
Note: CFs, Collective Farms; SFs, State Farms.
[a] These averages differ from those in table 2.2 because after 1966 farms were progressively consolidated in size and reduced in number. In 1990, for example, there were only 411 SFs and 3,170 CFs in Romania, compared to 621 and 4,301 in 1966. Statistical yearbooks after 1966 do not contain the numbers of farms by county necessary for this calculation.
[b] Excludes Banat. Farm sizes in the Banat resemble those of the Regat, rather than of the Transylvanian plateau.

price scissors that Transylvanian associations found so debilitating. Some of these association leaders began to farm in a commercial manner (even if abusively), with better chances of success than those in Transylvania. Even in the south, however, associations might function as transitional forms, in ways I describe next.

Associations as Heirs of Socialism

In this chapter I have shown how the leaders of the Vlaicu Association, an entity spun off from the infrastructure of the collective farm, strove to gain control over means of production in an environment of high risk and uncertainty; how conflicts arose between their strategies and those of smallholders; and how they ended by further devaluing the capital under their management, including land (left unworked), inadequately maintained tractors and buildings, and the asset value of CF inventory sold without distributing the proceeds at once. I have indicated that the resources these leaders drew on to succeed in farming were largely those with which they emerged from the socialist period: the expertise acquired in the socialist education system and in the experience of working in socialist farms, as well as the networks of contacts all CF staff developed as part of that experience. These resources gave them forms of capital that individual households lacked—precisely because of the socialist experience—and enabled them to think in longer time spans than smallholders could. External conditions prevented that, however, forcing most associations into shorter-term coping strategies.

Although their socialist past endowed association personnel with certain benefits, it also bequeathed to them a major liability. Former CF members quite reasonably suspected that the new form was just another kind of CF, out to exploit them. We might say that socialism gave its CF personnel social and cultural *capital* but not much *credit*. The rare exceptions, such as Vinerea, confirm the point. Collective farming in Romania was among the worst in the former socialist bloc, and in Transylvania, at least, it left a legacy of alienation from anything resembling it. In chapter 5 and this one we have seen different forms of that alienation.

The Legacy of a Complex Symbiosis

There were other legacies, however, that my ethnographic material brings into focus. Among them was the murky boundary between the organization and its households. Villagers who had previously taken from the CF what they believed was theirs now sought to milk the Association, also theirs in a sense. They expected to use its equipment even for land they withheld from it. In the absence of proper storage, they used it to store their grain by "forgetting" to come and pick up their in-kind payment; many I spoke with believed they had a right to store in its granary (their collective good) grain from their other land too. They brought it their conflicts to resolve, got it to do their crop rotation, and had it cultivate their worst land. They even expected to procure from it its hard-won inputs ("Oh, please! Only two or three sacks of fertilizer!") just as before, calling Nica "nasty" and "unfriendly" when she refused. Although most of the literature on recombinant property has been written from the vantage point of managers, here we see it in the repertoire of smallholders too.

Beyond this, collective farms worked via a complex symbiosis between the organization and its member households, the former engaging mainly in capital-intensive grain (and some livestock) farming, the latter in labor-intensive cultivation and animal-rearing on small usufruct plots (see, e.g., Creed 1998; Kideckel 1993b; Lampland 1995). The two forms depended on one another: without household labor, the capital-poor collective could not complete its work; without the collective, households could not raise the cattle, pigs, and fowl they fed on thefts and in-kind payments from the CF. The rationalities behind these two productive organizations differed, making their relationship constantly tense. After 1989 that symbiosis was broken and then recreated. Village households used national laws to destroy the collectives; CF personnel created a new shell in which those households could work. Once again, a capital-intensive, organization-based grain-farming adaptation coexisted with a labor-intensive, household-based one emphasizing livestock. Each required the other, although not for the same reasons as before. Indeed, this same symbiosis characterized the feudal period and its immediate aftermath as well.[36]

Let me dwell for a moment on the different rationalities that took shape after 1989. In chapter 5, I introduced Sandu, a factory worker who had recently retired to work his land full-time. We were discussing one day in 2000 why the Association had foundered. After the usual litany about unfavorable prices, he offered this opinion:

> The land is *sick*! After all these years of communism, it's sick! They forced it to produce as much as possible, at ever greater heights, and they filled it with poisonous chemicals. It's just like with a trained athlete: if you push him past the limit, fill him full of hormones and other pills, after five years he'll be no good any more. Land is the same. It needs to be given manure—natural products, not chemical fertilizer—and not forced to produce the maximum possible.

Sandu offers a vision of agriculture as a form of interaction, based not just on mastery [*stăpânire*] but on nurturance of a creature-like thing that can be sick and well. This imagery is not peculiar to Vlaicu: Gail Kligman, working in northern Transylvania, found the same thing,[37] as did Margaret Paxson (n.d.) for Russia. But it was certainly not the vision animating the practices of the Association.

Sandu's observation suggests that we see the Association as the primary point at which very different ways of thinking and acting about land, different sets of capacities and endowments, are forced together. Oversimplifying, we can characterize these ways for a moment as contrasting visions of farming practice. The first way thinks of land as an object, a resource that has to be expertly managed; the second sees it as a kind of being that requires both mastery and care. The first treats labor as a cost; the second does not. For the second vision, labor is an aspect of self, to be devoted to one's own enterprise and withheld from others (such as associations) as much as possible; this view enables smallholders to raise livestock, a time- and labor-consuming activity that associations cannot afford. The first involves a stringent calculation of returns, especially after the introduction of capitalist accounting standards into Romania in 1994. By contrast, the second calculates only loosely, including all sources of income (such as pensions) and not just the returns from agricultural activity. The first type plans for the medium and long term; the second tends to the short term, thinking only from year to year. Although the first sees waiting until spring to buy one's inputs as irrational in inflationary conditions, the second sees it as part of a different calculus: you use grain in the winter to feed livestock and then sell what you have to, in order to buy the inputs that your household composition and winter weather conditions indicate will be needed. If winter weather indicates a bad season, then you sell less grain, thereby affording fewer inputs, so as to feed your animals through another year.

Accompanying these variants, as I observed earlier, is variation in the kinds of endowments with which people emerged from socialism. The cultural capital of smallholders included a certain respect for technology but very little experience and knowledge of it; their social networks did little for them in working their land. Agronomists such as Nica emerged, in contrast, with a good understanding of modern agriculture and the technology that enables dominating nature, as well as a network of contacts to help them solve problems in using that technology to the full. We would be mistaken, however, to emphasize this polarity and to cast it as a matter of traditional versus modern. Rather, the efforts of villagers and Association leaders to act within the constraints of the macroeconomy fall along a continuum of possibilities, loosely clustered into these groupings. Smallholders did not reject modern technology altogether: they simply could not afford to pay for it. For plowing they much preferred tractors to livestock, and if they could (or if they felt they must), they might try new types of seed, complex herbicides, and so on. Some occupied hours of their agronomist's time with questions about the best kind of seed or the proper time for applying herbicide. In this sense, the Association served as a limited extension service, spreading knowledge about alternative methods of cultivation.

The different sets of rationalities do not come from more traditional versus more modern mentalities but from differing organizations of resources and differing tolerances for risk. In addition, they fit alternative dispositions toward the preceding collective farm. The group of people who benefited from collective farming—those trained as specialists and employed as managers—found plenty to criticize in it but did not question socialism's basic farming orientation, with its emphasis on modern technology. The group of people most oppressed by socialist agriculture rejected much of that orientation, which represented to them a neglect of particularity in favor of abstraction. In other words, the seemingly traditional cluster was rejecting socialist agriculture, using an idiom *we* read as traditional. That is not good news for the successors of socialist agriculture, the associations, and it returns us yet again to the socialist legacy behind their failure: their deficit of trust.

Associations as Transitional Forms

Associations continue another socialist legacy in addition to the symbiosis of different orientations to agriculture. In socialist planning, collective farms were always envisioned as a transitional form, an unfortunate compromise that would disappear once they received the same level of capital investment as state farms. Associations took up this role of collectives and began consummating it, but not quite according to the socialist plan. Many of my specialist respondents, including Anda and Nica, saw associations in these transitional terms. What might this mean?

On the basis of my admittedly narrow material, I suggest that associations helped to polarize the field of agricultural producers into poor rural households and commercial farmers. By planting more of the costly wheat than cheaper crops and by farming at a technological level beyond the means of most smallholders and then requiring their members to bear the costs, they sometimes contributed to a process of impoverishment that national policy was already causing for smallholders who were not in associations. This was particularly true when bad weather kept the better technology from producing higher yields sufficient to offset the higher costs to members. A state farm director made a similar argument when I asked why he expressed such antiassociation sentiments: "Because it's a transitory form, and while it exists it impoverishes people. Look at them! The leaders give 300 kg/ha to the owners, who thus can't raise themselves up at all!" The same view in another guise came from Vlaicu's wealthiest smallholding family, who had some of their land in the Association because they had too little labor to work all of it. In 1999 even before the Association collapsed, they told me, "Our problem is that at first the Association did very well, so we didn't buy equipment, but now it's more expensive." In 2000 they extended this thought: "We don't want an Association any more. We liked it at first, because we thought 'We're old, how can we work this land?' But now we're sorry, because without it we'd have bought all the equipment we needed." These people were on the threshold of becoming commercial farmers, but they saw the Association as having jeopardized that possibility. If it did so for them, how much more so for villagers of lesser means?

Impoverishment was indeed the outcome wherever association leaders stole their members blind, as repeated exposés in the Romanian media revealed. The case I have explored here, however, shows the same result even from hardworking and apparently honest leaders, who tried to help their members get along and then lost sleep when they failed. The problem was not (only) with unscrupulous leaders but with the structural circumstances of associations as the principal option available to smallholders after Law 18/1991. To prevent even worse exploitation, the Iliescu government tied the hands of the most powerful agrarian actors—the directors of state farms and Agromecs—by forbidding the former to privatize and the latter to rent land. Associations exploited smallholders on a pettier scale, barely visible even to their well-intentioned leaders, which permitted smallholders the illusion that their ownership was meaningful.

Just *how* meaningful was the subject of a reflection from Anda, as we discussed the Association's passing. After saying, "I never got the feeling that people really *wanted* it to work" (see the second epigraph of this chapter), she added,

> I thought that each of them would have the sense of property and would feel this on their own skin. But no: it was easier for them to come and go, expecting *me* to have the sense of *their* property—*me* to tremble with fear at the prospect of hail, drought, and so on. If they've gotten this land for free and it causes them no pain, then it was pointless to give them land. Only if [ownership] hurts does that mean it wasn't pointless.

We can perhaps excuse the uncharitability of this arresting comment about the joys of ownership and what makes it effective, because in making it Anda was also facing her own dashed hopes, as an activity to which she had devoted uncommon effort came to naught. Her comment underscores that ownership is more than a property title—it is an experience, often bitter, for which people's long years in the collective left them unprepared. What she neglected to mention was that the causes of much of that bitter experience lay in the macroeconomic environment.

I have claimed that associations furthered the polarization of rural inhabitants, but I have spoken so far only of impoverishment. Its other face was that associations, with their many unresolvable dilemmas, created breathing room for a commercial agriculture still in the process of forming. In part for the reasons I have given in this chapter, associations offered nascent commercial farmers little competition. By accustoming villagers to the idea of land leasing and thereby contributing to the development of a land market, however, associations contributed, instead, to making smallholders potential renters to such farmers. After their Association fell apart, Vlaiceni cast about anxiously for someone to come and work their land for them, regardless of the pay. For the 2000–2001 season, about half of the Association's 200 ha ended under the management of just such a person, a supertenant (of the sort to be described in chapters 7–8) who paid them 300 kg/ha. The unintended effect of association activity was to prepare the field for people like that to enter.

This said, I think it is mostly a mistake to see associations as failing because of competition from more efficient farmers. Throughout the 1990s those more efficient farmers were still struggling to get on their feet; few were in a position to offer anyone a serious challenge. Over a longer term, perhaps, they might have outcompeted any associations that still remained, in Transylvania or in Romania more broadly; during that decade, however, the "properly functioning markets" that would support their rise did not yet exist (see Bromley 2000). Mainly, associations were in competitive interaction with something else: the "inefficient" smallholders for whom they worked. In trying to keep costs down, they were hoping to break even and distribute the rest to shareholders (or pocket it themselves), not to accumulate more than some other association. They were not competing to get land from anyone except village households. When members withdrew land, it was usually not to give it to a more efficient competitor but for alternative options of a lesser kind: to work it, to give it in sharecropping arrangements that would return a bit more of their crop, or to sell it altogether. Only at the decade's end did commercial farmers offer a better alternative, but by then the Association was moribund for other reasons.

I propose, instead, that association agriculture failed precisely because it grew out of collective farms. The same structural space existed both before and after 1991: a space of rural production that the state served minimally, always sacrificing it to the needs of industry and planning for its eventual demise. This past, with its consequently disastrous CFs, meant first of all that associations began with a trust deficit—an absence of social capital, in Putnam's (1995) use of the term—that was far greater in Romania than in most other socialist countries, where collectives had fared better. As a sign of that deficit, after 1989 CF members all across Romania (although not in Vlaicu) had destroyed the CFs in fury. The second aspect of associations' socialist past was that insofar as agriculture received any attention after 1989, the chief beneficiaries were the state farms, just as before. In short, associations that collapsed for reasons similar to Vlaicu's show the ongoing values and priorities of socialist agriculture. Starting from a less well-endowed base, associations never contained enough accumulated value to become serious players in a market economy. Their accumulations were squandered in inflation, noncompetitive auctions, and excessive bank interest rates, if not in outright larceny by the unprincipled among their own staff. The result was a great monetary devaluation of agricultural assets all across the board.

In this, however, associations were the early subjects of the same processes that later afflicted state farms. Associations were one kind of transitional form; state farms were another, having an entirely different trajectory, rooted, once again, in their place in the hierarchy of socialist agriculture, as chapter 7 shows.

CHAPTER 7
THE DYNAMICS OF DECAPITALIZATION
THE FATE OF VLAICU'S STATE FARMS

Paradoxically, privatization is to a large extent not so much a process by which assets in the state sector become revitalized but a managed process of decline and retirement of a . . . substantial portion of these assets.
(Frydman and Rapaczynski 1994; 200)

What should have been happening here is a change in property form, from state property to individual property. Instead, we have the destruction of property values. It's as if you wanted to pour liquid from a ten-liter jug into a one-liter bottle. You do it, you're very happy you saved that liter, but you say nothing about the nine that were lost.
(State farm director whose farm has just been sold for a pittance)

In August 2000 I accompanied my friend Traian[*] Oproiu, director of State Farm 2, or SF2 (state farms had numbers, not names, in the socialist period), to the auction at which SF1, the state farm run by his cousin and business associate Radu, was to be sold. On the block was only the farm complex: the headquarters of SF1, some ten buildings occupying seven hectares of the farm's total 141 ha.[1] According to Law 18, any land on which buildings had been constructed during the socialist period was state property and its owners would receive land elsewhere—that is, the buildings would not be torn down. The remaining area, of course, belonged to Vlaiceni, who had been collecting dividends from the farm since 1991; they alone could sell that area, as individual owners, but only after it had been titled. Although Radu and Traian had hoped to be able to buy the farm themselves—that plan folded as the farm's debts mounted and Parliament produced no law for privatizing state farms—Radu was cheerful that at least someone was buying it. He hoped the buyer would be an Italian, Giovanni, who had expressed interest in the farm's location and with

* Pronounced "tra-YAHN."

An Italian bought one of Vlaicu's collective farm buildings, tore it down, and is setting up a furniture factory.

whom they had struck up a relationship. Even though Giovanni wanted to use the farm buildings not for agriculture but to manufacture parquet flooring, he was willing to hire Traian and Radu to work the land of any Vlaiceni who wanted him to. There were a number of Italians buying into Vlaicu's state farms: after the passage of a 1999 law that subjected state-owned forests to privatization, foreign wood processors and furniture makers suddenly developed great interest in Hunedoara's forested mountains.

The reason for the auction was that the director of the bank that handled the two farms' accounts had decided to call in a loan she had made to SF1 in 1994, even though they thought they had eight years to pay it off. But since the neoliberals had come to power and begun pushing the credit risks of loans onto the banks that had made them, all banks were coming under scrutiny and needed to remove some of their bad loans. The bank director had already sued for payment and won; today's auction would execute the court's judgment. For SF1's debt, the collateral was not the whole farm complex but two apartment blocks in which SF1 had housed its wage workers. These included Vlaicu's twenty-four families of Roma and other poor people who had been left without income when SF1 began to fail in 1997.[2] The bank, however, had insisted on auctioning not just these two buildings but the entire farm complex.[3] The starting price of

SF1 had been set at 2,286,000,000 lei (a figure Traian and Radu found much too low).[4]

The August auction was in fact the second one held for this farm; at the first, no buyer had shown up. Therefore, according to the normal procedure for privatizing Romania's state-owned enterprises (SOEs), the starting price in August was dropped substantially, in hopes of finding a buyer. This time the bidding would open at 1.5 billion lei, a full 33 percent lower than the initial price. To both Traian's and Giovanni's surprise, another potential buyer appeared at the August auction: a pair of Chinese from Hong Kong who had already spent large sums to buy the biggest state farm in the county and had started wood-processing factories (as well as a silk factory and a Chinese restaurant) elsewhere in Hunedoara. They had a reputation for getting what they wanted. Also present at the auction were the bank director and her legal counsel, Traian's accountant, Giovanni and his Romanian partner, the court executor who ran the auction, and a few other hangers-on like myself, for a total of fourteen people.

Although the Chinese began aggressively enough, they withdrew after only a few bids. Giovanni thus walked away with the farm for a total of 1,535,000,000 lei—at that time, worth approximately $75,000 (or 500 times Traian's monthly salary, equivalent to $150), a derisory price for these ten buildings. Traian was appalled: "He's bought this entire farm infrastructure for a third of what a German might spend on a house!" The tiny sum would barely cover the part of SF1's total debt that the bank had called in. The rest would now have to come from the sale of the other farm (SF2), whereas Traian had hoped to throw the entire debt of both halves onto Giovanni—for whom, he thought, it would seem a paltry sum.[5] Although Traian suspected the bank director of having taken a bribe from the Chinese to drop the starting price so low, he did not realize all the determinants of that price. The most important was the World Bank's advice to the Romanian government that it was more important to give state firms away than to quibble over the unresolvable question of asset evaluations, which would delay interminably the assignment of stable ownership rights and the reversal of Romania's economic decline.[6] He and Radu had become caught up in a process of devaluation whose parameters were well beyond their reach or that of any single bank director.

This auction (about which more later) leads us into a rather different world from that of collectives and their successor associations: the world of the third main entity that emerged from socialist agriculture, state farms. This was a world with which villagers had had relatively little contact before 1989, even though the farms were on village territory. Vlaiceni might on occasion steal some hay from state farm land for their cows at home or some corn for their chickens, and a few might do occasional wage work there; otherwise, their contacts with SF directors were infrequent, except in the rare case in which the director happened to live in the village itself. Therefore, the problems of trust and credibility that I raised in connection with the transformation of collective farms into associations afflicted the process of privatizing state farms rather less, at first.

For broader comparative purposes, it is important to recall the variation among countries of the former socialist bloc in how much land they had in state farms (see table 2.2, in chapter 2). First was the Soviet Union (68 percent of all land), then Romania and Czechoslovakia (30 percent each); Hungary, East Germany, and Poland had the least. These last three were less likely to have scenarios such as the ones I describe here, although we might find analogs there among chairmen of collectives, instead (e.g., see Lampland 2002). In East Germany, according to the Buechlers (2002, 300), with only 8 percent of the land in SFs that were heavily bureaucratized, it was CF managers who had more autonomy and experience making things work. The weight of land in state farms and of agriculture in Romania's budget gave the state farm lobby real power in Bucharest that one would be unlikely to find in Budapest or Warsaw.

This chapter shows a trajectory for state farms similar to the trajectories of individual households and associations, lagged by a few years. In describing those units, I did not have to go very far from Vlaicu. Chapter 5 was primarily about interactions among villagers or between them and Agromecs; chapter 6 was primarily about village-level relations that intersected with a fairly narrow range of other local institutions (Romcereal, fertilizer factories, Agromecs, local banks, and so on), with the occasional personal connection extending more widely. To show the trajectory of state farms, however, takes us well beyond these fairly local settings—even though the actual state farms were embedded in such settings, and in important ways. The difference reflects the different socialist property forms from which state and collective farms emerged after 1989.

As in the previous two chapters, I organize my description around the interconnected phenomena of risk, time horizons, capital endowments from the previous regime, and devaluation. Like the events I have already recounted, these too took place in a climate of constant uncertainty, concerning not just the prices for inputs and commodities but also whether state farms would be privatized or not. Law 18 had decollectivized only the CFs, leaving SFs intact, but no one knew for how long. The risks state farm directors faced were initially cushioned, however, by their continuing in their earlier mode, in which SOEs enjoyed soft budget constraints; they were not immediately crippled by the price scissors that so endangered smallholders and associations. At least for the early years, their losses did not put them out of business but were absorbed by the state budget. In some cases, this enabled their directors to build up a base for privatizing the farms they ran. Given budgetary cushions and the hoped-for privatization of SFs, directors planning to continue in agriculture could take a fairly long-term view. (Many chose instead to plunder the resources of their farms as much as possible, however, and then move on to something else.)

The events I narrate take us from a fully functioning and successful state farm to the moment of its auction as it teetered on the brink of bankruptcy. At each point in this slow hemorrhage of its financial value, its director sought to keep it alive through infusions of great effort and ingenuity, based in his endowment from socialist times. He exploited far-flung networks, expanding these to include possible foreign buyers who might help him remain with the farm if it were sold, and he made full use of his knowledge both of the changing politics of agriculture in Bucharest and of techniques for obtaining the best possible yields. None of these measures could overpower the many mechanisms of devaluation at work in bankrupting his farm, among them interminable delays in privatization while Bucharest politicians and state bureaucrats sought to manipulate that process to their own benefit.

Privatizing Romania's State Farms

Privatizing state farms was a very different proposition from dismantling collectives. To begin with, state farms participated, alongside all other SOEs, in that most privileged form, state property. They had been fully governed by the national planning process—unlike CFs, whose existence was framed by the locales from which they derived their land even though they too were part of national plans. In addition, because SFs were generally formed from land that had been nationalized or confiscated, their owner, technically speaking, was "the whole people," not just the local villagers whose land it had been. Unlike collectives, state farms often had large investments—plantings of vineyards or orchards, complex installations for growing hops or vegetables, huge irrigation systems, and so on (see table 1.1, in chapter 1). One could not privatize a firm laden with collective investments and belonging to the whole people simply by giving the land in it back to original owners. There were other values to consider, such as what would happen to all the socialist wealth that SFs contained.

Finally, the two kinds of farms were differently organized, and the differences affected their extrication paths. CFs were grouped into communes and then into multicommune organizations subordinated to their county's Agriculture Department, itself part of the Ministry of Agriculture. SFs bypassed the commune altogether and were grouped in what I call *state-farm systems* (SFSs), several per county; these were further aggregated into *trusts* comprising multiple counties. Besides the directors of farms and farm systems, the state farm organization included directors of institutions that linked the various segments together—such as the entities that gathered animal fodder used to supply multiple SFs, or the state procurement centers (later to become Romcereal), which received crops from both CFs and SFs and redirected them to food-processing industries.

Because the heads of these various entities were very powerful, after 1989 they formed highly consequential lobbies at the level of national policy-making. As state enterprises, SFs' postsocialist transformation presented very different problems from those of the collapsing CFs: the process implicated not just officials based primarily in villages, communes, and (occasionally) counties but the entire bureaucracy that continued to manage state property and later, ostensibly, to privatize it. Therefore, any SF director after 1989 participated in circles and events of much larger scope than did anyone formerly attached to collectives. Their insertion into the national economy meant that even in their very localized contexts of action, SF directors were forced to think more globally—and were drawn into more global forces—than any specialist directing a post-CF association would be. The structural position of state farms as heirs to a specific kind of socialist entity makes their story very different from those told in chapters 5 and 6.

There is no good account of the national politics of state farm privatization for Romania; I can offer only some elements of one. They begin with the Iliescu government's decision to protect the status of SFs as state enterprises, arguing that SFs would feed Romania's population while the shift to private agriculture was taking place in the former collectives. In 1991, therefore, people who had land in the SFs were made not owners, as were those with land in CFs, but shareholders. There was at first no talk of their removing their land from SF management. Shareholders were to receive dividends from the proceeds of the farm, if there were any. The Ministry of Agriculture set these at a minimum of 300 kg of wheat (or cash equivalent) for every hectare one had in the state farm's perimeter; this figure was later raised, although many state farms were by then in such financial trouble that they could not pay more.

By 1994, extensive pressure from various quarters produced a Law on Land Rental (Law 16/1994) specifying, inter alia, that people with land in state farms should consider themselves not shareholders in the SF corporation but real owners of the land, and that in five years they would have the opportunity to withdraw their land from the state farms if they wished. In short, state farms would eventually be privatized. Over the next several years, however, Parliament proved unable to determine whether and how that would occur. As von Hirschhausen observes, "The state had too much invested in state farms to relinquish control over this productive apparatus, and thereby risk their massive devaluation" (1997, 73). The balance of power was almost equally matched between, on the one hand, powerful politicians and wheat speculators in southern and eastern Romania, who wanted unmediated access to the products of continued state farming, and, on the other, various groups that pushed for privatization (including the neoliberal parties, the IMF and World Bank, and some state farm directors).

A key player in this battle was senator Triță Făniță, from southern Romania. In socialist times he had worked in the Ministry of Agriculture and then become director of Agroexport, a firm engaged in grain commerce on the international market, which he turned into a business lucrative both for himself and for the secret police to whom he paid protection money. After 1989 Făniță moved into big-time grain speculation, which included flooding the Romanian market with foreign wheat (for which he received a commission) and undercutting internal production. He then become involved in politics and was elected to Parliament for the Agrarian Democratic Party of Romania (ADPR), the party of the agrarian elite. From the vantage point of the chairmanship of the Senate's Agriculture Committee he was able to influence legislation concerning the future of state farms, which he and people of like mind hoped to keep in existence for as long as possible so as to exploit the SFs' productive capacity for personal gain. An ally of Iliescu's PRSD, the ADPR entrenched itself firmly at all levels of the Ministry of Agriculture; it also worked to keep SFs intact and to continue some form of centralized procurement (von Hirschhausen 1997, 57). When the PRSD lost to the neoliberal DC in 1996, however, the ADPR entered the new coalition government. Still representing the state farm lobby, Făniță continued to obstruct passage of a privatization law for state farms from this new vantage point. Only in 2001 was a law passed. This lengthy delay allowed the SFs to hemorrhage much of their accumulated value by accruing huge debts and arrears (Mungiu-Pippidi and Althabe 2002, 177–78).

For the first several years, SF directors adopted one of several options.

1. Some engaged in grain speculation or ran their farms chiefly for their own benefit, maintaining them as state rather than private firms and giving minimal dividends (if any) to the land's putative owners. Complex procedures at length enabled SF directors to separate their farms from the larger state-farm systems into which they were grouped in each county. This permitted them independent action but was not yet full privatization. The farms remained state-owned enterprises.

2. Some directors conducted spontaneous privatizations, buying up or otherwise acquiring farms that were strictly speaking not yet available; they hoped these privatizations would hold once the legal framework was established. The director would cease participating in his SF system and use the SF's buildings and equipment as if they were his own, working the land that was in transit to private ownership. As a new farm proprietor, he might acknowledge the claims of prior landowners, giving them some sort of payment.

3. Some SF directors encouraged former landowners not to wait for five years but to claim rights to their SF land at once and then offered to work it for them in some kind of leasing arrangement.

4. Some waited for the rules for SF privatization to be clarified, meanwhile working their farms as best they could within the existing SF system and its practices. However, as state-farm systems increasingly collapsed, this path became very difficult, leading to devaluations and failures. At this point, foreign investors and others could profit from their problems and buy the farms at auction. (This was the path taken by Traian and Radu.)

With the election of a neoliberal coalition in 1996, the pace of privatizing increased, although Parliament still could not agree on how to do it for state farms. Debate focused on whether sitting directors would be allowed to buy their farms or not. If yes, it was argued, that would privilege the old communist agrarian elite; they were in the best position to monopolize units they already controlled and might privatize in a manner detrimental to the welfare of SF shareholders. If no, then the buyers might be nonelites unlikely to have appropriate farming knowledge; the result would be to exclude people who actually knew how to manage this kind of enterprise, in a climate in which few other such people were likely to present themselves. SFs might then become the property of buyers (often foreign, in partnership with a Romanian who legalized the affair) who had no interest in agriculture and who planned—like Traian and Radu's Giovanni—to use the SF infrastructure for something else entirely. Although in some respects this might make good business sense, to villagers and larger farmers it felt unnatural.

Any privatization of a state enterprise was managed by a body called the State Property Fund, or SPF, set up in 1991. Comparable organizations were set up in most Eastern European countries, such as the State Property Agency in Hungary and the Treuhandanstalt in eastern Germany.[7] For any specific case, such as Radu's farm, the SPF created an administrative council and a board called a Shareholders' General Assembly to oversee the process. The assembly consisted of three or more people, appointed by members of two official bodies (the State Property Fund and its corresponding Private Property Fund) from among their cronies; these people often had no connection whatever with the firm in question and no knowledge about its production processes. Conspicuously absent from the assembly were any of the small shareholders, such as the people who had worked in that SOE (or had land in that state farm) and held coupons entitling them to some share in it. These assemblies created the impression for western lending agencies that shareholders were represented and that the SOE's board was diversified beyond parochial interests.

In fact, however, such councils and assemblies were an opportunity for middle-level members of the old Party networks to provide income for one another: with each privatizing SOE, every council and assembly member received a fee for attending each of the obligatory monthly meetings, plus an honorarium that amounted to a whopping 20 percent of the salary of the director, as well as transportation and expenses. The connection between their incomes and the income of the firm's director was the main factor driving the constant increases in the salaries of state-enterprise directors (including those in SFs) during the 1990s. With many firms to be privatized, there were many such councils, generating interlocking directorates based in reciprocal favors. These councils and assemblies also permitted higher authorities to maintain surveillance over SOEs and keep a finger on the pulse so as to preempt spontaneous privatizations where these might prove inconvenient. One restive SF director, disgusted with the meddling of his council, gave me the following analogy: "Let's say you and I each have a family. Any time there's a problem in my family, you insist on sending someone over."

In other words, for bodies such as the State Property Fund and its associated shareholders' assembly, the state enterprises that western accounting firms judged worthless in budgetary terms were loaded with assets of the kind most important to former Party bosses: opportunities for political patronage, reciprocity, and enrichment. Under these circumstances, it is hardly surprising that privatization of SFs, and of SOEs more generally, proceeded so slowly; the bureaucrats in SF systems, in the SPF, in assemblies, and in administrative councils had no interest whatever in killing the goose that laid them golden eggs. To push for privatization would end their interlocking directorates and mutual back-scratching. Instead, they sought ways of postponing the chance that these asset-rich entities would hive off into independence.

Initially, one means to this end was for the SPF to assign a privatizing SOE an excessively high monetary value. SOE directors, as well as higher bodies such as the SF systems, collaborated in this (if they did not, indeed, initiate it) by seeking high evaluations of fixed assets so they could obtain from their bank-director friends mammoth loans, guaranteed by the evaluations assessed for their firms. Many of them squandered or pocketed these loans, thus contributing to a chain of bank failures.[8] Then, following the 1996 election of the neoliberals in place of the privatization-resistant postcommunists, evaluation trends shifted. Now, under strong pressure from the World Bank and IMF, the new government stepped up the process of privatizing state enterprises so as to staunch the drain of subsidies from the state budget into SOEs. This was a serious matter: an official at the Ministry of Agriculture informed me in 1997 that state farms had eaten up subsidies worth 30 trillion lei! Because it was difficult to find buyers for firms bearing such excessive evaluations, these international agencies pushed the Romanian government to sell firms at whatever price it could get, even if that did not reflect their potential value. The point was, in the World Bank–IMF view, to put property rights in the hands of responsible individuals as fast as possible and give up trying to determine what the firms were actually worth.

The result was a vast devaluation, in budgetary terms, of the wealth accumulated under socialism. From this time on, firms were assessed at sometimes astoundingly low figures, with the actual sale price potentially even lower. Sometimes the evaluations were low because potential buyers had given the evaluators large bribes to ensure a cheap price. Sometimes it was because bureaucrats wanted to buy the firms for themselves: low evaluations benefited SOE directors and other powerful persons, who could purchase the firms for a song. Although the assets thus acquired might not impress a foreign investor, there might be ways of profiting from them nonetheless, if only by dismantling them to sell on the international scrap-metal market—for which Eastern Europe and especially Romania were providing a rich supply. Whatever the reason, the values assessed for state enterprises, including state farms, were political values that did not reflect a firm's economic potential. It is thus important to realize that the devaluation was, for the moment, largely budgetary; the firm might still have value politically. The disjunction between budgetary and political valuings is evident if we note that a low price on the books was likely to be shadowed by a bribe that would greatly increase the real price.

There were a number of mechanisms for these devaluations, which took place not only in Romania but all across the former socialist bloc (see, e.g., Lampland 2002; Staniszkis 1991a; Stark 1996). One was for the director of the firm to set up a side company into which the SOE's assets were gradually drained, leaving nothing in the SOE for evaluators to find. Another was to put constant pressure on a firm's resources, forcing it to sell off items of equipment or other goods in order to meet its continued costs. The obligatory monthly council/assembly meetings did this also, by multiplying manyfold the sums the SOE had to pay in addition to the (sizable) directors' salaries. Yet another mechanism was ghost auctions—a buyer would express interest in a firm, an auction would be announced, the buyer would not show up nor would anyone else bid on the firm, and the process would be reiterated. The price would drop by 10–25 percent each time, until the buyer finally presented himself and bought the firm for much less than its initial evaluation. Insider information and bribes to bank officials or to the court executors conducting such auctions could easily ensure that a desired firm would go through one or more iterations until its price was acceptable to a hopeful purchaser. That had been Giovanni's procedure in buying Radu's SF. In Romania, these means of squandering state assets increased in 2000, when the neoliberals, facing inevitable electoral defeat, issued a government decree that all SOEs should privatize even where the legal framework for doing so was incomplete, as with state farms.

From what I have said, we see that the interests of the bureaucrats managing the privatization process were fairly unambiguous: they wanted first to delay it with high evaluations and then, under the neoliberals (1996–2000), to collude in lowering the prices and thus collect huge bribes or prime assets for themselves. The interests of individual SOE directors, on the other hand, were more contradictory. A high evaluation would enable them to secure bigger bank loans for modernizing their firms or some other purpose, whereas a low one would enable them to buy the SF cheap, if that became possible. If it did not, their interest would depend on what exit strategy they envisioned. Should they hope to establish a partnership with an eligible buyer who would keep them on as the effective manager, they would prefer high evaluations if they needed to repay debts or take out loans, but low ones if they themselves and not their presumptive partner were actually paying the purchase price.

Some directors (although perhaps not many) had yet another interest at stake, namely, their sense of dignity and their attachment to the results of their work. This was Radu's reaction to the low sale price of SF1: it assaulted his sense of pride in a farm that had once performed admirably. Traian, too, arguing in 1999 for a higher sale price for SF2, observed, "I'm the one with a moral connection to this farm, the one who feels embarrassed when people come to look at it and find a mess." In 2000, explaining why he still had not resigned even though his SF was totally inactive, he said, "I personally have nothing to lose by resigning, but I don't want to just drop everything and walk away. I want to have someone to leave it to." For both men, the devaluation of their state farms struck at the heart of their self-image as excellent farmers. Here we see once again, although in a different context, the values expressed by smallholders in chapter 4: an identification of character and self-concept with evidence of skilful work.

The common stereotype of state farm directors has no place for this sort of pride in accomplishment. That stereotype is of grasping, corrupt agrarian elites depriving lowly villagers of their due and manipulating information to take advantage of any opportunity for gain. Throughout the 1990s myriad television and newspaper reports propagated that image, as did villagers in ordinary conversation. Aside from sometimes characterizing real persons, however, the stereotype of the grasping and corrupt SF director may also have been propagated by bureaucrats higher up, who resented those SF directors prepared to strike out on their own and wanted to turn other Romanians against them. SF directors were in the unenviable position of appearing as villains all around: to villagers, who did not understand the pressures they were under, and also to higher-level bureaucrats, who feared the loss of valuable political assets if SF directors became independent.

There may be some regional variation in the truth of this stereotype, which haughty Transylvanians associate especially with Romania's more "balkan" Regat—perhaps with good reason. As I show in chapter 6 (table 6.3), Regat SFs were much bigger than those in Transylvania—by over one thousand hectares in the case of arable land. This gave Regat directors more economic weight than those in Transylvania and greater power relative to villagers. In consequence, I suspect that there was little competition among Regat SF directors for land to rent. By contrast, the smaller farms, less fertile soils, and greater population density in Transylvania created much more competition among their directors, who had to seduce village owners away from other potential tenants and might therefore treat villagers somewhat better. Whether for this reason or some other, the Transylvania SF directors I happened to encounter did not seem as ruthless as the stereotypes. They managed to persuade me of the tremendous obstacles they faced, thus enabling me to present the dilemmas of state-farm privatization with sympathy. Because it is unlikely that my associates were unique, the picture I present might be more broadly generalizable to other SF directors (Transylvanian ones, at least), calling into question the widespread public image of them as monsters.

Vlaicu has an unusually large number of state farms in its perimeter, but their directors are rather easily identifiable. In chapter 6 the easy identification of individuals was less of a problem because the two principals had left Vlaicu for distant places. Here, I try to protect my subjects by modifying and concealing some information, as well as blending into this account information received from SF directors in neighboring settlements. Thus, not everything I say about Traian and Radu is strictly true of them, but overall the picture I present is fully in keeping with the possibilities open to SF directors like them in this period of Transylvania's history.[9]

State Farms in Vlaicu

In 1948, Vlaicu's agricultural surface totaled about 1,287 ha.[10] Soon thereafter a proto–state farm (SF Aurel Vlaicu) was formed, which by 1950 contained 365 ha from several settlements.[11] From this farm were split off two other farms, one specializing in medicinal plants (1972) and one a vineyard (1980). The area under state management grew by bringing in land from the CF to create a chicken farm and a fifth SF, a fishery. In decollectivization figures from 1992, Vlaicu's entire surface area is given as 1,439 ha, 803 of it in SFs: the chicken farm held 27 ha, the fishery 100 ha, the medicinal plant farm 141 ha, the vineyard 132 ha, and the original farm, which now specialized in pigs, 405 ha. All these farms held land from other villages in addition to Vlaicu—that is, they all straddled the administrative boundaries of villages, communes, and even counties.

Vlaicu's five SFs participated in a larger SF system containing eleven farms, each specializing in some agricultural product: hops, dairy products (supported by grain-farming), vegetables, fruits, fowl, pigs, and so on. The system was centered in Simeria, a city to the west; I refer to this administrative center as *SFS-Simeria* (State-Farm System Simeria), or *the center*. During the socialist period, several of these farms did reasonably well, especially the pig and medicinal plant farms. The former had won performance prizes, and the latter was the only one in its SF system to have run a budgetary surplus every year from its creation until 1996. Success did not always mean surpluses, however, for state-set prices mostly prevented those, and savvy farm directors knew that a surplus one year could mean a raised target the next.

As of 1991, the directors of these and Vlaicu's other farms expected to continue with their jobs for the foreseeable future because the privatization of SFs was not then on the political agenda. They continued under the same arrangements with SFS-Simeria as before. Among those were that farm directors did not manage their own budgets, nor, in theory, did they have to procure their own supplies or find their own markets (in fact, however, directors often had to scramble for resources and markets on their own, like anyone else in the economy of shortage). They were supposed to receive from the center timely delivery of the necessary inputs (gas, seeds, fertilizer, 'cides, etc.), which the center bought with the pooled incomes of all the farms. They then delivered their produce to Romcereal, whence it entered into wider plans for feeding the population; the income went directly to SFS-Simeria, where no account was taken of who had produced it. The surplus of one would go to rectifying the deficits of the others. All sums borrowed for investments in any one farm came from the budget of the system as a whole.

Thus, from 1991 to 1994 state farms had fewer of the difficulties I have described for both individual households and associations. I can cover in a few short sentences their processes of mobilizing land, labor, and inputs, which it took me the better part of two long chapters to describe for those other production entities. SF directors were embedded in far-flung networks of both horizontal and vertical connections and benefited from the most expert knowledge and the best agricultural technology available in Romania. The land in the five SFs was captive and would remain so for the foreseeable future. Directors required minimal labor because much of the work was mechanized and capital- rather than labor-intensive. Only the medicinal plants farm required much manual labor, which came from the workers it housed in two apartment blocks and paid from the center's budget. Although the center was not always timely in its deliveries, it initially provided the SFs with most of their basic material inputs and investments. Like anyone who dealt with Romcereal, the SFs were constrained to accept the state price for their goods but were mostly spared the problem of finding markets.

Beginning with the Land Rental Law of 1994, however, all these advantages began gradually to crumble, as SFS-Simeria ceased to perform its duties, leaving its directors high and dry. In the next section, I describe at length the dynamics of the devaluation that ensued. My principal teachers were Traian and Radu, as well as several other former or present SF directors associated with their SF system and with SFs in neighboring Şibot, Romos, and Vinerea.

From Showcase State Farm to the Auction Block

Trained as agronomists, both Traian and Radu had worked for their entire lives in the socialist agricultural sector. Thus, both were deeply implicated in state-based agricultural production and had many contacts of a sort that far exceeded the social capital of anyone else in Vlaicu. Radu had spent many years as director of SF1, which produced raw material for the Romanian pharmaceutical industry. Traian had held several positions in socialist agriculture and its state-based successors; in the 1990s he was first the director of a large state concern nearby, then Radu's chief agronomist at SF1, and finally director of SF2 in 1997. Two years later he and Radu combined their two farms into a single entity (al-

A state farm near Vlaicu, which used to grow hops for Romania's beer industry (photo by author).

though it was still two farms from the point of view of creditors and privatizers). The story of their farms' devaluation begins with Radu.

The State Pulls Out, but Not Enough

An unusually conscientious and energetic person, Radu had built SF1 from scratch into a top-notch facility (using state investments, of course), which throughout his tenure, unlike other farms in the SF group, had reliably earned a surplus.[12] Owing to both his success and the nature of his crop, Radu's budget was very large, among the largest in the entire county even though at 141 ha his farm was relatively small. He was the darling of the SFS-Simeria central office, because with his surplus each year they could cover most of the debts of the other farms. The other SF directors, Radu complained to me, would sell some of their goods directly and pocket the earnings, thus producing a "loss" while he turned in a gain. Although he did not say as much, his surplus resulted in part from the specificity of his crop, which could be marketed only in bulk to a specific buyer, not in small pocketable increments. SFS-Simeria sold the entire product directly to pharmaceutical firms, so the money never flowed through his hands at all.

When the 1991 land law was passed, its main effect on Radu was that he was

now expected to pay his new shareholders—villagers from Vlaicu and other settlements who claimed land within the perimeter of SF1—the Ministry of Agriculture's prescribed 300 kg of wheat (or cash equivalent, at the state price) per
hectare of land claimed. In 1993, this did not pose an excessive burden: at the
state price of 100 lei/kg, it meant paying 3.9 million lei from an income of 140
million. The next year he chose to pay far more than the established minimum,
giving villagers 1,000 kg/ha and telling me, "We had good profits, so we should
give our shareholders more." (The sum did not come out of Radu's pocket, in
any case, but out of the surplus his crop brought the center that year.) Villagers
were happy to have received the equivalent of a month's top industrial pension
for having done absolutely nothing.

Even after the prospect arose of shareholders' recovering their land, Radu
was not concerned. His aim was to run a privatized SF1 either as its owner,
should this be possible, or as its administrator for some other, perhaps foreign,
buyer. He thought it unlikely that his shareholders would actually want to pull
out their land, owing to the special installations necessary for growing his crops,
including an underground irrigation system and numerous pipes sunk in
meter-square concrete blocks across the farm's surface. It seemed unlikely that
former owners would want to recover their land in tiny cement-and-pipe-
ridden parcels. Owing to his long record of making money with his farm, he expected that villagers would prefer to receive the handsome cash dividends he
would be able to pay and would not, therefore, sue to recover their individual
parcels. He knew he would eventually have to repair parts of the installation,
which was aging, and more immediately would have to buy new tractors and
other equipment to replace the rusting pieces among his inventory. Nonetheless, the farm was running a surplus and would continue to do so, he hoped, as
long as the process of privatizing it did not drag on too long.

Radu had two main problems. One was that, like all SF directors, he paid
dividends from a total harvest that he did not fully control; therefore local mayors implementing Law 18 took great advantage of him by assigning him more
shareholders than actually had land in his SF. The mayors then used those additional shareholders' actual land to solve a problem case or for some nefarious
purpose. I have described this elsewhere (Verdery 1994), speaking of SFs as
"rubber sacks." When Radu at length obtained an old map showing every parcel by owner and challenged the mayor's list, the mayor was furious: "It's your
business to pay people, not to verify who should be paid!" Being a rubber sack
would have posed no problem if SFS-Simeria had been functioning as it was
supposed to. Once it stopped supplying its state farms with inputs, however, directors needed every bit of income to cover their own costs and maintain their
infrastructure. Each unwarranted name on their list of shareholders meant in-

come they were not using on their farm. Whereas the true shareholders were draining the farm's productive potential by not reinvesting their dividends in it, the false shareholders were draining it even further. In this way, local mayors contributed to undercutting the SFs' operating budgets.

Radu's second problem was that because Law 18 had not touched the state farms at all, they continued to work under the old arrangements. His remained attached to the ten others in the larger SF system and was prevented from functioning independently. If he needed gas for plowing, money to pay his workers, fertilizer, seed, or other inputs, he had to apply to the SF center for them; when the bureaucrats there got around to it, they might send what he had requested. During the socialist period he had usually gotten what he asked for, but after 1989, with the long-term prospects of SFs in question, the bureaucrats at SFS-Simeria lost interest in running the farms and began to diversify their portfolios (we might say), using for other purposes the money that was supposed to keep the group's farms running. They also ceased to find markets for the SFs' products—yet still required SF directors to send all their revenues to the center and apply there for inputs. The revenues disappeared into the central office and the inputs arrived more and more haphazardly. Thus began a long saga for the directors, involving much ingenuity, determination, and discouragement.

For example, as of 1996, Radu had not received fertilizer from the center for five years. Because he did not have his own bank account, he could not simply go and buy some, as would Anda of the Vlaicu Association. Instead, he worked out deals with the director of a dairy SF, who sold him manure at well below the usual price (he would reciprocate with some favor later). He did not have to pay for it; because the whole SF group budget was pooled, he had only to write on a piece of paper that his colleague had transferred the asset to him and the cost of it would be deducted from his totals at the end of the year.

This system of accounting had advantages and drawbacks. On the one hand, if Radu needed bank loans to start his production cycle (and many SFs did), the weight of the SF group as a whole, with its tremendous infrastructure to serve as collateral, made him a credit-worthy borrower. Without the SFS, his farm might not be judged credit-worthy on its own. Thus, inclusion in an SF group was a condition of an individual SF's ability to produce. On the other hand, all such borrowing—by both individual SFs and the central office—entered into the system's total pool of debts. In the socialist period these had few consequences for any individual farm, but, beginning in 1995, the center began to divide its debts among the constituent farms in proportion to their budgets.

Therefore, although Radu had kept away from banks and mobilized his resources by other means—thus adding nothing to the SFS's debts—he was nonetheless assigned a hefty share (owing to his large budget) of the burgeoning arrears being racked up by SFS-Simeria as a whole. Other SF directors sought loans and credits ostensibly to modernize their farms, perhaps using the money to repay loans taken earlier. SFS-Simeria itself took out huge loans to start a milk-processing business, but much of the money reportedly went for bribes, payoffs, and their own incomes; that debt, too, was apportioned among the constituent SFs. Given the rate of inflation (300 percent in 1993, gradually settling into a regular 30–40 percent rate thereafter), the value of a loan might be shed simply by waiting a while; this was how some Vlaiceni had bought tractors. But the high interest rates and stiff penalties for nonpayment of debts more than offset this advantage.

In fall 1993, Radu, who had run a large surplus, asked for money to buy inputs now for the following season, when they would be more expensive. The center refused. In March 1994, when he asked again for his inputs, they told him to wait a few weeks and they would have the money to buy what he needed—but he needed it now. Thus, for the first time Radu was forced to take a loan to begin production. Throughout that season Radu found himself more hindered than helped by the SF center. When he complained about not having any money to pay his workers, the center told him to sell off a tractor to meet his payroll. They were not helping him to find markets for his crops, telling him to do it instead because he had the appropriate contacts. Because he lacked inputs, he was unable to work 15 ha of land in Şibot, but when he proposed renting the land to a commercial farmer there, the center declined, saying, "It's not yours to give to others." Radu's comment later: "So it's better to have nothing grow on it than to let me take a bit of initiative." Gradually he came to believe that the center really had no interest in his success but was prepared to destroy his productive potential, having spent years profiting from his results. Then, as soon as he started to sink, they would plunder his fixed capital. He decided that the moment to privatize was now, while he still had any fixed capital at all, and he began making inquiries.

Although some SF directors had already sought to pull their farms out of the SF group and work on their own, when the center got wind of Radu's interest in doing so they let him know they would never permit it. Presumably, the income he provided them, even if decreasing, was still useful; moreover, he thought, they would rather run his valuable farm into the ground so they could profit either from buying it themselves or by taking a bribe from some other potential buyer.[13] That is, Radu's farm represented an asset to the center in two forms: as a producer of surpluses against the system's debts and as a defunct firm that still had all its buildings intact, in a good location that could tempt a future investor. To be sure Radu got the message that he could not make it on his own, they stopped sending him gasoline deliveries, thus crippling his ability to harvest on time.

In 1994 as we discussed the possibility of his gaining his independence, Radu told me of a conversation he had had with his superiors in Simeria:

I told the director I didn't have enough gas, enough fertilizer, enough pesticide this year because he didn't give it to me, but still I had all this profit. He replied, "You can break off relations whenever you want." But what does this mean? It means I can try to privatize. They'll send people to evaluate my fixed capital and will put a mammoth price on it. I have a colleague who's decided to try it, and I keep my ear to the ground, say to the director, 'You know, X is thinking of privatizing,' and the director says, 'But who's going to let him!! Aren't we the ones who'll set the evaluation?' So they make you stand still. You can't leave the SF system, and you can't give any extra to your shareholders.

A colleague who managed to privatize a vegetable farm confirmed this: "When Radu raised the possibility, they [Simeria] said, 'We'll show you!'"

From this time on, the center's "negligence" compelled Radu to engage in one after another creative scheme to finance his operations. He asked the head of the pharmaceutical firm with which he had long done business to give him credits worth half the value of his crop for 1995. This would enable him to avoid another bank loan if the center did not serve him and to pay his workers through the full season. (The idea did not pan out.) Already he had reduced his expenditures for labor by hiring pensioners and the unemployed, because one was exempt from payroll tax (31 percent) for these kinds of employees.[14] On occasion he rented out his tractors and drivers to villagers for 60 percent of the Agromec cost so as to make extra money to buy gasoline.

It is likely that Radu was far from the norm of SF directors, although the problems he encountered were common to all of them. As early as 1994 he was having insomnia, trying to figure out how not to go bankrupt. In a sense, he was a bad socialist manager: he did not play the game of soft budget constraints but acted as if they were hard, and he failed to milk the system. He had a market-economy perspective according to which assets and liabilities are the same budgetary concepts that they were for international accountants. Even in the socialist period he had thought in these terms, generating a yearly surplus on his farm while most of his fellow directors were seeing budgetary losses as an asset. In their view, gain was a liability, simply swallowed up in a pooled account and in no way rewarded. For this reason, when Radu and a colleague proposed in 1994 that all directors in the SF system request subaccounts with budgetary autonomy, all rejected it; they benefited too much from having their losses covered by the group arrangement.

In 1996, Radu turned in a surplus to SFS-Simeria; it would be his last. The market for his product in Romania was collapsing as foreign pharmaceuticals entered partnerships with Romanian ones and required would-be suppliers to make very costly investments in new equipment, which he could not possibly make. Because several firms he had dealt with no longer bought from local growers, in 1996 Radu could not sell his whole crop. He tried to bribe a potential buyer with an expensive fur coat but was told, "You come with a fur coat! To get our business, you come with 5,000 deutsche marks or 5,000 dollars!" (an immense sum in Romania then). But how was he to do that with no control over his own purse? Three years later he still had 1.5 billion lei worth of unsold crops in his warehouse—enough to pay off his mounting debt, if only he could find a buyer.

In 1997 things changed significantly in one respect: Radu, Traian, and another director pushed for the division of SFS-Simeria into its constituent farms, although all would continue to be SFs. Their argument, which the other SF directors now bought, was that because the entire SF system was so far in debt, the center gave no one anything any more; therefore, directors had no reason to pay their revenues to the center but should keep their incomes for their own use. Henceforth, although they were still state farm employees and could not keep their earnings, they would pay their own salaries and expenses for inputs from what they could make by selling their product, only then turning the remainder over to the center.

The change was more helpful to some directors than to those specializing in industrial crops. Dairy products, animals, and many fruits and vegetables can be sold year-round, bringing in a constant stream of income that can be used to buy seed, fertilizer, pesticides, and gasoline for plowing, as needed. Cereals too can be stored and then marketed in small batches throughout the year. Radu's crops, by contrast, could not simply be taken to market every Saturday or sold at will but were usually sold in bulk at the end of the growing season—if at all. It made no sense to continue growing an unsalable product; instead, Radu now planted his entire surface to the more marketable tobacco, wheat, barley, and sugar beets. He selected the crops carefully: for all but the barley there was a guaranteed market, and for tobacco the government not only guaranteed purchase but also gave credits to start the production cycle. This plan put Radu in the same position as other SF directors with more readily marketable products: he could spend a day at the marketplace whenever he needed cash, selling as much as two tonnes of grain by the bag. (Unlike Anda and Nica in chapter 6, he had no councilors there to dictate his price, so he always sold his product.) For him, it was a great liberation not to have to beg the center for every leu and then wait six months for them to respond. He could give his crop in kind to shareholders or sell it piecemeal to pay them cash; he could use his new cash income to pay for additional inputs, for workers' salaries, and for at least some degree of upkeep on the farm buildings and other inventory.

The need for creative financing continued, however. When the center failed to send money for gasoline, for example, he called on the director of a firm that bought scrap metal for sale on the international market, to whom he offered some still-usable irrigation pipes.[15] Selling as few as possible (to keep from destroying his irrigation system altogether), he received enough cash for a month's supply of gas, which he used to put pesticide on his crop before it was totally consumed. Meanwhile, having no cash, he was paying his workers by assigning them hayfields to reap for animal feed. (The workers too found the pipes irresistible, dismantling them to sell as scrap so as to complete their unpaid wages.) As time passed, to cover expenses and meet his payroll, he had to sell more and more scrap metal, then some farm equipment, thus unwillingly decapitalizing the farm into which he had put many years of intense and dedicated effort—and which he had hoped to buy before it was completely ruined. He had to be careful, however, lest he be visited by the Financial Guard, ever vigilant to clever subterfuges to which the center might alert them. He did not want to end his directorship in jail.

From 1997 on, Radu and Traian struggled to derive income from their two farms, which they combined into one in 1999. Their wide network of contacts and kin proved invaluable. For instance, in 1997 a brother-in-law, director of a Belgian-Romanian joint venture, arranged a contract for them that included supplying them with seed and other inputs; the firm then bought the entire crop at a price that covered the remaining costs. Although Radu's yields had been so good that he received a premium, the next year the firm decided to import its material after all. Other connections helped them obtain gas and herbicide on credit from people they knew. Radu acknowledged that contacts of this kind had been essential to getting him through some very difficult times, and that they would stand him in good stead if he and Traian ended up striking out on their own. Their tie with SFS-Simeria, however, was undermining not just their farm but their social capital as well. For example, Liviu, a good friend from Radu's university days, sold herbicides and pesticides and asked if Radu would buy some. Because Radu could not buy directly, he told Liviu to make a contract through SFS-Simeria. At the end of the season, however, the center did not pay Liviu, and Radu was unable to repay the sum himself even though he had a large surplus because the bank would not give him access to the money. A couple of years later, the original bill for 4–5 million was now 11 million, and Liviu was angry. So was Radu, whose lifetime friendship with Liviu had been destroyed.

By 1999, with no SF privatization law in sight, the uncertain future and their financial difficulties caused the cousins to leave a portion of their SFs' land unworked: like the Vlaicu Association, they simply did not have the money to cultivate it. For two years their pay to shareholders had stagnated at 300 kg/ha. Radu explained, "We're supposed to pay shareholders from our surplus, but we had none!" Combining their farms had now saddled them with regular meetings of their SPF-imposed shareholders' assembly and administrative council, each requiring them to pay out one-and-a-half times Traian's salary for every member.[16] At that point it was around 5 million lei/month, very large by Romanian standards (his council had raised it to increase their honoraria), and all this money had somehow to come from their operating budgets, to which the center contributed nothing. To pay for his meeting in summer 1999, Traian even had to sell some pigs. It was partly to fund these unnecessary gatherings that they could no longer pay their SF shareholders and had to give their workers hay to reap instead of a cash wage.

One final point illuminates Traian's and Radu's fortunes during this time: they were in the losing faction of politics in their state-farm system. Not all SF directors received as little help and as much obstruction as they did. The SFs attached to Vlaicu were largely united in opposition to the center in Simeria, whereas those in Geoagiu and Romos were its allies. Traian's explanation involved shady deals, nepotism, and sexual favors to one of the center's officials. Regardless of the truth, there had clearly been long-term disagreement between SFS-Simeria and most of Vlaicu's SF directors, beginning with the tenure of one of these as head of a multi–state farm fodder complex. From that vantage point, he could see better than other SF directors exactly what game SFS-Simeria was playing and could encourage his colleagues to resist it. Perhaps Vlaicu's location at the county border also contributed to their resistance: SF directors there had regular contact with those in neighboring Alba county, where the state-farm system was encouraging successful SF privatization rather than thwarting it.

Planning for a Privatized Future

Why, readers might ask, were these two directors working like dogs and having insomnia to eke out a living from their ever-more-bankrupt farms when other specialists were privatizing spontaneously or plundering their SFs? Why did they not simply resign or do the same? There are two sure answers to this question and a third likely one. The first answer is that even though it was impossible to privatize right then, as long as there was some hope of buying their farms Radu and Traian strove to keep these sufficiently valuable as to be worth picking up later. Directors who did not want to keep on farming were more likely to plunder their SFs. As Traian put it, launching oneself into commercial agriculture from the platform of even a run-down state farm would be cheaper than starting up completely from scratch. This would be true even if they bought the farm through someone else. Especially given the lousy conditions for bank credits, it was preferable to wait, producing what they could by using the SF infrastructure, rather than buying their own new equipment. Here, incidentally, his judgment differed from that of the World Bank, which saw the firms as of no value, good only for giving away.

Meanwhile, they would try to upgrade the farms as much as they could, paying for that with any revenues they made. To do so had the advantage of reducing the farm's balance to zero and keeping any surplus out of the mismanaged coffers of SFS-Simeria; they could use all their excess cash for these modernizations or to purchase future inputs before sending the center what was left. Directors with a disaggregable product could earn enough for piecemeal improvements. They could sell fish, a few pigs or calves, a load of apples, or some vegetables so as to buy a lightly used piece of equipment in place of their farm's dilapidated one, to repair buildings, and to replace broken windows. Although observers often assumed that the money from these petty sales went into directors' pockets, this was not necessarily true; some directors used it to keep viable the farms they hoped to buy. The assets would have been purchased, of course, from the farm's budget, not their own pockets—the farm was still state property, even if no longer part of the SF group.

A second reason—essential to the success of the first—for their continuing to run their farms was to grow enough to pay their shareholders at least something. Their logic was that any post-SF commercial strategy would necessarily include a period of renting from new owners the same land they had worked when those people were their SF's shareholders (see also Lampland 2002, 44). To some SF directors in Romania the shareholders did not matter, particularly to those directors in regions with huge SFs, who had no competition for the land in their farms and thus no need to court smallholders' favor. But eastern Hunedoara was different. There, several kinds of commercial farmer were gradually gaining a toehold. To farm for a living, they would need to rent land from villagers, eventually including that in the state farms when its shareholder-owners would at last be able to claim it. This was the kind of commercial farmer who took over much of the surface that the Vlaicu Association could not work, as of autumn 2000.

One such person was Dora Filip, a former SF director who had been forced out and had taken some of her tenancy relations with her. She regularly paid the equivalent of 1,000 kg/ha of wheat to those from whom she rented, while Radu—with all the costs of running an SF that Dora no longer had—was struggling to maintain a comparable level precisely so his shareholders would want to become his landlords later on. The shortage of land in this region, relative to the number of agronomists interested in farming it, generated a level of competition that Radu and Traian feared would put them out of the running. If they could not satisfy their shareholders, these would all give their land to someone who paid better. In 2000 they managed to pay their shareholders 200 kg of wheat per hectare and 400,000 lei from corn sales.

Although at first Radu and Traian presented their concern for the shareholders as a humanitarian one ("they need income, we have a surplus, and we should give them some of it"), this other motivation at length emerged very clearly. When I asked Radu in 1997 why he was planting all this tobacco, for example, he replied, "To pay my shareholders, so they'll let me rent their land if the chance arises. A few locals will take theirs out, but I hope enough will be left for us to run a decent farm." Three years later, in a more pessimistic frame of mind, he lamented that Vlaiceni would not be trying to break up SF1 if he had had conditions adequate for paying them well earlier. Instead, the opposite had happened: SFS-Simeria had drained his funds, and people were alienated. "Now they'll be a lot less interested in my privatizing and renting their land."

If we put these comments together with the argument in chapter 5, we find two intersecting systems of value: smallholders sought to use land in order to collect people who would provide labor, whereas Traian, Radu, and other SF directors used dividends in order to collect people who would provide land. Both needed to accumulate people—to build social capital—but toward different ends. Like the Association, SF directors now faced a trust deficit, although for very different reasons. By continuing to work their SFs to pay shareholders, Traian and Radu were hoping to create trusting relations with village smallholders. Without that kind of social capital, they risked having a farm infrastructure but no land to work.

I have suggested previously that there might be a third, unarticulated reason for them to continue farming their SF. In all likelihood, they also kept their farms going to profit from the ambiguity of property rights in creating their own new farms, as their other colleagues in the state sector reportedly did.[17] Whether in agriculture or in industry, directors of SOEs often created their own private firms on the side, supporting those parasitically from their state subsidies. Many observers have described just this pattern for various formerly socialist countries, as managers of SOEs sought to shuck liabilities onto the state and create their own smaller, more viable firms (see, e.g., Cornea 1995; Eyal, Szelényi, and Townsley 1998; Frydman, Murphy, and Rapaczynski 1998; Lampland 2002; Stark 1996). Although Traian and Radu denied doing this (for fear of the Financial Guard, they said), their denials were implausible. Radu himself acknowledged that in order to supplement his salary each year, he raised four or five calves on the side, which happened to live at SF1 (the income from selling them went to building up his private farm). In addition, Traian looked embarrassed when I asked him if he had used gasoline from his SF to plow villagers' fields for extra cash—although he volunteered that by staying on at SF2, he continued to benefit from the SF informational system. Beyond this, one of their close friends, a former SF director now farming commercially, answered in this way to my asking why the cousins had not quit their farms: "Because of the free seed, fertilizer, gasoline, and herbicide for the 18–20 ha they cultivate on their own." They had to struggle to acquire the seed for the SF, of course, but once they got it with their SF funds, they might borrow it freely. Finally, there was my visit with another good friend of theirs, Dinu, whom I had just asked how he got herbicide for his garden. Dinu said, "However we can . . ." and then changed the subject. "We went to Radu's last night to celebrate his birthday . . ." I completed the sentence, "And all of you came back with herbicide, right?" to much assenting mirth.

There were a number of ways in which one's position in a state farm could serve one's nascent private enterprise. For example, at a fairly innocent level, SF staff might send a tractor and driver over to plow their private farm, use SF fertilizer and herbicides on it, maybe bring over an SF employee or two to help with the harvest, and store some of their own crop in the SF's buildings. Perhaps a director might sell some SF sheep and use the money as a loan to buy himself some land; he would then work it and might even repay the loan. He might buy himself a tractor partly with SF funds, using it to plow for both the SF and himself. More ambitiously, SF directors might take out loans for modernizing their SFs, pay the interest out of their (state) budgets, and use the loan money interest-free to buy themselves a tractor. News reports in Romania were full of incidents in which directors drained the state subsidies for their state firms straight into the budgets of their private ones. What were liabilities from the viewpoint of the SF budget—workers' wages, run-down equipment, expenses for inputs, and loans—provided assets for the parasitic private farm, which thus threw these costs back upon the state as owner of the SF. David Stark (1996) describes even more complex schemes for Hungary, calling the phenomenon "recombinant property." Traian and Radu were doubtless recombining SF assets and liabilities with their own, even if on a fairly modest scale.

The main people in a position to do this kind of symbiotic self-starting were those who managed state property and who could transform their position in that failing system into advantage in a new one. The important point about such practices, however, is not so much whether they were scandalous and illegal (although many clearly were) but their link with two features of how state property had functioned: through a complex system whereby administrative use-rights devolved onto SOE directors as integral to their jobs, and through the fuzzy boundaries among socialism's various property forms (state, cooperative, personal, and private) with goods moving easily among them. As I explain in chapter 1, fuzzy property boundaries had always characterized socialism's political economy, with its great fungibility of resources. This fact, together with directors' administrative rights to use the public resources under their control as they saw fit, positively invited directors to continue this practice with their state and private firms.

Such practices continued into the 1990s. Moving resources back and forth between different kinds of activity was not only normal, it could happen in both directions. For example, as directors such as Radu waited for the chance to buy their loss-making SFs, they might support those farms with auxiliary activities on their own. One man, for instance, kept his farm running by bringing used electricity meters from Germany, resetting the clocks to zero, and then exporting them to Moldova and Ukraine for $25 each. This enabled him to stave off bankruptcy and keep the farm viable (if barely) so its hoped-for transition into his private ownership would be smooth. Another one made rental contracts with villagers along the perimeters of his farm, then paid the owners 1,000 kg of wheat per hectare, and used the remaining 2,000–2,500 kg/ha to shore up his SF budget. Traian raised first-class boars at home and used them to maintain the quality of his herd at the SF. Although the traffic from state to private activity was no doubt considerably heavier than the reverse, we should not lose sight of the weak property boundaries that made this practice so easy. It was good commonsense management.

Selling the State Farms

As it turned out, no amount of tinkering would keep these farms running until their directors could privatize them, for they were on an inevitable slide into bankruptcy. While energetic directors waited year after year for a law privatizing SFs, the assets of their farms were being progressively devalued as productive enterprises. This took a number of forms, most of them already mentioned. Directors were forced to leave some land uncultivated, they could not afford fertilizer or other things to build up the soil, and they had to pay out to keep their shareholders on board rather than saving income for reinvestment. Because the center had supplied no funds for inputs, they were reduced to selling serviceable irrigation pipes and still-useful equipment as scrap metal. Being denied control of their budgets, they could not buy their own inputs at the cheapest price. This plus inflation diminished their reserves of working capital.

Their farm had to continue paying the costs of maintaining apartments for idle workers because the workers themselves had no income to pay rent, and the government did not want to create a social problem by having Roma thrown out of apartments all over Romania. Although Radu and Traian had tried to maintain their farms in good repair and Traian had bought some newer equipment for his, by 1998 they could no longer afford to do this. Radu was now having constant nightmares.

Most upsetting, in their view, was the systematic plundering of state assets by the people above them. First there was the State Property Fund, with its interlocking committees of cronies and its huge honoraria for mandatory meetings. In addition to these honoraria, SPF committee members got their own large salaries, plus 10 percent of the value of any state property privatized (that money thus became unavailable to reduce the property's debts). Once the sale prices of privatizing firms began to plunge, SPF bureaucrats assured themselves of comparable income by taking bribes in order to arrange outcomes (or so people in Radu and Traian's position, along with many Romanian investigators, believed). "This is where the real pillaging of our assets began," Traian protested. "These people are like locusts on our farms!" Then he continued with a diatribe against those who accused directors of SOEs of trying to bankrupt their firms so as to buy them cheap. If all state farms are going bankrupt, he observed, that suggests there's something systemic at work: controlled prices, imposed debts, impossible bank interest rates, penalties for nonpayment, byzantine privatization rules that bleed firms dry, and so on. "Why should we take the blame for struggling to keep our small boat afloat, while bank directors perpetrating mammoth rip-offs go unremarked?" The point is important because although it may well be true that some SF directors continued drawing salaries while running their farms into the ground so as to buy them for a song, there could be other scenarios as well. A director might hope to keep his farm going while *other* people ran it into the ground—perhaps because doing so provided them with valuable political capital.

Other means of plundering came from problems specific to their own state-farm system, resulting from a matter mentioned earlier: the imposition of its debts on all eleven farms regardless of whether the farms had contributed to the debt or not. In 1995, after extended borrowing by both the individual farm directors and the SFS-Simeria bureaucrats and with rumors of privatization in the air, the center developed a plan for handling this debt. The total debt was about 1 billion lei; the plan was to pay it off by auctioning the largest farm, SF7, which was worth that amount. But the bank did not get around to doing the auction, preferring instead to accumulate more interest on the loans of the unsold farm. When the SF directors decided to separate their farms from the center in 1997, its response was to apportion its immense debt among the constituent farms, arguing that because the system had kept no evidence of the credits taken by farm, only for the SFS as a whole, it had no way of knowing who should be paying what interest. When the bank finally did auction SF7 (in 1999), the interest on its debt was so high that the bank took the entire sale price and the constituent farms got nothing; thus, each remained with its share of the collective debt. As for the combines, butchery, dairy complex, and other items that SFS-Simeria's bureaucrats had bought with the original loans, SF directors were convinced that the bureaucrats had kept those, sold them, and pocketed the money.[18]

The debts left to the constituent SFs were what finally brought down Traian's and Radu's farms. Because neither had contributed to incurring the debt, they decided not to pay it—that is, they refused to accept their place in a state farm collective and to recognize the liabilities assigned them by the next level up. This decision saved them considerable monthly payments (thereby enabling them to continue operating their farms); yet with it they also racked up, over the next four years, penalties for nonpayment that swelled their debt from 200 million to 900 million lei and the total level of indebtedness of both farms to 3.2 billion lei by summer 2000. Included in these were fines and penalties for their having failed to pay employment tax on their own and their employees' salaries.

The debts posed several problems for future planning. They made Radu and Traian ineligible for loans to repair their farms. In consequence, they were assessed numerous fines for violating newly upgraded standards—a cable improperly installed twenty-five years ago, allegedly of substandard product quality, and other things they could not afford to fix, so the fines were repeated. The debts also made it impossible for them to think of buying the farms through some other person because they could not imagine finding the money to pay both the evaluation and the debts—which, according to their privatization statute, they said, would have to be covered by the sale price. They did not want to end up buying a whole lot of scrap metal at an astronomical price and then after that have to take out bank loans to modernize the farms.

Yet another problem concerned their credit-worthiness, which Radu feared had been compromised, obstructing any loans they might want later. Their credit-worthiness was diminishing not just as a function of the farm's ongoing loss of value, and not just because SFS-Simeria had assigned them so much debt with the proportional interest payments, but because of the entire system of centralized accounting the center had used. "My credit rating has been ruined by centralization," he told me in 1997. Two years earlier he had had huge profits and had discussed with two banks the possibility of taking out credits independently of the SFS; both had said yes immediately. Now he feared they would not be so eager. In that year (1995), Radu's costs for producing wheat had been 280,000 lei/ha, whereas those of other SF directors had been up to twice this amount. But instead of showcasing him, the center had made him inflate his costs on paper, so the bank would not see such huge differences among the farms. The center insisted on spreading everyone's costs across the whole group, he said, because it did not want the bank to realize that cheaper production was possible and therefore to cut back on the loans that kept the bureaucrats in clover. For Radu this cost-spreading was very damaging. If he sought a loan for privatizing, the official books would show only an enormous production cost and huge debts. How then would he be able to obtain a loan? He confessed that he had only one hope: having kept his own private records for his farm, he could take them to the bank and pray that the director would be impressed. The centralized organization of SFS-Simeria, he concluded, had prevented him from showing what a good farmer he was: "It clipped my wings."

What was Traian and Radu's calculation during this time? From 1994 through 1999, they continued to believe that if they waited and kept their farms in good condition, they would be able to purchase one or both from the state. At first they were terrified that SF1 would be evaluated at some enormous price they could not afford, owing to the valuable buildings and location. They would be buying seven hectares worth of very expensive scrap iron and financing it with high-interest loans—in other words, they would be buying liabilities rather than assets. This did not make a lot of sense. But as time passed and it became clear that the State Property Fund cared less about how much it got for SOEs than it did about either postponing their privatization or selling them for a trifle plus a bribe, the problem became rather the reverse: the farms' assets would have depreciated so badly that Traian and Radu would not be able to use the farms as collateral to raise the loans needed to modernize them.

By 1999, the cousins had become convinced that they had only one solution: to sell one or both farms to someone else and stay on as managers. They planned to find a buyer for one farm and work through him to continue farming, perhaps gradually taking over the other themselves. This new plan involved a shift in their view of the asset evaluation. Now, instead of fearing a high evaluation they could not afford, they wanted one high enough to pay off the debts. It was a long-term plan, and it depended on their finding a buyer whose purchase price would cover the debts of both farms, so they might take over one of them debt-free.

Given their location, right on a major international highway between Hungary and Turkey, they occasionally received inquiries from possible buyers. One of these was Juan, a Spaniard who had developed an interest in Transylvania because he employed migrant labor (of the kind mentioned in chapter 5) from this very region. In spring 1999, Juan approached the cousins to find out if SF1 would be sold, and they decided to cultivate him. Juan was not interested in farming (he planned some sort of manufacture) but he liked the location and the buildings, and he was not averse to having Traian and Radu work the surrounding land if he should buy. Radu used the occasion of his July 1999 council and assembly meetings to raise the question of a possible sale and to discuss the appropriate price.[19]

After lengthy discussion, all agreed that Traian should start negotiating at 2.5 billion lei, reduce the price for each piece of equipment that Juan did not want, and use the proceeds to reduce the debts.[20] Traian and Radu were pleased with this result. "Usually," Traian said, "the SPF makes all the arrangements for sale, including covert deals with buyers to hold ghost auctions until the price comes down 20–30 percent. They won't let me do the negotiating, but I'm the one who suffers if they sell at a low price, because then I can't cover my debts. I want a high price, they want a low price so they can get rid of it." In the event, however, the victory was hollow because Juan decided the price was too high and backed out.

A year later they were still in the same bind, except the debts had ballooned.[21] Fortunately they had found another potential buyer—the Italian, Giovanni, mentioned at the beginning of the chapter. Giovanni planned to buy SF1 and then maybe SF2 later, keeping the cousins on to work the land for Vlaiceni who wanted that. Meanwhile, the State Property Fund had ordered them to have the two farms reevaluated; the 2.5 billion market value for SF1 was now raised to 6 billion, but, to the cousins' alarm, the SPF chose to stay with the lower figure despite intervening inflation. As we have seen, Giovanni bought SF1 at auction in August 2000 for the paltry sum of 1,535,000,000 lei, one-third of the starting price for the first (ghost) auction. This was far from enough to cover the two farms' debts, which would now have to be covered from the sale of SF2. In other words, the cousins would not be able to take over the other farm because they had not received enough from selling the first one to pay the debts of the second.

The men were deeply shaken by the failure of their plan to secure SF2 debt-free. But more than this, Radu was profoundly upset that the place in which he had invested so much work over two decades had been sold for so little. In my postmortem with them and some others in their line of work, Radu complained that no one seemed to care about receiving a good sale price for state properties. "It's just like when some peasant sells a cow because he no longer has hay to feed it. It might be worth 7 million, but he accepts 5 million simply to be rid of it. Today we were sold just like a cow." (Someone corrected him: "No, like a pair of tennis shoes.") To these people, the idea that some actor in this drama might not want a good price was unfathomable. They had years of experience in agriculture, and they believed their farms were worth something; where the World Bank saw only liabilities, Traian and Radu saw assets. In that discussion, Traian made the observation in the second epigraph of this chapter: instead of a change from state property to individual property, what was happening was the destruction of property values.

Although it is not central to my purposes in this chapter, I would like to continue with the fate of SF1 so as to show the property morass into which buyers (especially foreign ones) could unwittingly step. Giovanni had bought SF1 as cheaply as possible, excluding the equipment for drying the medicinal plants; it remained in four of the buildings, and other items such as tractors remained as well. But when he ordered Radu and Traian to take it all away, he discovered that the buildings' construction made the drying equipment impossible to remove. In addition, as the state's representatives, the two men were obliged to protect any state property that remained after a sale, for if they did not, the SPF could sue them; therefore, they could not simply move the tractors outdoors in the rain. In Traian's succinct summary, "It's his house but the state's furniture." Giovanni's stinginess had boxed him in. In effect, the asset he had bought was a *location*; four of the buildings he now owned would have to be torn down, and the others were full of unremovable objects belonging to the Romanian state— liabilities to him, although assets to Traian and Radu. He had not even paid for the roads and power lines, which meant that Traian, as the state's representative, could block his access and his electricity. Because Giovanni had also not bought the pipes in their concrete, someone else did and began to cut out the pipes to sell as scrap metal, leaving no way to pull up the concrete blocks. Now Traian used his control of the roads to prohibit access to the owner of the pipes. Here we see the situation Michael Heller (1998) refers to as an "anti-commons," in which multiple ownership claims preclude using the object in question.[22]

The saga with Giovanni was not yet over. With the failure of their plan to free SF2 of debts by selling SF1 well enough to cover them, Traian and Radu persuaded Giovanni to buy SF2 also. The auction was set for October 3, 2000. Proceeding as he had before, Giovanni treated October 3 as a ghost auction and did not show up, waiting for the price to drop further as it had with SF1. But a month later, before another auction could be scheduled, the neoliberal government lost the elections and one of the first acts of its successor was to put all sales of state farms on hold. As a result, Traian had to stay on as director of SF2 (Radu had retired with the sale of SF1) and the debts were mounting even higher. I asked him why he did not resign. "There's no one to resign to!" he exclaimed. "The government is completely changing the arrangements for state farms, moving them out from the SPF and into the Ministry of Agriculture and creating a whole new organization and procedure. I tried to put my resignation on the desk of the director of the Agriculture Department and he said he was not competent to accept it; neither would the director of the SPF."

At this point, Traian stopped all activity at SF2; his goal was to take out no loans for production, so the level of indebtedness would not reach the assessed value of its capital. Even now they had not completely given up hope of buying SF2, despite having been immobilized by their SFS center and prevented from gathering momentum for a launch into independent commercial farming. Their preoccupation with the debt proves that intention because had they not hoped to take over one or both farms, the debt would have been of no concern—something for the state, not them, to worry about. So far, however, instead of taking over a farm they saw as valuable, they had watched its value being drained away. "What's been happening here," Radu concluded, "is privatization by destruction." Their only alternative now was to build up the small farm they had been creating on the side, partly through the SF.[23]

In discussing these events with me much later, Traian explained their motivations in more general language. "Romania's privatization laws didn't favor specialists," he said, "but bureaucrats. Our entire strategy was to force privatization to include us." There was more to it, however, than keeping up the farm's value:

> I didn't want to be seen in the area as powerless, as someone who can be pushed around. When I rented the 300 ha that Şiboteni had in my SF, I didn't want the center to come and take all my wheat so I couldn't pay people. I had to prove to the guys in Simeria that I'm not Dopey Oproiu. My family has always been respected in this area. I live here, and I want to keep people's respect as a man of character. So instead of selling tractors, the way the center hoped, I gradually sold all the pigs but kept my fixed assets intact. Ours was the only SF they didn't manage to bankrupt! I never let them bury me in debt. I thought of it as like being a father: you have to work very hard to get your daughter to the altar still a virgin. In the same way, I worked very hard to get my farm intact to the auction block, and I'm proud of that.

In this arresting metaphor, Traian makes it clear that the fate of his farm was a matter of honor with him, of maintaining the social capital that constituted his family reputation.

As a postscript, in June 2002 another Italian expressed interest in buying SF2, agreeing to pay 5 billion for it (he had an EU grant to set up a business in Romania). After a ghost auction the price fell to 2.4 billion, and a second ghost auction brought it to 1 billion—an amount that Traian and Radu could now envision being able to muster themselves with the proceeds of their private farm, if only they could produce the 40 percent down payment. Trying to get their finances together, they went to check when the third auction would take place—only to learn that it had already happened! Evidently someone had bribed someone else to hold not a ghost auction this time but a secret one.

The buyer was not their Italian, however, but a pair of men from near Vlaicu who had become commercial farmers. They had somehow managed to displace the previous buyer of SF1's pipes, which they extracted for sale as scrap iron; the proceeds enabled them to buy SF2 debtfree before the Italian knew what had happened. Then their connections secured them a loan from the EU's Phare Programme that would pay the costs of modernizing the farm. By September 2002, then, SF2 was in Romanian rather than foreign hands, but not those of Radu and Traian.

The Dynamics of Devaluation

In my conversations with state farm directors, their view of the SF center was always negative: its bureaucrats were scheming and gave no thought to the directors' hard work, it was always getting its hands on and pocketing resources others needed or deserved, it was run by people who had no conscience and lived by the old mentality of communist cadres, and so forth. Without dismissing these possibilities, I think the center's behavior too emerges from within the constraints affecting all economic actors in 1990s Romania. SFS bureaucrats too were living with tremendous uncertainty. The skills they had honed as bureaucrats gave them few prospects in a market economy, the grounds for stable future prosperity in Romania were depressingly nebulous, and their clearest path to safety meant keeping the state property form alive as long as possible so as to live off it parasitically, looting its wealth. The budgetary devaluation of state farms was less important to them than using these to maintain their retinues of allies and clients—their political capital. Many directors of SOEs behaved in the same way. But the difference between those bureaucrats and most SF directors of my acquaintance was that the latter had emerged from socialism with a marketable skill the former lacked. Both groups had an extensive capital of connections (the bureaucrats much more so), but specialist knowledge would give SF directors who chose to use it a possible livelihood unavailable to their bureaucratic superiors.

Meanwhile, these bureaucrats engaged in the destruction of budgetary value, in a chain that went from top to bottom. By plundering state assets, draining state farms of their revenues through frequent meetings, and forcing liabilities—such as the SFS debts—onto those beneath them, they compelled the latter to engage in desperate creative financing or their own forms of plunder. As a result, those even lower down in the food chain received smaller and smaller dividends at a time when they too needed all the income they could get. Conscientious and ambitious state farm directors strove against the odds to keep from going under; the less creative, scrupulous, or energetic behaved like their superiors. The Traians and Radus worried about maintaining social relations of trust with the people whom they saw as their future meal ticket, but their intentions fell victim to the behavior of those above them. These same directors were also compelled to devalue their assets further by dismantling irrigation systems or special installations and selling them, along with used equipment, on the scrap-metal market by day, while their unpaid employees came to do the same at night. In addition, they cast about for ways of escaping the liabilities being devolved onto them by throwing those onto the state or, in Traian and Radu's case, onto a foreign investor. (If foreign investment in Romania was scarce, perhaps this sort of tactic was a reason.)

The chain does not end there because, according to Anda and Nica of the Vlaicu Association, it was the privileged position of state farms in the pecking order that contributed to the collapse of those below, described in chapters 5 and 6. The 1990–96 government's subvention of state farms had diverted enormous funds that might have gone instead to associations and small cultivators. Because banks had all along seen the SFs, with their extensive collateral, as better credit risks than individual farmers or producers' cooperatives, those lesser actors had been prevented from improving their inventory or launching their production. As Anda said, "If I go to the bank and a state farm director goes too, he'll get the loan. He takes it out very casually, because the farm isn't his; if its debts get too big, he can just walk away. I could have used the money better." Also part of the banks' calculations, of course, was not just who was credit-worthy but who were their friends and cronies, and these were less likely to be small independents than people already important in the state sector.

Networks and connections—accumulations of social capital—thus kept resources from reaching the lower levels of rural society; they were captured by those above. The overall picture is one of assets in the form of credits, loans, salaries, honoraria, and interest on debts moving from the government through the banks into the pockets of the State Property Fund, state farm bureaucracy, and sometimes SF directors, to the detriment of other specialists and small cultivators. Although the recipients might invest the money in productive assets (such as Simeria's milk-processing installation), it was at least as likely that they would use it for consumption, such as building fancy villas, or to distribute to political allies, such as in the interlocking directorates of the SPF. Having incurred large debts, these people would then parcel them out from their own budgets onto the SF directors below. There the debts might join with others that those directors had incurred so as to improve farms they hoped eventually to buy. The result is that assets—whether productive or consumptive—tended to remain at the top of the hierarchy while the progressively lower levels acquired liabilities.

In his discussion of recombinant property, David Stark proposes two variants (1996, 1012). In one, assets are devolved onto satellite firms and liabilities are centralized as much as possible in state hands—the variant he explores for Hungary. In the other, assets are centralized and liabilities devolve onto lower units. This variant seems to fit the cases I have been describing, although, taken as a whole, Romanian actors were throwing off liabilities in any direction they could: onto smallholders, onto SF directors, onto state organizations, and onto foreigners. As the U.S. Enron scandal showed in 2001, however, a tendency to centralize assets in oneself and throw liabilities off onto other actors is not unique to Romania or Eastern Europe in the 1990s. What I have discerned in the interaction of Radu and Traian with their state farm system suggests the intersection of different rationales, those of people operating on the basis of an emerging market view of assets and those still operating on the model of clientelism and political capital. That is, what Radu saw as an asset with declining budgetary worth held for his superiors ongoing political possibilities. In this sense, running SFs into the ground may have been merely the effect (for Radu) rather than the goal of the actions of SFS-Simeria bureacrats having few resources for market success.[24] It is crucial, however, not to make the mistake of thinking of assets and liabilities solely in a budgetary sense. That is, we should not presume we know *ex ante* what counts as an asset, or we will miss the asset value Traian saw in getting SF2 to the "altar" intact and upholding his family reputation.

What has the present chapter contributed to the themes of this book? It has taken one of the key aspects of a property analysis—the value of the property object—and shown that there was no stable value to the kind of property that was the state farm (see also Alexander 2004). One man's asset was another's liability; each sought to capture what he saw as desirable and peel off the rest. Just as in chapters 4 and 5, assessments of market value were far from capturing other values the object might hold—as means of displaying one's competence, of sustaining one's family's reputation, or of accumulating people and building political capital. In the chaotic Romanian environment, for western advisors to imagine they could create responsible and accountable actors by assigning private property rights was sheer lunacy. None of these points is new, but the details through which I have documented them are. These help us to understand better the form of peripheral capitalism that began taking hold in Romania in the 1990s, including the nature of the risks SOE directors faced and the resources and strategies they had for coping with those. It took special endowments to be able to find the asset in a liability, to redefine a string of losing situations as a set of possibilities, in the manner of Traian and Radu.

During the decade of the 1990s, state farm directors were exposed to much less financial risk than were smallholders and associations. Initially, the price scissors had no effect on SFs because the state protected their budgets. Once SF centers ended regular supplies of inputs, some directors had to scramble for ways to obtain those, but if they failed their farm's future was not at stake, as was true for smallholders and association leaders. Even if a state farm was swimming in debt, its director could resign and walk away with no penalty. The debt did not follow him; it clung to him only if he hoped to continue a relationship with his farm later on. The principal uncertainty an SF director faced—and it was a big one—was what he would do if his SF folded. Hence the drive to accumulate smallholders from whom he could rent and to worry about his credit-worthiness.

Directors who intended to start farming on their own faced a risk environment similar to those of smallholders and associations, but one considerably mitigated by two things: their greater expertise and connections (the fruits of their time in socialist agriculture), and the possibility of using their SF infrastructure to ease them into their own farms. When observers condemn the way directors of SOEs drained state assets out of their subsidized firms and into parasitic private businesses—and the practice was, indeed, often condemnable—they may be forgetting that in postsocialist conditions, in postsocialist Romanian conditions especially, this was the only route toward private capital formation. Anthropologists and historians have shown repeatedly how pre- or noncapitalist systems incubate capitalist development, for example, through creating semiproletarians whose small farms subsidize below-subsistence wage work. In this light, directors of state-owned enterprises occupied crucial sites that articulated socialism with whatever would succeed it. Like associations, they were transitional forms, but, unlike associations, they had a future.

Owing precisely to the state budget that cushioned them against risk, SF directors had the luxury of thinking across longer time spans than did smallholders. Although this luxury faded as the decade wore on and directors had to struggle to keep their farms running with less help from the center, they were never reduced to thinking one season at a time, like smallholders. Delays in legislation for privatizing state farms forced them to keep their options open; their salaries as state farm directors facilitated that. Beyond this stable income, the fuzzy property boundaries separating their state farms from their own potential enterprises not only enabled them to protect the latter from risk but also encouraged them to think in terms of a gradual shift from one livelihood to the other. This long-term view informed their timing in purchasing land (they could withstand the devaluation described in chapter 5 until land prices hit rock bottom); it enhanced their ability to respond to medium-run market shifts in the relative prices of grains and livestock; and it made them readier to take on personal debts—such as for buying large equipment or farm buildings—because no matter what happened, they still had their salaries.

In this respect, however, time and timing had a particular contour: no matter how far into the future they might plan, the medium-run trend toward devaluation forced SF directors to seize an opportunity whenever it might appear, rather than when they were ready for it. They could not hold out indefinitely or they might miss the crucial moment for crossing the threshold into another form of livelihood. Any undue interruption in their accumulating their own capital reserves could be very costly in the longer run. As Dan, whom we meet in chapter 8, said after a lawsuit that cost him a lot of money, "I've lost my start." SF directors moving into commercial agriculture therefore had to work flexibly across several time horizons—thinking, as one of them put it, like chess players: "I have to ask myself, When the state farm is broken up what will I do? I have to accumulate now, make plans. I think of it as a chess game with several possible moves at any one time, so I try to create several options and keep them all open."

Nonetheless, we must remember that unlike smallholders, SF directors had been given not only a chess board but a number of pieces with which to play and some partners as well. This was the benefit they brought from having occupied a place of greater privilege under socialism: the management of state rather than collective property. In the next chapter we examine further what kinds of games they were able to play.

CHAPTER 8
FROM DEBTS TO *DALLAS*
VALUE TRANSFORMATION AND THE RISE OF SUPERTENANTS

It's a good thing we used to watch *Dallas* so often. That's where we learned what we need to know about privatization—all JR's struggles to gain 51 percent control. Now we understand! We recall very clearly one episode in which Jock is telling Ray, "You still haven't learned not to work for others." It really stuck in our minds. So we began asking ourselves, "Why should we work for others?"

(Couple who left a state farm to start their own)[1]

At our age, the forties and fifties, we should be at the height of our powers. We've done our apprenticeship, and now we should be in charge. But no! We have to start all over again. Firms want to hire only people under thirty-five. Ours is the sacrificial generation. A life should have a beginning, a middle, and an end, a rising and falling curve. Our beginning was an end, our middle a beginning, and we won't have the middle at all.

(Former local bureaucrat)

Toma Mezei was born in Vlaicu in the late 1960s into a family that had a respectable status prior to 1959 (his grandfather had about 5.5 ha in 1948). He completed officers' training in the Romanian military and a few years later earned an engineering degree, after which he worked in a factory near Vlaicu. In 1990 he and a colleague decided to quit their factory jobs and open a bakery. He explained his reasoning to me. From a newspaper article on layoffs and plant closings by General Motors in the United States, he concluded that the market was saturated with technological products; thus, for the next while, agriculture would lead the economy, and the food industry was where he should go.

A year later he started his own family association and bought at auction one of Vlaicu's CF barns. At the time its price seemed astronomical, but he was sure he could eventually cover it with proceeds from his bakery, which was doing well. He acquired some implements and began to work about 12 ha belonging to his kin; later he took in more land, luring some Vlaiceni from the big Association by paying them more. On it he grew some wheat for his bakery but, more important, animal fodder, with an eye to entering the meat-processing business. Because he worked through Romcereal, he began having difficulties when it stopped serving people. "Since this is the only remaining link in the chain that favors the agricultural entrepreneur, that is advantageous to anyone, of course it's being wiped out," he observed to me caustically, in a 1994 tirade against the government's privatization policies.

Toma had a number of other plans in mind, which included building a mill and getting into the export of raw and semiprocessed materials, particularly timber. He believed he could maintain more control over the prices and disposability of his product with those than by making finished goods, whose style might be soon outmoded. Although he declined to tell me the source of wheat for his bakery, the Romcereal director (his competitor) claimed that Toma had gone to Bucharest and, through a well-placed kinsman, managed to get on the list of private bakeries that were allowed to buy wheat at the state-controlled rather than the free market price—a privilege generally reserved for firms in the state sector such as Romcereal. In addition, he took wheat from villagers and brought them bread twice a week in exchange. This hardly helped his bakery, however, because he found the wheat of inferior quality; he was doing it, he said, as a favor to Vlaiceni. (Perhaps he was hoping to create goodwill for possible tenancy relations later.)

When I asked Toma in 1994 what he saw as the main obstacle to privatizing, he emphasized not external conditions but "mentality": "The biggest handicap is ten years—for me, but for others, a lifetime—of people telling you what to do. Now no one tells you what to do, and many people find this very demoralizing." A smart, commercially minded man of independent spirit, he began with few connections in the world of agriculture and very little expertise, but he planned to make a living from it and his other ventures. He bought a tractor and a combine, with which he worked for Vlaicu's smallholders. Throughout the 1990s, he remained flexible in responding to what he saw as risks and opportunities—many of them outside agriculture. Like everyone else, he had troubles: difficulty finding labor (it was he who brought in prisoners to harvest his corn; see chapter 6), problems with expensive herbicide that did not work, floods, people moving land in and out of his association the way they did with the big one, and so on.

Although Toma bought a bit of land, by 1997 he was saying it was not a good investment; by 1999 he was worried that animals were not either. Yet he remained committed to agriculture. In 2000 he was poised to become a larger-scale tenant farmer, convinced that despite the competition, the problems smallholders were having and the demise of the Association meant there was more than enough land to go around. When property titles were finally given out for land in state farms (autumn 2000), Toma was mobilizing people whose land he might work. Having been elected delegate to the commune council, he had influence over how the land was to be measured; he made certain that his owners' parcels were consolidated into large blocks, cooperating with others like himself to divide the surface among them efficiently. (In late 2001, gossip had it that he had declared the earlier titling all wrong and was doing it again, this time even more in his favor.)[2]

Toma Mezei represents a new kind of actor on the village scene. If the message of chapters 5–7 is that in Transylvanian conditions during the 1990s it was very difficult to make a living from agriculture, there were also a few exceptions and he hoped to be one of them. He brought to this endeavor the leadership experience he had gained in the military and in his engineering job—that is, the benefit of training and leadership in the socialist state sector—and a powerful kinship connection in Bucharest, which might mitigate some of the risks he encountered. By acting fast in 1990, he started to accumulate capital in the food industry while that was still possible; he turned inflation to his advantage by using his capital to buy early the buildings and equipment he would have found too costly later on.

Able to formulate a diverse plan of action across multiple time horizons, Toma differed from the state farm directors of chapter 7 in three main ways: he had no training in agriculture, he had relatively low-level managerial experience, and having quit his job in 1990 he lacked the cushion of continued state employment. This made him more vulnerable to risk than he might otherwise have been. By diversifying his activities, however, he sought to reduce that risk—the effect not just of having many strings to his bow, but of using those multiple activities (as his cousin explained to me) to mask expenses and profits by moving money around. It is a strategy readers should bear in mind for the other cases I describe.

By the year 2001 it was possible, although not easy, to make a living from agriculture. In this chapter I present examples of people such as Toma who were trying to launch themselves into commercial agriculture, some of whom appeared to be making a go of it.[3] These people were able to create economic value in agriculture in part because they had more extensive resources than those discussed in chapters 5 and 6. Coming largely from state farms or from positions of responsibility in other kinds of state enterprise, these are the people whom socialism had privileged and who could best parlay that privilege into successful farming. By the late 1990s, a few of them (including Toma) were in the process of becoming the supertenants I introduced in chapter 5. The supertenants' niche opened up because Romanian decollectivization had created tiny farms owned by people unable to work them, who would therefore be looking for others to do so (see also Giordano and Kostova 2000, 173, for Bulgaria). Supertenants differed from other kinds of tenants in that they had much more wealth in terms of the expertise and connections necessary to make a go of farming, and this enabled them to find value in land and bring it to fruition.

This conclusion is not new; many other scholars have found the same thing—that prior endowments enabled socialism's agricultural elites to become commercial farmers through tenancy arrangements (e.g., Giordano and Kostova 2000; Lampland 2002; Maurel 1994b; McFaul 1996; Milczarek 2000; Swain 1995). Going even further, Giordano and Kostova (2000, 172–73) suggest that in Bulgaria, the large number of absentee owners positively evoked this commercial strategy. The argument is appropriate to Romania as well. Many of these accounts explain such successes with the concepts of social and cultural capital (in addition to those just mentioned, see Elster, Offe, and Preuss 1998; Eyal, Szelényi, and Townsley 1998; Sandu 1999; but contrast Berdahl 1999). Those concepts seem to illuminate for a variety of Eastern European countries why many of socialism's elites became those of postsocialism, especially in agriculture. To speak of social and cultural capital is to address matters sometimes treated under the rubric of *path dependency* (e.g., Begg and Meurs 1998; Meurs and Begg 1998; Stark and Bruszt 1998)—what aspects of the past are shaping present and future developments—but to stress some variables not usually considered under that rubric. My task in this chapter is to compare several examples in detail to reveal the underlying processes at work.

To maintain analytic drive in my discussion, I often bring in these concepts. By *social capital* I mean (following Lampland 2002, 35, 48) social relationships and connections—both horizontal and vertical—that are valuable assets in one's career. An essential ingredient in these relations is trust; I emphasized this ingredient in chapters 6 and 7, in discussing why the Association failed and why Traian and Radu were so worried about paying shareholder dividends. Aspiring commercial farmers needed to win the trust of those from whom they hoped to rent—that is, trust was a means of collecting people with land. Where trust proved difficult to establish, these farmers would have to buy land, something not all could or wished to do. Another aspect of social capital is reputation, which might be linked with a family's position prior to 1945 and could serve to create or sustain trust. Traian's effort to uphold his reputation (chapter 7) shows precisely this concern. I use *cultural capital* to refer to education and expert knowledge, routines, information, and experience in managing a farm and handling large sums of money. As I noted in the Introduction, Eyal, Szelényi, and Townsley (1998) see cultural capital as the most important element in being able to convert the social and political capital of the prior era into present value; for them, cultural capital also includes a habitus of entrepreneurship. For Romania, however, I believe social and political capital retained a significance perhaps greater than in Central Europe—those scholars' research region (cf. Stoica 2004). At the same time, I point to forces that were undermining these prior capital endowments.

Why should it be, as I argue, that those associated with socialism's privileged property form—state property, and particularly state farms—had an edge in becoming commercial farmers? Although most staff of both SFs and CFs had advanced education, in Romania, the president of a CF was often a party hack who did not himself have this kind of expertise (the farm was run by agronomists who were not its heads), whereas the head of an SF almost always did. Expertise and connections thus converged in SF directors more often than in those who ran CFs. The latter might have important party and professional contacts in the capital, as did the head of Vlaicu's CF, but owing to the administrative organization of the SF system (not bounded by communes and counties) the range of contacts for SF heads was wider. CF chairmen had an abundance of relations with their members, the kind of relation that would have, if anything, negative consequences for them after 1989. That is, social capital could be a negative as well as a positive asset. By contrast, in the early 1990s the relations of SF directors with villagers were more likely to be neutral (even positive, if they paid their shareholders dividends). In addition, the managerial experience of CF heads was more limited because they managed smaller budgets with minimal subsidies or investments, and they used less complex technology; this gave them less opportunity to experiment or take risks. SF directors might take more risks because they knew they would be bailed out, whereas CFs simply fell further into debt. In short, the greater endowment of state farms in all respects (see table 1.1, in chapter 1) translated into greater social and cultural capital for their directors.

I would not generalize this argument to all of Eastern Europe—or even all of Romania—because the situations of state and collective farms varied by country and internally as well. For example, in East Germany, as the Buechlers (202, 300) argue, state farm directors had less autonomy and experience in making things work than did those in cooperatives. Lampland (2002, 49) makes the same point about CF managers in Hungary, their autonomy augmented by socialist Hungary's unusual economic policies. Both these countries, however, had the bulk of their land in collective farms, with state farms a very small presence. In Romania, with fully 30 percent of its agricultural land in state farms, I believe SF directors emerged from the socialist period with far more resources than those in CFs.[4] Scholars such as McFaul (1996) for Russia and Milczarek (2000) for Poland find the same pattern. Precisely how these directors converted that advantage into economic success, in comparison with people of other kinds, is the subject of this chapter.

Trajectories into Commercial Farming

I indicate in chapter 5 that a small number of Vlaiceni had set out on an entrepreneurial trajectory involving agriculture. The resources they drew on varied tremendously from one person to another. Although I focus mainly on three cases, I present several others more briefly so as to show some of this variation. Because there are few such people in rural communities, I have taken steps to disguise them as best I can without completely distorting their situation. My aim is to ask what enabled these people to think about farming commercially; how they amassed the resources for it; what networks, expertise, and experience they drew on; in terms of what time horizons they operated; and what their future prospects seemed to be as of late 2001. I distinguish among those without advanced agricultural training, those having it but lacking state jobs, and those specialists who retained their state positions as they began their own farming business. As with chapters 6 and 7 I include perhaps excessive detail because there is no published ethnography of the processes I describe.

Farmers Lacking Advanced Expertise or Extensive Connections

The Dara family had a long history of commercial ventures in Vlaicu and a reputation for deal-making. In the early 1900s, one of them, Ignatie, had owned a bar and been active in commerce with livestock; he and his son had suffered for this during collectivization. Ignatie lost a modest 3.5 ha to the CF, and his son began working there as a low-level technician. A grandson, Matei, served as a collection agent for products Vlaiceni grew on their usufruct plots and, after 1989, he continued this activity for petty sales of perishables destined for a state processing center in Deva. With Matei's help, his daughter and her husband Nicolae opened a bar; in addition, they fenced off a small pond that they rented from the commune, charging people a fee to swim there. The family repossessed land-holdings of about 8 ha, which they worked themselves.

The various businesses must have done well, because in 2000 Nicolae tried to buy at auction a former CF barn in which he intended to raise livestock. Although he was outbid, he now began publicizing his interest in working land for smallholders left stranded when the Association fell apart. Without experience in farming or the necessary implements, however, and without a strong reputation that might win him the villagers' trust, Nicolae was unlikely to make a go of this activity any time soon, unless he used patently illegal means. Lacking both cultural and social capital relevant to successful agriculture, his prospects were not good. His trajectory is nonetheless worth noting for its hint of a family disposition toward entrepreneurship (cf. Szelényi 1988), the variety of petty activities involved, and the role of commerce (the distribution of perishables, the bar, and the fishpond) in initiating his accumulation.

Some of the same elements appear in another case, that of Andrei Maior. The Maiors were venits, living in Vlaicu since the 1960s. Not liking to work for a boss, Andrei had entered a special status permitted during socialism—that of small independent craftsman. He worked as a cabinet-maker, amassing good money. In 1990, he was quick to invest some of it in agricultural equipment bought from an Agromec, before inflation would wipe out his savings. Because his family had received no land except their household garden, he initially used the equipment to work land for Vlaiceni, at rates just under those of the Agromec. He supplemented this with a lucrative business hauling goods with his truck (his was the only one in Vlaicu), a service for which people paid well; at length he opened a small convenience store. All these activities enabled him to buy some land, on which he decided in 1999 to produce some food items for his store. Together with his son, Andrei also rented some land belonging to absentee owners on a kind of contract several venits were using: each year's rent would go toward buying the land. By June 2001 he had bought about 7 ha and was renting another 18 for a total of 25 ha, which he thought was probably enough land for him. He was farming it very intensively, at an estimated cost of 10–11 million lei/ha, he said. No other venit was doing this well; he developed a reputation for being clever and hard-working.

An unusually shrewd businessman, Andrei maintained diverse activities while waiting to see which would pan out. Their diversity was a way of protecting himself against the risk associated with any one. His earlier experience as an independent tradesman doubtless contributed to his ability to identify opportunities, and his timing was excellent: he was always the first to try something, before its profitability went down. Although he himself was not well endowed with agricultural knowledge or social capital, he worked like an ox, sent his son to agriculture school, and planned to build up the tenancy angle with him in the future. Moreover, his wife Emilia had held office jobs in both the CF and a nearby SF so she had some of the connections that enabled them to find used equipment early, at good prices. Their main complaint was that they had no place to store grain so as to profit from price fluctuations, and this slowed their growth. Andrei shared three things with Nicolae Dara and Toma Mezei: none of them now held state jobs, all treated agriculture as one of several activities, and the pace of their accumulations was well behind that of the people I consider later in the chapter. But Andrei had extensive managerial experience (albeit in a different domain), a son with agricultural training, and a wife with connections, all of which put them ahead of the other two and would help them realize value from farming.

Some of these same traits are found in my next example, Luca Avramescu. Although Luca's ancestors had been on the poor side of middling, they had a reputation for diligence and rectitude, which he continued. A brilliant student, he earned an engineering degree in the 1980s and moved to an important factory job nearby, where he rose to a prominent position. Added to his managerial experience (and a state-sector job that mitigated his exposure to risk) was a small side business he set up in 1990 to repair household appliances. In 1991 his family recovered 4.6 ha, which, along with the 5 ha of two ailing relatives, gave them almost 10 ha. Luca's parents were not well, however, and could not easily work much land. At first they gave most of it to the Association, with which they soon became disenchanted.

Then Luca had a piece of luck: he became unexpectedly wealthy when his father-in-law died in 1992, leaving a large savings account. He immediately used it up buying a tractor and a few implements so as to work his family's land himself. As he explained to me, "It seems a pity to let a capital of 10 ha go to waste. Why shouldn't I give it a try?" He bought more implements with a low-interest bank loan—easily repaid, because of inflation and his two incomes. In obtaining it, he had the help of two high school classmates who worked at the bank through which these state-subsidized loans were channeled; they let him know before the loans were even announced and put him at the top of the list, ahead of all the SF directors who usually got these funds. (Although he did not owe this connection to his important state-sector job, that job made him the sort of fellow with whom classmates would want to keep in touch.) He began to read voraciously in technical manuals about agriculture and set to work, relying on his newly acquired knowledge and that of his parents.

Because his two jobs in town were very time-consuming, Luca could come only on weekends and could not spend a lot of time searching for inputs. He therefore used wage labor for the corn he planted and made contracts with Romcereal, taking advantage of its credits, inputs, and guaranteed purchase (even if at lower-than-market prices). In addition to grain, he planted some fodder crops and some potatoes, which he marketed in town himself. His production costs were initially low: being unincorporated, he paid no salaries, he bought gasoline "on the side" at a reduced price, and he did not use expensive substances such as herbicide and pesticide. In 1994 he calculated that his income from farming had almost doubled his monthly salary in his firm. And this was after he had withheld from sale 3,000 kg of wheat and 5,000 kg of corn for his parents to use as animal feed—they had two cows and a horse, as well as several pigs.

In addition, Luca worked out a clever way of increasing his yields without overly raising his production costs: he used a great deal of fertilizer by tinkering with his Romcereal contract. Anyone who contracted wheat received free fertilizer (a substance very difficult to find) at the rate of five 50-kg sacks/ha, against an obligatory contract of at least 1,000 kg of wheat per hectare, sold at the state price. He figured out that he could provide 15,000 kg of wheat and was not interested in marketing any of it on his own, so he contracted for 15 ha of wheat even though he had planted it on only 6 ha. This gave him 2.5 times the amount of free fertilizer he would otherwise have received, and his yields went up correspondingly—to an average of 5,500 kg/ha as against a normal average of 3,000–3,500. Although the maneuver was of dubious propriety, no one stopped him; indeed, when someone in the Romcereal office began asking questions about how he could contract this much, others defended him as "our serious client."

In 1996, Luca began planting less corn and using herbicide because the price of day labor had gone up. Also, he had had bad results with his workers not cutting the cornstalks, and it was simpler not to have to organize and oversee that work. To compensate for the change, he planted sugar beets, potatoes, and pulses, for rotational purposes. He sold his corn at a very low price to the moribund chicken farm near Vlaicu and was concerned that selling it in the future was going to take him more time than he had. In part for that reason and in part because of price trends, he began keeping more corn at home and raising pigs instead. He constructed a much larger pigsty and then hired someone to tend the animals. The very expensive herbicide (and occasional pesticides) he now used came from Romcereal on credit, repaid at the harvest. By these various devices, in 1996 he was content with his farming arrangements, which were still doubling his salary at work.

In 1997 he continued in more or less the same way, though he began keeping his books in dollars because the figures had become meaningless for comparative purposes if kept in lei. But he was worried, for soon Romcereal would not give inputs on credit and this would complicate things for him greatly. Whereas Romcereal had somewhat sheltered Luca from risk, now he was being thrown completely onto himself; he would have to mobilize all his inputs from his own resources each season. In 1998 for the first time he made no profit at all. By 1999 Luca was finding agriculture ever less profitable, owing to the loss of his guaranteed market and, he suspected, unfettered import of government-subsidized wheat from Hungary: "There's no one to take it to. We're at the mercy of traffickers and speculators." He calculated that he could make a "modest profit" only if he got yields of at least 3,200 kg/ha for both wheat and corn; without all the extra fertilizer, that was no longer easy. He stopped keeping track of his expenses, convinced that he was no longer making money. When his parents died, he said, he would give up this work.

A major problem was that with the neoliberal government's removal of such supports, Romanian agriculture was trying, as he put it, to match the prices of the Chicago Board of Trade without the subsidies U.S. farmers received. "Agricultural policy here is not set in a visionary and coherent way," he observed. "It's done for immediate political gain. The group that is most powerful gets what it wants for the moment—this is why things keep changing. They get a policy that fixes them up for now, and later they need something different." But from his viewpoint, the main thing preventing better results was the lack of marketing structures. "I have the knowledge and endowment adequate to get very good results, but not if I can't sell." The grain purchasers he managed to find often delayed paying him, so his earnings were already worth less when he finally received them. On the whole, Luca's starting from industry rather than agriculture had endowed him with little of the social capital that might help him find markets or lower his production costs; he was having to rely on his intelligence and on cultural capital he had acquired largely on his own.

In 2000 I found Luca less pessimistic. His wheat yield had been unusually high—4,800 kg/ha—and owing to bad weather elsewhere in the country prices started heading up. Anticipating this, bakers were posting ads to buy large quantities at a good price, so he sold his entire harvest to a single baker. He calculated that his income from agriculture had been 17 percent of his total income for the year—thus, at least something. What Luca nearly forgot to tell me about, however, was the 5.5 million lei in coupons that he had received from the election-conscious neoliberal government—these covered the entire cost of his wheat seed and fertilizer, plus half the herbicide. Without the coupons, he would barely have broken even. Meanwhile, he had resigned his factory job and hired on as manager of a foreign-owned agricultural concern. His new job would bring him into much closer contact with other agricultural specialists—to start making the connections his factory background had not given him—and this might affect his thinking about his family's farm.

Luca's careful record-keeping affords us a glimpse of a trend we have seen in chapter 5 and see again later: between 1994 and 2000, he moved from very little to substantial reliance on chemical inputs (treated seed, fertilizer, herbicides, and pesticides). The effect on his production costs was marked, as is evident from the structure of his expenditures. Whereas in 1994 his largest cost was labor and his smallest was chemical inputs, by 2000 it was chemicals that cost him the most—a whopping 40 percent of his total production costs (see table 8.1). The more his situation pushed him toward these inputs, the more risk he took on from an imported commodity whose price increases were fast outstripping all but gasoline. In the absence of subsidies this trend could lead to his withdrawal from agriculture.

Luca Avramescu was teetering on the brink of becoming a commercial farmer. Although he had not started with much expertise, he was extremely bright and had soon begun to impress agronomists with his knowledge. He was fortunate in his timing, for he managed to buy early most of the implements he needed at what soon became very small cost. He owed this in part to his high school contacts that brought him government credits and in part to his off-farm income. Thus independent of the Agromec, Luca could make good money even with Romcereal's low grain prices while benefiting from its guaranteed purchase and system of advances against the harvest. As long as Romcereal functioned, his initial lack of connections with suppliers or buyers did not matter. His managerial experience and connections grew with his new job, but, by summer 2002, he had grown unhappy with that job and was planning to strike out on his own, perhaps with another Vlaicean who had the pull to help him navigate the perilous waters of privatization.

Throughout the 1990s, Luca subsidized his farm with his state job and repair business. Resembling all three people presented so far in coming to agriculture late, he at first saw it as mainly a side hobby that helped his kin. The others, however, saw it as a central component of their multiple income-generating activities.[5] Only as of 2000 did farming become his central preoccupation; at that point, his connections began to catch up with the knowledge he had acquired. He and the other people discussed so far differ from those I consider now, for whom agriculture was and had long been their main way of life. I begin with one who emerged from the collective farm staff and then move on to three who came from state farms.

Table 8.1
One farmer's expenditure profile for 1994 and 2000[a]

Year	Gas/Oil	Seed	Chemical Inputs	Harvesting	Total
1994	18	36	8	38	100
2000	8	21	40	31	100

[a] Numbers represent percentages of total costs for that season.

Farmers with Special Expertise and Experience in Agriculture

Former Collective Farm Staff

Zucu Popa had training and extensive experience in agriculture and had worked for years on the veterinary staff of Vlaicu's collective farm. In 1990, Zucu's family recovered about 3 ha, plus some land in a state farm. Having lost his job in the CF, he decided he was sick of having someone else always telling him what to do; together with his parents, he decided to set up a small dairy farm. He persuaded one of the CF agronomists to join him—the only CF staff member to go out on his own—but Zucu ended up doing all the work. In 1991 he bought one of the CF barns at auction, stocking it inexpensively with some CF cattle (to which he had direct access) that remained after the herd was distributed to former members. He paid the million-leu total for start-up with his family's large savings (not yet devalued by inflation) and a bank loan, but when the interest on the latter rose from its original 13 percent to 70 percent within three months, Zucu sold some animals to pay off the rest of the loan. His goal was to buy about 10 ha of land and a tractor, which he thought would make him self-sufficient.

Owing to state controls on the price of dairy products, Zucu had problems from the very start. He had a guaranteed market through a state processing center, but it did not pay well, nor had he the time to spend marketing dairy products in town. Unlike Lila and Dan Bucur (discussed later), who also bought a barn but had other work and could wait for milk prices to improve, Zucu had no other work once the CF died; he had no choice but to begin no matter how unfavorable the conditions. To feed the cattle, he worked his land and took in a bit more, using tractorists from Vlaicu instead of the more expensive Agromec. He had virtually no contact with Romcereal or other state institutions other than the milk center. In hopes of keeping afloat as milk prices continued to stagnate, he started raising pigs, which sold better. Nonetheless, overwhelmed by the production costs, each season he had to sell a cow or two in order to produce food for the others, until gradually the herd was reduced to a handful. As he put it in 2000, "They ate each other up." By 1999 the farm had failed. When I asked him why, he pointed to the price controls that kept dairy products so low relative to production costs.

This venture had benefited initially from Zucu's work in socialist agriculture, but his land base was inadequate for amassing enough money to conduct his new venture profitably, and he had no cushion against risk. Having obtained a barn and some cows, he had exhausted most of his resources, which he could not renew as long as prices were controlled. In part Zucu's problem was the platform from which he had started: as mid-level staff of the collective farm. He knew about dairy cattle and this gave him the illusion that he could manage such an enterprise, but he could not make a long-term plan with several complementary lines of action, as did Toma Mezei, that would enable him to weather the riskiest period until commodity prices stabilized at a higher level. Like most mid-level CF personnel, his horizons and contacts did not extend much beyond the village, as did those of CF chairmen or agronomists (such as Nica of chapter 6)—the kinds of people who started associations. Zucu had no other resources to help with marketing or to support his activity while he got on his feet. In short, despite his initial advantage, his farm met the same fate that most other Vlaiceni were facing, in part for similar reasons.

Staff Emerging from State Farms They Had Left

I now turn to three cases whose trajectory is rooted in their having managed state farms. All three had wide contacts enhancing their access to information, to alternative sources of inputs, and to markets. All benefited from the experience of having managed large budgets at low risk, a situation they enjoyed into the 1990s until SF privatization came onto the agenda. All began their side business while still employed in the state sector; thus, they had salaries to fall back on if their venture should fail. In addition, all benefited from the two specific features of socialist property forms that I have pointed to in chapter 7: the devolution of administrative use-rights onto the directors of SOEs and the fuzzy boundaries between state property and their private ventures. In this respect, SF directors had an advantage over the leaders of collective farms, who, having lost their jobs, no longer had fuzzy property boundaries with which to develop their own enterprises, only the opportunity to cheat the smallholders whose land they managed if they formed associations. SF directors were the kinds of people most likely to become what I call supertenants, capable of working large amounts of others' land without the risks of actual ownership. I devote most of my time to one of these cases, prefaced by the other two so as to highlight contrasts.[6]

I refer in chapter 7 to Dora Filip, who had been a technician at and then briefly director of a Vlaicu state farm, SF3. Born in neighboring Vinerea, Dora did not live in Vlaicu; her local connections were with Vlaiceni who owned land in her SF. She lacked a university degree but had good mid-level training and deep familiarity with agriculture, enabling her always to obtain very good results. After 1989 her SF had a very similar trajectory to Traian's and Radu's, described in chapter 7: decreased support from the center required her increasingly to fend for herself. She too had endless problems with mayors trying to turn her surface area into a rubber sack for dividends to people not deserving them. Unlike Radu, however, she was always careful to show no surplus, only losses, which the surplus from farms such as Radu's would then have to cover.

She took out loans to upgrade her facilities, adding to the large SF system debt I discuss in chapter 7.

Like Traian and Radu, Dora was eager to collect clients for the future and tried to keep rents up for that reason—usually between 800 and 1,000 kg of wheat per rented hectare. Her long-term plan was to build up her SF, buy it, and, by working extra land from villagers, go into the meat-processing business. That is, all her accumulation would come from work in agriculture, her specialty. When I asked how she chose that path, she described a trip she had taken to Hungary right after 1989. Having never been outside Romania, she was stunned to see how much better organized Hungarian agriculture was and how much more disciplined its workforce. Her connections abroad were consolidated when her daughter married an Austrian.

Closer to home, she was very well connected with people in Deva, at the Agromecs, at Romcereal, and elsewhere. This was fortunate, because in 1996 she was fired for malfeasance (rumor had it that she had taken the fall for people higher up in the SF system). Taking with her the owners from whom she was renting 130 ha, she began to farm these on her own, with much discretionary help from her contacts at Romcereal and the Agromec. In 1997 she earned a 100-million-leu profit using the special cheap credits they offered her—and was appalled to find that this fell far short of the cost of the agricultural implements she had hoped to purchase. Nor would she be able to acquire in short order the 100 ha of land she intended to buy.

Dora now began diversifying her activities, engaging in some questionable practices with privatization vouchers for the local Agromec; she hoped to take it over when it would eventually go bankrupt. Having nothing but an inexpensive apartment as collateral, this was the only way she could see to obtain machinery for expanded land rental. She admitted to me that although she felt liberated by no longer having an SF to run, it had indeed helped her to accumulate a bit on the side and she missed that now. Also, she found it frightening to be exposed to so much risk and was having insomnia: "An SF director can sell a cow if he needs money for a debt, but I can't." Hoping to shed some of that risk onto the smallholders, she rented only their best land and promised them nothing if it should be flooded.

In the end, Dora's socialist-era connections were inadequate to her needs. Her trajectory shows the consequences of relying too long on the possibility of privatizing her SF; that is, she had trouble thinking outside the confines of that form and assumed that her existing social capital would carry her through every problem. Therefore, she failed to acquire the necessary equipment for herself before the price scissors widened. Her connections helped her only as long as the state institutions (such as Romcereal and the Agromec) were functioning, but once that ceased, those contacts were useless. Outside the state framework, she could not accumulate enough to outfit herself for independent farming—to buy land and equipment, build storage space, pay rising production costs, and still make a profit. Contributing to this was the fact that without infrastructure all she could grow was grain, a commodity that could be immediately unloaded to state warehouses but in the Transylvanian context was the worst-paid agricultural product. She decided to take a different route to success, maneuvering herself into a place on a land commission, from which she might more easily obtain land of her own. Note, however, that at no point did she cease to regard land as a source of value.

One of Dora's competitors in the supertenant market was Ion Olaru, whom I met in 1997. Born in neighboring Gelmar but residing in a town about 40 km distant, Ion had excellent university training and had been employed for a number of years as chief agronomist of a large state farm in a different SF system. His family, one of the most respected in Gelmar before 1945, repossessed over 9 ha in Gelmar and asked him to work it for them, despite the long commute. Friendly with the people in the bank from his SF days, he told me, he was able to secure a low-interest loan for buying equipment and in 1993 purchased a tractor, two seeders, and a plow.[7] Soon thereafter, he bought additional used equipment from the more prosperous farming areas in the western Banat, where farmers bought used German tractors from Hungary and then sold their older ones eastward.

In 1995 Ion left his state farm and (using his SF connections) found a job in the county Agriculture Department. From this vantage point he had superb access to information about changes in government policy, newly available technology or credits, and so forth—not to mention, of course, the state salary that protected him somewhat from the risks he faced. He decided to expand his activities in Gelmar by renting up to 100 ha from villagers there, taking advantage of the fact that Gelmar's fields, unlike Vlaicu's, had been consolidated. At first he planted corn to feed pigs, but given their low sale prices and the closure of a nearby pig SF (a possible market), he switched to sunflower seed and sugar beets, crops for which the state would supply start-up credits. That freed him of entanglements with banks, which he had found a source of great uncertainty. "Let's say I begin an undertaking with a 58 percent interest loan, and I plan it on a three-year investment cycle. Within two months, the interest is 165 percent, and there's no way I can pay it off because I don't expect results for three years. I'm not likely to take these kinds of chances!" He was fortunate that his wife's brother in Germany could help with financing, so he could buy a building for storage. "Unlike some people," he said, "we had start-up capital."

Amid rusting Agromec equipment destined for the scrap-metal market, a supertenant's new used combine.

A supertenant's equipment inventory, sheltered in an old collective farm structure he has bought.

Ion also complained about problems with the quality of the inputs available locally. He had bought treated seed, but plant maladies appeared anyway because the seed company had taken shortcuts (or had approved substandard seed when it happened to come from their friends); thus, a farmer could pay a lot for seed that did not do its job, jeopardizing his future. In addition, Romanian herbicides often did not work because they were adulterated. Although foreign ones were unthinkably expensive, he told me, "We're too poor to buy cheap! From now on, I buy only the most expensive imported products because they increase my chances of getting a really good result." Because no one in Gelmar could believe, however, that he was actually spending the unimaginable sums he claimed to spend on Pioneer seed, doubts arose in the minds of some of those who rented to him (whose receipts were partly a function of his costs).

By 1997 Ion was moving toward more specialized crops so as not to compete with every peasant doing grains. He planted more sunflower seed, sugar beets, and potatoes but avoided the lucrative tobacco, for want of labor.[8] Using his contacts from the Agriculture Department, he procured inputs—the most up-to-date available—at much lower prices than most of his peers, but he complained of trouble finding markets and this reduced his profits. And he also protested that the level of government taxation was virtually forcing growers like him into tax evasion.[9] Otherwise, given the lack of state supports, the burgeoning cost of inputs, and the low price of grain, the income tax of 40 percent or more would preclude agricultural livelihood altogether.

For a time, Ion was competing with Dora and found her hard to beat. Dora, he objected, had had the advantage (until she was fired) of using state-supplied materials and equipment for which she did not have to pay, thus enabling her to give better rents in her private business—as much as 1,000 kg/ha, while Ion could give only 700, sometimes less. After Dora was forced into business on her own, her connections at Romcereal and the Agromec had provided her with similar breaks. Ion found Dora's advantages "unfair competition," forgetting his own advantage from his city job. His response was to court Gelmareni by other means, seeking to gain their trust. He believed that Dora's luck could not hold, and if he could only keep going another two or three years she would fail—as indeed happened. Meanwhile, his special attractions included (as he put it) how good his crops looked, compared with Dora's (that is, a better "visible economy"); his being from a well-respected Gelmar family with a reputation for integrity, something Dora did not have; his ability to pay his urban members cash without delay after the harvest; and the extra services he was willing to provide, such as plowing for his members if they also had some land not in his association—even hauling their produce directly to their doors. In other words, Ion competed according to the values of the smallholders that I describe

Landlord and tenant. The tenant is on the left, with his equipment behind him (photo by author).

in chapter 5. Facilitating his social capital of trust was that Ion lived far away, not in Gelmar, and this meant villagers would not see things that might make them suspicious. Gelmareni would not have understood, for instance, that when he bought an extravagantly expensive house in the city, it was mainly because he needed a valuable possession to use as collateral for bank loans each year, having no title yet to his family's land and not wanting to risk his agricultural equipment for such a purpose.

By 1999, Ion had shifted almost entirely to specialized crops, cultivating seed varieties specific to Transylvania (which sold much better than regular crops) and planting only as much grain as was necessary for in-kind payment of rents. In addition, he had bought special potato seed from Holland that had given extraordinary yields, although the cost of producing them was equally extraordinary: 26 million lei/ha in 1998 and 35 million in 1999 (as against about 7 million for grain). To sell his crop, he made contracts with hospitals and canteens; his wife, deeply implicated in the business, took the rest to market herself. Potatoes suited Transylvanian conditions and thus reduced exposure to competition from southern and western Romania, where it was too hot to grow them. Now his ambition was to buy a foreign tractor and combine, much superior to Romanian ones, he felt—they used less gas and did not keep breaking down. Formerly he had been afraid of banks, but he was now realizing that debts were an advantage because inflation ate them up, so he was prepared to borrow for these acquisitions; their price, however, left him reeling.

When I spoke with Ion in 2000, things were harder than before but he was still afloat, his agricultural income equaling his official salary. For storage he had bought an old CF barn—at astronomical cost—from the Italian who had gotten it cheap at auction a few years before. To manage his increased exposure to risk he had taken a number of steps. First, he continued to limit his tax burden, and he apportioned his losses (such as the losses from 30 ha of inundated crops) among all those from whom he rented. Second, he had changed his formal job to one that gave him even better access to cheap inputs, thereby holding down his spiraling production costs. Third, he had bought some land (about 15 ha), although he was not really interested in going that route, preferring tenancy arrangements. I no longer heard about the more ambitious plans he had spoken of earlier—going into food processing, becoming a food wholesaler, and so on. His planning frame had constricted. Nevertheless, in 2001 I learned that he had left his salaried job altogether and was living entirely from agriculture.

During one of my conversations with Ion in 1997, he had expressed his regret at not having the money for the technology he needed. Technology was his obsession—indeed, an admiring competitor attributed his good results to his being an excellent farmer "who respects the proper technology." Ion's exactitude in this regard had caught him, however, in the price scissors involving not just Romanian commodities but foreign ones. To avoid the defects of Romanian products, he had put himself in the worst possible situation: producing for Romanian consumers but buying western inputs at western prices in the belief that the increased yields justified the expense. It was a risky strategy because the never-ending devaluation of Romania's currency (to support the many loss-making state industries still not privatized even in 2001) was making Ion's exposure to foreign prices ever more dangerous. Adding to his risk was the likelihood that foreign companies were dumping their wares, as his friend who sold foreign inputs had begun to realize from witnessing the battle by Ciba-Sandosz to capture the Romanian market. Once they had succeeded and raised their prices again, they might ruin people such as Ion, technologically sophisticated farmers working modest surfaces on a very small margin.

This kind of scenario is not, of course, unique to Romania: it happens all over the world, bankrupting farmers in emerging markets. But the consequences I wish to note for this local setting are those for the farmer's tenancy relations. In chapter 6 I argue that because associations worked at a higher technological level than smallholders might on their own and then deducted the costs of that technology from members' returns, they contributed to impoverishing the smallholders whose land they worked. This may be even truer for cases such as Ion's. A supertenant using the most expensive technology in the world (and especially if he is also selling his harvest in bulk at low state prices, for lack of time to find better markets) exposes the owners to vastly greater risk than those people would ever have assumed themselves. Perhaps his yields would be so much larger as to cover the higher costs completely, even bringing the land's owners substantial reward. But that was unlikely, given that the rents were fixed, not proportional to yields. If his crop were compromised, moreover, he would spread those very high risks among his smallholders.

Ion's story shows an expert seeking a market niche with cash crops dependent on foreign technology. His information-rich state job, highly specialized knowledge, and vast web of connections both drove up his pretensions and enabled him to hold down as much as possible the costs of equipment and production at that high level. These were qualities shared by many state farm directors. Familiar with complex technology, accustomed to thinking in terms of large budgets, and wealthy in connections that could lead them to cost savings and sometimes to new markets, they had the best chance to make it as commercial farmers.

Nonetheless, Ion may have pushed the envelope too far.[10] In the Romanian context, his dependence on tenancy relations might enable him to spread some risk, but it also constricted his space for maneuvering, given that his tenants could always move to other supertenants operating at somewhat lower levels of expenditure. In the final section, I describe one such state farm director, equally endowed with Ion's advantages, whose strategy for moving into commercial farming was somewhat different. Once again, to protect my respondents, the picture I provide is a composite.

Staff Emerging from State Farms They Still Managed

In chapter 7 I describe at length the story of Traian and Radu, attempting to keep their SFs alive for eventual privatization, and I hinted at ways in which their jobs might have helped them build up their own farming business on the side. This indeed happened after their state farms were sold and they took up work on their own. Now I wish to explore that trajectory for another state farm director, Lila Bucur, and her husband Dănilă, known as Dan, by which they moved from running a state farm to becoming supertenants engaged in commercial farming on their own. Lila had served for a number of years as director of yet another Vlaicu state farm, SF4. Before that, she had worked in various posts in the state agricultural sector and was widely respected. So was Dan, who had also been employed in state agriculture and had many connections; in the 1990s he held one such job, from which he was gradually disengaging. Because the couple collaborated closely on all ventures, I sometimes refer to SF4 as "their" state farm. Both had university training, tremendous energy, and a great deal of initiative; both were excellent farmers. Moreover, Dan was a very charming fellow with a flair for making friends. In a word, they entered the 1990s well endowed with social and cultural capital. Although they lived not in Vlaicu but a short distance away, they had kin in the village and would further localize themselves by purchasing buildings there.

The Bucurs' situation resembled that of Traian and Radu in many particulars. Because SF4 was a fairly good farm, they—like Dora, Traian, and Radu, with whom they were on friendly terms—hoped to be able to privatize it. They too reasoned that it would be cheaper to launch themselves into commercial farming from a state farm base than from scratch, as Dora was having to do. SF4 did well enough to enable reasonably good returns for shareholders, and they hoped this would win them future tenancy arrangements. In addition, SF4 was caught in the same infelicitous situation as those other farms, having also been apportioned a large share of SFS-Simeria's debt. Its product was disaggregable, like Traian's, which enabled them to sell items for the farm's needs without going through the center. Like Traian and Radu but unlike Ion and post-1996 Dora, they were directing their state farm simultaneously with their gradual move into commercial farming.

Lila and Dan enjoyed one post-1989 form of capital resembling Dora's and Ion's but in much greater measure: foreign social capital. Whereas Dora had traveled to Hungary and had a daughter in Austria and Ion had a brother-in-law in Germany, the Bucurs had traveled to Western Europe on several occasions. First, they became friendly with some Austrians, who invited them for a visit in 1990—their first trip abroad. The visit was life-altering for them. As they looked around at the well-kept and productive small farms to which they were taken, they vowed to aim for something like this themselves. For that reason, they clung even more tenaciously than their state-farm colleagues to the thought of privatizing SF4 and cared even more fervently about maintaining good shareholder relations. Their foreign social capital developed further through some Belgians who came to visit the area; unlike other Vlaiceni, Dan spoke some French. Over the decade, the Belgians came often and the Bucurs traveled to visit them, managing to purchase through them a used combine. Maintaining this foreign social capital interfered a bit, however, with his kinship relations, for his kin grew tired of having to cook for these people all the time and his elderly aunt felt neglected, avenging herself with bouts of illness precisely when the Belgians were to arrive. These ceased as soon as her nephew included her in the festivities.

Although fully immersed in their state farm, the Bucurs anticipated a future as independent farmers and started to plan for it. Wary of banks, they preferred to find other ways of raising money. Already in 1990 Dan had noticed that beer was nowhere to be found and decided he should try to rectify this; he worked out a deal with the local German priest to rent and maintain a truck belonging to the German organization in Orăştie. His connections in the Agriculture Department in Deva helped him navigate the ocean of bureaucratic requirements for establishing a limited liability company, and he paid for the authorizations and the first shipment of beer by selling some fattened livestock. With the truck he drove to three Romanian beer factories and supplied beer to local restaurants and bars. He found it a very lucrative activity, bringing him at first about 300,000 lei/month—a huge sum of money, at the time—but ended it later when the arrangement became less advantageous.

In 1991, they used some of this accumulation to buy a seeder, a small building, and a barn when Vlaicu's CF began auctioning off its patrimony. Although they confessed to me that the sums involved were frighteningly large, they had seen large budgets before and would manage to cover the price of the barn with a few months' beer transport, plus some loans from their kin. They developed a long-term plan: with their earnings from beer they would open a bar in the small building and then use the proceeds from that to set up a bakery and eventually a dairy farm, with butchering on the side. When the bar in fact opened (under the supervision of a partner), it too brought a good return. Now they began to think about buying some equipment for farming the 10 ha their kin had recovered.

Instead of going to the bank for a loan, however, they put their money in the Caritas pyramid scheme, about which they had learned from a relative who had gotten the promised eightfold return in three months. This scheme, as I argue elsewhere, enabled many Romanians to imagine previously unimaginable sums of money and to accumulate some as well, if they were lucky (see Verdery 1995). Dan and Lila invested the full proceeds of their relatives' 1993 wheat harvest. Then, having learned that the price of tractors was about to go up again, they took the money out three months later, increased eightfold. They were fortunate because soon thereafter the scheme collapsed, taking everyone else's money (including mine) down with it. Borrowing a bit more from their kin, they bought their tractor in 1993 with 3.4 million lei—about five times Lila's annual salary. Very important in this story is that by obtaining their equipment through the pyramid scheme, they avoided speculation as to what illegalities might be enabling them to make so much money.

At this point they began thinking seriously about their planned dairy farm, but given the low price of milk they decided to wait, leaving the barn unused. They started their bakery but found that here, too, state-controlled prices made it a losing proposition for the moment. Instead, they used their barn to begin raising pigs, fed from their relatives' 10 ha, and sold them in the market rather than to Vlaiceni. "If I sell to villagers, they all have a reason why I should give them a better price than I want to. To avoid problems with them, I'd rather sell to strangers," Dan explained. He was finding his local social capital an encumbrance.

Dan and Lila often expressed concern about their public image. When they bought their first piece of land, they were glad that it was off at the margins of Vlaicu, where it would be less visible to Vlaiceni. Later, when the Association began to fall apart, they generally did not offer its members their services: "Let them come to us, and then we can leap to their rescue. If we go ask for their land, they'll say we're greedy." The episode with Caritas and the tractor was yet another example. "You have to remember that under the communists, the term 'businessman' [*afacerist*] was a term of opprobrium, meaning someone who was dishonest," they reminded me (the word connoted "speculator" or "racketeer," alongside "businessman"). "People still have this mentality, and it makes privatization even harder—especially in the middle of a small community." Dan fretted that villagers inevitably would not believe he could obtain a corn yield of 8,000 kg/ha (smallholders' yields were at best 3,000–4,000) without stealing from somewhere. Thus, he aimed to expand very slowly so his progress would not raise suspicions of shady dealings: "Instead of going 120 kilometers an hour, we can get somewhere by going 90, and that's what we plan to do."

All these concerns, I believe, were part of their strategy for gaining villagers' confidence and trust, toward the possibility of future tenancy arrangements. At a party we all attended, they were explicit about these concerns. Lila observed, "We have to behave differently these days," as Dan was telling of an exchange with the former CF agronomist now heading Şibot's association: "He has the habit of talking down to villagers, and I told him, 'You have to be more polite with them, because any day now we'll depend on them for our livelihood. If they don't give us their land, we're sunk. It's their land, we need them if we're going to have a future.'" Conscious of competition from Dora, who was still paying her owners 1,000 kg/ha, as well as of the better rate paid by Ion, they were constantly anxious about the precarious budget of SF4. Because they hoped to buy it, they wanted to reinvest its proceeds in upgrading the facilities but feared losing their tenancy prospects if dividends dropped too low. As we see in chapter 7, this problem plagued other SF directors who hoped to rent land, too.

Meanwhile, in 1994 they decided they needed not just the small tractor they had already bought but also a larger one, partly for themselves and partly to use on Lila's SF. She went to the bank to pick up the forms for a loan she hoped their friends at the Agriculture Department would help them obtain; but reading the fine print and grasping the principle of variable interest rates, she renounced this plan. Moreover, she bridled at the necessity of paying a commission (a bribe) of as much as 15–20 percent to obtain the loan at all. Instead they bid at auction on a used tractor from the Agromec (perhaps assisted by their good relations with the Agromec director). Although I did not ask about the source of their funds, it was clear that the tractor's use would straddle the fuzzy boundary between SF4 and their emerging private farm.

That enterprise was now growing as a few Vlaiceni came to ask the couple to rent their land; in 1996 the Bucurs worked about 15 ha in addition to their family's, in 1997 about 20 ha, and in 2000 about 35 ha. Beyond this, they had begun buying some land of their own. The rhythm of their purchases varied with their hopes for privatizing their state farm: when those prospects looked good they would hold off buying land, and when the prospects waned they bought as much as they could. Although they were coy about the amount they had acquired by 2001, I believe the figure was around 25 ha. Their intention, as they had explained it in 1997, was that if buying SF4 did not pan out, they would raise and sell pigs by working their own land and renting some from Vlaiceni; then they would move into meat processing. At each step they sought to control as much of the production process as possible, cutting out intermediaries who ate into their returns. Lila even developed a taste for taking produce weekly to the marketplace—both their own and the produce she needed to sell to keep things going at SF4. Here again, the boundaries between the two enterprises were fuzzy.

When I expressed surprise that they could do so well if SF4 was foundering, Dan explained that because it was impossible for them to get out from under SFS-Simeria's debts, they were putting most of their effort into their own activities, seeking only to pay some dividends and to make a few improvements to SF4 if they could. But if they tried to work it more intensively, they would need loans that might outstrip the value of its fixed assets, which they hoped eventually to take over. He insisted to me that they kept the budgets for SF4 and their own firm separate, and this may well be true. Nonetheless, what he forgot to mention was that for all this time, they were drawing two hefty salaries from their state jobs. This greatly reduced the risk entailed in their home activities because even if those failed they would still have income. Whereas their two salaries helped them accumulate for further purchases of equipment and inputs at home (true of Ion in Gelmar, too, but with only one salary), people such as Zucu and Dora post-1996 had no such cushion. If the privatization plan worked, Dan and Lila would also acquire risk-free any improvements they had made on SF4. Perhaps the lower risk contributed to their ability to think very long term and to entertain many options simultaneously.

Here, on a small scale, we have another example of what Stark (1996) calls "recombinant property." Even if (improbably) no other materials from the formal workplace were drawn into the private one, the state-sector salary was facilitating the Bucurs' side accumulations. Personnel of the former collective farms had no such advantage unless they found state-sector jobs after 1989; if they merely started associations or launched their own firms, they were much more vulnerable to risk than were state employees. This realization helped me to understand why Lila, like Traian and Radu, stayed on at her SF: even after SFs had been completely devalued, until they were sold they still remained a source of revenue for their directors. One further irony is that because administrative councils and shareholders' assemblies appointed by the State Property Fund received 20 percent of whatever salary the SOE director was then receiving, as I explain in chapter 7, these councils were constantly pushing up directors' salaries so as to receive a larger take. Therefore, the very people who were helping to bankrupt Traian's, Radu's, and Lila's state farms were also increasing the cushion of those farms' directors as private entrepreneurs.

By 1999, as it became clear that Lila's SF too, like those of Traian and Radu, would be auctioned for more than they could afford, she and Dan set about trying to find a foreign buyer with whom they could work. Eyal, Szelényi, and Townsley (1998, 142) refer to this as a "comprador" strategy, suggesting that foreign buyers often prefer to employ former socialist managers who have the necessary know-how and connections—a pattern found even with new West German owners in eastern Germany (see Buechler and Buechler 2002). Starting unsuccessfully with their Belgian friends, Lila and Dan lined up a serious prospect, Lauro (yet another Italian). His first question—"Where will you sell the products?"—led Lila to find two possible outlets: a privatized chicken farm and an alcohol factory some distance away, both of which would buy good corn in bulk at a reasonably good price. Because SF4's finances were in such parlous shape, Lauro agreed to finance a trial year (even though he had not yet bought the farm) by paying for the inputs. This, of course, enabled the couple to pay SF4's shareholders better returns than they could have otherwise, and they hoped villagers would remember that the next year. Lila expressed her worries about what would happen if this arrangement did not go well, revealing precisely the risk strategy I have outlined: "Then we'll have to go out completely on our own, take our own risks, get loans so we can work maybe 100 ha from the villagers we think we can get along with best."

Meanwhile, the couple was still raising pigs on their own farm and working land for their kin and other Vlaiceni. They had pulled back from specialty crops such as tobacco or the sunflower seed and sugar beets that Ion was doing in Gelmar because they knew too many cases in which the buyers of such products had cheated the growers. Instead, they concentrated on the traditional Transylvanian pattern: grains and fodder crops for animals. Well trained like Ion, on the other hand, they invested in expensive inputs, some of these foreign (such as Pioneer seed), and were deeply alarmed by the price increases. In summer 2000 Dan estimated their production costs as 6–8 million lei/ha—compare this with the Association's figure of 3–4 million for the same year—but he knew those would be proportionately much higher the following season. (In January 2001 he confirmed that the price of herbicide had doubled in just nine months.) They were once again diversifying their portfolio by opening a small store, reasoning, as Lila put it, "If we can't make money in production, we'll do commerce." Dan was convinced that the furniture factory being built (by yet another Italian) in the CF barn near his store would bring customers right to his doorstep. The store would occupy the small building that had earlier housed their bar, which they had had to close in 1997 because of a quarrel with their business partner, Ştefan.[11]

In autumn 2000, with the collapse of the Association, their situation changed abruptly. In addition to the rental arrangements they already had, they were besieged by Vlaiceni wanting them as tenants. Given their other activities, they took on only 100 ha for 2001, the most they thought they could manage. The decision had its costs, however. First, their storage facilities were now inadequate, so they rented the Association's granary on the argument that they were serving its members, but the Council soon withdrew its permission. Second, they found the Association's land—uncultivated for three years—in such poor condition that it required large quantities of inputs, especially herbicides, that were ever more expensive. Now they too were depending on the government's coupons, without which they would barely have broken even, and even so their yields on that land were poor. They began scaling back their expectations, using a local variety of corn rather than Pioneer and doubting that they could take so much land for 2002.

Although the tenancy relations they formed beginning in the late 1990s might indicate that their various investments in creating trust were paying off, it was also true that villagers now had few viable options for working their land. Ion was busy with Gelmar, Dora was gone, as were most sharecroppers, and other aspiring supertenants could not yet absorb all the land people wanted to have worked. Thus, smallholders had to accept Lila and Dan's terms, and these were not generous. The rental contracts specified a fixed rent of 300 kg/ha of wheat for the first year and increasing increments for the next two, up to 500 kg/ha. To justify the 300 kg rent, Dan said it was an amount they would always be able to meet, given the escalating costs of inputs. If the harvest were good, they could add a bit more (as indeed they did). The gap was nonetheless very wide: 300 kg/ha was 7–10 percent of the Bucurs' usual wheat harvest, far from the 33–50 percent other Vlaiceni were telling me they expected—ignorant of the punishing expenditures of farming at the Bucurs' high technological level.

In sum, the couple was putting most of the risk of harvest fluctuation onto the owners and keeping the difference (which in the end they could use to buy these very same people's land when it became too burdensome to own). Although smallholders grumbled that the amount was too low, by this time many were just grateful to have the land worked at all (see also Szelényi 1998, 14). Lila and Dan were not, of course, the only people throwing risk onto owners, as I have already shown with Ion and Dora. We can raise again the same question posed concerning Ion: Because the Bucurs worked at a much higher technological level and at much greater expense per hectare than smallholders would, yet the owners gained little from the added yields because the rent was fixed, might the low level of that rent be subsidizing the supertenants while impoverishing the owners?

The examples of these various supertenants suggest that leasing might in fact be more profitable than owning. Leasing enables shucking off the risks and liabilities that owners are forced to bear, liabilities that in this period of Romania's history were substantial. That very conclusion began to dawn on agricultural economists after a decade of privatization: creating private property rights to land might be less desirable, after all, than leasing use-rights to it (e.g., Hagedorn 2000; Hagelschuer 2000). Milczarek (2000, 21) too suggests that the winners in SF privatization were SF managers who could rent land cheaply. This view conforms to late twentieth-century developments in intellectual property-rights regimes worldwide, wherein leasing rather than owning was becoming the rule (see, e.g., Parry 2004). It conforms as well with socialism's quasi-use-rights system, which had amply shown the benefits of being able to throw onto the state/owner liabilities such as infrastructure maintenance.

In this light, it is perhaps puzzling that Dan and Lila were buying land, stepping up their purchases in case the deal with Lauro did not work out. They imagined eventually having a farm of their own with 50–100 ha, no longer relying on tenancy arrangements. At SF4 they were now making rental contracts with the villagers about to become owners, knowing that the rental law gave right of preemption to the tenant (i.e., themselves) should the owner decide to sell. "We're at a special conjuncture," Dan explained. "Now is the time to buy land. It's cheap, but no one else can afford to buy it." In 2001 Lila told me of a Vlaicean, Valeria, who needed cash urgently and offered her a piece of good land. "We went to the market together, I sold five piglets and gave Valeria the money; then Valeria bought a cow with it!" Another vanished hectare. Later she added, "It costs the same amount to work a hectare—10 million—as it does to buy one!" Between August of 2000 and January of 2001 they bought 3.5 ha at about 800 deutsche marks/ha and another 13.2 at 1,100 marks/ha—about

$550/ha. This amounted to a year's pay for an office secretary, one-half year's for a well-paid skilled worker, or the price of a really good dairy cow at that time.

But why were they loading themselves down with all the risks of owning, rather than continuing to pass most of the risk off onto the smallholder? Why did they see ownership of land as diminishing risks that the latter-day partisans of use-rights see them centralizing dangerously in themselves? Their strategy ran counter to the rationale of capitalist corporations: obtain control, and spread the risk among the shareholders who own the firm. Dan and Lila were going in the opposite direction, and ethnography enables us to see why this might make sense.

First, they would say, individual ownership, which they had been largely denied under socialism, had a positive value that no economist's reasoning can easily demolish. Augmenting its value was their special competence, which enabled them to be effective owners, unlike most smallholders. Second, they resisted the idea of giving away part of their work, which is how they understood renting. Third, Dan said, once production costs on a hectare nearly equaled the price of that hectare, leasing ceased to make sense. And finally, in the context of high instability and uncertainty with respect to both values and risks, the couple saw their profits as surer the more production factors they brought under their direct control before prices rose further; this was best done by owning. Owning their tractors freed them of usurious machinery rentals; given the ever-widening price scissors, if they did not buy their tractor today they might not be able to afford it tomorrow. Owning their land also freed them of uncertainty about whether enough villagers would stick with them as tenants when they felt compelled by economic instability to pay such modest rents. Given the ridiculously low price of land, if they bought today they could buy more than if they waited until later, when their profit margin might have decreased. From this viewpoint, ownership reduced risk.

For supertenants such as the Bucurs, then, ownership meant something very different from its meaning for smallholders. For the latter, ownership that had initially promised mastery had ended by loading them with risks they had trouble escaping. Pressed constantly toward cash outlays by the labor shortage, they had seen their land lose both cultural and economic value. Having nothing else in their "portfolio," they were not in a position to diversify it. For the Bucurs, by contrast, ownership meant maximizing their control over the few factors they could control, even at the expense of centralizing risk in themselves. They could do so because they had significant resources for managing that risk: expertise, salaries, connections, and information the ordinary villager lacked, which led them to cost savings, markets, and additional resources. Lila and Dan could therefore see continued value in farming.

It is to this that I refer with the phrase *value transformation* in my chapter title. How were Lila and Dan transforming value? First, they were buying land others found too burdensome or insufficiently rewarding and no longer culti-vated, and once they bought it that land was producing crops and income. In-deed, given the price of land and their farming methods, they could pay off the entire purchase price in two or three years, after which everything it produced would be to their gain. In addition to these purchases, by renting the land of Vlaiceni whom the Association had abandoned, they were revalorizing it eco-nomically as a productive asset. Buying land increased its value for them further because they saw this as lowering their exposure to risk, in a context in which they were having to learn new budgetary practices.

Second, they used the proceeds to buy from the Association another CF barn, which had sat unused for a decade, deteriorating. Once repaired, it would hold their equipment and their larger harvests.[12] In November 2000 Dan and Lila paid for it one hundred times the sum that they had paid for an identical one in 1991, but given that the nonfood consumer price index in this period had increased by more than 50,000,[13] the barn's economic value had plummeted. Their repairing and using it would diminish that trend. Similarly, they had also bought at auction some old equipment from SF3 that likewise was unused and deteriorating but would now be brought into more productive circuits. In this way, they had returned to profitable use a number of objects of economic value caught in the larger political processes of devaluation.

These examples of creating value accord with a capitalist perspective, the principal transformation of value that privatization programs aimed for: to cre-ate private property rights that would enable farmers to allocate production factors more efficiently. Although there is considerable overlap between this view and the way Lila and Dan thought about their activity, we might point to other revaluations, too. The most important is that the Bucurs saw their work on the land as giving them a chance to manifest their talents and their character, to show what they could really do—something they felt the socialist organiza-tion of agriculture had hindered. (Recall Radu's comment, in chapter 7, that state-farm accounting practices had "clipped his wings.") Finally they would be able to reveal their personal capacities by farming well under nonsocialist con-ditions. This was not the same as the visible economy of smallholders because, although the couple of course wanted to be seen as good farmers, they hoped in some ways to be invisible, so as to reduce villagers' envy. Dan preferred distant plots that would be out of view, fearing that if he took numerous piled-high cartloads through the center of the village and then distributed paltry rents, people would suspect him of stealing their rightful due. For the Bucurs, visible mastery could boomerang and undermine the economic success that was more important to them.[14] This marked a substantial transformation of the value of land, no longer a matter of specific parcels beautifully worked.

In becoming commercial farmers, Lila and Dan combined aspects of the biographies of other people considered in this chapter. They started accumulating through petty commerce, like the small entrepreneurs with whom I began, and they maintained such activities alongside their farming for much of the decade. Together with Toma Mezei and Andrei Maior, they kept many options open at once, shifting their efforts and resources from one to another option according to the prevailing economic winds. Eyal, Szelényi, and Townsley refer to this as "standing on many legs" (1998, 152). In addition, they acquired important pieces of equipment early on. They used expensive technology, like Ion Olaru, but did not go as far as he in crop specialization, believing they could accumulate enough by raising and selling livestock without going over to crops as phenomenally risky as Ion's Dutch potatoes. Even so, like Ion and like Luca Avramescu, they were becoming captive to an alarming trend: increased reliance on expensive imported inputs in highly unstable market conditions.

How had Dan and Lila's origin in state agricultural institutions facilitated their success? It had supported them with salaries when other income was uncertain, and it had endowed them with technical knowledge, managerial experience, and extensive connections. Moreover, Dan observed, because their professional training was broad rather than hyperspecialized, they were able to cope in many circumstances (cf. Burawoy and Lukács 1992, chap. 4.). Finally, their SF origins had given them a platform—continued state employment—from which to ease into private farming, enabling them to benefit from the fuzzy property boundaries at the bottom of the hierarchy of administrative estates.

Conditions of Success in Transforming Value

What do these cases suggest about the routes to commercial farming in postsocialist Transylvania? A number of possibilities appear in the material I have presented, among them the opening of borders to foreign travel; the amount of land one's family recovered (most of these people had at least 6–8 ha of land to use as the basis for a private farm); an ability to find markets that would pay better than the state price; the role of serendipity, as with the Belgians who took a liking to Dan; and so on. I emphasize four others: supplementary income, crop specialization, aspects of timing, and forms and sources of capital endowment. All of these were critical to a person's ability to mitigate risk and to find or create value in agriculture, a site (as I have shown in chapters 5–7) of so much devaluation.

One important condition of success was that no one, whether individual households or state farm directors, could get ahead in agriculture without other sources of income: pensions, infusions of cash from abroad, or salaries from official jobs. These incomes protected their recipients against the tremendous risk and uncertainty deriving from government policy and the world economy, and I believe they help to explain why Dora and Zucu went out of business while Ion, Lila, and Dan did not. Outside income is important to sustaining agriculture in many other parts of the world, not just the formerly socialist bloc. What may be peculiar to these cases is the role played by state incomes (pensions and state salaries) in enabling people to survive in a sector the postsocialist governments systematically undervalued. In the case of the smaller entrepreneurs—Toma, Luca, Andrei, and the Daras—their extra income flowed from petty commerce, which provided an independent source of accumulation, even though on a modest scale. Lila and Dan, too, recognized the importance of this, opening their store as they were moving away from their salaried jobs. All these people knew the value of a diversified portfolio—a condition of which was, of course, having something already in the portfolio to diversify from. The larger point, as Stark and Bruszt (1998, 132) put it, is that firms take risks not when they are pushed to the wall but when they are buffered.

A special form of outside income that gave its recipients a leg up was contacts with or (better) financing from people abroad. Dora, Dan, and Lila had connections in Austria and Belgium, whence they obtained advice and help with equipment. In addition, part of Dan and Lila's production costs in 1999 was paid by their prospective Italian buyer, Lauro. Two other examples are Ion, who received some start-up capital from his brother-in-law in Germany, and Radu (chapter 7), whose contract with Belgian brewers in 1997 and 1998 entailed their supplying some of the inputs. A final instance is Cornel, a big-time local operator, who bought a CF barn in Vlaicu and installed a flour mill in it. For many years, Cornel (not from Vlaicu) had run a restaurant on the highway nearby, and he had a wealth of connections with foreign entrepreneurs who had stopped there for a meal. Some had agreed to join him in various ventures, which included timber exploitation and buying the Agromec Dora was interested in.

A second condition for long-run success in agriculture, in Transylvania at least, may have been an ability to escape reliance on marketing grain. In Transylvanian conditions, growing and marketing grains has rarely been as profitable as feeding them to animals. In a fully unified internal market, the difference should be even more pronounced, for Transylvanians cannot compete with cereal production in Romania's southern and eastern plains (never mind in Hungary or other foreign countries). I believe it is only because distribution channels remained so imperfect during the decade of the 1990s that Transylvanians were able to sell their grain on the market at all. Should those channels be improved, that is, should a market economy develop further, Transylvanian farmers will survive only if they can specialize in pigs, dairy products, potatoes, fruits, and other items particularly suited to the region's growing conditions.

Third, in an environment of constant inflation with the costs of inputs of all kinds outstripping agricultural commodity prices, an early start on acquiring the basic infrastructure—especially equipment and storage space or farm buildings—was crucial. Wegren (1998a, 209–10) observes this for Russia: the earlier a private farm was created, the more likely its survival because it would have gotten going before subsidies collapsed. Particularly important in my data was early acquisition of tractors and other equipment that eliminated recourse to the overpriced Agromecs. What was essential was to spend any accumulated savings while they still had value that would otherwise have evaporated in inflation. The relative wealth of Hunedoarans enabled more people to buy implements early than might be true elsewhere (and may account for why there were more supertenants and fewer associations there than in poorer Alba county[15]). Every one of my successful cases had a tractor by 1993; more generally, every one had embarked on a strategy of accumulation. A pyramid-scheme pay-out (that bought the Bucurs their tractor), prior savings spent before inflation ate them up (as with Andrei Maior's equipment purchases), a sudden windfall (such as Luca's inheritance), a gainful commercial activity begun early (such as Dan's transport business or Toma's bakery), and so on separated those who had prospects in 2000 from those who did not. Instances of the latter include Dora, as well as the Vlaicu Association with its relatively late acquisition of tractors. Thus, timing was a crucial ingredient in making a successful farm. It was not, however, a sufficient condition—nor were any of the others taken separately. The example of Zucu's failed dairy farm shows that even a person who specialized in livestock and bought his building early would not necessarily make it as a farmer.

Timing was not just a matter of an early start. Throughout these four chapters I have spoken of the different time horizons within which Vlaicu's actors could act. I suggested that the policy environment and other conditions under which smallholders struggled to work their land made it impossible for them to think more than one or at most two seasons ahead—that is, they operated with a fairly short temporal horizon. This caused constant problems for the leaders of Vlaicu's Association, who sought to create medium- to long-term viability for their organization while their members and governing council constantly pulled them toward the shorter term. As I put it in chapter 6, for the Association the short-term view ultimately trumped the long. Smallholders, prevented by their circumstances from planning long term or even simply waiting, therefore saw their land transformed from a positive to a negative economic asset, a process that undermined other values it held for them.

The situation was different, however, for state farm directors and other would-be commercial farmers. With their varied resources, their cushions from risk, and (unlike the Association) their independence from smallholders' temporalities, they could work with the longest time horizon of all. Thus, they could keep multiple options in play—or simply wait. For people such as Lila and Dan or anyone else who believed that owning land had a future, waiting was a prime ingredient in transforming land into a source of value.[16] We see this at many points in the Bucurs' calculations. They bought a small building and waited until they had the money to stock it; they waited again while their bar was closed, opening a store when their finances permitted it later. They bought a barn but were prepared to wait for milk prices to rise—a luxury Zucu Popa did not have. Once it was clear that milk prices would never rise, they went over to pigs instead, and these provided them with most of the money with which they bought land as the decade ended. Hoping to privatize their state farm, they waited to buy land, but then saw that land's devaluation made it so cheap they would be fools not to buy it. At every point, they assumed that land had value and would continue to have value in the future; it was for them to seize the "special conjuncture," as Dan put it, when they could use their substantial resources to acquire values that circumstance had caused others to lose.[17]

On the other hand, there could be too much waiting, as with the sale of SFs only after their value had been reduced to nothing. We saw the negative effects of delay in Radu and Traian's refusal to pay the debt assigned them, which in the end damaged their plans for buying SF2; Dora's delay in buying equipment, certain as she was that she would acquire that with her state farm; and the State Property Fund's delay in selling off state firms and Agromecs until their inventory had been completely plundered. In this last case, superior bodies were manipulating time to their own advantage, which became disadvantageous for those below them. Another example was the bank's delay in auctioning the farms of the SF system, so as to obtain more interest. The ability to synchronize one's timing so as to seize opportunities—and the good fortune not to be caught in others' efforts to do the same—was essential to being able to transform objects and relations that were losing their value into objects and relations newly valuable.

The final set of conditions I discuss is the forms of capital necessary to success in farming. Naturally, having enough money to start up was helpful, but few had that form of capital. At a time when economic assets were highly unstable, political, social, and cultural assets took on even greater importance than they already had in socialism. They included the positions, competences, knowledge, and general experience I have emphasized in the sketches I have presented as well as networks, relations of trust, and family reputation. In my examples, some combination of these various forms (educational credentials for some, independent managerial experience for others) was vital to the success of these rising commercial farmers. Here we see the absurdity of the World Bank's often-expressed interest in supporting the "dynamic farming element" in the rural population while shutting out the "old rural elite," as if these were two completely separate groups.

Rather than reiterate points I have already made, however, I reflect here briefly on the durability of these forms of capital through the decade, to emphasize the precariousness of even the state farm director's edge. Assets derived from socialism would not necessarily stand one in good stead for long—and here we encounter a major shortcoming of capital theory, such as Putnam's (1995) or Bourdieu's (1997, 1984). For example, Bourdieu treats the societies for which he analyzes forms of capital and their convertibility as having relatively stable structures and rules of the game.[18] But in postsocialist contexts, precisely that stability was absent: research into postsocialism necessarily begins with the assumption not of stability but of rupture, requiring us to modify Bourdieu's method (see Eyal, Szelényi, and Townsley 1998). For him, forms of capital exist only in relation to specific fields, in which one or another form of capital has value and one's competence in it can be deployed (Bourdieu and Wacquant 1992, 98). Although action within these fields is in flux, the fields themselves are less so.

That was not true, however, of 1990s Eastern Europe, where capitals, fields, and rules were in flux continually. As Eyal, Szelényi, and Townsley (1998, 24–36) formulate the matter, economic capital had been of relatively little value in socialist societies, cultural capital was becoming increasingly important, and social capital institutionalized as political capital was dominant. The events of 1989–1991 threw that hierarchy of values and their associated capitals up for grabs, along with the fields in which they operated. People had to reshuffle their portfolios, we might say, and their ways of doing so were diverse, both by country and among persons and social groups. For example, previously valued political capital were less useful in those countries where substantial change occurred (Hungary, Poland) than in those like Romania and Slovakia, where more of the previous structures and groups remained in place. Eyal and colleagues find almost no support for the political capitalism hypothesis—that old elites become new elites by converting their political capital into wealth—but their data come from Hungary. In contrast, I find that hypothesis intuitively apt for Romania, where much of the old apparatus continued in power, valorizing its political capital and social networks in familiar ways (see also Stoica 2004).

Among the people I have described in this chapter, there were no substantial concentrations of political capital in the sense of office or position. Their attempts to accumulate wealth and sustain an upward trajectory rested on converting social and cultural capital, derived from socialism's hierarchy of values. But various forces tended to undermine those capitals over time. For example, the specialist knowledge with which farm managers entered the decade proved inadequate to the rush of foreign inputs they found themselves using. Their managerial experience in socialist agriculture might have accustomed them to handling large budgets and making business plans, but they had to alter their practices and routines substantially if their farms were to succeed in a market environment with wholly new forms of risk (see, e.g., Dunn 2004). Information, always ephemeral, was likely to be more so in the post-1989 context as policies changed repeatedly; one's connections to it were unstable too because people often changed jobs (as did Ion Olaru) and ceased to be sources. Being director of a fertilizer factory did not guarantee holding onto that position, so anyone with ties to such a person could not count on the connection over time. Whereas in June 2000 you could get good information from the county Agriculture Department or the Office of the Cadastre, when you next looked for them in 2001 those offices had been collapsed into some other bureaucracy. Moreover, as competition among aspiring commercial farmers increased, people in one's old network might no longer be as willing to share information as they had been before.

During the time of my research, I saw several permutations in the social ties of the farmers I was closest to, indicating potentially unstable social capital. Competition, again, might have been one reason: two couples I knew, the ablest farmers in eastern Hunedoara and close collaborators in their work, had a permanent falling out whose hidden underpinnings, I believe, were professional jealousy. Owing to the rising cost of inputs, people might be less willing to share those, whereas such sharing had been a staple of their relations before. The decomposition of SF systems might cause directors' social ties to fray further, as with Radu's friend Liviu (chapter 7) when the center failed to honor its subordinates' contracts. Again, some of the relations suited to socialism worked less well in the new egalitarian climate. Finally, as Lampland (2002, 47) suggests, managers' networks under socialism were forged through endless meetings with their fellows, gathered in the county capital. With the end of socialism came an end to those meetings and with them an end to the means for sustaining the relationships. Never mind that people attempting to farm were now so busy that they had much less time to socialize on their own. Under such circumstances, the trust that underlay the ties could begin to dissipate and social capital to become devalued. Gerald Creed (2002) demonstrates this point nicely for rural Bulgaria.

In sum, I am suggesting that although the people most likely to make a go of commercial farming had to begin with sources of cultural and social capital that were particularly likely to accompany managing a state farm, the bases of those forms were not durable. As the decade wore on, people had to build new networks, acquire new knowledge and experience, and place their trust in new associates—a trajectory best illustrated here by Luca Avramescu. That too was part of the process of value transformation.

Some readers may find in the vignettes of chapter 8 evidence that an individual with an entrepreneurial spirit could succeed at commercial agriculture by outcompeting other, less efficient forms. They might see Ion, Lila, and Dan as heroic figures, battling the postsocialist odds to create market agriculture in Romania. By emphasizing such people's state subsidies—their prior training and experience and their creative use of state resources—I have already indicated my doubts about such an interpretation. Although I too have much admired the energy, ingenuity, and dedication of the people described in these pages as they struggled to accomplish something in a very unpropitious setting, I see them as the fortunate beneficiaries of a huge web of relationships and processes that sustained their chances. Supertenants becoming commercial farmers and smallholders giving up cultivating are not two separate outcomes, the result of some people knowing how to farm efficiently and others not. It is, rather, the effect of a complex system of interdependencies, involving many people caught up in all the organizational forms I have described in chapters 5–8. None of those forms is a bounded, self-contained isolate. This system of interdependencies in fact constitutes the final and most important condition for success in commercial farming; I summarize it in my final chapter.

CONCLUSION
PROPERTY PROCESSES AND EFFECTS

[Land restitution] illustrated ... that the replacement of a social project based strictly on ideology with another project based just as strictly on ideological criteria cannot succeed as long as it completely ignores reality.
> *(Pasti, Miroiu, and Codiță 1997, 50)*

Weren't we told that capitalism—being almost "natural" in humans— would appear magically from the morning mist if only governments would get out of the way?
> *(Bromley 2000, 2)*

In 1989, Vlaicu's physical landscape consisted mainly of huge fields, each planted to a single crop and uninterrupted by individualizing markers (fences, walls, or rows of shrubbery). In its social landscape were five state farms, with their staffs and wage workers, having relatively few connections with villagers. There were also the collective farm staff and its member households, the latter being linked through dense horizontal networks of kinship and neighborliness into three clusters of mutual aid: locals, Germans, and venits. Work in the collective farm cross-cut these clusters, but even so, venits tended to work in the dairy farm while locals and Germans more often worked in the field brigades on vegetables and grains. Although few kinship connections united people across these clusters, relations among them had become fairly tolerant. German-Romanian intermarriages were increasing, and more frequent marriage outside the village was diluting its core of proud locals. Differentiation among households was limited to occupation (farmers and skilled or unskilled industrial workers) and to displays of consumption, within a fairly narrow range. Not even CF staff were distinguished by markedly greater wealth, although they clearly dominated the members and wage workers. Owing to the difference in *political* status, however, some members sought patronage ties with CF staff, competing for favor so as to receive better land for their usufruct plots, better assignments for their field labor, eyes closed to their appropriation of produce, tickets for good health spas, or more workdays than they had actually put in.

By 1995 both the physical and the social landscapes had been profoundly transformed. The collective farm was gone, some of its buildings now being owned by individual Vlaiceni and others taken over by a new entity, the Association. Of the CF staff present in 1989 only one remained, the rest having dispersed to other jobs. Whereas beforehand Vlaicu's fields had lain in great unbroken expanses, now almost half of the area was an intricate patchwork of small strips distinguished from one another by different crop patterns. The remaining land was still in large fields, worked by state farms, with which over ninety families now had close connections through shareholders' dividends. The CF member households of before were split into two distinct categories: those with land (mostly locals) and those without (mostly venits, Roma, and some '45ers). In addition, there was a tiny cluster of Germans with their own association. Connecting the groups and replacing the former patronage links were hierarchical relations of labor, accompanied by greater hostility than had previously existed among these different categories of villagers, and relations of tenancy linking villagers with the Association. Quarrels over land had frayed the horizontal ties between kin and neighbors, while claiming land had consolidated vertical ties linking ancestors and heirs. In place of the earlier tolerance between Germans and Romanians was antagonism, particularly from the Romanian '45ers; the gradual improvement in relations between locals and venits during the 1980s had been reversed.

By 2001 the situation was once again radically changed. Four of the five state farms had been sold and their shareholders had begun receiving title to the land in them. Many villagers had gone from being reconstituted peasants to rentiers, leasing their land to supertenants. The Association had been reduced to a carcass—a couple of buildings and two tractors, being picked over by a few locals bent on acquiring its unused assets for themselves. Smallholders who could not work their land entered a different kind of hierarchical relations from before, with the commercial farmers. The intricate patchwork of tiny strips was being consolidated into larger uniform pieces again: supertenants worked multiple adjacent parcels according to a unified cultivation plan and created a landscape more akin to that of socialism than to peasant smallholding. Labor relations across the local-venit line had dwindled as venits bought land of their own and cooperated more intensely among themselves or worked occasionally for the larger farmers. Beginning to feel themselves on the ascendant, the venits I spoke with complained about locals less than they had before, cooperating where appropriate with those who were their neighbors and happily awaiting the day when they would outweigh the locals in village affairs. Conflict over land had abated somewhat, although the quarrels continued to rankle.

In brief, decollectivization had completely transformed the entire field of social relations in which both people and land were embedded, and the situation was still in flux. From appropriation based in state delivery contracts it had created appropriation through price controls, low rents, and transnational chemical companies. As I show in Part I, the process effectively created owners; what it had *not* created for most Vlaiceni, as I show in Part II, was effective owner*ship*. Nor had it stabilized the value of the property object—land—or other parts of the agricultural infrastructure. Decollectivization had also shaped new linkages among groups and individuals, loosely based in the hierarchy of linkages from the socialist period. I have implied this by ordering chapters 4–8 according to the increasing range of these linkages outward from Vlaicu, an order that fit the previous hierarchy of forms. As I suggest at the end of chapter 8, the new linkages enabled commercial farmers to transform land's value. The predictable result was social and economic polarization; I have shown just how that result occurred.

In this final chapter I bring together various parts of the analysis of the previous ones. I begin by putting all the interconnections among different groups on the table at once, asking for each of the various groups I have introduced what were their conditions of existence, what social relations linked them to the others, and what were the consequences of decisions taken by each for others around them. The answers will clarify my argument that commercial farmers such as Ion, Lila, and Dan were not just capable and hard-working individuals (which indeed they were) but precipitates of extended networks of relationships, whose overlapping linkages formed a single interactive field. Following this, I briefly summarize what the chapters reveal about decollectivization as a whole with respect to property, value, and institutions (the themes of my Introduction), indicating the main effects of that process for villagers like those in Vlaicu.

Rural Groups in Interaction

In roughly ascending order of the capital endowments that socialism had bequeathed to them, the groups or actors I consider are: village Roma; venits and other landless households, such as the Rusus and the Mogas of chapter 5; locally resident smallholders who received land in the restitution process, such as Iosif Borza, Victoria Iancu, and others also introduced in chapter 5; urban-based Vlaiceni who had received land; the Vlaicu Association; the Germans' Cervenka Society; state farms and their directors, such as Dora Filip and Radu Oproiu; and commercial farmers such as the Bucurs, Ion Olaru, and Luca Avramescu. These interacted either directly or indirectly with a number of state-based entities: the Agromecs, the Simeria state farm system, Romcereal, the county Agriculture Department, various banks, and so on. I begin with Roma and move most of the way up this hierarchy, looking for links and reciprocal influences that developed over the decade and helped some people to move into commercial agriculture.

Vlaicu's Roma existed in the village because of the state farms, which had brought them in (along with others) as wage workers. Receiving no land, they became gradually more dependent on wage work for villagers once the SFs began to disintegrate and needed them less. Singly and in family groups they weeded and harvested corn for a percentage of the crop and would work for smallholders, the Cervenka Society, and commercial farmers, preferring the latter two because the pay was generally better.[1] Because they were likely to leave any job for another that paid more, their choices for work most often kept them away from those smallholders who had no additional income and could not afford to cultivate well. They remained dependent on SFs (or the state) for their residences and on SFs or Agromecs for unauthorized access to scrap metal. Although local Roma did not monopolize this trade, they contributed to it.

Venits and other landless villagers relied on urban jobs or pensions (where those existed) and, like Roma, on sharecropping or day-labor arrangements with smallholders, the Cervenka, and commercial farmers. They depended at first on smallholders who did *not* have faith in the Association—that is, they benefited from the Association's legitimacy deficit. Like the Roma, for day-labor and harvesting arrangements they preferred Germans, commercial farmers, and the better-endowed smallholders with more promising harvests. Their choices contributed, as did those of the Roma, to the smallholder labor crisis; that, in turn, pushed the smallholders toward more reliance on cash and on the Association, each of which would prove impoverishing. Later in the decade, venits depended on smallholders and—especially—urbanites less for land to work than for land to buy; they increasingly relied on one another for labor exchanges and other mutual assistance, so as to work their small patches with minimal recourse to cash. These ties augmented the exchange relations some continued to have with their villages of origin, which helped them to keep and sell livestock and then buy land. Also important, their keeping livestock depended on access to Vlaicu's common pasture (retained as such since feudal times), open to anyone who paid pasturage fees. After 2000 it was the only land that was still common property.

People in the third category, village-resident smallholders, were enmeshed in complex relations with virtually all the groups I have listed. Without labor from Roma, venits, and their own kin and neighbors, many could not have stayed afloat; others depended similarly on the Association. Without the services of the

Agromec or people owning tractors, their land would have lost productivity from poor plowing. To meet their production costs, some depended on credits and markets through Romcereal, while it lasted, and others on state pensions or the industrial salaries of family members, all vulnerable during this time. Very few involved themselves with banks, other than the handful who bought tractors that way. As the decade progressed, some villagers came to depend on the venits and commercial farmers who created a land market, enabling them to sell land they could no longer afford to work because the labor crisis pushed them toward high-cost inputs. Others found themselves dependent on supertenants to work land that the Association and other villagers would no longer take.

In their relations with the Association, smallholders' behavior had important effects, beginning with which land they chose to give the Association and how much pay they expected from it. By keeping their best land for themselves and giving it their worst, by increasing its tractors' wear and tear and gasoline consumption for travel to numerous far-flung parcels, and by requiring immediate returns rather than reinvesting for the next season, they helped to undermine the organization's viability. In addition, they took on only small amounts of labor for corn, thus compromising proper soil rotation and diminishing yields. A result was to push the leaders toward greater independence in decision-making, and that cut into owners' rights of control. Smallholders later aggravated this trend by refusing to pay the Association for necessary inputs, such as pesticide and herbicide, which many of them did not use on their own fields either. The result was a deterioration of the soil worked by both them and the Association. As I argue in chapter 5, however, given the price scissors these decisions were hardly choices.

What I have said of smallholders was even truer of urbanites, most of whom refused to take corn because they could not weed and harvest it as the Association required. Depending on the same set of actors as smallholders, urbanites faced similar constraints, but sooner. They began selling land earlier, providing much of what was available in the late 1990s for venits and commercial farmers to buy. Moreover, they provided this valuable resource precisely when it was cheapest relative to incomes. Their decisions to sell reduced both the Association's flexibility, which unsupervised absentee holdings had enhanced, and the labor that venits would provide to smallholders now that they too had land.

With the Vlaicu Association, the network of dependencies begins to shift. It depended entirely on receiving land from smallholders; after that, it relied on the same groups as the others did to provide labor for corn. Without the credits and guaranteed markets of Romcereal, it would have had great difficulty managing production in the early years. When Romcereal ceased to offer these credits and in the face of prohibitive interest rates, the Association required members to pay up front, effectively excluding those who lacked other sources of income. It continued to depend extensively on Romcereal for marketing, but for production it had to take out the occasional bank loan. For other inputs its leaders mobilized their contacts with suppliers, sometimes at considerable distance. Aggravating its problems, the members often used it parasitically, not cooperatively.

Another of its dependencies was on the machinery services of the Agromec, until it bought its own tractors in 1994. Delaying that purchase had important consequences for its members, creating one of the three ways in which the Association contributed to impoverishing them. Because it initially used Agromec services at very high fees (rather than immediately buying tractors, like the associations in Romos and Vinerea), it increased costs, which would come from members' returns. Buying those tractors diminished members' returns further, as did the Association's working at a higher technological level than did most smallholders. These cumulative drains on income worsened the perennial legitimacy problem that plagued the Association as an offshoot of the collective farm. Increasing poverty, in turn, at length inclined some members to sell their land, and among the beneficiaries were the aspiring commercial farmers.

Although the Association and these commercial farmers had few interconnections, the latter benefited in a very important way from the Association's mere existence. As Dan observed to me, it created breathing room for them to consolidate, as well as time to get on their feet so they could later profit from its collapse. It accustomed people to a kind of leasing that commercial farmers then extended, and its troubles lowered smallholders' expectations as to the level of rent they might receive for their land. By the time the Association disintegrated, SF directors and others planning to farm commercially had accumulated their equipment and developed their wide network of connections, while also seeking to create relations of confidence with smallholders from whom they might rent. None of these conditions obtained in the early 1990s; the Association enabled them to be created gradually.

The situation was somewhat different with the Germans' Cervenka Society. It too depended on receiving land from owners and on hiring wage labor because most of its able-bodied members lived elsewhere—that is, most Cervenkans were the equivalent of the Vlaicu Association's urbanites. Venits and Roma were happy to work for them, since the larger corn yields gave workers larger amounts for the same percentage take. Like the Association, the Cervenka depended heavily on Romcereal and the Agromec for all its inputs, credits, agricultural services, and markets. Once Romcereal ceased to function, the Cervenka ran into trouble. To reduce its reliance on the expensive Agromec by buying its own tractor, it entered a ruinous relationship with the German Forum, which held its foreign-currency mortgage; then it found buyers who failed to pay for the goods they took. Beginning in 2000, therefore, its members abroad began to sell land. That in turn reduced income both for paying off the tractor and for the Roma and others who worked its corn. At the same time, sizable chunks of good land now appeared on the land market for buyers with money. Otherwise, the Cervenka's main effect on the others was the effect of its coming into existence in the first place: it deprived fifty-six Romanian families of land and thus created a potential pool of village labor.

Near the top of the list of capital endowment in 1990 were state farms. At first these relied entirely on the state and state farm system for their inputs, salaries, and markets, and on banks for the loans some directors took out, either to pocket or to modernize farms they hoped to buy. That these loans went to them rather than to others (the result of decisions by banks, not the SF directors) was a reason why associations and smallholders had difficulty acquiring loans for equipment and production. By the middle of the decade, however, those SF directors who were not simply plundering their farms were struggling to find alternative sources: mobilizing networks of suppliers, securing special contracts with local or foreign firms, growing crops such as tobacco on contracts with guaranteed state purchase, and selling goods at weekly markets. Instead of problems with labor, they had the problem of paying their shareholders. Both the directors' difficulties in producing and marketing their products without help from the center and their occasional transfer of SF goods into private businesses contributed to reducing shareholders' dividends—yet another cause of rural impoverishment. Meanwhile, directors' salaries, inflated by their farms' administrative councils and shareholders' general assemblies, helped support their move into commercial farming.

When successful farmers emerged from this field of forms and relations, then, it was not just because they were talented and hard-working but because the field was already pulsating with possibilities created by impoverishment and the failure of alternative forms. If such farmers needed day labor, they found it in the un- or underemployed workers of state farms, Roma, and venits and other landless, who preferred that work to sharecropping for villagers. If they needed land to rent or buy, the failure of the Association, the burdens of smallholder farming, and the smallholders' labor crisis made land available for them. The price scissors made it available at low cost, as well. If they needed time to accumulate the assets a modern farm required, they received that time from two sources: the state farm system (for those who were in it), which initially cushioned their risks, and associations, struggling and finally failing to provide smallholders with adequate services and income. Meanwhile, the terms on which a commercial farmer replaced an association as a smallholder's tenant might further diminish that owner's resources and augment his risks.

In other words, a condition of commercial farmer's success was the gradual impoverishment of villagers, a process to which he himself, along with numerous other groups, organizations, and policies, had contributed. That is scarcely news for social science. In this context, however, the process has taken a course specific to postsocialist Romania, with its slow decomposition of socialist property forms. In particular, I submit that the principal motor of this process was not market competition and the greater efficiency of new commercial farmers, as some accounts claim (e.g., Lerman 2000a). It was government-driven pricing policies and other decisions, emanating partly from international quarters and partly from the preferences and compromises of Romania's not-fully-displaced communist politicians, that were undermining smallholder production and associations while state property continued in favor. These policies began the process of differentiation that associations and supertenants further advanced.

Briefly, what forces shaped those policies?

1. Pressure from international financial agents such as the International Monetary Fund, European Development Bank, and World Bank, which pushed for rapid privatization and an end to subsidies. This pressure was felt by the Romanian government, both postcommunist (PRSD, 1990–96, 2000–) and neoliberal (DC, 1996–2000) but especially the latter. Therefore protective tariffs and subsidies were reduced even as they were strengthened in Europe, and Romcereal—whatever its shortcomings—was broken up before anything was ready to take its place. In addition, the Bank's advice that the government should privatize by, in effect, giving state firms away contributed to the massive devaluation of state farm assets.

2. In both PRSD and DC governments the Ministry of Agriculture was relatively weak in financial terms (and sometimes even in the ministers' suitability—in the late 1990s, one was a priest, another an electrical engineer). That did not distinguish it from communist times, when agriculture was equally disadvantaged relative to industry, but its weakness now perhaps contributed to the drift and incoherence of policy because it could not lobby effectively for its sector.

3. The PRSD's desire to avoid labor strife and unemployment led it to hold down food prices from the very outset, rather than letting these rise to market levels, and to subsidize loss-making state industries—a major cause of chronic inflation. Despite the government's erratic attempts to deliver subsidies to agriculture as well, those policies created the widening price scissors between agricultural commodity prices and industrially based inputs. For over five years, agricultural commodity prices were held so low that rural producers could barely earn anything, much less accumulate so as to equip themselves better.

Any accumulations rapidly disappeared in inflation. The International Monetary Fund's macroeconomic stabilization plan aimed to halt inflation but also brought steep interest rates that prevented people from borrowing.

4. The PRSD's concern about having an adequate food supply and the strength of the state-farm lobby in the government led to preserving state farms as the collectives were disbanded. Thus, at least some SF directors had the opportunity to accumulate toward privatizing in a lower-risk environment than that faced by other actors—whereas other directors simply took over their farms outright, privatizing the last vestiges of socialism's administrative rights. The ongoing existence of state farms and their tremendous drain on the state budget deprived other rural actors of necessary financing, as well as keeping small owners in continued dependency.

5. Finally, the same government and lobby also kept intact the Agromecs, the state-owned successors to the machinery parks that had once served collective farms. This policy was equally if not even more consequential for the rural population. By distributing land without distributing equipment and by refusing to allow the Agromecs to rent people's land, the postcommunists created endless problems for combining the two factors. Here is how Traian of chapter 7 described the process:

> Property restitution failed because Law 18 gave people land without equipment, and then the land rental law prevented Agromecs from renting land. In this way the equipment was blocked. Over ten years it became completely devalued. The Agromec directors, meanwhile, were selling scrap metal—they sold the motors at night, when it would be hard to catch them—and destroying what could be useful to Agromec workers, who all put their privatization vouchers into their Agromec and got nothing for it. The directors got rid of them by pensioning them off or firing them, and that took them out of the arena. They couldn't organize to defend their shares because they were all from different villages. Of course the director gets his salary from selling scrap metal, with no thought for his workers, who put their assets into that Agromec. He just says, "It didn't work out."

It would have been far preferable to dismantle the Agromecs and give the machinery to associations (which would then have been able to pay members better) or sell it to individuals (who could then have plowed more cheaply for smallholders). Instead, the bureaucracy of Agromec directors, accountants, tractorists, and mechanics still had to be supported, and because the state was no longer prepared to do this, support had to come from fees set for their services. A county's Agromec directors decided jointly how much money they needed for oil, gasoline, parts, depreciation, salaries for their numerous personnel, and maintenance of their aging equipment; they then set their rates accordingly.[2] This was precisely the means whereby their predecessor agricultural machinery stations (AMSs) had caused collective farms to work always in the red: the fees for machinery services were set too high to permit otherwise. Collective farm members were therefore underpaid so as to support the AMS bureaucracy, and the same was happening now, as smallholders' incomes suffered. The overpricing affected far more people than those who directly used the Agromecs, because the fees were the basis for the price charged by people who plowed others' land with a horse or tractor.

I believe it is not too much to say that the fee-setting system of the Agromecs began a chain of events that contributed to the impoverishment of smallholders and jeopardized the situation of many associations. Although producers might avoid using the Agromecs, the effects of Agromec prices reverberated throughout rural areas, even after the rusting machinery had been stripped and sold as scrap metal. This one government decision—to keep Agromecs intact—had a disproportionate effect on devaluing smallholders' land and eventually delivering it into the hands of supertenants. That decision was thus crucial in altering social relations among groups in the countryside.

Property and Value after Socialism

What does this material contribute to thinking about postsocialism, particularly about my two principal themes: property and value? I hope I have shown the fruitfulness of conceptualizing property from several angles: as a political symbol and active force in the contemporary world, as a basis for appropriation, as social relations conjoining people and things, and as processes of determining the values those things hold. This is far more than the proverbial bundle-of-rights conception of property common to economists and lawyers, a conception they brought into their advisory work in Eastern Europe. Property is not just about bundles but about the entire process of bringing a good into use. If so, then creating ownership meant bundling not only rights but the prerequisites for their successful exercise. As German economist Konrad Hagedorn (2000) puts it, "The process of privatisation should no longer be conceived . . . according to its theoretical understanding as establishing *merely private property rights*" (emphasis in original). In these chapters I have argued that receiving property rights did not do much for people who, for a variety of reasons, could not turn them into what I call *effective* ownership. That kind of ownership depended on policies the Romanian government and international organizations did not make.

As a device for linking persons through things, property creates inequalities. It states what things one has to have to the exclusion of which other persons, in order to control the process of making and appropriating value. Vlaiceni entered the 1990s in the belief that if they controlled land they would control the necessary labor, as had been true before collectivization. But in contemporary agriculture, the thing that gives the most extensive control is owning not land but patents on chemical inputs. In local terms this means that control in agriculture no longer goes to those who own land but to those who have sufficient off-farm incomes for purchasing these complex inputs, and who can carry on in this way until they have accumulated enough in agriculture to give up their other jobs. Romania is far from the only place in which this is true (for just two examples, see G. Collier 1999 for Mexico, and J. Collier 1997 for Spain). The global context has transformed the possibilities and conditions for realizing value in such a way that smallholders can no longer do it. Inflation rendered their pensions insignificant, industrial restructuring fired family members whose wages had provided additional income, and too few of them had the wherewithal to start a side business that might support their cultivation. Only people with more substantial resources—preexisting cultural and social capital and continued state employment—were likely to make a go of it.

Thus, many smallholders became owners without efficacy. They also became owners of something that had lost much of the value it initially held for them. By 2001 land had ceased to be an important status symbol; it did not support the cultural values of mastery, autonomy, and diligence; it had lost its place in the visible economy; and it had become a negative economic asset. Its subsistence value depended increasingly on compromising their idea of good farming practice, and its economic value was being reduced to a small rent. (Although I am speaking of the majority of Vlaicu's smallholder locals more than of venits or emerging commercial farmers, even those groups led a precarious existence, on different scales.) These outcomes underscore the truth that the "thingness" of land as a property object, the values that inhere in it, and the kinds of persons who orient to each other through it are all context-driven (see Alexander 2004). A change in the context of people's lives meant a reconfiguration of those persons, things, and values.

I have argued throughout the book, however, that property is about more than things, persons, and relationships. Central to its workings in this case has been the combination of time, risk, and resource endowments—topics emphasized throughout Part II. The greater one's resource endowments, then the longer one's time horizon could be, the greater one's capacity to withstand risk, and the higher the likelihood of creating or transforming value. In this sequence, time is the critical link between the resources inherited from socialism and the possibility of postsocialist value creation. But, in Romania, time itself was also shaped by both the socialist hierarchy and the global economy. The country's national elites experienced their situation as one in which prospects for enrichment were fleeting, and their short-term scavenging accompanied by delaying tactics to maintain their advantage set the environment within which actors below them could plan. In general, I have shown, time was not on the side of Romania's villagers.

What were the main consequences of decollectivization as a property-remaking process? There are six that I think my material reveals: demodernization, deracination, delegitimation, devaluation, polarization, and new subjectification. Each of these processes is ongoing.

Demodernization. I argue in chapters 5 and 6 that contrary to those who see the choices made by Vlaicu's smallholders as evidence of return to a traditional mentality, I see those choices as largely compelled by their meager resources, owing to their place at the bottom of the hierarchy of socialist agriculture.[3] Although these people did indeed have ideas different from those of agribusiness, such as their belief that land needs nurturing and care, there was much they admired about modern farming even as they rejected its socialist implementation. Vlaiceni who reverted to horse-drawn plows were not choosing tradition; tractor services were more expensive. Even if they thought chemical fertilizer had been overused in the past, they did not reject it outright; many simply could not afford it or the costly herbicide that would have saved them the work of hoeing. If they had been given adequate prices for their commodities, most of them would not have returned to the farming practices of the 1930s. In the absence of such prices, however, they could not produce value—convert capital—if they had none to start with. Their circumstances forced these cultivators back into behavior resembling tradition that was not, in fact, traditional (cf. Kandiyoti 2002, 248). For this reason, I write of demodernization rather than retraditionalization. As for the seemingly traditional ideas they used to assert status, we should rather see those as among the very few resources available to them for creating valuable new identities in the present.

Deracination. I use this word to describe several processes. One is the way conflicts over land among kin and neighbors, as well as conflicts over labor between those with and without land, broke up prior social relations and uprooted especially the locals from their established networks. Another is that because notions concerning autonomy, mastery, and a reconnection with ancestors made landowning part of identity, to sell land (as people were doing by 2000) would be an admission of defeat and a rupture with their family's past.

It too would be a kind of social uprooting, like the one they had undergone with collectivization in the 1950s. This relates to a broader tendency of the decade—to disembed villagers of nearly all categories (locals, venits, and Germans) from place. Most visible in labor migration to Spain and Italy, the process was also more subtle, involving progressive abstraction from local particularities. It took several forms, replacing *localized* ideas about kinship, knowledge, and value (kinship as something that is performed, local knowledge as the basis for ownership claims, and land's value as part of competence and personhood) by more *abstract* ones (kinship as lines on a chart, official papers as the basis for ownership claims, and land's value as rent or market sale price). Throughout Part II I have shown that even that most concrete thing, land, a property object firmly embedded in local social relations, gave way to greater abstraction, as it was devalued by villagers' incorporation into imperfect markets. Land lost its specificity as it entered the large fields of supertenants, whence its product would return to its owners as bits of the average harvest and the standard rent, regardless of the quality of their parcel.

Hudečková and colleagues call attention to comparable outcomes from decollectivization in the Czech Republic. When people give up management of their land, these authors say, that loosens their tie to locality. Part of their sense of ownership is to participate in decision-making about their land, but this diminishes with the move to tenants, who make all the decisions themselves. Thus, owners may own their fields, but they cannot behave as owners *sovereign* (Hudečková, Lošt'ák, and Rikoon 2000, 104)—as masters. I would go one step further: people are disembedded from locality *again*. Socialist farming worked land as an abstraction having fungible properties. By means of collectivization, it uprooted people from land so they would willingly enter the industrial labor force. Decollectivization, by contrast, was to have produced a contrary movement, to reroot people, to fix them to space again by returning to them land that had very localized meanings. The result over time, however, at least in the material I have presented, was to erase land's particularities and make it an abstraction once more. We might say, then, that for these small owners, land lost value twice: once when it was seized from them by socialism and again when it was seized by the free market.

Delegitimation. In chapter 3 I argue that Mayor Lupu and his like compromised the very idea of a justly acquired hectare and, thereby, the legitimacy of the government that supposedly guaranteed it. At the beginning of the decade I heard constant talk in Vlaicu of people's getting or not getting their rights, something they felt entitled to. The million-plus court cases suggests the same: that people had claims they felt were justifiable and if necessary they would go to court—something very stigmatized under socialism—because they believed, or at least hoped, that they would receive justice. One question I routinely asked Vlaiceni during my 1993–94 research was whether they thought it was possible that Mayor Lupu, or anyone else who had abusively entered land belonging to someone else, would obtain title to that land. In other words, I asked if usurpation could become legitimate. Nearly all replied no: as long as you have documents [acte] for your land, you'll always win a lawsuit for it. Their firm belief in the power of historical documents was striking. The only one who said yes was an early member of the land commission; he knew that usurpation worked by occupying land that had no clear heirs to bring suit. Yet even he said that if the real owner brought suit, usurpation would not stand.

In the early 1990s, then, I found many believing that the apparatus of justice would protect property rights. I did not pose this question systematically later in the decade, but my strong impression from conversations was that people had given up expecting justice. If you did not bribe the judge, they said, you would never win—and in any case they found bringing suit too costly in both time and money. People commented often on the extra land the three members of the land commission had managed to get, which they were now selling without impediment. Ex-Mayor Lupu's presence in the floodplain was no longer even worth comment. And perhaps because many villagers had found the experience of owning to be a disappointment, especially as ownership of land became increasingly separate from control over it, those who felt mistreated were renouncing their suits. Finally, although only a few realized it (Anda, Traian, and Radu), the justness of restitution was also affected by the paradox I mention in chapter 1: that creating private property required first legitimating the socialist property that the 1989 "revolution" had declared illegitimate. My time spent in this one Transylvanian community suggests, then, that the process of obtaining property rights enhanced the legitimacy of neither the private property form nor the government that purportedly backed it.

Devaluation. Because this matter was my main focus in Part II, it requires little additional comment. Perhaps I might recast it in the terms of my title's "vanishing hectare," a metaphor for the effects of the context in which decollectivization occurred and the practices that implemented it. The way the commission implemented the law took hectares from locals, and the way it applied kinship took away the hectare of venits; the way supertenants abstracted a hectare's product made it vanish as a source of personhood, and the effects of government policies made it vanish as a source of income for all but a few. Other assets in addition to land vanished too: the assets of well-endowed and reasonably successful state farms, as well as many of those belonging to Vlaicu's collective. All these vanishings produced a loss of locality, evident in departures for labor in other places, and all of them reflect a transformation of land's value.

Polarization. By this I mean the division of people into groups of rich and poor. Did all this restructuring improve people's life chances?[4] From the point of view of neoliberal economists and international financiers, the story I have told has been a success story. Even if slowly, privatization was doing just what it was supposed to: drive out a lot of aging, inefficient, and unproductive farmers and make room for younger, more entrepreneurial, and productive ones oriented to the market. The GNP would go up because that is what happens when a few people grow most of the food and market all they grow, instead of having many people eating some of it themselves. That more people—especially elderly ones—fell below the poverty line was simply, the architects of privatization would say, one of those unfortunate things that sometimes happens on the road to a capitalist economy. The elder generation had to be sacrificed so the younger one could prosper in the jobs that would arise as agriculture forcibly financed the growth of industry.

For those of us who judge outcomes not by GNP but by improvement in the life chances of human beings, however, this story is largely one of failure and profound discouragement, especially when assessed in light of people's hopes and expectations. First, good folk have been driven into unhappy straits. Second, those few who were able to get ahead were those who started with some advantages already, advantages offered them under socialism by the work of the others. Third, those who suffered did so in vain because the industrial growth did not occur that was supposed to come from exploiting the countryside—and that would have improved the lives of their children. Because small-scale agriculture could no longer absorb the people displaced by Romania's collapsing industries, those offspring left their aging parents behind to enter the international proletariat seeking work in Western Europe. Even if this strategy might at length enable accumulating something so as to return home, the heartache and fear and struggle involved made it, in human terms, a terribly costly solution. Only someone whose friends have not suffered it could dismiss it as just a normal response to supply and demand.

New Subjectification. As Wegren observes in his book on agriculture and the state in Russia, a major effect of privatizing was to transform villagers' relations with the state. Decollectivization, he proposes, was "a change in the way the state exercises its power in the countryside" (Wegren 1998a, 16), providing an opportunity for the state to penetrate villages more thoroughly and in new ways. He points to new instruments of control (taxes and budgetary and credit instruments), new alliances with groups that benefited from reform, and increased potential for domination as individualizing relations to land heightened the costs of collective action and fragmented rural interests far more than during the socialist period. Wegner's perspective casts into relief the old connection between political docility and property stakes. I add to this that decollectivization simultaneously reduced the state's burden of supporting an unprofitable sector (by entrusting it to a rural bourgeoisie-in-formation) and sloughed off a large segment of the population from social welfare (by giving them land rights that made them into semiproletarians). It helped the state to throw two major liabilities onto groups in the countryside, leaving the population to cope somehow with the fallout.

Relationships and Interdependencies

Discerning that fallout is the work of ethnography, which reveals things that institutionalist and rational-choice analyses miss. For example, they miss how decollectivization produced land concentration primarily in the form of leasing (rather than ownership) in part because villagers identified with their patrimony and tried to hold onto it, or how petty antagonisms ricocheted back and forth between locals and venits to produce a labor shortage integral to villagers' impoverishment. Ethnography helps us to understand the emerging regime of value, in which *private property* becomes a catch-all concept that may explain everything in its generality but obfuscates the details of how privatization produced revaluation. These details include the specific managerial tactics that separated assets from liabilities in the course of revaluing land, tactics that shifted the liabilities primarily downhill at each hierarchical level (from higher officials to SF directors, and from them to smallholders), and from corporate groups to individuals. These details enable us to link the demands of the IMF and other world financial institutions for fiscal austerity in government, which redirected capital elsewhere, with the fact that local farmers did not have the cash to make their acquisition profitable. Through such details we see how responsibility for the failure of the transition to capitalism was assigned to individuals; yet the context in which they acted denied them the potentialities of a successful transformation, and the actors responsible for those conditions evaded accountability for their actions. This is the experience of the transition to market economies for huge numbers of people in postsocialist East-Central Europe and Russia.[5]

Some analysts might dismiss my argument by saying simply that Romanians did not "get the institutions right," and that all would have been fine had that happened. I find such a view remarkably naive. First, it overlooks the specific contexts in which those "right" institutions would be embedded: institutions are not "right" in the abstract but only in relation to contexts and possibilities. Moreover, institutions are not neutral; they favor some and disadvantage others, such that *who* institutes them has a great deal to do with who finds them "right." The market, that profoundly political creation, is the perfect example. Finally, the very notion of *institutional design* presumes a *tabula rasa* (Elster, Offe, and Preuss 1998, 19), in terms of both what is already in place and what happens while the newly designed institutions are being installed. People do not wait quietly for institutions to form at the top and percolate downward; they strive to realize their goals through practices that may then congeal into forms not necessarily consonant with those planned above. For instance, World Bank officials with whom I spoke in 1994 were striving to promote the growth of a new class of farmer-entrepreneurs while undermining the old agrarian elite, but meanwhile the latter were busily turning themselves into the former—and were effectively the only ones who could, given the other constraints the Bank itself was placing on rural capital formation.[6] In chapter 3 I offer another example, in which even as the "rule of law" was being made the framework for restitution, out in the countryside those implementing it were the first to violate its intentions.

Both institutions and individuals have been essential to the story I have presented in these pages, but they are not primarily what that story is about, nor do they adequately help us perceive its lineaments. Property transformation is above all a story of relationships and interdependencies: the relationships that constitute property and the interdependencies that fructify it; the relationships that provided smallholders with labor and the changing interdependencies that generated its shortage; the relationships that enabled commercial farmers to cobble together the resources for farming and the interdependencies that enabled them to succeed at it where others had not. Without a grasp of those kinds of relations—and without the ethnography that alone reveals them—property restitution remains a black box.

It is precisely recognizing these interdependencies that should arrest the impulse to shrug, dismissing privatization's unhappy victims, with "Too bad, it just didn't work out," or to fault them for being irrevocably stuck in socialism's habits. As I have said, the rise of supertenants and the failures of smallholding were not two separate outcomes occurring because some people know how to farm efficiently and others do not but, rather, the single outcome of activities and groups that were interdependent. So too are the supertenants of global finance interdependent with those whose values they obliterate in this era of massive revaluation. Some of those dispossessed world-wide, it is clear, have begun to tire of the relationship.

The Specificities of Postsocialism

Much of what I have said about post-1989 developments in Transylvania could be said of other emerging market situations too. In what respects do these postsocialist cases differ from similar outcomes in Latin America, say, or Africa? What is particular to their having emerged specifically from socialism? I close with several reasons why these cases are different.

First and most obvious, postsocialist economies were being radically modified from a completely different kind of system, something less true of other emerging market stories. They were being transformed from a modern society in which the idea of liabilities made no sense; thus, it was much more complicated than usual for actors to assess costs and risks, strive for efficiency, and so forth. To do so required that they adopt an entirely different way of thinking about their activities and budgets. In such a context, the notion of risks and the desperate efforts of social actors to pass them off onto others played a larger role than might have been true otherwise. The intensified concern with liabilities contributed to the massive devaluations I have emphasized throughout these chapters.

A second reason these cases are different is the resolute insistence, in the Romanian case, on returning to the past, the 1930s to 1950s, so as to redress the injustices of collectivization both materially and symbolically. Restitution thus conceived not only resuscitated some of the ideological forms of that era but produced in many communities the nightmare of creating hundreds of tiny parcels, difficult to measure and costly to work. It was possible to adopt a more forward-looking solution, as Hungary did, but in most of postsocialist Eastern Europe the impetus to undo collectives by reviving the past was powerful in a way one could scarcely imagine for nonsocialist contexts.

A third specificity is the peculiarities of socialist property forms (especially SOEs), with their hierarchies, administrative rights, and fuzzy property boundaries. These mechanisms gave socialist managers specific kinds of experience and latitude in moving resources across lines that, in a more fully marketized context, would be more rigid and better policed. Usually seen as "corruption," such practices should instead be viewed as directly continuous with the operating rules of socialist systems. To move resources across fuzzy boundaries was not necessarily illegal—indeed, it was often essential to the success of socialist enterprise.

A fourth is the kinds of capital endowment with which various sorts of people emerged from the socialist experience and what those enabled them to do. Socialism gave some people expert training, and it endowed some people with far-flung social networks. Those endowments, rather than differences in wealth, initially proved crucial in obtaining opportunities, supplies, and outlets for goods in the context of very imperfect markets.

A fifth postsocialist specificity is the peculiar kind of rentier society that resulted from decollectivization. Instead of many tenants seeking land from a few large owners—the more usual case, which we might associate with declining Latin American haciendas, for instance—, decollectivization produced many small owners chasing fewer large tenants. Initially, prospective tenants had to cultivate owners, finding ways of creating trust so the owners would choose them over some other tenant. Here another peculiarity intervened: the connection of some of these forms, especially the associations, with unpleasant socialist precedent impeded the creation of trust and made tenancy arrangements unstable in ways we might not find in nonpostsocialist contexts.

Sixth, also peculiar to postsocialism is the remarkable speed with which socialism's rural population was ensnared in the emergence of markets. This placed an unusual premium on time horizons and timing, as well as on keeping open perhaps more than the usual number of options, so as to move quickly from one set of resources to another. Speed made particularly evident the loss of value in things that had had worth only a couple of years before. It kept most people off balance most of the time. The resulting uncertainty led to widespread scavenging behavior that plundered social resources and diminished future prospects.

A final peculiarity is the great height of expectation from which the value of newly acquired assets was soon to crash. People in socialist countries built up a great illusion, a myth of the West, which they saw as a land of unimaginable prosperity in contrast to their lives in socialism—constrained, modest, and often grim. The collapse of the socialist system led them to expect that now, overnight, their lives would become like those in their myth, and westerners fanned this hope. For many Transylvanian villagers, receiving their land was a promise of the prosperity they associated with the years before World War II. In this book we see how that illusion was shattered.

APPENDIX

Inventory of Objects Moved from the Collective Farm Patrimony into the Vlaicu Association at Its Founding, 1992

Assets	Assessed value (in lei)
Motor for irrigation installation	9,810 lei
Irrigation nozzles and sprinklers	26,334
Irrigation water supply pipes	163,000
Water tank	25,300
Wooden desk (3)	3,000
Fodder preparation equipment	240,000
Hayloft (2)	474,000
Simple hayloft	90,000
Barn #III	726,667
Barn #IV	720,852
Milking machine	23,939
Rake feeder (2)	62,873
Fodder mill	124,363
Weigh-bridge	363,000
Bridges and roads	300,000
Silo surface (3 cells)	343,400
Wood-burning stove	1,000
Charcoal-burning stove	1,500
Reservoir	4,606
Kiosk	55,000
Weigh-bridge scale	20,924
Thousand-kilogram scale	3,384
Metal safe	50,000
Metal cabinet	800
Wooden cabinet	1,000
Well	3,343
Garage	55,948
Typewriter	2,319
Granary	185,000
Humidometer	7,622
PEB and Lindan (insecticides), 1,000 kg	9,000

Chairs (4)	400
Benches (2)	400
Tables (2)	400
Typing table	100
Table	300
Iron gate	10,000
Clothes tree	300
Wooden chests (2)	100
Telephone	300
Electrical transformer	23,939
TOTAL	3,994,223 lei

Addendum:	244,000
Therefore, total value given over to the Aurel Vlaicu Agricultural Society	4,238,223 lei

NOTES

Introduction

In thinking about the issues I discuss in this chapter, I have benefited greatly from my participation in two conferences: Changing Property Relations at the Turn of the Millennium, organized by Caroline Humphrey and me, and sponsored by the Wenner-Gren Foundation, April 2001; and the Workshop on Postsocialist Property Rights in Natural Resources, organized by Janet Sturgeon and Thomas Sikor in Lund, Sweden, May 2001. In particular, conversations there and elsewhere with Sara Berry, Jane Collier, Chris Hann, Caroline Humphrey, Marilyn Strathern, and Keebet von Benda-Beckmann contributed to my thinking, as did my graduate seminars in property at the University of Michigan. I am grateful to all the members of these groups for stimulating my ideas.

1. Not all were so hasty: even Jeffrey Sachs observed, "Ironically, the rush of investment bankers and Western experts who have been proposing privatization strategies in Eastern Europe have not addressed the real needs of the privatization process" (Lipton and Sachs 1990, 296).

2. Indictments of the effects of foreign aid are legion; for the former Soviet sphere, see Bruno (1998); Sampson (1996); Wedel (2000).

3. A small sampling of relevant works includes Aglietta (1987); Beck (1992); Bonefeld and Holloway (1991); Hardt and Negri (2000); Harvey (1989); Lash and Urry (1987); Offe (1985); Piore and Sabel (1984); Verdery (1996, chap. 1).

4. See, for example, Borneman (1997); Dagan (1998); Heller and Serkin (1999).

5. As an aside, I believe part of these developments was the emergence of new postmodern theories about signification, to supersede referential theories of meaning. Aurel Codoban, in a fascinating essay, expresses it thus:

> Postmodernism is the epoch of signs that have won their autonomy from reality, not the epoch of symbols or of reality as a symbol. Its emblem is virtual reality. In postmodern societies, exchange value . . . loses its dialectical and balanced interaction with use value, and its referential function departs from reality. Exchange value is overvalued, and by this rupture, it escapes, like the linguistic sign, from all its former obligations to designate something. (2003, 6)

Exchange value completely takes over, he says, while money loses its efficacy and becomes instead magicosymbolic, rather as in socialism. Further evidence of this kind of tendency was the proliferation of pyramid schemes, gambling, lotteries, and other magical attempts (sometimes even state-sponsored) to make money (see Comaroff and Comaroff 2000; Verdery 1995). A single inflationary and speculative tendency, then, underlies both the economic and the verbal inflation characteristic of the times. Without seeking to bring these all together conceptually, I believe their coincidence indicates that *something* was going on globally in the realm of valuation.

6. I am grateful to Peter Bernholz and Patricia Springborg for insisting on this point.

7. According to OECD (1992), the GDP per capita (Dollar Purchasing Power Parity, $PPP)

in the East European countries in 1989 was Czech Republic $7,878; Hungary $6,108; Bulgaria $5,710; Poland $4,565; and, at the end, Romania $3,445. Turnock's (1997, 90) adjusted per capita GDP for 1990 places Romania even lower than Albania.

8. My thanks to Dr. Gábor Hunya for a very useful discussion about this question.

9. See, for example, the collections edited by Beckmann and Hagedorn (Forthcoming), Swinnen (1997a, 1997b), Szelényi (1998), and Wegren (1998b); and the work of Frydman and his collaborators (1993, 1994, 1998), Meurs (2001), McFaul (1996), and Nelson and Kuzes (1994). Useful work also came from geographers based in France, particularly Maurel (1994a, 1994b, 1997) and von Hirschhausen (1997).

10. In chapter 2, I refer to a conference of agricultural economists in Berlin, which I was fortunate to attend. Arguments between institutionalist and political economy interpretations were a central theme of the conference.

11. For example, Abrahams (1996); Bridger and Pine (1998); Burawoy and Verdery (1999); De Soto and Anderson (1993); Hann (2002); Humphrey (2002b); Kideckel (1995a).

12. For example, Abrahams and Kahk (1994); Anderson (2000); Berdahl (1999); Buchowski (2001); Buechler and Buechler (2002); Creed (1998); Humphrey (1998).

13. This point was made in papers and discussion at the Wenner-Gren symposium "Changing Property Relations at the Turn of the Millennium," Ronda, Spain, April 2001. (See Verdery and Humphrey 2004b.)

14. For further discussion, see Verdery and Humphrey (2004a).

15. See, for instance, Demsetz (1967); Ostrom (1990); Rose (1994).

16. An excellent discussion of the relation of property to propriety in Locke is McClure (1996, pt.I).

17. This view began to change with the sudden eruption of intellectual property claims in the late twentieth century, partly as a result of new technologies capable of mining resources hitherto not considered as such.

18. Fustel de Coulanges 1864; Williams 1986; Myers 1989.

19. A whole series of Romanian words share the root *moş-*. They include *moş*, grandfather, or elder; *moaşă*, midwife; *strămoşi*, ancestors; *moşteni*, to inherit; *moşier*, landowner; and *moşia*, landed estate, or, as Henri Stahl puts it, "genealogical joint possession" (1980, 44). See chapter 4, for some contemporary Romanian ideas about the relation of persons to ancestors via land.

20. This positioning can be of many possible kinds—use or enjoyment of the fruits of some valued thing, exclusion of others from it, rights to alienate it, and so on. In positioning persons or actors with respect to values, property concepts may serve to (re)affirm the unitary character of those actors by objectifying them in some specific relation to a thing. For example, the concept of *clan territory* affirms the unity of people constituted as a clan by positioning them jointly in relation to the same object, a particular territory (cf. Myers 1989).

21. See Heller (1998), (1999); Heller and Serkin (1999); Dagan and Heller (2001). Michael Heller offers some very original insights into the property question.

22. This phrasing calls to mind Bourdieu (1977, 1980, 1984) and his multiple forms of capital, all of which rest on particular notions of value. Questions about the conversion of one form of capital to another are about how values become enchained or under what conditions value is redefined. When Bourdieu asks how actors appropriate the profits from deploying one or another form of capital, this could easily connect with questions about property—appropriation of valued things through particular sets of social relations. Although I prefer to use a simpler (and less precise) language and to write not of converting older capital to newly valued forms but merely of revaluation, I am nonetheless interested in Bourdieu's questions.

23. Emily Martin creatively links this development of an "asset society" with the emergence of new representations of persons as holders of a portfolio of assets and liabilities—such as their health or personality traits or pension plans, which they must competently manage (e.g., by proper diet and exercise, good habits such as not smoking, financial advice, and medication for psychological problems) (see Martin [1997, Forthcoming]). The measure of one's managerial capacities, adds William Maurer (1999), is no longer bankruptcy (reflecting ownership status) but insurability (reflecting level of risk).

24. It also involved prioritizing values of which profitability was only one. For example, a World Bank study of profitability in the Romanian mining industry recommended closing any mine in which it cost more than $2 to produce $1 worth of coal; thus the determining factor in such decisions was not the value of the firm but whether it required state subsidies—a rather different value (Jonathan Maack, personal communication, January 2001).

25. According to Mateescu (2002, nn. 18, 19), in 2000 a ton of scrap iron could be sold internally for about $60, and internationally for as much as $400. The trade flourished especially during 1998–2000, because there were no export quotas on it and exporters often received tax reductions. The losses to the Romania economy were staggering, amounting to millions of dollars for the theft and sale of railway and electrical cables alone. In 2001 the government tried unsuccessfully to regulate scrap metal collection points and to limit its export to all countries except European Union members.

26. In writing this section, I benefited from yet another in the long string of marvelous conversations I have had with Ashraf Ghani, through which he has generously improved my work over the years.

27. Both Gail Kligman and I, for example, had this very experience in conversations with employees in the Bucharest offices of the World Bank, IMF, and USAID.

28. A commune [comună] is an administrative unit that existed before the Communist Party came to power in Romania.

29. In addition to short periods during the summers of 1990 and 1991, I spent the academic year 1993–94 there and from three to six weeks almost every year thereafter through 2001 (see Verdery 1994, 1998, 1999).

30. I myself encountered it in 1993 when I was seeking permission from the county secretary to begin work on my project. After I told him where I planned to work, he replied something to the effect: "That's a bad start, because Geoagiu commune is atypical." He went on to catalog its problematic boundaries with neighboring communes, the state farms there, and the German minority in Vlaicu, outlining for me the implications of each for land restitution. He ended by concluding that no research done in Vlaicu could to be of general validity.

Part 1. Making, Unmaking, and Remaking Owners

1. These figures are calculated from data in Institutul Naţional de Statistică (2002, tables 20.2, 20.3, 20.55). The generalization holds whether or not we include the urban population in the total figure (as I do here). The difference is even sharper if we include in the figures for the Regat those from the Banat (with its Regat-like agrarian economy).

2. The Regat formed new owners disproportionately. After World War I, of all the agricultural land in what would become Romania, the Regat held one-third and Transylvania two-fifths (much of it forest and pasture), but of all land that was distributed by 1927, 56 percent went to peasants in the Regat and only 12 percent to Transylvanians (calculated from figures in Roberts 1951, 362–67).

3. See Noronha (1996). My thanks to Mr. Noronha for explaining the different titling systems to me. I also owe a debt to Ms. Emilia Ciascai, a notary for Hunedoara county, who taught me much about the contrasts between the two systems and about the particulars of the Transylvanian one.

4. This is, of course, a relative statement because agriculture did not provide anyone a good living in late-1980s Romania. It was not only in Transylvania that one saw cartoons heralding Ceauşescu's "new agricultural revolution" with pictures of carts and oxen rather than tractors.

5. One other village near Vlaicu, Romos, also had Germans (14 percent in 1966), descended from colonists brought into Transylvania in the twelfth century rather than from those colonized in the 1890s. The difference is significant for the level of farming technology they brought.

Chapter 1. Property in Socialism

I am grateful to the following people for helpful comments on this chapter: Julia Adams, Stephanie Platz, Julie Skurski, Margaret Somers, Ann Stoler (members of the Goil's Group); Alaina Lemon; students in my 1999 graduate seminar on property, especially Jennifer Dickinson,

Elizabeth Ferry, and Paul Nadasdy; and participants in the 2000 Law and Political Theory seminar at the University of Michigan led by Michael Heller and Don Herzog.

1. Land had been expropriated in 1918 as well, but in that reform, owners had received compensation, even though modest.

2. From Article 4 of Decision (*Hotărârea*) no. 1650, 18 June 1953, "Cu privire la statutul-model al Gospodăriei Agricole Colective." (See Iancu, Țârău, and Trașcă 2000, 263–64.)

3. This material comes from oral history interviews I conducted in the summers of 2000 and 2001 for a project entitled "Transforming Property, Persons, and State: Collectivization in Romania, 1948–1962," co-organized with Gail Kligman. The project was funded by the National Council for Eurasian and East European Research, the National Science Foundation, and the National Endowment for the Humanities, for whose support I am very grateful. In my transcription I have adhered closely to the words I wrote down as people were speaking (most interviews were not taped) but have included only a few portions, not always indicated my questions, and modified some details in the interest of protecting people's identities. Footnotes explain unfamiliar items in the text.

4. The most comprehensive discussion, covering all Marxist regimes, is Pryor (1992). For other histories in English from a variety of perspectives, see, for example, for the Soviet case, Conquest (1986); Davies (1980); Fitzpatrick (1994); Hindus (1931); Lewin (1968, 1985); Viola (1987). For Romania, see, for example, Cartwright (2001); Cătănuș and Roske (2000); Iancu, Țârău, and Trașcă (2000); Levy 2001; Parlamentul României (1992).

5. This is not to say, of course, that there was no bourgeois property in the countryside, as Lenin was at pains to show. See Lenin (1967) and the debate with the narodniks as to whether village inequality was from capitalist processes or from demographic ones (Chayanov 1966).

6. Creed (1998, 266); Lampland (1995, 39); Roberts (1951, 370).

7. The figures are from 1930. The average area distributed per recipient was 2.8 ha (Roberts 1951, 366–67, 370–71). Roberts (1951) and Mitrany (1930) provide detailed discussions of this reform.

8. In Poland, the Sejm passed a land reform bill following World War I, but it was not effectively implemented, leaving significant reform to 1945.

9. From *Anuarul Statistic al Republicii Socialiste România* (1984, 58); Mitchell (1998, 11, 150).

10. See Hann (1980, 1985); see also Creed (1998), for Bulgaria. These should be compared with Humphrey's (1983) findings for Russia—although those apply to a period more than a decade earlier than Hann's and Creed's work.

11. My sources for this discussion, in addition to interviews with lawyers, judges, and notaries in Romania, are Armstrong (1983); Brădeanu, Marica, and Stângu (1968); Butler (1988); Campeanu (1988); Feldbrugge (1993); Heller (1998); Knapp (1975); Lipetsker (1946); Lupan and Reghini (1977); Păunescu (1974).

12. I found documents of this kind in my research for the collectivization project mentioned in note 3.

13. Law 183 of 1949 made it an offense punishable by imprisonment and confiscation of all goods to disobey any law, *including the decrees or orders of local authorities*. Thus a decree obtained the force of law. (I thank Ion Hotoiu for pointing this out.) Gail Kligman (1998) describes this same pattern of decrees acquiring the force of law in the domain of reproduction.

14. I use herein the term *property*, but in the Romanian system if not in others, another important term is *patrimony* [*patrimoniu*]. Romanian legal texts define *patrimony* as the totality of rights and obligations having economic content that pertain to a jural person, or all such rights and obligations related to the [economic] activity of an organization. Like the term *property*, this one is often used to refer to the specific material goods that bear these economic values. Patrimony is indissolubly linked to the person—"every person, as a subject of the law, has only one patrimony, and any person has a patrimony throughout its legal existence" (Lupan and Reghini 1977; 4). That is, one cannot be a person without having a patrimony, a set of economically relevant rights and obligations.

15. These subdivisions into subjects and objects of property are not simply my own analytic grouping but that of the legal texts I have consulted.

16. In Soviet property law, collective farm (*kolkhoz*) households were accorded use-rights to

household property known in pre-Soviet times as *dvor* and carried over as a notion into the *kolkhoz*. Feldbrugge (1993, 244) sees this as a unitary entity for purposes of property rights. In the Romanian case, however, Brădeanu, Marica, and Stângu (1968, 107) state explicitly that the holder of this use-right is not the family or household itself but its individual members, collectively, as joint owners.

17. These are the subjects of ownership in other systems, such as those described by Gluckman (1943, 1965), Malinowski (1926, 1935), and Leach (1961).

18. Not every East European country had an organization of state and cooperative property identical to Romania's. For example, in socialist Hungary state farms occupied only 8 percent of the surface area and were never as important as cooperatives (occupying 71 percent), whereas in socialist Romania state farms were the most privileged agricultural organizations and occupied over one-fourth of the arable land. In Poland, by contrast, state farms were the only socialist presence in agriculture, whereas in Bulgaria the most important organizations were, instead, the agro-industrial complexes. The closest parallels with Romania's distribution of property forms are in Albania and Czechoslovakia.

19. The labor forces in SFs and CFs tended to differ also in their gender composition—workers in the SFs being more often men and in the CFs more often women—and in age, workers in the SFs being generally younger than those in CFs. Only in areas with high industrial employment did the SF labor force come closer to the CF's older, feminized profile because younger men worked in factories. This was the case in Romania's Hunedoara county, where Vlaicu is located.

20. SF employees had not only fixed salaries but many other benefits: supplemental payments for children, medical insurance, apartments, and sometimes meals as well. They could buy farm products at reduced prices (see Sarris and Gavrilescu 1997, 195). CF members had far fewer social benefits than SF workers—in Romania in the late 1980s, some 30–50 percent lower in value (Hunya 1987, 261–62).

21. In Romania, the plot was 0.15 ha per individual member or 0.3 per couple, provided both actually worked in the CF; in Bulgaria before the 1990s, it was 0.3–0.5 ha (Creed 1998, 7). In the statistics, sometimes the agricultural surface these plots occupied is reported in the category *private farms* and sometimes it is included with the figures for collective farm land. Because the land in plots could amount to as much as 10 percent of agricultural land, it is important to know how a given set of statistics treats this category.

22. In a work that puts the problem of property in socialism at the very center of discussion, Pavel Campeanu (1988) analyzes this in his usual trenchant fashion. When the Communist Party declared social ownership of the means of production, no institution existed that had the capacity to organize such ownership. State ownership was thus to be exercised by states that were in complete organizational disarray. How could the state own and effectively use a unitary fund of values? This problem, says Campeanu, produced the "ownership vacuum" whose consequence was that ownership became concentrated in the hands of the top party leadership.

23. The comparison is less outrageous than we might think; indeed, I am not the first to make it—Caroline Humphrey, in her magisterial study of Soviet collective farms (1983), does so as well. In both systems, one's relation to property was a function of one's sociopolitical status—for the Lozi, kinship status or proximity to the king, and for socialist bureaucrats, place in the party hierarchy of offices (the *nomenklatura*) (Humphrey 1983, 4–5). Equally apt is a comparison with European feudalism, where the allocation of rights to land was similar—Gluckman himself makes this point (1965, 76, 86–88, 168–69 n. 29). All three can be characterized as "tributary" systems, in Eric Wolf's terms (1982, chap. 2).

24. To be sure, there were significant differences between the Lozi and Soviet Russia, stemming from the immeasurably greater power of the Soviet state relative to its subordinates, compared with the modest powers of the Lozi king, and from the vastly greater productive capacity of socialist economies.

25. For example, two firms that regularly traded raw materials for production, such as a shoe factory and a factory that made leather coats, might not have clear boundaries around their inventory because the goods in any firm's fund of circulating capital were fungible, enabling timely

substitution of materials from other enterprises. Thus, determining the assets of either firm would be a complex process. To take a second example, the owner of a piece of land might have "donated" it to a collective farm, whose chairman then transferred the administrative rights to it to the director of a state farm, who might then have assigned it to a farm employee for a house-plot. Although each of these entities might treat the piece of land as its own—especially the employee whose house stood on it—and dispose of it as such, none of them had been registered as the owner because ownership had not in fact changed. With decollectivization, if the farm employee wants to sell his house, he has no title to the land under it—nor is it certain from whom he might obtain that title.

26. See, e.g., Armstrong (1983); Böröcz (1992, 1993); Csaki and Kislev (1993); Hill and Karner (1996); McFaul (1996); Staniszkis (1990, 1991a, and 1991b.)

27. See, for example, Burawoy and Lukács (1992); Hann (1980); Haraszti (1978); Rév (1987); Stark (1989); Swain 1985. For other countries, see Burawoy and Hendley (1992); Humphrey (1983); Sampson (1984). The most influential writing by Hungarian economists includes Bauer (1978); Kornai (1980); Laky (1979). Joseph Berliner's *Factory and Manager in the USSR* (1957), referring chiefly to the Stalinist period, is a classic in the genre.

28. This material could not be systematic, in any event. During my research in the socialist period, the heads of the collective and state farms held me at arm's length; indeed, in 1973 the officials of Hunedoara county explicitly advised me not to trouble myself with the workings of the Vlaicu collective farm, which was among the worst in the county. Leaving aside the inevitable gossip about farm life that was the staple of daily talk in my 1970s research, I learned considerably more about the farms *after* 1989 than I had beforehand.

29. These contracts were precisely the sign that the state was not the proprietor of collectives; otherwise the produce would simply have been delivered to procurement centers. (I owe this observation to notary Ion Hotoiu, from a discussion of the status of collective farm property.)

30. Here are some possibilities for the head of a collective farm. To begin with, he might create for himself a network of support that would ensure his continuing in his post no matter how many complaints farm members might lodge against him. When I asked my friends in 1970s Vlaicu why the obviously incompetent farm president of whom they complained so much continued in office year after debt-ridden year, the answer was that he had friends in high places. In addition, perhaps some of these same friends helped him to work things out when he failed (as he repeatedly did) to meet production targets and thus could not fulfill his contracts. Perhaps they even helped him to negotiate contracts that might be more lenient than those the state made with other, less generous presidents. They would have eased his passage through court, should he become involved in some kind of suit. If the Vlaicu collective farm was in disastrous shape, as I had been advised, then the president's liberal recourse to this fourth destination of its produce—the gift economy—may have been partly responsible for the farm's seemingly low output.

31. See, for example, Gregory (1982); Strathern (1988); Dunn (2004). I acknowledge a debt to Elizabeth Dunn, who continued to insist on the importance of gift exchange in socialist systems until I finally got the message.

32. The networks characteristic of the Soviet system had their precedents in pre-Soviet times. See the review article by Barbara Walker (2001) and the books discussed therein, especially Ledeneva (1998).

33. This section is a shortened version of my 1994 article "The Elasticity of Land," which contains more information on the processes discussed here.

34. In the work of scholars such as Cernea (1974), Creed (1998), Hann (1980), Humphrey (1983), Kideckel (1992), Lampland (1995), and Swain (1985), we find a rich picture of these processes in the management of collective farm property.

35. The decree specified that the exchanges were "obligatory for all owners whose lands are subject to consolidation" (Republica Populară Romînia 1956, 101).

36. Furthermore, Humphrey was told that there had not been one single case of theft, in this sense, in the preceding ten years! Creed reports similarly that theft from individuals was much less common than theft from collective resources in his Bulgarian village (Creed 1998, 197–98). For a superb discussion of theft in Romania, see Mateescu (2002).

37. "*Am plecat într-o noapte la furat*," was how she put it.

38. Until 1982, payment for farm work was in kind, but in that year a money wage was introduced (still tied to workdays). This was when theft from the CF really began to take off.

39. I began by asking what remained in their possession [*Ce v-a mai rămas*] after collectivization, and if they did not bring up the personal plot I would ask, "Whose was the personal plot?" [*Al cui a fost lotul particular*]. I drew this locution from the way people usually talked about land both in the 1990s and in the past—for example, "it was mine" (*a fost al meu*). Compare the discussion in Maurel (1994b, 66–71). She finds that Hungarian and Czech peasants mostly knew the land was not exclusively the property of the CFs.

40. Conscriptio Cziráky for Benczencz, in the Transylvanian section of the Hungarian State Archives, Budapest, Hungary. For further information about this conscription, see Verdery (1983, chap. 2 and accompanying notes).

41. See also the discussions in Swinnen (1997a), Swinnen, Buckwell, and Mathijs (1997), and especially Swinnen and Mathijs (1997, 340–41). Knapp (1975, 39) shows that socialist countries varied in the extent to which they rewrote their pre-existing civil codes. Concerning property law, he divides the countries into three groups: (1) those that adopted new civil codes after the communist takeover (the Soviet Union, Mongolia, Poland, Czechoslovakia, and Hungary); (2) those where precommunist civil codes were abrogated and replaced in piecemeal fashion by special laws that did not form a comprehensive new code (Bulgaria, Albania); and (3) those where older civil codes (1864, 1896) remained in force, but provisions concerning ownership were constitutionally modified and regulated (Romania and East Germany).

42. Linda Miller (personal communication, May 22, 2001); see also Sikor (2001, 17). I owe a debt to Dr. Miller for ongoing discussion of this matter and for her efforts to resolve it.

Chapter 2. Unmaking Socialist Agriculture

The first part of this chapter owes a debt to the participants in the symposium of the KATO Projekt, held in Berlin on November 2–4, 2000, and particularly to its organizers at the Humboldt University, Prof. Konrad Hagedorn and Dr. Volker Beckmann, who welcomed me into their discussions. The symposium brought together the main researchers in the field of East European agrarian economics from a number of European countries. Edited volumes, some of them including these same participants (e.g., Swinnen 1997b; Swinnen, Buckwell, and Mathijs 1997; Wegren 1998b), have also contributed to my sense of the broader questions, as have papers on the KATO web site (*www.KATO-projekt.de*).

1. Cited in von Hirschhausen (1997, 57), from a speech Roman delivered before Parliament while the law was being debated.

2. Iliescu's comment was, "*Este un moft chestiunea aceasta cu sfânta proprietate privată care stă la originea vieții sociale.*" The subsequent outcry led his office to explain that his concern was with the high degree of fragmentation that private property had generated in Romania, hampering agricultural production; in urging that owners of small plots join associations, his goal was better results for everyone.

3. For fuller discussion of some of these points, see Frydman and Rapaczynski (1994); Heller and Serkin (1999); Offe et al. (1993); Swinnen (1997b); Swinnen, Buckwell, and Mathijs (1997).

4. This plan would work only in those countries such as Czechoslovakia where privatization was carried on by sales and auctions, not by give-aways.

5. Sources for this discussion include Borneman (1997); Elster, Offe, and Preuss (1998); Hanisch and Schlüter (1999); Heller and Serkin (1999); Offe et al. (1993); Pryor (1992); Rabinowicz and Swinnen (1997); Swinnen and Mathijs (1997). Pryor, in particular, provides an excellent and very prescient discussion (completed in January 1991) of why decollectivization would be difficult and what kinds of problems should be expected.

6. See, for example, Chaudry (1993); North (1979); Polanyi (1944); Tinbergen (1958); Wade (1990). For transition literature, see Domański and Heyns (1995); Elster, Offe, and Preuss (1998); Frydman and Rapaczynski (1994); Islam and Mandelbaum (1993); Swinnen (2000).

7. My discussion is indebted to Csaki and Kislev (1993); Elster, Offe, and Preuss (1998);

Heller and Serkin (1999); Offe et al. (1993); Pryor (1992); Stark (1992); Swain (1996, 1998, 1999); Swinnen (1997b); Swinnen, Buckwell, and Mathijs (1997).

8. For example, Bulgaria assessed compensation for the nonland assets according to an algorithm that weighted people's land and labor contributions equally, at 50 percent. This formula rewarded labor more than did the formula in Czechoslovakia (as it then was), where the weights were 50 percent for land, 30 percent for other capital assets given to the collectives (plows, horses, cattle, etc.), and only 20 percent for labor performed in the farm. Thus, the former village poor in Czechoslovakia received a far smaller proportion of the value of farm assets than did the wealthy. The algorithm in Romania was 60 percent for land and 40 percent for labor—closer to the Bulgarian one. The most favorable of all to those without land was Slovenia, where nonland assets were distributed 100 percent according to one's labor in the collective (Swinnen and Mathijs 1997, 338).

9. Of the total amounts that the 1945 reforms made available for redistribution, in Poland 76 percent came from Germans, in Czechoslovakia 71 percent, in Yugoslavia 41 percent, and in Romania 24 percent (see Brus 1986, 584–91).

10. The points in this paragraph come from the contribution by Shlomo Avinieri in Offe et al. (1993). See also Borneman (1997); Heller and Serkin (1999); and Swinnen (1997b).

11. In discussing this matter with a Romanian judge of strong neoliberal sympaties, I was surprised to hear him defending Romania's use of the 1948 baseline as the most ethical solution because it gave land to as many people as possible.

12. See Cungu and Swinnen (1997b, 7) for Albania. The figure for Romania comes from *Agra Europe* for June 1997, p. 34 (see Chelcea 1998, 22–23). In a 1994 interview I held with a researcher at the Institute for Agrarian History in Bucharest, he claimed that although the World Bank was using an estimate of three to four parcels per reconstituted holding, he and his colleagues found seven to eight a more reasonable guess. Sarris and Gavrilescu (1997, 218), however, report from a 1994 survey that 33 percent of all private holdings were in three or four parcels, and 28 percent were in more than five.

13. The account in the following paragraphs is based on information from a number of sources, including Swain (1998, 1999), as well as the papers in Swinnen (1997b) and Swinnen, Buckwell, and Mathijs (1997).

14. However, Poland and Yugoslavia also had the task of modernizing private farming, which had generally been starved of credits and investment under the prior regime.

15. For information on Albanian privatization, see Bloch (1998); Cungu and Swinnen (1997a, 1997b); de Waal (1996, 2001). Sources on the Baltic countries include Davis (1997) and Meyers and Kazlauskiene (1998).

16. Bulgaria specialists with whom I discussed this believed that the percentage in cooperatives was much higher and that the government wanted to veil this evidence of socialist recidivism in the interest of its relations with international lenders.

17. From an interview conducted by Y. Konstantinov (2000, 19, 32).

18. I thank Dr. Arnd Bauerkämper for this information.

19. Information in this paragraph is from Hagedorn (1998, 212–28). See also Siebert (2000).

20. See, for example, Harcsa et al. (1998); Mathijs (1997); Stark (1992); Stark and Bruszt (1998); Swain (1996, 1998, 1999).

21. This does not mean that people never got back their original parcels—see Thelen (2001).

22. The literature on Russian agriculture is immense and I cannot do it justice here. My sources include Hivon (1998); Humphrey (1998, chaps. 9, 10); Lerman (1997); Perotta (1998); Van Atta (1993, 1997); Wegren (1998a, 1998b).

23. The reason is that in the 1930s, peasants used almost no costly inputs, whereas by 1990 it was no longer acceptable to plow with horses and oxen (whose dwindling numbers deprived the soil of manure), new pests had arisen that were resistant to the old forms of pesticide (e.g., copper sulfate), the labor force no longer existed to supply labor in the absence of herbicides, and so on.

24. See also Nickolsky (1998, 207), which gives a table showing the declining use of fertilizer in Russia, 1989–94. In 1994, the amount of mineral fertilizers used was 11.1 percent of the average

for 1986–90 and 39 percent of what was used in 1993. The amount of organic fertilizers used in 1994 was 29 percent of the average for 1986–90 and 61 percent of that used in 1993.

25. This emerged from discussion at the KATO conference referred to in the chapter Acknowledgments.

26. There is as of this writing no comprehensive account of Romanian politics during the 1990s. For orientation, see Jackson (1997); Mungiu-Pippidi (2002); Pasti, Miroiu, and Codiță (1997); Pop-Eleches (1999, 2001); Shafir (1997); Tismăneanu (1997); Tismăneanu and Kligman (2001); Verdery (1996, chap. 5); Weiner (2001).

27. The names of Romania's main parties changed several times in confusing ways. The initial National Salvation Front split into two parties, the splinter retaining the old name and the other faction becoming the *Democratic* National Salvation Front. Each then changed its name again, the former becoming the Democratic Party and the latter the Party of Romanian Social Democracy (PRSD; confusingly close to the Social Democratic Party of Romania); the PRSD was the major party in 1990–96 and again from 2000, under President Ion Iliescu. In 2001, the PRSD fused with the Social Democrats and suddenly began calling themselves the Social-Democratic Party (SDP). I use here the label PRSD, which covered it for most of the 1990s.

28. See chapter 1, plus Verdery (1991, chaps. 2, 6; 1996, chaps. 1, 7).

29. See, for example, Cartwright (2001, 141, 174–5); Kideckel (1995b, 48–9); Mungiu-Pippidi and Althabe (2002, 68–70); Stewart (1998, 74); von Hirschhausen (1997, 18).

30. See Rizov et al. (2001, table 2); von Hirschhausen (1997, 18–19). Rizov et al.'s table 2 combined with other figures also indicates that the hilly regions had the smallest percentage of arable land in their total agricultural surface.

31. Thanks to Daniel Lățea for this observation.

32. The law specifies that such people should receive some land if there is any in excess of the claims of former owners; it even invites land commissions to create excess land by subtracting a fixed percentage—the *reduction coefficient*—from the reconstituted holdings. But many Transylvanian villages had no excess land, either because the reduction coefficient was miscalculated or because resolving superimposed ownership claims used up all the village's surface.

33. This includes first cousins, second cousins once removed, parents' and grandparents' siblings—a fairly wide net. I discuss the complexities of kinship claims in chapter 4.

34. See Cartwright (2001, 118), who cites as his source for this figure a 1998 OECD report; see also Jackson (1997, 215), who cites the Economist Intelligence Unit.

35. Documents I consulted for the 1921 reform in Vlaicu showed continued work as late as 1942. Data for 1848/1854 from Drs. Aurel Răduțiu and Simion Retegan of the Institute of History, Cluj (personal communication); for 1921, Șandru (1975, 250–51). For Vlaicu, the file I consulted in the Deva branch of the State Archives is entitled "Inspectoratul Cadastrul Arad, Com AV, jud. Hunedoara, Faza I-III, nr. 8," in the inventory for the 1921 reform.

36. From *Ziua*, March 14, 1998. The government replied that the figures had changed along with the adoption of a new method of calculating the different categories, but in my own figures, collected from 1994 to 2000, totals vary constantly as well. As against the total of 9,168,386 ha of 1994, official figures for 1998 give about 9,350,000 ha. Even in the *Romanian Statistical Yearbook* for 1999, figures often do not add up (e.g., table 20.54, pp. 878–79). For another discussion about the discrepancy among statistics, see *România liberă* for November 18, 1998.

37. I thank Mr. D. Popovici, president of the Senate Commission for Agriculture, for the 1994 interview that clarified these issues for me.

38. Note that the government (as well as international organizations) saw farm fragmentation as an unmitigated evil, but to cultivators it offered advantages. See discussion in chapter 5.

39. I thank Mr. William Carter of the Bucharest USAID office (1994), who explained to me the mapping project and its difficulties.

40. The result has been, in the words of a notary in Deva (thus, a proponent of the Transylvanian system), completely chaotic. Owners have received new property deeds that both describe the terrain according to its neighbors *and* assign it a number, which will eventually be linked to maps still in the process of being created. These new numbers bear no relation whatever to the old ones, *and there is no way of making them do so.* The reason is that the topographic

numbers in the land registry are all adjacent, whereas the numbers in the new cadastre are ordered as in the Regat system: according to who shows up on what day. The first person to appear is number 1, the next is number 2—regardless of whether the parcels they own are adjacent or at opposite ends of the settlement. The only way out of this mess will be to make a concordance between the two numbering systems so that the history of parcels can be traced through time.

41. From Sarris and Gavrilescu (1997, 192) for the number of claimants; print-outs provided by the Ministry of Agriculture, for the rest.

42. These figures are from unpublished print-outs I obtained from the Oficiul pentru Cadastru și Organizarea Teritoriului Agricol (for 1997) and the Ministry of Public Administration (for 2001). A press communiqué of 1 January 2003 from that Ministry claimed that 91 percent of titles were complete. (Information courtesy of A. S. Alexe.)

43. This was even greater than the fragmentation evident in 1948, when 36 percent of all holdings were under 1 hectare.

44. See note 12. Von Hirschhausen (1997, 207) reports a Ministry of Agriculture figure of 18–20 million parcels for those 9.2 million ha but gives no source.

45. This high percentage—exceeded only by Albania—resulted from Romania's continued reliance on manual labor, unlike Bulgaria, for example, where there was much more substitution of mechanical for manual labor (Jackson 1997, 283–85).

46. Figures from *Evenimentul zilei*, March 26, 1998. Once people began losing their urban jobs, however, possession of even a small holding made a great difference for their economic prospects.

47. The first figure is from Mungiu-Pippidi and Althabe (2002, 138), the second from Sarris and Gavrilescu (1997, 193). According to government statistics, in 1998 56 percent of rural households were headed by pensioners and only 18 percent by active cultivators (Neményi 2000a, 123).

48. My sources for the material in this discussion include European Commission (1998); Jackson (1997); Lerman (2000b); Mungiu-Pippidi and Althabe (2002); Pasti, Miroiu, and Codiță (1997); Sarris and Gavrilescu (1997); Teşliuc (2000a, 2000b).

49. Figures from International Monetary Fund Staff Country Report no. 98/123 (November 1998), "Romania: Statistical Appendix" (table 18, p. 23). I thank Peter Bernholz for this information.

50. The debt figure is given in a news report in *Curentul* for November 29, 1998, the budgetary figure in *Adevărul economic* for April 12–19, 1999.

51. A World Bank consultant with whom I discussed these subsidies said this goal was overt in DC government discourse.

52. In that year, a coupon covered most of the cost of fall plowing in Hunedoara county (about 180,000 lei/ha; the following spring it was 210,000).

53. Emil Constantinescu, DC party leader, on the weekly agricultural TV program *Viața Satului* for April 17, 1994.

54. Personal communication, June 2002.

55. I thank Larry Watts, Stelian Tănase, and Steven Sampson for discussions on this topic.

56. Von Cramon-Taubadel (2002) too suspects the rhetoric, wondering why western countries were not as eager to liberalize their own agricultural markets as those of Eastern Europe. Instead, EU policy was highly protectionist and subsidized; its members engaged in dumping outside its borders (2000, 13–14), even as it decried protectionist impulses in Eastern Europe.

57. Two commercial officers for the U.S. Embassy as well as the ambassador himself stated this to me outright.

58. This amounted to about $11 million at that time (the total state budget for agriculture in 1996 was about 2.7 trillion lei) (report in *Evenimentul zilei*, March 13, 1998).

59. See *Evenimentul zilei* for April 13, 1998.

60. From the television program *Viața Satului* for November 28, 1993.

61. *Evenimentul zilei* for July 19, 1998.

62. Both PRSD and DC governments set up price subsidies supposedly effective at the moment of purchase or sale; instead, people would apply for the subsidies but the money would ar-

rive several months later, if at all. People with subsidized equipment loans would go to make their monthly payment at the bank only to discover that it had not yet received the subsidy, so they would have to pay the full market interest, hoping to recover the subsidy later. The same thing happened with subsidized products. Meanwhile, cultivators and suppliers or buyers would each strive to have the other be the one holding the bag.

Vlaiceni, for example, would sell their wheat to a baker for the market price plus the subsidy, but the baker would refuse to pay the subsidy, telling the cultivator to get the money directly from the state. Alternatively, villagers would opt *not* to market their produce, thus obtaining no added support for their next production cycle. Teşliuc (2000a, 94) reports that the amount of nonmarketed produce from the smallholding sector was very large, estimated for 1994–98 at 42 percent of the wheat crop, 61 percent of maize, 38 percent of hogs, 55 percent of poultry, and 68 percent of milk. The average farming family was producing 80 percent of its own food needs and contributing to the ability of urban families to draw about half of their consumption from their own sources. Meanwhile, as if justifying the PRSD's reasons for not breaking up state farms, SFs worked only 16 percent of the land but provided half of all marketed wheat and barley, and more than half of all pork and fowl. Only as of 1997 did those figures begin to decline.

63. *Evenimentul zilei*, July 19, 1998.

64. See Verdery (1994, 1101). See also Cartwright (2001, 150–55, 176–86), for other examples of this kind.

65. See, e.g., *Adevărul*, November 25, 1998; *Ziua*, September 21, 1998; *România liberă*, November 21, 1998; *Adevărul*, March 1997.

66. See Verdery (1991, chap. 6) for an explanation of this view.

67. See also Schlüter (2000) for a bargaining model aimed at explaining why the implementation of land-rights restitution so often departed from its design.

68. Others too have argued that states were weak in the transition—particularly for Russia but for some East European countries as well. See, for example, Fairbanks (1999); Humphrey (1991); Staniszkis (1999).

69. The minister at the time was Oancea. *Viaţa Satului*, March 13, 1994.

70. Scholars have made this point repeatedly (see, for example, Hanisch 2000; Lampland 2002; Schlüter 2000; Swain 1999).

71. Oral comment delivered at the KATO symposium in November 2000, Humboldt University, Berlin.

Chapter 3. How Hectares Vanished

An earlier version of this chapter was published by Sage Publications Ltd. in the journal *Ethnography* 3 (2002), pp. 5–33, under the title "Seeing Like a Mayor: Or, How Local Officials Obstructed Romanian Land Restitution." Michael Burawoy, Loïc Wacquant, and Paul Willis offered helpful comments in producing that version.

1. Divertis (1996). I have greatly compressed this lengthy and hilarious skit and translated very liberally. Apropos the theme of property: in granting me permission to use this extract, Divertis observed that I was the first person to offer payment for what everyone else was simply taking.

2. I participated in and observed the commission's work in two ways. (1) Tipped off by a member that a meeting was imminent, I would go to the office and sit by the phone (one of only three in Vlaicu) looking at it expectantly from time to time. No one, including the two committee members from Geoagiu, ever asked me to leave, although many villagers looked at me quizzically when they came in. (2) For four weeks I accompanied the committee on its rounds when it measured household gardens. This followed a rare day in which the mayor had shown up, giving me permission to be present for a problem case. The committeemen, seeing me there with the mayor, assumed I could come whenever I wanted, an assumption no one bothered to clarify (including me). Although at first the committeemen were a bit nervous at my accompanying them, they soon came to see my presence as a good thing because it suggested to Vlaiceni that they were doing nothing untoward. (Indeed, this activity spawned yet another rumor about what I was really doing in the village: I was spying on the committee for the mayor!) From this

opportunity I began to understand how much more complicated it would be to assign land out in the fields.

3. Some are from the commune archives in Geoagiu, others from the topographer who measured Vlaicu for the new cadastre. The archives, which I consulted in fall 1993, consist of a number of folders containing papers in a somewhat disorganized state, with few dates to indicate which pieces were earlier or later. As I was copying material from them, the office staff carried on a lively discussion around me about the inaccuracy of many of the figures. My thanks to the Geoagiu commune officials who put this archive at my disposal.

4. The land included in these figures is mainly arable land, pasture, and orchards.

5. I say "tentative" because the various population figures I received from the local police and the commune archives did not agree. (No one had bothered to count with care, for example, the number of Roma in Vlaicu's "Gypsy apartment building.") The figures from 1992 are 915 people in 270 houses; my own provisional census in 2000, conducted with the assistance of the accountant of the Vlaicu Association, gives me a total of 820, which includes an estimate for the numbers of people in four Roma apartments. In arriving at the figure of 274 households, I left out all houses in which no one was living at that moment, even though there might be an owner living in town.

6. In Romanian (as in Latin), the word *venit* is the past participle of the verb *a veni*, "to come." Nominalized in the plural it is *veniți*, "those who have come." This is one of several names that Vlaiceni use for people who have moved in (others are *străinași*, *veniturile*, and *venetici*, the last two having very pejorative connotations), but because *venit* is the easiest to pronounce and the least offensive, I use it here, in preference to the clumsy *in-migrants*. The term for "locals" is *băștinași*.

7. I obtained figures on restituted holdings as of 1995 from the Office of the Cadastre and Territorial Organization in Agriculture, Deva. I thank the director of that office for permission to copy the records for Vlaicu during my research in summer 1996. I took the raw figures and combined them in all cases in which I knew that specific allotments had been conjoined with other allotments in a single household. This procedure leads to a somewhat higher average holding (2.7 ha) than I reported in Verdery (2002). The chart includes both Romanians and Germans.

8. In Romanian the precollective labels were *bogat*, *mijlocaș*, and *sărac*.

9. This comes from the name of the village—Binținți, in Romanian, and Benzenz, in German—prior to its name change in 1926.

10. This was not true everywhere. Cartwright (2001, 153), for example, found that in the village of Mirșid, where he worked, the commission created holdings for Roma.

11. I add that I had been working in and visiting this community since 1973 and enjoyed relations of trust with a number of the people interviewed for this project.

12. For descriptions of this process in other places, see the papers in Abraham (1996); Buechler and Buechler (2002); papers by Creed (1995a, 1995b, 1999); Cartwright (2001); Humphrey (1998, chaps. 9, 10); Konstantinov (2000); the papers in Kideckel (1995a); Lampland (2002); Meurs (2001); Stewart (1998); Swain (1996, 1999).

13. Geoagiu's mayor gave a different explanation: Vlaiceni were so divided among themselves that they could not organize a collective action.

14. People had to join such cooperatives because the return of land was not accompanied by return of other means of production. Many elderly recipients of land had no way of purchasing the tractors, plows, seeders, and other implements needed for making use of their land.

15. One staff member was so exasperated at people's "coming and complaining about what they were getting" that she finally quit.

16. In 1992 the Association harvested 303 ha; in 1993, 233 ha; and in 1994, 207 ha. For the next several years it stayed at around 200 ha.

17. See Verdery (1994) for further discussion of these procedures.

18. I was unable to secure a reliable figure for the percentage of Vlaicu's surface that was returned to nonresidents. The Association's accountant estimated that it was about 60 percent or more of the total.

19. Comparing the amounts the later committeemen ended up with against the amounts

their families had owned in 1959 shows that all of them came out ahead, if those 1959 figures are accurate.

20. Exactly how many property titles had been finalized for Vlaicu remains unclear to me. In 1996 a commune official told me that between 80 and 95 percent of Vlaicu's titles had been awarded, but for the next five years no one would ever actually show me a statistic; in summer 2001, after the new mayor had proved as recalcitrant with numbers as his predecessor, the head of the county restitution office estimated it as 50 percent (after the new round of restitution—SF land—had begun).

21. See also comparable stories in Pasti, Miroiu, and Codiță (1997) and in Mungiu-Pippidi and Althabe (2002).

22. Although Mayor Lupu was generally courteous with me, he seemed uncomfortable with my presence and held me at arm's length. A villager told me that in one of his first council meetings as mayor he had remarked that owing to the revolution, "that American spy" would no longer be coming around. Because I found it impossible to get very far with him in interviews, I describe him in terms used by many others in whose judgment I have confidence.

23. This committee member had seen from his attendance at the commission meetings that the commission did not plan to give Germans any land. They therefore had time to gather their documents and find a lawyer to help them plan their strategy. The favorable judgment came partly from the speed of their suit (they appealed to the county board in less than a month, using a petition they showed me the day after the amounts to be restituted were posted in Vlaicu). As the lawyer who had helped them informed me, the judiciary was in such confusion and had so little precedent for such cases that anyone with a well-prepared case and good legal advice was likely to win.

24. Like many of my numbers, this one is approximate. The lists put at my disposal had names crossed off and added, as well as other marginal notations that made it impossible to know exactly how many households had lost out to the Germans.

25. This story has a more sinister, indeed tragic, side. The treasurer of Geoagiu commune hanged himself after irregularities were revealed in various officials' procurement of building material.

26. I have this opinion from the Deputy Minister for Public Administration, in 2002.

27. Prime Minister Văcăroiu on *Viața Satului*, November 28, 1993.

28. Interview with Vasile Lupu, vice president of the Chamber of Deputies, 1994.

29. "*Patru ani mandatul garantat?*" December 8, 1993. The interviewer added that most mayors they approached refused to speak with them on camera.

30. I did not have detailed knowledge of field cultivation but had the 1948 agricultural census, which contained the size of parcels and their ordering in space—a listing that several villagers found very useful. I had also reconstituted genealogies beginning in the mid-1800s. Perhaps unfortunately, I was not present in Vlaicu when this information was most urgently needed in 1991, although several people asked me later to explain kin ties they found implausible.

31. See de Waal (2001) for a discussion of the role of old men in reconstituting field boundaries in northern Albania.

32. For an illuminating discussion of the place of information in socialist systems, see Szakolczai and Horváth (1991).

Chapter 4. New Kin, New Serfs, New Masters

1. The quotation (from notes taken at the time) is from an interview I conducted with this official.

2. The argument for restituting not just to immediate offspring (the original proposal) but to kin as far as the fourth degree was that because the latter is the rule in Romanian inheritance law it should be honored now (information from an interview with Dr. Florin Scrieciu, one of the drafters of Law 18).

3. Personal communication. I thank him for his extended comments on the similarities and differences in restitution in Transylvania and the Regat.

4. Interestingly, in urban (as opposed to rural) settings the new attention to ancestors was

coming at a time when relations between actual parents and children were changing significantly. In socialism, these ties had been essential to the survival of younger families, whose parents' pensions were large enough to supplement their own income. In addition, retired parents often helped their children by caring for the grandchildren, and—crucially, in the Romanian context—by standing in the interminable lines to buy food, something their working children had less time to do. After 1990, however, these patterns changed. First, pensions were so small that far from supporting their children, older people had to find ways of working longer themselves. This reduced their availability for grandchild care. Moreover, because there were no longer any lines to stand in, the elderly lost that important role as well. Parents, having always been a resource, now became largely a burden—unless, of course, they happened to own land.

5. The expression used is *moși-strămoși*, "my grandparents and those before them."

6. This fact could have consequences for the intention of the framers of Law 18 to consolidate land by requiring that it first be offered to kin or neighbors—the very people with whom one was most likely to have a quarrel.

7. See, for example, Cartwright (2001, 145, 149).

8. I thank Daniel Lățea and Oana Mateescu for a stimulating discussion about the kin effects of Law 18. They suggest that—much as in demographic literature concerning the division of extended families—siblings tended to have a centripetal relation to the holding while spouses exerted centrifugal pressures. In the cases they are familiar with from southern Romania, they see a great "horror of division."

9. Sometimes this could mean being forced into paying—and cash was in very short supply—for something one would otherwise have acquired through the labor of kin. For example, a widow bickering with her cousins over land would have to spend money she did not have so as to buy expensive mortuary bread, rather than making it with her relatives. I was party to several discussions among Romanian Vlaiceni as they compared their own death rituals unfavorably with those of Germans, who—instead of putting on a huge, costly, and labor-consuming feast— "have a plate of sandwiches, everyone takes a sandwich and eats standing up for a few minutes, then everyone goes home." The tone of these comments contrasted with that of earlier times, when Romanians scoffed that Germans spent hardly any time with their dead and were too cheap to put on a proper mortuary feast.

10. I overheard these comments during the committee's rounds for measuring household gardens, as the different parties to a measurement argued why they and not someone else should be getting more. These justifications were thus offered in a context in which my presence was unlikely to distort people's reasoning.

11. Although figures for population density do not show this difference, it appears clearly if we divide population not by total land surfaces but by *arable* surfaces only.

12. Kaneff (1998), working in Bulgaria, reports that work was counted toward land entitlement, but Konstantinov (2000) found the opposite; in the region he surveyed, most owners understood ownership only in terms of hereditary rights and original ownership.

13. There was no intermarriage in the first generation because venits came already married, but as of the late 1990s a few offspring of locals families—to the distress of their parents—had married venit offspring.

14. His actual words were, "*Ne-am domnit!*" which could also be translated as "We've turned into lords."

15. *Property* reflects what is proper to oneself (think of the French *propre*). This *proper* includes both self and the notion of *propriety,* the two terms being used interchangeably in Locke's day. Similarly, *ownership* is rooted in the Anglo-Saxon *eigen,* "self." The German word for property, *Eigentum,* might be glossed as "selfdom."

16. It is possible that this idea is not found in other parts of Romania. For example, Chelcea (personal communication) informs me that he heard nothing like it in Ialomița in the south.

17. There were some younger villagers who seemed eager to play the status game based on land, but most were indifferent to it. They wanted higher education or to use what they already had so as to leave Vlaicu altogether.

18. This was explicit in the law, with its ten–year moratorium on sales, and implicit in the government credit policies I discuss in chapter 3.

Chapter 5. The Death of a Peasantry

This chapter benefited from comments of audiences present when I gave versions of it at the Departments of Anthropology at Cambridge University and University College London, the seminar at the Wissenschaftskolleg zu Berlin, the Max Planck Institute for Ethnology (Halle, Germany), and the Wenner-Gren conference on Changing Property Rights at the Turn of the Millennium, 2001. My thanks to all who participated in those discussions.

1. Venits' main advantage over locals was that because venit women had been overrepresented in the best-paid work force of the CF, the dairy farm, their pensions might be somewhat larger than local women's (although still derisory).

2. Even during the socialist period households were allowed to keep cattle. At first the number was limited, but by the late 1980s some households in Vlaicu had as many as six. Cattle-raising in Vlaicu after 1989 therefore began on the base already provided by this prior activity. In addition, in 1990 everyone received back from the CF the number of cattle they had given to it in 1959.

3. I was stunned to learn in 1994 from one Vlaicean who used his horse to plow for others that he charged almost as much as the tractorists—and they charged according to Agromec fees. When I asked why, he replied that a plowing job is a plowing job, and his horses need to eat just as tractors need gas. He too was riding the coattails of the Agromec. Over the decade, the price of horses rose steadily, as did their number—between 1990 and 1995, at a time when most other animals were decreasing, the number of horses rose by 18 percent (see Pasti, Miroiu, and Codiţă 1997, 53).

4. The Ministry of Agriculture claimed that a coupon would cover 35 percent of production and harvesting costs per hectare (see Chelcea 1998, 5). I note that the figure I give here (2.5 million/ha) is higher than it would be in the Regat—that is, coupons covered a larger percentage of production costs for Regăţeni.

5. In this case, I recorded his speech verbatim: "Eu subsemnatul *rog a mi se binevoi să primească....*"

6. For example, men who worked as tractorists for the state machinery parks might have their directors declare an old tractor worn out, in exchange for a nice pay-off.

7. In 1994 the number of tractors in Vlaicu was about eleven, in 1999, twenty-five, two of the earlier batch having been sold meanwhile. My figures are approximate because I did not do a complete census in either year but merely asked a number of people which Vlaiceni had tractors; even so, my numbers are higher than those given me by the county Department of Agriculture in 2000. Of these tractors, three were purchased collectively by producers' cooperatives. The available surface of Vlaicu in this period was around 600 ha; hence, at twenty-five, it was carrying far more tractors than were needed.

8. An agronomist with whom I discussed this was convinced the increase exceeded both inflation and the devaluation of the leu because the foreign manufacturers of these products had purposely sold them at low prices in the early 1990s until they had created a market; they then began raising the price once people were hooked. See also chapter 8.

9. According to the Romanian Ministry of Agriculture and Food (1998), between 1990 and 1997 fertilizer use dropped from 1.2–1.3 million tonnes to under 400,000 tonnes, or 30 percent of original levels (I thank A. L. Cartwright for this source). Swinnen (2000) gives an even lower figure of 20 percent. Pasti, Miroiu, and Codiţă see the decline very early—only 25 percent of the fertilizer used in 1989 was being used in 1994 (1997, 53–54).

10. Meurs and Begg (1998, 250, 256), for example, report that in Bulgaria, the prices of inputs increased between 6- and 25-fold, those of outputs only 5- to 10-fold; from 1989 to 1992 the national use of pesticides dropped by 64 percent and of chemical fertilizer by 74 percent.

11. The unevenness of inflation from year to year, however, could be as devastating as its rate. Beneath an overall rate of 40 percent per year might lurk one or two years so bad as to push people over the brink.

12. Even if I use the highest *market* price for 1997 as against the *state* price for 1995—that is, the most favorable comparison possible, for the seller—the increment is only 5.4-fold.

13. In the socialist period there was a good system of professional schools to train skilled workers, but those schools were accessible only to people living in the lowlands. Because uplanders rarely had access to more than eight grades of schooling, when they moved down for work they were nearly all hired as unskilled manual laborers. In that position, they were not able to make many connections with important people in the factory, and for this reason as well as their lack of skill they were the most vulnerable to firing after 1989.

14. Their hectare had cost them 4 million lei, and they compared this with the 100 million for which a fancy house had recently sold.

15. I counted twenty-one households, or 7.7 percent of all households (not 7.7 percent of the whole population) as neo-Protestants. Only one household is local. Most of Vlaicu's neo-Protestants are Seventh-Day Adventists, who gather regularly in the houses of one or another local member and form a tight community. (There are far more venits who are Orthodox, however, so the overlap between the two categories is far from perfect.) Chelcea reports (personal communication) from his research in Ialomiţa in southeastern Romania that in one village, neo-Protestants had formed their own association and received from it three times more grain than did villagers in the other associations.

16. According to Lăţea (personal communication), the picture I present may have been peculiar to Vlaicu or comparable localities; he found less of a labor crisis in his research in Oltenia (Regat). Moreover, to the extent that he saw anything similar, it was earlier in the decade; by the late 1990s, people—including young people—began returning to work on the land. It may be that more Vlaiceni were emigrating to work in Europe at that time and that the possibility for venits to buy land in Vlaicu was greater than it was in Oltenia.

17. An agronomist scoffed at this reasoning, saying these peasants just did not know about the latest chemical inputs.

18. In Romania these two roles generally went together—the couple who "married" you also baptized your children. The roles were called *naş* ("nash") and *fin* ("feen"), the *naş* being the sponsor or godparent. The relationship once bound the respective families as if they were linked by blood. It was considered as incestuous to marry the kin of your *naş* as to marry blood relatives. The relationship might even be inherited: my *naşi* would be the children of my parents' *naşi*. The best treatment of this subject is Hammel (1968). Romanian custom resembled that which Hammel reports for Serbia, although the fact that Romanian kinship practices are bilateral (rather than lineal like those of Serbs) makes for important differences. Already by the time of my 1973 fieldwork these forms were rarely encountered; people sought *naşi* among their factory foremen or other social superiors in the socialist order of things, not among the children of their parents' *naşi*.

19. Moreover, the Association required those who wanted corn or sugar beets to do the weeding themselves, so if labor was your problem, then the Association was only partly beneficial.

20. Their cultural capital, however, in the form of knowledge about farming, was probably much lower for Vlaicu conditions. Those locals who had worked land themselves or with their parents up until 1959 had acquired much of the relevant knowledge for local conditions. The mix of crops and the condition of the soil in hill villages differ markedly from those of the plateau.

21. The 1.6 million was not a lot of money—workers were being pensioned with 3 million at that point—but it was probably more than they could earn as day laborers doing backbreaking labor.

22. The result of these processes resembles what lowland-hill relations have been like ever since the feudal period. The hills were always a realm of relative freedom—freedom from feudal lords and from collectivization—but also of disadvantage: soils were poor, distances to market very great, and basic services such as health and education weak or nonexistent. There was always a flow of hill people into lowland villages, where they might end up on marginal lands, just as became likely after 1991. Finally, venits could buy land precisely because agriculture was such a devalued sector in comparison with other lines of work. Lest one see here a triumph for venits, I should observe that the land being sold in the late 1990s was often land of poor quality or in

poor locations, which was also what venits could most likely afford. Good-quality land was more costly; it went to the supertenants who were bent on accumulating land and found money to do so (see chapter 8). Thus, even as successful buyers they remained at the bottom of the heap.

23. One interesting sign was that in twenty-three years of visiting in Vlaicu, I had always been invited into the house and given food and drink, but during my visits in the summers of 1996 and 1997, for the first time, people were more likely to sit me on a bench outside and not invite me in. My uncharitable landlord explained it, "They want you to leave, because they're so exhausted."

24. As long as it remained impossible to register a land sale legally, people generally sold with a written contract and two witnesses, hoping the document would hold up once sale became legally possible.

25. See also chapter 2, the section on scandals. Here are a few local examples. Some villagers schemed to get more coupons than they should. They would ask their supertenant to certify that he was working their entire surface area, not just the smaller portion he was actually cultivating, so they could qualify for coupons for their whole surface rather than a mere part of it. New abuses from the coupon system included tractorists' agreeing to harvest wheat for coupons instead of cash, but accepting them at only 80 percent of their value and keeping the remainder; and the mafia that appeared in market towns to buy up coupons would pay no more than 70 percent for them. Notably, the coupon system further increased the gap between those with and without land.

26. I might generalize this point to suggest that objects whose materiality is essential to their value may attract more risk to the extent that they are individualized—but this is the very secret of their having value, in that particular system of evaluation.

27. Simion Retegan (personal communication) reports that for his natal area of Transylvania, villagers did seem to take satisfaction in being rentiers.

28. I refer not only to the Iron Curtain but also to weak investment in urban infrastructures and to other policies that effectively prevented a large number of rural dwellers from moving to cities (see Szelényi 1983).

29. See Verdery (1977, chap. 5). The only occupation that ranked lower in my occupational prestige scores was factory night-watchman.

Chapter 6. Credits and Credibility

I am deeply indebted for the generous collaboration of the two women who ran the Association, particularly Anda, who never tired of answering my questions. In countless hours of conversation over the period September 1993 to May 2001 they taught me most of what I know about the workings of the organization.

1. In many villages both in Romania and elsewhere, more than one such cooperative was formed. In Transylvania they might be divided ethnically, although not every biethnic village necessarily divided that way (as we see from Romos, near Vlaicu). More common was that the "better" families with more land would form their own, usually hiving off from the association that emerged from the CF. For other examples see Kaneff (1996, 1998); Kideckel (1995b); Konstantinov (2000); Maurel (1994b); Stewart (1998).

2. For this reason, the government statistics on the relative proportions of individual farms and associations greatly underreport the latter.

3. The delay probably resulted from the fact that the CF president, whom many villagers disliked, had insufficient authority to make a bold move; the first two agronomists were not from Vlaicu and soon left; the accountants, both women, were too low on the totem pole to set up an association; and only belatedly did someone who was capable of running one present himself. This was an agronomist who had married into Vlaicu and had worked in the CF many years earlier; he now found it convenient to return, so as to recover as much of his wife's family land as possible, for she was contesting the allotments of land she had received. By being in the Association, he was better able to impose himself on some of the contested fields, wresting them from the kin who, many thought, deserved them more.

4. Between 1992 and 2000 five of these people died and/or were replaced with others having slightly more experience in agriculture.

5. I do not have data on other associations that had to elect a council, but the likelihood that there would be many former officials is, in the opinion of my respondent, very high.

6. This is not to deny the goodwill of some of these council members and their skill in other areas of life.

7. In the media of the 1990s, there was a constant stream of stories about abuses that association leaders committed. Where such charges were true (and I am certain that many were), one might doubt that the organization had been formed primarily to help its members. During my stays in Vlaicu I continually heard complaints that the leaders and council were ripping off funds from the organization and engaging in other illegalities. Although this is possible, I do not believe it was extensive. Some of the councilors evidently engaged in nefarious practices, but the two women who ran it were, in my opinion, mostly honest. They often complained at having to resist their councilors' pressure to work illegally, by keeping certain expenses off the books. Much of what villagers would have seen as working the land for their own benefit had other, less uncharitable explanations (see my discussion of corn land). When Anda decided in 2000 to go to Spain, she could not have gone had two friends not lent her the $1,000 visa fee—indicating that she had not enriched herself unduly.

8. One of the main achievements of the socialist period had been great upward mobility from peasant status in villages out into urban jobs. The migrants had retained ties with their local relatives but had a low impact on the community as a whole. Law 18/1991 changed that, however, reincorporating all those migrants in ways that had far-reaching effects on the community. Depending on where they lived, urbanites might sometimes appear to help their kin with agricultural work.

9. Using 274 as the number of active village households and the 1996 figure of 113 member families, 55 member households (49 percent) were not resident locally and 58 households (51 percent) were; the latter were just 21 percent of all village households. These numbers indicate that 79 percent of village households were not Association members. More households were implicated in it, however, without being members themselves: those whose member-parents held current title to the land. Anda estimated that 60 percent of all households with land had some in the Association.

10. For example, she was asking two locals, A and B, which field was better for planting sugar beets: x, or y (owned by B). A said y and B said x, but it emerged later that B wanted her to *think* x was better because he did not want her putting beets on his field, y. She finally planted them on the land of some urbanites, who would not know about it, to avoid the hassle.

11. Complicating the whole arrangement was that villagers took home the corn, which was more profitable, while the Association had to pay the costs of cultivation from sales of the more costly wheat, with its lower sale price.

12. Statistic courtesy of the Department of Agriculture, Deva branch (figures for 1996).

13. The ratios for 1999 and 2000 are high because flooding affected wheat more than corn. The total amount of land cultivated had dropped and, thus, in those years an even larger area was not being prepared for rotation.

14. Readers might wonder where the land came from that was farmed in this way. It came from people who were Association members but who had paid nothing to have their land worked (or had paid for only part of their total) and so had no claim to anything grown on their parcel. If Iosif has 3 ha in the Association but pays me to work only 1, then I have 2 left to play with.

15. The use of prison labor was more widespread, such as for clearing up abandoned construction sites and for other forms of public works.

16. The farm director professed not to mind, telling me, "Those Association women work hard. I don't see this as competition." In addition, her own farm had less and less work for its employees.

17. Readers might notice that this entire discussion has been about grain, and the reason is the shortage of labor. Livestock require even more labor than corn; therefore, animals were the

special preserve of individual households—and were a reason why Association members held onto their labor for themselves. Raising animals was out of the question for an association that labor shortage and a trust deficit had already driven toward cash outlay.

18. Between 1992 and 1997, it moved an average volume of 426 metric tonnes. This is for wheat and barley only (corn was harvested by the members and taken directly home). Only in 1997 did the Association also move corn—201 tonnes—from the 30 ha it planted on its own.

19. The reason is the better conditions for large-scale grain-growing in the south. Intermediaries emerged more rapidly where harvests were much bigger, and also where CF personnel dominated production and could ally with intermediaries to fix procurement prices—the conditions that prevailed in Romania's southern and eastern plains.

20. Recall that in Romania, as in the Soviet Union into the 1950s but unlike most other East European countries, collective farms continued to be served by state machinery parks, entities independent of the CFs. CFs might manage to acquire the occasional bit of machinery on their own, but rarely the full complement of items necessary to farming their land.

21. As I indicate in chapter 5, these loans with state credits operated according to a variable interest rate, of which the state was supposed to pay some portion (in the case of this loan, 15 percent). The loan was at 110 percent interest when they first took it out, and in the next several months it dropped to 42 percent, then rose to 67 percent and then to 75 percent. The problem was that the state subsidy almost never arrived in time for the monthly payment. Thus, Anda had to be prepared to pay the entire amount, and then wait in hopes that the subsidy would arrive. When I described my fixed-rate home mortgage, they were astounded: "that means you can actually *plan ahead*!"

22. Information courtesy of the director of that Romcereal office, spring 1994.

23. Prices given are those my respondents quoted me and apply only to this region of Transylvania, not more broadly.

24. The government's motive seems to have been that bad weather in Romania might push the price of grain (and therefore of bread) to an unacceptably high level, from the political point of view, but Hungarian wheat was selling at about 800 lei/kg. The difference wreaked havoc on local budgets.

25. The specific 1997 figures were plowing 100,000 lei/ha, harrowing 48,000 (two or three times depending on the field), sowing 56,000, fertilizer 168,000/ha on average plus 15 percent interest to Romcereal, fertilizer application 17,200, herbicide application 32,200, herbicide 56,000, and seed (at 32 kg/ha) 198,400 plus 15 percent interest to Romcereal. The total was 723,800 lei/ha without the interest payments, plus an expected harvest fee of 400,000/ha, giving a grand total of 1–1.2 million. I do not have this detailed a breakdown for 1999, only the total plus these: herbicide plus application 450,000 lei/ha, seed 520,000 lei/ha, and harvesting 500,000 lei/ha.

For the 1999–2000 production year, in autumn they put 15 ha. of winter wheat for twenty-seven families—this was all the people who were prepared to pay for cultivation—plus 30 ha of corn in the spring. The 4 million lei/ha cost included, in September, 1.8 million for full preparation (from plowing to sowing, with 1 million for 15 ha of treated seed and 800,000 for gas plus part of the tractorists' salaries); in February 1.2 million for fertilizer, in May–June 320,000 for herbicide, and in July 700,000 for harvesting. These were the Association's exact costs for these items, with no markup.

26. Although the Association was forced to work poorly, nevertheless it was at least working this land. Significantly, it did not plant precisely where the few participants had land, but combined fields into a few larger blocks—thus, in its death throes it produced field consolidation. The effects of this consolidation, however, were uneven. They used land that was good for the crop in question, putting all the wheat in one area and all the corn in another. What this story hides is that the best land for a given crop was also usually the land of wealthier locals; thus, once again, hierarchy was reproduced.

27. "Pronounced chair-VENG-ka." This was the name of the settlement from which Benzenzers had moved into Vlaicu in the 1890s. Their using this name thus demarcates them unmistakably from all things local and Romanian—a reflection, I believe, of their disgust at having had to sue for their rights, which the local commission had not recognized.

28. When they sued the Geoagiu land commission in 1992 they did so jointly in their own names, not as an association (which they formed later).

29. The Cervenka excluded all Romanian Vlaiceni, although most Benzenzers were too embarrassed to tell me so outright. Several would have liked to include the "better" Vlaiceni, but they had been outvoted, on the argument that if the Cervenka were solely German, it would get more help from Austria and Germany. In a sense, however, it is incorrect to refer to the Cervenka as a *German* association because one of its most influential members was an urban-resident Romanian who had married into a German family.

30. Vlaicu's two associations had cordial relations but little sustained cooperation. Their two accountants got on very well together and would readily exchange the occasional favor; the Cervenka benefited frequently from Nica's advice, having no agronomist of their own. But it was difficult to cooperate on use of equipment because both needed the same equipment at the same time. There was discussion of joining together to buy a combine, but the cost was so high and the circumstances of each association so unstable that neither side was willing to push the idea.

31. Anda, comparing the machinery costs for the two associations, found that, starting in 1994, she and Gretchen had spent the same amount on equipment purchases, but she had bought twice as much equipment and retired her debt in three years while Gretchen had bought less and paid higher interest for five.

32. The Association had land of much higher soil quality, but it was precisely this land that was repeatedly inundated. "Better" land here refers to the lower risk associated with working it.

33. Personal communication, based on research in 1999–2000 in the Perm region of Russia.

34. One of my respondents insisted on yet another criterion that distinguished both Romos and Vinerea from the others: both were historically part of the territory Transylvania's Saxon Germans had occupied since the twelfth century. The peasants there had been free peasants, not serfs like those in Geoagiu, Vlaicu, and Şibot: "Those people are more disciplined, have more initiative, work better, have a stronger sense of property. These former serfs are more cunning, more envious; those others are better." I believe there were former serf villages whose associations worked well, but the idea was nonetheless an interesting one.

35. Personal communication. The two villages in which he concentrated his work are Dobrosloveni and Cezieni, Olt county.

36. After 1854, serfs became land-owning peasants, but both they and the other categories of rural people remained in some dependence on their former lords. Only in 1921, with the post–World War I land reform, were smallholders on their own, unconnected to larger estates until the 1950s. Thus, we might say that the present pattern is in fact the normal one and the brief intermezzo of smallholding in the period from 1921 to the 1950s a departure.

37. Personal communication.

Chapter 7. The Dynamics of Decapitalization

I am very grateful for the patience with which those I call Radu and Traian explained to me their problems with SFs 1 and 2, as well as the trust with which they invited me to several events relating to the farms' sale. Before publishing this chapter, I went through it line by line with Traian to confirm the details of my analysis.

1. The buildings consisted of huge drying and storage warehouses for the crops, shelters for machinery, a small apartment block to house seasonal workers, and the building that served as the farm office. Because the land under them belonged to the state, not to shareholders, a buyer could buy only this land and the buildings on it, not the full hectarage of the farm.

2. Not wanting to risk any of his productive assets such as equipment, Radu put down these apartment blocks because he could not yet put down the farm buildings (which had not yet been titled even to the state). As I mention in chapter 1, communist cadres had not bothered to enter any of their constructions into the land registers, believing that local ownership was no longer an issue. That failure, however, had serious consequences for the post-1989 period: anyone wanting to sell a building that had been constructed between 1948 and 1989 had first to have the building properly entered into the land register; only then could the item be used as collateral or sold.

3. The reason given was that the entire complex, apartment buildings and all, was registered under only one topographic number in the land register. To divide it into its component buildings would have been possible but very time-consuming.

4. I have evaluation figures from 1999 for the two farms SF1 and SF2 together, valued then at 5.9 billion. A sale price of 2.5 billion was proposed for SF2, which would leave 3.4 billion as a possible value for SF1. This fits with what SF1's accountant told me after the auction: that it should have been sold for at least 3 billion.

5. I was unable to obtain a clear picture of the total debts because the two farms had different budgets for purposes of evaluation and sale, but one budget for purposes of operation. The accountant spoke sometimes of a debt of 3.2 billion, sometimes of 1 billion. I believe the former was the debt of the two farms together, the latter of SF1 alone.

6. I have this information from the economic officer of the U.S. Embassy in Bucharest, 1994. As he put it, the World Bank was pushing hard for privatization and had decided that the only way to speed things up was to switch to a version of the Czech model, with mass privatization, not case-by-case as was occurring in Romania at the time. To accomplish this meant that people would have to quit worrying about valuation and about getting the top price for firms. He concluded with the observation he had heard directly from the World Bank's number two official (whom he did not name): it would be better to give firms away.

7. What is interesting in these cases was that these agencies had first to acquire all state property and then to manage its dissipation into private hands. True to the rule that bureaucracies once formed are not easy to dissolve, these state property agencies became more interested in keeping themselves going than in completing the task for which they were formed. Only in Germany was the Treuhand dissolved because the statute setting it up had authorized a specific period for it to complete its work.

8. A local bank executive with whom I discussed the matter of high asset evaluations gave the example of an SF director who obtained a 1 billion lei loan against a barn, which had been assessed at that figure but was in fact a ruin. The director of the bank in question had not confirmed the assessment (probably, my respondent suggested, because he pocketed something for not doing so). When the borrower defaulted, the bank found it had no value with which to cover the sum. It prosecuted the borrower for fraud and he was jailed. With the 1-billion-lei loan, he had built three enormous villas, and his comment at the end of the trial was that he would be the owner of the three villas, all for a bit of jail time!

9. My analysis in this chapter is based on numerous conversations with the following people: five SF directors from eastern Hunedoara, three other agronomists working in post-CF associations, several employees of the county's Agriculture Department and two in its Chamber of Commerce, the head of an Agromec, the head of Romcereal, and a bank executive. In addition, I was present for one meeting of an SF assembly/council and attended the auction of one SF. I did not interview anyone in the state farm central office (SFS-Simeria)—an unfortunate omission.

10. From "Recapitulația generală a tarlalelor din hotarul comunei Aurel Vlaicu." National Archive, Hunedoara branch, Fond Camera Agricolă Deva, dosar 49/1948, Aurel Vlaicu. See Verdery (1994) for a discussion of the reliability of this figure.

11. I do not have figures for the amount taken from Vlaicu specifically. The 365-ha figure is from the National Archive, Hunedoara branch, Fond Sfatul Popular al Regiunii Hunedoara, Secția agricolă, dosar 18/1950, n.p.

12. I use the term *surplus* to translate *beneficiu*, the term *profit* being inappropriate for this setting.

13. I do not have direct contacts to the people in this office and am imputing to them the motives revealed in innumerable newspaper stories and conversations on the subject.

14. The people who lost out in this move were the workers in the apartment blocks, mostly Roma.

15. The sale of irrigation pipes as scrap metal was a matter of sufficient concern to the Ministry of Agriculture that in 1994 (May 22) the ministry-sponsored television program *Village Life* [*Viața Satului*] raised it for discussion. (There may have been other discussions of the matter on

that program, not to mention in the press; I happened to see this episode of it.) Scrap metal was a huge industry in Hunedoara, with its high level of industrialization and many now-defunct factories. The prefect of Hunedoara county as of 2000 had been head of scrap metal in Valea Jiu-lui earlier in the decade.

16. They acquired the paraphernalia of the SPF in 1999, when they changed the status of their farms by combining them into a single agricultural society, a prelude to privatization.

17. These farms might come from pooling the Law 18 land received by them and their family members, from buying land even though it was not yet legal to do so, and from taking land on lease arrangements from villagers.

18. This is the view presented to me by Traian and Radu; I cannot verify it independently.

19. I was present for this pair of meetings (held concurrently) and was able to discuss them at length with Traian and Radu afterward. Their main achievements are revealing. During the discussion, the two men and the main representative of the shareholders' assembly and adminis-trative council (a man who appeared to be their ally) agreed that although Juan planned to buy only one or two buildings, Radu was to tell him that what was for sale was either nothing or the whole farm complex (i.e., the buildings and equipment, but not the remaining land that be-longed to shareholders). "You're not selling items, you're selling the entire farm complex," this man said. "You have two options: you sell him the whole thing and negotiate buying back what he doesn't want, or you sell him only the pieces he wants and you're left with the rest. The first option is to your advantage. Tell him the price for the entire farm, then buy back the items he doesn't want. Your advantage is that you know the prices for those items, but he doesn't." This solution would fetch a higher price for the farm complex (it would go toward paying off the debts) and would also enable Radu and Traian to buy at very low cost many of the items they would have wanted to keep had they privatized the farm themselves.

20. I did not fully understood the accounting behind this figure and was unable to clarify it on the spot. In the discussion, they agreed that although the official evaluation of the fixed capi-tal within the SF2 complex was 1.85 billion lei, its "actual market value" was over 2.5 billion, tak-ing into account the interlinkages among the components (such as a single electricity line for all the buildings, the irrigation system in the fields that was coordinated from the complex, etc.). The numbers listed on an evaluation dated 30 June 1999 were for the combined farms and broke down as follows: (1) debts 2,027,396[,000] lei comprising unpaid suppliers 344,249,000, debts to the state 643,812,000, social security 231,680,000, special funds 17,499,000, bank credits 282,631,000, bank interest 477,800,000, and other debts 29,725,000 and (2) assets comprising "so-cial capital" 4,941,600,000 and total fixed assets [*active*] 5,853,170,000. One year later I was told that the farms' combined debts were now 3.2 billion.

21. As SF1's accountant told me, "I just don't understand how the interest accrues so fast. Last year the bank interest was 400 million, and somehow another 600 million have been added on so now it's 1 billion!" Note, however, that the additional 600 million is not just interest but includes penalties on unpaid employment tax.

22. Exactly the same situation obtained with an SF that specialized in fruit trees. A foreign buyer had bought its buildings and wanted to cut down the trees. Because he had not paid for the trees, which still belonged to the state, he could not do this. Meanwhile, the land the trees were on belonged to the former owners. Thus, anyone wanting to work on the trees or cut them down was trespassing on the owners' land—who themselves could get no use from the trees, which be-longed to the state. The only way to privatize this SF would be for the state to give each of the trees to the person owning the land under it.

23. We might ask why they did not pick up and go to Spain, like Anda and many others from Vlaicu. I think the answer is that they saw themselves as too well educated for the menial labor they would have to do abroad. People with advanced specialist training did not clean toilets and pick olives, and they still believed they could accumulate more by finding the right path in Ro-mania within their specialty.

24. Liviu Chelcea suggests (personal communication) that there was something very partic-ular about the early 1990s, when people sought to grab anything they could from any source, es-

pecially the state. By later in that decade, cooler assessments were emerging in which stability of income sources counted more than their magnitude.

Chapter 8. From Debts to *Dallas*

I too have debts, chief among them being those to the people whose trajectories I describe in this chapter (some of whom I have known for decades). I thank them for their candor in providing rich material with which I could piece together my analysis; one of them also discussed my interpretation with me at length once it was written.

1. From about 1975 until sometime in the 1980s, *Dallas* was the only U.S. serial shown on Romanian television—doubtless because of the unattractive image it presented of U.S. capitalism. Shown at prime time on Saturday evening, it educated millions of Romanians into the practices some of them would later follow.

2. I was unable to confirm this possibly-correct rumor; I note, however, that village sentiment regarding people who were "raising themselves up" was not uniformly favorable, and gossip was one way of keeping them in their place.

3. These examples do not exhaust the number of such people in the village, although there were only a few others. In addition, some were trying to make money strictly through commercial activities not involving agriculture.

4. It is also possible that my argument applies less well to the Regat than to Transylvania because, as I show in table 6.3, the different sizes of SFs and CFs in these different regions and the greater importance of the grain-growing Regat to the national economy might have endowed CF heads there with more power. Moreover, according to agronomist friends in Transylvania, nearly all Transylvania's SF directors had university training but that was not uniformly true in the Regat, where they might be only technicians (with mid-level training).

5. Valeriu Rusu (chapter 5) was, like Luca, a trained engineer who learned his agriculture from books. Because he had lost his state-sector job and was unable to find another, he was compelled to take his agricultural livelihood more seriously than Luca did. He had lost a great deal of time by not having the wherewithal to buy a tractor early, but already by 2000 he was accumulating land at an impressive rate.

6. Another kind of person who might have gotten into the supertenant business was the directors of the Agromecs. One with whom I spoke had started just such a business early on. In 1992 he formed an association and rented some 275 ha from villagers in Vaidei, paying the owners 25 percent of the harvest. But in 1994 the land rental law prohibited Agromec directors from renting land, so along with the numerous other Agromec directors who had had the same idea, he had to renounce this plan.

7. There is an alternative story about how he obtained this equipment: that in his earlier SF job, he had declared the machinery used up and sold it to himself for a pittance. According to the person who gave me the story, it was for this reason that Ion was fired and had to find another state job. I cannot assess this story's veracity, but the pattern it describes was reported in many Romanian newspapers.

8. In Gelmar, he said, all the venits had gotten land, and all the locals had big industrial pensions; no one was willing to do menial labor on tobacco. In a crisis, such as when he ran out of money for a second herbicide application and had to do hand hoeing of sugar beets, he would go with a van to a city whose main industry had shut down, gathering pensioners and the unemployed; unlike village Roma, those people did not insist on being fed.

9. Among the most common practices used by people he knew were these. (1) One would register one's firm as renting, say, 50 ha and keep scrupulous books for that, while actually renting 125 ha. (2) One would pay employees more than one put on the books, so as to reduce employment taxes. (3) One would do everything possible so as to come out with zero profit, buying next year's inputs early and selling some of one's produce without receipts.

10. It is possible that state farm directors' long experience of relatively risk-free farming may have impeded their grasping fully the risks they assumed now.

11. The quarrel, worth its own separate chapter, included a radical difference of opinion as to

whether one person (Dan) could put all the capital into something and another person (Ştefan) manage it yet not be entitled to half the capital Dan had invested. "After all," Ştefan insisted, reflecting hallowed socialist sentiment, "he wasn't doing any of the work. It was my work that kept the place going. He never had time. So why shouldn't I own half the buildings?" The socialism cut both ways because, to my mind, Dan had behaved toward Ştefan rather in the old clientelistic way of the Party bureaucrat ("I did him a few big favors, so he owes me loyalty"). Dan calculated that the quarrel and its attendant lawsuit had cost him the price of a combine and thus gravely set him back.

12. The auction at which they bought it did not resemble the auction of Radu's state farm, in chapter 7. Three locals showed up, all of whom wanted the barn, and the Association had every interest in selling it well because members would benefit from the sale price. This was not one of those ghost auctions managed by the SPF with the requisite bribes because the barn was not state but collective property. It had originally belonged to the collective farm and then passed into the patrimony of the Association at no cost; there it remained the joint possession of Association members until they (through their leaders) decided to sell it.

13. I derive this estimate from the International Monetary Fund Country Report for Romania no. 98/123, 1998 (table 18, p. 23). The figures in the table run from 1990 to 1998; increases after that date would have further increased the figure I give here. I thank Peter Bernholz for providing me with the data.

14. Even so, smallholders continued to hold supertenants such as the Bucurs to their own standards. When Vasile Barbu, mentioned in chapter 5, took me to see his beautiful wheat, we passed by a field belonging to the Bucurs, and Vasile lost no time in pointing out how inferior it was to his own. "They take on too much and can't do it well," he remarked. He also indicated some corn fields that had been plowed with herbicide (Dan's practice), rather than hoed, showing how many more weeds there were in the former than among his own carefully hoed cornstalks.

15. I owe this observation to Iosif Crişan.

16. I am grateful to Elizabeth Ferry for suggesting this line of thought.

17. A note on their salaries: from the way Dan and Lila spoke, I suspect they saw land as a positive asset all along because they were making money at it, without calculating exactly how much their salaries contributed to their overall revenues. They also, incidentally, admitted to not calculating their own labor, rather like smallholders. Ion Olaru, by contrast, found this unprofessional.

18. This was questionable for Algeria, of course.

Conclusion

1. For example, if Lila had a corn harvest of 8,000 kg/ha and paid workers 20 percent for weeding and harvesting it (this happened occasionally when herbicide was ineffective owing to untimely weather), they received 1,600 kg for their work; if a smallholder had 3,500 kg/ha and paid at 30 percent, they took home 1,050 kg.

2. I mention in the introduction to Part II that the Geoagiu Agromec had on average one staff member for every 29 ha. It worked for two communes (Geoagiu and Romos) with a total agricultural surface of 3,200 ha, of which it covered 2,240 ha, or about 70 percent. The unit supported a staff of seventy-six people: seven administrative personnel (agronomists and accountants), fifty tractorists for forty-five tractors, and nineteen mechanics. (The Vlaicu Association, by contrast, worked 200 ha with two tractors and four people—one staff member per 50 ha.)

3. If I am correct in this conclusion, it should not be automatically generalized beyond Romania for the reasons I gave in chapter 1: the different amounts of land held in each form means that the forms have variable weight across the different countries.

4. I owe my phrasing here and below to Jane Collier.

5. I thank John Borneman for help with this wording.

6. I conducted a useless argument with three World Bank officials on precisely this point. They wanted to know how to serve the growth of dynamic farmers at the expense of the "red bourgeoisie" and found unpersuasive my example of people, such as those described in chapters 7 and 8, who were both.

GLOSSARY

Agromec The name given to the former agricultural machinery stations (AMSs) after 1989. For a fee, they would use their machinery to plow, plant, and harvest the land of new owners and associations, where needed.

AMS agricultural machinery stations. During the socialist period, these were units separate from collective and state farms, containing the agricultural equipment necessary to working land on contract for the collectives.

ADPR Agrarian Democratic Party of Romania. The party of agrarian elites, dominated by the state farm lobby in the Regat.

Association (Vlaicu Association). The producers' cooperative formed out of the collective farm to work the land of people lacking labor or equipment.

Cervenka Society The producers' cooperative formed by village Germans separately from the Association. Many of its members emigrated to Germany.

CF collective farm. Socialist agricultural enterprise in which ownership rights were nominally held by the member households who had "donated" land at its formation. In Romania, these were created during the period 1948–62, with the bulk of farms coming into being between 1958 and 1962. This was the form dismantled in Romania's 1991 Land Law.

Chiabur (kya-BOOR). The Romanian term used for wealthy peasants during the collectivization drive, equivalent to the *kulaks* of Soviet collectivization. These people might in fact own only a small amount of land; many acquired the label as a result of denunciations by villagers bearing a grudge against them.

DC Democratic Convention. The umbrella group formed in opposition to the main party of the former apparatchiks, the PRSD, which dominated Romanian politics after 1989. The DC's reform policies were neoliberal, much influenced by the International Monetary Fund and World Bank.

IMF International Monetary Fund.

Land Register (*Cartea Funciară*). The form of registering all transactions involving land in Transylvania, based in the Austro-Hungarian land registration system. It inscribed new owners in files that also verified prior ownership. During the socialist period very few transactions were entered into it, but after 1989 it became the prime means of verifying restitution claims.

Law 18 (*Legea Fondului Funciar,* or *Legea 18/1991*) The term by which Romanians refer to the land restitution law passed in February 1991.

Leu (pl. *lei*) The Romanian currency unit. Its value dropped throughout the decade; in 1989 it was about 20 lei to the dollar (USD), falling to 1,752 lei/USD in 1993, to

5,802/USD in 1996, to 10,825/USD in 1997, to 15,419/USD in 1998, to 25,055/USD in 1999, and to 31,369/USD in 2000, after which its value began to stabilize.

PRSD   Party of Romanian Social Democracy. Party dominated by former communists, led by president Ion Iliescu; under one name or another, it held power from 1990 to 1996 and then again after 2000.

Regat   ("Kingdom") This refers to the southern and eastern regions of modern-day Romania, which constituted a kingdom prior to World War I. At the end of that war, Transylvania was transferred from Hungarian to Romanian control; the territories of the previous kingdom were then referred to as the Old Kingdom (*Vechiul Regat*), or Regat for short. Inhabitants of the Regat are referred to collectively as Regățeni.

Rentiers   Smallholders who rented out their newly acquired land to be worked by others for a rental payment.

Romcereal   State monopoly organization that was formed from the previous procurement centers. Until 1997, it was used to funnel state credits for cultivation into rural areas and it bought up grain in bulk at the controlled state price, serving as a distribution channel in the absence of alternative arrangements.

SF   state farm. Socialist agricultural enterprise in which ownership rights were held by the state. In Romania, these were formed as early as 1948; they remained intact under the 1991 Land Law, the former owners of the land in them becoming shareholders until repossession of the land became possible in 1999. A law breaking up state farms was finally passed in 2001.

SFS-Simeria   State Farm System Simeria. Term I use to designate one of the multifarm groupings (this one centered in the city of Simeria, Hunedoara county) into which state farms were organized.

SPF   State Property Fund. The body set up in 1991 to manage the privatization of state enterprises, including state farms (but not collectives).

SOE   state-owned enterprise. Enterprise of the socialist period, fully owned by the state until SOEs were privatized.

Stăpân   (stuh-PÎN) Noun and associated verb [*stăpâni*] meaning "mastery, dominion, lordship, sovereignty"; villagers used it as a way of talking about effective ownership.

Supertenants   Individual farmers (or farm families), usually from the prior leadership of one or another socialist agricultural form, who had the capacity to work more than their own land and rented land from smallholders. Their much higher endowments of cultural and social capital, as well as their access to complex inputs and equipment, made them "super" relative to their landlords.

USAID   United States Agency for International Development.

Venits   (from the Romanian *veniți*) One of several terms that Vlaiceni used for people who had moved into lowland villages from the hills during the socialist period to work in industry. These people had donated no land to the collective and in many villages were therefore targets for exclusion when Law 18 was implemented, leaving them landless.

REFERENCES

Abrahams, Ray, ed. 1996. *After Socialism: Land Reform and Social Change in Eastern Europe*. Providence: Berghahn Books.

———. 2001. Out of the Collective Frying Pan? Ideals and Practicalities in the Reformulation and Restitution of Political and Property Rights in Post-Soviet Rural Estonia. Max Planck Institute for Social Anthropology Working Paper no. 34, Halle/Saale, Germany.

Abrahams, Ray, and Juhan Kahk. 1994. *Barons and Farmers: Continuity and Transformation in Rural Estonia (1816–1994)*. Report no. 3, University of Göteborg—Faculty of Arts Inter-European Research, Göteborg.

Adams, Walter, and James W. Brock. 1993. *Adam Smith Goes to Moscow: A Dialogue on Radical Reform*. Princeton: Princeton University Press.

Aglietta, Michel. 1987. *A Theory of Capitalist Regulation*. London: Verso.

Alexander, Catherine. 2004. "Values, Relations and Changing Bodies: Privatisation and Property Rights in Kazakhstan." In *Property in Question: Value Transformation in the Global Economy*, edited by Katherine Verdery and Caroline Humphrey. Oxford: Berg Press, forthcoming.

Anderson, David G. 1998. "Property as a Way of Knowing on Evenki Lands in Arctic Siberia." In *Property Relations: Renewing the Anthropological Tradition*, edited by C. M. Hann, 64–84. Cambridge, UK: Cambridge University Press.

———. 2000. *Identity and Ecology in Arctic Siberia: The Number One Reindeer Brigade*. Oxford: Oxford University Press.

Appadurai, Arjun. 1986. "Introduction: Commodities and the Politics of Value." In *The Social Life of Things: Commodities in Cultural Perspective*. Cambridge, UK: Cambridge University Press.

Armstrong, George M. 1983. *The Soviet Law of Property: The Right to Control Property and the Construction of Communism*. The Hague: Martinus Nijhoff.

Bauer, Tamás. 1978. "Investment Cycles in Planned Economies." *Acta Oeconomica* 21: 243–60.

Beaglehole, Ernest. 1931. *Property: A Study in Social Psychology*. New York: Macmillan.

Beck, Ulrich. 1992. *Risk Society: Towards a New Modernity*. Newbury Park: Sage.

Beckmann, Volker, and Konrad Hagedorn. Forthcoming. *Understanding Agricultural Transition: Institutional Change and Economic Performance in a Comparative Perspective*.

Begg, Robert, and Mieke Meurs. 1998. "Writing a New Song: Path Dependency and State

Policy in Reforming Bulgarian Agriculture." In *Privatizing the Land: Rural Political Economy in Post-Communist Societies,* edited by Iván Szelényi, 245–70. New York and London: Routledge.

Berdahl, Daphne. 1999. *Where the World Ended: Re-Unification and Identity in the German Borderland.* Berkeley and Los Angeles: University of California Press.

Berliner, Joseph. 1957. *Factory and Manager in the USSR.* Cambridge, Mass.: Harvard University Press.

Berry, Sara. 1993. *No Condition Is Permanent: The Social Dynamics of Agrarian Change in Sub-Saharan Africa.* Madison: University of Wisconsin Press.

Bloch, Peter C. 1998. "Picking up the Pieces: Consolidation of Albania's Radical Land Reform." In *Land Reform in the Former Soviet Union and Eastern Europe,* edited by Stephen Wegren, 189–207. London and New York: Routledge.

Bonefeld, Werner, and John Holloway, eds. 1991. *Post-Fordism and Social Form.* London: Macmillan.

Borneman, John. 1997. *Settling Accounts: Violence, Justice, and Accountability in Postsocialist Europe.* Princeton: Princeton University Press.

Böröcz, József. 1992. "Dual Dependency and Property Vacuum: Social Change in the State Socialist Semiperiphery." *Theory and Society* 21: 77–104.

———. 1993. "Simulating the Great Transformation: Property Change under Prolonged Informality in Hungary." *Archives Européennes de Sociologie* 34: 81–107.

Böröcz, József, and Ákos Róna-Tas. 1996. "Small Leap Forward: Emergence of New Economic Elites." *Theory and Society* 5: 51–81.

Bourdieu, Pierre. 1977. *Outline of a Theory of Practice.* Cambridge, UK: Cambridge University Press.

———. 1980. *The Logic of Practice.* Stanford: Stanford University Press.

———. 1984. *Distinction: A Social Critique of the Judgement of Taste.* Cambridge, Mass.: Harvard University Press.

Bourdieu, Pierre, and Loïc J. D. Wacquant. 1992. *An Invitation to Reflexive Sociology.* Chicago: University of Chicago Press.

van Brabant, Jozef M. 1998. *The Political Economy of Transition: Coming to Grips with History and Methodology.* London: Routledge.

Brădeanu, Salvator, Petre Marica, and Lucian Stângu. 1968. *Tratat de drept cooperatist-agricol.* 2 vols. Bucharest: Ed. Academiei Republicii Socialiste România.

Brewer, John, and Susan Staves, eds. 1996. *Early Modern Conceptions of Property.* London and New York: Routledge.

Bridger, Sue, and Frances Pine, eds. 1998. *Surviving Post-Socialism: Local Strategies and Regional Responses in Eastern Europe and the Former Soviet Union.* New York: Routledge.

Brooks, Karen, and Mieke Meurs. 1994. "Romanian Land Reform, 1991–1993." *Comparative Economic Studies* 36: 17–32.

Bromley, Daniel. 2000. Perspectives on Privatization during Transition. Lecture presented at the KATO Symposium, Berlin, Germany, November 2000.

Bruno, Marta. 1998. "Playing the Co-operation Game: Strategies around International Aid in Post-Socialist Russia." In *Surviving Post-Socialism: Local Strategies and Regional Responses in Eastern Europe and the Former Soviet Union,* edited by Sue Bridger and Frances Pine, 170–187. London: Routledge.

Brus, W. 1986. "Postwar Reconstruction and Socio-Economic Transformation." In *The Economic History of Eastern Europe, 1919–1975,* edited by M. C. Kaser and E. A. Radice, 564–641. Oxford: Clarendon Press.

Buchowski, Michał. 2001. *Rethinking Transformation: An Anthropological Perspective on Post-Socialism.* Poznan: Humaniora.

Buechler, Hans C., and Judith-Maria Buechler. 2002. *Contesting Agriculture: Cooperativism and Privatization in the New Eastern Germany.* Albany: State University of New York Press.

Bunce, Valerie, and Mária Csanádi. 1993. "Uncertainty in the Transition: Post-Communism in Hungary." *East European Politics and Societies* 7: 240–75.

Burawoy, Michael. 1985. *The Politics of Production: Factory Regimes under Capitalism and State Socialism.* London: Verso.

———. 2001a. "Review Essay—Neoclassical Sociology: From the End of Communism to the End of Classes" [with replies by authors reviewed]. *American Journal of Sociology* 106: 1099–120.

———. 2001b. "Transition without Transformation: Russia's Involutionary Road to Capitalism." *East European Politics and Societies* 15: 269–90.

Burawoy, Michael, and Kathryn Hendley. 1992. "Between Perestroika and Privatization: Divided Strategies and Political Crisis in a Soviet Enterprise." *Soviet Studies* 44: 371–402.

Burawoy, Michael, Pavel Krotov, and Tatyana Lytkina. 2000. "Involution and Destitution in Capitalist Russia." *Ethnography* 1: 43–63.

Burawoy, Michael, and János Lukács. 1992. *The Radiant Past: Ideology and Reality in Hungary's Road to Capitalism.* Chicago: University of Chicago Press.

Burawoy, Michael, and Katherine Verdery, eds. 1999. *Uncertain Transition: Ethnographies of Everyday Life in the Postsocialist World.* Boulder: Rowman and Littlefield.

Butler, W. E. 1988. *Soviet Law.* London: Butterworths.

Campeanu, Pavel. 1988. *The Genesis of the Stalinist Social Order.* Armonk: M. E. Sharpe.

Cartwright, Andrew. 2000. Against 'Decollectivisation': Land Reform in Romania, 1990–92. Max Planck Institute for Social Anthropology Working Paper no. 4, Halle/Saale, Germany.

———. 2001. *The Return of the Peasant: Land and Reform in Post-Communist Romania.* Dartmouth: Ashgate.

Cătănuş, Dan, and Octavian Roske. 2000. *Colectivizarea agriculturii în România: Dimensiunea politică, 1949–1953.* Bucharest: Institutul Naţional pentru Studiul Totalitarismului.

Cernea, Mihail. 1974. *Sociologia cooperativei agricole.* Bucharest: Editura Academiei.

Chaudry, Kiren Aziz. 1993. "The Myths of the Market and the Common History of Late Developers." *Politics and Society* 21: 245–74.

Chayanov, A. V. 1966. *The Theory of Peasant Economy.* Edited by Daniel Thorner, Basile Kerblay, and Robert E. F. Smith. Homewood: Irwin.

Chelcea, Liviu. 1998. "Agricultural Policy in Romania, 1998." Manuscript.

———. 2003. "Ancestors, Domestic Groups, and the Socialist State: Housing Nationalization and Restitution in Romania." *Comparative Studies in Society and History* 45 (4): 714–40.

Codoban, Aurel. 2003. "La 'transition,' simulacre postmoderne de nôtre modernité." *La Nouvelle Alternative* 8 (spring–summer).

Coleman, James S. 1990. *Foundations of Social Theory*. Cambridge, Mass.: Harvard University Press.

Collier, George A., with Elizabeth Lowery. 1999. *Basta! Land and the Zapatista Rebellion in Chiapas*. Oakland: Food First Books.

Collier, Jane Fishburne. 1997. *From Duty to Desire: Remaking Families in a Spanish Village*. Princeton: Princeton University Press.

Comaroff, Jean, and John L. Comaroff. 2000. "Millennial Capitalism: First Thoughts on a Second Coming." *Public Culture* 12: 291–343.

Commission of the European Communities, Directorate-General for Regional Policies. 1992. *Socio-Economic Situation and Development of the Regions in the Neighbouring Countries of the Community in Central and Eastern Europe*. Regional Development Studies, no. 2. Brussels: Commission of the European Communities,

Conquest, Robert. 1986. *The Harvest of Sorrow: Soviet Collectivization and the Terror-Famine*. New York: Oxford.

Coombe, Rosemary. 1998. *The Cultural Life of Intellectual Properties*. Durham: Duke University Press.

Cornea, Andrei. 1995. "Directocraţie remaniază guvernul." In *Maşina de fabricat fantasme*. [Bucharest]: Clavis.

Creed, Gerald. 1995a. "An Old Song in a New Voice: Decollectivization in Bulgaria." In *East European Communities: The Struggle for Balance in Turbulent Times,* edited by David Kideckel, 25–46. Boulder: Westview.

——. 1995b. "The Politics of Agriculture in Bulgaria." *Slavic Review* 54: 843–68.

——. 1998. *Domesticating Revolution: From Socialist Reform to Ambivalent Transition in a Bulgarian Village*. University Park: Pennsylvania State University Press.

——. 1999. "Deconstructing Socialism in Bulgaria." In *Uncertain Transition: Ethnographies of Everyday Life in the Postsocialist World,* edited by Michael Burawoy and Katherine Verdery, 223–44. Boulder: Rowman and Littlefield.

——. 2002. "Economic Crisis and Ritual Decline in Eastern Europe." In *Postsocialism: Ideals, Ideologies and Practices in Eurasia,* edited by C. M. Hann, 57–73. London and New York: Routledge.

Csaki, Csaba, and Yoav Kislev, eds. 1993. *Agricultural Cooperatives in Transition*. Boulder: Westview.

Cungu, Azeta, and Johan F. M. Swinnen. 1997a. "Agricultural Privatization and Decollectivization in Albania: A Political Economy Perspective." In *Political Economy of Agrarian Reform in Central and Eastern Europe,* edited by Johan F. M. Swinnen, 55–89. Aldershot, UK, and Brookfield: Ashgate.

——. 1997b. "Agricultural Privatisation, Land Reform and Farm Restructuring in Albania." In *Agricultural Privatisation, Land Reform and Farm Restructuring in Central and Eastern Europe,* edited by Johan F. M. Swinnen, Allan Buckwell, and Erik Mathijs, 1–21. Aldershot, UK, and Brookfield: Ashgate.

Dagan, Hanoch. 1998. *Unjust Enrichment: A Study of Private Law and Public Values*. Cambridge, UK: Cambridge University Press.

Dagan, Hanoch, and Michael Heller. 2001. "The Liberal Commons." *Yale Law Journal* 110: 549–623.

Davidova, Sophia, Allan Buckwell, and Diana Kopeva. 1997. "Bulgaria: Economics and Politics of Post-Reform Farm Structures." In *Agricultural Privatisation, Land Reform and Farm Restructuring in Central and Eastern Europe,* edited by Johan F. M. Swinnen, Allan Buckwell, and Erik Mathijs, 23–62. Aldershot, UK, and Brookfield: Ashgate.

Davies, R. W. 1980. *The Socialist Offensive: The Collectivisation of Soviet Agriculture, 1929–1930.* Cambridge, Mass.: Harvard University Press.

Davis, Junior. 1997. "Understanding the Process of Decollectivisation and Agricultural Privatisation in Transition Economies: The Distribution of Collective and State Farm Assets in Latvia and Lithuania." *Europe-Asia Studies* 49: 1409–32.

de Coppet, Daniel. 1985. ". . . Land Owns People." In *Contexts and Levels: Anthropological Essays on Hierarchy,* edited by R. H. Barnes, Daniel de Coppet, and R. J. Parkin, pp. 78–90. Oxford: JASO.

De Soto, Hermine G., and David G. Anderson, eds. 1993. *The Curtain Rises: Rethinking Culture, Ideology, and the State in Eastern Europe.* Atlantic Highlands, N.J.: Humanities Press.

de Waal, Clarissa. 1996. "Decollectivisation and Total Scarcity in High Albania." In *After Socialism: Land Reform and Social Change in Eastern Europe,* edited by Ray Abrahams, 169–92. Providence: Berghahn Books.

——. 2001. Laissez-faire at the Top, DIY on the Ground: Post-Socialist Property Rights in Albania. Paper presented at Workshop on Postsocialist Property Rights in Natural Resources, Lund, Sweden.

Demsetz, Harold. 1967. "Toward a Theory of Property Rights." *American Economic Review* 57: 347–59.

Divertis. 1996. "Unde nu-i lege e teoremă." On *Corabia speranței.* Audiocassette. Bucharest: Tempo Music.

Domański, Henryk, and Barbara Heyns. 1995. "Toward a Theory of the Role of the State in Market Transition: From Bargaining to Markets in Post-Communism." *Archives Européenes de Sociologie* 36: 317–51.

Donovan, Michael. 2001. "The Intimate Geography of Family Farms." *Comparative Studies in Society and History* 43: 273–97.

Dunn, Elizabeth. In press. "Audit, Corruption, and the Problem of Personhood: Scenes from Postsocialist Poland." In *Negotiated Universals,* edited by Wolf Lepenies. Berlin: Campus.

——. 2002. Accounting for Change. In *Critical Management Research in Eastern Europe: Managing the Transition,* edited by Mihaela Kelemen and Monika Kostera, 38–64. London: Palgrave Publishers.

——. 2004. *Baby Food, Big Business: The Remaking of the Polish Working Class.* Ithaca: Cornell University Press, forthcoming.

Elster, Jon, Claus Offe, and Ulrich Preuss. 1998. *Institutional Design in Post-Communist Societies: Rebuilding the Ship at Sea.* Cambridge, UK: Cambridge University Press.

Europa Publications. 1994. *The Europa World Year Book,* vol II. London: Europa Publications Limited.

European Commission, Directorate General for Agriculture. 1998. Working Document.

Agricultural Situation and Prospects in the Central European Countries: Romania. Manuscript.

Eyal, Gil, Iván Szelényi, and Eleanor Townsley. 1998 *Making Capitalism without Capitalists: The New Ruling Elites in Eastern Europe*. New York: Verso.

Fairbanks, Charles H., Jr. 1999. "The Feudalization of the State." *Journal of Democracy* 10: 47–53.

Feldbrugge, F. J. M. 1993. *Russian Law: The End of the Soviet System and the Role of Law*. Dordrecht: Martinus Nijhoff.

Ferguson, James. 1992. "The Cultural Topography of Wealth: Commodity Paths and the Structure of Property in Rural Lesotho." *American Anthropologist* 94: 55–73.

Fine-Dare, Kathleen S. 2002. *Grave Injustice: The American Indian Repatriation Movement and NAGPRA*. Lincoln: University of Nebraska Press.

Firoiu, D. V. 1976. *Istoria statului și a dreptului românesc*. Bucharest: Editura Didactică și Pedagogică.

Fitzpatrick, Sheila. 1994. *Stalin's Peasants: Resistance and Survival in the Russian Village after Collectivization*. New York: Oxford University Press.

Fortes, Meyer. 1961. "Pietas in Ancestor Worship." *Man* 91: 166–91.

Frydman, Roman, Kenneth Murphy, and Andrei Rapaczynski. 1998. *Capitalism with a Comrade's Face: Studies in the Postcommunist Transition*. Budapest: CEU Press.

Frydman, Roman, and Andrzej Rapaczynski. 1994. *Privatization in Eastern Europe: Is the State Withering Away?* Budapest: CEU Press.

Frydman, Roman, Andrzej Rapaczynski, and John S. Earle. 1993. *The Privatization Process in Central Europe*. Budapest: CEU Press.

Fustel de Coulanges, Denis Numa. 1980. *The Ancient City*. Baltimore: Johns Hopkins University Press.

Giordano, Christian, and Dobrinka Kostova. 2000. "Understanding Contemporary Problems in Bulgarian Agricultural Transformation." In *Bulgaria: Social and Cultural Landscapes*, edited by Christian Giordano, Dobrinka Kostova, and Evelyne Lohmann-Minka II, 159–75. Fribourg, Switzerland: University Press Fribourg.

———. 2002. "The Social Production of Mistrust." In *Postsocialism: Ideals, Ideologies and Practices in Eurasia*, edited by C. M. Hann, 74–91. London and New York: Routledge.

Gluckman, Max. 1943. *Essays on Lozi Land and Royal Property*. Livingstone, Rhodesia. Rhodes-Livingstone Papers, no. 10.

———. 1965. *The Ideas in Barotse Jurisprudence*. New Haven: Yale University Press.

Graeber, David. 2001. *Toward an Anthropological Theory of Value: The False Coin of Our Own Dreams*. New York: Palgrave.

Greaves, Thomas. 1994. *Intellectual Property Rights for Indigenous Peoples: A Sourcebook*. Oklahoma City: Society for Applied Anthropology.

Gregory, Christopher A. 1982. *Gifts and Commmodities*. London: Academic Press.

Grey, Thomas C. 1980. "The Disintegration of Property." In *Property*, edited by J. Roland Pennock and John W. Chapman, 69–85. New York: New York University Press.

Gross, Jan T. 1988. *Revolution from Abroad: The Soviet Conquest of Poland's Western Ukraine and Western Byelorussia*. Princeton: Princeton University Press.

Hagedorn, Konrad. 1998. "Concepts of Institutional Change for Understanding

Privatization and Restructuring of Agriculture in Central and Eastern European Countries." In *The Importance of Institutions for the Transition in Central and Eastern Europe*, edited by Klaus Frohberg and Witold-Roger Poganietz, 51–64. Kiel: Wissenschaftsverlag Vauk Kiel.

———. 2000. What to Learn? Evaluating the Privatization Experience in Transition. Lecture presented at the KATO Symposium, Berlin, Germany, November.

Hagelschuer, Paul. 2000. Was Können Wir Lernen? Eine Evaluierung der Restrukturierung Während der Transformation. Lecture presented at the KATO Symposium, Berlin, Germany, November.

Hallowell, A. Irving. 1955. "The Nature and Function of Property as a Social Institution." In *Culture and Experience*, 236–249. Philadelphia: University of Pennsylvania Press.

Hammel, Eugene A. 1968. *Alternative Social Structures and Ritual Relations in the Balkans*. Englewood Cliffs: Prentice-Hall.

Hanisch, Markus. 2000. Property Reform and Social Conflict—The Analysis of Agricultural Ownership Transformations in Post Communist Bulgaria. Paper prepared for the KATO Symposium, Berlin, Germany, November.

Hanisch, Markus, and Adam Schlüter. 1999. Institutional Analysis and Institutional Change—What to Learn from the Case of Bulgarian Land Reform? Paper presented at the FAO-IAMO Conference on Land Ownership, Land Market and Their Influence on the Efficiency of Agricultural Production in Central and Eastern Europe, Halle, Germany.

Hann, C. M. 1980. *Tázlár: A Village in Hungary*. Cambridge, UK: Cambridge University Press.

———. 1985. *A Village without Solidarity: Polish Peasants in Years of Crisis*. New Haven: Yale University Press.

———. 1993a. "From Production to Property: Decollectivization and the Family-Land Relationship in Contemporary Hungary." *Man* 28: 299–320.

———. 1993b. "Property Relations in the New Eastern Europe: The Case of Specialist Cooperatives in Hungary." In *The Curtain Rises: Rethinking Culture, Ideology, and the State in Eastern Europe,* edited by Hermine G. De Soto and David G. Anderson, 99–119. Atlantic Highlands, N.J.: Humanities Press.

———. 1998a. "Introduction: The Embeddedness of Property." In *Property Relations: Renewing the Anthropological Tradition,* edited by C. M. Hann, 1–47. Cambridge, UK: Cambridge University Press.

———, ed. 1998b. *Property Relations: Renewing the Anthropological Tradition*. Cambridge, UK: Cambridge University Press.

———, ed. 2002. *Postsocialism: Ideals, Ideologies and Practices in Eurasia*. London and New York: Routledge.

Haraszti, Miklós. 1978. *A Worker in a Worker's State*. New York: Universe Books.

Harcsa, István, Imre Kovách, and Iván Szelényi. 1998. "The Price of Privatization: The Post-Communist Transformational Crisis of the Hungarian Agrarian System." In *Privatizing the Land: Rural Political Economy in Post-Communist Societies,* edited by Iván Szelényi, 214–44. New York and London: Routledge.

Hardt, Michael, and Antonio Negri. 2000. *Empire*. Cambridge, Mass.: Harvard University Press.

Heller, Michael. 1998. "The Tragedy of the Anticommons: Property in the Transition from Marx to Markets." *Harvard Law Review* 111: 621–88.

——. 1999. "The Boundaries of Private Property." *Yale Law Journal* 108: 1163–223.

Heller, Michael, and Christopher Serkin. 1999. "Revaluing Restitution: From the Talmud to Postsocialism." *Michigan Law Review* 97: 1385–412.

Hill, Peter J., and Margé Karner. 1996. "Spontaneous Privatization in Transition Economies." In *The Privatization Process: A Worldwide Perspective*, edited by Terry L. Anderson and Peter J. Hill, 81–96. Lanham: Rowman and Littlefield.

Hindus, Maurice. 1931. *Red Bread: Collectivization in a Russian Village*. Bloomington and Indianapolis: Indiana University Press.

Hivon, Myriam. 1998. "The Bullied Farmer: Social Pressure as a Survival Strategy?" In *Surviving Post-Socialism: Local Strategies and Regional Responses in Eastern Europe and the Former Soviet Union*, edited by Sue Bridger and Frances Pine, 33–51. New York: Routledge.

Hoebel, E. Adamson. 1942. "Fundamental Legal Concepts as Applied in the Study of Primitive Law. *Yale Law Journal* 51: 951–66.

——. 1954. *The Law of Primitive Man: A Study in Comparative Legal Dynamics.* Cambridge, Mass.: Harvard University Press.

Hudečková, Helena, Mihal Lošt'ák, and Sandie Rikoon. 2000. "Reflections of 'Late Modernity' in Land Ownership in the Czech Republic." *East European Countryside* nr 6: 93–110.

Humphrey, Caroline. 1983. *Karl Marx Collective: Economy, Society, and Religion in a Siberian Collective Farm*. Cambridge, UK: Cambridge University Press.

——. 1991. " 'Icebergs,' Barter, and the Mafia in Provincial Russia." *Anthropology Today* 7: 8–13.

——. 1998. *Marx Went Away but Karl Stayed Behind*. Ann Arbor: University of Michigan Press.

——. 2002a. "Myth-Making, Narratives, and the Dispossessed in Russia." In *The Unmaking of Soviet Life: Everyday Economies after Socialism*, 21–39. Ithaca: Cornell University Press.

——. 2002b. *The Unmaking of Soviet Life: Everyday Economies after Socialism*. Ithaca: Cornell University Press.

Hunya, Gábor. 1987. "New Developments in Romanian Agriculture." *Eastern European Politics and Societies* 1: 255–76.

Iancu, Gheorghe, Virgiliu Ţârău, and Ottmar Traşcă. 2000. *Colectivizarea agriculturii în România: Aspecte legislative*. Cluj-Napoca: Presa Universitară Clujeană.

Institutul Naţional de Statistică. 2002. *Anuarul Statistic al Romăniei, 2000*. Bucharest: Institutul Naţional de Statistică.

Islam, Shafiqul, and Michael Mandelbaum. 1993. *Making Markets: Economic Transformation in Eastern Europe and the Post-Soviet States*. New York: Council on Foreign Relations.

Jackson, Marvin. 1997. "Political Economy of Agricultural Reform in Romania." In *Political Economy of Agrarian Reform in Central and Eastern Europe*, edited by Johan F. M. Swinnen, 283–320. Aldershot, UK, and Brookfield: Ashgate.

Johnson, Simon, and Zanny Minton-Beddoes. 1996. "The Acquisition of Private Property Rights in Ukrainian Agriculture." In *Reforming Asian Socialism: The Growth of Market Institutions*, edited by John McMillan and Barry Naughton, 253–70. Ann Arbor: University of Michigan Press.

Kandiyoti, Deniz. 2002. "How Far Do Analyses of Postsocialism Travel? The Case of Central Asia." In *Postsocialism: Ideals, Ideologies and Practices in Eurasia,* edited by C. M. Hann, 238–57. London and New York: Routledge.

Kaneff, Deema. 1996. "Responses to 'Democratic' Land Reforms in a Bulgarian Village." In *After Socialism: Land Reform and Social Change in Eastern Europe,* edited by Ray Abrahams, 85–114. Providence: Berghahn Books.

——. 1998. "When 'Land' Becomes 'Territory': Land Privatisation and Ethnicity in Rural Bulgaria." In *Surviving Post-Socialism: Local Strategies and Regional Responses in Eastern Europe and the Former Soviet Union,* edited by Sue Bridger and Frances Pine, 16–32. New York: Routledge.

Kennedy, Michael. 2002. *Cultural Formations of Postcommunism: Emancipation, Transition, Nation, and War.* Minneapolis: University of Minnesota Press.

Kideckel, David. 1990. The Politics of Decollectivization in Romania After Ceauşescu. Working Papers on the Transitions from State Socialism, no. 90.9. Cornell University Center for International Studies, Ithaca, N.Y.

——. 1992. "Peasants and Authority in the New Romania." In *Romania after Tyranny,* edited by Daniel Nelson, 69–83. Boulder: Westview Press.

——. 1993a. "Once Again, the Land: Decollectivization and Social Conflict in Rural Romania." In *The Curtain Rises: Rethinking Culture, Ideology, and the State in Eastern Europe,* edited by Hermine G. De Soto and David G. Anderson, 62–75. Atlantic Highlands, N.J.: Humanities Press.

——. 1993b. "The Social Impact of the Transition." In *Romania: A Strategy for The Transition in Agriculture,* vol. 2, 117–96. Washington, D.C.: World Bank.

——. 1993c. *The Solitude of Collectivism: Romanian Villagers to the Revolution and Beyond.* Ithaca: Cornell University Press.

——, ed. 1995a. *East European Communities: The Struggle for Balance in Turbulent Times.* Boulder: Westview.

——. 1995b. "Two Incidents on the Plains in Southern Transylvania: Pitfalls of Privatization in a Romanian Community." In *East European Communities: The Struggle for Balance in Turbulent Times,* edited by David Kideckel, 47–64. Boulder: Westview.

Kligman, Gail. 1998. *The Politics of Duplicity: Controlling Reproduction in Ceauşescu's Romania.* Berkeley and Los Angeles: University of California Press.

Knapp, Viktor. 1975. "Socialist Countries." In *International Encyclopedia of Comparative Law,* Vol. 6, edited by Frederick H. Lawson, 35–67. New York: Oceana.

Konstantinov, Yulian. 2000. "Bulgaria: Property Registration and Cadastre Project. Social Assessment Part, Final Report." Manuscript.

Kornai, János. 1980. *Economics of Shortage.* Amsterdam: North-Holland Publishers.

——. 1992. *The Socialist System.* Princeton: Princeton University Press.

Kotkin, Steven. 1995. *Magnetic Mountain: Stalinism as a Civilization.* Berkeley: University of California Press.

Laky, T. 1979. "Enterprises in Bargaining Position." *Acta Oeconomica* 22: 227–46.

Lampland, Martha. 1995. *The Object of Labor: Commodification in Socialist Hungary.* Chicago: University of Chicago Press.

——. 2002. "The Avantages of Being Collectivized: Comparative Farm Managers in the

Postsocialist Economy." In *Postsocialism: Ideals, Ideologies and Practices in Eurasia,* edited by C. M. Hann, 31–56. London and New York: Routledge.

Lash, Scott, and John Urry. 1987. *The End of Organized Capitalism.* Madison: University of Wisconsin Press.

Leach, Edmund S. 1961. *Pul Eliya, A Village in Ceylon: A Study of Land Tenure and Kinship.* Cambridge, UK: Cambridge University Press.

Ledeneva, Alena. 1998. *Russia's Economy of Favors: Blat, Networking, and Informal Exchange.* Cambridge, UK: Cambridge University Press.

Lenin, Vladimir. 1967. *The Development of Capitalism in Russia.* Moscow: Progress Publishers.

Lerman, Zvi. 1997. "Experience with Land Reform and Farm Restructuring in the Former Soviet Union." In *Agricultural Privatisation, Land Reform and Farm Restructuring in Central and Eastern Europe,* edited by Johan F. M. Swinnen, Allan Buckwell, and Erik Mathijs, 311–32. Aldershot, UK, and Brookfield: Ashgate.

——. 2000a. Perspectives on Future Research in Central and Eastern European Transition Agriculture. Lecture presented at the KATO Symposium, Berlin, Germany, November.

——. 2000b. "Status of Land Reform and Farm Restructuring in Central and Eastern Europe: A Regional Overview." In *Structural Change in the Farming Sectors in Central and Eastern Europe.* World Bank Technical Paper no. 465. Washington, D.C.: World Bank.

Levy, Robert. 2001. *Ana Pauker: The Rise and Fall of a Jewish Communist.* Berkeley and Los Angeles: University of California Press.

Lewin, Moshe. 1968. *Russian Peasants and Soviet Power: A Study of Collectivization.* Evanston: Northwestern University Press.

——. 1985. *The Making of the Soviet System: Essays in the Social History of Interwar Russia.* New York: Pantheon.

Lipetsker, Mikhail. 1946. *Property Rights of Soviet Citizens.* Moscow: Soviet News.

Lipton, David, and Jeffrey Sachs. 1990. *Privatization in Eastern Europe: The Case of Poland.* Brookings Papers on Economic Activity, 2. Washington, D.C.: Brookings Institution Press.

Lowie, Robert. 1920. *Primitive Society.* New York: Liveright Publishing Company.

Lupan, Ernest, and Ionel Reghini. 1977. *Drept civil: Drepturi reale principale.* Cluj: Universitatea Babeş-Bolyai, Facultate de Drept.

Malinowski, Bronislaw. 1922. *Argonauts of the Western Pacific.* London: Routledge.

——. 1926. *Crime and Custom in Savage Society.* New York: Harcourt, Brace & Company.

——. 1935. *Coral Gardens and Their Magic.* London: Allen and Unwin.

Mandel, Ruth, and Caroline Humphrey, eds. 2002. *Markets and Moralities: Ethnographies of Postsocialism.* New York: Berg.

Martin, Emily. 1997. Colonizing Minds: Managing the Mental in Late 20th Century U.S. Paper presented at CSST Seminar, University of Michigan.

——. Forthcoming. *Bipolar Expeditions.* Princeton: Princeton University Press.

Marx, Karl, and Frederick Engels. 1968. *The Communist Manifesto.* New York: New York Labor News.

Mateescu, Oana. 2002. Making Persons, Placing Objects: Narratives of Theft in Southern Romania. Manuscript.

Mathijs, Erik. 1997. "Process and Politics of Agrarian Reform in Hungary." In *Political Economy of Agrarian Reform in Central and Eastern Europe*, edited by Johan F. M. Swinnen, 237–68. Aldershot, UK, and Brookfield: Ashgate.

Maurel, Marie-Claude. 1994a. "Terre, capital, travail: Vers de nouveau rapports sociaux en Europe centrale." *Cahiers Internationaux de Sociologie* 96: 7–32.

———. 1994b. *La transition post-collectiviste: Mutations agraires en Europe centrale*. Paris: Editions L'Harmattan.

———. 1997. *Recomposition de l'Europe Médiane*. Paris: Sedes.

Maurer, William. 1997. *Recharting the Caribbean: Land, Law and Citizenship in the British Virgin Islands*. Ann Arbor: University of Michigan Press.

———. 1999. "Forget Locke? From Proprietor to Risk-Bearer in New Logics of Finance." *Public Culture* 11: 365–85.

Mauss, Marcel. 1965. *The Gift: Forms and Functions of Exchange in Archaic Societies*. Translated by Ian Cunnison. New York: Norton.

McCay, Bonnie J., and James M. Acheson. 1990. *The Question of the Commons: The Culture and Ecology of Communal Resources*. Tucson: University of Arizona Press.

McClure, Kirstie. 1996. *Judging Rights: Lockean Politics and the Limits of Consent*. Ithaca: Cornell University Press.

McFaul, Michael. 1996. "The Allocation of Property Rights in Russia: The First Round." *Communist and Post-Communist Studies* 29: 287–308.

Meurs, Mieke. 2001. *The Evolution of Agrarian Institutions: A Comparative Study of Post-Socialist Hungary and Bulgaria*. Ann Arbor: University of Michigan Press.

Meurs, Mieke, and Robert Begg. 1998. "Path Dependence in Bulgarian Agriculture." In *Theorising Transition: The Political Economy of Post-Communist Transformations*, edited by John Pickles and Adrian Smith, 243–61. London: Routledge.

Meyers, William H., and Natalja Kazlauskiene. 1998. "Land Reform in Estonia, Latvia, and Lithuania: A Comparative Analysis." In *Land Reform in the Former Soviet Union and Eastern Europe*, edited by Stephen Wegren, 87–108. London: Routledge.

Milczarek, Dominika. 2000. Privatization of State Farms in Poland—A New Institutional Approach. Paper prepared for the KATO Symposium, Berlin, Germany, November.

Miller, Peter, and Nikolas Rose. 1990. "Governing Economic Life." *Economy and Society* 19: 1–31.

Mitchell, Brian R. 1998. *International Historical Statistics: Europe, 1750–1993*, 4th ed. London: Macmillan and New York: Stockton Press.

Mitrany, David. 1930. *The Land and the Peasant in Rumania: The War and Agrarian Reform*. New Haven: Yale University Press.

Moore, Sally Falk. 1986. *Social Facts and Fabrications: "Customary" Law on Kilimanjaro, 1880–1980*. Cambridge, UK: Cambridge University Press.

Mungiu-Pippidi, Alina. 2002. *Politica după comunism*. Bucharest: Humanitas.

Mungiu-Pippidi, Alina, and Gérard Althabe. 2002. *Secera și buldozerul: Scornicești și Nucșoara. Mecanisme de aservire a țăranului român*. Iași: Editura Polirom.

Munn, Nancy. 1986. *The Fame of Gawa: A Symbolic Study of Value Transformation in a Massim (Papua New Guinea) Society*. Cambridge, UK: Cambridge University Press.

Murrell, Peter. 1992. "Conservative Political Philosophy and the Strategy of Economic Transition." *East European Politics and Societies* 6: 3–16.

———. 1993. "What Is Shock Therapy? What Did It Do in Poland and Russia?" *Post-Soviet Affairs* 9: 111–40.

Myers, Fred. 1989. "Burning the Truck and Holding the Country." In *We Are Here: Politics of Aboriginal Land Tenure*, edited by Edwin N. Wilmsen, 15–42. Berkeley: University of California Press.

Nadasdy, Paul. 2002. "Property and Aboriginal Land Claims in the Canadian Subarctic: Some Theoretical Considerations." *American Anthropologist* 104: 247–61.

———. 2003. *Hunters and Bureaucrats: Power, Knowledge, and Aboriginal-State Relations in the Southwest Yukon.* Vancouver: University of British Columbia Press.

Neményi, Ágnes. 2000a. "Rural Households in Romania—Structure, Income, Consumption." *East European Countryside* nr 6: 121–28.

———. 2000b. *Rural Restructuring and the Sustainability of Farming in Romania and Bulgaria.* SOCO Project Paper no. 71. Institut für die Wissenschaften vom Menschen, Vienna. Available at: http://www.iwm.at. Accessed May 2003.

Nelson, Lynn D., and Irina Y. Kuzes. 1994. *Property to the People: The Struggle for Radical Economic Reform in Russia.* Armonk: M. E. Sharpe.

Nickolsky, Sergei. 1998. "The Treadmill of Socialist Reforms and the Failures of Post-Communist 'Revolutions' in Russian Agriculture: Is There an Alternative?" In *Privatizing the Land: Rural Political Economy in Post-Communist Societies*, edited by Iván Szelényi, 191–213. New York and London: Routledge.

Noronha, Raymond. 1996. Romania: The Rural Planning and Development Agency (ADAR) and the Land Market and Rural Development. Paper prepared for a World Bank Report. Manuscript.

North, Douglas C. 1979. "A Framework for Analyzing the State in Economic History." *Explorations in Economic History* 16: 249–59.

Offe, Claus. 1985. *Disorganized Capitalism: Contemporary Transformations of Work and Politics.* Edited by John Keane. Cambridge, Mass.: MIT Press.

Offe, Claus, Frank Bonker, Stephen Holmes, Shlomo Avineri, George Sher, and Ulrich Preuss. 1993. "A Forum on Restitution: Essays on the Efficiency and Justice of Returning Property to Its Former Owners." *East European Constitutional Review* 2:30–40.

Organisation for Economic Cooperation and Development (OECD). 1992. *Reforming the Economies of Central and Eastern Europe.* Paris: Organisation for Economic Cooperation and Development.

———. Centre for Co-operation with Non-Members. 1998. *Agricultural Policies in Emerging and Transition Economies, Monitoring and Evaluation 1998.* Paris: Organisation for Economic Cooperation and Development.

———. 2000. *Review of Agricultural Policies: Bulgaria.* Paris: Organisation for Economic Cooperation and Development.

Ostrom, Elinor. 1990. *Governing the Commons: The Evolution of Institutions of Collective Action.* Cambridge, UK: Cambridge University Press.

Otiman, Păun Ion. 2002. *Agricultura României la cumpăna dintre secolul XX și secolul XXI.* Timișoara: Ed. Agroprint.

Parlamentul României. 1992. *Dosarul colectivizării agriculturii în România, 1949–1962.* Bucharest: Camera Deputaților al Parlamentului României.

Parry, Bronwyn. 2004. "Bodily Transactions: Regulating a New Space of Flows in Bio-Information." In *Property in Question: Value Transformation in the Global Economy*, edited by Katherine Verdery and Caroline Humphrey. Oxford: Berg Press, forthcoming.

Pasti, Vladimir, Mirela Miroiu, and Cornel Codiță. 1997. *România: Starea de fapt*. Vol. 1, *Societatea*. Bucharest: Nemira.

Păunescu, Daniela. 1974. *Drept cooperatist*. Bucharest: University of Bucharest Law Faculty.

Paxson, Margaret. 2002. Symbolic Topographies of Social Memory in the Village of Solov'ovo. Manuscript.

Perrotta, Louise. 1998. "Divergent Responses to Land Reform and Agricultural Restructuring in the Russian Federation." In *Surviving Post-Socialism: Local Strategies and Regional Responses in Eastern Europe and the Former Soviet Union*, edited by Sue Bridger and Frances Pine, 149–69. New York: Routledge.

Pine, Frances. 1998. "Dealing with Fragmentation: The Consequences of Privatisation for Rural Women in Central and Southern Poland." In *Surviving Post-Socialism: Local Strategies and Regional Responses in Eastern Europe and the Former Soviet Union*, edited by Sue Bridger and Frances Pine, 106–23. New York: Routledge.

Piore, Michael J., and Charles F. Sabel. 1984. *The Second Industrial Divide: Possibilities for Prosperity*. New York: Basic Books.

Polanyi, Karl. 1944. *The Great Transformation: The Political and Economic Origins of Our Time*. Boston: Beacon.

Pop-Eleches, Grigore. 1999. "Separated *at* Birth or Separated *by* Birth? The Communist Successor Parties in Romania and Hungary." *East European Politics and Societies* 13: 117–47.

———. 2001. "Romania's Politics of Dejection." *Journal of Democracy* 12: 156–69.

Povinelli, Elizabeth. 2002. "Shamed States." In *The Cunning of Recognition: Indigenous Alterities and the Making of Australian Multiculturalism*. Durham: Duke University Press.

Putnam, Robert. 1995. "Bowling Alone: America's Declining Social Capital." *Journal of Democracy* 6: 65–78.

Pryor, Frederic L. 1992. *The Red and the Green: The Rise and Fall of Collectivized Agriculture in Marxist Regimes*. Princeton: Princeton University Press.

Rabinowicz, Eva, and Johan F. M. Swinnen. 1997. "Political Economy of Privatization and Decollectivization of Central and East European Agriculture: Definitions, Issues and Methodology." In *Political Economy of Agrarian Reform in Central and Eastern Europe*, edited by Johan F. M. Swinnen, 1–31. Aldershot, UK, and Brookfield: Ashgate.

Republica Populară Romînia. 1956. *Legislația civilă uzuală, II*. Bucharest: Editura Științifică.

Rév, István. 1987. "The Advantages of Being Atomized." *Dissent* 34: 335–50.

Rizov, Marian, Dinu Gavrilescu, Hamish Gow, Erik Mathijs, and Johan F. M. Swinnen. 2001. "Transition and Enterprise Restructuring: The Development of Individual Farming in Romania." *World Development* 29: 1257–74.

Ries, Nancy. 1997. *Russian Talk: Culture and Conversation during Perestroika*. Ithaca: Cornell University Press.

Roberts, Henry. 1951. *Rumania: Political Problems of an Agrarian State*. New Haven: Yale University Press.

Romania, Ministerul Agriculturii și Alimentației. 1998. *Evoluția sectorului agroalimentar în România. Raport, anul 1997*. Bucharest.

Róna-Tas, Ákos. 1998. "Path-Dependence and Capital Theory: Sociology of the Post-Communist Economic Transformation." *East European Politics and Societies* 12: 107–31.

Róna-Tas, Ákos, and József Böröcz. 2000. "Bulgaria, the Czech Republic, Hungary and Poland: Pre-Socialist and Socialist Legacies among Business Elites." In *Elites after State Socialism: Theory and Analysis*, edited by John Higley and György Lengyel, 209–27. Boulder: Rowman and Littlefield.

Rose, Carol M. 1994. *Property and Persuasion: Essays on the History, Theory, and Rhetoric of Ownership*. Boulder: Westview.

Sahlins, Marshall D. 1972. "The Original Affluent Society." In *Stone Age Economics*. Chicago: Aldine-Atherton.

Sampson, Steven L. 1984. *National Integration through Socialist Planning: An Anthropological Study of a Romanian New Town*. Boulder: East European Monographs.

———. 1996. "The Social Life of Projects: Importing Civil Society to Albania." In *Civil Society*, edited by Chris Hann and Elizabeth Dunn, 121–42. London: Routledge.

Șandru, Dumitru. 1975. *Reforma agrară din 1921 în România*. Bucharest: Editura Academiei.

Sandu, Dumitru. 1999. "Drumul antreprenorial: Fără încredere dar cu relații." *Sociologie românească* 2: 123–46.

Sarris, Alexander H., and Dinu Gavrilescu. 1997. "Restructuring of Farms and Agricultural Systems in Romania." In *Agricultural Privatisation, Land Reform and Farm Restructuring in Central and Eastern Europe*, edited by Johan F. M. Swinnen, Allan Buckwell, and Erik Mathijs, 189–228. Aldershot, UK, and Brookfield: Ashgate.

Sawyer, Suzana. 2004. "Crude Properties: The Sublime and Slime of Oil Operations in the Ecuadorian Amazon." In *Property in Question: Value Transformation in the Global Economy*, edited by Katherine Verdery and Caroline Humphrey. Oxford: Berg Press, forthcoming.

Schlüter, Achim. 2000. Institutional Change in Transition: Restitution, Transformation and Privatisation in Czech Agriculture. Paper prepared for the KATO Symposium, Berlin, Germany, November.

Scott, James C. 1998. *Seeing like a State: How Certain Schemes to Improve the Human Condition Have Failed*. New Haven: Yale University Press.

Scrieciu, Florin, and Xenia Chercea. 1996. *Legislația in agricultură și industria alimentară*. Bucharest: WEGAFOR.

Shafir, Michael. 1997. "Romania's Road to 'Normalcy.'" *Journal of Democracy* 8: 144–58.

Siebert, Rosemarie. 2000. "Socio-economic Changes in the East German Countryside." *East European Countryside* 6: 111–20.

Sikor, Thomas. 2001. "Agrarian Differentiation in Post-Socialist Societies: Evidence from Three Upland Villages in North-Western Vietnam." *Development and Change* 32: 923–49.

Simis, Konstantin M. 1982. *USSR—the Corrupt Society: The Secret World of Soviet Capitalism*. New York: Simon and Schuster.

Stahl, Henri H. 1958–65. *Contribuții la studiul satelor devălmașe romînești*. 3 vols. Bucharest: Editura Academiei.

——. 1980. *Traditional Romanian Village Communities*. Cambridge, U.K.: Cambridge University Press.

Staniszkis, Jadwiga. 1990. "Patterns of Change in Eastern Europe." *East European Politics and Societies* 4: 77–97.

——. 1991a. *Dynamics of the Breakthrough in Eastern Europe*. Berkeley and Los Angeles: University of California Press.

——. 1991b. "'Political Capitalism' in Poland." *East European Politics and Societies* 5: 127–41.

——. 1999. *Post-Communism: The Emerging Enigma*. Warsaw: Institute of Political Studies, Polish Academy of Sciences.

Stark, David. 1989. "Coexisting Organizational Forms in Hungary's Emerging Mixed Economy." In *Remaking the Economic Institutions of Socialism: China and Eastern Europe*, edited by Victor Nee and David Stark, 137–168. Stanford: Stanford University Press.

——. 1992. "Path Dependence and Privatization Strategies in East Central Europe." *East European Politics and Societies* 6: 17–54.

——. 1996. "Recombinant Property in East European Capitalism." *American Journal of Sociology* 101: 993–1027.

Stark, David, and László Bruszt. 1998. *Postsocialist Pathways: Transforming Politics and Property in East Central Europe*. Cambridge, UK: Cambridge University Press.

Stephens, Sharon. 1986. "Ideology and Everyday Life in Sami (Lapp) History." In *Discourse and the Social Life of Meaning*, edited by Phyllis Pease Chock and June R. Wyman, 205–31. Washington, D.C.: Smithsonian Institution Press.

Stewart, Michael. 1998. "'We Should Build a Statue to Ceaucescu [sic] Here': The Trauma of De-Collectivisation in Two Romanian Villages." In *Surviving Post-Socialism: Local Strategies and Regional Responses in Eastern Europe and the Former Soviet Union*, edited by Sue Bridger and Frances Pine, 66–79. New York: Routledge.

Stoica, Augustin. 2004. "From Good Communists to Even Better Capitalists: Entrepreneurial Pathways in Post-Socialist Romania." *East European Politics and Societies* 18 (1). Forthcoming.

Strathern, Marilyn. 1988. *The Gender of the Gift: Problems with Women and Problems with Society in Melanesia*. Berkeley and Los Angeles: University of California Press.

——. 1999. *Property, Substance, and Effect: Anthropological Essays on Persons and Things*. New Brunswick, N.J.: Athlone Press.

Swain, Nigel. 1985. *Collective Farms Which Work?* Cambridge, UK: Cambridge University Press.

——. 1995. "Decollectivising Agriculture in the Visegrad Countries of Central Europe." *Labour Focus on Eastern Europe* 51: 65–85.

——. 1996. "Getting Land in Central Europe." In *After Socialism: Land Reform and Social Change in Eastern Europe*, edited by Ray Abrahams, 193–215. Providence: Berghahn Books.

——. 1998. "A Framework for Comparing Social Change in the Post Socialist Countryside." *East European Countryside* 4: 5–18.

——. 1999. "Agricultural Restitution and Co-operative Transformation in the Czech Republic, Hungary, and Slovakia." *Europe-Asia Studies* 51: 1–25.

Swinnen, Johan F. M. 1997a. "The Choice of Privatization and Decollectivization Policies in Central and Eastern European Agriculture." In *Political Economy of Agrarian Reform in Central and Eastern Europe,* edited by Johan F. M. Swinnen, 363–98. Aldershot, UK, and Brookfield: Ashgate.

———, ed. 1997b. *Political Economy of Agrarian Reform in Central and Eastern Europe.* Aldershot, UK, and Brookfield: Ashgate.

———. 2000. Ten Years of Transition in Central and Eastern European Agriculture. Paper prepared for the KATO Symposium, Berlin, Germany, November.

Swinnen, Johan F. M., Allan Buckwell, and Erik Mathijs, eds. 1997. *Agricultural Privatisation, Land Reform and Farm Restructuring in Central and Eastern Europe.* Aldershot, UK, and Brookfield: Ashgate.

Swinnen, Johan F. M., and Erik Mathijs. 1997. "Agricultural Privatisation, Land Reform and Restructuring in Central and Eastern Europe." In *Agricultural Privatisation, Land Reform and Farm Restructuring in Central and Eastern Europe,* edited by Johan F. M. Swinnen, Allan Buckwell, and Erik Mathijs, 333–73. Aldershot, UK, and Brookfield: Ashgate.

Szakolczai, Árpád, and Ágnes Horváth. 1991. "Information Management in Bolshevik-Type Party-States: A Version of the Information Society." *East European Politics and Societies* 5: 268–305.

Szelényi, Iván. 1983. *Urban Inequalities under State Socialism.* Oxford: Oxford University Press.

———. 1988. *Socialist Entrepreneurs: Embourgeoisement in Rural Hungary.* Madison: University of Wisconsin Press.

———, ed. 1998. *Privatizing the Land: Rural Political Economy in Post-Communist Societies.* New York and London: Routledge.

Teşliuc, Emil. 2000a. "Agricultural Policies: Achievements and Challenges." In *Economic Transition in Romania: Past, Present and Future,* edited by Christof Ruhl and Daniel Dăianu, 91–137. Bucharest: Imprimerie Arta Grafică.

———. 2000b. "Romania." In *Agricultural Support Policies in Transition Economies,* edited by Alberto Valdés, 48–64. World Bank Technical Paper no. 470. Washington, D.C.: World Bank.

Thelen, Tatjana. 2001. "Post-Socialist Entrepreneurs in Rural Hungary: Social Continuity and Legal Practice in Mesterszállás." *Acta Ethnographica Hungarica* 46: 315–42.

Thomas, Nicholas. 1991. *Entangled Objects: Exchange, Material Culture, and Colonialism in the Pacific.* Cambridge, Mass.: Harvard University Press.

Tinbergen, Jan. 1958. *The Design of Development.* Baltimore: Johns Hopkins University Press, for the International Bank for Reconstruction and Development.

Tismăneanu, Vladimir. 1997. "Romanian Exceptionalism? Democracy, Ethnocracy, and Uncertain Pluralism in Post-Ceauşescu Romania." In *Politics, Power, and the Struggle for Democracy in South-East Europe,* edited by Karen Dawisha and Bruce Parrott, 403–51. Cambridge, UK: Cambridge University Press.

Tismăneanu, Vladimir, and Gail Kligman, eds. 2001. "Romania after the 2000 Elections." Special Issue of *East European Constitutional Review* 10.

Tompson, William. 1999. "The Price of Everything and the Value of Nothing? Unravelling the Workings of Russia's 'Virtual Economy.'" *Economy and Society* 28: 256–08.

Turnock, David. 1986. *The Romanian Economy in the Twentieth Century.* New York: St. Martin's Press.

——. 1997. *The East European Economy in Context: Communism and Transition*. London and New York: Routledge.

Van Atta, Don. 1993. *The "Farmer Threat": The Political Economy of Agrarian Reform in Post-Soviet Russia*. Boulder: Westview.

——. 1997. "Agrarian Reform in Post-Soviet Russia." In *Political Economy of Agrarian Reform in Central and Eastern Europe,* edited by Johan F. M. Swinnen, 321–37. Aldershot, UK, and Brookfield: Ashgate.

Verdery, Katherine. 1977. Ethnic Stratification in the European Periphery: The Historical Sociology of a Transylvanian Village. Ph.D. diss., Stanford University.

——. 1983. *Transylvanian Villagers: Three Centuries of Political, Economic, and Ethnic Change*. Berkeley and Los Angeles: University of California Press.

——. 1991. "Theorizing Socialism: A Prologue to the 'Transition.'" *American Ethnologist* 18: 419–39.

——. 1994. "The Elasticity of Land: Problems of Property Restitution in Transylvania." *Slavic Review* 53: 1071–109.

——. 1995. "Faith, Hope, and *Caritas* in the Land of the Pyramids, Romania 1991–1994." *Comparative Studies in Society and History* 37: 625–69.

——. 1996. *What Was Socialism, and What Comes Next?* Princeton: Princeton University Press.

——. 1998. "Property and Power in Transylvania's Decollectivization." In *Property Relations: Renewing the Anthropological Tradition,* edited by C. M. Hann, 16–80. Cambridge, UK: Cambridge University Press.

——. 1999. "Fuzzy Property: Rights, Power, and Identity in Transylvania's Decollectivization." In *Uncertain Transition: Ethnographies of Everyday Life in the Postsocialist World,* edited by Michael Burawoy and Katherine Verdery, 53–81. Boulder: Rowman and Littlefield.

——. 2001. "Ghosts on the Landscape: Restoring Private Landownership in Eastern Europe." *Focaal* 36: 145–63.

——. 2002. "Seeing like a Mayor, or How Local Officials Obstructed Romanian Land Restitution." *Ethnography* 3: 5–33.

Verdery, Katherine, and Caroline Humphrey. 2004a. "Introduction: Raising Questions about Property." In *Property in Question: Value Transformation in the Global Economy,* edited by Katherine Verdery and Caroline Humphrey. Oxford: Berg Press, forthcoming.

——. eds. 2004b. *Property in Question: Value Transformation in the Global Economy*. Oxford: Berg Press, forthcoming.

Viola, Lynne. 1987. *The Best Sons of the Fatherland: Workers in the Vanguard of Soviet Collectivization*. Oxford: Oxford University Press.

Vitebsky, Piers. 2002. "Withdrawing from the Land: Social and Spiritual Crisis in the Indigenous Russian Arctic." In *Property Relations: Renewing the Anthropological Tradition,* edited by C. M. Hann, 18–95. Cambridge, UK: Cambridge University Press.

von Cramon-Taubadel, Stephan. 2000. Perspectives on Liberalisation during Transition. Paper prepared for the KATO Symposium, Berlin, Germany, November.

von Hirschhausen, Béatrice. 1997. *Les nouvelles campagnes roumaines: Paradoxes d'un "retour" paysan*. Paris: Belin.

von Hirschhausen, Béatrice, and Florence Gerbaud. 1998. "La 'question agraire' ou la renaissance d'un vieux défi." In *Les teritoires centre-européens: Dilemmes et défis,* edited by Violette Rey, 141–66. Paris: La Découverte.

Vultur, Mircea. 2002. *Collectivisme et transition democratique: Les campagnes roumaines à l'épreuve du marché.* [Québec]: Les Presses de l'Université Laval.

Vysokovskii, Aleksandr. 1993. "Will Domesticity Return?" In *Russian Housing in the Modern Age: Design and Social History,* edited by William Craft Brumfield and Blair A. Ruble, 271–308. Cambridge, UK: Cambridge University Press.

Wade, Robert. 1990. *Governing the Market: Economic Theory and the Role of Government in East Asian Industrialization.* Princeton: Princeton University Press.

Walker, Barbara. 2001. "(Still) Searching for a Soviet Society: Personalized Political and Economic Ties in Recent Soviet Historiography." *Comparative Studies in Society and History* 43: 631–42.

Wedel, Janine R. 2001. *Collision and Collusion: The Strange Case of Western Aid to Eastern Europe.* New York: Palgrave.

Wegren, Stephen. 1998a. *Agriculture and the State in Soviet and Post-Soviet Russia.* Pittsburgh: University of Pittsburgh Press.

——, ed. 1998b. *Land Reform in the Former Soviet Union and Eastern Europe.* London and New York: Routledge.

Weiner, Annette. 1992. *Inalienable Possessions: The Paradox of Keeping-While-Giving.* Berkeley and Los Angeles: University of California Press.

Weiner, Robert. 2001. "Romania, the IMF, and Economic Reform since 1996." *Problems of Post-Communism* 48: 39–47.

Williams, Nancy M. 1986. *The Yolngu and Their Land: A System of Land Tenure and the Fight for Its Recognition.* Stanford: Stanford University Press.

Wolf, Eric R. 1982. *Europe and the People without History.* Berkeley and Los Angeles: University of California Press.

World Bank. 1997. *Romania: Agricultural Sector Adjustment Loan Report,* no. P-7113–RO. Washington, D.C.: World Bank.

——. 2001. *World Bank Reports On-line. www.worldbank.org/2001/[country date]/aag.* Accessed 9/13/01.

Woodruff, David. 1999. *Money Unmade: Barter and the Fate of Russian Capitalism.* Ithaca: Cornell University Press.

——. 2002. Negotiable Balance: The Political Construction of Capitalism's Legal Institutions. Manuscript.

INDEX

10, 11, 21, 170–71, 179, 188, 290, 342–43, 368n22. *See also* capitalist economic integration; cultural capital; international organizations; investment; mode(s) of production; political capital; social capital

capital endowments, from socialist period: 343, 348–55, 360; and associations, 129–31, 232, 239, 251, 268–69; and commercial farmers, 312, 313, 321–22, 323–24, 330, 339; and postsocialist specificities, 363–64; and SF directors, 276–77, 305, 308, 309, 352; and smallholders, 190, 192, 227–28

capitalist economic integration, 11, 26–27, 74–75, 308, 361–62; and agricultural subsidies, 105, 107; and devaluation of agriculture, 231; and effective ownership, 270–71; and imported inputs, 264, 326, 327–28, 339; influence of international finance on, 78, 79–80, 109, 353–54; and SF privatization, 275

capitalist economies, 7, 20, 337, 389n1

Caritas (pyramid scheme), 201, 331, 332, 341

Cartea Funciară. See land register

Cartwright, Andrew, 13, 103, 139, 378n10

cash crops. *See* specialty crops

Ceaușescu, Nicolae, 8, 11, 94, 105, 113

center-local relations, 91, 148, 157; and communes, 145–46; politics of, 95, 104, 108, 113, 114–15; and restitution, 120, 139–40

certificate (provisional property title [*adeverință*]), 88, 97, 101, 121–22, 135–36

Cervenka Society, 216, 259–62, 348–55, 385n27, 386n29

Chelcea, Liviu, 160, 388–89n24

cherry-picking, 23

chiabur (wealthy peasant), 127, 169, 175

China, 47

Ciba-Sandosz, 328

'cides. *See* herbicides; pesticides

clacă (work party), 214

claims (to receive land): criteria for, 165–66, 167, 170, 182; establishing, 138; number filed, 101; language of, 119, 155, 159, 161–62, 167, 170, 181, 380n12. *See also* proofs

class formation, 19, 159, 347, 361; associations and, 269–70; commercial farmers and, 335–36; and local-venit conflict, 167, 169, 211; and red bourgeoisie, 99, 112, 390n6; restitution and, 81–83, 125, 144, 171, 183, 374n8; in Vlaicu, 35, 118–19, 122–25, 195. *See also* commercial farmers/agriculture; dispossession; impoverishment; polarization; supertenants

clientelism, 60, 65, 162, 305, 335; in associations, 264–65; in CFs, 346, 372n30; of political officials, 111, 146–50, 157, 281, 307; and

labor supply, 63, 214; in socialism, 60–63, 70; and SF directors, 188, 324. *See also* exchange; reciprocity

Codiță, Cornel, 13, 227–28, 381n9

Codoban, Aurel, 367n5

coercion, 42–43, 44–46, 52, 103, 127. *See also* violence

Coleman, James, 10

collateral (for bank loans), 106, 206, 274, 289, 323, 327, 386n2

collective farms and state farms, compared, 52–55, *55*, 82–83, 85–93, 277–78; international comparisons, 82–83, 88, 314–15; by size, *86*, 121, *265*; in Transylvania, 34

collective farms (CFs), 188–89, 321–22, 347; in agricultural economy, 185–86; average size of, *265*; chairmen of, 322, 372n30; destruction of, 87, 89–90, 96, 125, 267, 272; labor force of, 167, 168; land management in, 63–69, 197; ownership status of land in, 71–74; patrimony of, 42, 233, 251, 263, 266, 331, 365–66, 390n12; personnel of, 232; process of dismantling, 125–31, 157, 232, 234–35; as socialist property, 52–55; strategies of, 188–89; "theft" in, 65–69, 266; in Vlaicu, 120, 125–40, *126*. *See also* collective farms and state farms, compared

Collectivisme et transition democratique (Vultur), 13

collectivization, 5, 25, 34, 41–47; comparative, 43–46; implications of, 69–70; and land reform, 35; resistance to, 44, 200; in Soviet Union, 45–46; in Vlaicu, 42–43, 172

Collier, Jane F., 165

commerce, small-scale. *See* commercial farmers/agriculture

commercial farmers/agriculture, 18, 89, 115, 195, 348–55; associations and, 239, 266, 271; characteristics of, 310–12, 315, 316, 317, 321, 324, 330, 389n5; competition among, 265, 284, 295–96, 311, 324, 326–28, 344–45; conditions for success of, 339–45, 348, 352–53; degree of expertise of, 315–39; and intergenerational conflict, 179, 227; kin ties of, 310, 311, 312, 320, 330, 334; and land market, 209–10, 295–96; relations with villagers, 323, 326–27, 332, 338–39, 364; SF directors as, 189, 322–29; and SF privatization, 186, 295, 309; strategies of, 310–12, 315–39. *See also* cultural capital; networks, of commercial farmers; social capital; supertenants

commodification, 22, 25, 74–75, 360

commune, defined, 369n28

communism. *See* socialism

Communist Manifesto (Marx and Engels), 48

Communist Party (general), 28, 51, 113, 371n22. *See also* Romanian Communist Party

compensation, 82, 162; algorithms for, 83. *See also* justice; reparations

"comprador" strategy, 334

confiscations. *See* nationalization

conflict, 13, 39, 113–14, 228; class, 172, 175–77, 211, 215–16, 218, 347; ethnic, 103, 142–45, 261; generational, 151–52, 161, 179–81, 379–80n4; intravillage, 46, 102–3, 139, 154–55, 163, 183, 357, 378n13; with kin, 46, 102–3, 120, 163–66, 183, 357, 379–80n4

conflict, locals/venits, 181–83, 215–18, 361; as class conflict, 175–77; over land, 131, 133, 167–70, 210, 347; and social status, 171–72

connections. *See* networks; social capital

consolidation (of fields), 82, 199, 264, 347; and Association, 230, 240, 263, 385n26; in Cervenka Society, 260; in CFs, 42, 63–64; Law 18 and, 99, 133; and "old sites," 162, 182; by supertenants, 347; in Vlaicu, 143. *See also* court cases; lawsuits

Constantinescu, Emil (Romanian president, 1996–2000), 105, 223, 376n53

consumption, 205, 208, 346; of elite villas, 110, 144, 147, 171, 306,

contestation, 27, 64, 151; proofs required for, 154; and socialist property, 64; in Vlaicu, 117–20, 143

contracts: by CFs, 54, 61, 66; for land sales, 383n24; for leasing land, 225, 241, 243, 245, 335–36; for produce, 249, 254, 317, 318, 327

cooperative farms, 42n.a, 231–32. *See also* collective farms

cooperative property, 50–51, 316; creation of, 52, 53; defined, 50n.e; property rights in, 71–73

cooperatives. *See* associations; cooperative property; socialist property

corn, 213; and Association, 230, 384n11; and crop rotation, 243, 247, 249, 318, 350; labor requirements for, 244–49, 260

cornstalks (*tulei*), 245–46, 318

"corruption," 9, 59, 279, 363, 387n8; as protectionism, 24–25; and restitution, 130–31; scandals, 110–13; and SF privatization, 281–85, 290, 295, 299–300. *See also* bribery

county boards, 100, 127. *See also* land commissions

coupon system (subsidies), 107, 110–11, 223, 319, 376n52, 381n4, 383n25

court cases, 97, 118, 163, 358–59. *See also* lawsuits

Court of Accounts, 110

credits, 105–9, 306; international influence on, 259; Romcereal and, 253–54, 255, 257, 350. *See also* loans; prices; subsidies

credit-worthiness, 300–301, 308

Creed, Gerald, 11, 12, 344, 372n36

crop rotation, 197, 201, 204, 318; in Association, 242–43, 384n13; in Cervenka Society, 260; and labor, 220, 230, 244–49. *See also* corn; wheat

Csanádi, Máriá, 26

Cugir (city and commune), 37–38

cultural capital, 10, 262, 313, 343; of commercial farmers, 316–17, 322, 339, 344–45; defined, 313; and entrepreneurship, 10, 313–14; importance of, 342–43; of SF directors, 75, 308, 314; of smallholders, 268; of venits, 382n20. *See also* capital endowments; expertise

cultural property, 22

Czechoslovakia, 45, 85, 87, 276; compared, 85–86; restitution in, 83, 374n8

Czech Republic, 88, 90, 225, 367–68n5

Cziráky conscription, 68

Dăianu, Daniel (Romanian finance minister), 108

Dallas (TV series), 33, 310, 389n1

debt: as asset, 327–28; forced onto others, 306–7; of SFs, 299–300, 302, 330, 387n5; of SFSs, 289–90, 330, 333

decapitalization, 187, 298–99. *See also* devaluation

decollectivization, 39, 70–76, 78, 373n5; comparative, 12–13; defined, 3, 13; effects of, 93, 186, 231–32, 347–48, 357–61; politics of (general), 78–84, 86–90, 96–104, 113–15; politics of (in Vlaicu), 116–157; rationales for, 79–80; in Romania, 94–115

Decree 151/1950, 63–64

deed. *See* titling

delays: in Association, 252, 351; in restitution process, 111, 117, 182; in SF privatization, 275, 277, 305, 308–9, 342; in SOE privatization, 281, 283; in titling land, 139, 147, 163, 165, 243

delegitimation. *See* legitimation

Deloitte and Touche, 5

Democratic Convention (DC), 107, 279, 375n27, 376–77n62. *See also* neoliberals

demodernization (of agriculture), 110–11, 191, 357; by Association, 258, 268–70; in Cervenka Society, 262; Law 18 and, 102; smallholders and, 226–28

deracination, 357–58

devaluation, 23–24, 282–83, 303; of agricultural

sector, 224, 272; causes of, 12, 363; of CF assets, 234; of labor power, 4; of land, 114, 183, 191, 204, 205–9, 220, 223–26, 258, 337, 354, 356, 358; mechanisms for, 282–83; of nonland assets, 290, 293, 298, 338, 354, 359; of SF assets, 187, 276, 279, 294, 298–300, 301, 304, 305–7, 334, 353, 359; and vanishing hectares, 359–60. *See also* revaluation

dignity, 9, 155, 304

directorates, interlocking, 299, 306–7

dispossession, 32, 70, 362, 387n14; decollectivization and, 22, 39, 76. *See also* impoverishment; polarization

distribution channels, 209, 235, 259, 285–86; and agricultural policy, 92, 377n62; and grain market, 340–41; Romcereal and, 185, 253–54; in socialism, 232; weakness of, 251, 319, 326, 340–41, 354. *See also* markets

Divertis (Romanian comedy team), 116–17

dividends (from SFs), 98, 121, 204, 278, 352; mayors manipulate, 141, 143, 306, 322; and supertenant strategies, 288–89, 295–96, 313, 330. *See also* shareholders

"dividuals," 173

"donation" (of land to collectives), 42–43, 44–46, 50, 52, 54, 103, 371–72n25

dumping, 108, 328, 376n56, 381n8

Dunn, Elizabeth, 19–20, 24–25

East Germany, 209, 45, 89–91, 280; compared, 85–86, 88; SFs in, 53, 85, 276, 314.

economy: GDP, per capita, 109, 367–68n5; informal, 20; of shortage, 60–63, 285; transformation of, 79, 101–2, 191, 278, 280–81, 303–4, 361, 363; and unemployment, 376n46; "visible," 178–81, 223–25, 326, 338, 390n14

elites, 46, 214, 278; competition among, 9, 11, 12, 51, 60, 75, 94, 95, 265, 284, 326; information controlled by, 111, 284, 288; local, 46, 129, 133–57, 312; of socialism, 8, 9, 10; subvert central plans, 31, 59, 95, 113, 120, 144, 166–67, 170, 362; trajectories of, 11, 12, 297–98, 313–14, 322, 323, 329, 343; village, 96–97, 127–29, 166, 182; and villagers, 32, 65, 68, 106, 149, 155–56, 284, 389n2. *See also* agrarian elites; class formation; elites, abuse by; networks, of elites

elites, abuse by, 34, 279, 288, 358–59; in associations, 266, 270, 384n7; in restitution process, 102, 110, 111–12, 137–39; in Vlaicu, 140–45, 154

Elster, Jon, 6

embeddedness, social, 165, 173, 286, 348

emigration, 359–60, 384n8, 388n23; and labor shortage, 218–19, 358; from Vlaicu, 33, 124, 144, 195, 225–26

Engels, Friedrich, 40

entrepreneurship. *See* commercial farmers/agriculture

equality/equity, 158, 172; as basis for land claims, 170; as political goal, 80, 82, 84, 98, 159, 166, 182

equipment, agricultural, 190, 206, 211, 301; and Agromec prices, 187, 341; and Association, 238, 251–53, 263, 365–66; and associations, 233, 378n14; and commercial farmers, 324. *See also* tractors

Erdei, Ferencz, 175

Ernst and Young, 5

estates of administration. *See* administrative estates

estates of production. *See* production, estates of

ethnic relations, 80, 103; and associations, 383n1; German-Romanian, 142–45, 260, 346, 379n23, 380n9, 385n27, 386n29; restitution and, 83–84, 103, 133–35, 374n9, 379n23; in Transylvania, 34; in Vlaicu, 37, 118–119, 133, 143–44, 182, 260, 331, 346–47, 351. *See also* Germans

ethnography, 115, 178, 192, 337; and neo-institutionalism, 28, 164, 361–62; and property in socialism, 59–60, 65–68. *See also* research methods

European Bank for Reconstruction and Development (EBRD), 5, 78, 94, 114

European Development Bank, 353

European Investment Bank, 4–5, 94

European Union, 7, 78, 107, 109; Phare Programmes of, 12, 100, 305

exchange: among communist cadres, 60–63, 69, 76, 162, 177–78. *See also* labor; land exchanges; reciprocity

exchange value, 21, 367n5

expertise: in Association, 250, 252, 253, 256; in associations, 260–4; and commercial farming, 315–39; as cultural capital, 305, 308, 344; lack of, 382n17; vs. managerialism, 236, 352; and risk management, 337, 339; in SFs vs. CFs, 314; and social status, 224, 227, 388n23; of venits, 382n20. *See also* cultural capital

expropriations: by communists, 40, 52, 53, 123, 142; pre-communist, 45, 83–84, 97

Eyal, Gil, 313–14, 334, 339, 343

Fame of Gawa, The (Munn), 25

Făniță, Triță (Romanian senator and entrepreneur), 104, 279

farm size/type, 85, 86, 89–93, 265, 389n4

fertilizer, 93, 318; and cultivation strategies, 201, 203–4, 211, 212–13, 245; decline in use of, 381n9, 381n10; mineral vs. organic, 197, 201, 203–05, 211, 267, 374–75n24. *See also* inputs; manure

field consolidation. *See* consolidation

finance capital. *See* capital

financial blockage, 28

financial institutions. *See* banks; international organizations

fini (godchildren), 214, 382n18

floods, 199, 200, 209, 250, 257, 259, 311, 384n13, 386n32

foreign connections. *See* social capital, foreign

foreign investment. *See* investment, foreign

"'45ers," 119, 123, 133, 142–45, 182, 240, 260, 352

fourth degree. *See* kinship

fragmentation (of fields), 82, 87, 373n2, 374n12, 376n44; advantage of, 199; in Association, 136, 230, 240, 260, 261; and land market, 99; and "old sites," 101, 136, 162; in Vlaicu, 125, 133–134. *See also* consolidation

Frydman, Roman, 18, 70, 81

Fustel de Coulanges, Numa Denis, 14, 368n18

gardens, household, 168–70, 182, 194

gasoline, 107, 110, 199, 207, 255, 289–91

Gelmar (village), 37, 389n8

gender: in Association, 236; and class relations, 167; and labor, 167, 168, 381n1; and power relations, 160, 252–53, 264

genealogical joint possession, 368n19

generation gap, 214, 236, 264, 360, 379–80n4, 380n16

Geoagiu (commune), 37–38, 125–29, 126

Gerbaud, Florence, 96

German Federal Republic, 90–91, 209

Germans, 216, 240, 259; in Eastern Europe, 83–84; in Romania, 34; technology brought by, 37, 369n5; in Vlaicu, 37, 118–19, 122, 133–35, 142–45, 182, 386n29. *See also* Cervenka Society; ethnic relations

"gift economy," 62, 63, 66, 75, 103

globalization, 4–8, 362

Gluckman, Max, 14, 15, 55–58, 59, 371n23

gosudar' (sovereign), 178

gosudarstvo (state), 178

governmentality, 24

Graeber, David, 21, 22

grain. *See* corn; wheat

granary, of CF/Association, 234–35, 237–38, 335

Great Britain, 5

Gross, Jan, 26

gypsies. *See* Roma

Habsburg Empire, 34, 35

Hagedorn, Konrad, 114–15, 355

Hallowell, A. Irving, 14

Hanisch, Markus, 78

Hann, C. M., 12, 14, 47

hectares, vanishing: devaluation and, 359–60; forms of, 32; restitution and, 97–98; values and, 191; and venits, 166–67; in Vlaicu, 116–57, 336–37

Hegel, G. W. F., 172

Heller, Michael, 19, 56, 74, 303

herbicides, 26, 54, 61, 297, 326; Association and, 208, 256, 257; cost of, 207, 230, 255, 311, 335; and cultivation strategies, 196–97, 201, 203–4, 211, 212–13, 220–23, 244–45; and labor shortage, 197, 205, 208, 223, 230, 318, 374n23. *See also* inputs

hiding land, 64–65

hierarchies: of administrative estates, 55–59, 57, 70, 339; of property forms, 21, 51–57. *See also* socialist hierarchies

historical justice. *See* justice

hoarding, 59, 60–63, 64–65

Hoebel, E. Adamson, 14

Holmes, Stephen, 6

Homorod (village), 37, 204–5

horses, 102, 211, 213, 227, 374n23, 381n3. *See also* livestock

Hudečková, Helena, 177, 225, 358

Humphrey, Caroline, 12, 56–57, 60, 62, 67, 371n23, 372n36

Hunedoara (city), 38

Hunedoara (county), 207, 232, 265, 341; competition for rental land in, 295; and industry, 36–38, 191, 197, 217–18; and scrap metal trade, 187

Hungarians, in Romania, 34

Hungary, 34, 44–45, 59, 87; CF managers in, 314; compared, 85–86, 88; decollectivization in, 84, 91, 280; GDP, per capita in, 367–68n5; recombinant property in, 297, 307; SFs in, 85, 276; trade with Romania, 255, 318–19

ideology, 71, 113, 158, 346; of private property, 4, 14–17, 114, 361, 364

Iliescu, Ion (Romanian president, 1990–96, 2000–04), 13, 94–96, 104, 118, 217, 373n2

implements, agricultural. *See* equipment, agricultural

impoverishment, 13, 218, 352, 361; and agricultural policy, 269–70; Association and, 351; associations and, 271, 328; commercial farmers and, 352–53; of smallholders, 336, 349, 355. *See also* dispossession

impropriation, 35, 370n7, 386n36. *See also* restitution

impunity: of local officials, 146; of SF directors, 308. *See also* sanctions

industry, 7, 70, 78, *84*, 166; pensions from, 38–39, 197, 207; restructuring of, 9, 36, 124, 171, 176, 194, 217–19, 356; and social capital in agriculture, 319; in socialist period, 11, 36, 41, 84, 123–24, 191, 231–32; subsidies to, 24, 93, 105, 108, 328, 353. *See also* economy, transformation of; price scissors

inflation, 185, 193, 259, 367n5; and devaluation of CF assets, 130, 234; and interest rates, 27, 354; and consumer price index, 105, 338, 376n49, 390n13; pensions and, 197, 220, 356; and production costs, 206–9, 255; and savings, 190, 316; and SF privatization, 298; strategies for, 331, 341; and subsidies, 93, 105–6, 353; and timing, 204, 341

information: control of, 111, 153, 156, 284, 288, 329, 337, 344, 388n19; lack of, 147, 150–51, 251; necessary for restitution claim, 153, 155; networks needed for, 121, 297, 322. *See also* knowledge; proofs

inheritance, 102, 103, 160–62, 163, 171, 193; law, 379n2

inputs (for crop production), 196–97, 233, 253–56, 322, 326; and agricultural policy, 92; capital, 205–9, 212, 250–56; chemical, 197, 318–20, 356; cost of, 197, 240, 292, 318–20, 335, 341, 381n10; difficulty of acquiring, 20, 93, 102, 105–6, 110, 193, 197–98, 203–4, 268–69, 290, 298; distribution channels for, 107, 285–86; imported, 326; as source of value, 7–8; "theft" of, 201. *See also* equipment, agricultural; Romcereal

institutional design. *See* social engineering

institutions, 26–28. *See also* neoinstitutionalism

insurance (for crops), 249, 255

interdependency (of social groups), 345, 348–55, 361

interest rates: associations and, 264, 350–51; fluctuating, 27, 106, 206, 385n21; IMF and, 106, 354; and input purchases, 196–97; and SF privatization, 299–300

International Monetary Fund (IMF), 3, 94, 114; conditions set by, 78; influence of, 4, 109; macroeconomic stabilization plan of, 106, 354; pressure on Romania, 12, 353; and Romcereal, 107, 254; and SF privatization, 279, 282

international organizations, 18, 79, 92, 361; conditions set by, 78; influence of, 109, 259; loans

from, 94, 100; pressure on Romania, 353, 387n6, 390n6; and SF privatization, 281, 282

întovărășire (preliminary cooperative), 42

investment, 211, 306, 311, 316, 383n28; in agriculture, 277, 286, 287, 295; in CFs/SFs, *55*, 314; generational conflict over, 181

investment, foreign, 79, 292; commercial farmers and, 334, 340; and Romanian economy, 8, 12, 94; and SF privatization, 280, 288, 303, 388n19; in Vlaicu, 275, 277, 301–2. *See also* Italian investors

irrigation works, 187, 288, 387–88n15

Italian investors, 273–75, 283, 334, 340

Italy, emigration to, 226, 358

justice, 80, 91, 120, 155, 159, 160, 169, 358–59

Kaneff, Deema, 380n12

khoziain (proprietor, master), 56–57, 178, 264

khoziaistvo (domain), 178

Kideckel, David, 12, 13

kin: and commercial farmers, 310, 311, 312, 320, 330, 334; connections, 153, 163–65, 379n30, 380n8; cooperation among, 165, 211, 214, 215, 380n9

kinship, 151, 158–66, 343, 368n19; conceptions of, 165–66; criteria for, 162; decollectivization and, 13; four degrees of, *161*, 379n2; and land claims, 132–33, 153, 182–83; and Law 18, 97, 375n33; as performative, 165–66, 358; ritual, 214, 382n18; in socialism, 379–80n4; "too much," 166, 167; transformation of, 159, 161, 163–66, 347, 358

Klaus, Václav (Czech prime minister), 3

Kligman, Gail, 268, 370n13

Knapp, Viktor, 57

knowledge (general), 150

knowledge (concerning land claims), 131, 150–51; claims to, 118, 120, 127, 151–52, 171, 233; held by villagers, 135–36, 149, 151–52; official, 150–56, 358; struggles over, 150–56

kolkhoz (collective farm), 43

Konstantinov, Yulian, 139, 380n12

Kornai, János, 47, 60

KPMG, 5

labor, 159, 166, 182, 213, 371n19; bargaining power of, 217, 218, 349; in CFs, 167, 234; competition for, 216–17, 248–49, 349, 357, 384n16, 390n1; cost of, 203, 318; devaluation of, 4; hierarchies in, 347; migrant, 257, 301–2; and personhood, 174–75, 268; and property, 174–75; in SFs, 124; supply, 133, 190; wage, 124, 215, 219–23, 317, 351, 380n9 labor mobilization: in Association, 248; in Cervenka Society, 260; on CFs, 68; commercial farmers and, 352, 389n8; and networks, 62, 63; and prison labor, 248, 384n15; on SFs, 291; smallholders and, 194, 201–5, 212–20

labor shortages, 36, 124, 197, 212–22; and Association, 199–200, 242, 244–49, 382n19; and commercial farmers, 311, 337, 389n8; comparative, 382n16; and crop rotation, 230; and livestock raising, 384–85n17; and smallholders, 212–13, 215, 219–23, 349; and specialty crops, 326; venits and, 191, 215–17, 361

"La Jigoaia," 140–44

Lampland, Martha, 12, 175, 314, 344

land: as abstraction, 224–25, 358; and ancestors, 16–17, 155, 159, 167, 171, 357, 368n19, 379–80n4; assigning, 135–40, 151; Association control over, 239–43; concentration of, 224, 361; conflict over, 36–37, 215–16, 242, 268, 347; cultivation of, 192–205, 212–13, 220–23, 225, 238; elasticity of, 64–65; forcible occupations of, 96, 127, 142, 144, 148, 164, 280; meanings of, 9, 22, 31, 170–81, 191, 224–25, 270, 337, 357; measuring/remeasuring of, 99–101, 117–18, 120, 135–37, 148–49, 162; as negative asset, 191, 203, 209, 220, 224, 342, 356; as object, 16–17; and personhood, 17, 63–64, 172–74, 178, 179; process of obtaining, 142–44, 153–56; quality of, 211, 212, 220, 243, 259; and social status, 171–72; uncultivated, 93, 203, 209, 257, 258, 262, 294, 298, 335, 384n13. See also consolidation; fragmentation; soil quality

land claims. See claims

land commissions, 27, 100, 120; abuse by, 155, 156, 162, 210, 378–79n19; commune, 100, 127

land committee. See village committee

land exchanges, 136; in socialism, 42–43, 63–64, 71, 111, 141, 371–72n25

landless villagers, 125, 131, 144, 166–67, 171, 194, 348

land market, 90, 93, 98, 167, 223; associations and, 271, 352; commercial farmers and, 333, 336–37; competition in, 295–96; and contracts, 383n24; effect of subsidies on, 109; and emigration, 219; and fragmentation, 99, 112; urbanites and, 182, 350; venits and, 170, 182, 191, 210–12, 240

land reform, 14, 45; 19th century, 386n36; post–World War I, 35, 97, 375n35, 386n36; post–World War II, 123, 145, 167, 374n9

land register/land registry book (Cartea Funciară), 97, 132, 153, 156, 252; topographic numbers in, 154, 375–76n40, 387n3

land registration, 34, 386n2; forms of, 35–36

land value, 21, 224, 226; commercial farmers and, 342, 352; decollectivization and, 25, 92, 348; and input use, 204; leasing and, 217; and meanings of land, 170–71, 223; supertenants and, 313, 336–37; venits and, 181

Lățea, Daniel, 160, 192, 264–65, 382n16

Latvia, 88, 89

law, 71–74; categories of, 49; -governed state, 79, 359; inheritance, 379n2; invocation of, in argument, 119, 120, 149, 169–70; property, 370–71n16, 373n41

Law 7/1996 (Law of the Cadastre), 100

Law 16/1994 (Law on Land Leasing), 186, 188, 278–79, 286, 389n6

Law 18/1991 (Law on Land Resources), 96–104, 168, 273; associations and, 270; complexity of, 132; drafting of, 98–100; effects of, 101–4, 120, 183, 287–88, 384n8; and field consolidation, 133; implementation of, 100–101, 111, 112, 117; implementation of, in Vlaicu, 132–40, 288; and kinship, 160–62, 166, 167, 375n33; and land cultivation, 195, 225; and political capital, 146–47; priorities promoted by, 159; and reserve land, 375n32; right of preemption to tenant, 336; sanctions for implementing, 145; SFs unaffected by, 276

Law 36/1991 (Law on Agricultural Societies and Other Forms of Association in Agriculture), 235

Law (Decret Lege) 42/1990 (On Measures to Stimulate the Peasantry), 96, 125, 220

Law 69/1991 (Law on Local Government Autonomy), 145

Law 169/1997 (Modification and Completion of the Law on Land Resources, no. 18/1991), 98

Law 183/1949, 370n13

lawsuits, 66, 90, 99, 142, 169; involving Germans, 135, 143–44, 259, 260–61, 379n23; among kin, 163, 164; over CF/Association granary, 234–35, 237–38; and proofs, 152–55; and restitution process, 139. See also court cases

Leach, Edmund, 14

leasing, 32, 217, 388n16; associations and, 271; commercial farmers and, 335–36; contracts for, 225, 243, 245, 335–36; and land concentration, 361; and liabilities, 93; vs. ownership, 10, 336; and SF privatization, 122; smallholders and, 115, 191, 193; supertenants and, 201, 223, 224–25, 347

"legacies" of socialism. See path dependency; socialism and postsocialist society

Legea Fondului Funciar. See Law 18/1991

legitimation, 27, 79, 149–50; compromised, 157; decollectivization and, 358–59; deficit of, in Association, 235, 237–38; restitution and, 73–74, 145; state and, 108

Lenin, Vladimir, 370n5

Lewandowski, Janusz (Polish privatization minister), 7

liabilities: assets as, 220, 262; forced onto others, 23–24, 93, 305–7, 336, 361; seen as assets, 23–24, 114, 115, 199, 297, 303, 307; in socialism, 60

liquidation commissions, 100, 127, 129–35, 251

Lithuania, *88*, 89

livestock, 267, 268, 381n2; feed for, 213, 317–18; labor requirements for, 384–85n17; production cost of, *321*; sale of, 194, 196, 201–3, 205, 207, 209–210, 295, 319, 321, 324, 331–33, 336, 339, 342; and Transylvanian farming, 34, 36; and venits, 168, 215, 349. *See also* horses

loans: bank, 110, 274, 289, 252, 290, 317, 324, 327, 387n8; collateral for, 206, 252, 274, 327; debt and, 300–301; difficulty obtaining, 93, 172, 204, 206, 332–33, 352; foreign, 94, 100, 105, 261–62, 305; and SF privatization, 106, 110, 306

local government, autonomy of, 145–46

locality, 173, 225–26, 358, 359–60

locals (*băştinaşi*), 122–23, 191, 216–17, 219; in Association, 242; property rights of, 226; relations with venits, 166–70, 346, 380n13. *See also* conflict, locals/venits; venits (in-migrants to Vlaicu)

Locke, John, 16, 172

Losták, Mihal, 177, 225, 358

Lowie, Robert, 14

Lozi kingdom, 56–57, 371n23

"Lupu law," (Law 169/1997), 98

Lupu, Vasile (Romanian senator), 99

"mafias." *See* elites

Maine, Henry, 14

Making Capitalism Without Capitalists (Eyal et al.), 10

Malinowski, Bronislaw, 14, 47

managers: behavior of, 60–65, 75–76, 279–80, 361; and "theft," 58–59

manure/manuring, 201, 204, 205, 207, 211

Marica, Petre, 371n16

market, for land. *See* land market

markets, 109, 322, 377n62; Association and, 236–37, 249, 250, 254, 255, 257; "emerging," 328, 363; imperfect, 231, 238, 271, 358; Romcereal and, 262, 351; SFs and, 286, 292; in socialism, 232. *See also* land market

Marriott hotel chain, 8–9

Martin, Emily, 368n23

Marx, Karl, 21, 40, 48, 175

master/mastery (*stăpânire*) (as value in landowning), 57, 177–79, 183, 268, 337–39; land cultivation and, 183, 191, 356357; and leasing, 225; and social status, 175; and "visible economy," 178–81, 223–24

Mateescu, Oana, 192, 369n25

Maurer, William, 14–15

Mauss, Marcel, 17

McFaul, Michael, 314

means of production: Association control over, 196–97, 237, 239–53, 266; cost of, and inflation, 206–9; Law 18 and, 102; smallholders and, 110–11, 190, 205–9. *See also* inputs

meat-processing industry, 311, 323, 333

media: effects of, 96; and scandals, 111–12, 270

Meurs, Mieke, 381n10

Milczarek, Dominika, 314, 336

Miller, Linda, 72

Miller, Peter, 24

Miroiu, Mirela, 13, 227–28, 381n9

mir (Russian village community), 44

mode(s) of production, 371n23; articulation of, 11, 20, 267–69, 308; in socialism, 47–59

"monetary overhang," 206. *See also* savings

Moore, Sally Falk, 14

morality, 22, 74–75; property and, 16, 283

Morgan, Lewis Henry, 14

Mungiu-Pippidi, Alina, 13

Munn, Nancy, 22, 25

Narodniks, 370n5

naşi (godparents), 214, 382n18

nationalization, 5, 40, 41, 52

national minorities. *See* ethnic relations

native land claims, 17–18

neocolonialism, 3–4, 15, 19, 109

neoinstitutionalism, 9–10, 26–28, 164, 361–62

neoliberals, 9, 114, 274; and agricultural policy, 353–54; and coupon system, 107, 110–11, 319; and EU policy, 376n56; and industrial restructuring, 217–18; and SF privatization, 279–80, 283, 303. *See also* Democratic Convention (DC); political parties

neo-Protestants, 212, 382n15

networks, 10, 27, 70, 106, 343; of agronomists, 322; and banks, 110, 206; of commercial farmers, 311, 317, 320, 322, 323–24, 326, 331, 344; and "corruption," 25; of elites, 140, 141, 145–46, 153, 188, 192, 250, 252, 256; of exchange partners, 62–63; interlocking directorates, 299, 306–7; and risk management,

networks (*continued*)
337; of SF directors, 250, 281–82, 286, 289, 291, 297; and SFs, 54, 306; smallholders and, 191–92, 227; as social capital, 173, 204, 256, 262, 268, 305, 308; and subsidies, 106; of village committee, 137–39. *See also* exchange; reciprocity; social capital

Noronha, Raymond, 226–27

notaries, 30, 98, 122, 150, 154–55, 163

Nouvelles campagnes roumaines, Les (Hirschhausen), 13

objectification, 368n20

obligation, 22, 60; and labor mobilization, 213–14; networks of, 61–63

Offe, Claus, 6

off-farm incomes, 11, 197, 339–40, 356. *See also* pensions

Office of Economic Cooperation and Development (OECD), 367–68n5

"old sites," 99, 136; conflict over, 143, 245; fragmentation and, 101, 162, 182; and restitution process, 74, 82, 90, 91

Olt (county), 264–65

Orăştie (city), 38, 207

ortaci (labor partners), 214

Otiman, P. I., 13

"outside committeemen," 127, 137, 149, 151, 152

ownership, 22, 44, 102, 176; and character, 173–74; history of, 35, 44; of patents, 7–8; vs. leasing, 336; title, 87–89; by "the whole people," 32, 40, 48–52, 54, 69, 71, 277. *See also* ownership, effective; personhood; private property; property

ownership, effective, 31, 104, 212; associations and, 270–71; commercial farmers and, 337; decollectivization and, 9, 348, 358; defined, 178; and mastery, 176–77; obstacles to, 20, 92, 205–6; property rights and, 355–56; smallholders and, 110, 183, 224, 356

"ownership vacuum," 371n22

Party of Romanian Social Democracy (PRSD), 95, 170, 182, 223; and agricultural policy, 353–54, 376–77n62; policy on SFs, 278, 303; support for private agriculture, 104–9, 112–13, 217, 373n2; transformations of, 375n27

Pasti, Vladimir, 227–28, 381n9

pasture, common, 196, 349

path dependency, 11, 313. *See also* socialism and postsocialist society

patrimony: of CFs, 42, 251, 263, 266, 331, 365–66, 390n12; defined, 370n14

patronage. *See* clientelism; elites

Păunescu brothers, 8–9

Paxson, Margaret, 268

pay. *See* remuneration

pensions, 130, 161, 379–80n4; and inflation, 197, 220, 356; intergenerational conflicts over, 161, 179–81; as support for cultivation, 11, 201, 204

personhood: jural, 49–50, 59, 235; labor and, 268; land cultivation and, 191; and "theft," 69. *See also* property, and personhood

pesticides, 196, 208, 374n23, 381n10

petitions: to enter collective farm, 43, 97, 127, 132, 153, 200; for return of land, 103, 132, 151

Pioneer seed, 203, 326, 335

Pişchinţi (village), 37

plan: bargaining, 59, 60; in socialism, 52, 60

plows/plowing, 102, 106, 190, 193, 196, 198, 201, 212–13. *See also* Agromecs; Romcereal

Poland, 5, 43, 45, 89, 314; compared, 85–86, 88; GDP, per capita in, 367–68n5; SFs in, 53, 276

polarization (of social groups), 24, 112, 125, 383n25; Association and, 351; associations and, 269, 271; decollectivization and, 76, 82, 348, 360; smallholders and, 194, 226. *See also* class formation; impoverishment

policy, agricultural, 217, 224, 318, 321; and agricultural subsidies, 24, 185, 376–77n62, 381n4; associations and, 264, 272; comparative, 90–93; and effective ownership, 9, 355–56; effects of, 185, 207, 227, 269–70, 318–19, 353; influences on, 353–54; instability of, 20, 185; international organizations and, 28; in Romania, 104–15; Romcereal and, 253–54; and time horizons, 341–42; and vanishing hectares, 359–60

political capital, 10, 18, 313–14, 343–44; of commercial farmers, 324; of commune officials, 120, 146–47, 157, 171; and SF privatization, 281, 282, 284, 299, 305, 307; in socialism, 343. *See also* capital endowments

"political capitalism" (hypothesis), 10, 343

political economy: as perspective, 12; of socialism, 47–52, 55–63

political parties: identity of, 112; privatization and, 279; relations among, 94–95, 159; scarcity of resources for, 80, 98; transformations of, 375n27; as "unruly coalitions," 95. *See also* Agrarian Democratic Party of Romania; Democratic Convention; neoliberals; Party of Romanian Social Democracy

politics, electoral, 95, 104–9, 145, 223, 319; of restitution, 80–84, 98–99; and SF privatization, 283, 303; transformation of, 22, 94–95,

104, 145, 279–80. *See also* decollectivization,
politics of
Post-Communism (Staniszkis), 12
postcommunists (PRSD). *See* Party of Romanian Social Democracy
postmodernism, 367n5
postsocialism: specificity of, 353, 363–64. *See
also* socialism and postsocialist society
Postsocialist Pathways (Stark and Bruszt), 10
Povinelli, Elizabeth, 16–17
power: gender and, 160, 252–53, 264; of local
officials, 91–92, 95, 112, 114–15, 139–40,
144–50, 182; organization of, 26, 48–69,
177–78, 263–64; in socialism, 48–69, 177–78
prices, 255–56, 259, 282–83, 320; administrative,
54, 63, 187, 236–37, 355; and agricultural policy, 92, 105–9, 254, 319; at Agromecs, 186–87,
227, 253, 261, 355, 381n3; of auctioned SFs,
275, 301–04; and inflation, 105, 206–08, *208*,
338, 341; of inputs, 193, 381n10; of land,
208–210, 209, 217–18, 337–38, 382n14; of services, 186–87, 381n3; state controls on, 105,
108, 227, 255, 321, 331. *See also* credits; devaluation; price scissors, production costs; subsidies
price scissors, 7, 206–9, 259, 350; agricultural
policy as cause of, 92–93, 353; Association
and, 238, 255; associations and, 262, 265–66;
in Bulgaria, 381n10; commercial farmers
and, 323, 328, 337; price controls and, 105,
185; SFs and, 276–77
PricewaterhouseCoopers, 5
prison labor, 248, 384n15
"private plots." *See* usufruct plots
private property, 3, 15, 31, *128*; creation of, 5,
75–76, 79–80, 104, 336; in Hunedoara, 36;
and ideology, 4, 113–14, 361, 364; and Ion Iliescu, 77, 373n2; legitimation of, 157; as "natural," 4, 17, 47–48, 114, 364; in socialism, 36,
40–41, 50–53, 63–64, 69, 168; as symbol, 4, 31,
88–89
Private Property Fund, 281
privatization, 3–4, 9–13, 18, 22–23, 311; bureaucrats favored by, 277, 281, 282, 290, 299, 304,
306; in capitalist countries, 78; forms of, 5–6,
373n4, 387n6; and globalization, 4–8; process of, 275, 298–300, 302, 305–7, 386n1,
388n16; and property ideology, 17; in socialist period, 59, 75, 77; of state farms, 273–309;
vouchers, 82, 91, 211, 323, 354
production, estates of, 66, 70
production costs: of Association, 250, 255,
385n25; chemical inputs, 318–20; of commercial farmers, 316, 317, 336–37; dependent

on farm type, 256; imported inputs and,
327–28; in Regat, 265–66; of smallholders,
206–9, 350; of wheat, 301
proofs (for land claims), 103, 111, 153–56, 359;
forms of, 97 132, 150–51; in Transylvania,
35–36, 153. *See also* claims
property, 14–20, 226; administrative vs. legal
regulation of, 48–49, 70–74; and anthropology, 14–15; anti-commons, 290, 303, 388n22;
as bundles of rights, 14, 19, 75–76, 226, 355;
conceptions of, 181, 268, 307, 380n15; defined, 6, 14–19, 48, 49, 177; and democracy,
16; and identity, 48, 83, 113–14, 172–78,
283–84, 357; and morality, 16, 283; as "native
category," 15–17; objects of, 49, 50, 370n15;
and personhood, 158, 159, 170, 172–78, 193,
223–25, 304, 338, 368n20; as process, 13–14,
19, 47, 48, 55–69, 183, 346–64; and rights, 16,
56–57; and socialist capital endowments,
356–57; subjects of, 49–51, 370n15; as symbol,
15, 17–18, 79, 88, 113–14, 363; transformation
of, 78, 79–81, 358; types of, 49, 50–51, 53,
371n18; value and, 20–25, 31, 356; ways of analyzing, 55–56, 226, 307, 355–57. *See also* private property; property in socialism; property, recombinant; socialist property
property, recombinant, 10, 24, 307; and commercial farmers, 330, 333–34; and fuzzy
boundaries, 58–59; and SF privatization,
296–98, *297*, 308; smallholders and, 267
property ideology, 4, 14–17, 114, 361, 364
property in socialism, 13–14, 18, 40–76, 289, 358;
and administrative rights, 297–98; and associations, 266–67, 269, 271; fuzzy boundaries
of, 10, 74–75, 135, 298, 363; and legitimation,
157; and postsocialist specificities, 363; and SF
privatization, 276, 277, 308–09, 322, 333
property law, 370–71n16, 373n41
property regimes, 18–19, 49
property rights, 35, 71–73, 368n20; bundles of,
19, 75–76; and effective ownership, 4, 355–56;
intellectual, 7, 22, 336; locals and, 226; restitution of, 5–6, 14, 191
propriety, 16
protectionism, 24–25, 109, 376n56
Pryor, Frederick, 13, 92, 373n5
Putnam, Robert, 10
pyramid schemes, 27, 201, 331, 332, 341, 367n5

quotas (requisitioned produce, during collectivization), 42, 65, 172

Rapaczynski, Andrzej, 18, 70, 81
rational-choice analysis, 361

rationalities (in farming), 63–64, 224, 239, 267–69, 296, 307, 337

reciprocity, 22, 61–63, 70, 214–15, 256, 289

redistribution, 57, 62

reduction coefficient, 133, 375 n32

Regat (kingdom), 33–36, 98, 104, 182, 376 n40. *See also* Transylvania and Regat, compared

relations, social. *See* clientelism; kinship; networks; social capital

remuneration, 233, 293, 354; in Association, 199, 235, 237, 240, 243, 252, 257, 263; in Cervenka Society, 260, 261; of CF members, 54–55, 61, 66–68, 355, 373 n38; of day laborers, 382 n21

rent. *See* leasing

rentiers, 225–26, 347, 364, 383 n27

rent-seeking, 81. *See also* "corruption"

reparations, 115, 172, 363. *See also* compensation

research methods, 28–31, 284–85, 369 n30, 370 n3, 372 n28, 373 n39, 377–78 n2, 387 n9

reserve land, 122, 133, 135, 139, 143, 375 n32

resistance: to abuse by superiors, 111–12, 143, 174, 294; during collectivization, 44, 53, 70, 127, 269; to decollectivization, 90, 191; to privatization, 75–76, 282; to sharecropping, 215; to socialism, 364; "theft" as, 66–69

resources, scarcity of, 16

restitution, 5–6, 14, 111, 115; baseline dates for, 83–84, 374 n11; comparative, 77–115; effects of, 97, 124–25, 158–59, 170, 177, 357–62; forms of, 81–82; as genealogical practice, 160–61; magnitude of, 97–98; organization of, 100, 127, 129–*130*; problems with, 34, 35–39, 64, 65, 70–76, 80–84, 121, 363; and reconfiguration of value, 25, 357; 10–ha. cap on, 98, 133; venits excluded from, 133, 166–67, 215–16

restoration of past, 77, 83, 102, 155

restructuring. *See* industry; unemployment

Retegan, Simon, 383 n27

retraditionalization. *See* demodernization

Return of the Peasant (Cartwright), 13

revaluation, 6, 23–25, 223–26, 338, 361. *See also* devaluation; value

Ries, Nancy, 192

right of direct/operational administration. *See* administrative rights

rights, 5, 14–19, 56; and effective ownership, 4, 20, 31, 78–79, 92, 104, 183, 355–56; property as bundles of, 19, 75–76;. *See also* administrative rights; property rights

Rikoon, Sandie, 177, 225, 358

Riles, Annelise, 14–15

risk, 6, 19–20, 113, 185, 269; and agricultural

policy, 92, 108, 254, 340; in Association, 238, 242, 251; in capitalism, 337; commercial farmers and, 316, 318, 322, 328–29, 333–34, 337; and demodernization, 269; protecting against, 198–200, 203, 207–8, 231, 312, 322; property and, 356–57, 383 n26; redistribution of, 187–89, 203–4, 256, 274, 323, 336, 363; and SF privatization, 276, 308–09, 314, 352–53; sources of, 27

Rogers, Douglas, 264

Roma, 299, 347–55; and labor, 201, 204, 214, 216–18, 260; land holdings created for, 378 n10; in Vlaicu, 124, 274

Roman, Petre (Romanian prime minister, 1990–96), 12

Romania, 84, 228, 314, 276; agricultural reforms in, 87; associations in, 232; compared, 85–86, 88; economy of, 8–9, 20, 84–85, 94, 101–2, 104–12, 369 n25; GDP, per capita in, 367–68 n5; in global economy, 12, 94, 105, 115, 357; international pressure on, 20, 96, 100, 107–09, 207, 282, 353, 390 n6

Romanian Communist Party, 8, 43, 80, 94–5, 96

Romanian National Bank, 106

Romanian Orthodox Church, 212, 382 n15

Romcereal (state procurement center), 30, 107, 320, 350; and Association, 254–56, 257; collapse of, 185, 254, 257, 259, 262, 311; and commercial farmers, 317, 318, 326; and distribution channels, 253–54, 286; and interdependency, 349–55; scandal involving, 110

Romos (commune), 37–38, 286, 369 n5

Rose, Nikolas, 24

Rusan, Achim, 153–54

Russia, 63, 268; collectives in, 43, 44, 82; decollectivization in, *88*, 91–92, 314, 341

Russians, 84, 89, 118–19

Sachs, Jeffrey, 3, 367 n1

Sahlins, Marshall, 16

sanctions, 148; in Law 18/1991, 100–101, 145

savings, 103, 237, 317, 321; generational conflict over, 181; and inflation, 190, 206, 316, 341; in socialist period, 105

scandals, 110–13

scavenging, 12, 110–11, 113, 187, 281, 357, 388–89 n24

Scott, James, 46

scrap metal, 12, 23, 124, 187, 298, 349, 354, 369 n25, 387–88 n15

second economy. *See* economy, informal

seeds, 7, 102, 205, 256, 326; as cash crop, 249,

state farms (SFs) (*continued*)
socialist property, 52–55; strategies of, 32, 187–89; in Vlaicu, 37–38, 285–86. *See also* collective farms and state farms, compared; dividends; shareholders

state-farm systems (SFS): accounting in, 281–82, 291; collapse of, 280, 307; and commercial farmers, 352; debt of, 289–90, 330, 333; and interdependency, 349–55; organization of, 277–78, 301, 304; politics in, 294; in Vlaicu, 285–86

state-owned enterprises (SOEs), 57, 186, 277, 298; dismantling of, 78; evaluating assets of, 74, 282–83, 301; privatization of, 75–76, 275, 281, 283, 296, 334; soft budget constraints in, 276; subsidies to, 105, 282. *See also* socialist property; state property

state ownership. *See* state property

state procurement centers. *See* Romcereal

state property: and administrative rights, 50, 51, 277–78, 297–98, 303; agencies, 387n7; vs. cooperative property, 50–51; creation of, 52, 53; defined, 273; and "ownership vacuum," 371n22; and socialist hierarchies, 41. *See also* property in socialism; socialism; socialist property

State Property Agency (Hungary), 280

State Property Fund (Romania), 280–81, 299, 302, 303, 306–7, 334, 342, 390n12

status, social, 156, 175, 227; emigration and, 388n23; land and, 171–72, 179, 191, 356, 380n16; property and, 371n23; and SF privatization, 304; venits and, 168; in Vlaicu, 346

strategies, 108, 157, 215, 341; in Association, 241, 242–43; in associations, 266–67, 311; "comprador," 334; for crop rotation, 244–49; for cultivation, 58, 195–207, 212–13, 220–23; multiple, 312, 316, 320, 323, 331, 333, 335, 339, 340, 342, 364; for redistribution of risk, 187–89, 203–4; of smallholders, 220–23, 226–27; smallholders vs. Association, 250–53. *See also* delays; time/timing

Strathern, Marilyn, 14–15, 172, 173

subjectification, 360–61

subjects, jural, 49–51

subsidies, 106–9, 282; agricultural, 91, 92, 264, 319; to CFs, 314; EU and, 376n56; to industry, 328, 353; and timing, 385n21. *See also* credits; industry; loans; policy; prices

subsistence agriculture, 76, 89, 92, 191, 377n62; industrial restructuring and, 124, 171; problems of, 205–9; in Vlaicu, 195, 200–205. *See also* demodernization

supertenants, 201, 216, 347, 364; Agromec directors as, 389n6; associations and, 271; defined, 195; emergence of, 76, 312–13; and interdependency, 362; and land value, 239, 336–37; and leasing, 223, 224–25, 347; SF directors as, 322–29; and vanishing hectares, 359

surpluses, 287, 288, 290, 292, 322; defined, 387n12; forced transfer of, 5, 360

surveyors, 100, 129

Swain, Nigel, 87

Swinnen, Johan F. M., 92, 93, 381n9

symbiosis, of property forms, 266–69, 348–52

Szelényi, Iván, 10, 92, 313–14, 334, 339, 343

tariffs, 92, 255, 259, 264

taxation, 107–8, 233, 326, 328

tax evasion, 326, 389n9

technology, 269, 286, 314; commercial farmers and, 256, 328–29, 339; as cultural capital, 268; for farming, 189, 277, 369n5; Germans and, 37, 369n5; and labor shortage, 244, 249. *See also* expertise

tenancy. *See* supertenants

Teşliuc, Emil, 108–9, 377n62

"theft," 58, 177–78, 275–76, 373n37; in CFs, 55, 65–69, 267; and associations, 254, 266–67, 270; of CF assets, 372n36; property as, 40; and scrap metal trade, 369n25; by sharecroppers, 201

Thomas, Nicholas, 22

time horizons. *See* time/timing

time/timing, 108, 227, 364, 385n21; and Association, 231, 237, 240, 241, 243, 252, 263, 268; and commercial farmers, 312, 316, 320, 323, 331–32, 333, 341; and demodernization, 226; in Law 18/1991, 97; manipulation of, 342; and personhood, 173; property and, 356–57; and redistribution of risk, 187–88, 204; and SF privatization, 276, 308–9;and successful associations, 264

titling/titles, 87, 97, 135, 163, 311–12; authority to award, 145; delayed, 101, 104, 108, 144–47, 182; empty, 72; systems of 35–36, 132

Tompson, William, 23

topographers. *See* surveyors

topographic numbers, 154, 375–76n40, 387n3

Townsley, Eleanor, 313–14, 334, 339, 343

tractors, 102, 206, 213, 337; and Agromecs, 211, 341, 351; in Association, 351; imported vs. Romanian, 327; in Vlaicu, 206, 381n7

trade, terms of, 105. *See also* price scissors

"traditional" agriculture. *See* demodernization; resistance

transnational firms/companies (TNC), 7–8, 12, 328